SECOND EDITION

Tourists
and Tourism

Posing for the tourist camera, Peru. (Photo by George Gmelch)

SECOND EDITION

Tourists and Tourism

A Reader

Sharon Bohn Gmelch

University of San Francisco
and
Union College

WAVELAND
PRESS, INC.
Long Grove, Illinois

For information about this book, contact:
    Waveland Press, Inc.
    4180 IL Route 83, Suite 101
    Long Grove, IL 60047-9580
    (847) 634-0081
    info@waveland.com
    www.waveland.com

7   6

To Sheila Otto, Teresa Meade, Pat McNamara,
Tom Curtin, and George Gmelch—
my adventurous friends and traveling companions.

Tourists
and Tourism

Masked Peruvian warns tourists about touching Cusco's Incan walls. (Photo by Sharon Gmelch)

Contents

Two:
When Tourists and Locals Meet   89

Three:
Authenticity and the Marketing of Culture   185

Tourist photography outside the Sun Yatsen Memorial Hall in Guangzhou, China. (Photo by Sharon Gmelch)

Preface and Acknowledgments

Tourists and Tourism was inspired by the anthropology course I teach on tourism and by a desire to bring together a collection of engaging readings that capture the diversity and importance of tourism research. Although no collection can hope to cover everything, I have tried to achieve a balance between theory and case studies from different parts of the world. I have also sought articles from international specialists in a range of disciplines including anthropology, sociology, history, geography, folklore, and journalism. Although domestic tourism is discussed in several articles, the focus is on international travel and—as befits my interests as an anthropologist—on the cross-cultural encounter and impact. Appendices provide information on the authors, recommended films, and examples of behavioral guidelines written for tourists. The second edition contains nine new articles and three that have been revised and updated, as well as an expanded list of recommended films.

Many people have helped make *Tourists and Tourism* possible—foremost among them are the authors who contributed their articles and insights. With the first edition, I received valuable help from Union College librarians Donna Burton, Bruce Connolly, Mary Cahill, and David Gerhan. Deb Ludke, Elizabeth Daigle, Amanda Haig, and Farida Siddiqi provided secretarial support and also commented on many of the essays as did Pat Mahoney, Morgan Gmelch, and students in my Tourists and Tourism courses. For the second edition, about two dozen colleagues generously took the time to respond to a survey I sent asking for feedback on the first edition. I especially wish to thank Robert Wood and Phyllis Passariello for their detailed remarks and other assistance. Diane Royal, at the University of San Francisco, carefully read every article I considered for inclusion in the second edition. Her help and insightful critiques were extremely valuable. I also wish to thank Katie Newingham for reading and reacting to many of these articles, providing yet another student perspective. Both editions have also benefited from the suggestions of my colleague and husband, George Gmelch. Lastly, I thank Tom Curtin and Jeni Ogilvie of Waveland Press for their unfailing good cheer and desire to make the second edition an even more appealing and valuable collection both for students and for the specialists who teach them.

One:
Tourism and the
Tourist Experience

Japanese tourists from the same company enjoy a cruise down the Li River in China in 1989. (Photo by Sharon Gmelch)

I

Why Tourism Matters

Sharon Bohn Gmelch

I became interested in tourism while directing an anthropology field school for students in Barbados, a popular tourist destination.[1] Each year, this small Caribbean island "hosts" four times as many tourists as its 275,000 population.[2] The impact of tourism is visible everywhere, from the beach-front hotels with fantasy names like "Glitter Bay" that line the west coast to the scantily clad, sunburned visitors who wheel carts down grocery-store aisles or stand awkwardly in bank lines next to neatly groomed and fully clothed Bajans. Tourists often do seem out of place, if not "vulgar, vulgar, vulgar," as Henry James once wrote.

My students were always horrified when they left the villages where they lived and were mistaken for "tourists." The insensitivity and ignorance tourists sometimes displayed embarrassed my students, and they were eager to disassociate themselves. After all, they were in Barbados to work, not play. They were learning the culture and living with local people, not lying on the beach and being served by them. They felt their experiences were deeper and obviously more valuable than those of tourists.[3] Ironically, tourists often draw similar distinctions amongst themselves: "*I* am a traveler, *you* are a tourist, *he* is a tripper" [emphasis added] (Waterhouse 1989). The reason students in Barbados were classified as tourists (their foreign accent and, for most, white skin) and their reactions to this raise some initial questions about tourism. Where do most tourists come from? What kind of engagements with local people do they seek? What impact does their presence have on the people and places they visit?

3

Tourism's Global Reach and Economic Impact

Worldwide, tourism employs one in every 12 workers and accounts for 11 percent of global gross domestic product (GDP).[4] In some countries, the figures are higher. In Barbados, for example, tourism employs 21 percent of the labor force and accounts for 15 percent of the island's GDP and 57 percent of its foreign exchange earnings.[5] Tourism is also the top foreign exchange earner in communist Cuba (Medea 1998). According to the United Nations' World Tourism Organization, by 2020 growth in the tourism and travel industry is projected to reach 1.6 billion tourist arrivals a year with receipts of US$2 trillion. Considering this, it is not surprising that many less-developed nations view tourism as the road to development and prosperity.[6] Even Arab governments (besides the long-established destinations of Tunisia, Egypt, and Morocco) are now promoting tourism.

But international tourism is a fickle form of development. Nations have little control over events that can cut off the tourist flow overnight. Whether and where people travel depends largely on economic factors, namely the cost of a trip and a person's ability to afford it. Eighty percent of international tourists are citizens of the 20 richest nations. Citizens from just five—the United States, Germany, Japan, France, and the United Kingdom—account for five of every ten international trips and half of all global spending on tourism. They have the leisure time, discretionary income, and easy access to transportation to make this possible. This profile is changing, however. Before long, Asia will dominate tourism due to the region's growing economies and populations (Smith and Brent 2001).[7] Before the global economic meltdown that emerged in 2008, it was predicted that by 2020, China would rank fourth in terms of the number of citizens who travel abroad as tourists and first as an international destination. (France currently holds this distinction.)

Tourists demand not only affordable and appealing places (both "sites" and "sights") to visit; they also demand safety. They need to feel confident that their trip and chosen destination are not unacceptably more risky than staying at home. Since 1970, international tourism has experienced several precipitous declines following crucial events such as the oil crisis of 1975, the Gulf War in 1991, the U.S. terrorist attacks of September 11, 2001, and the global financial crisis of 2008. Domestic and regional events can also keep would-be tourists at home: the Chinese government's harsh reprisal against pro-democracy demonstrators in Tiananmen Square in 1989; the murder of tourists in Cairo and Luxor, Egypt, in 1997; and the takeover of Bangkok's airports by antigovernment protesters in 2008.

Tourism has enormous social implications globally. It represents the largest movement of people ever across national borders, eclipsing emigration and immigration, refugee flight, pilgrimage, and business and educational travel. In many locations, tourists significantly outnumber residents during peak seasons. In the course of a year, they may nearly double the population of a country (as in Ireland) or even quadruple it (as in Barbados).[8] In some nations, like the United States and India, most tourism is domestic; that is, the tourists are fellow Americans or Indians rather than foreigners. Regardless of where they come from, however, any large influx of people to a particular place has a significant effect on its population, its natural and built environment, its infrastructure and services, and—through the creation of tourism attractions and venues—its cultural and national identity. More will be said about these later.

A Brief History

Tourism, defined broadly as temporary travel for the purpose of experiencing a change, is not new.[9] Elites in Imperial Rome traveled to the isle of Capri or cities like Pompeii and Herculaneum for holidays. Travel for pleasure is also historically linked to other quests: the pursuit of profit (trade and commerce), of spiritual renewal (pilgrimage), of knowledge (e.g., the "Grand Tour"), of adventure (early exploration), and of health. Most cultures have long-established traditions of hospitality: rules and etiquette on how to treat the strangers who show up at your door (i.e., providing food, shelter, and protection).

Much early tourism was linked to pilgrimage. For many of the medieval pilgrims in Chaucer's *The Canterbury Tales*, the trip to St. Thomas Becket's shrine was as much a holiday as a pilgrimage. I became aware of the connection between pilgrimage and tourism when I visited the shrine of Knock in western Ireland, the site of an apparition of the Virgin Mary, Joseph, and St. John the Evangelist in 1879. I was unprepared for the casual jollity of the pilgrims on the train from Dublin and taken aback by the commercial bustle of Knock's main street, as people who had finished their prayers jostled with vendors to buy all manner of sacred and secular souvenirs—from plastic figurines of the Virgin Mary meant to be filled with holy water to tacky T-shirts. In pilgrimage, we see important features of tourism: the welcome change of scene, the freedom from everyday routines and responsibilities, the excitement of the journey, and playful permissiveness of a "liminoid" experience[10] (Turner and Turner 1978). Today, many secular tourist sites are also, deep down, places of pilgrimage: from the nearly sacred, such as the Vietnam Memorial in Washington, D.C., and the Dachau concentration camp outside Munich, to the completely secular like the Baseball Museum and Hall of Fame in Cooperstown, New York, or the Tokyo Disneyland.

Touristic travel is also associated with health. Many spa towns developed throughout Europe during the eighteenth century. Barbados's salubrious sea breezes made it a popular health destination in the nineteenth century and even earlier; in 1751 George Washington brought his half-brother Lawrence there hoping he would recuperate from tuberculosis (he died on the voyage home). Tourist destinations boasting hot springs, pure mountain air, and warm seas are still linked to health and recuperation—both physical and mental. When we think about tourism, we tend to forget this long history. The earliest form of tourism most of us are familiar with is the "Grand Tour" of the seventeenth and eighteenth centuries when young English elites, and some Americans, polished their education by exposing themselves to European architecture, art, geography, history, and culture. Visits to Paris and major Italian cities such as Florence, Venice, Naples, and Rome were especially important. Guidebooks and a fledgling tourism industry developed to meet the needs of these visiting elites and their tutors as they traveled across Europe.

The development of large-scale or mass tourism, however, only became possible with improvements in transportation. Many tourism destinations were promoted by railways and shipping companies in cooperation with private entrepreneurs. Thomas Cook, a British temperance worker turned entrepreneur, used the railways and, later, steamships to take people on guided excursions first within England and later to the Continent and beyond (e.g., up the Nile and across the Holy Land). After the success of his first organized railway temperance excursion between Leicester and Loughborough in 1841, he realized people's fascination with railway travel and their need for a specialist agent who could organize complex journeys that covered several railway lines and issued tickets at favorable rates (Brendon 1991). This led to the formation of a travel agency that still bears his name. Tourism through the Inland Passage to southeastern Alaska was instigated by steamship companies in the late 1800s to fill their ships during the summer. Totem poles made by Northwest Coast natives were restored and new ones commissioned in order to market the region to tourists; the poles were positioned along railway lines and ferry routes and at ferry terminals to evoke the region's exotic Indian heritage and wildness (Jonaitis 1999). With the rise of jet travel in the 1960s (which dramatically cut travel times) and the increased use of private automobiles in North America and Europe—aided by higher salaries and more generous vacation times—both international and domestic tourism flourished. The age of mass tourism had begun.

The Study of Tourism

Tourism began to receive sustained academic attention from social scientists in the 1970s (Cohen 1974, 1979; MacCannell 1973, 1976; Smith 1978), following the development of mass tourism. But many academics at first appeared to regard the study of tourism as barely respectable.[11] One reason may be that tourism is basically about relaxation and play; it stands in marked contrast to work and therefore it seemed frivolous and not worthy of serious study. Sport as a subject of inquiry suffered from the same stigma and marginalization. (Furthermore, both tourism and sport are largely of the body, not of the mind and intellect.) In the case of tourism, there may also have been reluctance on the part of anthropologists to acknowledge that the "exotic" people they studied were also visited by other outsiders called "tourists." Fieldwork in a foreign culture is a rigorous rite of passage into anthropological "adulthood," and anthropologists may not have wished to acknowledge the extent of their group's outside contact or their own similarities to tourists (Crick 1995). Fredrick Errington and Deborah Gewertz (1989) discuss some similarities, but also the fundamental differences, between tourists and anthropologists.

In anthropology, research on tourism began to flourish at the same time a major paradigm shift was taking place (Gupta and Ferguson 1997); that is, anthropologists ceased treating cultures as bounded in place and time, cut off from outside influences and change. They became more interested in processes and in the encounters that link people. Today, popular culture is disseminated globally by all sorts of media (e.g., Internet, television, film, cell phones) and has reached even the most remote peoples that anthropologists study. Tourism is an increasingly important influence in this transmission. While it is still possible to visit a H'mong village in the northern highlands of Vietnam, watch people dressed in hand-dyed indigo clothing plant rice in terraced fields that have been maintained for generations, and focus on how different and timeless it all seems, we know that the life of the H'mong is far from static. If we made the effort, we would soon learn that family members of the villagers we watch live as far away as Los Angeles and that the people working the fields are also involved in setting up a sustainable tourism project.[12]

Why tourism is worthy of serious study (e.g., its scale, scope, economic importance) should be clear from what has already been said. Another feature that makes it of particular interest to social scientists is the way it brings consumers (i.e., tourists) and producers (e.g., local providers, ethnic Others) into intimate contact with each other. In this regard, tourism is very different from most modern industries. Think about what it is like to be a tourist compared to being a consumer who buys groceries at the supermarket or a pair of jeans at the Gap. When we buy bananas or Levis, we seldom think about who produced them or where they came from. When we travel, in contrast, we meet and interact directly with the local people who make the products, services, and experiences we consume, and although we may not realize it, we probably also end up interacting with many of the people who produce the products we purchase at home. Increasingly, the things we buy at home are made by the people we visit abroad—workers in Vietnam, Thailand, the Philippines, Indonesia, China, and Mexico. As tourists, we experience their local economies, observe their standard of living, and develop at least some empathy and interest in their lives.

Research on tourism has focused on two themes: its origins and impacts (Stronza 2001).[13] When examining origins, the focus has been on the reasons people travel and what determines where they go. People travel for many reasons, including the desire for change or difference, the opportunity to relax on a cruise or experience the tactile pleasures of the beach, a craving for adventure by visiting distant and "exotic" peoples and locales, the wish to experience "wilderness" or pristine nature, an interest in history or culture, a search for meaning or for a renewed sense of identity, the desire for thrills and danger—from organized adventure tourism (e.g., white-water rafting, bungee-jumping) to visits to active war zones. A seldom-mentioned motivation to travel is the desire of parents to interest their children in the world around them; many families take trips to expose children to interesting and significant places—historical, cultural, and natural. People often combine tourism with other activities: study, business, and increasingly, medical procedures.

The factors that determine where people travel are similarly complex. Some sites have widely recognized historical, cultural, or natural importance—many of which UNESCO has validated as "world heritage" sites. Cost and safety are important considerations for most tourists. After that, much depends on how effectively local resorts, tour operators, and government tourism boards have marketed locations through brochures and Web sites. Destinations are advertised like any other "product" through photographs and language that create appealing images and fantasies. Tourists also have their own pre-established ideas about certain places. Many sites, such as Hard Rock cafés, are famous for being famous. What began in London in 1971 as a café decorated with Americana and rock 'n' roll memorabilia has become an international "brand" of restaurants, hotels, and casinos (now owned by the Seminole Tribe of Florida) visited by tourists in multiple locations.

Other sites become attractive based on associations created by literature and film. Prince Edward Island is a popular destination for Japanese tourists because it is the fictional home of Anne Shirley, the beloved heroine of Lucy Maude Montgomery's 1908 novel *Anne of Green Gables* (and a popular television miniseries). Anne's spunk and determination endeared her to the Japanese beginning in 1954 when the book was translated and introduced into the junior high curriculum. Tourists from all over the world still visit Anne Frank's house in Amsterdam, the World War II site made vividly real in her published diary. Similarly, tourists in Salzburg, Austria, still flock to take the *Sound of Music* tour nearly 50 years after the musical's release. *The DaVinci Code,* released in 2006, prompted a temporary partnership among British, French, and Scottish national tourism agencies that, in collaboration with SONY Pictures and the high-speed rail service Eurostar, developed a "Seek the Truth" tour program to promote tourism that offered tourists a chance to "follow in the footsteps" of the film's characters. The 2009 Oscar-winning *Slumdog Millionaire* spawned new interest in travel to India, especially Mumbai, but also renewed the ethical controversy about "slum" or "poverty tourism." Status considerations also play a role in where tourists decide to go: some destinations have more cachet than others within a tourist's home society. The reasons some places have greater status may be based on their associations with "high culture," celebrities, remoteness, expense, and a host of other factors. In 2009, Hungarian-born software developer and "space tourist" Charles Simonyi made his second visit to the International Space Station: "list price" for the trip—US$35 million.

Tourism's Economic Impact

The economic impact of tourism on a country (or region or locality) depends on many factors including the scale of tourism, the size of the country, the complexity of its economy, and who controls and profits from the industry. Tourism can contribute significantly to local economies by creating jobs both during the development phase and in hotels and related businesses once it is established. It also provides opportunities for local people to become independent entrepreneurs (e.g., starting a guesthouse, making souvenir crafts, serving as unofficial guides). George Gmelch (2003) examined tourism work in Barbados through oral histories and found that most people liked their jobs, although most did not intend to stay in them permanently. At the regional and national levels, tourism can also bring improved infrastructure and services that benefit the local population, including better roads, water, and electricity.

But not everyone benefits equally from tourism development. Many locals have no direct economic involvement in their area's tourism industry. The formal-sector jobs that are typically available in tourism (e.g., maids, waiters, gardeners, bartenders) are low paying and seasonal and provide little long-term security, benefits, or opportunity for advancement. Foreign employees or expatriates usually fill higher-paid managerial positions. In the Galapagos, most of the islands' tourism labor force is recruited from mainland Ecuador. These newcomers benefit more from tourism than do locals and now outnumber them, creating social tensions. The jobs that local people create for themselves in the informal sector of the tourist economy—such as unlicensed tour guides, "taxi" operators, and street vendors—are even less remunerative and secure than formal-sector jobs. Local elites generally benefit far more from tourism development than other citizens since they are far more likely to have the capital, connections, and know-how to take advantage of emerging opportunities (van den Berghe 1994; Smith 2004).

Most research on the impacts of tourism—whether by anthropologists, cultural geographers, sociologists, or activists—has, in fact, stressed the negative. Much of tourism's profits never reach destination countries due to the foreign ownership of tourism's key players. One study of "leakage" in Thailand estimated that 70 percent of all money spent by tourists left the country via foreign-owned tour operators, airlines, and hotels, and through the purchase of imported drinks and food.[14] Polly Pattullo (2005) estimates that the Caribbean as a whole loses from 70 to 90 percent of every dollar earned from tourism. All-inclusive resorts in developing countries that offer tourists a prepaid package of airfare, accommodation, entertainment, food, and other services pump even less money into the local economy; tourists have little reason to leave the resort since they have paid for everything in advance. Cruise ships, which are in essence floating all-inclusives, likewise contribute little to the local economy, and they are getting bigger and offering more onboard entertainment all the time. Royal Caribbean's *Oasis of the Seas,*

Informal sector entrepreneur, a Qalandar man, tries to profit from tourism at the expense of India's now threatened sloth bears. (Photo by Sharon Gmelch)

launched in 2009, has sixteen decks with 2,700 staterooms. It is divided into themed "neighborhoods" (e.g., "Boardwalk," "Youth Zone") and contains a putting green, two rock-climbing walls, a zip line, a carousel, and a fresh water pool (with synchronized swimming and diving performances in the evening), in addition to other resort amenities.

Infrastructure developments such as international airports and deep-water harbors that are built by governments to support tourism—often with loans from international organizations like the International Monetary Fund (IMF) and World Bank—siphon off money that could be used for other projects like schools and hospitals that would better serve the local population. They must also be maintained largely through local taxes. Moreover, when services like water or electricity are in short supply, priority is usually given to guaranteeing the tourists' comfort (and future business) instead of that of local people.

International airports, deep-water harbors, large-scale resorts, golf courses, and game parks and nature preserves often displace local people who may have been unwilling to move and have been unfairly compensated for their land and homes. Three percent of the island of Barbados is now devoted to golf courses used primarily by visitors; some of these also have attached gated communities that physically exclude the local population. Large tourism projects of this kind often remove important agricultural or grazing land and fishing grounds from use. Sally Ann Ness (2003) has documented the plight of the many Filipinos who were resettled in the 1990s to make room for the huge Samal Island Tourism Estate adjacent to Mindanao. The Philippine government projected the creation of thousands of jobs, but training programs fell far short of what had been promised to the local people, and the actual development of the huge complex has been repeatedly delayed and scaled back. Most relocated residents have no opportunities for jobs; have no access to their land, which they previously used for agriculture, or to fishing grounds; and have received few of the promised new services. As in this example, too often tourism's impact is asymmetrical.

Tourism and the Environment

Wherever the carrying capacity of the environment is exceeded by too many visitors or too much tourism development, the environment is damaged. Because tourists generally seek the most beautiful or unique environments to visit—often the most fragile—the local environment can be degraded easily. For example, each year 300,000 tourists wearing shoes and hiking boots—compared to 500 Inca in bare feet or sandals—visit Machu Picchu in Peru, trampling the trails and causing land slippage of .4 inches a month according to Japanese geologists. The number of tourists in the Galapagos has grown from 40,000 in 1990 to over 140,000 in 2006. The risk of introducing new invasive species they create is an even bigger threat to local biodiversity than their numbers. Diving boats and cruise ships often damage coral reefs. One study of the effects of a single cruise ship anchor dropped for just one day over a coral reef found that it destroyed an area half the size of a football field. Yosemite, one of America's most popular national parks, now has more than 30 miles of roads covering its small valley floor (seven miles by one mile) over which a million cars, trucks, and buses travel each year, adding noise, pollution, and congestion to other environmental damage.

Tourism depletes natural resources. It takes an especially heavy toll on local water supplies (i.e., for use in hotel laundries, showers, pools, landscaping, and golf courses). Tourists easily use twice as much water as do locals. One golf course in a tropical country like Thailand requires 1,500 kg of chemical fertilizers, pesticides, and herbicides a year and can use as much water as can 60,000 rural villagers. Similarly, the wood needed to support one trekker for one day in Nepal equals that used by a Nepalese family of five for a week (Gurung and De Coursey 1994). In the Annapurna area, the forest is being cut down at an estimated rate of 3 percent per year to build hotels, lodges, and furniture and to provide fuel for cooking, hot showers, and campfires. In the Caribbean, wetlands, mangroves, and beaches are destroyed for hotels, yacht harbors, deep-water harbors for cruise ships, and other tourism infrastructure. Their loss destroys fish, crustacean, and bird habitats and damages shorelines and offshore corals, often with serious consequences during hurricane season (Pattullo 2005).

Tourism creates pollution, often in surprising ways and places. Oxygen canisters, food containers, and other debris now litter Mount Everest. Trekking groups in Nepal leave fields of human excreta, toilet paper, and litter behind. Cruise ship passengers produce about 3.5 kilos of garbage per day, compared to .8 kilos for the residents of the Caribbean countries they visit. Some cruise lines still dump garbage and oil illegally at sea. Tourists account for 60 percent of air travel and of the ozone depleting substances that jets emit. Tour buses left idling in very hot or cold climates in order to keep the air conditioning or heat flowing for tourists' comfort exacerbate air pollution. As a result of the noise pollution caused by scenic helicopter flights, natural stillness can be found in only one-third of the Grand Canyon. So many visitors used snowmobiles in Yellowstone National Park in the winter of 2000 that researchers found that engine noise was heard fully 90 percent of the time at eight popular tourist sites, including Old Faithful geyser. Visual pollution occurs when tourist destinations are overbuilt or resorts are prominently situated on mountainsides and along coastlines, with only tourists' and not the locals' views in mind.

Ecotourism is an increasingly popular form of tourism. It refers to tourism in natural areas that contributes both to the conservation of the local environment and to an improvement in the lives of local people. According to Martha Honey (1999), true ecotourism has several characteristics: it is small-scale, has minimal environmental impact, promotes environmental awareness on the part of tourists and their local hosts, financially benefits the local community, respects local culture, and supports human rights and democratic aspirations. Not all tourism destinations or ventures that bill themselves as ecotourism, however, meet all these criteria. Many tourism operators use the "green" label as a form of niche marketing (just as some food merchandisers intentionally misuse the "natural" label).

"Alternative" tourism is similar to ecotourism in that it refers to tourism projects that are managed for the common good and place human and local ecological needs on a par with profits. Richard Butler (1992) offers a cautionary critique of alterative tourism, however, pointing out that it is not always or in all ways better than more conventional mass tourism. For example, even small-scale alternative tourism projects can result in fairly dramatic long-term change. Such projects usually place tourists and locals in more intense contact than mass tourism does, and their interactions usually occur in more sensitive areas such as the home and village versus the beach and hotel lobby. Alternative tourists usually visit more fragile areas, placing pressure on vulnerable resources. Such projects often take place the year round and thus can have a greater impact on local people and the environment than seasonal mass tourism even though the number of tourists involved is smaller. Although alternative tourists tend to stay in an area longer, they spend less money than do mass tourists. Moreover, there is a limited market for alternative tourism, and visitors are not likely to return to the same destinations as mass tourists often do. Butler concludes that alternative tourism should be considered only as a complement to mass tourism; it can never replace it. Furthermore, it must be carefully planned and controlled and should be regarded only as one way to supplement the incomes of rural people in marginal areas.

Community-based tourism and "responsible" tourism are newer initiatives that support ecotourism and alternative tourism principles as well as the concept of sustainable development (cf. Smith and Brent 2001). Community-based tourism refers to tourism ventures that local community groups—including indigenous groups—manage and operate so that the income earned from tourism directly benefits community members, reinforces their cultural identity, and provides opportunities for sustainable development. Responsible tourism shifts the burden and ethical responsibility to tourists by encouraging individual travelers to examine the reasons they plan to travel and to take personal responsibility for minimizing the negative impact they have if they decide to go (McLaren 1998; Pattullo and Minelli 2006). Increasingly, tourists are involving themselves in philanthropic projects that benefit the places they visit; many of these have conservation or environmental goals.

The Social and Cultural Impact

Relatively little research has examined the effect travel has on tourists. Most research, instead, has concentrated on its impact on people living in the places tourists visit. Tourism's social and cultural impacts are diverse and not always easily separated from the effect of other outside influences. Clearly, when too many tourists visit a destination, especially if they do so year-round and are not confined to certain areas (e.g., the beach), local people can feel overwhelmed. Carrying capacity is about more than just the physical environment; it also has psychological and social dimensions for both locals and visitors. Locals in many destinations would prefer to cater to elite rather than mass tourists because they can make as much money without the hassles of large numbers. Once tourists feel that the quality of their experiences has deteriorated as a result of overcrowding or locals' less than hospitable attitudes toward them, they can vote with their feet—often with serious economic consequences for the tourism-dependent populations they leave behind.

Local people react to tourists in many ways, not only in response to their numbers and behavior, but also based on preconceived ideas about them. It is worth remembering that the images and stereotypes locals have of tourists can be as distorted or ill informed as the tourists' views of them. After all, many ideas people acquire about others come from television and film. As I sat in a small rural pub in Ireland many years ago, I wondered what the somber farmers around me—all wearing dark work suits and mud-covered Wellington boots—were thinking about Americans as they watched *Dallas*, then a popular prime-time television series, with its depictions of ostentatious wealth, ruthless backstabbing, and casual sex.

Most encounters between tourists and local people are short-lived and instrumental, usually involving the sale of a commodity or service or an exchange of information. (Local guides are an important exception.) How

Indian vendor eyes photographer while a tourist contemplates a purchase. (Photo by George Gmelch)

locals react to the tourists they interact with has a lot to do with their own role in the tourism industry. Business people in cities and towns, for example, tend to dislike backpackers because they spend so little money compared to other tourists, while rural villagers may not mind. The nature of tourist–local exchanges, however, is not all predicated on money. Some locals actively seek engagement with tourists in order to practice their language skills or simply because they are curious.

So-Min Cheong and Marc Miller (2004) have pointed out the power local tourism brokers and agents have to control what tourists do. In a very real sense, tourists—even though they come from powerful countries and usually have more wealth than most locals—as visitors in a foreign country are relatively powerless. When they wander into more private or "backstage" areas, local people often attempt to elude them. Jeremy Boissevain (1996, 2004) has discussed some of the common strategies locals use, including hiding, fencing their property, keeping group or community events secret, and reacting aggressively as well as organizing protests against tourism. The Suri of Ethiopia are often offended by tourists' behavior and treat them aggressively—taking their cameras, demanding payment, and sometimes threatening them physically (Abbink 2000). Other groups like the Pueblo Indians (Sweet 1991) use humor, management strategies, and regulations (that are enforceable on their reservation with the help of Native police) to keep tourists in line and preserve their privacy.

In many parts of the world, tourists increasingly confront signs that explain local customs and lay out the rules for visiting. Examples include being told to remove one's shoes, not to give candy to children, and not to

Rules for tourists at a community-based tourism project near Sa Pa, Vietnam. (Photo by Sharon Gmelch)

photograph sacred objects. Ads in newspapers produced for tourists in Barbados have tried clever jingles: "We value your business and we know that you're cool, but please leave exposed tummies around the pool" (Wirthlin 2000). Increasingly, organizations and ethnic minority populations are publishing tourism guidelines that they distribute to visitors and post on their Web sites. The Himalayan Tourist Code, for example, was developed by Nepalese tour operators and nongovernmental organizations (NGOs) working with the British-based NGO, Tourism Concern. Among other things, tourists are told to ask permission before taking photographs, to respect local etiquette by not wearing revealing clothing or kissing in public, and to never touch religious objects. The Kuna Indians of Panama's San Blas islands have drawn up a comprehensive "Statute on Tourism in Kuna Yala," which attempts to ensure Kuna control of tourism development and to define their own terms for interaction with outsiders (Snow 2001).

Tourism has been blamed for introducing or exacerbating many social ills: everything from drugs, crime, and prostitution to bad language, bad manners, and bad art.[15] In fairness, however, it is difficult to disentangle the social effects of tourism from other global influences, notably the spread of Western popular culture and consumer values through largely American-owned and produced media (e.g., satellite television, films, music videos, the Web). Many researchers have discussed tourism's "demonstration effect"—its tendency to create in local people of modest means, the desire to have the same lifestyle and belongings that tourists have. By raising the expectations of people in less-developed nations who do not yet have the resource base or opportunities to acquire what wealthy visitors possess, tourism can contribute to feelings of deprivation and a search for ways to "get rich quick"—activities like street crime, drug dealing, hustling, and gambling. The term "jineterismo" was coined in Cuba to describe those who try to latch onto tourism dollars: beggars, freelance tour guides, hustlers, and drug dealers. Barbadian police report that the first four drug arrests on the island (for marijuana) occurred in 1971, just as mass tourism was getting underway; three of the four people arrested were tourists (Gmelch and Gmelch 2001[1997]). Today, in many parts of the world, drug traffickers use tourism's infrastructure—planes, ships, casinos, offshore banks, and hotels—to transport, launder, and invest drug money.

Some tourists' sexual taste for "exotic" others has fueled a demand for young women and men and children in the developing countries tourists visit, drawing local people into prostitution (Brennan 2002). Specialized tour operators in the tourists' home countries and abroad offer package tours for the purpose of exploiting erotic nightlife. Local governments are not innocent here; some, like Thailand, have marketed their population's beauty and availability.[16] Child prostitution is a growing problem in many tourist destinations. Bangkok-based End Child Prostitution in Asian Tourism (ECPAT) estimates that a million children are involved. According to the World Tourism Organization (WTO), a study of 100 schoolchildren in Kalutara, Sri

Lanka, found that 86 had their first sexual experience at ages 12 and 13, the majority with foreign tourists. Recent legislation in the United States, Germany, Britain, Sweden, and other countries has made it a crime to travel abroad for the purposes of having sex with a minor, and tourists who do so have been prosecuted.

Some forms of sex tourism are arguably less exploitative then others, as when young Japanese and Western women travel abroad and explore their sexuality with men in the host society (Kelsky 1996). Much depends on the circumstances—the extent to which local people have real alternatives and give informed consent—and on the nature of the inequality (e.g., age, gender, economic) that exists within the relationship. On tourist beaches in many countries, local men actively seek out sexual partners from among tourist women who may have had no prior intention of having an "affair" or "romantic fling" while on vacation. In some situations, they manipulate racial stereotypes to their advantage and play on the tourist's desire not to appear prejudiced (Gmelch and Gmelch 2001[1997]).

To attract tourists, destinations have to differentiate themselves from other places. One way they do so is to market local heritage and culture and any visible cultural diversity that exists. New Orleans, for example, markets its African American–influenced musical heritage (Atkinson 2004). Barbadian businesses use images of dread-locked, spliff-smoking Rastafarians on T-shirts and other tourist goods to highlight and create a "no worries," feel-good image for the island. Vietnam highlights its 53 ethnic minorities in promotional literature to give it added exotic appeal, and so do the many guidebooks that market the country: "To see them [the H'mong] in their traditional style of dress—layers of indigo-dyed, brilliantly embroidered cotton; elaborate headdresses; and silver adornments—is to feel yourself caught in a time warp," states a recent Fodor guide (Kaufman 2001:114). If the groups in question are still somewhat isolated; have interesting architecture, clothing, crafts, or art; maintain "exotic" traditions such as tattooing or lip plates; or practice dramatic courtship, initiation, marriage, or funeral rituals, so much the better.

When local people become the objects of the "tourist gaze" (Urry 1990) and are watched and photographed while doing even the most mundane things, their lives are dramatically altered. The "love market" of Sa Pa in northern Vietnam provides one example; historically a Red Dao tradition, the market draws ethnic minority people from within a two-day walk of Sa Pa. They come to sell their wares, buy what they need, socialize, and for some, seek marriage partners. Courting couples who meet at the market serenade each other with impromptu and highly personalized songs that tell of their attraction for the other person, their domestic abilities, and strong work ethic. Today, the market is losing its courtship function as couples feel too much on display and now meet elsewhere in order to avoid tourists (Pham et al. 1999). Conversely, some people capitalize on the love market's fame, volunteering to perform their songs for tourists in exchange for money.

Red Dao women, Vietnam. (Photo by Sharon Gmelch)

When local rituals and celebrations are marketed as tourist "spectacles" by local entrepreneurs or government tourism boards they can lose their importance to local people. When the Chambri of Papua New Guinea opened their initiation ceremony to tourists, they unwittingly turned it into a performance that was losing its meaning for initiates (Errington and Gewertz 1989). Davydd Greenwood (2004) has reassessed some of the conclusions he drew in a much-cited 1977 work on the impact of tourism on the *alarde* celebration in Hondarribia, Spain. The ceremony reenacts the town's historic victory over the French in 1638 and reinforces its Basque identity and solidarity in a richly symbolic ceremony that once involved most of the population. After it was marketed to tourists by municipal authorities, local people's participation declined dramatically. Today, however, it has acquired a new political purpose and value.

Much has been written about the impact of tourism on cultural authenticity and the fact that societies frequently "stage" and "manufacture" culture for tourists. Edward M. Bruner (2001) discusses the ways in which American popular culture and global media influence Maasai performances for tourists. New dances, songs, and festivals are created all the time to provide tourists with entertaining "cultural" or "folkloric" performances. A state-supported dance troupe entertained my students and me in a mountain village in Vietnam in 2002, performing "traditional" folk songs and dances that had just been created and that they were performing for the first time. Similarly, the

Barbados Tourism Board created "Crop Over" (referring to the end of the sugarcane harvest) in 1974 as a national celebration to promote tourism in the slack summer season. While it is true that small-scale celebrations had taken place in the past on individual plantations at the end of the harvest, this was an entirely new and lavish festival modeled after Carnival in Trinidad. The medieval pilgrimage to Santiago de Compostella, the reputed burial place of the Apostle James, was revived in modern times by the Catholic Church, Spanish Tourism Board, and Council of Europe, which adopted it as a European Heritage Trail. Recently, a controversy broke out in Romania over a proposed Dracula theme park at Sighisoara, the medieval Transylvanian town that was home to the mid-fifteenth-century historical Vlad Dracul (not the mythical Dracula that Bram Stoker created in 1897). The debate was whether to mangle Romanian history (and seriously disrupt the local environment to provide needed tourism facilities) by promoting the fictional vampire or to leave things as they were and lose a moneymaking venture.

Terms like "authentic" and "traditional" are frequently used with reference to the aspects of culture marketed to tourists. Most tourists like to think that what they are seeing is "real" in the sense of being old and an internally generated part of local culture. The hula, for example, was once a sacred temple dance that celebrated the procreative powers of the Hawai'ian chiefly class. Today, it has been thoroughly co-opted by and commodified for tourism and is performed in entirely secular contexts (Desmond 1999). Yet, to tourists it is a signifier of authentic Hawai'ian culture—a real and unmediated dance that is "a genuine performance of an age-old tradition rather than something merely undertaken for the tourist" (Urry 2001:5). Some tourists are very concerned with authenticity. I have listened as visitors to the Sitka National Historic Park in southeastern Alaska question the Tlingit crafters who work there about the "authenticity" of the materials they use and the art they create—telling the silversmith that his grandfather could not possibly have used the metal carving tools he uses today and telling the weaver that her ancestors could not have possessed the colored glass beads she works with. Western tourists often regard any change toward the "modern" or contemporary—whether it occurs among ethnic minorities in their own society or in the less-developed countries they visit abroad—as negative. As MacCannell (1999) has pointed out, however, authenticity exists whenever people have significant control over their lives and play an active role in determining what changes occur in their society. He provocatively asks which is more real or "authentic": is it the town that decides on its own to tear down historic buildings to build a golf course for tourists or the town that is prevented by the government from making any changes in order to artificially preserve its ancient townscape? Traditions and culture are constantly reworked and reinterpreted to fit the needs and reality of each generation. Tourism is now part of that reality in most parts of the world.

Of course, not all tourists care about tradition or authenticity. Many are perfectly happy with completely artificial environments and activities as long as they are clean and entertaining. Some prefer simulations like ethnic theme parks, living museums, and other reconstructions to the real thing. I was shocked at first when I overheard a middle-aged tourist tell her husband after stepping off the small submarine that had just taken us on a 100-foot dive over Barbados's outer reefs: "Sure, it was good. But the submarine at Disneyland was better." She preferred an artificial reef, fake fish, and a mock submarine that runs on a circular track in a few feet of water to the real thing. Some people actually seek out inauthenticity—the more glaring and kitschy, the better. Las Vegas immediately comes to my mind (although many could argue that it is "authentically" American), but so do the roadside attractions that I call "folk tourism" like Carhenge in Nebraska—an imitation Stonehenge constructed out of up-ended cars. As suggested earlier, local peoples often don't care whether or not their performances are authentic, that is, old and internally generated. The Balinese, for example, often incorporate touristic performances into their culture; the "frog dance," created for tourists in the 1970s, is today performed at Balinese weddings (Bruner 1996). Similarly, Barbadians have fully embraced the "Crop Over" festival.

Tourism has wide-ranging ramifications and is an important agent of globalization as well as an adjunct of other global processes (e.g., combining tourism with business or seeking cheaper medical treatment abroad). However, in contrast to the popular understanding of globalization as a process that eliminates differences between cultures, tourism can have the opposite effect. Governments and the tourism industry's many agents work hard to highlight, if not create, local differences by aggressively re-imaging, reconstituting, and appropriating heritage, culture, and place in order to present and emphasize a location's uniqueness and to distinguish it from other possible tourist destinations (Sofield 2001). Thus, despite the uniformity that does occur as a result of applying international standards in accommodations, travel arrangements, and service, tourism does not necessarily destroy cultural differences. It also offers opportunities that many local people want.

Source: Written expressly for *Tourists and Tourism*.

Notes

[1] I co-directed an anthropology field school for Union College undergraduates every other year between 1983 and 2008 with my colleague, George Gmelch. For most of these years, we ran the program in Barbados before moving it to Tasmania.

[2] According to World Tourism Organization (WTO) figures, Barbados in 2002 received 497,899 "stopover" tourists (–1.8 percent from the previous year) and 529,319 cruise ship passengers (up 0.3 percent).

[3] The exception might be the small number of tourists who are regular visitors to the island and have established long-term friendships with local people.

[4] Gross domestic product is the market value of all goods and services a country produces in a year. It is the standard measure of the overall size of an economy. Global GDP averages the gross domestic product of all countries. According to the World Travel and Tourism Council

(WTTC), the travel and tourism industry generates US$4,495 billion in economic activity and provides 207,062,000 jobs globally.

[5] These are World Bank figures for 2000. The WTO has adopted global standards for measuring the economic impact of tourism. This measure is referred to as the "tourism satellite account." It calculates tourism's contribution to a country's GDP and balance of payments, how many jobs it creates, and how much capital investment and tax revenue it generates.

[6] See Vision 2020, a WTO publication (http://pub.unwto.org/WebRoot/Store/Shops/Infoshop/Products/1243/1243-1.pdf).

[7] Among the most developed nations (MDCs), only the United States and the United Kingdom will have population increases over the next 50 years; the rest will decline. As Smith and Brent (2001) also point out, virtually all industrial nations, including China, now have adopted a maximum 40-hour workweek, encouraging more leisure time. The electronic technology that has created jobs and prosperity in Asia, the United States, and Europe also provides more discretionary income. Increasingly, too, travel is recognized as a human right, which encourages still more travel.

[8] The figures for Barbados include both land-based tourists and those who visit the island abroad cruise ships.

[9] Valene Smith defined the tourist as "a temporarily leisured person who voluntarily visits a place away from home for the purpose of experiencing a change" (1989:1).

[10] Liminoid situations are those in which people's everyday obligations are suspended and a relatively unconstrained "communitas" or social togetherness is encouraged. Travel—whether for tourism or pilgrimage—creates a situation of relative anonymity and freedom from collective scrutiny during which the normal social conventions under which people live are relaxed (Turner and Turner 1978).

[11] Some of these earlier studies include Mitford 1959; Nuñez 1963; Forster 1964; and Boorstin 1966 (cited in Cohen 1984).

[12] My students and I participated in such a sustainable tourism project in the fall of 2002 in the H'mong village of Sin Chai. It was introduced to the village and coordinated by International Union for the Conservation of Nature (IUCN), an NGO working out of Hanoi. We were the third small group of tourists to arrive in the village in which five families had opened their homes to two or three overnight guests. Other activities included tours through the village, a cultural performance, personal exchanges in which tourists and local people teach each other some language or clean up trash together, and guided nature hikes up Mount Fansipan (also spelled Phanxipan).

[13] Cohen's (1984) review article of the sociology of tourism identified eight conceptual approaches to tourism that largely hold true today. Research has looked at tourism as: (1) commercialized hospitality, (2) democratized travel, (3) a modern leisure activity, (4) a modern form of pilgrimage, (5) an expression of culturally specific meanings on the part of tourists from different backgrounds, (6) an acculturative process, (7) a type of ethnic relations, and (8) a form of neocolonialism.

[14] Thai Institute for Development and Administration, Bangkok, 1990. Quoted in World Development Movement Web site: www.wdm.org.uk/resources/reports/climate/planetruths27092008.pdf.

[15] Tourism has different impacts on the arts. It is blamed in many parts of the world for causing a deterioration in local crafts and arts by encouraging simplifications (e.g., in design and materials) in order to produce items more quickly and bastardized styles and performances (like the limbo) to appeal to tourist tastes. But tourism can also be credited with creating a demand for quality visual arts and for supporting the performing arts by providing more venues and work for local dancers, singers, and musicians.

[16] Tourism cannot be blamed for the introduction of prostitution in most countries, although it clearly increases the demand and changes its form. Jones (1982), in a study of Bali, found that most customers at brothels were Balinese and other Indonesians, while those who fre-

quented women on the beach and call girls were tourists. He found that the physical relations prostitutes had with tourists also differed from those they had with locals: with tourists, most of whom were Western, there was more foreplay, more mouth-to-mouth kissing, and more attention to the breasts as an erotic zone.

References

Abbink, Jon G. 2000. "Tourism and Its Discontents: Suri–Tourist Encounters in Southern Ethiopia." *Social Anthropology* 8(1):1–17.

Atkinson, Connie Zeanah. 2004. "Whose New Orleans? Music's Place in the Packaging of New Orleans for Tourism," in *Tourists and Tourism,* 1st ed., ed. Sharon Bohn Gmelch, pp. 171–182, Long Grove, IL: Waveland Press.

Boissevain, Jeremy. 1996. "Introduction," in *Coping with Tourists: European Reactions to Mass Tourism,* ed. J. Boissevain, pp. 1–26. Oxford: Berghahn Books.

———. 2004. "Coping with Mass Cultural Tourism: Structure and Strategies," in *Tourists and Tourism,* 1st ed., ed. Sharon Bohn Gmelch, pp. 253–266. Long Grove, IL: Waveland Press.

Brennan, Denise. 2002. "Globalization, Women's Labor, and Men's Pleasure: Sex Tourism in Sosúa, the Dominican Republic," in *Urban Life: Readings in the Anthropology of the City,* 4th ed., ed. George Gmelch and Walter Zenner. Long Grove, IL: Waveland Press.

Brendon, Piers. 1991. *Thomas Cook: 150 Years of Popular Tourism.* London: Secker & Warburg.

Bruner, Edward M. 1996. "Tourism in the Balinese Borderzone," in *Displacement, Diaspora, and Geographies of Identity,* ed. Smadar Lavie and Ted Swedenburg. Durham, NC: Duke University Press.

———. 2001. "The Maasai and the Lion King: Authenticity, Nationalism, and Globalization in African Tourism," *American Ethnologist* 28(4):881–908.

Butler, Richard. 1992. "Alternative Tourism: The Thin Edge of the Wedge," in *Tourism Alternatives: Potentials and Problems in the Development of Tourism,* ed. Valene Smith, pp. 31–46. Philadelphia: University of Pennsylvania Press.

Cheong, So-Min and Marc Miller. 2004. "Power Dynamics in Tourism: A Foucauldian Approach," in *Tourists and Tourism,* 1st ed., ed. Sharon Bohn Gmelch, pp. 239–252. Long Grove, IL: Waveland Press.

Crick, Malcolm. 1995. "The Anthropologist as Tourist: An Identity in Question," in *International Tourism,* ed. Marie-Françoise LaFant, John Allock, and Edward M. Bruner, pp. 205–223. London: Sage.

Cohen, Erik. 1974. "Who Is a Tourist?: A Conceptual Clarification." *Sociological Review* 22(4):527–255.

———. 1979. "A Phenomenology of Tourist Experiences." *Sociology* 13:179–201.

———. 1984. "The Sociology of Tourism: Approaches, Issues, and Findings." *American Review of Sociology* 10:373–392.

Desmond, Jane. 1999. *Staging Tourism: Bodies on Display from Waikiki to Sea World.* Chicago: University of Chicago Press.

Errington, Frederick, and Deborah Gewertz. 1989. "Tourism and Anthropology in a Post-Modern World." *Oceana* 60:37–54.

Gmelch, George. 2003. *Behind the Smile: The Working Lives of Caribbean Tourism.* Bloomington: Indiana University Press.

Gmelch, George, and Sharon Bohn Gmelch. 2001[1997]. *The Parish Behind God's Back: The Changing Culture of Rural Barbados.* Long Grove, IL: Waveland Press.

Greenwood, Davydd. 2004. "Culture by the Pound: An Anthropological Perspective on Tourism and Cultural Commoditization," in *Tourists and Tourism,* 1st ed., ed. Sharon Bohn Gmelch, pp. 359–371, Long Grove, IL: Waveland Press.

Gupta, Akhil, and James Ferguson. 1997. *Culture, Power, Place: Explorations in Critical Anthropology*. Durham, NC: Duke University Press.

Gurung, Chandra and Maureen De Coursey. 1994. "The Annapurna Conservation Area Project: A Pioneering Example of Sustainable Tourism?" in *Ecotourism: A Sustainable Option?*, ed. Erlet Carter and Gwen Lowman, pp. 177-94, New York: John Wiley and Sons.

Honey, Martha. 1999. *Ecotourism and Sustainable Development: Who Owns Paradise?* Washington, DC: Island Press.

Jonaitis, Aldona. 1999. "Northwest Coast Totem Poles," in *Unpacking Culture: Art and Commodity in Colonial and Postcolonial Worlds*, ed. R. Phillips and C. Steiner, pp. 104–21. Berkeley: University of California Press.

Jones, David. 1982. "Prostitution and Tourism," in *The Impact of Tourism*, ed. F. Rajotte Pacific. Trent University, Canada: Development in the Environmental and Resource Studies Programme.

Kaufman, Deborah. 2001. *Vietnam: Completely Updated Where to Stay, Eat, and Explore: Smart Travel Tips from A to Z*. New York: Fodor's Travel Publications.

Kelsky, Karen. 1996. "Flirting with the Foreign: Interracial Sex in Japan's 'International' Age," in *Global/Local: Cultural Production in the Transnational Imaginary*, ed. Rob Wilson and Wimal Dissanayake, pp. 173–192. Durham, NC: Duke University Press.

MacCannell, Dean. 1973. "Staged Authenticity: Arrangements of Social Space in Tourist Settings." *American Journal of Sociology* 79(3):580–603.

———. 1976. *The Tourist: A New Theory of the Leisure Class*, New York: Schocken Books.

McLaren, Deborah. 1998. *Rethinking Tourism and Ecotravel*. West Hartford, CT: Kumarian Press.

Medea, Benjamin. 1998. "Chasing the Good Life." *New Internationalist* 301:26.

Ness, Sally Ann. 2003. *Where Asia Smiles: An Ethnography of Philippine Tourism*. Philadelphia: University of Pennsylvania Press.

Pattullo, Polly. 2005. *Last Resorts: The Cost of Tourism in the Caribbean*. London: Tourism Concern/Earthscan.

Pattullo, Polly and Orely Minelli. 2006. *The Ethical Travel Guide*. London: Tourism Concern/Earthscan.

Pham Thi Mong Hoa, Lam Thi Mai Lan, and Annalisa Koeman. 1999. *The Impact of Tourism on Ethnic Minority Inhabitants of Sa Pa District, Lao Cai: Their Participation in and Attitudes toward Tourism*. Hanoi, Vietnam: International Union for Conservation of Nature.

Sofield, T. H. B. 2001. "Globalization, Tourism and Culture in South East Asia," in *Interconnected Worlds: Tourism in Southeast Asia*, ed. Cheok Teo, Chang Chin, Chuang Tou, and K. C. Ho, pp.103–120. London: Butterworth Heinemann.

Smith, M. Estellie. 2004. "The Role of the Elite in the Development of Tourism," in *Tourists and Tourism*, 1st ed., ed. Sharon Bohn Gmelch, pp. 359–371, Long Grove, IL: Waveland Press.

Smith, Valene, ed. 1978. *Hosts and Guests: The Anthropology of Tourism*. London: Blackwell.

Smith, Valene, and Maryann Brent. 2001. *Hosts and Guests Revisited: Tourism Issues of the 21st Century*. New York: Cognizant Communications.

Snow, Stephen. 2001. "The Kuna General Congress and the Statute on Tourism." *Cultural Survival Quarterly* Winter: 17–20.

Stronza, Amanda. 2001. "Anthropology of Tourism: Forging New Ground for Ecotourism and Other Alternatives." *Annual Review of Anthropology* 30:261–83.

Sweet, Jill D. 1991. "'Let 'Em Loose': Pueblo Indian Management of Tourism." *American Indian Culture and Research Journal* 15(4):59–74.

Turner, Victor, and Edith Turner. 1978. *Images and Pilgrimage in Christian Culture*. New York: Columbia University Press.

Urry, John. 1990. *The Tourist Gaze: Leisure and Travel in Contemporary Societies*. London: Sage.

———. 1995. *Consuming Places*. London: Routledge.

———. 2001. "Globalizing the Tourist Gaze." Department of Sociology, Lancaster University at www.comp.lancs.ac.ek/sociology/soc079ju.html.

van den Berghe, Pierre. 1994. *The Quest for the Other: Ethnic Tourism in San Cristobal, Mexico*. Seattle: University of Washington Press.

Waterhouse, Keith. 1989. *Theory and Practice of Travel*. London: Hodder & Stoughton.

Wirthlin, Karin. 2000. Tourism and Barbados: An Examination of Local Perspectives. Masters Thesis, Colorado State University.

2

Secular Ritual: A General Theory of Tourism

Nelson H. H. Graburn

Tourism, defined by the sentence "a tourist is a temporarily leisured person who voluntarily visits a place away from home for the purpose of experiencing a change" (Smith 1989:1), may not exist universally, but in many ways it is functionally and symbolically equivalent to other institutions—calendrical festivals, holy days, sports tournaments that humans use to embellish and add meaning to their lives. In its special aspect—travel—tourism has its antecedents in other seemingly more serious institutions such as medieval student travel, the Crusades, and European and Asian pilgrimages.

It is my contention that tourism is best understood as a *kind of ritual*, one in which the special occasions of leisure and travel stand in opposition to everyday life at home and work. This general theory applies to all forms of tourism. Therefore, we have to understand the nature of tourist travel and experience in terms of the *contrasts* between the special period of life spent in tourist travel and the more ordinary parts of life spent at home while working. Tourism experiences are meaningful because of their difference from the ordinary and they reflect the home life from which the tourists stem. Thus, any one kind of tourist experience (e.g., a week in Paris) can mean something very different in the life of tourists from, for example, urban New York, metropolitan Tokyo, or rural California. Indeed, for some people a week in Paris would be too ordinary and boring, whereas for other people, from very

25

different social backgrounds, it might be too daunting and exciting and they would never undertake such a vacation. Thus, we can see that the tourists' gender, class, occupation, and life stage are all significant in determining where tourists choose to go and what they think of the experience when they have been there.

Tourism: Rituals of Reversal

The ritual theory of tourism proposes that the motivations and compensations of tourism involve "push" and "pull" factors. Tourists leave home because there is something that they want to get away from, and they choose to visit a particular place because they believe that they will experience something positive there that they cannot easily experience at home. This kind of explanation involves the "ritual reversal" or "ritual inversion" of some aspects of life. Simple examples would include the winter migrations of eastern Canadians to the Caribbean and of Scandinavians to the Mediterranean, when these northerners seek some warmth away from home, or when lower-middle-class Californians go to large hotels in Las Vegas or Reno at any time of the year and "live it up" by occupying large, well-appointed rooms and being served lavish meals (Gottlieb 1982). Middle-class Japanese who vacation in the hotels of Southeast Asia in the wintertime seeks both touristic goals: seasonal warmth and a luxurious style of life (Beer 1993)—inversions of their cramped lives in cold Tokyo.

The felt needs of tourists, the things that they look for and forward to in their travels, are never the complete opposites of their home class position and lifestyle. For instance, erudite people don't want to become ignorant, although they may want a relaxing break, and good athletes don't try to become physically incompetent. The felt needs are indeed the product of, or an inherent part of, the values of the home class and lifestyle. Scandinavians and Canadians value sunshine and warmth; American college professors value culture and history and may seek more of it on their vacations; many obese people value thinness and may visit a special reducing establishment; and gourmets may partake of simple foods in their travels, but never bad foods—not willingly! So the temporary reversal sought is rarely an antithesis of their values but is a product of their cultural background, and the promised reward is supposed to satisfy the need in a direction of further enhancement of these values, not turn the tourist into an entirely different kind of person.

The claim that tourism is a secular ritual, embracing goals or activities that have replaced the religious or supernatural experiences of other societies, was strongly suggested by a recent television advertisement in the San Francisco Bay area (1997). It showed exciting scenes of young, fit people diving off cliffs into the sea, skiing down steep slopes, bungee jumping, and so on. At the end of these came a voice-over, "If you want a religious experience, why don't you try a religious experience!" as the scene moved to a shot of the Protestant evangelist the Reverend Billy Graham, who was about to bring his crusade to the area.

Tourism, Ritual, and Time

Tourism in the modal sense emphasized here is but one of a range of choices or styles of recreation or vacation. All of these ritualized breaks in routine define and relieve the ordinary. There is a long tradition in anthropology of the examination of these special events and institutions as markers of the passage of time. Vacations involving travel (i.e., tourism) are the modern equivalent for secular societies to the annual and lifelong sequences of festivals and pilgrimages found in more traditional, God-fearing societies. Fundamental is the contrast between the ordinary/compulsory work state spent "at home" and the extraordinary/voluntary metaphorically "sacred" experience away from home.

The stream of alternating contrasts provides the meaningful events that mark the passage of time. English anthropologist Edmund Leach (1961) suggested that celebratory events were the way in which people without clocks and calendars used to measure the passage of time, implying that those who have scientific calendars and other tacit reminders such as newspapers, TV, and radio rely only on the numerical calendar. I believe that even "scientific, secular" Westerners gain greater meaning from the personal rather than the numeric in life. We are more satisfied and better recall loaded symbols marking the passage of time: for example, "that was the year we went to Rome" or "that was the summer our dog drowned at Brighton Beach" rather than "that was 1988," because the former identify the nonordinary, festive or sorrowful, personal events.

Our two lives—the sacred/nonordinary and the profane/workaday/at-home—customarily alternate for ordinary people and are marked by rituals or ceremonies as should be beginnings and ends of lives. For instance, after a period of work we celebrate with TGIF (Thank Goodness Its Friday), "happy hours," and going-away parties, to anticipate the future state and to give thanks for the end of the mundane. The passing of each year is marked by the annual vacation (or by Christmas or a birthday); something would be wrong with a year in which these events didn't occur, as though we had been cheated of time! These repetitive events mark the cyclical passage of time just as in traditional Christian societies weeks would be marked by Sundays and churchgoing and the year would be marked by Easter, Harvest Festival, Advent, Christmas, and so on. These rituals have been called rites of increase or rites of intensification in agricultural or forager societies (Durkheim 1912), but are generally better thought of as *annual cycle rites*. The types of holidays and tourism that fill these may be family occasions at home, but when they involve travel (e.g., weekends spent skiing or fishing, weeks spent on the beach or even longer trips traveling abroad), they are usually of the seasonal or "annual vacation" type, a form of re-creation, renewing us and making the world go round.

Life is not only cyclical with the same time-marking events occurring again and again, but it is also progressive or linear, as we all pass through life by a series of changes in status, each of which is marked by different but similarly structured rituals. These life-stage marking events are called *rites of passage* and were first analyzed by French folklorist Arnold Van Gennep (1960); it is his model that we shall follow in our analysis of tourism as ritual. Just as rites of passage (e.g., births, graduations, marriages, and funerals) are usually more significant rituals than ordinary cyclical events such as birthdays, Thanksgivings, or *Días de los Muertos*, so rites-of-passage-type tourist experiences may be unusually intense (e.g., semesters abroad, honeymoons, or retirement cruises). But in the relatively individualistic, informal lives of the contemporary Euro-Americans, many rites of passage as kinds of tourism may be purposely self-imposed physical and mental tests (e.g., college-aged people trekking across continents trying to go as far as possible with little expenditure) (Cohen 1973, Teas 1988) or when recently broken-up, divorced, or laid-off middle-class persons take "time off" for long sailing, walking, or cycling trips or other adventures (Frey 1998, Hastings 1988).

The Structure of Ritual and Tourism

For the present discussion our focus is consciously on the prototypical examples of tourism, such as long-distance travel to famous places or to visit exotic peoples, all in unfamiliar environments. However, even the most minimal kinds of tourism, such as a picnic in the garden, contain elements of the "magic of tourism." The food and drink might be identical to that normally eaten indoors, but the magic comes from the movement and the nonordinary setting. Conversely, a very special meal in the usual but specially decorated eating place may also, by contrast with the ordinary, be "magic" enough for a special celebration.

The alternation of sacred and profane states and the importance of the transition between them were first shown by the French sociologists Hubert and Mauss (1898) in their analysis of the almost universal ritual of sacrifice. They emphasized the sequential process of leaving the ordinary, that is, the sacralization that elevates the participants to the nonordinary state where marvelous things happen, and the converse of desacralization and return to ordinary life. "Each festival [each tourist trip, we contend] represents a temporary shift from the Normal-Profane order of existence into the Abnormal-Sacred order and back again" (Leach 1961:132–136). The flow of time has a pattern, represented in figure 1.

Each festive or tourist event is a miniature life, with a happy anticipation, A–B, an exciting middle, C–D, and a bittersweet ending, D–F. The peri-

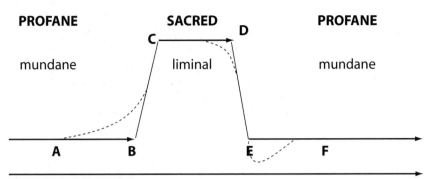

Figure 1: *The Ritual of Tourism* (modified from Feyerabend 1997:11)

ods before A and after F are the mundane, everyday life, expressed in "That's life." The period C–D, the metaphorically "sacred," the "liminal" (see below) out-of-the-ordinary period, is the time of pilgrimage, travel, and tourism. These holidays (formerly "holy days") celebrated in vacations and tourism might be expressed as: "I was living it up, really living . . . I've never felt so alive." These changes in moral and spatial states are usually accompanied by aesthetic changes and markers. This is most obvious in the case of religious rituals and rites of passage, where colorful dresses and strikingly decorated settings are accompanied by chanting, singing, and music. In tourism, too, there may well be aesthetic and sensory changes, in clothing, settings, and foods, and even in touch and smell in the case of tropical beach holidays or Japanese hot springs tourism (Graburn 1995b).

Entries and Exits

The experience of being away on vacation (or going on pilgrimage) has important effects on the life of the traveler *outside* of the actual time spent traveling. Just as there are rituals of preparation, cleansing oneself, changing garments, perhaps putting on perfumes, or getting into the right frame of mind before undertaking religious rites such as pilgrimages, sacrifices, or Christian communion, so for the tourist and travelers there are rituals of preparation. These routinely involve not only planning, booking, and getting new clothes, gear, or luggage, but also social arrangements such as getting someone to water the garden, to look after the house and pets, to collect the mail, to leave numbers for emergencies, and often having parties for saying goodbye.

All of these necessary actions produce the pleasure of anticipation in the period A–B and the weeks and months before the actual takeoff B–C, but the feelings are also ambivalent. There may be misgivings about having made the right decisions, having laid out so much money, or having chosen the right traveling companions. There is also the remote possibility that one is saying goodbye forever, especially for long journeys to more distant places for greater lengths of time, as well as for the elderly or infirm either as travelers or those left behind. [For instance, when I went to graduate school in Canada (by ship), my mother at home in England died unexpectedly before I had my first trip home.] Nevertheless, this period of anticipation is extremely important: the pleasure being looked forward to itself shines on many of the preparations and is often what people "live for" in their workaday lives.

Going home, the journey D–F, the reentry process coming down from the "high" C–D, is equally important and fraught with ambivalence. Most people are reluctant to end a vacation, to leave the excitement and new friends, and to have to go back to work. In fact, a desire to get home and end the vacation might be seen as an admission that it didn't turn out to be as good as expected—that the recreation did not recreate. Some travelers even have twinges of sorrow during the period C–D, for instance on reaching the furthest point away from home (Frey 1998), as they anticipate "the beginning of the end," the loss of new friends, or of the "paradise" visited.

The work of Berkeley undergraduate Amanda Feyerabend (1997) on the rituals and experience of the reentry and the reincorporation into normal society explains what is called *reverse culture shock*. The term is a corollary to the notion of *culture shock*—the feeling of strangeness and inability to cope—that travelers feel when first in unfamiliar environments, such as tourists at point C in figure 1. The reverse of this is the unhappiness felt when the tourist first gets back into his/her home and working environment (the period E–F in figure 1). Feyerabend's informants suggested that while their normal home and work lives might be quite satisfying most of the time, life suffered by comparison with the excitement, the out-of-the-ordinary special experiences that they had just left behind; thus, the lowered state of feelings at E–F is a relative measure of happiness.

Feyerabend also found that, in general, the length of time this ambivalent reverse culture shock lasted was approximately *half the length of time* the traveler had been away. For instance, after a two-day weekend of skiing in the nearby Sierra Nevada range, Berkeley students felt the next day (Monday) was a real letdown, but they would feel okay by Tuesday. On the other hand, a student who returned from a year abroad in a foreign country might feel ill at ease and not quite at home for the whole next semester back in the United States.

The Tourist Experience: Liminality and Communitas

Van Gennep (1960), building on the work of Hubert and Mauss, gave us the model commonly used for the analysis of rituals in general. While Hubert and Mauss emphasized the micro-rituals of preparation, separation, and reincorporation in their look at sacrifice, Van Gennep focused on the central period of the ritual, C–D, and the nature of the participants' experience. In his analysis he labeled the "sacred" out-of-the-ordinary period "liminal," meaning "on/over the threshold," following the European custom where a groom has to carry his bride over the threshold of their new home. At this liminal point the participants are neither in nor out, or as Victor Turner (1974) put it, they are "betwixt and between." In some societies this special period is likened to a temporary death; the person in their old status dies, then follows the liminal period where they are bracketed off from ordinary time (or their ordinary place in the case of tourism), out of which they are reborn with their new status, e.g.,

Bachelor → [groom at wedding ceremony] → husband
Single   → [bride at wedding ceremony] → wife

Victor Turner (1974) and Edith Turner (Turner & Turner 1978) further examined this period of liminality in African rituals and Christian pilgrimages, and they noted: "If a pilgrim is half a tourist, then a tourist is half a pilgrim" (1978:20). Turner stressed that for the participants (those to be transformed in the ritual or the travelers as pilgrims and tourists), the normal social structure of life, work, and family roles, age and gender differences, and so on tends to become looser or disappear. This leveling he called "anti-structure" though, of course, these participants are always surrounded by others carrying out their usual structured roles (e.g., priests or shamans at rituals, and guides, hoteliers, and food workers for pilgrims and tourists). Turner suggested that this leveling of statuses ideally sought outside of home and work structures produces a special feeling of excitement and close bonding among the participants, which he called *communitas*. This state is often signaled by a reduction in marked differences, with all pilgrims wearing the same clothes or all Club Med clients in their beachwear, and with people addressing each other as equals and sharing the same foods, drinks, accommodations, pleasures, and hardships. While consulting for Club Med, I explained this ritual model to a number of *chefs de villages* and GOs *(gentils organisateurs)* who replied with a flash of understanding: "Of course, and the hard part of our job is to keep our customers 'up' in the state of communitas for their seven days nonstop!"

This liminal state, this special human feeling of communitas, may be examined and understood in a variety of ways. In lay language, "going on a trip" usually refers to a journey but it can refer to an "altered state of consciousness" (ASC) brought on by drugs or alcohol, and a special religious or magic experience; "trip" literally means away from the ordinary. Such experience may be called a "high" after which there is a "letdown" or a "come down" (i.e., period C–D followed by D–F in figure 1), and a "high" is opposed to a feeling of depression or a "low," the negative ASC experienced in period E–F. The special state of consciousness experienced during a "trip" was illuminated when I was discussing Feyerabend's findings with my under-graduate class on tourism. Some students pointed out that the reverse culture shock (E–F), lasting half as long as the period of absence (C), paralleled the students' common belief that the time it takes to get over a serious love affair or a broken friendship is half as long as the relationship lasted, putting the "magic" of tourism and pilgrimage into the same emotional category as love and friendship!

Variations on a Theme: Different Strokes for Different Folks

Our analysis of tourism as ritual and the equation of the feelings and meaning of the trip with other human experiences does not mean that all tourism experiences are the same any more than all rituals are the same. Turner and others have characterized the state of communitas as being "high," "liminal" (or liminoid when not part of a truly religious experience), a state of homogeneity, equality, and humility among the participants, a period of transition, magic, or otherworldliness. For today's tourists, the vacation away from home might be described as above, but also may be described as "away," "timeless," a time of freedom, play, mindless spending, and attention to the past or the future (cf. Dann 1996).

The range of tourist experiences has best been outlined by Israeli sociologist E. Cohen in his "Phenomenology of Tourist Experiences" (1979a). Here he takes into account the equation I have suggested between today's tourism and more spiritual pursuits such as pilgrimage, by placing such serious pursuits at one end of his continuum. At this serious end, the traveler is seeking a very important or "sacred" experience or place "out of this world," a sacred center spiritually more important than anything at home. These "existensional" tourists or pilgrims are on a true exploration and many are so moved by the experience attained or the place visited that they stay there and never go home or, in a more practical sense, they never want to go home. Thus, American Jews, having visited Israel, may emigrate there; North American mainlanders may retire to Hawai'i or San Franciscans to the Mendocino County coast. The nature of such tourists' experiences may well be spiritual rather than patently religious; one may feel deeply moved by "communing with nature." Others, atheist or agnostic, might follow the old European pilgrimage way through northern Spain, the Camino de Santiago, and have profoundly moving, even life-changing experiences both along the way and on reaching the cathedral in Santiago (Frey 1998).

At the other end of Cohen's continuum are the mere diversionary or recreational tourists, who never seriously doubt their commitment to their home lifestyle, but just want a simple change—perhaps a change of climate or season, a temporary change of recreation or sports—and have very little desire to explore or seek new experiences. And in the middle of the continuum are the more exploratory tourists, who may make considerable efforts to go to out-of-the-way places, may try to learn foreign languages, or may live temporarily like foreign peoples. These "experiential" and "experimental" tourists are fascinated by difference, like to get close to others, and like to immerse themselves in different environments (e.g., jungle ecotourists, Middle Eastern *souks*, or visitors to remote Nepalese villages). Such people, often young adults without much money or work experience, but probably well educated by their home standards (Cohen 1973, Teas 1988), have the exploratory urge and the *cultural self-confidence* (Graburn 1983) to get out of their shell and experiment with different lifestyles.

Plus ça Change, Plus c'est La Même Chose (The More Things Change, the More It's the Same Thing)

This chapter claims that tourism is a manifestation of a need for a change, and that the change the tourist seeks depends on what perceived touristic attractions would satisfy something not fully met at home. In this concluding section, this general proposition is explored by some specific cases, pointing in particular to the social historical contexts.

In the contemporary Western world and in modern Japan, tourism is the opposite to work; it is one kind of that recent invention: re-creation. It is a special form of play involving travel and "getting away from it all" (i.e., from work, including homework and housework). There is a symbolic link between work + staying and play + travel. Most people feel they ought to go away when they have holidays, and never to go on a vacation might be an indication of sickness or poverty, or extreme youth or old age. Able-bodied adults who don't take holidays might be thought of as poor, unimaginative, or the "idle rich." For the middle classes, this going away on holiday is supposed to be a worthwhile, even a stimulating, creative, or educational experience (see below); for such people, staying at home can be "morally excused" by participating in some creative activity, such as remodeling the house, redoing the garden, or seriously undertaking painting, writing, or sports.

Sociologist Dean MacCannell (1989) has powerfully expressed another instance of this theory in *The Tourist: A New Theory of the Leisure Class*, claiming that the educated middle classes are the sector of our present population who are the most alienated, contrary to Marx's nineteenth-century assertions. MacCannell shows that the urban and suburban middle classes feel that their lives are overly artificial and meaningless, lacking deep feelings of belonging and authenticity. These are thought to exist elsewhere, especially in the simpler lives of other peoples such as family farmers, manual workers and craftsmen, and "primitive peoples." This missing authenticity is thought to lie, above all, in the past, as indicated by English geographer David Lowenthal (1985) in *The Past is a Foreign Country*. Thus, historical, cultural, and ethnic forms of tourism have become increasingly popular, all of them catering to one form or another of modernity's nostalgia for the premodern (Graburn 1995b). MacCannell also shows us that the producers of tourist packages and displays understand these longings and are capable of "manufacturing" authentic Others and Pasts, so that the unfortunate tourists are once more faced with the artificial and commercial in their quest for "reality" and the untouched. One popular arena for getting in touch with the true and the pure is Nature itself, which is often sought in its wilder forms by Euro-American campers, backpackers, and ecotourists, and in more managed versions by the equally alienated urban Japanese (Graburn 1995a). The world's tourist industry, in its advertising and its packaged offerings, must paradoxically create the illusion that the tourists are, by purchasing their services, getting satisfaction of their needs.

While MacCannell's work is a brilliant analysis of educated Westerners, it is not a universal theory. Many people in Europe and North America are not necessarily seeking the particular ritual inversion from "fake to authentic culture"; indeed, it has been shown that this "moral" concern with authenticity correlates with years of education. This search for the pure and the Other, which Urry (1990) has called the "Romantic" gaze, is supplemented by a more direct, communal, and, some would say, unsophisticated (perhaps a better term is unpretentious) kind of enjoyment he calls the "Collective" gaze. The latter is typical of the "working classes," who are more gregarious and derive as much pleasure from the company they keep as the places they visit. Indeed, R. Campbell (1988) has shown that city bus drivers often return to their places of work on their days off, just to socialize with their coworkers. Similarly, Japanese *salarymen* and other groups of male workers often go on trips together, leaving their families at home. Hence, Japanese women often travel in single-sex groups, and children travel in school groups.

The research focus on the "gaze"—the visual practice of sightseeing—has also been challenged by those whose research shows that the changes desired may be sensual or tactile. Selänniemi (1994) found that Scandinavians wintering in the Mediterranean or elsewhere in the "south" want a thoroughly Scandinavian vacation, but one in which they can soak up the sun, lie on the beach, or play simple sports. Jokinen and Veilola (1994) have criticized tourism theorists in general for overemphasizing the visual, the sightseeing quest, because that is the touristic goal of the educated class to which the tourism theorists themselves belong.

In conclusion, this chapter has taken care in using the ritual model not to see all tourism as one individual might experience it, nor should it be expected that ritual reversals are all-encompassing. In fact, tourists on holiday are seeking specific reversals of a few specific features of their workaday home life, things that they lack or that advertising has pointed out they could better find elsewhere. Other than obtaining some straightforward goals, whether they be warmth for northerners, weight loss for the overweight, history for the culturally hungry, or immersion in nature for bored urbanites, tourists generally remain unchanged and demand a lifestyle not too different from that at home. Rarely do the timid become bold, the neat become messy, the educated become dumb, the monolingual be come polyglot, the frigid become sexy, or the heterosexual become gay, except when these are the specific goals of the trip. Gottlieb (1982) has shown how tourists may play "Queen [Peasant] for a Day" with temporary changes in life or class style, and E. Cohen (1973, 1979b) and Frey (1998) have described some of the more rigorous touristic choices for the young or the alienated moderns, but most tourists on their seasonal and annual vacations want to enjoy their own chosen pursuits and come back refreshed as better versions of their same old selves.

Source: From *Hosts and Guests Revisited: Tourism Issues of the 21st Century*, Valene Smith and Maryann Brent (eds.), 2001. Reprinted with permission of the author and Cognizant Communications.

References

Beer, J. 1993. *Packaged Experience: Japanese Overseas Tourism in Asia.* Doctoral dissertation, University of California, Berkeley.

Campbell, R. 1988. "Bushman's Holiday—or the Best Surprise is No Surprise." *Kroeber Anthropological Society Papers* 67/68: 12–19.

Cohen, E. 1973. "Nomads from Affluence: Notes on the Phenomenon of Drifter Tourism." *International Journal of Comparative Sociology* 14:89–103.

———. 1979a. "A Phenomenology of Tourist Experiences." *Sociology* 13:179–201.

———. 1979b. "Sociology of Tourism." [Special Issue] *Annals of Tourism Research* 1–2.

Dann, G. 1996. *The Language of Tourism.* Wallingford: CAB International.

Durkheim, E. 1912. *Elementary Forms of Religious Life*, trans. J. Swain. London: Allen and Unwin.

Feyerabend, A. 1997. "Coming or Going: An Examination of Reverse Culture Shock in the 'Tourism as Ritual' Theory." (unpublished paper) Berkeley: University of California.

Frey, N. 1998. *Pilgrim Stories: On and Off the Road to Santiago.* Berkeley: University of California Press.

Gottlieb, A. 1982. "Americans' Vacations." *Annals of Tourism Research* 9:165–187.

Graburn, N. 1983. "The Anthropology of Tourism." [Special Issue] *Annals of Tourism Research* 10.

———. 1995a. "The Past in the Present in Japan: Nostalgia and Neo-traditionalism in Contemporary Japanese Domestic Tourism," in *Changes in Tourism: People, Places, Processes*, ed. R. Butler and D. Pearce, chapter 4. London: Routledge.

———. 1995b. "Tourism Modernity and Nostalgia," in *The Future of Anthropology: Its Relevance to the Contemporary World*, ed. A. Ahmed and C. Shore, pp. 158–178. London: Athlone Press.

Hastings, J. 1988. "Time Out of Time: Life Crises and Schooner Sailing in the Pacific." *Kroeber Anthropological Society Papers* 67/68: 42–54.

Hubert, H., and M. Mauss. 1898. *Sacrifice: Its Nature and Functions*, trans. W. Halls. London: Cohen & West.

Jokinen, E., and S. Veilola. 1994. "The Body in Tourism: Touring Contemporary Research in Tourism," in *Le Tourisme International entre Tradition et Modernité*, ed. J. Jardel. Nice, France: Actes du Colloque International, Laboratoire d'ethnologie.

Leach, E. 1961. *Rethinking Anthropology*. London: Athlone Press.

Lowenthal, D. 1985. *The Past is a Foreign Country*. Cambridge: Cambridge University Press.

MacCannell, D. 1989. *The Tourist: A New Theory of the Leisure Class*. New York: Schocken Books.

Selänniemi, T. 1994. "A Charter Trip to Sacred Places—Individual Mass Tourism," in *Le Tourisme International entre Tradition et Modernité*, ed. J. Jardel, pp. 335–340. Nice, France: Université de Nice, Laboratoire d'ethnologie.

Smith, V. 1989. "Introduction," in *Hosts and Guests: The Anthropology of Tourism*, 2nd edition, ed. V. Smith, pp. 1–17. Philadelphia: University of Pennsylvania Press.

Teas, J. 1988. "'I'm Studying Monkeys; What Do You Do?'—Youth and Travelers in Nepal." *Kroeber Anthropological Society Papers* 67/68: 35–41.

Turner, V. 1974. *Dreams, Fields, and Metaphors: Symbolic Action in Human Society*. Ithaca, NY: Cornell University Press.

Turner, V., and E. Turner. 1978. *Images and Pilgrimage in Christian Culture*. New York: Columbia University Press.

Urry, J. 1990. *The Tourist Gaze: Leisure and Travel in Contemporary Societies*. London: Sage.

Van Gennep, A. 1960 [1909]. *The Rites of Passage*, trans. M. Vizedom and G. Caffee. Chicago: The University of Chicago Press.

3

The Global Beach

Orvar Löfgren

To the Beach

Once I found a postcard in a secondhand shop. It was manufactured in New York, probably in the fifties, and carried the simple text: "By the beautiful sea." It is a good example of the universalization of the beach experience, the making of a truly global iconography and choreography of beach life. It is one of those many postcards without any hint of the "local," just sand, sea, and carefully arranged groups of beach visitors. Pictures like these turn up in any card rack along the coasts of the world. No surprise that I found it in Sweden.

What is a beach, what can a beach be used for? In the 1990s the Lego toy producers developed a transnational holiday world called *PARADISA* in the Esperanto of the global toy industry. If you bought kit number 6410 (and were over the age of six) you would be able to construct your own beach, with the following basic ingredients: 1 palm tree, 2 bathing huts, 1 parasol, 2 deck chairs, 1 surfboard, 1 fishing rod, 1 speedboat, 1 portable cassette player, 1 beach bar (complete with waiter and exotic drinks), 1 male and 1 female vacationer in swimsuits. This bricolage of props and activities comes from different settings and epochs all around the world and now, integrated and globalized, becomes a familiar place to play at being a teenager, a grownup, a tourist.

The concept of beach covers a lot of territory and history. The range of beach life is amply demonstrated along a coast like that of California. In northern California there is the constant search for a beach of your own, a small cove, protected by cliffs and rocks. As the tide moves out, strings of small beaches suddenly become available to couples or single families—*nota bene*, if public access is possible. The idea of this kind of beach is that it belongs to nobody but you. Intruders are a provocation, they should move on to find their own beach. This beach is yours, you can collect shells and drift-wood, build a castle in the sand, knowing that in a few hours it will be gone, washed away. The other end of the scale would be a beach like the famous Los Angeles beach studied in the 1970s by the sociologist Robert Edgerton (1979). This "Southland," as he labeled it, attracted 400,000 visitors on a fine summer day.

Beaches come in all forms and fashions, finding their position along this continuum from the Robinson Beach, where there is just you, sand, water, and maybe a couple of palm trees, to the lively holiday beach, à la Coney Island or Blackpool. But any of these beaches represents a sedimenta-tion of cultural traditions, from the eighteenth-century history of seashore invalids to the 1990s cult of *Baywatch*. For the eighteenth- and early nine-teenth-century pioneers the beach was mainly an access to the ordeal of sea bathing, getting a quick dose of the healthy sea breeze and saltwater. The beach served for quiet strolls or as a site for sunset watching, but the idea of the beach as a playground was still far away.

In this global history some beaches occupy a limited stretch of sand but take up a huge mental space. These are the famous beaches that less famous beaches often try to emulate. There is the early example of the Lido outside Rome, later on the Murphys' beach, La Garoupe, at Antibes. "Romantic Rio can be yours" is the headline of a 1946 ad from Pan Am, which shows two women leisurely resting in the sand. The text continues, "In Rio de Janeiro it is summer! And by clipper Rio's Copacabana Beach is just a weekend away from the United States."[1] For Mediterranean package tourists the beach of Las Palmas on the Canary Islands had a strong image, just like Miami Beach in Florida or Malibu in California.

The Tropical Dream

The props of the *PARADISA* beach have their own history. Already in the making of the Riviera, palm trees became a must, and this tropical plant has steadily expanded north. The collapsible deck chair was borrowed from the decks of ocean cruisers, while the bathing hut has many national variations.

But the whole concept of paradise relies above all on the romance of the South Pacific and the tropical beach. The global notion of the beach as paradise began in the cult of Hawai'i and Waikiki Beach next to Honolulu. The site of Hawai'i is special. For a very long period it continued to be a fan-tasyland. The first modern resort hotel was built in 1901, but as late as 1955 the yearly number of tourists barely reached 100,000 and it was only with the arrival of cheap jet flights that Hawai'i became a mass destination. Until the 1950s Waikiki remained a beach experience for a small, mainly American elite. The power of the Hawai'ian imagery above all had to do with the fact that this was the first really mass-mediated paradise: a landscape not only to experience through colored postcards and illustrated magazine features but also a landscape set to music. As early as 1915 the tune "At the Beach of Waikiki" was a great hit at the Panama-Pacific Exposition in San Francisco (Grant 1996:60). Tin Pan Alley versions of Hawai'ian sheet music started spreading around the world and their colorful covers established the image of the tropical beach, hula girls with flowers in their hair and palm trees swaying gently in the breeze, or just a pair of lovers admiring the silvery moon and the mountain silhouette of Diamond Head. Tropical nights on the beach became a new romantic fantasy, and as Hawai'ian music on gramophone records complemented sheet music, everybody could create their own Waikiki atmosphere at home in the living room or even down at the local beach. It was the ultimate romantic beach serenade, with mass-distributed landscape sound and images. During the 1930s Waikiki became the first radio beach; there were countless shows broadcast from "the beach at Waikiki," and mass-syndicated radio shows like "Hawai'i Calls" at times were heard on 750 radio stations worldwide (Grant 1996:68).

During the Second World War tourists vanished from the Waikiki Beach, which was taken over by the hundreds of thousands of soldiers stationed in Honolulu or passing through. Discussions of tourism rarely mention the fact that masses of working-class men got their first experience of the exotic during the war, albeit in rather strange circumstances. Most of the GIs in Honolulu never came closer to their Polynesian dream girls than the offer of "Two Pictures with Hula Girl" for 75 cents, and then the hula girls usually weren't local Hawai'ians but Puerto Ricans or mainlander girls. The local women did not live up to the fantasy images of slender hula bodies, which the men brought with them from back home (Bailey and Farber 1992:212).

Many of the GIs came back later to Hawai'i and the South Pacific with their families as tourists. During the 1950s active mass media marketing furthered the fantasyland of the Pacific beach as an appetizingly exotic Eden of sensual women with inviting smiles. "Every man's vision of delight," as the *National Geographic* aptly called a 1962 feature on Tahiti. During the postwar period this influential magazine consistently pictured the Pacific as a friendly and secure paradise (Lutz and Collins 1993:133).[2]

On Waikiki the Hollywood presence had been strong since the 1920s. Movie moguls and stars simply had to spend a vacation in one of the fashionable resort hotels, and the result was a strong Hollywood interest in Hawai'ian settings, which culminated in the 1950s with movies like *From Here to Eternity* and Elvis's *Blue Hawaii*. In those years the favorite prize on an American quiz show was often a romantic trip to Hawai'i for two (Grant 1996).

By the time the mass tourists started flying in with the firmly established romance of Waikiki Beach among their baggage, the actual beach experience with its jungle of high-rise hotels, overcrowded beaches, and traffic congestions had difficulties in living up to these images.

After Waikiki with its groves of coconut palms any serious beach had to have palm trees, like the PARADISA version. Another element on the PARADISA beach also had a Waikiki past: the surfboard, but it made the global beach through a detour to California (Grant 1996).

When the tourists started visiting Waikiki Beach, surfing was almost gone as local tradition, and mainland Americans helped revitalize it. Local surfers became one of the great sights at the beach. They produced all kinds of stunts, from surfing dogs to night surfing with torches, but they also brought the experience to the tourists. Visiting Hawai'ian teams took the sport to California in the early twentieth century, but since few tourist seashores have good surf, the sport's diffusion was slow. Until the 1950s surfers made up a relatively small subculture, mainly confined to southern California.[3] Wearing swimming shorts, T-shirts, and sandals, they spent most of their summer on the beach and out in the surf, often staying overnight in the car and having improvised beach parties in the evenings. They also went on "surfing safaris" to distant beaches with great surf.

Surfing went global through the media, but in rather unorthodox ways. In the late fifties and early sixties low-cost surfing films were made and shown in high-school auditoriums and similar places. Surfing attracted attention in novels and later Hollywood movies, but the big breakthrough came when "surfing music" was transformed into an international success by some southern California musicians. When the Beach Boys (named after the famous surfers on Waikiki Beach) had several surfing songs in the top ten during 1962 and 1963 the craze was already a fact. The number of surfers grew and, more important, a new image of teenage beach life spread around the world to the tunes of "Surfing Safari" and "California Girls": blond and tanned youth, jumping into their open cars to drive down to the beach for a summer of endless parties. Surfboards no longer had to be part of the surf scene, other than as a suitable backdrop, and the surf scene was no longer seen as a Hawai'ian but a Californian innovation.[4] In the 1960s it also produced another global export: why not arrange a real California beach party down at the local beach or in your own backyard? It became an avant-garde form of informal socializing.

Beach Basics

Three basic elements make up the global beach: sand, sun, and sea. What are their characteristics? How did these three ordinary elements turn beaches into a global phenomenon?

Sand is usually not a popular terrain for human activity. It is hard to walk in, it gets into your clothes, eyes, and food. It moves too easily in the wind. The early seashore visitors who used the beach mainly as a vista or for a slow walk avoided the sandy dunes and made only quick expeditions over the banks when going into the water. People who went for a serious swim preferred other kinds of beaches. Sand was a strange and alien material, difficult to shape and control.

It was only when the swimming and sunning beach developed that sand acquired its new qualities. It became an extremely sensual element, caressing the body. From now on a real beach should have sand, and preferably either white or golden yellow, it should also look clean, virginal. The sand combined the fluidity of water and the warmth of the sun.

Once vacationers started to make contact with this new element, they found that it had all sorts of uses. Already during the early twentieth century sand and children were well linked. In northern Europe the sandbox was developed for children. Children needed sand; sand was good for them. It turned into a medium for play, and in suburban gardens and urban playgrounds small sand dunes, fenced in by planks, materialized. At the beach the sand brought out the child in the adult. Grown-ups joined the kids in fooling around with sand, building sand castles, canals, sculptures, covering each other in sand. Digging became a favorite pastime and in some cases led to stranger activities.

The craze for sandy beaches had some far-reaching consequences. Above all it began a burgeoning export of sand, not any sand, but the kind of perfect beach sand that does not occur just anywhere. All over the tourist world beaches have been constructed with the help of truckloads of sand. One of the first experiments was made in Monaco, where Elsa Maxwell was hired to promote tourism and came up with the idea of a rubber beach to be spread with sand. It didn't turn out to be such a good idea (Blume 1994:75). Cannes and other resorts along the Riviera imported sand from the French west coast, where it had the right quality.

The discovery of water as a hedonistic element was also slow. Body motions changed from slowly lowering yourself into the water to "taking a plunge," from controlled restraint to childish euphoria. People started to run rather than walk into the sea. All new kinds of water movements developed. In the water you could float, glide, stroke, paddle, dive, crawl. Again it was a chance of returning to the simple pleasures of childhood. Exploring water was like entering a different universe:

> there is the wonder of buoyancy, of being suspended in this thick, transparent medium that supports and embraces us. One can move in water, play with it, in a way that has no analogue in the air . . . . One can become a little hydroplane or submarine, investigating the physics of flow with one's body. (Sacks 1997:45)

You could also enjoy water from land. Water made you mellow, as the visitors to Southland Beach put it. The languid movements, the rhythm of the surf had a calming, soothing effect, and the endless horizon proved to be a perfect medium for daydreaming. Its vastness opened up a wide space for wandering thoughts and fantasies. Out there, past a distant ship on its way to an exotic destination, are other worlds. The philosopher Bachelard sees a connection between the immensity of the seashore landscape and the depth of "inner space." Staring at the horizon, your eyes glaze—you are looking at nothing and at a hidden world at the same time (1994:205–09). Contemplating the ocean and trying to represent its magic also calls for a new language, as in the description of Waikiki Beach from 1929: "Far out to the opalescent horizon stretches the ocean in broad bands of jeweled color—turquoise, sapphire, emerald, amethyst; and curving around it like a tawny topaz girdle presses the hard, firm sand of the shore."[5] At midday, as at sunset and in moonlight, Waikiki offered the perfect tropical beach: new combinations of light and colors, in the meeting of sky and ocean.

After learning to handle the water in new ways, tourists took the next step. They cultivated the art of sunbathing. A tanned body was previously a sign of manual labor and vulgarity: only bodies exposed to the sun in outdoor labor were tanned. As late as the 1920s Swedish magazines carried ads for lotions that would help you to get rid of a tan and regain the white, fashionable complexion, but a few years later the new fashion of sunbathing had spread to most of the Western world. (In some cases the same lotions that once promised to whiten the skin now offered a safe way of getting "the brown, beautiful summer tan.")[6]

Sunbathing as a hedonist project originated in Germany, already in the late nineteenth century, but the great expansion came when a new generation of war-weary youth craved a new life after 1918. The Englishman Stephen Spender was attracted to this movement and described the sun as "a primary

"By the beautiful sea": in this postcard from the 1950s, the photographer has choreographed his models' posture to demonstrate the properly relaxed beach body. (Courtesy of Orvar Löfgren)

social force in Germany": "Thousands of people went to the open-air swim-ming baths or lay down on the shores of rivers and lakes, almost nude, and sometimes quite nude, and the boys who had turned the deepest mahogany walked among those people with paler skins, like kings among their court-iers" (quoted in Fussell 1980:140).

Nudism and sunbathing were often linked in this pioneer period, as a utopia of modern and natural living. In Germany "Free Body Culture" (*Freikörperkultur*) camps started up, and from his experience in such a camp Kurt Barthel was one of those who brought nudism to the United States. Here the emphasis was to be more on tanning and informality than on athletics. Sunlight was seen as the cure for everything. Nudist camps developed all over the United States, often viewed with great suspicion (and curiosity) by the surrounding society. A promotional movie was made in 1933, called *Ely-sia Valley of the Nude.* "The Sunshine Park" in New Jersey became the head-quarters of the American Sunbathing Association, where there were hopes for developing a whole "Nude City," but nudism never really caught on. "Nudists bodies are free, but their souls are in corsets," as one critic of the movement put it, and nudists spent as much time fighting one another as bat-tling the ignorance of the public.[7]

The cult of sunshine did catch on, though, transforming vacations and beach life. Sometimes it made tanning rather than swimming the most impor-tant pastime on the beach. "Sunshine is healthy" was the new advice, but the British writer Evelyn Waugh, as usual, was critical. In 1930 he wrote for the *London Daily Mail:* "I hate the whole business . . . . All this is supposed to be good for you. Nowadays people believe anything they are told by 'scientists,' just as they used to believe anything they were told by clergymen" (quoted in Fussell 1980:141).

The health arguments soon faded as the sun became a liberating force, a highly sensual communion with nature. The sun warmed both your body and your senses, you should be drenched in it. It made you both beautiful and sexy. A new color scheme was developed, a cult of *bronzage* as the French term was. The romance of Polynesia was part of the picture. Natives like hula girls or surfing beach boys were not black, they were just perfectly tanned.

The skills of acquiring the perfect bronze tan developed into a more and more complex art, comprising ointments, tanning hints, and the rituals of rub-bing down. As an Australian newspaper advised its readers, "It turns out to be all too easy to obtain the uneven coloration deprecatingly termed a 'farmer's tan.' It takes time and commitment to get the all-over allure of deep and enduring brownness" (quoted in Fiske 1989:47). The term "sunbaking" replaced "sunbathing" in Australia, to mark this commitment (still quite seri-ous in 1982; and in the United States the comic strip *Doonesbury* mocked and immortalized Zonker's quest for the perfect tan). At the beach you learned to massage yourself and your partner with all kinds of lotions, developing new forms of body consciousness as well as redefining acceptable and unaccept-able forms of nudity.

No sooner was the art of tanning safely institutionalized than the first warnings appeared. In the 1980s cancer patrols started to patrol beaches over the world, offering to protect you from the dangers of the sun. In some sunny parts of the world tanning was no longer the thing, but on the whole pale Northern tourists kept working on their *bronzage.*

Beach Bodies

The beach is very much the site of the making of the modern body. Wherever you look there are bodies, all kinds of bodies, old and young bodies, fat and thin, swimming or sleeping bodies, running bodies, bodies doing somersaults or rolling in the sand. Life at the modern beach becomes bodywork: exposing the body to sun, water, winds, and sand—as well as the critical eyes of others. On the beach you learn a lot about bodies, your own and others'. After three-quarters of a century of bodies in scant swimwear and various degrees of exposure we may have become so blasé that we don't realize what a revolutionary experience this has been.

One genre may help us recapture some of this early impact. It is what George Orwell called, in an essay from 1942, "the penny or two-penny postcards with their endless succession of fat women in tight bathing-dresses" (1968:183–94). He was thinking of a specific comic postcard tradition that developed in Britain and elsewhere with the focus on beach bodies and beach situations. Orwell had an eye for popular culture but found it hard to repress his middle-class reactions to these images:

> Your first impression is of an overwhelming vulgarity. This is quite apart from the ever-present obscenity, and also apart from the hideousness of the colors. They have an utter lowness of mental atmosphere, which comes out not only in the nature of the jokes but, even more, in the grotesque, staring, blatant quality of the drawings . . . every gesture and attitude, are deliberately ugly, the faces grinning and vacuous, the women monstrously parodied, with bottoms like Hottentots. (1968:183)

Of course Orwell is able to see these postcards as a cultural phenomenon that represents a different kind of humor and lifestyle from his own. The cards tell us something of the making of a new body-oriented beach culture, which certainly isn't one of middle-class constraint and decorum. First, there are all kinds of bodies parading here, fat, ugly bodies and broad backsides, as well as vulgar forms of bodily contact: the slapping of backs, the pinching of bottoms, unrestrained public kissing and hugging. Second, they draw attention to other bodily functions, such as gluttonous overeating, getting blind drunk, or frantically searching for the restrooms. So many activities that should occur in privacy go on here in the wrong place, at the wrong time. These are bodies lacking any form of moderation: loud laughs, large gestures, swelling forms. In some ways they represent guerrilla warfare against middle-class taste and self-control, and they do this in a liberating, shameless

"The water is so clear you can see the bottom quite distinctly."

Beach bottoms, backsides, buttocks, behinds, and bums—such was the dominating obsession in the British comic postcard tradition of the 1930s. (Courtesy of Orvar Löfgren)

way. These voluptuous ladies bending down to expose their enormous backsides and the men floating on their big bellies in the water are not hiding their "vulgar" bodies. They are on the beach to enjoy themselves: "Having a great time, wish you were here!" In this world backsides, buttocks, behinds, bums, and bottoms are always good for a laugh, as is any form of nudity. (The nudist camp jokes were among its basic ingredients.)

The point I want to make about the symbolism of this world is that it celebrates bodies enjoying themselves, bodies that definitely do not live up to the rigorous standards that later came to dominate beach culture.

Some bodies are there on the beach to enjoy themselves—other bodies are there to be judged. In the 1920s the concept of bathing beauties appeared, with an endless string of beauty pageants that chose the beach as their stage (Cohen, Wilk and Stoeltje 1995). Starlets and models posed for photographers against the blue sea, and women's magazines started running advice on getting bodies ready for the beach season. Stern dieting programs later became part of this regime, creating the terror of pre-beach flab. And ads for men urged them to start building bodies during the winter to make sure some hunk on the beach didn't try to steal their girlfriend or trip them up in the sand. "Hey skinny—yer ribs are showing!" was the catching start of the 1950's ads about beach humiliations, in which Charles Atlas promised to make you into a new man for next summer, in only fifteen minutes a day.

In some settings the monitoring of the perfect body became so strong that some people stayed away or found other, less demanding beaches. But beach bodywork was not only about exposing sand, sea, and sun as well as different forms of motion. The languidness of swimming also influenced body movements on land. People learned to walk and move very differently on the beach. There was some kind of magic and liberating transformation occurring the moment your feet hit the sand.

The new beach bodies also demanded beachwear, a term that first appeared in 1928 on the Riviera beaches together with the two novelties of beach pajamas and beach gown, while items like beach bags and beach sandals appeared a few years later.[8]

Beach Etiquette

JIM: Wenn man an einem fremden Strand kommt, ist man immer zuerst etwas verlegen.

JAKOB: Man weiss nicht recht, wohin man gehen soll . . .

JIM: When a person lands at a strange shore, he is always a bit embarrassed at first.

JAKE: He doesn't rightly know, where he is to go to . . .

Brecht's lines from *Mahagonny* on the awkwardness of coming to an unknown beach would hold very true for most large beaches of the world. They hold an astonishing mix of people. Southland Beach is a good example. Here groups of different ages and classes and cultural and ethnic identities mingle. Inner-city people and tourists who are new to the city, strangers, sit close together on the same strip of flat sand, in full exposure, with very little protective clothing. It is a mass confrontation that in many other settings would be volatile. But still the beach works. Even strangers soon make themselves at home.

The beach is supposed to be an arena of relaxation, of minding your own business, of doing what you want. But behind such notions of anarchy or individualism is heavily regimented behavior. The French sociologist Jean-Claude Kaufmann's (1995) study of topless bathing on French beaches illustrates this very clearly. Many of his beach informants stated strongly, "Here on the beach everybody does what they want," but a world of unwritten rules and regulations allowed them to do so. People knew exactly where the borders were, how to look, how to dress and undress, how to move their bodies.

The rules were especially clear in the sensitive field of topless bathing, where women turned out to have very precise ideas about the propriety of this French tradition: when, where, and how to let go of the top piece. Kaufmann's choice of topic may sound esoteric, but it unearthed a whole universe of ideas about privacy, individualism, social relations, and gender.

One of his main arguments is that the beach is a laboratory for the sophistication of the gaze. People he interviewed often said, "I don't spend any time looking around, I am in my own world." There is, of course, no way you cannot look. People on the beach are constantly testing different ocular techniques, consciously or unconsciously switching between different ways of seeing: watching, staring, glancing, scanning, looking from the corner of your eye, pretending not to look, making brief eye contact, looking away.

There was constant observation of how other people handled these techniques and very quick registration of those who broke the rules. Topless women in particular monitored the male gaze as well as that of other females. "When bodies are naked glances are clothed," as the sociologist Erving Goffman once put it.[9]

All this doesn't come naturally. The ways in which people observe at the beach have changed over time.[10] The colonizing gaze of the Victorians would today be considered most provoking and unsophisticated. The degree of learning ocular competence also becomes obvious when kids constantly have to be told, "Don't stare." You have to learn to discipline the ways you look at others in a suitably disinterested way: observing but never staring.

The beach was also the place for another important innovation: sunglasses, which developed new forms of hiding yourself and at the same time offered new opportunities for unobtrusive observation.

A beach is, as we have seen, a very special arena, often with clear boundaries. The kind of behavior that is okay down by the water is not okay in the parking lot or on the other side of the beach road. Beach life may seem banal, but these banalities express very basic conceptions about private and public, decent and indecent, individuality and collectivity. Most of the rules regulating beach behavior have never been written down, many of them can hardly be verbalized, and yet—down at the beach—people know.

Unlike many other arenas, beaches bring classes together, sometimes in an uneasy coexistence, sometimes in strikingly unproblematic ways. They offer the chance to observe, very close at hand, "those other people" at play. The history of British tourism emphasizes this role of the beach as one of the few "neutral grounds" that allowed the working class to enter the vacation scene much earlier than in many other nations. As the historian John K. Walton describes the situation in the late nineteenth century, "At the seaside rich and poor, respectable and ungodly, staid and rowdy, quiet and noisy not only rubbed shoulders . . . they also had to compete for access to, and use of, recreational space" (1983:190–91). He overstates the classlessness of the beach, but a striking theme in early twentieth-century beach life is the idea of make-believe. Music-hall songs talked about "Beach Sultans" and on the comic postcards you could see working-class girls exclaiming: "At home I might be nothing, but here I am at least something!" The seaside visit was that special place, "a geography of hope," which stood out as a highlight in the British working-class year (Sprawson 1993:19).

In a similar manner a place like Coney Island became an arena of social confrontations. In the middle of the nineteenth century it was still a desolate beach, visited by a few wealthy families in search of fresh air and solitude. By the 1870s it had developed into New York's leading resort. By 1900 up to a half million New Yorkers visited the beach and its amusement parks on summer weekend days. By then it offered what has been called a "linear visual study in American class structure" with different social groups distributed along the shore. While certain areas kept a middle-class focus, others catered for the working class. Some spots had a reputation as a hangout for underworld figures or attracted a socially mixed male audience of the "sporting" subculture (Towner 1996:211).

Beaches like Coney Island and Blackpool fostered endless debates about beach morals and beach rules as different lifestyles overlapped or clashed. On some global beaches debates take new, multicultural, forms.

Beach Blankets

> I grow up bathing in sea water
> But nowadays that is bare horror
> If I only venture down by the shore
> Police is only telling me I can't bathe anymore.
>
> (quoted in Pattullo 1996:83)

This Calypso text from Barbados is one of many comments on the conflicts about beach access in the Caribbean. Here, as in most other tourist regions of the world, beaches are public, but in reality local access has been constrained. Seaside resorts may try all sorts of tactics to monitor visitors. Tourists' complaints of being hassled by vendors or "beach boys" cruising for single female tourists led to an increased policing of beaches, as in the Barbados case, which opened up a discussion of who and what belongs on the beach. On many Caribbean islands, the natives feel that they have been forced out of the best beaches, or as a local paper put it, "The day could come when the ordinary Jamaican doesn't know what a good beach looks like" (Pattullo 1996).

So who owns the beach? A Canadian travel ad from 1958 says: "Want to own an ocean?" There is a picture of a family on a beach blanket in the middle of vast empty space, an image of perfect order and relaxation, but most tourist beaches tend to be crowded, though, which has led to all sorts of tactics for creating private space. When Robert Edgerton interviewed Los Angeles beachgoers, the vast majority argued that the first thing they did was to carve out space on arrival by rolling out their towel and arranging their private belongings: "I pick out my little plot of sand and set down my towel. For the next few hours that is my own little world; it belongs to me" (1979:150). To cross over this private territory or to sit down next to it was considered a provocation and rarely happened. Beach etiquette thus starts with the micro-rituals of installation, of making yourself at home, and at the same time marking a physical and mental distance from others.

Another common ritual of signaling privacy is to immerse yourself in some activity as soon as you have arranged your belongings, to bury yourself in a book or lie down in the sand. The strong sense of privacy even on a crowded beach also has to do with the techniques of daydreaming. By closing your eyes you are signaling that you are in your own private dream world, far away.

After such initial moves you can become more active later on. Some complain of beach life being too private, with people going to great lengths not to communicate with those close by. "It's like being in an elevator where nobody talks," one woman complained to David Edgerton. Those who consistently break these rules of privacy and noncommunication are small kids and dogs.

Against this complex regimentation of the private sphere the clash with beach vendors or beach boys on distant vacation beaches become more understandable. These are locals who don't know the rules the tourists have brought with them from back home. In Los Angeles many white middle-class visitors also complained about Chicano families: they did not understand the need to keep their distance.

On the whole, Southland visitors stressed how easy it was to be on the beach. "I feel so safe here, people are mellow, the environment makes people behave. . . . It may be one of the places a woman can go alone and yet feel safe," were some of the comments.

The ability of the beach to produce this mellowness is a statement that turns up again and again: "Waikiki at that time was a very, very healing place. You would come there because you instinctively knew that's where you needed to be if you wanted a rest, if you needed to get well. The waters were beneficent, the breezes were soothing, the whole vibration of the place was something that just drew you in" (quoted in Timmons 1986:34).

My Home Is My Sand Castle

On some German beaches you may spot a sign telling you that it is absolutely forbidden to build sand castles. This may, to an outside visitor, seem like a harsh attitude to a harmless occupation, but then you have probably not seen what a German sand castle may look like. We are not talking about miniatures here but the old tradition of building a secluded, circular wall around your beach territory, to protect yourself from the wind and the regards of others. These structures are nothing like the improvised shelters you might make out of a ring of stones, which appear on beaches all over the world. On a real German sand castle beach you may have to maneuver your way past castle after castle, and then it might also feel like walking through an art show, because the German tradition puts great emphasis on decoration, as Harald Kimpel and Johanna Werckmeister (1995) point out in their history of the phenomenon.

The tradition of placing yourself inside a sand castle was well established in the nineteenth century. It probably started as a way of claiming space on the beach and also as a protection against the often chilly winds of German beaches. The tradition soon triggered off competition and the idea of building a more perfect and more beautiful structure around yourself. Some of the structures had elegant patterns accomplished with shells or wreckage, and many had sand sculptures.

Subtexts underlined the ways in which sand castles became personalized statements: "Young ladies welcome," "The unfinished," "Kalifornien," or "Castle Sansoucie." Less poetically they could be called "Düsseldorf," announcing your hometown, or just presenting the occupants "Irmgard und Egon." The changing aesthetics and namings mirror different periods of beach life. The nastier ones are some of the sand castles from the 1930s, as the one with Hitler's portrait in sand and the title "Unser Führer." This sand castle is photographed surrounded with happy beachgoers in swimwear doing the Heil Hitler salute.

As I pointed out earlier, German tourists have often had a bad press, and the sand castle–building habit contributed to it. When German tourists after the Second World War started traveling abroad they brought along their building tradition, not always aware of the kind of signals they were sending. In countries like Holland and Denmark, where the same beaches had been occupied by Nazi troops, surprised Germans found their castles trampled down when they returned to the beach the next morning. Local youths had demolished them during the night.

An earlier source of conflicts was the tradition of putting up flags on the beach. This was a late nineteenth-century tradition, found not only in Germany, but in this young nation travelers often took along flags when they went abroad. The tradition led to international conflicts, as locals saw it as a symbol of aggressive Germanness, the quest for *Lebensraum.* On one of the beaches in Denmark where there were many German castles and flags, local Danes went out and removed the flags. German tourists protested, and in the end the two governments had to exchange stern notes.

Apart from its place in the stereotype of "typical German tourist," the sandcastle tradition had quite another aspect. One castle from 1913 bears the inscription in small shells: The Club of Work-Shy. This imposing artwork must have taken many hours of hard work to build, but the whole idea of the sand castle is that of nonwork, it is work for pleasure, where you work off a lot of childish energy and creativity. You invest hours in building something that the wind and the tide will wash away. As the German authors point out, the investment may have to do with the fact that relaxation at the beach often produces boredom and restlessness: let's do something!

Seasides and Poolsides

Time isn't the great healer.
Poolside seats are.

This 1997 slogan of an American resort chain is part of a move away from the beach.[11] In many coastal settings, sand and seawater have become less important. An appetizing destination must advertise its beach, but when you get there you often find out that there are very few people in the water: it is too cold, too windy, too polluted. The sand is sticky or full of cigarette butts. The tourists have withdrawn to the safer territory of the hotel pool, but they have brought with them all the necessary skills developed at the beach.

If you look up "swimming pool" in the *Encyclopedia Americana* you get "a tank constructed of cement, wood, steel, plastic, fiberglass or other material and used for swimming, or pleasure bathing." Behind this minimalistic definition lies a gradual development that has made the pool rather than the beach a focus of much vacation life. Pools have an impressive history, but in the Western world there is a long void from the Roman era to their reintroduction in the nineteenth century.[12]

Down at the old boardwalk of Santa Cruz, California, you may view the ruins of the old giant swimming pool building from 1907, but the first tank was built next to the beach in the 1860s. In nearby San Francisco the even bigger Sutro Baths were developed in the 1890s. They covered three acres on the western headlands of San Francisco, with saltwater and freshwater pools, palm trees, a tropic beach, restaurants, galleries, and an amphitheater. The baths could accommodate ten thousand swimmers a day and were in use until 1966, when they were dismantled (Croutier 1992:159, Sprawson 1993:268).

In other big cities like Chicago and New York public swim baths were often introduced to encourage working-class cleanliness, but the public pools soon became popular playgrounds. By 1911 Chicago's outdoor pools were so popular that groups were marched in by the hour, supplied with swimsuits and towels, and then ordered out of the water one hour later, to make room for the next group in line (Crantz 1982:72).

The waning popularity of these giant baths during the twentieth century had to do with the scale on which different groups and classes mixed. The future of the seaside pools turned out to be the more private hotel pools, often developed as alternatives to overcrowded beaches or polluted coastal waters. In the early 1950s a hotel developer at Waikiki surprised the world by developing a complex away from the high-cost beach locations but with its own hotel pool (Grant 1996:82). A new concept was born. Most hotel pools developed out of the Californian model, the testing ground not only for pool styles but also for pool etiquette. In southern California's roaring 1920s private pools became part of Hollywood stardom, but the real expansion came in the 1950s and 1960s, with new and cheaper techniques (Baldan and Melchior 1997, Elving 1972, and Spawson 1993).

During the 1980s hotel pools became more and more elaborate, as designers developed veritable water lands, with artificial sand beaches, waterfalls, slides, and lagoons. Water spectacles have become an increasingly important part of hotel aesthetics and entertainment.

The vacation pool culture shows an immense degree of standardization. The same azure blue nuance, imitating tropical beaches, similar pool shapes, springboards, chairs. We move our bodies according to a well-established choreography, pull our stomachs in before climbing onto the diving board, or nonchalantly rest one of our arms on the side of the pool as we make poolside conversation from the water, just the way we have seen in countless advertisements for Martini.

Today the pool is a condensation of the beach and seashore: a much better managed version, nice water temperature, no sand between the toes, close to the hotel bar. The restricted space makes for new kinds of conflicts. All over the world people sneak down to the pool in the early morning to wrap a towel around a chair in a good position for basking in the sun. During the day they move their chairs around, group and regroup them, and then leave them for dinner in a frozen sociogram of the day's interaction.

Life's a Beach

Maybe it is the mix of activities and possibilities with an aura of luxurious living that has made beach and poolside life such a vacation success. Here you oscillate between very different vacation modes. Frolic in the water, daydream with the help of the horizon or a Walkman, float on your back in sand or water, drink cold beer or cappuccino, fool around with the sand, mas-

Alone together: reading on a global beach. Nusa Dua, Bali, Indonesia.
(© 2003 Martin Benjamin)

sage your own body or that of your partner with suntan lotion, and not least important: who could have guessed that the beach or pool chair would become one of the most cherished reading places in the world? Everywhere people are buried in their books, magazines, mysteries, and thick paperback novels with sunscreen smudges. The beach has become a great read.

The fact that this is a territory for the pursuit of hedonism also means that it often becomes a place of boredom. Modes of awareness drift in and out: dozing, daydreaming, sitting up to take in the scenery, registering activities around you, reflecting on the behavior of others, becoming self-conscious when moving through the beach landscape or diving into the pool.

You learn so much at the beach without ever noticing that you're a vacationer in constant training. The global beach has an ability to detach itself from its immediate surroundings, which means that you can travel the world and usually feel quite at home on any beach. Changing beach aesthetics make the landscape more and more minimalistic, as two ads in the *New Yorker* from 1996 illustrate. The first for Australia shows a couple walking along a sandbank completely surrounded by water, a small island of sand, and nothing else. Apart from a small parked airplane, there is total stillness. Another ad for the Bahamas shows just a deck chair in the sunset, vast areas of sand, and a few palm trees in the distance. Nothingness, emptiness, seclusion, not a single soul, getting away from it all.

In his analysis of an Australian beach John Fiske (1989) focuses on the structuralist notion of the beach being in-between, an anomalous zone between nature and culture. But the old slogan from the 1968 Paris student revolt is more telling: "The beach is under the street!" Just start breaking up the tarmac and you'll find the world of sand. However great its distance from city life, the holiday beach keeps its polarity to city life and work. Urban culture's competence of handling privacy and communication in crowds of strangers makes the beach as a global project possible.

The global beach is a fact, but there are still the fine distinctions of class and ethnicity. People on Southland Beach complain of outsiders not sticking to the local rules and feel affronted at Chicanos who bathe with their clothes on, as well as at the Swedish woman who performs the classic Scandinavian tradition (and feat) of changing into swimwear with the help of a scanty beach towel. And in many settings the locals are still not very happy about the ways in which tourists expose their bodies on the beach. The tradition of going into the water fully clothed is still strong in many parts of the world.

There is a constant tension between the beach as an individual experience and the beach as a cultural arena, impregnated with rules, routines, and rituals. When Jean-Claude Kaufmann tries to sum up his beach observations he finds himself saying things like: the beach does this or that, the beach thinks, the beach prefers . . . There was an unconscious cultural collectivity of beach life to set against the fact that individuals often experience the beach as a liberating space, a space to break habits, not make them. This ambiguity catches rather nicely the cultural complexities of beach life.

The beach may seem to standardize vacation life, and yet the closer you look at beach experiences, the more personal they seem. Let me end the chapter with a quote from the Swedish novel *The Beach Man*, which travels between distant beaches:

> First down the stairs is as usual the old couple from Rotterdam . . . they unfold their piece of Balinese cloth, seventeen years old. *Got*, how time passes, and arrange sandals, clothes, water bottle, books, towels, bags, lighters, a pack of Salem, according to a choreography, which has been perfected and made permanent after—I don't dare to think—how many vacations at the beach together. . . .
>
> They bring out a tube of Piz Buin from a plastic bag and rub it on each other's backs, in silence and without gestures, as if they were taking turns to wipe the kitchen table, that's all. They look out toward the sea. He makes a short comment and gets a surprised smile back. They make themselves comfortable, getting the right angle to the sun. He puts two fingers on her hip and she gives his hand a brief pat: their parting ritual, because from now on they will be alone, each with their own sun. (Kihlgård 1992:7)

Source: From *On Holiday: A History of Vacationing*, 1999. Reprinted with permission of the author and University of California Press.

Notes

[1] The text goes on to assure you that personnel speaking both Portuguese and English will meet you at the airport and take care of your needs; quoted in Bilstein (1994:117).

[2] Over in Europe there was a similar craze for Pacific romance, a "polynesification" of European beach life, as the French sociologist Jean-Didier Urbain (1994:151) has called it.

[3] See the discussion in Finney and Houton (1996) and Timmons (1986:42).

[4] See the discussion in Irwin (1977:84).

[5] Frances Parkinson Keyes, "Hawaii Gets Under their Skin" (quoted in Timmons 1986:43).

[6] See Andolf, "Turismen i historien" in Löfgren et al. (1989:79) and Stilgoe (1996:355–58).

[7] For an overview of the nudism movement see Ilfled and Lauer (1964).

[8] See under "beach-" in the *Oxford English Dictionary.*

[9] Quoted in Edgerton (1979:152). See also Douglas, Rasmussen, and Flanagan (1977), which discusses nudity and privacy on a southern California beach.

[10] See the discussion in Snow and Wright (1976:960–75) and in Peiss (1987:115–38), where the gendering of the beach also is analyzed.

[11] Advertisement for Omni Hotels, *New York Times*, 15 June 1997.

[12] On the history of pools see Elving (1972) and Sprawson (1993).

References

Andolf, Göran. 1989. "Turismen i historien," in *Längtan till landet Annorlunda: Om turism i historia och nutid,* ed. Orvar Löfgren et al., pp. 355–58. Stockholm: Gidlunds.

Bailey, Beth, and David Farber. 1992. *The First Strange Place: Race and Sex in World War II Hawaii.* Baltimore: Johns Hopkins University Press.

Baldon, Cleo, and Ib Melchior. 1997. *Reflections on the Pool: California Designs for Swimming.* New York: Rizzoli.

Bilstein, Roger E. 1994. *Flight in America: From the Wrights to the Astronauts,* 2nd edition. Baltimore: Johns Hopkins University Press.

Blanchard, Gason. 1994. *The Poetics of Space.* London: Beacon Press.

Blume, 1994. *Cote d'Azur: Inventing the French Riviera.* London: Thames and Hudson.

Cohen, Colleen B., Richard Wilk, and Beverly Stoeltje, eds. 1995. *The Beauty Queens on the Global Stage: Gender, Contest and Power.* New York: Routledge.

Crantz, Galen. 1982. *The Politics of Park Design: A History of Urban Parks in America.* Cambridge: MIT Press.

Croutier, Alex Lyle. 1992. *Taking the Waters: Spirit, Art, Sensuality.* New York: Abbeville Press.

Douglas, Jack, and Paul K. Rasmussen, with Carol Ann Flanagan. 1977. *The Nude Beach.* Beverly Hills, CA: Sage.

Edgerton, Robert B. 1979. *Alone Together: Social Order on an Urban Beach.* Berkeley: University of California Press.

Elving, Phyllis. 1972. Sunset Swimming Pools, 4th edition. Menlo Park, CA: Sunset Publishing.

Finney, Ben, and James D. Houton. 1996. *Surfing: A History of the Ancient Hawaiian Sport.* San Francisco: Pomegranate Art Books.

Fiske, John. 1989. *Reading the Popular.* London: Routledge.

Fussell, Paul. 1980. *Abroad: British Literary Travelling between the Wars.* New York: Oxford University Press.

Grant, Glen. 1996. *Waikiki Yesteryear.* Honolulu: Mutual Publishing.

Ilfled, Fred Jr., and Roger Lauer. 1964. *Nudism in America.* New Haven, CT: College and University Press.

Irwin, John. 1977. *Scenes.* Beverly Hills: Sage.

Kaufmann, Jean-Claude. 1995. *Corps de femmes: Regards d'hommes.* Paris: Nathan.

Kihlgard, Peter. 1992. *Strandmannen.* Stockholm: Bonnier.

Kimpel, Harald, and Johanna Werckmeister. 1995. *Die Strandburg: Ein versandetes Freizeitsvergnugen.* Marburg: Jonas Verlag.

Löfgren, Orvar et al., eds. 1989. *Langtan till landet Annorlunda: Om turism i historia och nutid.* Stockholm: Gidlunds.

Lutz, Catherine A., and Jane L. Collins. 1993. *Reading National Geographic.* Chicago: University of Chicago Press.

Orwell, George. 1968 [1942]. "The Art of Donald McGill," in *The Collected Essays, Journalism and Letters of George Orwell,* pp. 183–94. London: Penguin Books.

Pattullo, Polly. 1996. *Last Resorts: The Costs of Tourism in the Caribbean.* London: Cassell.

Peiss, Kathy. 1987. *Cheap Amusements: Working Women and Leisure in Turn-of-the-century New York.* Philadelphia: Temple University Press.

Sacks, Oliver. 1997. "Water Babies: The Boundless Possibilities of Being in the Water." *New Yorker,* 26 May 1997:45.

Snow, Robert, and David Wright. 1976. "Coney Island: A Case Study in Popular Culture and Technical Change." *Journal of Popular Culture* 9:960–75.

Sprawson, Charles. 1993. *Haunts of the Black Masseur: The Swimmer as Hero.* London: Vintage.

Stilgoe, John R. 1996. *Alongshore.* New Haven, CT: Yale University Press.

Timmons, Grady. 1986. *Waikiki Beachboy.* Honolulu: Editions Ltd.

Towner, John. 1996. *An Historical Geography of Recreation and Tourism in the Western World.* Chichester: John Wiley and Sons.

Urbain, Jean-Didier. 1994. *Sur la plage: Moeurs et coutumes balnéaires.* Paris: Payot.

Walton, John K. 1983. *English Seaside Resort: A Social History, 1750–1914.* New York: St. Martin's Press.

4

Sightseeing and Social Structure: The Moral Integration of Modernity

Dean MacCannell

The Place of the Attraction in Modern Society

Modern society constitutes itself as a labyrinthine structure of norms governing access to its workshops, offices, neighborhoods, and semipublic places. As population density increases, this maze of norms manifests itself in physical divisions, walls, ceilings, fences, floors, hedges, barricades, and signs marking the limits of a community, an establishment, or a person's space.[1] This social system contains interstitial corridors—halls, streets, elevators, bridges, waterways, airways, and subways. These corridors are filled with things anyone can see. Erving Goffman has studied behavior in public places and relations in public for what they can reveal about our collective pride, shame, and guilt. I want to follow his lead and suggest that behavior is only one of the visible, public representations of social structure found in public places. We also find decay, refuse, human and industrial derelicts, monuments, museums, parks, decorated plazas, and architectural shows of industrial virtue. Public behavior and these other visible public parts of society are tourist attractions.

Sightseeing and the Moral Order

The organization of behavior and objects in public places is functionally equivalent to the sacred text that still serves as the moral base of traditional society. That is, public places contain the representations of good and evil that apply universally to modern existence in general.

A touristic attitude of respectful admiration is called forth by the finer attractions, the monuments, and a no-less-important attitude of disgust attaches itself to the uncontrolled garbage heaps, muggings, abandoned and tumble-down buildings, polluted rivers, and the like. Disgust over these items is the negative pole of respect for the monuments. Together, the two provide a moral stability to the modern touristic consciousness that extends beyond immediate social relationships to the structure and organization of the total society.

The tours of Appalachian communities and northern inner-city cores taken by politicians provide examples of negative sightseeing. This kind of tour is usually conducted by a local character who has connections outside of the community. The local points out and explains and complains about the rusting auto hulks, the corn that did not come up, winos and junkies on the nod, flood damage and other features of the area to the politician who expresses concern. While politicians and other public figures like Eleanor Roosevelt and the Kennedys are certainly the leaders here, this type of sightseeing is increasingly available to members of the middle class at large. *The New York Times* reports that seventy people answered an advertisement inviting tourists to spend "21 days 'in the land of the Hatfields and McCoys' for US$378.00, living with some of the poorest people in the United States in Mingo County, West Virginia."[2] Similarly, in 1967, the Penny Sightseeing Company inaugurated extensive guided tours of Harlem.[3] Recent ecological awareness has given rise to some imaginative variations: bus tours of "The Ten Top Polluters in Action" were available in Philadelphia during "Earth Week" in April 1970.

This touristic form of moral involvement with diverse public representations of race, poverty, urban structures, social ills, and, of course, the public "good," the monuments, is a modern alternative to systems of in-group morality built out of binary oppositions: insider vs. outsider, us vs. them. Traditional societies could not survive unless they oriented behavior in a "we are good—they are bad" framework. Although some of its remains are still to be found in modern politics, such traditional morality is not efficacious in the modern world. Social structural differentiation has broken up traditional loyalties. Now it is impossible to determine with any accuracy who "we" are and who "they" are. The modern world cannot survive if it tries to orient behavior in a traditional "we are good—they are bad" framework. As we enter the modern world, the entire field of social facts—poverty, race, class, work—is open to ongoing moral evaluation and interpretation. This craziness of mere distinctions forces the modern consciousness to explore beyond the frontiers of traditional prejudice and bigotry in its search for a moral

identity. Only "middle Americans" (if such people actually exist) and primitives—people whose lives are "everyday" in the pejorative, grinding sense of
the term—may feel fully a part of their own world. Modern humanity has
been condemned to look elsewhere, everywhere, for authenticity, to see if we
can catch a glimpse of it reflected in the simplicity, poverty, chastity, or
purity of others.

The Structure of the Attraction

I have defined a tourist attraction as an empirical relationship between a
tourist, a *sight*, and a *marker* (a piece of information about a sight). A simple
model of the attraction can be presented in the following form:

[tourist / sight / marker] attraction

Note that markers may take many different forms: guidebooks, informational
tablets, slide shows, travelogues, souvenir matchbooks, etc. Note also that no
naturalistic definition of the sight is possible. Well-marked sights that attract
tourists include such items as mountain ranges, Napoleon's hat, moon rocks,
Grant's tomb, even entire nation-states. The attractions are often indistin-

The Austin used by Thich Quang Duc, the first Buddhist monk in Vietnam to commit
a protest suicide through self-immolation in Saigon in 1963. It is kept at his home
monastery at the Thien Mau Pagoda near Hue. A photograph of the incident is on the
windshield. (Photo by Sharon Gmelch)

guishable from their less-famous relatives. If they were not marked, it would be impossible for a layperson to distinguish, on the basis of appearance alone, between moon rocks brought back by astronauts and pebbles picked up at Craters of the Moon National Monument in Idaho. But one is a sight and the other a souvenir, a kind of marker. Similarly, hippies are tourists and, at home in the Haight Ashbury, they are also sights that tourists come to see, or at least they used to be.

The distinguishing characteristic of those things that are collectively thought to be "true sights" is suggested by a second look at the moon rock example. *Souvenirs* are collected by *individuals*, by tourists, while *sights* are "collected" by entire societies. The entire United States is behind the gathering of moon rocks, or at least it is supposed to be, and hippies are a reflection of our collective affluence and decadence.

The origin of the attraction in the collective consciousness is not always so obvious as it is when a society dramatizes its values and capabilities by sending its representatives out into the solar system. Nevertheless, the collective determination of "true sights" is clear cut. The tourist has no difficulty deciding the sights he ought to see. The only problem is getting around to all of them. Even under conditions where there is no end of things to see, some mysterious institutional force operates on the totality in advance of the arrival of tourists, separating out the specific sights that are the attractions. In the Louvre, for example, the attraction is the *Mona Lisa*. The rest is undifferentiated art in the abstract. Moderns somehow know what the important attractions are, even in remote places. This miracle of consensus that transcends national boundaries rests on an elaborate set of institutional mechanisms, a twofold process of sight *sacralization* that is met with a corresponding *ritual attitude* on the part of tourists.

Sightseeing as Modern Ritual

Erving Goffman has defined ritual as a "perfunctory, conventionalized act through which an individual portrays his respect and regard for some object of ultimate value to its stand-in" (1971:62). This is translated into the individual consciousness as a sense of duty, albeit a duty that is often lovingly performed. Under conditions of high social integration, the ritual attitude may lose all appearance of coercive externality. It may, that is, permeate an individual's inmost being so ritual obligations are performed zealously and without thought for personal or social consequences.

Modern international sightseeing possesses its own moral structure, a collective sense that certain sights must be seen. Some tourists will resist, no doubt, the suggestion that they are motivated by an elementary impulse analogous to the one that animates the Australian's awe for his Churinga boards. The Australian would certainly resist such a suggestion. Nevertheless, modern guided tours, in Goffman's terms, are "extensive ceremonial agendas involving long strings of obligatory rites." If one goes to Europe, one "must see" Paris; if one goes to Paris, one "must see" Notre Dame, the Eiffel Tower, the Louvre; if one goes to the Louvre, one "must see" the *Venus de Milo* and, of course, the *Mona Lisa*. There are quite literally millions of tourists who have spent their savings to make the pilgrimage to see these sights. Some who have not been "there" have reported to me that they want to see these sights "with all their hearts."

It is noteworthy that no one escapes the system of attractions except by retreat into a stay-at-home, traditionalist stance: that is, no one is exempt from the obligation to go sightseeing except the local person. The Manhattan-ite who has never been to the Statue of Liberty is a mythic image in our soci-ety, as is the reverse image of the big-city people who come out into the country expressing fascination with things the local folk care little about. The ritual attitude of tourists originates in the act of travel itself and culminates when they arrive in the presence of the sight.

Some tourists feel so strongly about the sight they are visiting that they want to be alone in its presence, and they become annoyed at other tourists for profaning the place by crowding around "like sheep." Some sights become so important that tourists avoid use of their proper names: in the Pacific Northwest, Mount Rainier is called "The Mountain," and all up and down the West Coast of the United States, San Francisco is called "The City."

Traditional religious institutions are everywhere accommodating the movements of tourists. In "The Holy Land," the tour has followed in the path of the religious pilgrimage and is replacing it. Throughout the world, churches, cathedrals, mosques, and temples are being converted from reli-gious to touristic functions.

The Stages of Sight Sacralization

In structural studies, it is not sufficient to build a model of an aspect of society entirely out of attitudes and behavior of individuals. It is also neces-sary to specify in detail the linkages between the attitudes and behavior and concrete institutional settings.

Perhaps there are, or have been, some sights that are so spectacular in themselves that no institutional support is required to mark them off as attrac-tions. The original set of attractions is called, after the fashion of primitives, by the name of the sentiment they were supposed to have generated: "The Seven Wonders of the World." Modern sights, with but few exceptions, are not so evidently reflective of important social values as the Seven Wonders must have been. Attractions such as Cypress Gardens, the statue of the Little Mermaid in the harbor at Copenhagen, the Cape Hatteras Light and the like, risk losing their broader sociosymbolic meanings, becoming once more mere aspects of a limited social setting. Massive institutional support is often required for sight sacralization in the modern world.

The first stage of sight sacralization takes place when the sight is marked off from similar objects as worthy of preservation. This stage may be arrived at deductively from the model of the attraction

[tourist / sight / *marker*] attraction

or it may be arrived at inductively by empirical observation. Sights have markers. Sometimes an act of Congress is necessary, as in the official designation of a national park or historical shrine. This first stage can be called the naming phase of sight sacralization. Often, before the *naming phase*, a great deal of work goes into the authentication of the candidate for sacralization. Objects are x-rayed, baked, photographed with special equipment, and examined by experts. Reports are filed testifying to the object's aesthetic, historical, monetary, recreational, and social values.

Second is the *framing and elevation* phase. Elevation is the putting on display of an object—placement in a case, on a pedestal, or opened up for visitation. Framing is the placement of an official boundary around the object. On a practical level, two types of framing occur: protecting and enhancing. Protection seems to have been the motive behind the decision recently taken at the Louvre to place the *Mona Lisa* (but none of the other paintings) behind glass. When spotlights are placed on a building or a painting, it is enhanced. Most efforts to protect a sacred object, such as hanging a

Sight sacralization: Domestic and foreign tourists queue to see Ho-Chi-Minh's body in Hanoi, Vietnam. (Photo by Pat Mahoney)

silk cord in front of it, or putting extra guards on duty around it, can also be read as a kind of enhancement so the distinction between protection and enhancement eventually breaks down. Tourists before the *Mona Lisa* often remark: "Oh, it's the only one with glass," or "It must be the most valuable, it has glass in front." Advanced framing occurs when the rest of the world is forced back from the object and the space in between is landscaped. Versailles and the Washington Monument are "framed" in this way.

When the framing material that is used has itself entered the first stage of sacralization (marking), a third stage has been entered. This stage can be called *enshrinement*. The model here is Sainte Chapelle, the church built by Saint Louis as a container for the "true Crown of Thorns" that he had purchased from Baldwin of Constantinople. Sainte Chapelle is, of course, a tourist attraction in its own right. Similarly, in the Gutenberg Museum, in Gutenberg, Germany, the original Gutenberg Bible is displayed under special lights on a pedestal in a darkened enclosure in a larger room. The walls of the larger room are hung with precious documents, including a manuscript by Beethoven.

The next stage of sacralization is *mechanical reproduction* of the sacred object: the creation of prints, photographs, models, or effigies of the object which are themselves valued and displayed. It is the mechanical reproduction phase of sacralization that is most responsible for setting the tourist in motion on his journey to find the true object. And he is not disappointed. Alongside of the copies of it, it has to be The Real Thing.

The final stage of sight sacralization is *social reproduction*, as occurs when groups, cities, and regions begin to name themselves after famous attractions.

Tourist attractions are not merely a collection of random material representations. When they appear in itineraries, they have a moral claim on the tourist and, at the same time, they tend toward universality, incorporating natural, social, historical, and cultural domains in a single representation made possible by the tour. This morally enforced universality is the basis of a general system of classification of societal elements produced without conscious effort. No person or agency is officially responsible for the worldwide proliferation of tourist attractions. They have appeared naturally, each seeming to respond to localized causes.

Nevertheless, when they are considered as a totality, tourist attractions reveal themselves to be a taxonomy of structural elements. Interestingly, this natural taxonomic system contains the analytical classification of social structure currently in use by social scientists. A North American itinerary, for example, contains domestic, commercial, and industrial establishments, occupations, public-service and transportation facilities, urban neighborhoods, communities, and members of solitary (or, at least, identifiable) subgroups of American society. The specific attractions representing these structural categories would include the Empire State Building, an Edwardian house in Boston's Back Bay, a Royal Canadian mounted policeman, a Mississippi River bridge, Grand Coulee Dam, an Indian totem pole, San Francisco's Chinatown, a cable car, Tijuana, Indians, cowboys, an ante-bellum mansion, an Amish farm, Arlington National Cemetery, the Smithsonian Institution, and Washington Cathedral.

Taken together, tourist attractions and the behavior surrounding them are, I think, one of the most complex and orderly of the several universal codes that constitute modern society, although not so complex and orderly as, for example, a language.

Claude Lévi-Strauss claims that there is no such system in modern society. I think it is worth exploring the possible base of this claim, which is by no means confined to Lévi-Strauss's offhand remarks. Erving Goffman has similarly suggested that:

> ... in contemporary society rituals performed to stand-ins for supernatural entities are everywhere in decay, as are extensive ceremonial agendas involving long strings of obligatory rites. What remains are brief rituals one individual performs for another, attesting to civility and good will on the performer's part and to the recipient's possession of a small patrimony of sacredness. (1971:63)

I think that the failure of Goffman and Lévi-Strauss to note the existence of social integration on a macro-structural level in modern society can be traced to a methodological deficiency: neither of them has developed the use of systemic variables for his analysis of social structure. In my own studies, I was able to bypass Lévi-Strauss's critique by working up the very dimension of modernity that he named as its most salient feature: its chaotic fragmentation, its *differentiation*.

Interestingly, the approach I used was anticipated by Émile Durkheim, who invented the use of systemic variables for sociological analysis and who named tourist attractions ("works of art" and "historical monuments") in his basic listing of social facts. Durkheim wrote:

> Social facts, on the contrary [he had just been writing of psychological facts], qualify far more naturally and immediately as things. Law is embodied in codes ... fashions are preserved in costumes; taste in works of art ... [and] the currents of daily life are recorded in statistical figures and historical monuments. By their very nature they tend towards an independent existence outside the individual consciousness, which they dominate. (1938:30)

Until now, no sociologist took up Durkheim's suggestion that "costumes," "art," and "monuments" are keys to modern social structure. The structure of the attraction was deciphered by accident by the culture critic Walter Benjamin while working on a different problem. But Benjamin, perhaps because of his commitment to an orthodox version of Marxist theory, inverted all the basic relations. He wrote:

> The uniqueness of a work of art is inseparable from its being imbedded in the fabric of tradition. This tradition itself is thoroughly alive and extremely changeable. An ancient statue of Venus, for example, stood in

a different traditional context with the Greeks, who made it an object of veneration, than with the clerics of the Middle Ages, who viewed it as an ominous idol. Both of them, however, were equally confronted with its uniqueness, that is, its aura. Originally the contextual integration of art in tradition found its expression in the cult. We know that the earliest art works originated in the service of ritual—first the magical, then the religious kind. It is significant that the existence of the work of art with reference to its aura is never entirely separated from its ritual function. In other words, the unique value of the "authentic" work of art has its basis in ritual, the location of its original use value. (Benjamin 1969:223–24)

Setting aside for the moment Marxist concerns for "use value," I want to suggest that society does not produce art: artists do. Society, for its part, can only produce the importance, "reality," or "originality" of a work of art by piling up representations of it alongside. Benjamin believed that the reproductions of the work of art are produced because the work has a socially based "aura" about it, the "aura" being a residue of its origins in a primordial ritual. He should have reversed his terms. The work becomes "authentic" only after the first copy of it is produced. The reproductions *are* the aura, and the ritual, far from being a point of origin, *derives* from the relationship between the original object and its socially constructed importance. I would argue that this is the structure of the attraction in modern society, including the artistic attractions, and the reason the Grand Canyon has a touristic "aura" about it even though it did not originate in ritual.

Attractions and Structural Differentiation

In the tourists' consciousness, the attractions are not analyzed type by type. They appear sequentially, unfolding before the tourists so long as they continue sightseeing. The touristic value of a modern community lies in the way it organizes social, historical, cultural, and natural elements into a stream of impressions. Guidebooks contain references to all types of attractions, but the lively descriptions tend to be of the social materials. Modern society makes of itself its principal attraction in which the other attractions are embedded. Baedeker wrote of Paris:

Paris is not only the political metropolis of France, but also the center of the artistic, scientific, commercial, and industrial life of the nation. Almost every branch of French industry is represented here, from the fine-art handicrafts to the construction of powerful machinery . . .

The central quarters of the city are remarkably hustling and animated, but owing to the ample breadth of the new streets and boulevards and the fact that many of them are paved with asphalt or stone Paris is a far less noisy place than many other large cities. Its comparative tranquility, however, is often rudely interrupted by the discordant cries of the itinerant hawkers of wares of every kind, such as "old clothes" men, the vendors of various kinds of comestibles, the crockery-menders, the "fontaniers" (who clean and repair filters, etc.), the dog barbers, and newspaper-sellers. As a rule, however, they are clean and tidy in their dress, polite in manner, self-respecting, and devoid of the squalor and ruffianism which too often characterize their class. (1990:xxix–xxx)

Georg Simmel began the analysis of this modern form of social consciousness which takes as its point of departure social structure itself. Simmel wrote:

> Man is a differentiating creature. His mind is stimulated by the differences between a momentary impression and the one which preceded it. Lasting impressions, impressions which differ only slightly from one another, impressions which take a regular and habitual course and show regular and habitual contrasts—all these use up, so to speak, less consciousness than does the rapid crowding of changing images, the sharp discontinuity in the grasp of a single glance, and the unexpectedness of onrushing impressions. These are the psychological conditions which the metropolis creates. With each crossing of the street, with the tempo and multiplicity of the economic, occupational and social life, the city sets up a deep contrast with the small town and rural life with reference to the sensory foundations of psychic life. (Wolff 1950:410)

Simmel claims to he working out an aspect of the *Gemeinschaft Gesellschaft* distinction. It would be more accurate to say that he is describing the difference between everyday life impressions, be they rural *or* urban, and the impressions of a strange place formed by a tourist on a visit, a vantage point Simmel knew well.[4]

Baedeker's and Simmel's stress on the work dimension of society is also found in touristic descriptions of New York City, which is always in the process of being rebuilt, and the waterfront areas of any city that has them. Similarly, Mideastern and North African peoples have traditionally made much use of their streets as places of work, and tourists from the Christian West seem to have inexhaustible fascination for places such as Istanbul, Tangiers, Damascus, and Casablanca, where they can see factories without walls.

Primitive social life is nearly totally exposed to outsiders who happen to be present. Perhaps some of our love for primitives is attached to this innocent openness.

Modern society, originally quite closed up, is rapidly restructuring or institutionalizing the rights of outsiders (that is, of individuals not functionally connected to the operation) to look into its diverse aspects. Institutions are fitted with arenas, platforms, and chambers set aside for the exclusive use of tourists. The courtroom is the most important institution in a democratic society. It was among the first to open to the outside and, I think, it will be among the first to close as the workings of society are increasingly revealed through the opening of other institutions to tourists. The New York Stock Exchange and the Corning Glass factory have specially designated visitors' hours, entrances, and galleries. Mental hospitals, army bases, and grade schools stage periodic open houses where not mere work but good work is displayed. The men who make pizza crusts by tossing the dough in the air often work in windows where they can be watched from the sidewalk. Construction companies cut peepholes into the fences around their work, nicely arranging the holes for sightseers of different heights. The becoming public of almost everything—a process that makes all people equal before the attraction—is a necessary part of the integrity of the modern social world.

Tourist Districts

Distinctive local attractions contain (just behind, beside, or embedded in the parts presented to the tourists) working offices, shops, services, and facilities: often an entire urban structure is operating behind its touristic front. Some of these touristic urban areas are composed of touristic *districts*. Paris is "made up" of the Latin Quarter, Pigalle, Montparnasse, Montmartre; San Francisco is made up of the Haight Ashbury, the Barbary Coast, and Chinatown; and London of Soho, Piccadilly Circus, Blackfriars, Covent Gardens, the Strand. Less touristically developed areas have only one tourist district and are, therefore, sometimes upstaged by it: the Casbah, Beverly Hills, Greenwich Village. An urban sociologist or an ethnographer might point out that cities are composed of much more than their tourist areas, but this is obvious. Even tourists are aware of this. More important is the way the tourist attractions appear on a regional base as a model of social structure, beginning with "suggested" or "recommended" *communities, regions,* and *neighborhoods*, and extending to matters of detail, setting the tourist up with a matrix to fill in with discoveries of typical little *markets, towns, restaurants,* and *people*. This touristic matrix assures that the social structure that is recomposed via the tour, while always partial, is nevertheless not a skewed or warped representation of reality. Once on tour, only the individual imagination can modify reality, and so long as the faculty of imagination is at rest, society appears such as it is.

The taxonomy of structural elements provided by the attractions is universal, not because it *already* contains everything it might contain but rather, because the logic behind it is potentially inclusive. It sets up relationships between elements (as between neighborhoods and their cities) which cross the artificial boundaries between levels of social organization, society, and culture, and culture and nature. Still, the resulting itineraries rarely penetrate lovingly into the precious details of a society as a Southern novelist might, peeling back layer after layer of local historical, cultural, and social facts, although this is the ideal of a certain type of snobbish tourism. Such potential exists in the structure of the tour, but it goes for the most part untapped. Attractions are usually organized more on the model of the filing system of a disinterested observer, like a scientist who separates passion from its object, reserving passion entirely for matters of method; or like a carpetbagging politician who calculates his rhetoric while reading a printout of the demographic characteristics of the region he wants to represent. In short, the tourist world is complete in its way, but it is constructed after the fashion of all worlds that are filled with people who are just passing through and know it.

The Differentiations of the Tourist World

Functioning *establishments* figure prominently as tourist attractions. Commercial, industrial, and business establishments are also basic features of social regions, or they are first among the elements from which regions are composed. Some, such as the Empire State Building, the now-defunct Les Halles in Paris, and Fisherman's Wharf in San Francisco, overwhelm their districts. Others fit together in a neat structural arrangement of little establishments that contribute to their district's special local character: flower shops, meat and vegetable markets, shoe repair shops, neighborhood churches. Unlike the Empire State Building, with its elevators expressly for sightseers, these little establishments may not be prepared for the outside visitors they attract. A priest who made his parish famous had this problem, but apparently he is adjusting to the presence of tourists:

> For a time, in fact, St. Boniface became an attraction for tourists and white liberals from the suburbs. Father Groppi recalled that he had sometimes been critical of the whites who overflowed the Sunday masses at St. Boniface and then returned to their suburban homes.
>
> "But now I can understand their problems," he said. "They come from conservative parishes and were tired of their parish organizations, the Holy Name Society and that sort of nonsense."[5]

Under normal conditions of touristic development, no social establishment ultimately resists conversion into an attraction, not even *domestic establishments*. Selected homes in the "Society Hill" section of downtown Philadelphia are opened annually for touristic visitation. Visitors to Japan are routinely offered the chance to enter, observe, and—to a limited degree—even participate in the households of middle-class families. Individual arrangements can he made with the French Ministry of Tourism to have coffee in a French home, and even to go for an afternoon drive in the country with a Frenchman of "approximately one's own social station."[6]

A version of sociology suggests that society is composed not of individuals but groups, and *groups*, too, figure as tourist attractions. Certain groups work up a show of their group characteristics (their ceremonies, settlement patterns, costumes, etc.) especially for the benefit of sightseers:

> At an open meeting yesterday of Indian businessmen, government officials and airline representatives, Dallas Chief Eagle, spokesman and director of the new United States Indian International Travel agency, said the cooperative hoped to be able to offer low-cost group tours to German tourists by June.[7]

Other groups, even other Indian groups, militantly resist such show-manship, even though their leaders are aware of their touristic potential, because this kind of behavior *for* tourists is widely felt to be degrading.[8] Given the multichanneled nature of human communication, these two versions of the group (the proud and the practical) need not be mutually exclusive. The following account suggests that a member of one of our recently emergent self-conscious minorities can do her own thing and do a thing for the tourists at the same time:

> New Jersey, Connecticut, and even Pennsylvania license plates were conspicuous around Tompkins Square yesterday, indicating that the Lower East Side's new hippie haven is beginning to draw out-of-state tourists.

> "You go to where the action is," a blond girl in shorts said through a thick layer of white lipstick. The girl, who said her name was Lisa Stern, and that she was a freshman at Rutgers University, added: "I used to spend weekends in Greenwich Village, but no longer." However, Lisa didn't find much action in Tompkins Square Park, the scene of a Memorial Day clash between about 200 hippies and the police . . . Yesterday there was no question any more as to a hippie's right to sit on the grass or to stretch out on it.

> Some tourists from New Jersey were leaning over the guardrail enclosing a patch of lawn, much as if they were visiting a zoo, and stared at a man with tattooed arms and blue-painted face who gently waved at them while the bongo drums were throbbing. (Hoffman 1967:3)

Other groups—the Pennsylvania "Dutch," the Amanas, Basques, and peasants everywhere—probably fall somewhere in between resistance and acquiescence to tourism, or they vacillate from self-conscious showiness to grudging acceptance of it.

Perhaps because they have a human being inside, *occupations* are popular tourist attractions. In some areas, local handicrafts would have passed into extinction except for the intervention of mass tourism and the souvenir market:

> Palekh boxes are formed from papier-mâché and molded in the desired shape on a wood form. A single artist makes the box, coats it with layers of black lacquer, paints his miniature picture, adds final coats of clear lacquer and signs his name and the date. Each box represents two to three days' work. Some of Palekh's 150 artists work at home . . . I watched Constantine Bilayev, an artist in his fifties, paint a fairytale scene he might have been doing for his grandchildren. It illustrated the story of a wicked old woman with a daughter she favored and a step-daughter she hated. She sent the stepdaughter into the woods to gather firewood, hoping harm would befall the girl. Instead, the stepdaughter triumphed over every adversity. (Chapman 1969:29)

In addition to this cute side of occupational sightseeing, there is a heavy, modern workaday aspect. In the same community with the box makers, there are *real* young ladies triumphing over adversity while serving as tourist attractions. The report continues:

But the main attraction of this city of 400,000 people is the Ivanovo Textile Factory, an industrial enormity that produces some 25,000,000 yards of wool cloth a year. The factory represents an investment of US$55 million. The factory's machinery makes an ear-shattering din. Ranks of machines take the raw wool and convert it into coarse thread, and successive ranks of devices extrude the thread into ever-finer filaments. The weaving machines clang in unison like a brigade on the march—Raz, Dva, Raz, Dva, Raz, Dva as an unseen Russian sergeant would count it out. The 7,500 workers are mostly young and mostly female. A bulletin board exhorts them to greater production in honor of the Lenin centenary.

Along with handicraft and specialized industrial work, there are other occupational attractions including glassblowers, Japanese pearl divers, cowboys, fishermen, Geisha girls, London chimney sweeps, gondoliers, and sidewalk artists. Potentially, the entire division of labor in society can be transformed into a tourist attraction. In some districts of Manhattan, even the men in gray flannel suits have been marked off for touristic attention.

Connecting the urban areas of society are *transportation networks*, segments and intersections of which are tourist attractions. Examples are: the London Bridge, the Champs Elysées, Hollywood and Vine, Ponte Vecchio, the Golden Gate, Red Square, the canals of Venice and Amsterdam, Broadway, the Gate of Heavenly Peace, the Rue de Rivoli, the Spanish Steps, Telegraph Avenue, the Atlantic City Boardwalk, the Mont Blanc tunnel, Union Square, and New England's covered bridges. Along these lines is the follow-

Gondoliers ferry tourists through the canals of Venice. (Photo by George Gmelch)

ing comment on an attraction that is not well known but for which some hopes have been raised:

> The city of Birmingham recently opened its first expressway. To do so it had to slice a gash through famed Red Mountain in order to complete construction and get people in and out of the city in a hurry. To the drivers of Birmingham the freeway means a new convenience, but to the thousands of visitors the giant cut at the crest of the mountain has become a fascinating stopping place . . . a new and exciting tourist attraction.[9]

In addition to roads, squares, intersections, and bridges, *vehicles* that are restricted to one part of the worldwide transportation network also figure as attractions: rickshaws, gondolas, San Francisco's cable cars, and animal-powered carts everywhere.

Finally, the system of attractions extends as far as society has extended its *public works*, not avoiding things that might well have been avoided:

> A London sightseeing company has added a tour of London's public lavatories to its schedule. The firm, See Britain, said the lavatories tour will begin Sunday and cost five shillings (60 cents). It will include lavatories in the city and the West End. A spokesman said visitors will see the best Victorian and Edwardian lavatories in the areas with a guide discussing the style of the interiors, architecture, hours of opening and history.[10]

The presentation of the inner workings of society's nether side is, of course, the Paris sewer tour.

Although tourists need not be consciously aware of this, the thing they go to see is society and its works. The societal aspect of tourist attractions is hidden behind their fame, but this fame cannot change their origin in social structure. Given the present sociohistorical epoch, it is not a surprise to find that tourists believe sightseeing is a leisure activity, and fun, even when it requires more effort and organization than many jobs. In a marked contrast to the grudging acquiescence that may characterize the relation of the individual to industrial work, individuals happily embrace the attitudes and norms that lead them into a relationship with society through the sightseeing act. In being presented as a valued object through a so-called "leisure" activity that is thought to be "fun," society is renewed in the heart of the individual through warm, open, unquestioned relations, characterized by a near absence of alienation when compared with other contemporary relationships. This is, of course, the kind of relationship of individual and society that social scientists and politicians think is necessary for a strong society, and they are probably correct in their belief.

Tourist attractions in their natural, unanalyzed state may not appear to have any coherent infrastructure uniting them, and insofar as it is through the attraction that the tourist apprehends society, society may not appear to have coherent structure either. It is not my intention here to over-organize the touristic consciousness. It exhibits the deep structure, which is social structure that I am describing here, but this order need never be perceived as such in its totality. Consciousness and the integration of the individual into the modern world require only that one attraction be linked to one other: a district to a community, or an establishment to a district, or a role to an establishment. Even if only a single linkage is grasped in the immediate present, this solitary link is the starting point for an endless spherical system of connections that is society and the world, with the individual at one point on its surface.

Source: From *The Tourist: A New Theory of the Leisure Class*, [1976] 1999. Reprinted with permission of the author and University of California Press.

Notes

[1] Detailed microstudies of social structure are provided by Hall (1969) and Sommer (1969).
[2] *New York Times*, 30 June 1969, p. 1.
[3] Ibid., 22 May 1967, p. 39.
[4] See Simmel's essay on "The Stranger" (Wolff 1950:410).
[5] *New York Times*, 12 April 1970, p. 34.
[6] From my fieldnotes.
[7] *International Tribune* (Paris), 26 March 1971, p. 7.
[8] Interestingly, behavior *for* tourists is only felt to be degrading by members of already exploited minorities. Middle-class hippies and radicals seem to enjoy working in front of the camera. Perhaps leaders of exploited minorities teach non-cooperation with tourists because this is one of the only areas in which members of these minorities can dramatize self-determination.
[9] News release dated 27 April 1970 from "Operation New Birmingham," a civic group, quoted in "Images of America: Radical Feeling Remains Strong in the Cities." *New York Times*, 24 May 1970, p. 64.
[10] "For Tourists Who Want to See All," *International Herald Tribune,* 4 November 1970.

References

Baedeker, Karl. 1900. *Paris and Environs*. 14th rev. edition. Leipzig: Karl Baedeker Publisher.
Benjamin, Walter. 1969. *Illuminations*, ed. Hannah Arendt, trans. Harry Zohn. New York: Schocken.
Chapman, Irwin M. 1969. "Visit to Two Russian Towns." *New York Times*, 23 February 1969, section 10.
Durkheim, Émile. 1938. *The Rules of Sociological Method*, trans. S. A. Solovay and J. H. Mueller. New York: Free Press.
Goffman, Erving. 1963. *Behavior in Public Places: Notes on the Social Organization of Gatherings*. New York: Free Press.
———. 1971. *Relations in Public: Microstudies of the Public Order*. New York: Basic Books.
Hall, Edward T. 1969. *The Hidden Dimension*. Garden City, NY: Anchor Books.
Hoffman, Paul. 1967. "Hippie's Hangout Draws Tourists." *New York Times*, 5 June 1967.
Sommer, Robert. 1969. *Personal Space: The Behavioral Basis of Design*. Englewood Cliffs, NJ: Prentice-Hall.
Wolff, Kurt H., ed. and trans. 1950. *The Sociology of Georg Simmel*. Glencoe, IL: Free Press.

5

Let's Go Europe: What Student Tourists Do and Learn from Travel

George Gmelch

The idea that travel is educational has been around a long time. From the late seventeenth century onward, the sons of the rich and powerful were sent on a "Grand Tour" of Europe not only for pleasure but also to learn about its history and culture. In the process, these young elites would improve and develop themselves: "A man who has not been to Italy," remarked essayist Samuel Johnson in the 1770s, "is always conscious of an inferiority, from his not having seen what is expected that a man should see" (in Lofgren 1999). Visiting the Mediterranean, particularly Italy and Greece, was considered especially valuable since the region had not yet been transformed by industrialization. These early "tourists," therefore, could journey back in time and explore the roots of Western civilization. It is the Grand Tour that gave us the word "tourism."

Mark Twain also recognized the connection between travel and education, declaring that "travel is fatal to prejudice, bigotry, and narrow-mindedness . . . broad, wholesome, charitable views of men and things cannot be acquired by vegetating in a little corner of the earth all one's lifetime." Much more recently, *New York Times* op-ed columnist Nicolas Kristof (2006) proposed that universities grant a full semester's course credit to any incoming freshman who had taken a gap year to travel around the world. Kristof also suggested that American universities switch to a three-year on-campus academic program and require all students to live abroad for a fourth year, ideally three months in each of four continents: Latin America, Asia, Africa, and Europe. The cost of a year of travel, he claimed, "would be far less than the annual cost of attending college and students would get far more." No university that I'm aware of has yet implemented Kristof's proposal but nearly all encourage their students to travel, and most have "international programs" designed for students to study abroad. Once students are abroad, their academic schedules are often arranged to maximize the time they have to tour.

The study-abroad program in Innsbruck, Austria, in which I taught, provides the basis of this article. All classes finished each week at noon on Thursday, so that students could get a head start on their weekly three-day jaunts around Europe.[1] When I first arrived in Innsbruck in the summer of 1993, I, too, believed that travel offered all kinds of educational benefits for students.[2] As an anthropologist trained to take field notes, I believed that my students would learn even more from their travels if they kept a journal—the next best thing. Having to write about their daily experiences would force them to reflect on the people, places, and customs they encountered as tourists. To this end, I required students in both of my anthropology classes to

Innsbruck, Austria. (Courtesy of University of New Orleans)

keep detailed travel journals. Nevertheless, when I collected and began reading their entries, I was startled at how shallow their engagements were with
the people and places they visited. The few observations they made were, on
the whole, naïve and simplistic; the students didn't seem to be learning much
of anything. Yet, it was clear from class discussions that the students valued
their travel experiences highly; most believed they learned more by being
tourists than from their on-campus classes, including my own.

The contradiction between what I read in their journals and the students' claims about the educational value of their travel piqued my curiosity.
What really happened when they went on the road as tourists?[3] To find out, I
asked them to record all their movements and activities in "travel logs." They
made very brief notations every 15 minutes—from the time they got up in the
morning until they retired at night—about what they were doing (e.g., "on
train") and the number of people they were with. Students then calculated at
the end of each three-day weekend, how much time they had spent on each
activity (e.g., waiting for trains, riding trains, riding buses, sightseeing, shopping, drinking, eating, etc.). My intent was not to collect "data" from my students—I hadn't yet thought of writing this paper—rather I thought that the
travel logs would help them see the patterns in their travel (and perhaps the
folly in some of it). Only toward the end of the term, as I reviewed the material they turned in did I begin to think that it revealed something significant
about what students really learn when they travel.[4] In searching the scholarly
literature later, I discovered that while a significant amount had been written
about the educational impacts of study-abroad programs (Kauffmann et. al.
1992 provides a useful review), hardly anything had been written specifically
about what students learn as tourists or travelers.

What follows is an attempt to do just that. First, I describe what my students did when they traveled. Then, and more significantly, I explore the
ways in which their travel was educational and offer an explanation as to why.

Students on Tour

At the end of classes each Thursday afternoon, the students, packs on
their backs, set out for the Innsbruck train station to begin their weekend
sojourn. With Eurail passes' unlimited travel, they visited countries throughout Western Europe and parts of Central Europe. They went wherever the
trains could conveniently take them, but their preferred destinations were
places other students had recommended, which also happened to be the
places featured in popular guidebooks like *Let's Go Europe*. The most popular destinations in Italy, for example, were Venice, Florence, and Rome; in
Austria, they were Vienna and Salzburg; in Germany, they were Munich and
Berlin; and so on.

They traveled frequently, never staying long in one place. Their travel
logs showed that they visited an average of 1.7 countries and 2.4 cities per

weekend. This means that the average student spent slightly over one day in each of the cities he or she visited. (They stayed longest in the beach resort areas of the French and Italian Rivieras and at Interlaken's adventure tourism sites.) Their city-a-day tourism approach can be attributed to several factors. Many wanted to see as much of Europe as they could during their brief time abroad. They were not sure when, if ever, they would come back. Amanda expressed the sentiments of many students when she explained, "I wanted to be able to go home and say that I saw as much as I could in the six weeks that I was here." There was also some competition among the students, especially the men, to see how much of Europe they could cover with their Eurail passes. For many students, getting to know the places well mattered far less than being able to say that they had been there. The tendency to "map hop," as some students referred to it, was also motivated by their desire to get maximum value from their Eurail passes, for which they each had paid about $500. They traveled hastily, despite the program director's advice to get to know the places they visited and "not to run up the mileage." One consequence of their highly mobile form of tourism was that they spent a lot of time waiting in train stations and sitting on trains. Over an average three-day or 72-hour weekend, the students spent 18.7 hours on trains and three hours in stations waiting for them—in other words they spent nearly a third of their time in transit.

Despite all the time spent in transit, the journey itself was much less important to students than the destination. Few reported or were observed by others to spend much time looking out the window. Karen wrote about her traveling companions: "They want to run to the goal and run back." Another student reflected: "I seem to be preoccupied on most train rides, if not sleeping, reading, or writing, just talking or laughing with friends. Now that I look back, I wish that I had paid more attention to the places that we were passing through because I think that probably a lot more would have come out of it." But there were an equal number of students who had no regrets. Michelle, who calculated that she had spent five full days sitting on trains since arriving at Innsbruck, wrote:

> Some of my most striking moments occurred on the trains—the train strike in Milan, sleeping in couchettes with complete strangers, being hot as hell, the French man that molested Betsy and me, the beautiful scenery in Switzerland, random thoughts, open windows, mountains . . . sleeping with Andrew, not knowing what stop to get off.

Decisions about where to go next were often made on the spur of the moment. If students were disappointed with a place once they reached it, they were inclined to return to the train station and pick a new destination. They often chose where to go based on where the next available train was heading. If, for example, they were thinking of going to Florence but the wait for the train to Milan was half as long, they would be just as likely to hop on the train for Milan.

As the term progressed, many students slowed down, staying longer in the places they visited. Often, they became critical of those who continued to travel excessively. Betsy, who had visited eight countries in her first three weekends in Innsbruck, commented: "Americans approach their leisure activity like work . . . they exhaust themselves running about trying to get in as much as they can. I am guilty of this too, but I now try to spend some time pondering where I am." And Julia wrote in her journal: "I wonder if we really enjoy the museums and sights that we see. It seems that too often we are too concerned about where to go next, and how we will get there, and that we don't always appreciate where we are at the time."

At the end of the term, Julia wrote: "I need to go back and stay for a longer period of time in each place. Everywhere we went everyone would ask why we only stayed for one day. And now I am wondering the same thing. For most Americans it seems to be enough to visit a place, take a few pictures and say to their friends and relatives, 'Been there, done that.'"

Traveling Companions

Students also recorded the number of companions they traveled with in their travel logs. The average group size during journeys was 5.2 students, shrinking to 4.6 once they arrived at a destination. Why such large groups? For most students, this was their first time abroad and they were understandably nervous about traveling alone or even in pairs; they found security in numbers. Over the summer, as they learned their way around and became more confident, the size of tour groups declined by a third. The shrinkage was also the result of the frustrations many students experienced when looking for accommodation, going to restaurants, and visiting places in large groups. "I've discovered that it is better to travel in small numbers!" wrote Stephen. "Not only is it a pain to appease a large crowd, but you had to listen to constant complaining. . . ." Some students saw other liabilities to large groups, as Stephanie noted while on a train to Amsterdam:

> As I head for the city of 24-hour decadence I have realized that we create our own little culture here and that may not be entirely good. Don't get me wrong. I've had fun. But our student culture isolates us from absorbing and trying to fit in to the cultures that we are visiting. Even in Innsbruck we tend to go out in flocks, mostly to local bars at night and the same bars over and over again. And more often than not, the places we choose are tourist magnets where we don't have any chance of meeting people in the country we are in. I think it will be important for me to come back to Europe with just one or two people.

Some students admitted that they often followed the "herd" rather than deciding for themselves how they really wanted to spend their time. Ben wrote about his companions during a trip to Munich. Though only a freshman, he was the only one in the group who had been there before: "I said,

'Let's go to the Hofbrauhaus' and everybody followed. I felt like the Pied Piper." About her stay in Cannes, Andrea wrote: "We ended up at the Miss Cannes pageant. How, I don't know. Sara and Charles were following the music and paid thirty francs to get in, so we all followed along. . . ."

Walking around European cities in groups definitely limited the students' opportunities to interact with local people. In groups, they spend most of their time interacting with each other and far less time observing their surroundings. Their conversations, even when standing before great works of European art, architecture, or scenery, were often about people, places, and events back home rather than where they were at that moment. Local people also are less inclined to start a conversation with a group of students, especially boisterous Americans, than they would if it were just one or two individuals. In perhaps the most comprehensive study of American students studying in Europe, J. Carlson and colleagues found that "the most important medium for personal experience in the host country was conversation with host nationals" (1990:11). Clearly, by traveling alone or in pairs students could enhance the educational value of their trips. Most of my students eventually realized this, but still were not ready to give up the security of the group (although some said they hoped to do so in the future). Megan, who had spent most of the summer traveling with five companions, wrote about the one day she had spent on the road away from the group:

> I really enjoyed the Italian Riviera. It was only Jennifer and me, and we met a lot of different people. On the train ride back I was by myself and literally took in everything—the people I saw, how they acted, a baby on the train yelling, everyone annoyed at him, and I was too until the baby made me think of my niece and I laughed. Women talking to a couple and kissing cheeks. A couple leaving one another on the train. They were kissing and it made me so sad that they were leaving each other that I cried. Looking out the window at the gorgeous Mediterranean Sea and cliffs. . . . Being by myself I had lots of emotions going on inside of me that I hadn't felt before.

But few students ever traveled alone, and those who did were invariably traveling to meet someone else—a friend, pen pal, or relative who was also in Europe. Being on their own usually made students anxious. Before going to London to visit a college friend, Amanda wrote in her journal, "I'm very excited and nervous. I'll be in Europe all by myself. I'll have to make all the decisions without having to consult anyone. This will be an experience of independence."

Daily Routines of Student Travelers

What do students do once they have arrived at a destination? Most followed the recommendations of earlier students. They also consulted their guidebooks and got advice from local tourist offices. In Salzburg, they walked around the old town, climbed the hill to the castle, and took the *Sound of Music* tour; in Venice they went to St. Mark's Square, rode the canals in a gondola or vaporetto, and visited the glass shops; in Munich they looked at paintings in the Alte Pinakothek or technology in the Deutsches Museum, visited the Englischer Garten, and spent an evening in the Hofbrauhaus drinking beer with other tourists; in Florence they went to the Uffizi and the Academic museums (the latter mainly to see the *David*); and in Budapest they visited the castle district, the free museums, and because goods and services were cheaper there than elsewhere, they ate well, and the female students went to spas for massages, pedicures, and facials.

Early in the term the students rushed to the great cities of Western Europe—Paris, Munich, Venice, and Vienna—where they engaged in cultural tourism—visiting museums and galleries and looking at great architecture. Toward the end of the term, the students' interests shifted to recreation sites—the beach resorts of the Italian and French Riviera, and Interlaken, Switzerland, which offered paragliding, white-water rafting, and horseback riding. The number of museums they visited declined by more than two-thirds during the last half of the term. When I asked students about this in class, some said, with others nodding or murmuring in agreement, that they'd had their fill of museums and churches. About staying on the French Riviera toward the end of the term, Jane wrote: "Laying out seems to be the only incentive these days! Whatever happened to sightseeing?"

Besides going to the prescribed attractions, the students spent their days walking the streets, looking at buildings, stepping into churches to gaze at the art and stained glass windows, sitting on benches and watching people go by,

Students in the one of Innsbruck's museums. (Courtesy of University of New Orleans)

resting in parks, and talking among themselves. And like tourists everywhere, they took photographs: an average of 16 pictures per weekend. Most students did not yet have digital cameras, so this number is far less than it would be today. Many of their photos were of themselves and their companions posed in the foreground of the places they visited. When I asked why a postcard wouldn't be as good, one student said: "A photograph is proof that you've been there. You took it and it's got you and your friends in it."

There was nothing remarkable about the students' eating habits, except that 1.5 times per weekend they went to an American-style or franchise restaurant (e.g., McDonald's, NY Bagels, and Pizza Hut). Their interest in American franchise restaurants was strongest when they were in countries like Hungary, where none of the students spoke the language and waiters then spoke little or no English, making it difficult to decipher the menu. In Budapest, a group of students took a 30-minute taxi ride across the city merely to find a NY Bagels. Food was one of the subjects students were required to write about in their journals and, almost invariably, it was the women who wrote the most. They wrote not only about the different kinds of foods they saw but also about what dishes they ordered for dinner. The women were more willing and interested in trying new foods. The men were more inclined to write about European beer and how it differed from American beer than about the food they ate.

Time was also spent shopping. Female students set aside time specifically to shop, but students of both sexes made a habit of looking at the goods displayed in shop windows as they walked around. For many women, shopping was an integral part of traveling; they could always tell me what the best buys were in each country or city they visited—leather and jewelry in Italy, Hummel figurines in Germany. Many looked for "bargains," which they defined as high-quality goods at lower prices than they would find at home. They also shopped for mementos or souvenirs of the places they visited and for presents to take home to parents and friends. The amount of time spent shopping declined over the summer as their funds ran low and as they purchased the requisite number of gifts or ran out of luggage space.

In the late afternoon, students returned to their hotel or hostel to nap. In the evenings, after going out to dinner, they spent most of their time drinking and fraternizing in bars. The travel logs showed that only 14 percent of the students routinely did something other than go to bars in the evening. The students stayed out late (after midnight), and often reported going to bed drunk and exhausted. In her journal, Elizabeth characterized her companions as "young students who come to Europe to spend their parents' money by getting drunk in as many different cities as possible." Another described a recurrent dream she had in which she broke down crying from exhaustion: "Sometimes I feel like I just need to stop everything and sleep for several days non-stop. It would probably help if we all just eased up on the drinking and eating poorly."

College students enjoy their independence. (Photo by Andrea Tehan)

Education? If so, What Kind?

It should be evident from the descriptions above that most students do not learn much about European history and culture. Certainly not as much as their parents and professors would hope. As noted earlier, when reading student journals I was surprised by the superficiality of their engagement with the cultures they visited and how little meaningful contact they had had with local people. In the words of one of my Innsbruck colleagues, "Europe is for the students a big shopping mall in which to hang out, not a place to challenge one's cultural categories." Perhaps. But there was also evidence that touring and living in Europe for a summer did have a significant positive impact on students.

At the end of the term, I asked each student to read his or her own journal while imagining that someone else had written it and then to describe how the author had changed, if at all, since arriving in Europe. Two broad areas of change emerged from these reflective accounts. First, a large majority of the students believed that the experience of having gone abroad on their own and then traveling extensively through Europe without the supervision of parents or other adults had given them more self-confidence.[5] Some typical declarations were: "I now have the confidence that I can handle any situation I encounter in some way, even if I am alone, unable to communicate easily and unsure of the culture . . ." and "I've learned that I don't need any pretenses, that if I just be myself people will still like me." One student used her reaction to an incident in London as evidence of her growing self-confidence. She was in Trafalgar Square where she and her companions wanted a picture of themselves sitting on top of a large stone lion:

> I was wearing my navy silk shorts outfit and slippery sandals. I was having difficulty getting up on the lion when a young girl asked me if I would like some help. So here I am flailing about trying to get up on this lion with this girl pushing up on my butt. My silk shorts came totally up my butt and a crowd of people are standing below, right beneath me. I was so embarrassed when I finally got up, but I was psyched. . . . It was not only a physical victory; it was also a mental victory. I might finally be at the period where I can say "this is who I am, you can like me or not like me. . . ." Actually I am probably not at that point yet, but I am getting closer. I am not as paralyzed by my insecurities and fears as I was before this trip.

The other change that many students wrote about was having become more adaptable. They believed they were now better able to cope with the surprises, discomfort, and inevitable problems that arise when traveling. The terms they used to describe this change in themselves included being able to "survive," "cope," and "deal" with unfamiliar situations and minor adversity. For example, Emily wrote:

> This trip has made me more laid back. I always tended to need things on time and just the way I like it at home or else I became quite agitated. I suppose that is just part of being American. When you learn that things don't always go your way, and that you simply have to go with the flow. Here [Europe] you have to adjust to the differences . . . . Your train isn't always going to be on time; you may not want to go everywhere that your travel companions do; the locals may not speak English or be particularly thrilled to see you; and you will not get ice in your drink. I can deal with that now.

When Emily first arrived in Europe the limited hours that stores were open angered her, but five weeks later she noted: "I have learned to accept them . . . I now even think it's great that they close the stores on weekends, as it gives people time to spend with their families."

The students' perceptions of how they had changed were echoed by their parents, whom I interviewed later over the telephone. When I asked if they thought their son or daughter had changed while abroad, most said yes and talked about their being more "mature" and "independent." Typical of many, one mother said about her daughter: "She was just so self-assured when she got back." The phenomenon the students and their parents described is part of what developmental psychologists call "personal development," that is, the "unfolding, growth, evolution, expansion and maturation of the individual self" (Kauffmann et al. 1992:124). Personal development differs from "cognitive development," which has more to do with the acquisition of knowledge (e.g., what students actually learned about European cultures and places).

The students' personal assessments of how they had changed are consistent with the research literature on the impact of international study programs on students. For example, a study of 1,260 American Field Service students found that they became "less materialistic, more adaptable, more independent in their thinking, more aware of their home country and culture, and better able to communicate with others and to think critically" than a control group that did not go abroad (Hansel 1988:187). Even a short stay abroad with a homestay family can have a significant effect, as a study by Michael Stitsworth (1988) has shown. He administered a psychological inventory to 154 student exchangees before and after their one-month stay in Japan. He found personality changes in three areas: students developed less conventional attitudes, became more "adaptable" in their thinking (e.g., they showed more tolerance of uncertainty and ambiguity), and scored higher on measures of independence and autonomy than a comparison group that had stayed at home. Interestingly, he also found that students who paid for most of their trip themselves changed more than those who had paid only a small proportion. At least a dozen other studies have produced similar results (see Özturgut 2007).

What interested me even more than how the students had changed was why. After 20 years of taking students abroad on anthropology field programs (to Ireland and Barbados), I already knew that cross-cultural experiences had a big impact on students (Gmelch 1992, 2005). But I was never sure what exactly caused the change until an idea occurred to me while reading the Innsbruck students' journals. The journals showed that from the instant students left the familiarity of their Innsbruck dorm at the beginning of every weekend trip, they continuously confronted problems to solve— where to go, how to get there, where to stay, where to change money, where to find good but reasonably priced places to eat, what sights were worth seeing given their limited time, what places or areas of the city were unsafe and to be avoided, what goods were worth buying and where, and so on. In order to make good decisions, and to satisfy their basic needs, they had to learn how each local "system" worked. And to do so, they had to communicate with local people, asking the right questions and understanding the responses, sometimes given in a foreign language. They often had to ask the same questions of different people to assure that the information was reliable, much as anthropologists do in fieldwork. One student, after traveling in Hungary and Czechoslovakia, said he had become so adept at nonverbal communication and mimicking that he could not wait to get home to play charades. So it is not surprising that many students reported that their travels had given them the confidence to speak with strangers and to collect information.

Also, traveling is rarely predictable, and I believe students learn much from having to cope with the surprises, unexpected problems, and predicaments, such as missing a train connection, getting lost, and arriving in a town only to discover there is no available accommodation. Nineteen-year-old Megan describes the problems she and her companions encountered in a single journey across Budapest on public transportation:

> We took the Metro [subway] and trams, which were even more frustrating than the bus system. Along the way, we almost lost Susan, Kelly got her sunglasses stuck in the Metro doors, Susan almost had her purse stolen, and some weirdo put his face in my hair. But we made it to the bagel shop [NY Bagels].

During the term, a dozen students found themselves stranded in Italy by a train strike. They had to find a way to inform college administrators in Innsbruck that they were safe, learn about the strike in order to assess how long it might last, and look for alternative ways of getting back to Austria. For young adults traveling on their own in a strange culture, often for the first time, these are challenging life experiences.

Because the students travel in so many different countries and move so frequently—almost a new city every day—the challenges they face multiply. They have to find and arrange for travel, shelter, food, local transportation, and decide how best to spend their free time, not once but several times every weekend. Such challenges, of course, are compounded when the travel takes them across national borders. When students journey from Austria to Hungary, Italy, France, and Spain, they are crossing not just political boundaries but also cultural and language barriers, and therefore new social systems, new customs, and new meanings, the basics of which they must learn in order to get by. In some countries, women students face the additional problem of dealing with unwanted sexual advances from local men. Traveling in a foreign country also requires a certain level of organization. Students had to remember to bring and keep track of their passport, Eurail pass, student identification, money, and Travelers Cheques.

When I returned from Austria, I found support in the writings of development psychologists (e.g., Chickering 1969; Bruggemann 1987; and Kauffmann et al. 1992) for the idea that student tourists' personal development arises primarily from their having to cope with change and solve problems. Kauffmann and his colleagues (1992), for example, found that change and maturation in adolescents occurs most during "periods of discontinuity, displacement, and disjunction." Put differently, individuals acquire new understandings about life, culture, and self when they must deal with changes in their environment and circumstances. This is exactly what happens to student travelers.[6] Conversely, it is argued that little change occurs when students are in "situations of equilibrium," such as staying at home. Of course, other factors inherent in studying abroad also contribute to students' personal development. Being in a new school environment, for example, requires them to develop new social relationships; and the lack of the usual forms of recreation, forces them to find new ways to entertain themselves.

Conclusion

First, let's review the major points. When touring, American students traveled in groups, rarely stayed in any place for more than a day or two, often made decisions about where to go on the spur of the moment, and had little meaningful contact with local people. Their daily routines—when not on or waiting for trains—typically involved visiting recognized tourist attractions, shopping, taking afternoon naps, and staying out late drinking in bars or pubs. Over the course of the summer, their touring did change: they slowed down, becoming less mobile, moved about in slightly smaller groups, did less shopping, and became more interested in recreation than in seeing famous sites. Despite their very limited immersion in the cultures they visited, student tourism did have a positive impact. It resulted in the students becoming more confident, self-reliant, and adaptable. The primary reason for this appears to be the independent problem solving they were forced to engage in as a result of the daily challenges they faced getting around, satisfying basic needs, and coping with minor adversity in an ever-changing array of foreign places and often in a foreign language. Adapting to these challenges also meant the acquisition of at least some new cultural understandings.

How typical is the Innsbruck case? Since that summer, I have been with students on terms abroad to Japan and Vietnam, and while I did not "study" student travel in these locations as I had in Innsbruck, I was curious about their experiences and did gain some insights from reading their journals and hanging out with them. On these terms abroad, the students also traveled a good deal on their own, although nothing like the Innsbruck students. The high frequency and near frenetic pace of the Innsbruck students is probably due to the program being a six-week summer program rather than a full 15-week semester abroad, its central location in Europe with easy access to many other countries, and the students' possession of Eurail passes with virtually unlimited travel. But in other respects what I have described for the Innsbruck students seems applicable to student travelers on these other terms. Most significantly, the real education student tourists derive from their travel comes in the form of their own personal development and stems from the same causes as I described for the Innsbruck students. I think the words Hannah wrote at the end of her summer in Innsbruck are true for many student tourists, "Coming to Europe was a huge experience for me, bigger than anything I've ever done before. I'll never be the same because of it."

Source: Adapted from "Crossing Cultures: Student Travel and Personal Development," *The International Journal of Intercultural Relations*, 1997, 21(4):475–89.

Notes

[1] The most comprehensive study of American students studying in Europe found that students spent more than one month on the road during their academic year abroad (Carlson et al. 1990).

[2] I had previously taught anthropology field programs in Ireland and Barbados, but I had not taught a conventional term abroad before this. The Innsbruck program was run by the University of New Orleans, which still operates it today.

[3] The students were asked to divide their journal into chapters, each dealing with a different broad topic, including customs, food, people, language, stories, etc. It was suggested that the students try to write in several different chapters each day in order to encourage them to observe and write about a range of experiences. Some psychologists (Biggs 1992b; Cloninger, personal communication) assert that journals are a particularly effective means of understanding personal growth in students. Writing about students in cross-cultural situations, Donald Biggs argues that students think about and describe their study abroad experiences with "narrative forms of thought" and not with a logical, abstract, and/or context-independent mode of thought (1992b:7). Hence, journals are a conduit to understanding the development of the students' narrative thinking (these narratives or stories about life events influence and guide behavior).

[4] I also used a 20-item open-ended questionnaire to gather additional data on the students' experiences, and I did at least a dozen informal interviews with students, often during afternoon hikes. In fact, hiking proved to be an ideal setting for talking casually with them up about a broad range of subjects relating to their travel. I also accompanied students on several weekend trips, though these were organized by other professors and were not typical of the students' independent travel.

[5] Kauffmann et al. (1992:99) discuss the reliability and validity of students self-reports, notably the lack of uniformity in the students' responses and the difficulty of comparison between studies. For example, the meaning given to "self-reliance" by one researcher may be the same that other researchers refer to as "independence" or "autonomy." Similarly, "self-esteem" in some studies means the same as "self-confidence" in others. But Kauffmann (1992) and others note that other techniques for measuring personal development can also be problematic and that for some areas self-reports yield better data than standardized tests or questionnaires.

[6] Donald Biggs (1992a) arrived at a similar conclusion in his attempt to assess the benefits of study abroad for Cypriot students. He uses the term "surprises" to refer to the differences between the students' home culture and the host culture, which they encounter abroad. It is their exposure to these "surprises," "troubles," or enigmas, and the students' attempts at resolving them that become "potent influences" in their development.

References

Biggs, D. 1992a. "Psychological Issues in the Cross-cultural Exchange of Expertise and Training," in *Advances in Educational Productivity*, vol. 2, pp. 271–287. Greenwich, CT: JAI Press.

———. 1992b. "The Costs and Benefits of Study Abroad." Manuscript.

Bruggemann, W. 1987. *Hope within History*. Atlanta: John Knox Press.

Carlson, J. S., B. B. Burn, J. Useem, and D. Yachimowicz. 1990. *Study Abroad: The Experience of American Undergraduates in Western Europe and the United States*. Westport CT: Greenwood Press.

Chickering, A. 1969. *Education and Identity*. San Francisco: Jossey-Bass.

Gmelch, G. 1992. "Learning Culture: The Education of American Students in Caribbean Villages." *Human Organization* 51(3): 245–252.

——— 2005. "Lessons from the Field," in *Conformity and Conflict*, eds. J. Spradley and D. McCurdy. New York: Allyn & Bacon.

Hansel, B. 1998. "Developing an International Perspective in Youth through Exchange Programs." *Education and Urban Society* 20(2): 177–195.

Kauffmann, N. et al. 1992. *Students Abroad: Strangers at Home*. Yarmouth, ME: Intercultural Press.

Klineberg, O., and F. Hull. 1979. *At a Foreign University: An International Study of Adaptation and Coping*. New York: Praeger.

Kristof, N. 2006. *New York Times*, March 3.

Lambert, R. 1989. *International Studies and the Undergraduate*. Washington DC: American Council on Education.

Löfgren, O. 1999. *On Holiday: A History of Vacationing*. Berkeley: University of California Press.

Özturgut, O. 2007. "Study/Teach Abroad Programs for Higher Education Faculty." *Essays in Education* 22:42.

Piaget, J., and B. Inhelder. 1958. *The Growth of Logical Thinking from Childhood to Adolescence*. New York: Basic Books.

Stitsworth, M. 1988. "The Relationship between Previous Foreign Language Study and Personality Change in Youth Exchange Participants." *Foreign Language Annals* 21(2): 131–137.

Two:
When Tourists
and Locals Meet

A tourist shares his photographs with villagers in the Urabamba Valley, Peru. (Photo by Sharon Gmelch)

6

Tourism and Anthropology in a Postmodern World

Frederick Errington and Deborah Gewertz

As he drove from the airport in Wewak, Papua New Guinea, to his three-room guesthouse, Ralf warned us that with our arrival all fifteen beds would be filled. We were disappointed, for we had hoped to be largely alone there, as we occasionally had been in the past when we came from our Chambri Island field site to resupply in Wewak. Indeed, as we grumpily wrestled our heavy metal patrol boxes inside the door, his house seemed to be crawling with noisy, young tourists. Our annoyance was increased when one of them derisively asked us whether we always traveled so heavy, adding that he had just returned from two weeks of paddling from village to village along the Sepik River with only a small backpack. We promptly responded to this taunt. We said that we were anthropologists who had come not to travel but to stay; our boxes contained supplies sufficient for seven months of field research among the Chambri. Moreover, to ensure our victory in what was obviously a contest, we added that this was our fourth trip to Papua New Guinea during the past twenty years.

Thinking over the incident we were amused to see how easily these tourists had been able to pull us into competition over which, they or we, had had the more authentic experience with native people in Papua New Guinea. This had been a competition we had wanted to win, and we wondered whether we would have emerged triumphant if this had been our first trip.

91

After we had settled at Chambri, we might not have thought much more about these noisy young tourists—"travelers" they called themselves—with their search for the authentic and their competition with us—if it were not for the frequent arrivals of older and wealthier tourists. Although more easily accepting that we had surpassed them in their search for the authentic, the latter were largely unimpressed with our choice of a profession that was not only relatively poorly paying in their view but required the deprivation and discomfort of life in the jungles of Papua New Guinea. Unlike the travelers with their sporadic and low-budget arrivals, these tourists came to Chambri at regular intervals, transported in luxury on the Sepik in a cruise ship, the *Melanesian Explorer*. With their frequent visits, we realized that tourists now had a major role in Chambri life. Their presence, and that of the travelers—their reactions and those of the native people as members of each group observe and perform for the other—needs to be understood.

To this ethnographic focus, and prompted by our musings on our own relationship to these visitors, we add a more general theoretical discussion about the nature of anthropological authority. A number of contemporary writers would not have been surprised that we were so readily pulled into a comparison with these tourists (of both sorts). They have argued that, despite an ideology to the contrary, anthropologists are, in fact, little different from tourists (see Boon 1982; Dumont 1977; Hamilton 1982; Mintz 1977; and van den Berghe 1980). Perhaps the most forceful formulation of this view comes in a recent article by Crick (1985) who endorses and summarizes the recent critique that we have, as anthropologists, lost our authority because, like tourists, we do not reach an objective understanding of the other—what we do is for ourselves and in our own terms. (On the loss of ethnographic authority, see also Clifford 1988; Clifford and Marcus 1986; Crapanzano 1986; Strathern 1987, 1989; and Tyler 1986.)

Furthermore, Crick suggests, many field confessions reveal that anthropologists, far from immersing themselves and thereby acquiring competence in an alien culture, frequently spend much time avoiding interaction with native people by reading novels and dreaming of home (see Barley 1983). Semiotically if not linguistically maladept and chronically gauche, they both misunderstand what they are told and, in addition, annoy their informants who become little inclined to reveal themselves (Herzfeld 1983). And, often forced to employ interpreters and purchase information, anthropologists further distance themselves from the other.

Nor can anthropologists be readily distinguished from tourists since the former work and the latter play. According to Crick and others, tourists may be engaged in a modern secular ritual equivalent to a rite of passage or a rite of intensification. (See, for example, Cohen 1988; Graburn 1983; Lett 1983; and Pfaffenberger 1983.) Comparably, fieldwork may be a modern secular ritual for those seeking transformation from students into professional anthropologists.

Finally, at the most general level, it is argued that anthropologists, like tourists as products and agents of capitalist systems, objectify those they observe (Fabian 1983; Pratt 1986), regarding the other as available for their acquisition and use. In this process, the other, stripped of power and volition, becomes defined to meet Western standards of conceptual utility (Appadurai 1985; Asad 1973; Haraway 1985a; Spooner 1986).

Thus, according to this critique, the "I was there" of the anthropologist should carry little more ethnographic authority than that of the tourist. Ethnography, these writers contend, is like the tourist report; it is essentially self-interested fiction (Crapanzano 1986).

Although Crick allows that not all anthropologists or all tourists are the same (as we have indicated, many of the tourists in Papua New Guinea consider themselves not as "tourists" but as "travelers") and that there are differences between them, his general conclusion from this comparison is that anthropology, like tourism, is a game we play for our own purposes. This conclusion, however, does not disturb him particularly. Indeed, he thinks that the nature of anthropology as game has unfortunately been obscured by a scientism, which holds that social reality is an entity that may be perceived objectively through the application of value-free rules. (On misplaced scientism, see Bleier 1984; Haraway 1985b and 1986; Keller 1985; and Louch 1969.) Crick's is the postmodern perception that social life (including the disciplines that examine social life), in its fragmentation and multiplicity, is not *an* order produced by the enactment of *a* set of rules. Therefore, a much more accurate perception not only of anthropology but of social life more generally (including, of course, tourism) would be one that recognizes the importance in both of the continual negotiation of the rules in gamelike fashion. Freed from its pretenses, anthropology could itself become more ludic, he argues, and in so doing better convey the ludic in the game that constitutes social life.

We contend that one could regard social life as the product of continual negotiations and yet not share Crick's conclusion that anthropology should be more like play (no matter how important or pervasive play might be as a human phenomenon). We also contend that one could likewise reject scientism without accepting that anthropology be essentially ludic, simply one game of many, without substantial seriousness.

We doubt, in fact, that there can be much justification for anthropology if anthropologists are fundamentally like tourists. In this paper, therefore, while pursuing our ethnographic interest in the Chambri social field (which includes both tourists and anthropologists), we return to Crick's original comparison to examine the terms we share with those we met at Ralf's and elsewhere in Papua New Guinea, and those we did not. It will be our conclusion that, in a world in which it profoundly matters who controls the terms of the interactions—the negotiations—and who wins or loses, anthropology needs not a heightened sense of the ludic but of the political.

On Travelers

Ralf's guesthouse was inexpensive, costing PGK6.00 per night. (Kina is the currency of Papua New Guinea. In 1987, PGK1.00 = US$1.15.) In contrast, each of the three local hotels was by any standard expensive, costing approximately PGK100.00 per night. His guests were generally in their twenties, often on long-term excursions after they had completed university studies or military service. They stayed at Ralf's, not only because they rarely could afford the other accommodations, but also because they wished to distinguish themselves from those they regarded as tourists. They did not use money to insulate themselves from direct and significant experience—from the "real"—as did the "tourists." (On travelers, see, for example, Cohen 1989; Smith 1989; and Teas 1988.)

Ralf's accommodations were basic. Although he had electricity and running water, the shower was cold and the outdoor toilet, odorous. Strangers shared rooms with each other and with members of Ralf's family in what was his home. Ralf originally came from Germany to Papua New Guinea as a Catholic missionary. Although no longer a priest, Ralf had remained permanently in the country, as a citizen. He married a woman from a Sepik River village and was raising a family. Since Ralf had led an eventful life and seen much of Papua New Guinea, his guests felt that staying with him was memorable for it was in itself an authentic experience.

Most travelers arriving in the Sepik region brought with them a popular travel guide, *Papua New Guinea: A Travel Survival Kit* (Lightbody and Wheeler 1985), from which they learned, for example, that the Sepik is "the best known area of PNG for artifacts" (1985:44) and "has attracted little development and remains remarkably untouched by western influences" (1985:152). Nevertheless, Ralf's establishment was an important clearinghouse of information for them. In addition to the knowledge Ralf himself conveyed about where to go, how to get there, and what to take (he rented at low cost such absolute necessities for travel in the Sepik River area as mosquito nets), there was advice available from the other guests—especially those stopping at Ralf's as they returned from their trip on the Sepik.

Those returning furnished the new arrivals with accounts of recent adventures larded with travel tips. The new arrivals reciprocated in kind by telling of their own travel in other parts of Papua New Guinea or other remote parts of the world. In these accounts of adventure and advice there was a striving for verification. Virtually anyone who ended up at Ralf's could be recognized as intrepid, at least by comparison with the tourists. However, even among this relatively elite group, important distinctions were made about which among them was immersed most completely in native life. These preoccupations pervaded not only the conversation at Ralf's but also the observations that these guests wrote in notebooks Ralf provided for the edification of later visitors. As we shall see in the following excerpts from these notebooks, by recording what to visit and what to avoid, travelers conveyed the breadth of their experience, their fortitude, and their capacity to discriminate between the authentic and the inauthentic. Of particular interest to us are the criteria used in this discrimination.

1. An anonymous traveler wrote in April 1983:

> Watch out for Kanganaman and Parambei [villages along the Sepik] you might miss them. It is quite some paddling to get to Parambei. The *haus tambaran* [men's ceremonial house] in Kanganaman is sure worth seeing. They try to charge you for it. In both villages people are friendly because they are accustomed to the big spending Explorer tourist. Hardly any good carving left if you are looking for that. . . . Kapaimari, the Catholic school shortly after Kanganaman, you leave untouched. It is like other mission places—Timbunke, Ambunti. People very unfriendly; ready to rip you off. The smaller the village the better. Some places may get five white tourists a year. . . . Accommodation is no problem if you stay away from the tourist spots. Every village will put you up and sometimes even provide food free. Your visit is an honor for them—a change in everyday life . . .

This traveler assumed that tourist money and missionary activity spoiled local people by making them unfriendly and concerned only with acquiring money. Those so remote as to have escaped these pernicious Western influences retained a tradition of carving and hospitality. Moreover, they also recognized and appreciated the fact that this traveler was willing to leave the path beaten by the less enlightened members of his own European society to visit them. Such an encounter as an instance of intercultural communication was seen as reciprocally enriching traveler and villager alike.[1]

2. Two male travelers, one from Poughkeepsie, New York, and the other from Russian River, California, described villages along the Sepik in July, 1983:

> Japanaut: friendly; good resting spot. Yentchamangua: very friendly... free night. Korogo: very friendly; free night with Peter; his son is Ronny; one of the first houses up river; excellent haus tambaran; good for carvings... Yentchan: interesting haus tambaran; impersonal atmosphere; 5 PGKs [In 1983, PGK1.00 = $U.S.1.40] to sleep in haus tambaran... Kambrindo: friendly. Moim: uninteresting...; no carvings, at least they don't offer to show us some. Also had clothes ripped off here. Important notes: . . . If you want to buy artifacts, do it last, or in the morning. Show you are interested in the villagers; they are interested in you. Be friendly and they will not treat you like a tourist. Explain difference between tourist and traveler. They are really good people. Show pictures. Tell stories. Ask questions . . . We met people who hated the Sepik. Be respectful of haus tambarans and culture. Bargain but don't degrade. Be a traveler, not a tourist. It makes a big difference . . . Don't leave things in canoe at night. Even grungy clothes will disappear—something belong "masta" [a colonial Pidgin English term for white man.] Food: bring plenty. No one really offered us food since we brought our own. They did let us use their pots, pans, fresh water and utensils. . . . By the way, we had a fantastic time. Go for it, yea, to the max, far-fucking out!

These travelers categorized villages according to whether social encounters had been friendly and nonmonetary or impersonal and commercial. In addition, they were alert to the presence of features of interest such as a haus tambaran or carvings and implied that since insensitive tourists were attracted to these features, local people had become cynical and indifferent. It was the travelers who could, because they were sensitive and caring, reestablish warm, human (and inexpensive) relationships and enable villagers to manifest their essential goodness. Although such a project of redemptive encounter might fail to reclaim those who coveted even grungy clothes, these travelers found their experience eminently rewarding.

3. A family traveling on motorcycles left their account anonymous but nonetheless included a photograph of themselves on their motorcycles. Writing in December, 1984:

> As we travel as a family, two adults, two kids and two motorcycles, we had a different trip. Luckily for us we had got a Papuan friend here in Wewak and we went up to Ambunti [sub-provincial headquarters] with him in his motorboat free and slept in his house. Next day we borrowed his boat and went four hours up the Sepik River and turned up the April River to [the village of] Biaka where we lived with a family for two days free. The food we brought we gave to the wife and asked to have only native food during our stay. A bit hard to get sago down, but nice fish, taro and pumpkin and this was really an experience. Everything very "primitive." As gifts we had brought toys for children and these everybody enjoyed, adults as well as children. It was lots of fun. In return we got a grass skirt, pigs' teeth, a belt with tail and a cassowary knife, which we are really happy about. On way back we saw a witch doctor working in another village. A very outstanding experience.

These travelers had it all. They formed such a close friendship with a Papua New Guinean that he not only provided them with free accommodation but also loaned them his motorboat. They chose to spend their limited time in a single village where they developed reciprocal relations with a local family. Living under "primitive" conditions and encountering a witch doctor at work, they experienced Papua New Guinea life as it really was.

4. Two anonymous travelers wrote in July 1986:

> The next morning half the village turned out to watch us spin out into the Sepik. The younger group amused, the older alarmed. After an erratic half hour in which the three of us simultaneously attempted to use our own steering methods, we calmed down and zigzagged semi-proficiently to the village of Korogo . . . The villagers are building a new haus tambaran. The carvings are interesting, but photographs [of the haus tambaran] cost an exorbitant 5 dollars [kina] . . . We stopped at Aibom village [in the Chambri Lakes] where they are carving a new haus tambaran to watch an old woman potter making the clay cooking pots for which the village is famous. The lakes are well worth a trip, beautiful islands with highlands in the distance. Many birds and fish, lilies in the water. The

village of Chambri is huge [actually there are three villages on Chambri Island] with a large mission and interesting haus tambaran with oval windows. But it has become like a souvenir shop with chalked prices on the statues. There is a special house for visitors. No cooking facilities; two kina per person.

By lightheartedly demonstrating to a Sepik audience that they lacked competence in the basic skill of canoeing, these travelers showed themselves willing to establish relations of intimacy and equality with local people. Given their genuine interest in and appreciation of the people, it was lamentable that they, as if they were tourists, should be offered the culture—the haus tambarans and the artifacts—as commodities.

Ralf provided a place where travelers might appraise themselves and seek validation as unique, autonomous, and subjectively rich individuals. They were able to regard themselves as relatively unique and autonomous since few members of their society had either the desire or the self-reliance to travel in a place as distant and "undeveloped" as Papua New Guinea. Moreover, what they encounter there was experienced as further enhancing their already distinctive selves. For travelers, the encounter with what was seen as the "primitive"—the exotic, the whole, the fundamentally human—contributed to their own individuality, integration, and authenticity. Those who gathered at Ralf's also sought to affirm the extent to which they had embodied the values and the rewards of the successful traveler and, as we have seen, they competed as each tried to gain further distinction as being unique among this august body of fellow travelers. This competition concerned who had most fully encountered the most "untouched" people in Papua New Guinea. (In this competition, as we have noted, the anthropologist who lived for a major period in a remote village had the upper hand. Indeed, anthropologists are often drawn to the "remote" for many of the same reasons as are the travelers.)

The motives that impelled this competition frequently led to a politics that, while purporting to be (distinctively) radical in its rejection of conventional, materialistic Western values was—at least in the context of Papua New Guinea—relatively conservative. The principal value of Papua New Guineans to most of the travelers was that they be "untouched." (The radicalism at home and the conservatism abroad were experienced as consonant since travelers assumed that their own societies had become corrupt because earlier—more "primitive"—values were lost.)

Correspondingly, the principal lament of those travelers who found aspects of their trip disappointing was that the people had become spoiled. The social relationships between travelers and native people had become, like those in the West, essentially commercialized. The "primitives" they had expected to engage with had, in other words, become too much like us.

Those held most responsible for spoiling Papua New Guineans were "the big spending Explorer tourist[s]" (see account 1) who, representing the worse commercialism and superficiality of Western society, had through their insensitive use of money fostered the commercialization of social relations and the consequent development of a "souvenir shop" (see account five) atmosphere throughout the Sepik.[2] From the perspective of the travelers, the tourists not only reduced the value of the "primitives" by corrupting them, but also manifested their own corruption by remaining "content with [their] obviously inauthentic experiences" (MacCannell 1976:94).

On Tourists

Most tourists who visited the Sepik region had bought a packaged excursion that included four days on the river in the *Melanesian Explorer*. This was a relatively luxurious, air-conditioned tourist ship that cruised at 12–14 knots and contained European amenities, including in-room plumbing and showers, a full bar, a video recorder with tapes of Papua New Guinea peoples and a library with over 100 books on the country.[3] The Travel Corporation of America, which provided tours to the South Pacific that had the option of a swing through Papua New Guinea, furnished the *Melanesian Explorer* with most of its passengers. Their travel brochure described the Sepik River cruise as follows:

> Eighth thru 12th days—Tuesday thru Saturday—Sepik River Cruise: Board our cruise ship Tuesday evening and begin our journey to one of the world's most remote and fascinating areas, the Sepik River region. We cruise in air-conditioned comfort aboard the *Melanesian Explorer*. Our trip through the lower and middle Sepik visits villages such as Kamindimbit, Timbunke, and Tambanum. Off the main river, we use speedboats to travel the tributaries and the Chambri and Murik Lakes. Life along the Sepik has been virtually untouched by western ways.
>
> The villagers hew canoes from gigantic logs and set off on fishing and hunting trips, bringing back food, exotic feathers, shells, skins and animal bones to use as headdresses, adornments and ritual implements.
>
> You will have time to explore the many villages, and the House Tambarans, some of which are enormous and display a wealth of art. We are able to buy magnificent ritual masks, statues, and artifacts of these artistically gifted people. We will witness traditional sing-sings and get-togethers for joyous events or mourning, in the lives of these primitive people. (Travcoa n.d.:35)

This text promised an encounter with the "primitive." Tourists visiting the Sepik did wish to have this encounter although, as we will see, their reasons were somewhat different from those of the travelers. Most of the tourists from the *Melanesian Explorer* that we met, as they visited Chambri by speedboat or after we joined the ship itself for portions of two of its cruises, were prosperous middle-aged professionals—physicians, lawyers, scientists. Older and much better established in life than the travelers, they sought not the "pure primitive" but the "primitive" on the edge of change.

A tourist brochure promised: "You will have time to explore the many villages, the House Tambarans, some of which are enormous and display a wealth of art. We are able to buy magnificent ritual masks, statues, and artifacts of these artistically gifted people." (Photo by Deborah Gewertz and Frederick Errington)

An experienced guide on the *Melanesian Explorer* cautioned us that in the lectures we would give (in exchange for our board and room) we should be careful not to overemphasize the extent to which change had already taken place. For example, tourists interested in "black magic" should not be informed that old Chambri men had begun tape recording their magical spells so that these spells would not be forgotten when they died. The tourists "don't mind a little change," she said, "but would hate to know that the natives are sophisticated enough to tape their own chants."

One *Melanesian Explorer* tourist, a woman from New Jersey, told us that her Sepik trip had been wonderful although she had been, along with others, puzzled about how to characterize it. She said that it was "not a fun trip; not exactly educational; it was like stepping back in time, but there are modern things too." In a like vein, one physician from Chicago, in stating her reason for coming to Papua New Guinea, said that it was about as far away from her hospital as she could get, and that it is a place that "will be completely changed in ten years; one has to see it now as it really is." Another physician said that he was glad to have seen the Sepik "before," he added wryly, "people like us spoil it, as we have in so many other tourist places."

One group of these tourists told us with satisfaction of an unscheduled visit by the ship to a lower Sepik village where they came across a group of men trying to raise PGK4,000.00 to purchase what would be a collectively-owned truck. The PGK200.00 they had thus far raised was displayed on a mat around which the men sat. The tourists joined this group by contributing some PGK60.00. Their names, along with those of the native contributors, were duly recorded in a notebook. Then, probably in recognition that the tourists would not be able to make reciprocal claims for assistance, they were given two live chickens.

Because this stop was unscheduled, the tourists knew that these men were pursuing their own interests rather than engaging in a staged production. (See MacCannell 1976:91–107 for an interesting discussion of authenticity in tourist settings.) They found the mixture of old and new engaging: the villagers were cooperating in a traditional way to pursue nontraditional objectives, even though they were a long way from realizing their goal. (As one tourist commented to us, "My goodness, we contributed almost a third of what they had; they'll never get to where they want to go.") Certainly in the view of these affluent professionals, the villagers appeared naive: they were sadly naive in hoping to raise the money needed for their car[4] and charmingly naive in believing that a gift of live chickens was appropriate reciprocity to the Europeans. This naiveté marked these villagers as still on the edge of change and left them sufficiently open that they would reveal their real lives to the passing tourist.

We were told of another encounter by two members of a group that, before joining the *Melanesian Explorer*, had visited the home of "the daughter of a chief" in the Highlands of New Guinea.[5] She had been married to an Australian but had divorced him to return to her home territory and marry a Papua New Guinean. Now living on the outskirts of her natal village in a nice house, she had her own car in which she drove her children to school. Although well educated, having been trained as a teacher, she was not using her skills to help her people progress. The first tourist to tell us this story was incensed by the young woman's selfishness in not helping her people advance to her level of development. A different evaluation of this woman came from another tourist who was impressed by the attractiveness of her home, the clarity and precision of her English and the beauty of her mixed-race children. Both of our commentators agreed, though, that the sophistication of this woman relative to other Papua New Guineans must be the product of her special position as the daughter of a "chief" and as the former wife of an Australian. Although others would, and indeed should, follow in her path, she was in her cultivation still very unusual.

Another tourist we met, a physicist, saw himself as a catalyst for change. He had been impressed by the accuracy of what he regarded as the largely intuitive knowledge of physical principles possessed by Papua New Guineans. He commented to us with excitement and admiration that villagers had been able to modify their traditional canoes to accommodate the additional weight and speed provided by outboard motors in a way that duplicated the configuration of a Western-designed speedboat. He was impressed by certain projections internal to slit-gong drums, which, he said, served to amplify the sound in the same way as did the bridge of a violin. However, his dismay was apparent when he encountered some bamboo scaffolding surrounding a haus tambaran under reconstruction. This scaffolding did not employ triangular bracing. Speaking in English and describing the success of the Chinese in Hong Kong with high-rise bamboo scaffolding, he gestured toward the haus tambaran in an effort to convince a passing youth that this scaffold would have been easier to construct and safer to use if diagonal supports had been employed. He believed with obvious sincerity that he could significantly help Papua New Guineans in their further development by conveying to them an important principle of construction that they had not yet discovered for themselves.[6]

Of all the villages he and the other tourists on the cruise visited, Korogo was their favorite. They said that it was the first village they had seen in which the houses were ordered. By this they meant that the houses were laid out in a geometric lattice with a wide central avenue. There were also plantings of ornamental shrubs around a number of the houses. These the tourists referred to, only partly in jest, as "formal gardens." Many were particularly impressed by a house whose roof was under construction. Three-foot sections of sago-leaf thatch were stacked neatly in piles along the length of the house and adjacent to each section of roof. The concern with efficiency that this planning seemed to demonstrate was interpreted as indicating the advent of a "division of labor," a specialization of skills and work. In Korogo, the tourists thought that they had discovered a progressive community about to replicate Western patterns of development—a community on the edge of modernity.

The motives of the older and professionally successful tourists in coming to the Sepik were quite different from those of the young travelers who, as we have already noted, wished to engage with the "primitive" as a means of personal development. The tourists on the *Melanesian Explorer* wished to engage with the "primitive" partly to demonstrate that personal development had already successfully taken place. Whereas travelers wished for the "primitive" to remain frozen in time, tourists had a much more positive attitude toward change. Although many of our conversations with travelers concerned the extent to which Papua New Guinea had changed and was thereby spoiled, many of our conversations with the tourists focused on the obstacles that had to be overcome before change was possible. Tourists asked us whether college-educated Papua New Guineans would be able to reject beliefs in sorcery, and to persuade others to reject these beliefs. They urged us to persuade the Chambri to give up the "barbaric" practice of scarification during ceremonies of male initiation. They speculated about the marvelous transformations that could be made in Papua New Guinea, a country rich in natural resources, by people of vision and enterprise (such as the Israelis).

The view that Papua New Guinea should eventually develop was consistent with the interest of these tourists in validating the system in which they, as prosperous professionals, had achieved success. However, the tourists in addition wanted to be assured that they had come before this rapid transformation of the "primitive" world was complete: they viewed the "primitive" as an increasingly rare prize to be witnessed and captured before it was too late. But since they wanted to be among the last to do this, they also wanted assurance that they had come in time. They wished to use their money to enjoy life and see the out-of-the way portions of the world, and they wanted assurance that this world was still worth seeing.

The competition of most interest to these tourists was not with the other tourists who had chosen to visit the Sepik, but was with their peers at home where it would focus on efforts to display themselves as having led unusually full, interesting and successful—distinctive—lives (see Bourdieu 1984). Moreover, unlike the travelers, tourists—at least after the first sounding-out—did not find it important to compete with us as anthropologists. They did not envy our research conditions in Papua New Guinea—in a remote village without running water and plumbing—or our standard of living as academics at home. On those few occasions when we thought they were vying with us for distinction, the competition concerned the universities we were affiliated with as students and as teachers. (Thus, one tourist, after discovering that we were living at a Chambri Lake village as academic researchers rather than as missionaries, immediately volunteered how pleased she was that her daughter had just decided to attend M.I.T., an institution favored by members of her family for generations.)

It was not surprising that travelers felt antagonism toward the tourists: it was antagonism between the unformed and the well-formed and, we need add, between those who had time and energy and those who had money and experience. The older tourists were viewed by the younger travelers in what were perhaps Oedipal terms: the older tourists consumed and spoiled the "primitive" in such a way that it was difficult for those who were, in generational terms, their children to be nourished and to develop. Certainly the travelers took more notice of the tourists than the tourists did of the travelers. We did, though, hear occasional and somewhat wistful comments from the tourists about the enterprise of the youthful travelers: one anesthetist (who, perhaps significantly, had come to the Sepik as part of the affluent adventure of sailing around the world in a yacht) said that 20 years ago she and her husband would have been among those she had seen paddling along the Sepik River. An orthopedic surgeon and his wife, likewise, said that, if they didn't have the money to travel in comfort, they wouldn't, at their age, want to travel at all.

On Anthropologists

Many of these data would seem to substantiate Crick's case. Indeed, we recognized from our interaction with both varieties of tourists that we were motivated in some of the same ways as they. We readily understood the terms of comparison between us and the travelers concerning relative authenticity of experience and between us and the *Melanesian Explorer* tourists concerning relative professional status, earning capacity, and taste. And, of course, the outcome of these comparisons—more favorable in the first than in the second instance—was not a matter of indifference to us. Such could be expected. All of us were products of the same sociocultural system; all of us, despite differences in age, possessed largely comparable views of person, of self.

Yet, tourists (of both sorts) have little impetus or competence to go beyond self-reference: the significance of the other is largely in what it does for oneself. Although anthropologists may share some of the personal objectives that have led tourists to Papua New Guinea, the comparative data we have collected since the nineteenth century make us reject the epistemology on which the tourists rest their politics. Tourists are essentially unilinear evolutionists who find the world filled with chiefs and witch doctors, and their self-referential tales are based on—indeed require—partial, simplified, and often completely erroneous information. However ultimately incomplete the understanding anthropologists have of the other, we are, to judge by our Papua New Guinea experience, incomparably better informed.

We can use our superior understanding (and we really must emphasize that no tourist seriously attempts to understand a Papua New Guinea kinship, exchange, or cosmological system) to convey what the world looks like to the natives and how our world affects theirs. We can document and explicate moments of resistance, capitulation, confusion, and indifference. We can place their lives and ours in sociohistorical, cultural, and systemic context. Thus, if we cannot easily differentiate our personal motivation from that of tourists, we can differentiate our politics from theirs. What can distinguish anthropologists from tourists is that we can and must be political in terms, not self-referential and individualistic, but comparative and systemic.

Let us illustrate this argument that anthropologists do have something of distinctive importance to say by describing, as a modest example, an event in which anthropologists, tourists, and Chambri took part. As will be apparent, each had very different perceptions to report.

The Hazing

It was already mid-afternoon and the feast that Maliwan had arranged as part of the ritual to take place on the sixth day after his sons had received their initiation cuts had been over for some time. Everyone was waiting for the next ritual event. Maliwan was circulating inside the men's house, assuring an increasingly impatient audience of initiators that the tourists would be arriving soon. He was hoping to attract many tourists to Chambri during what would be a month-long course of events focused on the initiation. Indeed, he was counting on charging them admission fees of PGK10.00 per person or

PGK50.00 per group to defray a significant portion of his costs, expected to exceed PGK1,000.00.

Early in the initiation he had been disconcerted when a group of tourists from the Karawari Lodge (a luxury hotel set on one of the Sepik's tributaries) refused to pay. When their European guide translated Maliwan's policy to them, one exclaimed with tones of outrage, "Ten Kina! What a rip-off!" and the rest—clearly hot and tired—grumbled their agreement. When they left, claiming to have looked only at the artifacts in the men's house and not at the initiates, their guide had pressed PGK3.00 into Maliwan's hand. Maliwan was furious: he told us and other Chambri that he had been doing this tourist work a long time and was not to be tricked by a young man who gave him PGK3.00 rather than the amount he had set. He said that the tourists and the guide think they can treat those of us in Papua New Guinea as if we were of no importance. They spend lots of money to come here and take pictures that they will sell for large amounts of money. He simply did not believe them— staying as they were at the Karawari Lodge—when they claimed they could not afford to pay the PGK10.00 admission. If they don't want to pay, they can simply leave.

This unpleasantness was an exception: Maliwan usually had satisfactory encounters with tourists. Over the years, he had been especially careful to cultivate a good relationship with the owner and the guides of the *Melanesian Explorer*. And he had persuaded them to bring their tourists regularly to Chambri, where they could enter a traditional men's house (which Maliwan managed) and purchase artifacts. (Few of the 443 adults living at Chambri during the period of our most recent research were able or willing to subsist without money, and most saw tourism as the key to their postindependence economic viability. Although some money came into Chambri through the sale of produce, including crocodile skins, and in the form of remittances sent by relatives working in urban centers, most of the money acquired in the course of a year by men living at Chambri was derived from the sale of artifacts: the total from sales of artifacts comes to approximately PGK10,000, according to our 1987–88 data. Extensive as this contemporary reliance on money had come to be, the acquisition of money was, nonetheless, regarded as requiring the exercise of ancestral knowledge to "pull" tourists to Chambri and to impel them to purchase artifacts. Hence, the presence of tourists at Chambri was interpreted not as testimony to the transformation of Chambri tradition but to its persistence and strength.) In the present instance, Maliwan had even arranged with the *Melanesian Explorer* guide, who had guaranteed admission payment, to coordinate the major events of the initiation with the schedule of the ship. As a consequence, the ceremonies of the sixth day were to take place on the seventh, which meant that he had to convince members of the appropriate initiatory moiety to delay their hazing of the initiates for a day. Thus, as he circulated after the feast, he was anxious to reassure the other Chambri men that the delay had been justified, that the tourists were coming. But they were nowhere to be seen and clearly Maliwan was nervous.

Finally, to his evident relief the sounds of the two big speedboats that convey the tourists from the Sepik River anchorage of the *Melanesian Explorer* up the tributary to Chambri were heard.

Once the twenty-five or so tourists arrived in the men's house, many began to take pictures of the initiates who had been posed to show their partially healed cuts. Then the initiates, together with uninitiated clan brothers—some older and younger than they—were instructed to sit down in the middle of the men's house floor. As the tourists crowded around them, Maliwan asked us to advise the tourists that there was going to be a loud noise above them from the second story of the men's house. He did not want the tourists to be alarmed by the noise that would mark the awaking of Kwolimopan, the ancestral crocodile who had previously "eaten" the backs of the initiates.

As the four hazers approached the seated initiates, Maliwan instructed them to talk not in Chambri but in Pidgin English, which it was assumed the tourists could understand. Their performance, which consistently amused the Chambri audience and, periodically, even the initiates themselves, began when they offered fish and sago to the initiates but then pulled the food away and themselves ate portions. Next, they offered the initiates fish bones, fruit stalks, and other inedible scraps from a platter while shouting: "You don't know how to eat; you eat just like pigs, just like ducks; you don't have any shame."

While the initiates glumly contemplated their "food," there came the thundering from above as men jumped up and down on the floor of the second story, shaking loose a great cloud of dust. No sooner had the dust begun to settle, than water was poured through the floor, soaking the initiates and their platter of refuse, turning the dust covering the food into mud. The hazers walked among the initiates shouting "hurry up, hurry up" as they insisted that some of the water-soaked rubbish be consumed. (In fact, Kwolimopan's bull-roarer had been kept in this water and the water had thereby become filled with his power.)

Betel nuts were next offered the initiates and then taken away with the words, "You eat betel nut as if you were a woman, as if you were your little sister." Oversized spatulas covered with ashes instead of the lime normally consumed with betel nuts were shoved into their mouths. Burning banana leaf cigars—an inch in diameter and a foot long—were stuffed into their mouths and then pulled away, showering them with sparks, while the hazers harangued them: "You want to smoke; here, smoke! Your papa is giving this to you; smoke this big one, you rubbishman. You beg for cigarettes and betel nuts all the time, well here they are; take them; are you enough for them?"

Then a large female carving was brought out and was thrust on top of the initiates with the challenge: "Are you enough to make carvings and place them in the men's house for the tourists to buy?" Large pieces of firewood, including one with embers, were pushed down on them as they were asked: "Are you enough to bring firewood to the men's house?" A broom and a large bark dustpan were pushed down on the their faces with the words: "Are you enough to sweep out the men's house?" Several grass-cutting knives were pressed against them with the question: "Are you enough to cut the grass around the men's house?" Finally, the initiates were asked derisively if they had more than the understanding of their mothers—if they were enough to sire children.

All of these questions were meant to convey that the initiates should uphold Chambri custom. Chambri custom, especially as it concerned appropriate adult male roles within the men's house, was presented in a quite literal way as heavy, as not to be taken lightly. Such custom based on collective authority, an authority embodied by the four hazers, could be made to cover virtually all aspects of life. Thus, reference was made to a rule that men are not supposed to smoke or chew betel nuts until they have been scarified. Although this rule is normally ignored nowadays, it was presented as one that could be made binding if the assembled men chose to make it so.

This assertion of collective male power had lasted about twenty minutes when one of the hazers said in Pidgin: "The law is finished now; we will stand up and the tourists will take pictures of us." Then all four of the hazers moved behind the initiates and stood in a row, facing the tourists, who were then instructed: "Clap your hands. The rule of Kwolimopan is over; it's finished now; we have completed it. OK, you can take pictures of us now. Clap your hands." The tour guide informed the tourists in English that they should applaud and had been invited to take pictures.

The tourists did applaud, and most took a picture or two—although with some reluctance. They seemed somewhat annoyed and confused at this point. The hazers had suddenly defined the performance as staged, at least in part, for tourists rather than for the Chambri themselves and this called into question its authenticity. Moreover, by instructing the tourists to applaud and to take pictures of them, the hazers were extending to the tourists the same kind of control that they had exercised over the initiates: just as the initiates were not allowed to express their own autonomy with respect to activities that are usually defined as matters of individual volition—to smoke or chew betel nut—so too the tourists were commanded to express appreciation and interest. This occasion threatened to become for the tourists not simply a performance, but a performance out of control.

A fair number of tourists had left before this point in the performance and were outside photographing the Chambri women who were singing "take it, take it; listen, listen"—songs that enjoined the initiates to do as they were being told. It was very hot inside the men's house; with the shaking of the floor, it was very dirty—the tourists were anxious about their camera lenses after the dust had poured down. They seemed to find the hazing too violent, too aggressive, too prolonged; one woman looked askance at the cut that had opened on the initiate's arm when he had been pushed down by a burning piece of firewood.

By the end of the performance, those still remaining in the audience felt vulnerable, uncertain of their safety. Not only had the performance been violent, but they were no longer sure what the objectives and boundaries of the performance were. However, they were somewhat reassured when one of their number, an impressively large German man, asserted control by over-complying with the hazers' command to take pictures of them. He waded through the seated initiates, very much as the hazers had done, and took a series of extreme close-ups of each hazer's face.

The picture-taking concluded, Maliwan sent the initiates outside into an enclosure attached to the men's house. He was eager to clear the men's house so that the tourists could look at and purchase the carvings. Out in the enclosure, the hazers shook hands and talked with the initiates, some of whom were angry at the treatment they had received. One, for instance, was upset because several of his cuts had opened during the turmoil of the performance. He had enlisted the help of another initiate in cleaning up the blood so as not to further disturb the cut. Looking at them, a passing hazer said—in combined reassurance and disdain—that it was nothing to be worried about.

In this initiation, and in others we have seen with no tourists present, the initiates were made to appear not only ridiculous but impotent. Their escape was precluded; participants were forced to do as they were instructed yet nothing they could do was right. They were, in other words, placed in a multiplicity of double binds, a circumstance well designed to convey complete powerlessness—a powerlessness itself compounded in that they were unable to perform even the normal routines of life.

The hazing, however, was as well a means of conveying power to initiates. In particular, it was by having dirt and the water of Kwolimopan dumped on them and the garbage just served, and then being required to eat of that soggy garbage that the initiates incorporated into themselves important aspects of power—the power of Kwolimopan. As a result of this, they were released from most of the initiatory taboos—for instance, they might once more eat and scratch themselves in a normal manner, rather than with the use of tongs. In this Chambri version of what is a familiar theme of initiation throughout the world, the experience of powerlessness would seem to be an important step in the acquisition of adult status.

What was the effect of the presence of an audience of tourists—both men and women—on this ritual? Hazing, as we have described it, would be most effective when it completely precluded any escape on the part of the initiates. It seemed to us, though, that the presence of the tourists, by introducing another sort of audience, gave the initiates a partial escape from their double binds. Because the initiators were to some extent playing for another audience, the hazing was no longer a closed Chambri show.

Significantly, the hazers in this initiation were clearly trying to be funny, and that even the initiates frequently laughed. Certainly, based on our own and Chambri recollections of other initiations, hazing as an occasion for the display of virtually absolute power with respect to the initiates was not normally experienced or remembered by the initiates as funny. Moreover, on this occasion, there was a concern that the tourists might become frightened—they were warned, for instance, about the great thump that was to take place over their heads. Also, there is no doubt that the incorporation of the tourists into the proceedings made the hazing shorter—time had to be allowed for them to purchase artifacts. (As we have seen, the tourists thought even the modified performance was too frightening and lengthy.)

In addition, the distinction that the ritual of hazing imposed between those having and not having power—between those who could exercise adult volition and those who could not—and between those inside the men's house and those outside—between men and women—became somewhat blurred by the presence of the tourists, by the presence of these wealthy men and women from outside the Chambri system.

Thus, not only did the presence of the tourists dilute the display of absolute power and diminish the clarity of the distinctions that were made in terms of the social and spatial distribution of power, but their presence also reduced the duration and intensity of the hazing. The consequence, we think, of this partial leavening of ridicule was the emergence of comic elements.[7]

But this comic was not characterized by a complete amiability. Although the initiates found some humor in the double binds in which they were placed, they were, nonetheless, rendered substantially powerless. And if the presence of tourists had partially deflected the force of the display from the initiates, the tourists themselves became partial targets. They were transformed from spectator to performer and a portion of their volition (and distance) stripped from them, as they were commanded to applaud: they were required to assent, whether they had liked it or not, to a performance in which as the final act they too became victims.

Such a display of control over the tourists in an initiation staged in part as a tourist attraction would have especially appealed to Chambri. Certainly it would offset the vulnerability that Chambri might feel now that they were offering for sale not only artifacts but major cultural events such as the initiation itself.

Whether or not the Chambri were conscious of the sources of their satisfaction at turning the tables on the tourists, we do not believe they realized they were changing important elements of the initiation as it affected the initiates. To be sure, the world that these initiates were entering—a world in which adult capacities could now be measured through such activities as selling artifacts to tourists—was continually changing with respect to patterns of authority and valuation of Chambri custom. Yet, it seems to us that many of these changes had come about as the culmination of events like the initiation just described. An event of this sort had effects that, because they were unintended and unforeseen, were likely for some time to be unperceived. Understanding of what was in the process of happening was likely to be inhibited if there were no recognition that anything had happened. In particular, the Chambri did not understand that if they continued to sell their initiations (and perhaps other ceremonies) as tourist attractions, they would themselves no longer find them convincing and effective.

The tourists (including the travelers) were more aware than the Chambri that the tourist trade was an important component in change. They lacked, however, sufficient knowledge of both cultural particulars and cross-cultural patterns to understand in any sort of detail either the effect or the process of change. As far as we could observe, they understood practically nothing about the Chambri nor, significantly, did more than a very few want to learn from us anything except the most readily assimilated facts about the initiation or other aspects of Chambri life. Apart from knowing that the scars in some way marked manhood and that Maliwan was staging the initiation for his sons, the ceremony was, and remained, virtually opaque to them. They were, in most cases, uninterested in our simplified explanations of even the most noticeable events as the drenching of the novices and their "food" with Kwolimopan's water. But what is the importance of our having reported on this hazing? We have provided the most complete and accurate inscription this moment will probably ever have. The understanding of these moments in their contexts has political consequences because it enables us to talk knowledgeably about such intersecting matters as the nature of the world political economy, the reasons that tourists come to Papua New Guinea, and the effects on and the response of the Chambri—including their capacity to resist, adapt, transform. (Ortner 1984 and Fernandez 1985 make a similar point.) For anthropologists to work toward reaching *and* conveying an understanding of such matters (even when specific events have a ludic form) strikes us as serious, but not as value-free, business.

Anthropology in a Small Place

In a recent novel, *A Small Place*, Jamaica Kincaid writes a powerful critique of tourism and tourist economies. She does this by caustically (certainly nonludically) describing the postmodern malaise—the fragmentation of experience and relationships—that leads Europeans to visit places like Antigua.

> From day to day, as you walk down a busy street in the large and modern and prosperous city in which you work and live, dismayed, puzzled . . . at how alone you feel in this crowd, how awful it is to go unnoticed, how awful it is to go unloved, even as you are surrounded by more people than you could possibly get to know in a lifetime that lasted for millennia . . . I mean, your dismay and puzzlement are natural to you, because people like you just seem to be like that . . . But one day, when you are sitting somewhere, alone in that crowd, and that awful feeling of displacedness comes over you, and really, as an ordinary person you are not well equipped to look too far inward and set yourself aright, because being ordinary is already so taxing, and being ordinary takes all you have out of you, and though the words "I must get away" do not actually pass across your lips, you make a leap from being that nice blob just sitting like a boob in your amniotic sac of the modern experience to being a person vis-

iting heaps and death and ruin and feeling alive and inspired at the sight of it . . . to being a person marveling at the harmony (ordinarily, what you would say is the backwardness) and the union of these other people (and they are other people) have with nature. (Kincaid 1988:15–16)

Kincaid does not specifically discuss anthropologists as among those who are, in the words of another analyst of sightseeing in the postmodern world, "striving for a transcendence of the modern totality, a way of attempting to overcome the discontinuity of modernity, of incorporating its fragments into unified experience" (MacCannell 1976:13). Presumably, she would agree with Crick and others who have noted that Western anthropologists are products of the world economy and subject to the same influences as the (Western) tourists. However, in her view, it would be the postmodern nature of this experience that would make anthropologists similar to tourists and, like them, pernicious influences and miscomprehending presences in places like Antigua. As she objects to the tourists reading Antiguan lives as the harmonious opposite of their own, she would, we think, object to anthropologists reading those lives as the fragmented equivalent of their own. Antiguans, in her presentation, are not postmodern: they are angry and oppressed. Moreover, in Jamaica Kincaid, they have a powerful indigenous voice that is able to combine intimate knowledge of Antiguan sociocultural particulars with that of world systems.

Under circumstances as these, it seems to us, if anthropologists are going to have anything of importance to say about these small places, we need to move, not in the direction of indulging our own postmodern sensibilities of, as Crick puts it, "anything goes" (1985:86) but of developing an anthropology of non-post-modern people: we need to develop an anthropology that has a voice as politically informed as that of Jamaica Kincaid. If she had explicitly extended her critique to encompass anthropologists, it would not have been to tell us to be more ludic, more poststructuralist, more self-involved. Whatever our own feelings of malaise, of rulelessness, of anything goes, we should not indulge them at the expense of the world, particularly as we work in places (like Chambri) where such a voice as hers has not yet emerged to correct and perhaps supersede our own.[8]

Source: From "Tourism and Anthropology in a Post-Modern World," *Oceania*, 1989, 60:37–54. Reprinted with permission of the authors.

Acknowledgments

We wish to thank the National Endowment for the Humanities, the American Council of Learned Societies and Amherst College for supporting our most recent field trip to the Chambri during 1987. We also wish to thank the Department of Anthropology of the Research School of Pacific Studies at the Australian National University for sponsoring our field trip to the Chambri during 1983. Gewertz has made two previous trips. On the first, from

1974 through 1975, she was supported by the Population Institute of the East-West Center, the National Geographic Society and the Graduate School of the City University of New York. The second, during the summer of 1979, was paid for by the National Endowment for the Humanities and by Amherst College. Gratitude is expressed to each of these institutions, as it is to the Wenner-Gren Foundation for Anthropological Research, which allowed Gewertz to investigate archival material during 1981.

Notes

1 To be sure, many anthropologists (including ourselves) have been influenced by similar expectations and assumptions. Indeed, anthropologists often minimize references to tourism, missionization, and other indications of "development" in their ethnographic accounts: these, it is thought, make "their" people and, by extension, themselves less distinctive and, hence, less valuable. Such elisions could, however, be regarded as obscuring the nature of the world system.

2 Missionaries as well are regarded as a source of corruption but of quite a different sort.

3 The owners of the *Melanesian Explorer* plan to replace their present ship with a far more luxurious one, equipped, for instance, with phones in each cabin that allow direct dialing worldwide.

4 In fact, considerable sums of money, sufficient to buy large trucks, can be raised in this way.

5 Perhaps basing their view of "primitives" on their stereotypes of Native Americans, many tourists, even when we attempted to explain the achieved leadership of big men, refused to change their views that Papua New Guinea social organization focused on chiefs.

6 Although not used on this scaffolding, triangular bracing is common and was, for instance, employed on a small bridge we had crossed earlier that morning.

7 In this analysis, the emergence of the ludic was something of an accident: it had not been the Chambri intention to allow the initiates respite from their double binds.

8 The construction of ethnographies on the basis of dialogues might appear to be an anthropological responsibility under these circumstances prior to the emergence of an indigenous voice strong enough to command outside attention (Clifford 1986). However, we have argued that one of the difficulties in constructing such ethnographies is that, at least in the Sepik and in much of Melanesia, people wish the anthropologist to present not a dialogue—a plurality of voices—but a monologue, an inscription of a particular partisan view (Errington and Gewertz 1987). Although the voice of a Chambri comparable to Jamaica Kincaid might also promulgate a particular set of local interests, the politics expressed would under these circumstances be his or her responsibility, not ours.

References

Appadurai, Arjun. 1986. "Theory in Anthropology: Center and Periphery." *Comparative Studies in Society and History* 28:356–61.

Asad, Talal, ed. 1973. *Anthropology and the Colonial Encounter*. London: Ithaca Press.

Barley, N. 2000 [1983]. *The Innocent Anthropologist: Notes from a Mud Hut*. Prospect Heights, IL: Waveland Press.

Bateson, Gregory. 1946. "Art of the South Seas." *The Arts Bulletin* 2:119–23.

Bleier, Ruth, ed. 1984. *Science and Gender*. New York: Pergamon Press.

Boon, James. 1982. *Other Tribes, Other Scribes*. Cambridge: Cambridge University Press.

Bourdieu, Pierre. 1984. *Distinction: A Social Critique of the Judgment of Taste*. Cambridge, MA: Harvard University Press.

Clifford, James. 1986. "Introduction: Partial Truths," in *Writing Culture*, ed. James Clifford and George Marcus, pp. 1–26. Berkeley: University of California Press.

————. 1988. *The Predicament of Culture*. Cambridge: Harvard University Press.

Clifford, James, and George Marcus, eds. 1986. *Writing Culture*. Berkeley: University of California Press.

Cohen, Erik. 1988. "Traditions in the Qualitative Sociology of Tourism." *Annals of Tourism Research* 15:29–46.

————. 1989. "Primitive and Remote." *Annals of Tourism Research* 16:30–61.

Crapanzano, Vincent. 1986. "Hermes' Dilemma," in *Writing Culture*, ed. James Clifford and George Marcus, pp. 51–76. Berkeley: University of California Press.

Crick, Malcolm. 1985. "Tracing the Anthropological Self." *Social Analysis* 17:71–92.

Dumont, Jean-Paul. 1977. "Review of MacCannell." *Annals of Tourism Research* 4:223–225.

Errington, Frederick, and Deborah Gewertz. 1987. "On Unfinished Dialogues and Paper Pigs." *American Ethnologist* 14:367–76.

Fabian, Johannes. 1983. *Time and the Other*. New York: Columbia University Press.

Fernandez, James. 1985. "Exploded Worlds." *Dialectical Anthropology* 10:15–26.

Gewertz, Deborah, and Frederick Errington. 1990. *Twisted Histories, Altered Contexts: Representing the Chambri in a World System*. Cambridge: Cambridge University Press.

Graburn, Nelson. 1983. "The Anthropology of Tourism." *Annals of Tourism Research* 10:9–33.

Hamilton, Annette. 1982. "Anthropology in Australia," in *Anthropology in Australia: Essays to Honour 50 Years of Mankind*, ed. Grant McCall, pp. 91–106. Sydney: Anthropology Society of New South Wales.

Haraway, Donna. 1985a. "Manifesto for Cyborgs: Science, Technology, and Socialist Feminism in the 1980s." *Socialist Review* 80:65–108.

————. 1985b. "Teddy Bear Patriarchy." *Social Text* 4:20–64.

————. 1986. "Primatology is Politics by Other Means," in *Feminist Approaches to Science*, ed. Ruth Bleier, pp. 77–118. New York: Pergamon Press.

Herzfeld, Michael. 1983. "Signs in the Field." *Semiotica* 46:99–106.

Keller, Evelyn Fox. 1985. *Reflections on Science and Gender*. New Haven: Yale University Press.

Kincaid, Jamaica. 1988. *A Small Place*. New York: Farrar Straus Giroux.

Lett, J. W. 1983. "Ludic and Liminoid Aspects of Charter Yacht Tourism in the Caribbean." *Annals of Tourism Research* 10:35–56.

Lightbody, Mark, and Tony Wheeler. 1985. *Papua New Guinea: A Travel Survival Kit*. Victoria: Lonely Planet Books.

Louch, A. R. 1969. *Explanation and Human Action*. Berkeley: University of California Press.

MacCannell, Dean. 1976. *The Tourist*. New York: Schocken Books.

Mintz, Sidney. 1977. "Infant, Victim and Tourist: The Anthropologist in the Field." *Johns Hopkins Magazine* 27:54–60.

Ortner, Sherry. 1984. "Theory in Anthropology since the Sixties." *Comparative Studies in Society and History* 26:126–166.

Pfaffenberger, B. 1983. "Serious Pilgrims and Frivolous Tourists." *Annals of Tourism Research* 10:57–74.

Pratt, Mary Louise. 1986. "Fieldwork in Common Places," in *Writing Culture*, ed. James Clifford and George Marcus, pp. 27–50. Berkeley: University of California Press.

Smith, Valene. 1989. "Introduction," in *Hosts and Guests*, ed. Valene Smith, pp. 1–17. Philadelphia: University of Pennsylvania Press.

Spooner, Brian. 1986. "Weavers and Dealers," in *The Social Life of Things*, ed. Arjun Appadurai, pp. 195–235. Cambridge: Cambridge University Press.

Strathern, Marilyn. 1987. "Out of Context: The Persuasive Fictions of Anthropology." *Current Anthropology* 28:251–281.

————. 1989. *Partial Connections*. Maryland: University Press of America.

Teas, J. 1988. "'I'm Studying Monkeys; What Do You Do?'—Youth and Travelers in Nepal." *Kroeber Anthropological Society Papers* 67/68: 35–41.

Travcoa. n.d. *Tourist Brochure*. Travel Corporation of America.

Tyler, Stephen. 1986. "Post-Modern Ethnography," in *Writing Culture*, ed. James Clifford and George Marcus, pp. 122–140. Berkeley: University of California Press.

van den Berghe, Pierre L. 1980. "Tourism as Ethnic Relations." *Ethnic and Racial Studies* 3:375–392.

7

Tourism and Its Discontents: Suri—Tourist Encounters in Southern Ethiopia

Jon Abbink

Tourism as an "Avant-Garde" of Globalization

The tourism "industry" is the largest business in the world and has, apart from its economic significance, a growing social and cultural impact on the local societies and places visited. The transformative role of tourist activity in society and culture deserves closer attention. In its present form, tourism is the expression of a particular kind of consumer identity with a notable globalizing impact. It emanates largely from societies that are relatively powerful and wealthy. Communities and places visited by tourists undergo unforeseen changes due to these foreign visitors' unrelenting presence. While both positive and negative aspects can be recognized, in most cases a process of skewed or unequal exchanges between tourists and locals is evident. Furthermore, these need more extensive empirical study in emerging contexts of globalization (which is here defined as a transformative process of intensified contacts—via mass and electronic media and migration—between human collectivities and communities in the economic, political, and cultural domains, forging new and more pervasive interrelations and dependency between social and cultural units of varying scale).

115

This chapter is a reflection on the encounter of foreign tourists with the Suri or Surma[1] people of southern Ethiopia, a relatively small ethnic group only recently "discovered" by the tourist industry, and on the "exoticizing" impact this encounter has. The chapter reflects back on the preconceptions and prejudices that tourists and other outsiders bring to bear on local peoples subject to their gaze. Next to describing the encroachment of tourism among these people, I intend to give a cultural critique of tourism, developed on the basis of Suri views.

Seeing tourists at work was a phenomenon that initially disturbed me while doing field research.[2] The first question, of course, might be why an ethnographer should feel disturbed. Some critics will jump in to say: "Because there are 'hidden similarities' between tourists and anthropologists, as affluent Westerners or uninvited guests, among a culturally different group—similarities that generate some kind of guilt and insecurity about the epistemological basis of the latter's research activities." We can respond to such a remark with a qualified yes: there is, on one level, a similarity in that the tourist visit and the ethnographic praxis are both strategies for "framing the exotic" (Harkin 1995:667). But on this trivial level anthropologists can also be said to share characteristics with pilgrims, businesspeople, or missionaries, or anybody entering a, for him/her, new social setting—a common experience even for people in their own society. Furthermore, this argument leaves us not much wiser about *what is actually happening* in such "inter-cultural encounters," about their different shapes, or about their historicity.[3] An anthropological understanding of tourist–"native" interactions needs to aim at explaining the preconditions, the structure and meaning of the tourist encounter, with reference to the interests and cultural models that are articulated in that setting.

In many respects, tourism itself imposes a dominant global "exotopic strategy," or an "appropriation of otherness" (Harkin 1995) to deal with cultural difference. Due to its ubiquitous presence in the media, in advertising, and in international business, the imagery and discourse of travel and tourism tends to exclude or push away other viewpoints. It can be said to be a hegemonic system of representation that functions as part of an (unconscious) *ideology* of globalization. As such, tourism deserves much more empirical and theoretical exploration, as Nash has suggested in a very useful overview (1996:179). However, in contrast with previous tourism studies "the voice of the other [i.e., those visited by the tourists] needs to be given its due" (p. 196). In this article, responses of the Suri people towards tourists will be considered.

The Suri, an agro-pastoralist group of about 28,000 people in the utmost southwest of Ethiopia, are an interesting case because the prime attraction for the tourists is not the geographical area or natural setting (rivers, forests, mountains, game parks, etc.) but the Suri *themselves*, as a "real primitive, untouched tribe."[4] This is how they are advertised on Web sites and in travel brochures. The Suri are indeed a marginal group in Ethiopia, and, although faced with manifold problems, they retain a high degree of sociocultural integrity. But any idea of their being untouched or isolated is incorrect. They have been involved in wide-ranging regional trade-flows of cattle, gold, arms, ivory, and game products at least since the late nineteenth century, and for the past two decades, they have been affected by the Sudanese civil war and by Ethiopian state efforts to incorporate them politically, economically, and socially. The production of their reputation of "primitiveness" and "remoteness" is in the first instance a phenomenon or problem to be explained from the perspective of the tourists, since they are the creators and consumers of images of "authentic experience" and of "exoticism" that are carefully screened and constructed. These images function as commodities like any other to be bought and sold, and a growing part of the tourist industry is thriving on them. In exploring some aspects of the tourist encounter, this chapter will contend that especially when people instead of nature or buildings are the object of such commoditized images, tourism often leads to friction or conflict.

The Semiotics of Tourism

Theorizing on tourism has been done within a variety of frameworks, among them, neo-Marxism (MacCannell, 1976, 1984), semiotics (Culler 1981; Urry 1990; Harkin 1995), and socio-cultural psychology (Smith 1994; Chambers 2010). It is less interesting to present a list of possible motives of tourist behavior, such as nostalgia, quest for the unknown, breaking the daily routine, rediscovery of the self, and so forth, than it is to inquire into some of its formal, systematic aspects (see MacCannell 1976; Cohen 1979, Urry 1990). Recognizing that there are several different types of tourists or "modes" of tourist experience (cf. Cohen 1979:183), it might be possible to identify some of these formal aspects. In this respect we follow some leads of Michael Harkin's very interesting semiotic approach (Harkin 1995).

In a semiotic perspective one can say that tourist experiences, especially of tourists of the type discussed in this paper, are initially marked by an "anxiety about authenticity" (p. 653). Tourists expect a kind of credibility and genuineness about the objects, places and people they visit. Tourists also expect the latter to be contained in a system "whereby a set of signs marks the object as authentic," so that their attention can be focused. The tourists can thus be given an orientation vis-à-vis their own framework of familiarity related to their own society. In other words, the alterity of the other landscape or the other people should be appropriated (p. 655). This implies a hegemonic strategy, domesticating the exotic (p. 656). This semiotic enterprise, of course heavily supported by photography, is evidence of the search of tourists for predictability in a context of new meanings. Culture difference as such is not problematic in such a scheme, but it should be marked clearly. The tourists expect such a minimal semiotic frame wherever they go.

Identity and Difference in the Contested Field of Global Encounters

In the encounter of Suri and tourists, extremes meet. Suri have always been at the margins of the Ethiopian state, even though they nominally have belonged to it since 1898. They were wary of outsiders—Ethiopian soldiers, traders, and administrators; Italian colonizers; and visiting white tourists. A politically and economically largely self-sufficient society, they always tried to assert their way of life and group identity toward others. Questions of identity and difference have thus been a vital issue in all their relations with non-Suri.

In the past 15 years, the Suri have been visited not by mass tourism but by a "select" crowd of tourists who have seen all the regular mass-tourist destinations and who like to think of themselves as "adventurers and explorers." In the 1980s, a few travel agencies in Italy, the USA, the UK, France, or Germany (and several expatriate Italian and American travel agents with an office in Addis Ababa) started advertising the Suri as a destination for this category of "explorer"-tourists. This attracted small groups of Western and later also Japanese and other tourists for an adventurous or exotic vacation "off the beaten track." In the case of the Italians, one travel agency used a slogan indicating that the tourists could retrace the historical routes of some nineteenth-century Italian explorers of southern Ethiopia (like Cecchi, Vannutelli, Citerni, and Bottego). The reputation of the remarkably informative 1938 *Guida dell'Africa Italiana Orientale*, the publication of which was one of the first acts of the Italian occupation force in the country (1936–1941) to legitimize and "normalize" its presence there, also played a significant role in creating Ethiopia as an Italian "tourist destination" (Consoziazione Turistica Italiana 1938). In recent years, tours were booked on which the visitors could take a plane to the grass airstrip near the small capital of the southwestern Maji district (the airstrip marked with a sign saying, "The Wonderland Route," put there by Ethiopian Airlines) and then make a walking excursion with pack-mules and native porters into the Suri area. There the tourists lodged in tents, looked at the local people, took photographs of them, and engaged in some typical tourist bartering for material objects (the Suri lip-plates and ear-discs) as souvenirs. After spending a few days, they left as they had come.

As we can see, the tourist interest in the Suri is undoubtedly based in part on "exoticism," the idea of going to a remote, isolated wilderness area "where hardly any whites had set foot" and where people are assumed to live in "pristine conditions of nature." This may go back to the renewed fascination in the (post)modern industrial world with the "radical others" outside industrial culture—and this time, due to the techno-economic conditions of globalization, it can be pursued as a mass-phenomenon. There is also a lingering heritage of the colonial gaze. As Bruner and Kirshenblatt-Gimblett (1994:435) note: "Tourism gives tribalism and colonialism a second life by bringing them back as representations of themselves and circulating them within an economy of performance." In the early 1980s—before the tourist influx—the Suri were already known to a wider public, through folklore and tourist-guide texts (for an Ethiopian one see Donovan and Last 1991[1980], as an exotic, strange, primitive people at the ends of Ethiopia (which was in itself a relatively unknown tourist destination). The Suri appearance was also fascinating: the women and girls wore big clay or wooden discs in their pierced lower lip and earlobes, and the virtually naked males had fine physiques and remarkable body scarifications and decorations made with bright natural paints.[5]

Young Suri woman with clay lip plate in Korum, Ethiopia. (Photo by Jon Abbink)

The coffee-table book (Beckwith and Fisher 1990) and *National Geographic* article (Beckwith and Fisher 1991) by photographers Carol Beckwith and Angela Fisher summarized this image of difference in a telling way. Their work contains a series of excellent photographs of the Suri, albeit only on some aspects of their way of life. The pictures evoke the impression of a very out-of-the-way and self-contained, "happy" culture of complete African "others," in a somewhat romanticized way. The shots also appeal to the image of a remote, well-integrated and proud culture—almost the "noble savage" of old—and indeed, they help to *create* this image.[6] We see here a typical contemporary representation of a "tribal group" for the public eye of modern-industrial society, the genre of the exoticist, postcolonial photography of "natives." Needless to say, apart from granting that they may contain useful information and evoke fascination, what the pictures convey to us is incomplete.[7] They are not meant to be informative and analytic, but primarily evocative and aesthetic. We see that the image created by them is—as always with visual representations—in large part a reflection of the preoccupation or selective interests of the observers. As the photographic evocation of the Suri makes clear, both in professional and tourist form, difference and contrastive identity are essential elements in the encounter of opposites. Indeed, there is no effort, or intention, by either Suri or tourist to come to a "mutual exchange" or "understanding" between tourist and "native," except a purely businesslike one, even if the wish to do so is sometimes rhetorically expressed (the photographic act is a major ingredient of the touristic appropriation of the Suri, a point further discussed below).

The inherent bias in the representation of the Suri, and of the tourist–Suri relationship (particularly acute in their case, as we shall see) is of course neither new nor surprising. It is rooted in the very encounter of "whites and natives" in non-Western parts of the world, conditioned as it is by tacit epistemological canons of colonial experience or by a still, in essence, colonializing gaze. The Horn of Africa is no exception. A brief historical retrospect makes this clear.

The Image of the Suri since 1897

Following the various, scarce descriptions of the Suri in travel and colonial literature, one sees that the image of "primitiveness" was an inherent ideological element of the colonial penetration of the Sudan-Kenya-Ethiopia borderlands from the start.

The first to mention the Suri was the Russian officer A. K. Bulatovitch who was traveling with a contingent of Ethiopian emperor Menilik II's army on a campaign in the Southern Käfa area in January–April 1898 (see Bulatovitch 1900, 1902). There they met a people resembling, he said, the "Sciuro" (in reality, they were the Me'en, a neighboring agro-pastoral people; for a brief survey, see Abbink 2002b). However, the author notes that the natives extracted their lower incisors, and the inserting of lip and ear discs by the women he described is even now a distinctive custom of the Suri.

After Bulatovitch, the Suri are mentioned again in an article by a member of the British border demarcation commission in 1909. C. Gwynn met whom he called, the "chief of the tribe" at Turmu, an escarpment north of Mt. Shulugui (or Naita), a big border mountain between Sudan and Ethiopia. Gwynn said that the tribe's women wore "indescribably hideous" wooden or leather discs in the lower lip (Gwynn 1911:127). Like all travelers after them, these two European observers felt the need to comment on the lip-plate custom and its, for them, unaesthetic appearance. This physical detail overrides all other information on this group, and emphasizing it has set a pattern reflected in all popular articles and tourist brochures written about the Suri since, including the book and article by Beckwith and Fisher (1990, 1991).

From 1936 to 1941, Fascist Italy occupied Ethiopia and reports on the Suri came from Italian visiting travelers/businessmen or researchers (Viezzer 1938; Marchetti 1939; Rizetto 1941). The mining engineer C. Viezzer was probably the first who described them and to publish photographs.[8] He pictures the Suri as a group living in very "primitive conditions," without cattle, cultivating poorly with primitive tools (Viezzer 1938). He praises their colorful body-painting and general physique, but predictably abhors the female custom of inserting wooden or clay lip-plates in the lower lip. He was one of the first to take photographs of this decoration, thus initiating the act so often repeated by visitors and tourists today. Viezzer also describes some rituals he observed, such as the spectacular burial of the wife of a chief. The language of the Tirmaga (a subgroup of the Suri) strikes him as primitive: "guttural sounds, animal-like, absolutely incomprehensible" (pp. 424–425). Viezzer's picture of the Tirmaga-Suri is, of course, very incomplete, and characterized by a predominantly negative or condescending evaluation of their way of life, fed by the author's own ignorance of how such a society works.

F. Rizetto (1941) also stayed among the (Tirmaga-) Suri, but for a longer period. His report contains more factual information on the group and adds some qualifications about their character as a people. One can frequently hear an echo of his remarks on "Suri character" among their present-day highland neighbors. For example, Rizetto notes, perhaps echoing local highland dwellers' opinion, that they are "ignorant, violent, thievish, arrogant and revengeful." But, he says, they are also proud of their country and their freedom. They go naked, but are generally of good build and health (Rizetto 1941:1204). They live isolated, in blissful ignorance of the world outside, and on a primitive, timeless level (pp. 1205, 1209).

In 1938, the Suri were studied by M. Marchetti, an Italian working for a private company at the time. He passed four months in the Suri area and describes their three original subgroups, then known as Tirma, T'id and Zilmamo, in fairly detailed terms. Marchetti, though no social scientist, is the first to try to present a more balanced, matter-of-fact survey of Suri society, refraining from extreme evaluative statements about their character or level of cultural or intellectual development. He gives information on settlement patterns, cultivation practices, material culture, ornaments, food consumption, supernatural beliefs and customs related to marriage, burial, and, what he called, the "stick fight." Nevertheless, toward the end the author concludes his description with remarks about the "low level of social life" of the Suri, who are also "absolutely infantile as to mentality and intelligence" (for instance, he said, their counting system "was underdeveloped") and they have "a rather simple language," their speech accompanied by expressive mimic, and often repeating words (Marchetti 1938:71). They are said to miss an oral historical tradition transmitted from parents to children—they only retain memory of the most recent events. Despite a good start, we again see the account ending in questionable, evaluative statements based on outsider values—not very informative about Suri culture itself.

After 1941 there were few foreign or Ethiopian visitors in the Suri area. The Ethiopian government had a nominal presence until 1988 (when the few police and soldiers left the area), some intermittent tax collection, and a short-lived American mission post in the 1960s with an elementary school (up to fourth grade) and a small clinic. None of these intersections left any lasting imprint on the local society, and no reports are available from this period up to 1990.

The Suri have been part of a neglected and marginal region of Ethiopia, without roads, facilities and government services. The area was viewed as a poor and unhealthy malarial lowland, where no Ethiopian would go of his or her own free will. The Suri people were considered as "uncivilized nomads" without fixed abode. The Maji area served as a place of internal exile. Under the Mengistu-government (1977–1991), army commanders who had failed in the civil war were sent there to spend their days as civil servants.[9] In the wider regional context, however, the Suri were never isolated. In the early decades of the twentieth century, they were connected to the cattle, game, and ivory trade in Ethiopia and Kenya. In the 1980s they smuggled in automatic weapons from Sudan and got involved in the gold trade (panned in rivers in southern Ethiopia) and in a network of Sudanese and Ethiopian traders. During the decades since 1991, a closer involvement of the Suri with the Ethiopian authorities is notable (Abbink 2002a, 2009a).

In the early 1980s the Suri were "rediscovered" as a piece in what was stereotypically known as the "museum of peoples" of Ethiopia.[10] Some tourist agencies started organizing individual or small-group trips to the Maji area, including the Suri country. Some of the tourists came with a guide of the Ethiopian National Tour Operators (NTO, a state agency), and some with a personal guide from a private travel agency. Recent travel guidebooks on Ethiopia make mention of the "colorful" Suri people, describing their primitive material conditions but also their body-paintings, their lip- and ear-plates, and their spectacular ritual stick-dueling contests. Practical conditions for the tourists were difficult, but this was part of the attraction: to chart an allegedly unexplored culture at the margins of civilized society.

In fact, tourist trips regularly had to be cancelled due to security reasons. Until this day, foreign visitors, upon arrival in the area, may be officially forbidden by the local authorities to go to where the Suri are because of fear of disturbances.[11] Nevertheless, during the 1990s and 2000s, many hundreds of tourists have visited the Suri, and this flow will continue in the near future.

A ceremonial stick duel in progress among the Chai Suri. (Photo by Jon Abbink)

The Suri and the Tourist: Exchanges and Confrontations

The interaction of Suri and tourists is usually more of a "confrontation" than normal social interaction. Obviously, the language difference is the first problem. The Suri are mostly monolingual, and very few of the Ethiopian guides speak the Suri language in more than a rudimentary fashion. "Conversation" takes place by means of gesticulation and shouting. Prior to the contacts with tourists, the Suri had only known white foreigners in the shape of Italian soldiers in the 1930s and American missionaries in the 1960s. Their experience with them was much better than with the tourists, basically because, as some Suri said, "they were there for a long time" [several years] and "tried to get along with us. They traded things, like food-stuff, cattle, sheep, and tried to talk with us." However, the Suri quickly found out that the tourists of today were quite different from these earlier foreigners. Below, we look at the interaction from the two ends of the dyad.

The Suri View

The responses of the Suri men and women and the older and the younger generations, are remarkably similar. No doubt, the tourist presence will, in the near future, create a subgroup of Suri youngsters that can make a living on tourism, and thus, this new generation will suppress any feelings of disdain. But at present, the Suri are rather uniform in their display of bewilderment and irritation toward the foreign visitors. Two kinds of behavior strike the Suri as most characteristic of the tourists: their taking photographs all the time and their behaving in a childish, rude and incomprehensible way, to the point of being bizarre.

Photography is of course a quintessential activity or posture of a tourist. It was noted by Susan Sontag in her pioneering book *On Photography,* that from the point of view of the tourist, the "very activity of taking pictures is soothing, and assuages general feelings of disorientation that are likely to be exacerbated by travel. Most tourists feel compelled to put the camera between themselves and whatever is remarkable that they encounter" (Sontag 1977:10). While this is true in a general sense for all sorts of tourists, in the case of the explorer-tourists among the Suri, there is the desire for "authentic documentation" of the otherness of these people (and occasionally for commercially marketable pictures).[12] However, Sontag has definitely hit on a defining element of the tourist: as a traveling person she or he wants to make sense of his or her experience and needs to "frame" it in some way and relate it to his or her own world. This calls to mind Harkin's analysis of the tourist experience as a quest for framing and structuration of meaning through the management of a set of signs rooted in the tourist's own life-world.

One aspect of the photographic act is especially pertinent to the Suri case. As Susan Sontag has noted: "To photograph is to appropriate the thing photographed. It means putting oneself into a certain relation to the world that feels like knowledge—and therefore, like power" (1977:4). The Suri being photographed are aware of this more than any other people and act accordingly: they say that no one should have this power over them, or if so, it should be compensated for by means of an appropriate monetary transaction.

Sontag also made the, by now very familiar, point that there "is an aggression implicit in every use of the camera" (1977:7). This is easy to observe in the Suri–tourist exchanges. If an argument ensues over a specific photographing act, as is often the case, reactions very often take on an aggressive form: people are manhandled and those photographed try to get hold of the camera. In the case of one Japanese tourist group visiting in 1989, cameras were forcibly taken from them, thrown on the rocks, and destroyed. Suri irritation at cameras and photographing has nothing to do with the fear often ascribed to non-Western people that their "soul" or "well-being" is being taken away. Nothing of the kind. In this as in other things, the Suri are rationalists; they are well aware of how a camera works and what comes out of it. They only resent being "turned into an image or a souvenir" (Sontag

1977:9), which is taken away, and being limited in their interaction as adult humans with tourists whom they thought were other adult humans.

During fieldwork, observing interactions between tourists and Suri—always stunted because of translation problems and the insecure interpretation of gestures—I often noted Suri responses like the following: "You are not going to shoot me just like that, first give me the green leaves (money)!"[15] "For every one of us in the picture you pay us one note, now!" Turning toward me, they said: "Are they all like that, bothering us before they have done their duty and given us things? Tell them to cooperate!" "What is their aim, what is it they do? If we are being fooled, we will not allow any picture taken here!" "Can we deal with people who behave unfair?"

Such remarks illustrate the Suri dislike of the absence of equal exchange with the tourists. The apparent value tourists attach to taking pictures of them, but not taking their time and not communicating to them, bred deep irritation. Suri often forbade tourists outright from taking pictures or even sitting in their village; they also asked what they knew were outrageous prices for some of their cultural items (lip-plates, wooden stools, leather decorations, calabashes) when tourists expressed any interest in buying them. In doing so, the Suri also ridiculed the tourists' wish to have everything. For instance, some tourists even wanted the special ivory bracelets worn by male members of the chiefly clan but did not know that these can never be sold, and even if they heard about this would not desist.

Similar abrasive responses have been noted among the Mursi, the people neighboring the Suri, who are culturally very much alike. For instance, in response to his question of what they thought that tourists were doing, anthropologist D. Turton quotes the following remarks from Mursi friends: "*You* tell us: why do they shoot [photograph] us? . . . They can't speak our language so we can't ask them why they are doing it. . . . They come with Ethiopian guides who just sit in cars. After the tourists have taken their photos, they drive off. We say: 'Is it just that they want to know who we are, or what?' We say: 'They must be people who don't know how to behave.' Even old women come and totter about taking photos. 'Is that the way whites normally behave?' That's what we say. Goloñimeri [the Mursi name for Turton], what are they doing? Do they want us to become their children, or what? What do they do with the photographs?" Finally: "This photography business comes from your country—where the necklace beads grow. You whites are the culprits. Give us a car and we'll go and take pictures of you" (Turton 1994:286).[14] The only difference between Mursi and Suri is perhaps that the latter are in general more annoyed and aggressive in actually demanding money for the photographs and they actively obstruct their being photographed if the tourists try to duck payment.[15]

Photography is an essential element of the tourist gaze (cf. Urry 1990:140)—it expresses the token appropriation of the objects, landscapes, or people. The photographic act thus illustrates the underlying tourist concern with the visual, the aesthetic representation of experience. Here lies the link with the characteristic tourist desire for the consumption of ever new images and experiences, which makes the tourist the quintessential expression of postmodern consumer identity. As Sontag (1877:24) already noted, "Needing to have reality confirmed and experience enhanced by photographs is an aesthetic consumerism to which everyone is now addicted." In semiotic terms, for the tourist the picture becomes not only the visual sign of "having been there" but also of having captured the "reality" of the signified.

In the literature it has often been remarked (cf. Urry 1990:10) that tourist behavior exemplifies license, a release from everyday obligations and norms—"liminal" behavior. The manners and "civilizational standards" of tourists sometimes may or may not be greatly at variance with local mores, especially in very divergent cross-cultural settings. But the very structure of the encounter is a determining factor in bringing out behavior among tourists that is beyond "normal" bounds. The temporality, displacement, language difference, and perception of "distance" seem to cancel out the need for meaningful or respectful social contact, or some element of reciprocity. In the tourist game, a relationship is a commodity, and as the fleeting encounter of people will not ever be repeated, freedom from reciprocal norms seems guaranteed. Restraint or respect according to the local norms is secondary. The people visited are, so to speak, just part of the landscape, not meaningful social partners: a landscape cannot (and should not) have an opinion about people, as Nietzsche once said. But what is usually not treated in much detail in the literature on tourist–native interaction, is the *actual* behavior of tourists in their contacts with locals and the effect this has on the latter.

From numerous interviews and observations, I noted that the Suri and other local people neighboring them (Dizi and village people, who usually act as guides and porters for the tourists) are always amazed if not shocked by the "dirty," "uncontrolled," and "shameless" demeanor of the tourists. For example, they say these people fart in public without inhibition, they often urinate and defecate in plain sight of the porters and the local people, males and females demonstratively kiss and embrace each other in public, others, often the couples, frequently argue and shout at each other. The Suri also note that the tourists quickly show anger and other emotions, like children. This is all contrary to local standards of decent or adult behavior. Perhaps this kind of behavior is in principle still unacceptable, or at least questionable, in the tourists' own society as well. But the point is that here, in the "liminal phase," which trekking represents, tourists think they can afford to dispense with ordinary standards and manners, because they suppose the natives have no such manners either. These "natives," however, were offended time and again, and their former image of the "polite" or "developed" foreigner became seriously dented. As a result, scorn and disdain are becoming the dominant feelings toward foreigners. Originally, the Suri (and the Mursi) approached white foreigners with some kind of awe or respect, expressed in their using the term *barári*, which means "having power" or "being hot," in the sense of "dangerous."[16] Today, this word is never used for any tourist.

The Tourist View

The other end of the dyad, the point of view of the tourists must also be considered. Here, the effect of the encounter is also upsetting. The main reason is that the Suri do not behave as the tourist frame of reference would expect them to behave. If the tourist encounter is seen as a kind of ritual, that is, as a form of "scripted play" with some predictability or at least markedness, then the Suri do not give evidence of wanting to recognize that script. Numerous incidents illustrate this pattern. I take a few from observations and interviews with tourists in 1990–1994. The base line in all these stories is the feeling of deception, indignation and anger.

- One group of Italian tourists (in 1994) came to a village to meet the Suri but were sent back after they refused to pay the money for photographs and the daily "tourist tax," because, they said, they had already paid that money to the NTO and for their visas. They were adamant; but so were the Suri, and as the latter had automatic rifles, the Italians did not insist and went back without having taken any pictures.

- In another incident in 1994, a small group of German tourists were threatened at gun point to give money, medicines, clothes, and razor blades. Some girls in the group panicked and dramatically started begging the Suri men not to shoot. Others started crying. In a state of shock, they left the area.

- One elderly American couple with a private guide whom I met shortly after their return from the Suri area in 1995 told me about their utter disappointment and indignation about having been subjected to constant shouting and pushing by the Suri, who incessantly demanded money and other things. They said that they had cut short their visit among them, and that they "had never met such impolite and rude behavior anywhere in the world."

- A Belgian tourist who was in the area in late 1994 was asked to pay huge sums of money because of his desire to take hundreds of photographs. His main interest was, as he phrased it to me, "to see and photograph naked tribesmen in their original state, untouched by outside civilization." He stated that he loved the country and people, and would stay long among them. But finally he just had to pay up, and only then could move through the area. Afterwards, he expressed to me his disappointment and his indignation at the efforts and financial sacrifices that he had to make to get his pictures. He said he loathed the Suri for their extreme monetary greed and would never visit them again.

- In 1990, a group of about 20 Japanese tourists were bathing in the Kibish River, which runs in Suri territory. When they came out, they found that all their clothes, cameras and bags had been stolen. Great indignation. No Suri claimed to have seen the thieves. After long deliberations with some local Suri spokesmen, some of the things were recovered. The tourists quickly left the Suri area, baffled and disturbed.

In Ethiopian terms, the Suri are exceptional in their response to tourists. Indeed, no group in Ethiopia routinely demands a sum of money from foreigners who come to visit them. In 1996, the Suri asked 150 *birr*[17] per tourist per day to be paid to their newly founded local "Surma Council," in addition to the money to be paid for individual photographs.[18] Nor do they mind being assertive, even aggressive, in their dealings with foreigners who come there for a few days. They say that this is their own country, so the people who visit them should pay just for being there, and they do not trust the motives of the tourists. Few local populations harass or threaten the tourists during their actual "meeting": in most places, the "realist illusion" is somehow kept up because of the material benefits that accrue. Obviously, the Suri also want the material benefits, driven by a logic introduced or made acutely relevant by the tourist presence, but underneath their attitude lies a deep irritation about the perceived power difference and arrogance of tourists not wanting to engage in meaningful contact and behaving like children. Their tactic is not one of terrorism, but it is one of intimidation; my own impression is that they would be even more violent if their religious leaders did not restrain them.

It is interesting to note that the travel agents who sell these trips do not warn their customers about such problems (except in very general terms, to make them appear part of the attraction of the trip): they do not intend to disturb the illusion of realism before they have dispatched their clients and cashed their cheques.

In analyzing staged Maasai performances for tourists on the farm of the British-Kenyan Mayer family, Bruner and Kirshenblatt-Gimblett (1994:467) remarked that "the Maasai and the Mayers are merely players in a show written by international tourist discourse." The Suri are an example of the opposite. They give clear evidence of a refusal to be incorporated as actors in the triadic tourist game (Suri–state agents/guides–foreign tourists). In a radical way they *refuse to act as a party in the relationship*, rejecting its terms and thus their inclusion into a system of meaning of others. In contrast to peoples who have been exposed for longer periods to external contacts and who are willing to see the advantages of an encounter with tourism—cf. the Balinese, the Maltese (Boissevain 1986), the Toraja (Volkman 1990) or the Maasai (Bruner and Kirshenblatt-Gimblett 1994)—the Suri consciously intend to keep the visitors at bay. If they do respond to them, it is in a remarkably exploitative way; for them, tourists are the last in a long line of visitors who intend to incorporate them into their scheme of things, be it the state administration, the colonial structure (the Italians), the army, tax gatherers, and so forth. They resist them like they have resisted the latter: by militant and aggressive self-assertion.

The Clash of Identities and the Reinforcement of Group Boundary

The meeting of Suri and tourists described above refers to a relatively new contact situation: before about 1988, the Suri were simply not visited by tourists, and they were not familiar with such a category of people. But the friction is probably common at all locations where tourists are now an established feature of the social landscape. A study of such a situation in its "pristine form" reveals an ultimately irreconcilable clash of cultural interests between the locals and the tourists, despite all the compromises and accommodations that develop later when it becomes clear that the tourists will not leave the place alone.

We might also say that in the encounter of Suri and tourists, "violence" is produced (cf. Mudimbe 1994): both symbolic (because of imposition and power difference) and physical (pushing and hitting, stealing of property, and threats, sometimes at gunpoint). The second could be seen as a response to the first. The tourists—though equipped with plenty of money and material goods—feel very tense, and come to see their being there as indeed having an element of force. The conditions of discourse and "exchange" are imposed, meaningful contact is precluded, and they are obliged to constantly and unpleasantly negotiate on commercial values: money for pictures and for objects; gifts of razors, soap, cloth; and so forth. There are no reciprocal terms of exchange known in advance but only exploitative ones, realized in what both parties know is a one-time encounter.

All this inhibits and structurally precludes normal social exchange and enhances antagonism. What the tourists do not immediately see is that this clash is *predicated upon their very motive of their coming there,* as adventurous would-be explorers, with their "social center" (Cohen 1979:183) elsewhere but who come to discover the unknown Other, a "remote primitive tribe." This explorer-experience goes back to an old Western *topos* and still functions as an ideological trapping cultivated by the travel agencies that market such trips. It may or may not be related to the cultural ambiguity of modern-industrial society with its lingering nostalgia for a lost past (Graburn 1995:166) and its residual feelings of alienation (MacCannell 1976). But more importantly it must be seen as part of the great tourist game of producing "realism" in an unambiguous, marked domain where people from both sides are expected to "follow the rules."

From the point of view of the tourists, their encounter with the Suri is a case of "failed framing": due to Suri resistance against the social model of subordinate exchange and the rendering of "services," most (though not all) tourists feel disoriented. They, as white visitors, are pushed back to their elementary identity as "intruders" and confront the limited power of their resources (money) and status (as "white, developed" people). Their illusion of authentic realism is punctured, and their image of a pristine tribe with its own codes and customs happily and generously shared with outsiders is shattered. One could say that the Suri have become so "authentic"—with their very original "rude, savage and uncontrolled" behavior—that they defy the tourist script to the point of breaking it up.

The Suri example shows once again that the confrontation of "otherness"—both for the tourist and for the local people visited—can reinforce group consciousness (see also MacCannell 1984). Increased contact between ethnocultural groups does *not* automatically produce mutual understanding or the management of difference; more often, it leads to the opposite.[19] In this case, of course, this is enhanced by the fact of spatio-temporal remoteness reproduced in the very encounter of locals and tourists: the latter will go back and are there *because* they cherish the fact that they are on the verge of going back to their social peers—which allows them to gaze at the differences separating them from those who will stay there in their full "otherness."

For the Suri, the encounter initially produces a redrawing of their group identity as "strangers" to the visitors. As remarked earlier, they are acutely aware of this fact. Their group consciousness—traditionally already characterized by high self-esteem, by a strongly shared normative culture centered on cattle, and by a tacit contempt for all others—is also reinforced by their actual dealings with tourists. Their disdain for them has underlined their conviction that only they themselves are, what they call, "real adult people" (in Suri: *hiri mù*). While they appreciate the ingenuity of some of the material culture items that the tourists bring and do not reject the money to be gained, they cannot take them seriously as persons. Inadvertently, therefore, their exposure to tourists may have brought about a revaluation of their own way of life.

The Suri, Tourism, and Development

Above, we noted that the Suri resist their unquestioned annexation into the tourist discourse, and in their encounter with the tourists develop more self-consciousness about the value of their own ethnocultural tradition. They do not aspire to "become like them." This phenomenon underlines Cohen's conclusions (1988:383) about the mixed effects of "commoditization" in tourism: some local cultural values may be negatively affected but others may be redefined or reinforced. It has to be noted, however, that much will depend on the extent and manner of outside interventions.

The relative autonomy and independence of the Suri way of life, and their ability to "resist" or "contest" the tourist challenge, will gradually erode, and social transformations will occur. Tourists will keep coming, there has been a foreign missionary station among them since 1990, and government political interference has become stronger since 1991.

The Suri will also find themselves increasingly connected to the global economy. This was most obvious in a recent National Parks Project. The European Union in the late 1990s financed a large, five-year development project in Ethiopia (of some 16 million European Currency Units, at the time ca. US$19 million) to upgrade and redevelop the national parks and game reserves in the south of the country, with the underlying aim of stimulating wildlife tourism from the EU to Ethiopia (on the basis of the example of Kenya). These plans, fuelled by global concerns about wildlife diversity and conservation as well as by the long-term commercial interests of the tourist sector, did not initially consider the position of the Suri and other local groups. Of course, the Suri experience with future game park tourism had some tangible benefits, certainly in the short-term: for example, the influx of significant cash. In the project plans, roads, clinics, schools and the drilling of water holes were also promised.[20] The Ethiopian authorities indeed built some schools and clinics, but these hardly materialized on the scale predicted. However, when the EU project (finances and labor) receded after some years—the project was phased out in 1999), the Ethiopian government was not able to uphold or increase the level of local services or infrastructure, and many of the improvements were withering away. Moreover, a largely nonlocal elite from the capital profited from the proceeds of tourism, not the average Suri.

In the EU plans, the park areas were seen as an "impressive wilderness" (the tourist image), with the implication that human populations had always been marginal to their existence—although the park areas had known human existence for thousands of years and indeed owed their state to prolonged human activity (Turton 1996:107). In this context we see two rather different views of what is "real." There was little detail in the plans about the effective integration of local people's (underestimated) knowledge about ecological management, or their need for living space, or the importance of cultural values; the globalist model of top-down planning aimed at "conservation" and "tourist management" seems to have taken precedence. It might be advisable for development-oriented people (government agents, NGO people, and those in the Game Park Project) not only to take into effective account the presence, attitudes and socio-cultural aspirations of local people but also to recognize their right (as the most ancient and most knowledgeable inhabitants of the area) to have their identity as active local *subjects* respected (see Turton 2002).

In view of the increasing global flows, local identity in general is becoming more and more fragile (cf. Appadurai 1995). If these local interests and sensibilities are not recognized in such globalist schemes and are drawn up largely based on a Western approach, problems will arise. If a real role for local populations is not envisaged, the latter can easily resort to ways of undermining game park tourism, for instance by killing the animals in the park and causing security problems for tourists and others. A new phase in the encounter between locals and external authorities and agencies was entered in 2004, when the African Parks Foundation (AFP), a Netherlands-based organization running wild-life parks in Africa for African governments, was hired by the Ethiopian authorities to take responsibility for the Nech'Sar, Mago, and Omo National Parks and to have them emulate the Kenya model of park tourism.[21] Despite a commendable commitment to wildlife and natural habitat preservation and a new round of benefits announced, the venture was controversial from the start due to displacement of local people from the parks, and the fear within AFP for human rights problems led to their withdrawing from the project in 2007.[22]

Globalization, Exotopy and Suri Identity

While tourism itself is a phenomenon of considerable antiquity, by the early twenty-first century global conditions allow a large portion of the post-modern industrialized world to indulge in it. The existence of diverging values will always cause tensions in the tourist–"native" encounter, and this holds not only in Ethiopia but in any other country, the developed West included (see the studies in Boissevain 1996).

The Suri experience tourism chiefly as a disturbance and as a hegemonic strategy to be resisted. They refuse to be "signs" (of primitiveness, backwardness, tribalism, etc.) in a system of meaning of tourists that allows no reciprocity. The tourist effort toward inclusion is resisted by radical self-assertion and obstruction, whereby the Suri subvert the script of tourist realism. They refuse to be wrapped and taken home. So far, tourism among the Suri has not undermined their society but reinforced local values and self-esteem. At the same time, they are introduced to the charged symbolism of material exchange through money: money is the new means by which their group culture and artifacts are commoditized and expressed. Lacking another means of meaningful communication in the encounter with tourists, they capitalize on money and thus are drawn into the idiom of "consumerism" themselves. This money aspect, in fact, has now consolidated itself as the only tolerable motive for engaging in tourist encounters and has, in recent years, tended to lessen the enmity in the encounter but without resolving its inherent contradictions.

Contemporary tourist identity is a characteristic global consumer identity that has far-reaching implications in a socioeconomic and moral sense. Tourism is an inevitable phenomenon, enhanced by conditions of modern technology and travel facilities, which diminish the costs of mobility and strengthen notions of virtual "simultaneity" of place and of experience. In view of the reactions tourism initially seems to evoke in the local settings it penetrates, it is also *inherently* problematic and conflictual, despite its highly ritualized character. The impact, role and motivations of tourists need to be re-evaluated continuously. For instance, at the present historical juncture, it is highly questionable whether tourists really search for authenticity, which they are said to lack in their own daily lives. This claim, made by MacCannell in his landmark book *The Tourist* (1976), has been challenged by, among others, Cohen (1979, 1988) and Urry (1990).

My interpretation is also that postmodern consumer tourists are much more cynical, and are very conscious (not to say arrogant), about the unassailable advance they, as members of a developed industrial/information-age society, have over people of the not so wealthy, or as they see it, not well-organized—or worse, "primitive" or "chaotic"—societies they visit. That tourists go there is a result of the commoditization of local culture or landscape in tourist discourse on the home front: a discourse of status competition that structurally negates initial personal motives of a "sincere interest in the other." Tourists' exploration of these other societies and people is thus primarily to be seen as an act of self-confirmation or congratulation toward social peers in their own society, and not of seeking "lost values" of an authentic or an affectively rewarding life in the exotope, the visited locations outside one's own familiar sociocultural space.[23]

Tourism is another act in the politico-cultural drama of hegemonic strife between the global poles variously defined as rich and poor, North and South, developed and underdeveloped. As we saw in the case above, the Suri will be made safe for mass tourism through the noble aim of wildlife protection. The question remains whether the Suri, and numerous local societies like them, subjected unwillingly to tourists, can marshal their few resources of "counterdiscourse" to enhance their interests and collective identity in this political arena where the local and the global meet, *or* can only resist temporarily before the onslaught of globalizing consumer patterns. Of course, the latter scenario seems more likely, however much one might regret it.

Source: Adapted from "Tourism and Its Discontents: Suri–Tourist Encounters in Southern Ethiopia," *Social Anthropology*, 2000, 8(1):1–17.

Acknowledgements

For support of research work in southern Ethiopia, I am grateful to the Royal Netherlands Academy of Science (KNAW), the Netherlands Organization for Scientific Research in the Tropics (WOTRO, WR 52-601), and the African Studies Centre (Leiden). I also am much indebted to the former directors of the Institute of Ethiopian Studies (Addis Ababa, Ethiopia), Prof. Bahru Zewde and the late Dr. Taddesse Beyene for their institutional support. I thank Prof. Wim van Binsbergen and Dr. Azeb Amha for their critical comments on an earlier version of this text.

Notes

[1] Especially among neighboring groups they are known as *Surma*. Most commonly used self-names are Chai and Tirmaga (two subgroups).

[2] Ambivalence toward tourists is of course not uncommon among social science researchers. Cf. Middleton 1991, who considers the tourists on the Swahili coast as "cultural illiterates" (1991:vii) and sees the tourist trade as "a final form of colonialism" and as "the most degrading exploitation of the Swahili coast" (p. 53).

[3] Neither would the persistent ambivalence of the tourist enterprise be explained: why do tourists get irritated by other tourists, and why is the general image of the tourist so invariably negative? (See the quotes on the first page of Urry's 1990 book.)

[4] In contrast to, for example, coastal tourism in Kenya (see Peake 1989; Sindiga 1996).

[5] Perhaps one can recognize here something of the "Riefenstahl syndrome."

[6] Since the publication of their books, and notably since the late 1990s, the photographic (mis)representation of the Suri has assumed dramatic proportions, as hosts of commercial photographers, journalists, artists, filmmakers, and others have visited the Suri and produced a never-ending series of exoticizing papers, books and documentaries on them. That these productions create any more understanding of Suri society is doubtful (see Abbink 2009b).

[7] Good explanatory text might have helped here, but G. Hancock's chapter on the Surma and related groups (in Beckwith and Fisher 1990) leaves much to be desired. The Beckwith-Fisher article of 1991 contains very little text.

[8] Although Arnold Hodson, British consul in Maji in the early 1920s, published a photograph of the "Kachubo"-Surma (these are the Kachepo or Baalé-Surma, living on the Boma Plateau in Sudan) in 1929 (see Hodson 1929:207).

[9] Also the under current regime the area is used to station demoted people.

[10] The Italian scholar C. Conti Rossini was the first to call Ethiopia "un museo di popoli" (a museum of peoples) in his book *L'Abissinia* (Rome 1929, p. 20).

[11] When I was in the field in 1994, a group of German tourists was called back by the authorities and had to fly back to Addis Ababa without having seen the Suri. Similar incidents were recorded in more recent years, although after c. 2002 the situation stabilized due to more government presence in the area.

[12] This was the case with the Beckwith-Fisher expedition of 1988, and of one Belgian tourist-photographer of my acquaintance, who toured among the Suri in 1994. Both came back with pictures that they used in publications, or that they were about to sell or publicly exhibit. This is also the case with most of the recent photo-books on the Suri.

[13] The Ethiopian one *birr* notes given are green.

[14] See also the Granada TV ("Disappearing Word") film on the Mursi, called *Nitha* (1991). The most recent film on the Mursi is *Fire Will Eat Us,* Granada TV for Channel 4 Television (UK), 2001.

[15] D. Turton (2004) also has addressed the impact of tourism among the related Mursi people, in a perspective quite similar (including the references to S. Sontag's work) first offered in the original version of the present chapter (Abbink 2000).

[16] This term is also applied to the innate "power" of their religious chiefs and to certain ritually important plants.

[17] In 1996 US$25 equalled 150 Ethiopian *birr.* In mid-2009 US$25 equalled 227 Ethiopian *birr.*

[18] That no Suri outside this council benefits from it is of secondary importance. In the past few years I heard that other Southern Ethiopian groups also started to ask for "tourist money."

[19] The conditions under which exposure to and experience with cultural differences *reinforce* group boundaries and generate antagonistic images or actual conflict are not yet well addressed in globalization studies (cf. Sindiga 1996:431).

[20] These were announced in the first (1993) program-document of the Agriconsulting Group that made a feasibility study for the Project.

[21] The project became the issue of polemics between the APF, the Ethiopian government, and the advocates of the local peoples, after news about the forceful eviction of locals from the projected park areas. See information at the Web sites: www.wrm.org.uy/bulletin/105/Ethiopia.html and www.iucn.org/about/union/commissions/ceesp/ceesp_alerts/evictions.cfm (accessed 20 February 2009).

[22] See: www.conservationrefugees.org and the APF statement there (accessed 20 February 2009).

[23] The numerous photographers and filmmakers who have discovered the Suri in the past decade (see note 6 above) are often genuinely fascinated by them but convert this into primarily commercial products. There are now at least a dozen well-produced photo-books on the Suri.

References

Abbink, J. 2002a. 'Paradoxes of power and culture in an old periphery: Surma, 1974–98,' in: D. Donham, *et al.*, eds. *Remapping Ethiopia: Socialism and After*, pp. 155–72. Oxford: James Currey - Addis Ababa: Addis Ababa University Press - Athens, OH: Ohio University Press.

————. 2002b. 'Me'en', in: C.R. Ember, M. Ember & I. Skoggard, eds., *Encyclopedia of World Cultures, Supplement,* pp. 200–4. New York - Farmington Hills, MI: Macmillan Reference USA - Gale Group.

————. 2009a. 'Conflict and social change on the Southwest Ethiopian frontier: an analysis of Suri society,' *Journal of Eastern African Studies* 3(1).

————. 2009b. 'Recycling exoticism: Western visualizations of the Ethiopian Suri people,' *Cahiers d'Etudes Africaines 49 (195).*

Appadurai, A. 1995. "The Production of Locality," in *Counterworks. Managing the Diversity of Knowledge,* ed. R. O. Fardon, pp. 204–225. London - New York: Routledge.

Beckwith, C. and A. Fisher. 1990. *African Ark.* London: Collins-Harvill.

————. 1991. "The eloquent Surma of Ethiopia," *National Geographic Magazine* 179(2): 77–99.

Boissevain, J. 1986. *Tourism as Anti-structure.* Amsterdam: Anthropological-Sociological Centre (Euromed Working Paper).

Boissevain, J. (ed.). 1996. *Coping with Tourists: European Reactions to Mass Tourism.* Oxford - Providence, RI: Berghahn Publishers.

Bruner, E. and B. Kirshenblatt-Gimblett. 1994. "Maasai on the Lawn: Tourist Realism in East Africa. *Cultural Anthropology* 9: 435–470.

Bulatovitch, A. K. 1900. "Dall'Abessinia al Lago Rodolfo per il Caffa," *Bolletino della Società Geografica Italiana* 38:121–142.

————. 1902. "Les campagnes de Ménélik," *Journal des Voyages et des Aventures de Terre et Mer,* 2me série, no.s 297–307, pp. 186–9, 206–7, 226–7, 241–3, 255–6, 274–5, 294–8 (Traduit et adapté par Michel Delines).

Chambers, E. 2010. *Native Tours: The Anthropology of Travel and Tourism,* 2nd ed. Long Grove, IL: Waveland Press.

Cohen, E. 1979. "A phenomenology of tourist experiences," *Sociology* 13: 179–201.

————. 1988. "Authenticity and commoditization in tourism," *Annals of Tourism Research* 15: 371–386.

Consoziazione Turistica Italiana. 1938. *Guida dell'Africa Orientale Italiana.* Milano: CTI.

Culler, J. 1981. "The semiotics of tourism," *American Journal of Semiotics* 1: 127–140.

Graburn, N. 1995. "Tourism, Modernity, Nostalgia," in *The Future of Anthropology: Its Relevance to the Contemporary World,* ed. A. Ahmed and C. Shore, pp. 158–178. London: Athlone Press.

Gwynn, C. 1911. "A journey in Southern Abyssinia," *Geographical Journal* 38: 113–131.

Harkin, M. 1995. "Modernist anthropology and tourism of the authentic," *Annals of Tourism Research* 22: 650–670.

Hodson, A. W. 1929. *Where Lion Reign.* London: Skeffington & Son.

MacCannell, D. 1976. *The Tourist: A New Theory of the Leisure Class.* New York: Schocken Books.

————. 1984. "Reconstructed Ethnicity: Tourism and Cultural Identity in the Third World," *Annals of Tourism Research* 11:375–391.

Marchetti, M. 1939. "Notizie sulle popolazioni dei Tirma, Tid e Zilmamo," *Archivio per l'Antropologia e l'Etnologia* 69: 59–76.

Middleton, J. 1991. *The World of the Swahili: An African Mercantile Civilization.* London - New Haven, CT: Yale University Press.

Mudimbe, V. 1994. "Race and science," *Transition* 64: 68–76.

Nash, D. 1996. "Prospects for Tourism Study in Anthropology," in *The Future of Anthropology: Its Relevance to the Contemporary World,* ed. A. Ahmed and C. Shore, pp.179–202. London: Athlone Press.

Peake, R. 1989. "Swahili Social Stratification and Tourism in Malindi Old Town," *Africa* 59: 209–220.

Rizetto, F. 1941. "Alcune notizie sui Tirma," *Annali dell'Africa Italiana* 4: 1201–1211.

Sindiga, I. 1996. "International Tourism in Kenya and the Marginalization of the Waswahili," *Tourism Management* 17: 425–432.

Smith, V., ed, 1994. *Hosts and Guests: The Anthropology of Tourism*. Philadelphia: University of Pennsylvania Press.

Sontag, S. 1977. *On Photography*. New York: Delta Books.

Turton, D. 1992. "Anthropology on television: what next?" In: *Film as Ethnography*, ed. P. I. Crawford and D. Turton, pp. 283–99. Manchester - New York: Manchester University Press.

———. 1995. "The Mursi and the Elephant Question." Paper for the *Participatory Wildlife Management Workshop*, Ministry of Natural Resources and FARM Africa, Addis Ababa, 16–18 May 1995, 29 pp.

———. 1996. "Migrants and Refugees. A Mursi Case Study," in *In Search of Cool Ground: Flight and Homecoming in Northeast Africa*, ed. T. Allen, pp. 96–110. London: James Currey.

———. 2002. "The Mursi and the Elephant Question," in *Conservation and Mobile Indigenous Peoples: Displacement, Forced Settlement and Development*, ed. D. Chatty and M. Colchester, pp. 97–118. New York–Oxford: Berghahn Books.

———. 2004. "Lip-plates and 'the People Who Take Photographs.' Uneasy encounters between Mursi and tourists in southern Ethiopia." *Anthropology Today* 20(3): 3–8.

Viezzer, C. 1938. "Diario di una carovana di missione geo-mineraria di Bonga-Magi-Tirma nell'Ovest Etiopico," *Rassegna Mineraria Mensile* (Materie Prime d'Italia e dell'Impero) XVII: 404–425.

Urry, J. 1990. *The Tourist Gaze: Leisure and Travel in Contemporary Societies*. London - Newbury Park - New Delhi: Sage.

Volkman, T. 1990. "Visions and Revisions: Toraja Culture and the Tourist Gaze," *American Ethnologist* 17: 91–110.

8

"Let 'em Loose": Pueblo Indian Management of Tourism

Jill D. Sweet

The Pueblo Indians of the American Southwest have developed creative and assertive techniques for interacting with tourists. Embedded in specific historic and cultural circumstances, these techniques help the Pueblo Indians survive the pressures of tourist contact, fortify their cultural boundaries, and exercise a degree of power over individuals who are, in most other situations, defined as the more powerful.[1] In this paper I examine two of the techniques that are central to Pueblo tourist management and Pueblo cultural maintenance.

Although there is considerable literature examining host/guest dynamics in situations of tourist contact,[2] only recently have researchers regarded indigenous hosts as powerful players in the process.[3] An intriguing analysis of host/guest dynamics offered by Evans-Pritchard (1989) treats the indigenous hosts as "subjects" initiating action, rather than merely "objects" acted upon and ultimately doomed by tourism. Although the issue of host control in these interactions is not her focus, Evans-Pritchard does examine Native American/tourist encounters and notes that, "armed with stereotypes of tourists, and aware of touristic stereotypes of Indians, Indians can exercise more control over frequently uncomfortable situations" (1989:102). She also observes that many Native Americans have much more experience dealing with tourists than tourists have dealing with Native Americans; this gives the latter an advantage in host/guest interactions (1989:99).

Using Evans-Pritchard's observations as a point of departure, I will focus specifically on the ways the Pueblo Indians control the tourists who enter their world. In particular, this paper examines the Pueblo/tourist inter-active techniques of secrecy and regulation. I also regard the techniques of burlesque and exportation as practices of tourist management, but these latter two techniques will not be dealt with here, since I have discussed them at length elsewhere.[4] An examination of the Pueblo situation will help research-ers understand both host/guest dynamics and an important dimension of cul-tural maintenance. It also will contribute to a better understanding of the reasons why some indigenous communities survive and even benefit from tourist contact while others experience only cultural disruption.

Research for this paper was conducted primarily at the villages of Acoma, Santo Domingo, San Ildefonso, and San Juan, New Mexico, during several field sessions between 1973 and 1989. The first two villages are Keresan-speaking pueblos, and the latter two are Tewa-speaking pueblos. All of these villages currently are visited by tourists.

The Pueblo Indian and Tourism in the Southwest

Long before tourists first arrived in the Southwest, the Pueblo Indians already had considerable experience with cultural others, including Navajo, Apache, and other nomadic tribes; Spanish explorers, colonists, and mission-aries; Anglo traders, settlers, entrepreneurs, missionaries, and military per-sonnel. Although many of these early contact situations were extremely difficult and often tragic for the Pueblo people, they prepared these Indians to be forthright and clever in their response to outside domination.

By the turn of the nineteenth century, the time was right for tourist interest in the Native American. Spicer observes,

> In most cases, after the native peoples were subjugated, strong sentiment grew up in the conquering nation regarding the injustice of the original conquest. The native survivors assumed a symbolic significance as reminders of a ruthless past and as representatives of a lost and better way of life, pre-urban and pre-industrial. Associated with this symbolism strong feelings developed for preservation of the native peoples and their ways . . . (1962:1–2)

The sentiments described above developed among some Anglo-Ameri-cans and encouraged visits to surviving native communities. Anglo tourists began "discovering" Pueblo Indians in the 1890s (Eickemeyer and Eicke-meyer 1895), and by the 1920s a tourist industry was flourishing in this region, with Pueblo people and villages regularly advertised as tourist attrac-tions. Large touring cars with Anglo female guides dressed in Southwest Indian garb began bringing groups of tourists to the Pueblo villages. Hotel lobbies, town plazas, and train stations became sites where Pueblo Indians displayed and sold their arts and crafts to travelers (Weigle 1989). The types of tourists who were and who continue to be attracted to the Pueblo people are what researchers call participants in "ethnic tourism."

Ethnic tourism is travel for pleasure that features activities such as visiting native villages, observing ceremonies, and shopping for indigenous arts and crafts (see Smith 1977). Swain defines ethnic tourism as "the marketing of tourist attractions based on an indigenous population's way of life" (1989:85). Van den Berghe and Keyes characterize ethnic tourism as fostering "the most complex and interesting types of interactions between tourists and natives. The native is not simply 'there' to serve the needs of the tourist; he is himself 'on show,' a living spectacle" (1984:343).

Ethnic tourists in the Southwest want to see, experience, and interact with the native inhabitants. They want to take pictures of Indians and purchase their pottery, jewelry, and textiles. Some ethnic tourists are satisfied by seeing Indians selling their wares in the Santa Fe plaza or by viewing a theatrical performance of Pueblo dance at a staged, commercial ceremonial, while others want to visit a reservation where they will see Indians doing "whatever they normally do," or where they might even catch a glimpse of a ritual that is still a vital part of the native religious calendar. Those who find the exotic experiences they seek may try to learn when the rituals are most likely to be held and may return to the reservation villages repeatedly. These more frequent visitors sometimes develop friendships with Pueblo families and are invited to share in the domestic feasting that occurs during village rituals. This is not a rare occurrence; many Pueblo families have what they call "Anglo friends" or "white friends" who regularly come to the open village rituals. While some of these friendships are lifelong and anything but superficial, Anglo friends never become fully accepted or formally adopted members of a Pueblo community. Most Anglo friends fit Evans's description of the "resident" tourist who retires, resides seasonally, or vacations regularly in one area (1978:43–44). These frequent visitors, as well as other tourists who come to the Pueblo reservations, typically do so by private automobiles and in small groups. Although bus tours occasionally stop at some pueblos, mass tourism is not yet common, and one-to-one contact between host and guest still occurs.

It is when the ethnic tourist comes to the reservation that the Pueblo Indians are able to control their visitors most effectively. This is possible primarily because of the Pueblo communities' history and political status. That is, through rights established by land grants, legislation, and legal cases, the Pueblo Indians maintain considerable independence and control over their communities and lands. In the mid-1930s, the United Pueblos Agency, the centralized federal administration of all New Mexico pueblos, acknowledged "that matters of purely internal nature were the exclusive jurisdiction of Pueblo officials" (1979:217). Relevant to tourism, Pueblo officials have the right to exclude visitors and to set the rules for acceptable behavior. They have the right to close the village to outsiders at any time. They also have the right to police their reservations and enforce their regulations. In short, the Pueblo communities determine what tourists may do or see while on the reservation and whether or not tourism will be encouraged, simply tolerated, or discouraged.

The fact that the reservations are still relatively isolated and removed from cities, towns, hotels, restaurants, and shops also permits control. Most villages remain out of the way, with considerable land surrounding them, which serves as a buffer. This makes the villages appealing to the ethnic tourist who enjoys adventure "off the beaten path," but, more importantly, it keeps the Pueblo communities from being engulfed by tourist facilities.

The Pueblo Indians' position on reservation tourism is clearly reflected in the Pueblo rejection of a 1975 nationwide American Indian Movement call to boycott the tourist industry. Typical of the Pueblo position, the governor of Santa Clara Pueblo, Lucario Padilla, announced that his village, where 50 percent of the residents depend on tourism for at least a portion of their livelihood, would not support the A.I.M. boycott. He explained,

> We realize the tremendous impact of the tourist trade upon the economy of the people within our pueblo . . . But, we must reiterate that anyone entering our pueblo as visitors must be aware of the responsibilities that accompany their roles as guests and act accordingly.[5]

With their long history of contact with others, their established independence, and their spatial isolation, Pueblo Indians were able to develop specific techniques for interacting with and ultimately controlling the behavior of visitors. The first of these techniques to be considered here is the Pueblo practice of withholding information. Secrecy is one way the Pueblo people protect their privacy, influence the behavior of visitors, and maintain the advantage in host/guest encounters.[6]

Secrecy

Many anthropologists who have worked within Pueblo Indian communities have noted the importance of secrecy. One scholar even suggested that "the central problem confronting any Pueblo scholar is secrecy" (Brandt 1980:123). While Pueblo secrecy has been discussed as an external device for the protection of the traditional religion and as an internal device for Pueblo leaders to maintain political control, Pueblo secrecy has not been analyzed until now as an advantage in host/guest interactions or as a vehicle for controlling tourists.[7]

Pueblo secrecy involves privacy and the protection of what is considered sacred space. There are sections of some Pueblo villages that are strictly off-limits to all visitors. Kivas—Pueblo sacred ceremonial chambers—are always closed to tourists in all but the Hopi and Zuni villages. As a result, most kiva rituals remain private. In addition, streets or sections of a village may be temporarily blocked off during the day because of funeral rites or the activities of the native religious societies. There are also days when an entire village is closed, with Pueblo males guarding the entrances and turning away any outsiders who might try to enter. Finally, some villages are closed routinely to all Anglo friends and other visitors after dark.

The rules of secrecy also control information concerning village rituals, which are either closed, open but unannounced, or open and announced. The closed rituals may be held in one of the kivas or in a temporarily closed village. The open but unannounced performances are held in the village plazas. If outsiders arrive, they are permitted to stay and watch as long as they are respectful and do not get too close to the action. Anglo friends may learn of these open but unannounced rituals from their Pueblo friends, who will offhandedly mention that "something is going on in the village tomorrow."

Village performances that are open and announced are those native events that have become associated with the Catholic calendar. For example, each village holds native dances in honor of its patron saint. Because these events are now part of the public Catholic calendar, their occurrence is predictable and local chambers of commerce, newspapers, magazines, radio stations, and even some Pueblo governors' offices announce them to the general public.

The inquisitiveness of Anglo tourists may pose problems for the Pueblo Indians, who have been taught since childhood that it is rude to ask questions directly. Furthermore, Pueblo Indians believe sacred knowledge may lose its power if it is openly discussed; therefore, it must be protected from the uninitiated. If an Indian is seen talking to outsiders in public, especially during a ritual performance, he may be ridiculed by his neighbors or accused of giving away sacred information. As a result of these attitudes and methods of internal social control, Pueblo people learn to distance themselves when confronted with questions. A question posed by a tourist may be met with a polite but very short response or a claim of ignorance, after which the Pueblo individual may quietly turn away from the visitor. Eye contact is usually avoided throughout the exchange; if the questioning persists, some Pueblo Indians will simply refuse to acknowledge the tourist's presence. Pueblo families often teach their Anglo friends that direct questions make them uncomfortable and probably will go unanswered, particularly if the questions are personal or concern native religious practices.

There were countless times that I observed Pueblo Indians withholding information from inquisitive tourists. I observed such an exchange, for example, at a February Basket Dance at the village of San Juan. About thirty members of the village were dancing in the plaza as other villagers and a few tourists watched. One male tourist asked a Pueblo woman, "Why are you [generic 'you'] dancing today?" She kept her eyes on the dancers and did not acknowledge that she heard the question, but the man repeated it. She then responded as if she did not understand the generic use of the word you: "I'm not dancing today." Hearing this subtly sarcastic response, several other Indians standing nearby began to smile and quietly chuckle. Next, the man said, "I mean, why is the village dancing today? Why are they dancing?" and he pointed to the dancers. "Oh," she said, not lifting her eyes from the dancers in front of her, "I think they must want it to rain." "Is that what this is?"

responded the man. "A rain dance?" Without waiting for a confirmation, he continued, "What do the baskets symbolize then?" "I don't know," she said. After a few minutes, he asked, "What about the songs? What are they saying?" But by now the woman had moved slightly away from the man and was ignoring his last questions. After a few minutes of waiting for a response, he gave up his quest for meaning.

This example not only illustrates the Pueblo Indians' reluctance to share information about native religious practices but also reveals how they often use a tourist's ignorance to make him appear foolish. MacCannell observed that host/guest relationships are inherently unequal (1984). The nature of this inequality, however, depends on whether one considers economics or local knowledge. In terms of economics, the native host often holds an inferior position to that of the tourist, but, as the above example illustrates, the native host has the advantage in terms of local knowledge. By withholding information, the Pueblo people have control over something ethnic tourists want—exotic cultural knowledge and experiences.

Controlling the desired knowledge and access to coveted experiences gives the Pueblo people a considerable advantage over tourists; they can choose to tell or not tell these visitors when and where Indian cultural events will be held. Further, they can decide just how far they will permit their visitors to enter the private regions of their villages.[8] Controlling knowledge and access also gives the Pueblo Indians an edge in interactions, because they are the ones "in the know." They can decide whether to translate and share any of the meanings contained in these events and whether the information given will be truthful. In addition, they can make ignorant tourists look foolish because of their lack of knowledge.

An example from Evans-Pritchard illustrates this last point further. During Indian Market, an annual event held in Santa Fe,

> . . . a lady was examining the silver balls on a squash blossom necklace. She turned to Cippy Crazyhorse [Cochiti Pueblo artist] . . . and in the slow, over-emphasized fashion intended for someone who does not really understand English, she asked "Are these hollow?" Cippy promptly replied "Hello" and warmly shook her hand. Again the lady asked, "Are these hollow?" pronouncing the words even more theatrically this time. Cippy cheerily responded with another "Hello." This went on a few more times, by which time everyone around was laughing, until eventually the lady herself saw the joke. (Evans-Pritchard 1989:95–96)

In addition to the interactional advantages gained by withholding information from outsiders, some Pueblo Indians keep certain information to themselves because they fear that breaking rules of secrecy will not only be met with disapproval by their neighbors and families, but may also result in supernatural misfortune. An incident at Santo Domingo Pueblo illustrates this dimension of Pueblo secrecy.

On an afternoon in May a number of years ago, a non-Indian companion and I decided to take a canoe trip down a portion of the Rio Grande. We chose a section of the river that flows through the Santo Domingo Reservation, with the idea that we would stop at the village and take some of the children out in the canoe. When we neared the back side of the village, we heard muffled singing, as if the singers were wearing masks. Knowing that in this village all masked performances are closed to outsiders and considered extremely private events, I decided we should continue on down the river rather than enter the village. The following day, I talked to a Santo Domingo friend about this river trip and my decision not to enter the village. She was relieved that we had not come up from the river, not only because I would have been in trouble with the authorities, but, more importantly, because something very bad would have happened to all of us. She kept asking me, "Weren't you terribly afraid?" and hinted that if I was not afraid, I certainly should have been. Fifteen years later, this Santo Domingo woman as well as other members of her family still bring up this incident, referring to it as a potentially dangerous situation.

The people of Acoma Pueblo have gone to great lengths to control where visitors can go, what they can see, and what they can learn when they visit the village. Acoma is located on top of a mesa; since the early 1980s, tourists have been directed to park their cars at the base of the mesa. Then they must purchase a ticket to ride a shuttle bus up the steep road to the mesa top. On reaching the village, the visitors are guided in small groups by one of several Acoma women who talk about the settlement's history and culture. Along the way, the guests are given several opportunities to purchase Acoma pottery. This arrangement permits the Acoma people to control their visitors while benefiting economically from tourism. Nevertheless, Acoma is closed for certain ritual events, and visitors are simply turned away at the base of the mesa.

Controlling what outsiders may see and know are important to Pueblo cultural survival. Key aspects of Pueblo Indian tradition are reserved exclusively for the Pueblo people. To be Pueblo is to share in these private domains. Furthermore, withholding information from visitors puts the Pueblo Indians in a position of power, since they hold what their guests desire. This control of knowledge distances us (the Pueblo people) from them (the Anglo tourists) and is central to the socially supported and ongoing maintenance of the culture. Pueblo secrecy is not simply a cultural quirk, but rather a deeply embedded technique for cultural survival.

Regulations

When tourists enter a Pueblo village, they find one or more signs providing them with information about village regulations. These range in quality and content from crudely painted signs that simply state restrictions on photography, sketching, notetaking, driving speeds, and a curfew for visitors to more sophisticated and professionally printed signs such as the one at the entrance of the Acoma Reservation. The Acoma sign reads,

PUEBLO OF ACOMA OFFICIAL NOTICE

You are entering the Pueblo of Acoma. All lands herein are governed by statutes enacted and/or adopted by the Acoma Tribal Council. Continued entrance beyond this point constitutes a knowing and voluntary consent on your behalf to abide by the laws of Acoma and to be held accountable to the Acoma judicial system for any violation of Acoma law.

As visitors get closer to the Acoma village, they find another sign; this one hand painted and titled "Pueblo Etiquette." Advice here is informal but certainly to the point:

Do not be loud or obnoxious. Keep a low profile at all times . . . When attending dances or ceremonies stay clear of dance performers . . . Stay off old structures like kivas and ladders . . . Hope you enjoy your tour and visit here at the Pueblo of Acoma. Thank you and come again.[9]

In each case, the message is clear: visitors must accept a new set of rules and obligations if they want to venture onto the reservation.

But posting village regulations is not the only way that Pueblo hosts attempt to control the behavior of tourists. An open and announced ritual event held at San Ildefonso Pueblo exemplifies other forms of control. Every January, San Ildefonso holds a Buffalo/Game Animal Dance for snow, health,

Managing tourists through regulations. (Photo by Roger Sweet)

hunting success, and to honor the pueblo's patron saint. This event includes an evening prelude dance on 22 January, followed by a dawn ceremony and a full day of dancing on 23 January. Because the village is only a twenty-minute drive from Santa Fe and since the dance is held on the same date each year, this event has become a popular activity for residents of Santa Fe and winter tourists interested in native culture.

The 1988 Buffalo/Game Animal Dance was particularly revealing in terms of village regulations and the control of tourists. That year, there were approximately thirty tourists and one hundred Indians waiting in the plaza for the evening prelude performance. As soon as the singers and dancers appeared, a female tourist began taking notes in a small notebook. She was very open about what she was doing, recording details of the performance and talking to her companion about the numbers of dancers and their regalia. One Indian man mentioned to her that she should not be taking notes, but she ignored the warning. Soon an assistant war captain approached the woman, asked her what she was doing, and took her notebook away.[10] As he examined the pages by the light of the nearest bonfire, the woman became indignant, claiming that her rights were being violated. In minutes, there were four

Buffalo/Game Animal
dancer at San Ildefonso
Pueblo, New Mexico.
(Photo by Roger Sweet)

tribal police, one war captain, and two of his assistants surrounding the woman. The war captain spoke to her calmly but firmly and confiscated the notebook. Throughout the incident, other tourists and Indians whispered, criticizing the woman's behavior. No one came to her defense. After all, there was a sign at the entrance to the village stating that sketching, notetaking, and photography were not permitted. Furthermore, rather than apologize or plead ignorance, the woman argued with the authorities. While incidents like this are rare, they communicate to all present that Pueblo communities are absolutely serious about their regulations.

While the number of tourists attending the 1988 prelude performance was typical of past years, the dawn ceremony on the following day attracted approximately 250 tourists—more than twice the number I had observed in previous years. The increase was probably due to the fact that in 1988 the event fell on a Saturday and the weather was relatively mild. Apparently, the village officials were prepared for the increase with an elaborate system of control. As car after car entered the pueblo, drivers were directed to park by the church on the west side of the village. There the tourists sat waiting; a village official with a megaphone repeatedly told them they must remain in their cars. Through a series of signals from the performers in the eastern hills, the message was relayed to the church lot that the ceremony was soon to begin and the tourists could now leave their cars. I could hear officials calling to each other, "OK, let 'em loose, let 'em loose!" In moments, all the tourists were out of their cars and walking to the east side of the village. When they reached the base of the eastern hills, they were directed to stand at one side of the road while all the San Ildefonso Pueblo people stood on the other side. Surprisingly, although a few tourists found the entire situation amusing and some commented on feeling like cattle being herded to pasture, I did not hear any serious complaints about these measures taken to control them.

When the dancers neared the village, the war captain insured that the tourists stayed back from their path. This was accomplished through subtle but dramatic intimidation. Wrapped in a large blanket and wearing symbolically transforming face paint over a very serious expression, the war captain appeared powerful, even superhuman. An occasional quiet request from him was all that was required to keep the crowd back.

After the dawn ceremony, the officials became more relaxed about the festivities. The sign prohibiting photography was removed, and camera permits were sold to many of the hundreds of tourists who arrived throughout the day. As this event illustrates, however, the Pueblo people make the rules and enforce them. It is their decision which events will be open to the public and if and when camera permits will be sold.

Village regulations are designed to minimize potential conflicts between hosts and guests and serve as reminders that the Indian hosts are in charge. They set the limits and ultimately define the nature of the contact. Pueblo officials enforce their regulations in several ways. Visitors may be denied entrance or escorted out of the village. They also may be fined, their film or notebooks confiscated. The regulations and methods of enforcement communicate clearly that tourists must abide by Pueblo rules if they want to visit. The regulations also distinguish insiders from outsiders, since the rules often are not the same for both groups. For example, at San Ildefonso before the game animal dancers appeared, tourists had to stay in their cars and wait, while village members could move through the pueblo freely or gather by a bonfire at the base of the hills.

While Pueblo regulations have the potential of annoying or offending some tourists, the ethnic tourists often are intrigued, because, by following these rules, they gain access to a "backstage" region—a small price to pay for authenticity. Furthermore, many Southwest ethnic tourists feel that, by cooperating, they are participating in Pueblo culture, faithfully following the "when in Rome . . ." principle. Most Southwest ethnic tourists accept the Pueblo rules and even applaud them, for they suggest that the Pueblo people have not "sold out."

Controlling members of the wider society represents a reversal of the usual power structure. This reversal surely gives the Pueblo people a welcome sense of strength and pride. Not only are they aware that non-Indians travel great distances to see them and their villages, arts, crafts, and rituals, but they know that as long as these visitors are on their reservation lands, the hosts are in charge and the non-Indians can be made to conform to village policies and Pueblo notions of proper behavior. The regulations also serve to protect and underscore Pueblo ways of life while distancing the non-Pueblo from the Pueblo. Hence, along with secrecy, the regulations control outsiders and contribute to cultural maintenance.

Discussion

Overall, the Pueblo Indians participate in the tourist industry with considerable success.[11] They have been able to control tourists who come to their reservations and keep important aspects of their culture private, while benefiting financially from tourism. By contrasting themselves with the tourists, the Pueblo Indians also have strengthened their definitions of themselves and their cultural boundaries. The significant factors in their success have been time, space, type of contact, and level of self-determination.

Compared to many other areas of the world, the transition to tourism came slowly in the Southwest, giving the Pueblo people time to adjust to their most recent invaders. There has been no sudden onslaught of mass tourism; the number of tourists increased gradually throughout the twentieth century. Slow growth in numbers of tourists has given the hosts a chance to develop techniques for tourist management (M. E. Smith 1982).

Space is another important factor in the Pueblo case. The Pueblo communities have a significant land base, with established villages that are still isolated and protected from tourist development. The Pueblo Indians secured ownership rights over much of their territory soon after first contact with Europeans. Formal land grants were established under Spanish rule and later were recognized by the United States government. Unless a Pueblo community decides on development, the Pueblo villages are not going to be surrounded by hotels and restaurants catering to tourists. As long as the villages remain isolated, aspects of Pueblo culture will be private and protected. The ability to keep at least some of the host's culture private has been cited as critical to host survival during tourist contact (V. Smith 1977:2).

The type of tourist contact—one-to-one rather than the more impersonal mass tourism—is also an important factor in assessing the Pueblo situation. When one-to-one contact is positive, genuine cultural exchange and mutual respect is possible. These positive encounters sometimes have resulted in the establishment of genuine friendships between Pueblo and Anglo families. Many Pueblo village rituals remain open, in part because Pueblo families like to invite their Anglo friends. Sometimes Anglo friends have acted as cultural brokers, helping Pueblo individuals with difficult situations involving unfamiliar aspects of the wider Anglo-American society. Nolan and Nolan observe that independent travelers who engage in one-to-one contact with native hosts "may serve as positive agents of cultural exchange rather than as individual hammer blows in an assault on the host culture. These visitors and their hosts may benefit from the traditional broadening aspect of travel" (1978:43–44).

While time, space, and type of contact are important in shaping the Pueblo case, the most significant factors are independent authority, self-determination, and a degree of power. Within the limitations set by the larger society, these indigenous people are influencing the behavior of visiting members of that larger society. Through the control of knowledge and the establishment and enforcement of specific rules, the Pueblo Indians are defining their world in their own terms and actively shaping their relationship with their visitors. By controlling those visitors, the Pueblo people are directing their cultural destiny and contributing to their own faith in the Pueblo way of doing things—a faith essential for Pueblo cultural survival.

Source: From *American Indian Culture and Research Journal*, 1991, 15(4):59–74. Reprinted with permission of the author.

Acknowledgements

Thanks go to the many Pueblo Indian families who welcomed me into their homes and permitted me to experience their moving and symbolically rich ritual dramas. Thanks also are due to colleagues Donileen Loseke and William Fox for reading and commenting on earlier drafts of this paper.

Notes

[1] Power is defined here as the ability to influence the behavior and/or thoughts of other individuals.

[2] See, for example, Farrell (1979), Forster (1964), Greenwood (1977), and Huit (1979).

[3] See, for example, Adams (1990), Johnston (1990), Chapin (1990), McKean (1989), and Swain (1989).

[4] Burlesquing tourists is an extension of the ancient Pueblo clowning tradition. Ritual clowns and other village comics burlesque tourists and even draw them into their plaza skits, making the visitors the fools. For more on this form of tourist management, see Sweet (1989). Another interesting technique is the exportation of dance segments away from the villages. By presenting dance segments in cities, arts and crafts fairs, state fairs, or commercial ceremonials, the Pueblo Indians satisfy the curiosity of large numbers of tourists without having to host these visitors in their villages. For more on exploration, see Sweet (1983, 1985).

[5] *The Santa Fe New Mexican*, 13 June 1975.

[6] One reviewer of this paper expressed a concern that the following discussion about Pueblo secrecy might be actually disclosing Pueblo secrets. I can only respond by stating that the Pueblo people are not secretive about being secretive. On the contrary, given the opportunity, they try to educate outsiders about their secrecy principles with statements such as, "We don't [won't or can't] talk about that" or "We like you because you don't ask questions" or "We can't talk now because they will think you are asking questions." I hope the following discussion of Pueblo secrecy will promote respect for and understanding of the Pueblo reluctance to share certain kinds of cultural information.

[7] For a discussion of Pueblo secrecy as external control, see Dozier (1961) and Spicer (1962). For secrecy as an internal device, see Brandt (1980).

[8] For a discussion of the "frontstage" and "backstage" behavior, see Goffman (1959).

[9] This hand-painted sign was noted in 1988. In 1989 it had been replaced by a printed sign, and the request that visitors "not be loud or obnoxious" had been omitted.

[10] War captains are village officers who, among other duties, oversee public ritual activities.

[11] I am not claiming that tourism among the Pueblo communities has been without problems. Occasionally, obnoxious tourists offend the Indians. Recently, there has been a controversy over the rights of Indians to sell native arts and crafts in the urban centers. For information on this controversy, see Sweet (1990).

References

Adams, Kathleen. 1990. "Cultural Commoditization in Tana Toraja, Indonesia." *Cultural Survival Quarterly* 14:31–34.

Brandt, Elizabeth. 1980. "On Secrecy and the Control of Knowledge: Taos Pueblo," in *Secrecy: A Cross Cultural Perspective*, ed. Stanton K. Tefft. New York: Human Sciences Press.

Chapin, Mac. 1990. "The Silent Jungle: Ecotourism among the Kuna Indians of Panama." *Cultural Survival Quarterly* 14: 42–45.

Dozier, Edward. 1961. "Rio Grande Pueblos," in *Perspectives in American Indian Culture Change*, ed. Edward Spicer, pp. 99–186. Chicago: University of Chicago Press.

Eickemeyer, Carl, and Lilian Eickemeyer. 1895. *Among the Pueblo Indians.* New York: The Merriam Company.

Evans, Nancy. 1978. "Tourism and Cross-Cultural Communication," in *Tourism and Behavior: Studies in Third World Societies*, ed. Mario Zamora, Vinson Sutlive, and Nathan Altshuler. Williamsburg, VA: College of William and Mary.

Evans-Pritchard, Deirdre. 1989. "How 'They' See 'Us': Native American Images of Tourists." *Annals of Tourism Research* 16:89–106.

Farrell, Bryan. 1979. "Tourism's Human Conflicts: Cases from the Pacific." *Annals of Tourism Research* 6:122–36.

Forster, John. 1964. "The Sociological Consequences of Tourism." *International Journal of Comparative Sociology* 5:217–27.

Goffman, Erving. 1959. *Presentation of Self in Everyday Life*. Garden City, NY: Doubleday.

Greenwood, Davydd. 1977. "Culture by the Pound: An Anthropological Perspective on Tourism as Cultural Commodification," in *Hosts and Guests: The Anthropology of Tourism*, ed. Valene Smith, pp. 127–38. Philadelphia: University of Pennsylvania Press.

Huit, Groupe. 1979. "The Sociocultural Effects of Tourism: A Case Study of Sousse," in *Tourism: Passport to Development?*, ed. Emmanuel de Kadt. New York: Oxford University Press.

Johnston, Barbara. 1990. "Save Our Beach Dem and Our Land Too!" *Cultural Survival Quarterly* 14:30–37.

MacCannell, Dean. 1984. "Reconstructed Ethnicity: Tourism and Cultural Identity in Third World Communities." *Annals of Tourism Research* 11:387–88.

McKean, Philip. 1989. "Towards a Theoretical Analysis of Tourism," in *Hosts and Guests: The Anthropology of Tourism*, 2nd edition, ed. Valene Smith, pp. 119–38. Philadelphia: University of Pennsylvania Press.

Nolan, Sidney, and Mary Lee Nolan. 1978. "Variations in Travel Behavior and the Cultural Impact of Tourism," in *Tourism and Behavior, Studies in Third World Societies*, ed. Mario Zamora, Vinson Sutlive, and Nathan Altshuler. Williamsburg, VA: College of William and Mary.

Simmons, Marc. 1979. "History of the Pueblos Since 1821," in *Handbook of North American Indians*, vol. 9, ed. Alfonso Ortiz. Washington DC: Smithsonian Institution.

Smith, M. Estellie. 1982. "Tourism and Native Americans." *Cultural Survival Quarterly* 6:10–12.

Smith, Valene. 1977. "Introduction," in *Hosts and Guests: The Anthropology of Tourism*, ed. Valene Smith. Philadelphia: University of Pennsylvania Press

Spicer, Edward. 1962. *Cycles of Conquest: The Impact of Spain, Mexico, and the United States on the Indians of the Southwest, 1533–1960*. Tucson: University of Arizona Press.

Swain, Margaret. 1989. "Gender Roles in Indigenous Tourism: Kuna Mola, Kuna Yala, and Cultural Survival," in *Hosts and Guests: The Anthropology of Tourism*, 2nd edition, ed. Valene Smith, pp. 83–104. Philadelphia: University of Pennsylvania Press.

Sweet, Jill. 1983. "Ritual and Theater in Tewa Ceremonial Performances." *Ethnomusicology* 27: 253–69.

———. 1985. *Dances of the Tewa Pueblo Indians*. Santa Fe, NM: School of American Research Press.

———. 1989. "Burlesquing 'The Other' in Pueblo Performance." *Annals of Tourism Research* 16:62–75.

———. 1990. "The Portals of Tradition: Tourism in the American Southwest." *Cultural Survival Quarterly* 14:62–75.

van den Berghe, Pierre, and Charles F. Keyes. 1984. "Introduction: Tourism and Re-created Ethnicity." *Annals of Tourism Research* 11:343–52.

Weigle, Marta. 1989. "From Desert to Disney World: The Santa Fe Railway and the Fred Harvey Company Display the Indian Southwest." *Journal of Anthropological Research* 45:115–37.

9

When Sex Tourists and Sex Workers Meet: Encounters within Sosúa, the Dominican Republic

Denise Brennan

There is a new sex-tourist destination on the global sexual landscape: Sosúa, the Dominican Republic. A beach town on the north coast, Sosúa has emerged as a place of fantasy for white European male tourists willing to pay for sex with Afro-Caribbean women. But European men are not the only ones who seek to fulfill fantasies. Dominican sex workers also arrive in Sosúa with fantasies: fantasies of economic mobility, visas to Europe, and even romance. For them, Sosúa and its tourists represent an escape: women migrate from throughout the Dominican Republic with dreams of European men "rescuing" them from a lifetime of foreclosed opportunities and poverty. They hope to meet and marry European men who will sponsor their (and their children's) migration to Europe. Yet, even though more and more women and girls migrate to Sosúa everyday, most leave the sex trade with little more than they had when they arrived.

This article explores this paradoxical feature of sex tourism in Sosúa, and examines why women continue to flock to Sosúa and how they make the

151

most of their time while there. Through the sex trade in this one tourist town, we see how globalization affects sex workers and sex tourists differently. In this economy of desire, some dreams are realized, while others prove hollow. White, middle-class and lower-middle class European visitors and residents are much better positioned to secure what they want in Sosúa than poor, black Dominican sex workers. Globalization and the accompanying transnational processes such as tourism and sex tourism not only open up opportunities but also reproduce unequal, dependent relations along lines of gender, race, class, geography, and history.

Why the Sex Trade? Why Sosúa?

Dominican women who migrate to Sosúa and its sex trade are seduced by the opportunity to meet, and possibly marry, a foreign tourist. Even if sex workers do not marry their clients, Sosúa holds out the promise of maintaining a transnational relationship with them, using new transnational technologies such as fax machines and international money wires. Without these transnational connections, Sosúa's sex trade would be no different than sex work in any other Dominican town. By migrating to Sosúa, women are engaging in an economic strategy that is both very familiar and something altogether new. I argue that they try to use the sex trade as an *advancement* strategy, not just a *survival* strategy. In short, these marginalized female heads-of-household try to take advantage of the global linkages that exploit them.

Though only a handful of women regularly receive money wires from ex-clients in Europe—and even fewer actually move to Europe to live with their sweethearts—success stories circulate among the sex workers like Dominicanized versions of the movie *Pretty Woman*. Thus, Sosúa's myth of opportunity goes unchallenged and women, recruited through female social networks of family and close friends who have already migrated, keep on arriving, ready to find their "Richard Gere." Yet what the women find is a far cry from their fantasy images of fancy dinners, nightclubs, easy money, and visas off the island. One disappointed sex worker, Carmen,[1] insightfully sums up just how important fantasy is to constructing the image of Sosúa as a place of opportunity: "Women come to Sosúa because of a big lie. They hear they can make money, and meet a gringo, and they come. . . . They come with their dreams, but then they find out it is all a lie."

Work choices available to poor Dominican women are determined not only by local factors, but by the global economy. Internal migration for sex work is a consequence of both local economic and social transformations and larger, external forces, such as foreign investment in export-processing zones and tourism. Just as international investors see the Dominican Republic as a site of cheap labor, international tourists know it as a place to buy cheap sex. In sex tourism, First-World travelers/consumers seek exoticized, racialized "native" bodies in the developing world for cut-rate prices. These two components—race and its associated stereotypes and expectations, and the economic disparities between the developed and developing worlds—characterize sex tourist destinations throughout the world. What do white men "desire" when they decide to book a flight from Frankfurt, for example, to Puerto Plata (the nearest airport to Sosúa)? I turned to the Internet for answers. Any exploration of the relationship between globalization, women's work choices in the global economy, and women's migration for work must now investigate the role the Internet has in producing and disseminating racialized and sexualized stereotypes in the developing world. The Internet is quickly and radically transforming the sex trade in the developing world, since online travel services make it increasingly easy for potential sex tourists to research sex-tourist destinations and to plan trips. I looked at Web sites that post writings from alleged sex tourists who share information about their sex trips.[2] In the process, they advertise not only their services but also Dominican women as sexual commodities. One sex tourist was impressed by the availability of "dirt cheap colored girls," while another boasted, "When you enter the discos, you will feel like you're in heaven! A tremendous number of cute girls and something for everyone's taste (if you like colored girls like me)!"[3] There is little doubt that race is central to what these sex tourists desire in their travels.

International Tourism: Who Benefits?

International tourism has not benefited poor Dominicans as much as many had hoped. Although development and foreign investment have brought "First-World" hotels and services to Sosúa, the local population still lives in Third-World conditions. The most successful resorts in Sosúa are foreign owned, and even though they create employment opportunities for the local population, most of the new jobs are low-paying service jobs with little chance for mobility. What's more, the multinational resorts that have moved into Sosúa have pushed small hotel and restaurant owners out of business. One such restaurant owner, Luis, comments on the effects of these large "all-inclusive" hotels (tourists pay one fee in their home countries for airfare, lodging, food, and even drinks) on the Sosúa economy:

> These tourists hardly change even US$100 to spend outside the hotel. Before the all-inclusive hotels, people would change between US$1000–2000 and it would get distributed throughout the town: some for lodging, for food and entertainment. Now, not only do any of the local merchants get any of the money, but it never even leaves the tourists' home countries—like Germany or Austria—where they pay for their vacation in advance.

Foreign ownership, repatriation of profits, and the monopolistic nature of these all-inclusive resorts, make it difficult for the local population to profit significantly. Tourism is one of the largest industries in the global economy (Sinclair 1997), and it is not unusual for foreign firms to handle all four components of a tourist's stay: airlines, hotels, services, and tour operators. I interviewed the general manager (an Italian citizen) of a German hotel, for example, whose parent company is a German airline company. Eighty percent of the hotel's guests are German, all of whom paid for their airfare, lodging, and food in Germany. Furthermore, this German company imported most of its management staff from Europe, as well as the furniture, fabrics, and other goods necessary to run the hotel. So much for opportunities for local Dominicans.

Marginalized individuals in the global economy frequently turn to migration and more recently to tourism as an exit from poverty. Both migration and transnational relationships with foreign tourists are perceived as ways to access a middle-class lifestyle and its accompanying commodities. A several decades-old history of migration between the Dominican Republic and New York (Georges 1990; Grasmuck and Pessar 1991) and the transnational cultural, political, and economic flows between these two spaces, have led many Dominicans to look *fuera* (outside) for solutions to their economic problems. A preoccupation with goods, capital, and opportunities that are "outside" helps explain how sex workers and other Dominican migrants can view Sosúa as a place of opportunity. These women would go to New York if they could, but they do not have the social networks (i.e., immediate family members in New York) to sponsor them for visas, nor the contacts to underwrite an illegal migration. Migrating internally to Sosúa is the closest they can get to the "outside." Without established contacts in New York, they have a greater chance to someday get overseas by marrying a tourist (no matter how slight a chance) than they do of obtaining a visa. In many ways, hanging out in the tourist bars in Sosúa is a better use of their time than waiting in line for a visa at the U.S. Embassy in Santo Domingo. Carla, a first-time sex worker, explains why Sosúa draws women from throughout the country: "We come here because we dream of a ticket" (airline ticket). But without a visa—which they could obtain through marriage—Dominican sex workers cannot use the airline ticket Carla describes. They must depend on their European clients-turned-boyfriends/husbands to sponsor them for visas off the island. They are at once independent and dependent, strategic and exploited.

A question I routinely posed to sex workers (and others have asked me, as an anthropologist working with women who sell sex) is why they decide to enter sex work rather than other forms of labor? The majority of these women are mothers with little formal education, few marketable skills, limited social networks, and minimal support from the fathers of their children. They are poor Dominican women who have few means to escape from poverty and the periodic crises they find themselves in. Within this context, sex work appears as a potentially profitable alternative to the low wages they could earn in export-processing zones or in domestic service—the two most common forms of formal employment available to poor women.[4] Many poor Dominican women must find work within the insecure and even lower-paying informal sector. Felicia and Margarita, two friends who had migrated to Sosúa from the same town, found that the employment opportunities available to them at home (e.g., hairstylist, waitress, domestic) did not sufficiently provide for their families. They summed up their dilemma this way: "If you have a husband who pays for food and the house, then you can work in jobs like hairstyling. Otherwise it's not possible to work in jobs like this." Maintaining the view that women's earnings are "secondary" or "supplementary," these women nevertheless became the primary breadwinners once they separated from their "husbands."[5]

Women can choose to enter the sex trade in other Dominican towns, so by choosing Sosúa they are choosing to work with foreign rather than Dominican men. The selection not only of sex work over other work options but also of Sosúa, with its foreign tourist clientele, over other Dominican towns demonstrates that sex work for these women is not just a survival strategy but rather a strategy of advancement. This "choice" of the sex trade *in Sosúa* presents an important counter example to depictions of sex workers (who are not coerced or forced into prostitution) as powerless victims of male violence and exploitation. Yet, without protection under the law, sex workers are vulnerable to clients' actions once they are out of public spaces and in private hotel rooms. They risk battery, rape, and forced unprotected sex. Sex workers in Sosúa, however, often discount the risks of violence and AIDS given what they see as the potential payoffs of financial stability or a marriage proposal. Recently, however, so many women have migrated to Sosúa from throughout the Dominican Republic that sex workers outnumber clients in the bars. Thus, in order to understand why women place themselves in a context of uncertainty and potential violence, we need to explore fully Sosúa's opportunity myth. How reliable are the payoffs and how high are the risks? Why might or might not women achieve "success" through sex work in Sosúa? Can these poor, single mothers benefit from globalization?

Sex Work: Short- and Long-term Strategies

Working with foreign tourists can represent considerable long-term financial gains for a sex worker and her extended family—far more than she could gain from factory or domestic work. Yet, not all women who arrive in Sosúa to pursue sex work want to build long-term transnational ties. Some have different long-term strategies, such as saving enough money to start a *colmado* (small grocery store) in their yard in their home communities. Others use sex work simply as a way to make ends meet in the immediate future. Those who hope to pursue long-term relationships with foreign tourists are often disappointed. Relationships go sour and with them their extended family's only lifeline from poverty disintegrates. For every promise a tourist keeps, there are many more stories of disappointment. Even the success stories eventually cannot live up to the myths.

Sex work yields varying levels of reward. Some women open savings accounts and are able to build houses with their earnings, while others do not have enough money to pay the motorcycle taxi fare from their boarding houses to the tourist bars. Why are some sex workers able to save, despite the obstacles, while most continue to live from day to day? Success at sex work in Sosúa depends both on a planned strategy and a real commitment to saving money as well as luck. I cannot emphasize enough the role chance plays in sex workers' long-term ties with foreign clients. Whether or not clients stay in touch with the women is out of their control. One sex worker, Carmen, was thus skeptical that the Belgian client with whom she spent time during his three-week vacation in Sosúa actually would follow through on his promises to marry her and move her to Europe: "I don't absolutely believe that he is going to marry me. You know, sure, when he was here he seemed to love me. But you know people leave and they forget." In fact, months later, she still had not heard from him. I helped Carmen write him a letter, which I mailed when I got back to the United States. It was returned to my address, unopened. Had she gotten the address wrong or did he give her a false address along with his proclamations of love and commitment to their living together?

Adding to the uncertainty and fragility of transnational relationships are other logistical obstacles to "success." Women must find ways to save money despite the drain on their resources from paying police bribes and living in an expensive tourist town where prices for food and rent are among the highest in the country. All of this combined with increased competition among sex workers for clients increases the likelihood of having to leave Sosúa with little or no money saved. Furthermore, the majority of women who arrive in Sosúa do not know what they are getting into. They have heard of police roundups and know that they must vie with countless other women like themselves to catch the attention of potential clients, but like most migrants they are full of hopes and dreams and believe that "it will be different for them." In gold-rush fashion, they arrive in Sosúa because they have heard of Sosúa's tourists and money, and they plan, without a specific strategy in mind, to cash in on the tourist boom. It only takes a few days in Sosúa to realize that the only hope they have to quickly make big money is to establish a transnational relationship. New arrivals see veteran sex workers drop by the Codetel office (telephone and fax company) every day, vigilantly looking for faxes from clients in Europe or Canada. If they want to receive money wires or marriage proposals from tourists overseas, they learn that they must establish similar ongoing transnational relationships.

Sex Workers' Stories

In order to explore how sex workers' time in Sosúa measures up to their fantasy images, I turn to three sex workers' divergent experiences. Their stories call attention to the difficulties of establishing a transnational relationship, as well as to its fragility. Through sex workers' accounts of their relationships with foreign men, we get a sense of just how wildly unpredictable the course of these relationships can be.

Elena and Jürgen: Building and Breaking
Transnational Ties through Sex Work

This story begins with Elena's release from jail. After being held for two days, twenty-two-year-old Elena went to the beach.[6] When I saw her, back at her one-room wooden house, she was ecstatic. At the beach she had run into Jürgen, who had just returned to Sosúa from his home in Germany to see her. They had been sending faxes to one another since he had left Sosúa after his last vacation, and he had mentioned in one of his faxes that he would be returning. He did not know where she lived, but figured he would find her that evening at the Anchor, Sosúa's largest tourist bar and a place tourists go to pick up sex workers. He brought her presents from Germany, including perfume and a matching gold chain necklace and bracelet. Elena was grinning ear to ear as she showed off her gifts, talking about Jürgen like a smitten schoolgirl: "I am canceling everything for the weekend and am going to spend the entire time with him. We will go to the beach and he will take me to nightclubs and to restaurants."

Elena began preparing for the weekend. Her two sisters who lived with her, ages fourteen and sixteen, would look after her six-year-old daughter, since Elena would stay with Jürgen in his hotel. She chose the evening's outfit carefully, with plenty of help from her sisters, daughter, and friend, a young sex worker who also lives with them since she has very little money. Elena provides for these four girls with her earnings from sex work. They all rotate between sharing the double bed and sleeping on the floor. Spending time with a tourist on his vacation means Elena would receive more gifts, maybe even some for her family, and would make good money. So they helped primp Elena, selecting billowy rayon pants that moved as she did and a black lycra stretch shirt with long sheer sleeves that was cropped to reveal her slim stomach. She was meeting Jürgen at the Anchor, where I saw her later on, and she stood out in the crowd.

As soon as Jürgen's vacation ended, he went back to Germany with a plan to return in a couple of months. Since he was self-employed in construction, he could live part of the year in the Dominican Republic. Elena was very upset when Jürgen left and could not stop crying. Maybe Jürgen represented more than just money, nice meals, and new clothes. I had often heard sex workers distinguish between relationships with tourists *por amor* (for love) or *por residencia* (for residence/visas) but Elena's tears broke down that distinction.

Unlike Carmen's relationship with her Belgian client, Jürgen kept his word to Elena and wired money and kept in touch through faxes. Even more surprisingly, he returned to Sosúa only two months later. Within days of his return, he rented a two-bedroom apartment that had running water and an electrical generator (for daily blackouts). He also bought beds, living room furniture, and a large color television. Elena was living out the fantasy of many sex workers in Sosúa: she was sharing a household with a European man who supported her and her dependents. Jürgen paid for food that Elena and her sisters prepared and had cable television installed. He also paid for Elena's six-year-old daughter to attend a private school and came home one day with school supplies for her. Occasionally, Jürgen took Elena, her daughter, and her sisters out to eat at one of the tourist restaurants that line the beach where the tourists sun themselves.

Elena had moved up in the world: eating in tourist restaurants, sending a daughter to private school, and living in a middle-class apartment were all symbols of her increased social and economic mobility. As a female head of household who had been taking care of her daughter and sisters with her earnings from sex work, Elena was now able to quit sex work and live off of the money Jürgen gave her. Sex work and the transnational relationships it had built altered Elena's life as well as the lives of those who depended on her. But for how long?

Jürgen turned out not to be Elena's or her family's salvation. Soon after they moved in together, Elena found out she was pregnant. Both she and Jürgen were very happy about having a baby. He had a teenage son living with his ex-wife in Germany and relished the idea of having another child. At first, he was helpful around the house and doted on Elena. But the novelty soon wore off and he returned to his routine of spending most days in the German-owned bar beneath their apartment. He also went out drinking at night with German friends, hopping from bar to bar. He was drunk, or on his way there, day and night. Elena saw him less and less frequently, and they began to fight often, usually over money.

Eventually he started staying out all night. On one occasion, a friend of Elena's (a sex worker) saw Jürgen at the Anchor talking with, and later on leaving the bar with, a Haitian sex worker. Elena knew he was cheating on her. But she did not want to raise this with Jürgen, explaining that men "do these things." Instead, she focused her anger on the fact that he was not giving her enough money to take care of the household. Ironically, Elena had more disposable income before she began to live with Jürgen. Back then, she could afford to go out dancing and drinking with her friends—not to look for clients, but just to have fun. Now, without an income of her own, she was dependent upon Jürgen not only for household expenses but also for her entertainment.

On more than one occasion I served as interpreter between the two during their attempts at "peace negotiations" after they had not spoken to one another for days. Since Elena does not speak any German or English, she asked me to help her understand why Jürgen was mad at her as well as to communicate her viewpoint to him. In preparation for one of these "negotiations," Elena briefed me on what she wanted me to explain to Jürgen:

I want to know why he is not talking to me? And why is he not giving me any money? He is my *esposo* [husband—in consensual union] and is supposed to give me money. I need to know if he is with me or with someone else. He pays for this house and paid for everything here. I need to know what is going on. You know I was fine living alone before, I'm able to do that. I took care of everything before, this is not a problem. But I need to know what is going to happen.

Since they were living together and Jürgen was paying the bills, Elena considered them to be married. To Elena and her friends, Jürgen, as an *esposo*, was financially responsible for the household. But Jürgen saw things differently. He felt Elena thought he was "made of money" and was always asking him for more. He asked me to translate to her:

I'm not a millionaire. I told Elena last week that I don't like her always asking for money. She did not listen. She asks me for money all day long. I don't want to be taken advantage of.

One day, without warning, Jürgen packed his bags and left for Germany for business. Elena knew this day would come, that Jürgen would have to return to Germany to work. But she did not expect their relationship would be in such disarray, and that he would depart without leaving her money (although he did leave some food money with her younger sisters who turned it over to Elena). In Jürgen's absence, Elena took her daughter out of the private school once the tuition became overdue and she started working part-time at a small Dominican-owned restaurant. When Jürgen returned to Sosúa from Germany a couple of months later, they split up for good. Elena moved out of their apartment back to the labyrinth of shanties on dirt paths off the main road. Her economic and social mobility was short-lived. She had not accumulated any savings or items she could pawn during her time with Jürgen. Jürgen never gave her enough money so that she could set some aside for savings. And all the things he bought for the apartment were his, not hers. When they vacated the apartment, he took all of the furniture and the television with him.

Elena's relationship with Jürgen dramatically changed her life; she was, after all, having his child. But her social and economic status remained as marginal as ever. Even though she was living out many sex workers' fantasies of "marrying" a foreign tourist, she still lived like many poor Dominicans, struggling day to day without access to resources to build long-term economic security. When she and Jürgen fought and he withheld money from her, she was less economically independent than she was as a sex worker, when she was certain to earn around 500 pesos a client. Although sex workers take on great risks—of AIDS, abuse, and arrest—and occupy a marginal and stigmatized status in Dominican society, Elena's status as the "housewife" of a German resident was fragile and constantly threatened.

Jürgen now lives, Elena has heard, somewhere in Asia. Elena is back living in the same conditions as before she met Jürgen. She has not returned to sex work and makes significantly less money working in a restaurant. Her older sisters now help take care of their younger sisters, and Elena sends what money she can, though less than in her sex work days, to help out her parents.

Luisa's Money Wires

Luisa is an example of a sex worker whose transnational connections were those other sex workers envied, but her "success," like Elena's, ended without warning. She, quite remarkably, received US$500 every two weeks from a client in Germany, who wanted her to leave sex work and start her own clothing store. She told him she had stopped working the tourist bars, and that she used the money to buy clothes for the store. Yet, when he found out that she was still working as a sex worker, had not opened a store, and was living with a Dominican boyfriend, he stopped wiring money.

At this juncture, Luisa was in over her head. She had not put any of the money in the bank, in anticipation of the day when the money wires might dry up. She was renting a two-bedroom apartment that was twice the size and rent of friends' apartments. And she sent money home to her mother in Santo Domingo, who was taking care of her twelve-year-old son. She also supported her Dominican boyfriend, who lived with her and did not have a steady job. Other sex workers called him a *chulo* (pimp) since he lived off of Luisa's earnings and money wires. They saw Luisa as foolish for bankrolling her boyfriend, especially since he was not the father of her son. She began hocking her chains and rings in one of Sosúa's half-dozen pawnshops.

As lucky as Luisa was to meet this German client at the Anchor, most of the women working the Anchor night after night never receive a single money wire transfer. Those who do generally receive smaller sums than Luisa did, on a much more infrequent and unpredictable basis. And as Luisa's story demonstrates, a sex worker's luck can change overnight. There is no guarantee that money wires will continue once they begin. Luisa had no way of knowing that she would lose her "meal ticket," nor can she be certain that she will ever find another tourist to replace him. Furthermore, women cannot count on earning money in sex work indefinitely. Luisa is in her early thirties and knows that over the next few years it will be increasingly difficult to compete with the young women in the bars (some are as young as sixteen and seventeen, most are between nineteen and twenty-five). Yet, once women make the decision to leave Sosúa and sex work, they face the same limited opportunities they confronted before they entered sex work. They are still hampered by limited education, a lack of marketable job skills, and not "knowing the right people." In fact, obstacles to economic and social mobility might have increased, especially if they are rumored to have AIDS. They might have to battle gossip in their home community and the stigma associated with sex work. After years of working in bars they might have a substance-abuse problem. And they return to children who have grown in their absence.

Carmen's Diversification Strategy

Carmen's story, compared to Elena's, is one of relative success, in which her relationship with Dominican clients figures prominently. In fact, supplementing uncertain income with foreign tourists by working with Dominican clients, as well as establishing long-term relationships with Dominican *amigos/clientes fijos* (friends/regular clients), supplies Carmen with a steady flow of income. Another sex worker, Ani, explains the function of *amigos*:

> You don't always have a client. You need *amigos* and *clientes fijos*. If you have a problem, like something breaks in your house, or your child is sick and you need money for the doctor or medicine, they can help.

For Carmen, working with Dominicans has proven much more reliable than establishing ties with foreign men. Carmen has saved enough money from four years in sex work to build a small house in Santo Domingo (the capital city five hours away where she will retire to take care of her mother and children). She has managed to save more money than most sex workers. I asked her why she thinks she was able to save money, while many of her friends don't have an extra centavo, and she answered,

> Because they give it to their men. Their husbands wait at home and drink while their women work. Not me. If I'm in the street with all the risks of disease and the police, I'm keeping the money or giving it to my kids. I'm not giving it to a man, no way. If women don't give the money to the men, they (the men) beat the women.

She is careful not to let the men in her life know how much money she has saved in the bank (unlike Luisa), or the sources of the money. She has a steady relationship in particular with Jorge, who is her economic safety net, especially in times of crises. She describes their relationship:

> He is very young [she scrunched her nose up in disapproval of this point]. He lives with his mother in Santiago and works in a *zona franca* [factory in an export-processing zone]. He gives me money, even though he does not make a lot. He bought me furniture for the new house.

At times, the money Jorge gives Carmen is the only money she has. By establishing a relationship with a Dominican man, she has been able to supplement her unpredictable income from sex work. Though the money he gives her is in smaller sums than transnational money wires other sex workers receive, like Luisa, it is money she can count on, on a regular basis.

Carmen not only has diversified her clients, focused on achieving one specific goal (building a house), but she also has clear personal limitations working in a dangerous trade. Since she has a serious fear of the police, she refuses to work when they are making arrests outside of the tourist bars where many of the sex workers congregate to talk, smoke, or greet customers entering the bars. At one point when the police seemed to be making more arrests than usual, Carmen quit going to the tourist bars altogether. Instead, she took a bus to a small Dominican town about thirty miles away to work in a bar that caters to Dominican clients. Thus, she developed an alternate plan to working in Sosúa when necessary.

By pursuing local Dominican clients as well as trying to establish trans- national connections, sex work is paying off for Carmen in the long term. Carmen refused to be seduced by the promise of a tourist enclave and the sweet talk of foreign tourists. Instead, she treated Sosúa as any other Domini- can town with "brothels" and set up a roster of local regular clients. Carmen's gains have been slow and modest. Nevertheless, she saved enough money to begin constructing a small house, though thus far it has taken her four years, and she still needs enough money for windows. But she will leave Sosúa with her future, and her family's, more secure than when she first arrived. Stories about modest successes like Carmen's are not as glamorous as those with transnational dimensions. Rather, stories of transnational relationships and quick, big money circulate among the sex workers, like those of Elena and Luisa. Their more immediate and visible ascension from poverty are regaled and fuel the illusion of Sosúa as a place to get rich quick.

Conclusion

Foreign sex tourists clearly benefit from their geographic position in the global economy, as they travel with ease (no visa is needed to enter the Dominican Republic) and buy sex for cheaper prices than in their home coun- tries. Dominican sex workers, in contrast, face innumerable constraints due to their country's marginal position in the global economy. Sosúa's sex trade is but one more site where, broadly, we can observe globalization exacerbating inequality and, more specifically, we can situate tourism and sex tourism as both relying on and reproducing inequalities in the global economy.

Like most prospectors in search of quick money, few sex workers who rush into Sosúa looking for a foreign tourist to solve their problems find what they were hoping for. It is of little surprise, however, that women, despite the obstacles to fulfilling their "fantasies" continue to arrive everyday. Women from the poorest classes have no other work options that pay as well as the sex trade with tourists in the short term. Nor do most other work options offer the opportunity to establish long-term relationships with foreign men. Although most transnational relationships are unlikely to alter sex workers' long-term economic and social status, they make far more financial gains than most women in the sex trade or other accessible labor options (such as domestic service or factory work).

Sex workers also slowly can make gains without transnational connec- tions. Though difficult to achieve, these gains might prove more durable than those resting on a transnational relationship. Carmen's transnational ties never paid off, and consequently she did not come into a lot of money all at once. But she still managed to save what she could over time. Her house represents security, but it does not catapult her out of *los pobres* (the poor). Her "success" is not on the same level as women with ongoing relationships with European men. But while these ties could dissolve at any time, Carmen's house will still be there. She looks forward to the day she completes her house and leaves Sosúa and its sex trade: "When I leave here I want to sit on the front porch of my new house with my mother and my children and drink a cold glass of juice. I want a peaceful life. No Sosúa, no men giving you problems."

Source: Adapted from "Globalization, Women's Labor, and Men's Pleasure: Sex Tourism in Sosúa, the Dominican Republic," *Urban Life: Readings in the Anthropology of the City*, 4th ed. George Gmelch and Walter Zenner (eds.), 2002, Waveland Press.

Notes

[1] I have changed all names.

[2] I did not join any of these sites, however. But, rather, looked at "satisfied customer" testimonials the sites post to try to entice new paying members.

[3] For more on the Internet and the sex trade see Brennan, Denise (2001), "Tourism in Transnational Places: Dominican Sex Workers and German Sex Tourists Imagine One Another," *Identities: Global Studies in Culture and Power* 7, 4 (1/01):621–63.

[4] These jobs, on average, yield under 1000 pesos a month, whereas sex workers in Sosúa charge approximately 500 pesos from foreign clients.

[5] Poor Dominicans are more likely to enter consensual unions than legal marriage. In fact, unless I specifically mention otherwise, sex workers are not legally married to their husbands. Yet since the women I interviewed referred to the men in their lives as "husbands" *(esposos)*, I also use this term.

[6] She paid 500 pesos (US$41.00) for her release—the standard bribe to the police.

10

Romance Tourism: Gender, Race, and Power in Jamaica

Deborah Pruitt and Suzanne LaFont

The United Nations identifies tourism as the world's fastest growing industry. It is the heart of development strategies in many less developed nations. Jamaica is one of the countries that has embraced the tourism industry as a path leading to economic prosperity and has focused on its growth and development for the past two decades.

Global economics means that most tourists are from the highly developed countries. The tourist's destination is often to poorer countries such as Jamaica that offer high value for their money and seemingly exotic locales. In contrast to these privileged travelers, most people in the world will never leave their native countries because poverty and/or visa restrictions preclude such luxuries as vacations. While the governments of the less-developed countries actively lure tourists, hoping to profit from the vast travel industry, many of the local people in these "tourist destinations" also try to benefit directly from tourism, either formally or informally, by offering a host of services to vacationers.

In recent years the contact between local peoples and tourists have received a great deal of attention (Altman 2001; Kempadoo and Doezema

165

1998). In Jamaica, these interactions are often between single women travelers and local men. Since the 1960s when the feminist movement fostered women's independence, expectations of freedom and mobility, and economic self-sufficiency, large numbers of single women have been traveling in pursuit of their own adventures—adventures that sometimes include sex, romance, and experimentation with new gender roles and power. Particular features of Jamaica and its image as a place to be "free" makes it a popular destination for such women.

Foreign women on the arms of local men in resort areas of Jamaica (and other parts of the Caribbean) are a regular part of the social landscape (de Albuquerque 1999). In this small-scale society, sufficient numbers of young men are involved in this activity that it is widely discussed and has recently become an issue for the media and the government-industry complex. It has been institutionalized to the point that the label "rent-a-dread" has been coined to refer to the men who get involved with foreign women. There are T-shirts, postcards, and cartoons making jokes about them. Popular songs also comment on these relationships. Such tourism liaisons are sufficiently common as to encourage at least one American tour operator to consider creating a promotional brochure complete with pictures of Jamaican men available as companions so she could broker the relationships from the United States before the women leave home. German women embark on these ventures frequently enough that an expression has developed in Germany that "The men go to Thailand and the women go to Jamaica" (Pruitt 1993).

But the interaction of foreign women and local men does not always end in Jamaica. In the small-scale tourism center where one author lived for two years, hundreds of local men have "gone foreign" with women who were vacationing. In fact, virtually all of the young men who sought their livelihood from informal tourism work during that period had or have gone to foreign countries with their tourist girlfriends at least once. Many of them are still living in Europe and all of them have ongoing relationships with foreign women.

Romance Tourism

Sexual tourism liaisons are diverse and multifaceted. Some are very short lived and could be termed superficial. We also see in Jamaica a particular kind of engagement between local men and tourist women that involves a complex set of desires, hopes, and fantasies that include romance, love, and the possibility of a long-term relationship in addition to sex. We use the term romance tourism to denote these particular qualities and to distinguish them from those of sex tourism.

Much more common and frequently studied are the sex-for-money exchanges that occur between male tourists and local women around the world. A survey of the Internet revealed hundreds of Web sites featuring travel agencies promising "sexual adventures" with women in Southeast Asia, Thailand, Russia, Eastern Europe, Central America, South America, Japan, and the Philippines. In contrast, none of the sites offered the sexual services of men to women (LaFont 2003). Although there is no doubt that some women travel to countries such as Jamaica specifically to engage in casual sexual relations with local men (Taylor 2001), sex tourism is primarily geared toward men and is quite formalized and widespread. It is often simply referred to as prostitution.

In Jamaica it is significant that neither actor in romance tourism relationships consider their interaction to be prostitution, even though others label it so. The actors place an emphasis on courtship rather than the exchange of sex for money. The purpose here is not to debate whether these men are prostitutes, but rather to convey the distinctive meaning these relationships hold for the partners and to acknowledge their definition of the situation. To refer to these relationships as prostitution and say that the participants are in "denial" (as some other authors have done) is to obliterate their reality and miss the subtle interplay of gender, money, and power. Gender is constitutive of these relationships, not ancillary to it. Gender roles are not simply being reversed. The nature of these relationships are shaped and defined by the fact that it is women who have the power, freedom, and money to engage in these liaisons. Romance is a dominant theme in Western culture and a central aspect of feminine sexuality. Not surprisingly, it is also a central aspect of many women's tourism relationships.

Romance tourism liaisons are constructed through a discourse of courtship and long-term relationship; an emotional involvement usually is not present in sex tourism. Both parties often share the ideal of a sustained relationship, though the meanings of such relationships are diverse. However, the framework of romance serves both parties as they seek to maximize the benefits they derive from the tourism relationship.

Tourists of Romance

The women who engage local men in romantic relationships span a wide range of nationalities, age, social, and economic backgrounds. The relationships are most often, though not always, cross-racial as well as cross-cultural in that the vast majority of tourists are classified as white, while the majority of the Jamaican population is of African descent. The duration of the women's stay is usually extended, lasting anywhere from a few weeks to a few months, and many are repeat visitors (Pruitt 1993). European women who often travel for periods of two to three months and come from countries with more relaxed immigration practices than those in North America are more likely to take local men back home with them. The women are seeking an "enriching" travel experience. They shun exclusive resorts in favor of locally owned guest houses, frequent local hang-outs, and socialize with the

local people. The milieu of romance tourism in Jamaica is in part a consequence of Jamaica's fame as the country that gave birth to the international
reggae counterculture. The burgeoning of adventurous travel and the global
spread of Jamaican reggae music has created a social environment within
which many tourists want to become more closely involved with local people, including having intimate relations with local men.

The desire for the "cultural" experience that the tourist woman seeks,
coupled with prolonged exposure to local society, demonstrates a readiness to
embrace, however superficially, the local culture. Such involvement contrasts
with the sexual liaisons of sex tourism. The Jamaican man is not merely a
sexual object, but rather becomes a woman's personal cultural broker. He
serves to ease her experience in his society and provide her with increased
access to local culture.

A foreign woman in Jamaica is assumed to be on vacation. If she is
without a male companion, it is often believed that she wants or needs a local
man to enhance her tourism experience. The frequency with which Jamaicans
have observed foreign women becoming involved with local men supports
this belief. It also relates, in part, to Jamaican notions of companionship and
pleasure and has resulted in what one local writer has called "the sexualization of routine encounters between a female tourist and a local Jamaican
male" (Henry 1988). Consequently, foreign women are frequently inundated
with offers from local men for companionship and a "bodyguard." One Canadian woman told the authors, "Guys at home are so confused, they don't
approach women directly very much. But you come down here [Jamaica] and
the men are dropping out of the trees like mangoes." The result is that many
women unexpectedly find themselves accepting the flattering offers they
receive. This might be the female traveler's opportunity to indulge fantasies
or explore a new aspect of herself by engaging in behavior that is unaccept-
able or unavailable at home.

Adding to the allure of the vacation romance are Caribbean ideals of
beauty. Light skin, straight hair, and Caucasian facial features are highly valued, and women who are considered overweight in their own cultures are
appreciated by many Jamaican men. Thus, foreign women who may not meet
Western standards of beauty find themselves being the object of amorous
attention by appealing local men.

Some women travel seeking companionship because they are unsatis-
fied with their relationships or the lack thereof at home. They travel with the
hope of finding an ideal mate and perhaps staying in Jamaica or returning
home with a partner. These women often express a frustration with men from
their own cultures as inattentive, preoccupied with careers, unemotional, or
confused about their male role (Pruitt 1993). However, many women are
unable or unwilling to establish permanent relationships with Jamaican men.
They sometimes settle for long-distance and part-time romances, returning to
the island year after year, while maintaining relationships through letters,
phone calls, and gifts of money and consumer goods.

The Caribbean man, who highly values proficiency at "sweet talk" (Abrahams 1983, Hubbard 2000), finds that his gender script for romancing women connects with her desire for romance. Ardent declarations of love, praises of beauty, and the like, which are a common part of a Jamaican man's repertoire, are seen as refreshing or passionate by the foreign woman who does not understand the culture. In the words of a Jamaican woman who runs a small guest house, the men "appeal to her emotions with flattery and compliments and do things for her to make her stay in Jamaica easier and more pleasant. They appeal to her sensual side by saying, 'Daughter [woman], if you come to Jamaica and never sleep with a Rastaman, the true, natural man of Jamaica, you never really experience Jamaica and yourself.'"

Courtship eases the interaction between local men and tourist women. It serves those women who are seeking "forbidden" experiences, romance idealism, or believe that sex should be linked to love. Western women draw from their cultural and gender script, assuming that Jamaican men hold the same ideals for intimacy. This pattern of social consumption also lies at the heart of romance tourism. The men are successful at elaborating on the tourist's imagination and thereby offering the promise of realization of her dreams.

Most Western tourist women in Jamaica are exposed to levels of poverty that are absent from their daily reality at home (Harrison 1997). "Third World poverty" is often perceived as noble in contrast to their hometown slums. Rural shacks may appear quaint, whereas ghettos are frightening. Reactions to poverty range from guilt and pity to the desire to help. This often brings people together despite striking socioeconomic differences. Fraternizing with local individuals of dramatically different social and economic status is seen as less threatening than at home. They develop a rapport and attempt to cross the boundaries of socioeconomic inequality. Consequently, many women romanticize their local lovers and hope to help him escape poverty. This tends to hasten the pace of the romance and add a "humanitarian" dimension to the relationship.

Racial, educational, age, and economic differences that constrain tourist women at home are often diminished or ignored during romance tourism. Thus, a rural, African-Caribbean man with little education and scant livelihood is often the companion of a foreign professional woman many years his senior. When necessary, the women pay for the man of their choice to accompany them to dinner, stage shows, discos, or trips around the island. In the light of obvious poverty, she frequently views her financial contribution to the relationship as relatively insignificant.

Women are also able to explore more dominant roles in the tourism relationship. The economic and social status the women enjoy provides them with security and independence that translates into power and control in the relationship. Some of the women say they enjoy the control they have in these relationships and express a preference for keeping a man dependent on them (Pruitt 1993). This ensures that he will be fully available to meet their needs and will not become distracted or otherwise occupied like the men in her own society.

Love and Money

The men hold their own ideals about the potential for emotional intimacy in relationships with foreign women. Many believe foreign women to be more tender and emotional than Jamaican women and imagine that they can experience an emotional and sexual intimacy in these relationships that is lacking in their lives, particularly as they are increasingly rejected by local women for their activities with foreigners.

Those men who desire a broader experience than that available in their immediate situation believe that a relationship with a foreign woman could also provide them with a way out of their limited circumstances. It has proven to be a successful strategy for many young men who seek opportunities and prosperity unavailable in the local society. The hope for economic benefits intertwines with emotional longing and fuels the men's romantic ideals for a relationship with a foreign woman.

Most of the men involved with female tourists can be seen as taking advantage of one of the few opportunities available to them. They generally come from that group of rural young people with little education and few social and economic prospects. The deprivation of opportunity in rural areas has led many young men to seek their livelihood directly from tourists (commonly referred to as hustling) by taking the role of guide or informal entrepreneur in the hopes of obtaining a few of the dollars tourists often spend liberally.

A steady flow of these young men who want to get out of rural areas move into the tourist developments and seek ways to make their living "hustling the tourists." In those regions where it is concentrated, tourism dominates the economy and has been billed as "The Answer" to Jamaica's economic future (Pruitt 1993). Yet, uneducated and unskilled young men living near resort areas are effectively cut off from formal jobs in the tourism industry. The prevalence of romance tourism has meant that increasing numbers of young men routinely view a relationship with a foreign woman as a meaningful opportunity for them to capture the love and money they desire. It is not uncommon to hear young men who come into the tourist areas from deep rural villages talk about their interest in "experiencing a white woman." The following is an excerpt from field notes.

> . . . It was a slow day, not many tourists were in town and none had ventured to Sunrise Beach that day. The guys were chatting about how slow things were.
>
> "Nothing's going on. No money is flowin'," Scoogie complained.
>
> "That's right. Nothing is happening around here. I just want to get me a white-woman and get out of here. Go to America and make real money," said Driver.
>
> "Yeah, you have to link up with a white-woman and get her to fall in love with you if you want a break . . ."

"Yeah man, you have to hook up with a white-woman. I mean look at Decker, Jah Red, Collin, even Punkie. All gone foreign just since this year," said Scoogie. . . . (Pruitt 1993:147)

The ability to earn a prosperous living has significance for the young Jamaican man far beyond basic needs for survival. Brodber describes the "pressure to establish one's maleness through the abilities to disperse cash" (1989:69). The Jamaican man's aspirations to the status of a "big" man (Whitehead 1992) involve money in each of the three elements—moral character, respectability, and reputation—which comprise that status. Evaluations of moral character are based in part on a man's generosity. Expectations of respectability include maintaining a household, while the reputation factor central to achieving status as a "big" man is based partially on virility displayed by sexual conquests and fathering many children (Handwerker 1989, Pruitt and LaFont 1997).

LaFont (1992:196) describes the expectations most Jamaican women hold of financial remuneration from men in exchange for sex and domestic duties by the woman with the result that "much of their [men's] role fulfillment is dependent on job opportunities and the economy." "No money, no talk" is a common expression in Jamaica. Here, the word "talk" refers to intimate relations between a man and a woman. Women expect that a man with whom they are having an intimate relationship will contribute financial support and that he will display an ability and willingness to do so early in the courtship. Thus, the road to women and reputation that verifies a young Jamaican male's manhood, and the status that follows, is constrained for the man with uncertain income opportunities.

In contrast, while his finances are important in his native culture, relations with foreign women do not depend on his ability to provide income. Her interests in him are not predominantly financial. Thus, he is able to acquire the desirable "reputation" of being successful with women without the financial outlay necessary in his own culture. This empowers the men's relations with foreign women while at the same time changing his experience of power and dominance.

While tourism acts as a catalyst for these men to manipulate gender identity as a strategy for economic access, it also places them in a subordinate role to women that is in conflict with their own gender ideals of male dominance. The independence and power the foreign woman enjoys from her financial means yields a control in the relationship that is inappropriate for Jamaican male aspirations. He chafes against her seemingly dominant position because, despite the discussions of male marginality (Chevannes and Brown 1998) and matrifocality (Gonzalez 1970), which refer to men's relationship within the domestic domain, his desire to be dominant in gender relations is intense. To maintain his reputation and avoid the appearance that the woman controls him, the Jamaican man without economic means continually seeks new ways to exhibit his dominion over women. During the tourist woman's holiday in Jamaica, the man has the power of local knowledge. He can control much of his female companion's circumstances in Jamaica, generally without her awareness. He actively acts as buffer between her and others who might influence her; he makes it clear that he "controls that thing" and a hands-off message is relayed to the other male hustlers. This, along with controlling the car she has rented and getting her to buy him material goods, all exhibit his dominion over her.

In order to compete in his community for the status associated with a reputation for success with women, young men play off the features of masculinity available in their culture that have the greatest appeal to foreign women. For most foreign women these are associated with the male Rasta.

The Rasta Appeal

The connection a Western woman develops with a Jamaican man is generally based on her idealizations of his embodiment of manhood, idealizations fueled by the discourse of hegemonic relations constructed through "race" in which the exotic and the erotic are intertwined (Said 1978). The exotic Other has been constructed as more passionate, more emotional, more natural, and sexually tempting. Stereotypes of black men and their sexuality, of non-Western peoples, and on real differences between the tourists' cultures and Jamaican culture promote the belief that Jamaican men represent the archetypal masculine. This is augmented by the men's displays of machismo drawn from their cultural gender scripts. These beliefs are held by Western women considered black as well as white, though black women may not be adhering to stereotypes of black men in general, but rather the black man who stands closer to his African heritage, in this case embodied in the Rasta identity.

Though by no means exclusively, those men with dreadlocks who are assumed to be Rastafarian receive substantially more attention from foreign women than do Jamaican men without locks. Dreadlocks, "locks," or "dreads," are the result of letting hair grow naturally without cutting or combing.

In Jamaica, dreadlocks developed as a symbol of the spiritually based Rastafarian culture of resistance. Since the 1930s, they have represented "stepping out" of the dominant cultural and social system that enslaved the African and continues to denigrate that identity. Dreadlocks are symbolic of the strength of the lion, and signify pride in African heritage and represent strength, anything that is fearful. As such, dreadlocks represent a power source for the Rastafarian. They also symbolize a commitment to a natural way of life, unmediated by Western standards and vanities. Dreadlocks are but one element of a system of symbols that includes a distinctive use of the Jamaican language, images of the lion, and displaying and wearing of the colors of red, gold, and green. Each of them is a "reflection of a form of resistance, linking these symbols to some concrete struggle among African peoples" (Campbell 1987:95).

Rastafarian wearing dreadlocks, symbolic of the strength of the lion. (Photo by Ellen Frankenstein)

Reggae music developed in this same manner as an expression of the Rastafarian spirituality and a vehicle for spreading the message of resistance with an exhortation to the international community to "live up" to standards of interracial justice and peace. The penchant foreign women have for men with dreadlocks is fueled by the mystique associated with the dreadlock singers of the international reggae music culture who project an image of the Rastaman as a confident, naturally powerful, and especially virile man. During the late 1970s, Rastafarian musician Bob Marley was the first to achieve international recognition and subsequently succeeded in capturing the attention of countercultural people across the world. Reggae music, dreadlocks, and Rastafari became synonymous for much of the international community so that, following the model of Marley's success, reggae musicians increasingly grew their hair in locks and adopted the presentation of the powerful Rasta "lion." Through the years, the music has attracted millions of Westerners disaffected by their own culture's systems of inequality and materialism, and enticed them to Jamaica. The pilgrimage to the roots of Rasta resistance climaxes each year in July with the music festival called Reggae Sunsplash.

Whether due to an agreement with the Rasta political philosophy and a desire to demonstrate lack of prejudice, or an attraction to the powerful masculinity projected by the Rastas, or both, men who assume the Rastafarian identity have proven to be a particularly popular with the female European and American tourists with a lust for the exotic. Since the 1970s, young men living in the tourist areas who grew their hair in dreadlocks have attracted special attention from foreigners in general and women in particular. Therefore, those men interested in trading with foreigners, whether selling handicrafts or marijuana (associated with Rastas and an important tourism commodity), or generally acting as companion to ease the way for foreigners through the largely informal society, have increasingly styled themselves as Rastafarian. They "locks" their hair, speak in the Rasta dialect, and develop a presentation that expresses the Rastafarian emphasis on simplicity and living in harmony with nature, in effect, constructing a "staged authenticity" (MacCannell 1973). The man with locks picks up and elaborates on aspects of the stereotype of the exotic Other, enhancing the contrast between himself and Western men, thereby strengthening his appeal to the Western women.

In turn, because these men with locks have increased contact with tourists, they become familiar with the foreign cultures, perhaps learning to speak a little German, or developing an expertise for guessing what types of experiences the specific tourists are seeking. Hence, they become more accessible to the foreigner. Those foreigners in search of an authenticity associated with nonindustrialized society (MacCannell 1976; Cohen 1979) are attracted to the Rasta images and impressions of unity associated with them. The Jamaica Tourist Board reinforced these impressions by using images of dreadlock musicians singing Bob Marley's song "One Love" in the 1991 television advertisement for Jamaica.

Leed (1991:218) describes travel as a "stripping away of the subjectivity rooted in language and custom, allowing travelers to become acquainted with a common nature, fate, and identity that persist beneath the diversity of cultural types and ideals." That motivation for travel intersects in Jamaica with the philosophy of Rastafari, which has at its foundation an emphasis on common identity and unity of spirit. The dread who approaches the tourist appears to offer travelers to Jamaica just that experience of "oneness."

A Rasta identity is attractive to the Jamaican man involved in the tourist hustle because it provides a model of masculinity that is not dependent upon disbursing cash. Rather, it developed around an articulation of the forces that prohibit the African-Jamaican man from achieving economic success. No one expects a Rastaman to be rich. He traditionally emerged from the ghettos of Kingston or the rural areas, and eventually took to the airwaves and concert stages to spread the Rasta message of African liberation. This is the chord Rasta has struck with thousands of men in Jamaica and throughout the African Diaspora, whether rural or urban: its capacity to represent his experience and provide a definition of manhood in Afrocentric terms, thereby providing an alternative to the dominant ideology that places Eurocentric achievement of occupational success and money at the center of the status system. The political philosophy that developed out of the Rastafarian movement of the 1930s through the 1970s included in its critique of the system of oppression of Africans the manner in which the African man's identity is obscured by the Eurocentric ideology of gender and race. The Rastas went on to develop a response by articulating an identity that affirms the black man's dignity and provides a language of opposition to a social system that denies his experience and seeks to obliterate his reality.

Local Consequences

While Rastafari appeals to many rural and urban young men, those who hustle tourists also see the opportunity for parlaying that identity into an opportunity to secure his fantasy of an emotional relationship and perhaps a more comfortable way of life. As Matthews (1977) noted, "Why should a young man in Barbados, for example, work long hours in agriculture when he can triple his income by hustling female tourists on the beaches? The fringe benefits of sex, good food, and night club entertainment are hard to resist."

Such relationships offer the young man with no economic means the avenue to the status associated with success with women, particularly amongst his new peer group of other hustlers. Those men who circulate through the tourist spots—those who work with tourists and those who hope for the opportunity to talk to one—become the community that accords status and prestige to the young men whose ambitions are frustrated by a system of inequality. This peer group becomes increasingly significant for the hustler as many locals shun him for dealing with foreigners, and he faces the generalized and institutionalized discrimination of those with dreadlocks.

While gaining reputation for success with women, the hustler forfeits the respect of the larger community. Anyone who chooses to spend much time with foreigners is subject to criticism and censure from the broader community for being "too much with white people." These men then become embroiled in a further opposition to cultural norms that hold that a man is not supposed to take money from a woman and are subject to persecution and shaming from others in the community. Locals ignore the nuances of the romance tourism relationship and consider the men prostitutes who are too lazy and irresponsible to work for a living. They are resented by many locals who work hard for measly wages while they watch the hustlers living luxuriously with tourist women.

The hustler's claim to be Rastafarian is viewed as superficial as he appropriates Rasta symbols for personal gain, yielding to the individualism of Eurocentric culture and failing to enter the spirituality of Rastafari that repudiates material accumulation and participation in the system of exploitative lifestyles. His internalization of the material ethic that Rasta rejects and his willingness to achieve it by trading in his sexuality with foreign women places him in opposition to the Rastafarian critique of the political economy of Western civilization.

Young men who sport dreadlocks while living amongst tourists have created ambiguity around the Rastafarian identity and the meaning of dreadlocks. As stated earlier, the term "rent-a-dread" evolved in Jamaica to refer to those men who are said to locks their hair in order to appeal to women tourists. When asked how one identifies a rent-a-dread, most locals will say something similar to, "Rasta is known by his works, his livity [manner of living]. If you see the guy around with a different white woman every week or so, then he is a rent-a-dread." The man responds from his cultural gender script for courting multiple women and, by professing his love for his companion, distinguishes himself from a prostitute.

The hustler draws on the language of resistance of the Rastafarian culture to generate a response to his critics. He criticizes non-Rastas for not repudiating the dominant system and ideology by becoming Rasta. The internal contradiction in this position reflects the ambivalence and multiple realities these men confront daily. Criticism from Rastas presents a more formidable challenge for the tourist hustler. His response will usually consist of an argument that Rasta means "One Love," and that Rasta does not subscribe to racial or color discriminations.

What the tourist generally does not understand is the context of origin of her particular dread. Anyone with dreadlocks represents Rastafari for many foreigners who are unaware of its unique history and culture, or who fail to see its symbols as signifiers rather than the thing itself and who have had contact only with those who hustle tourists and claim the identity. Whereas to "locks" one's hair was formerly a dramatic declaration of opposition to the Western system of exploitation, it now can mark an intention to maximize one's position within that system.

Nurturing this possibility requires making the most of the opportunities available so that some men maintain relationships with numerous women from different countries for years until one comes through with an airline ticket, or perhaps makes the decision to move to Jamaica herself and set up a household with her boyfriend.

Beyond Romance

Those who make a commitment to the romance tourism relationship find that romance turns the corner down the path of the hard work of getting along day after day in an intimate relationship between two people whose ideals and expectations have been formed in different cultures. If the women stay in Jamaica or take their boyfriends home with them, typecasts break down to personalities in the minutiae of everyday life. The relationship that extends beyond the casual vacation romance often loses its bloom and leads to disappointment and conflict. The fact that each partner has come to the relationship with a different agenda becomes more apparent as the economic dependency within the relationship becomes more evident.

The women, ignoring or ignorant of the conflicting purposes arising from such disparity of financial means, education, and exposure, are initially unaware of many of the dynamics underlying their relationships. Those who seek their ideal relationships eventually often feel used and disappointed by their partners who likely do not share their Western ideals of sexual equality. The following remarks by a German woman to her Jamaican boyfriend illustrate this attitude. "I came to meet you half-way to help you but you are still caught up in the resentment of the past between blacks and whites and you are not ready to meet me half-way."

Cast in the role of financial provider, the women may become enmeshed in an exchange relationship that did not define their initial impulses. These women often face insecurities about the man's commitment to her, fearing he might get involved with another woman who is in a better financial position to take care of him. Furthermore, if the woman decides to remain in Jamaica, unless she is independently wealthy, she may lose the financial advantages she brought to the relationship or grow weary of the economic demands placed on her. She will also learn that her "Rasta's" alienation within the community extends to her.

The challenges become even greater if the relationship moves to the tourist's country of origin where the man has little of the cultural capital needed to achieve the success he desires in Western society. The rural Jamaican man with little formal education is ill prepared for the demands of making a living in the postindustrial society. With the man's role as culture-broker and tour guide no longer necessary, educational, age, and racial differences that seemed inconsequential in the host country are magnified. His ability to contribute to the relationship in many ways has been diminished, and his difficulty in acculturation, learning the language and bureaucratic systems, as well as making a living, place further strains on the relationship. His "natural" persona may seem incongruous with the demands of life in the "artificial" North, and he will be judged by her family and friends without, or perhaps because of, his exotic backdrop.

Furthermore, by traveling to the woman's country, the man loses what independence he had in his homeland, and he leaves the peer group that verifies his exploits and provides him with reputation and status. Thus, he simultaneously loses the cultural rewards for his deeds while entering a greater dependency on the woman.

The economic relationship conjoined with an emotional one sometimes backfires on the man. While the relationship between a local man and a tourist woman may at first involve a substantial element of economic venture for the man, it also springs from his desire for his ideal emotional relationship with a "tender" woman. It is an intimate relationship involving all the inevitable issues of identity, connection, and power, compounded in this case by racial issues, cultural differences, and economic dependency. Unlike the sex/ money prostitutes, the Jamaican male hustler whose own culture idealizes romantic love may be caught in his own emotional web. Emotional attachments develop; hopes and desires are at work. While the man may be seeking a way out through a foreign woman, he is also vulnerable to being a mere instrument in her search for authenticity.

Tourist women often seem fickle, turning from one man, met early in their stay in Jamaica, to another man they later meet and find more desirable. These Jamaican men must cope with the insecurity of the status of one who represents an ideal type. The premise of the initial attraction is often feigned. To the extent that he has modeled himself to match an ideal, the relationship is not based on her choice of him in particular.

Many of the men describe feeling used by foreign women, only important to them so long as the desire for an exotic liaison lasts, or merely the instrument for her to have a "brown baby" to display her liberal ideas. The instances of children from these liaisons are noticeable but not easily quantified. The men are subject to being left behind as the woman returns home or moves on to new adventures. One interviewee expresses this sentiment succinctly: "I don't like the influence of tourism and being chased by white women. I realize that I can be used by these women. They go home and after a few months you are nothing. You never hear from them again." One of the authors heard a man say to his foreign girlfriend, "You are too emancipated. You think because you have money and education, you can come down here, buy everything and control man. But it can't work that way." When these resentments build, it is not uncommon for the man to resort to a common feature of his gender script for control over a woman and react with violence against the woman. This widespread use of the threat of violence by Jamaican men to maintain dominance is expressed in these lyrics of a popular song in Jamaica.

> Me, me, no woman can rule me.
> Now me is a man and me have me woman.
> But if she try to rule me, me have contention.
> She could get a broke foot and get a broke hand.
> And me rule she, she no rule me.
> If me tell her say A, she can't tell me B.
> And if me lift up me hand you know she feel it.
> (Shabba Ranks 1990)

Relationship between the tourist and local resident is generally based on stereotypes, each having preconceived but not well-formulated notions about the other and often dealing with each other not only as types, but as objects (Kempadoo 1999). Over time, the subjectivity of the partners overwhelms the simple objectified models each holds of the other. The disappointment from the failure of stereotypes to deliver their promise intrudes. The women often become dissatisfied with a partner with different ideas about loyalty and fidelity and who proves to aspire to the deluxe lifestyle that she believed him to refute as a Rastaman. The Jamaican who assumes that all tourists are wealthy may be disillusioned when he discovers that the object of his attentions is spending money freely in order to have a special vacation but is neither rich nor extravagant once the holiday is over.

Conclusion

Dissatisfied with the confines of cultural norms and expectations, people are willing, even eager, to experiment with and rewrite gender scripts. The constraining nature of gender ideologies (Gilmore 1990) invites response and resistance. Tourism creates a social space ripe with possibilities for change through the interplay between conventional scripts and new ideas. In a unique conjunction of need, hope, and desire, the romance relationships between tourist women and local men serve to transform traditional gender roles across cultural boundaries, creating power relations distinctive from those existing in either native society.

Travel has always offered a unique opportunity for self-discovery and potential transformation. Face-to-face contact with the Other and its concomitant challenge to cultural beliefs inevitably involves a confrontation with one's self qua self. While historically the purview of men and a "medium of peculiarly male fantasies of transformation and self-realization" (Leeds 1991:275), travel can now serve as a medium of female "self-realization." Travel has become part of the gendering activity of women as they seek to expand their gender repertoires to incorporate practices traditionally reserved for men and thereby integrate the conventionally masculine with the feminine.

Yet many women who seek more control in their relationships are simultaneously drawn to conventional notions of masculinity. Ideas about masculine power are central to women's attraction to local men, in particular the "natural" Rasta. Women's own gender scripts include a sense of appropriateness of the dominant male from a dualistic conception of man/woman constructed on hierarchical power relations. The farther women push the boundaries of feminine conduct to incorporate qualities conventionally defined as masculine, the more they confront internalized ideas about masculine power. The need for contrast through which to construct their identity draws them to the aspect of masculinity most closely associated with dominance, partially reproducing the dichotomy of gender from their cultural scripts. Thus, many women are drawn to the strength and potency of the masculine even as they experiment with the power they acquire through relative wealth.

Though not motivated by the search for a new gender identity per se, the men in these relationships manipulate their identity by expanding on features from their own cultural repertoire. The local men who associate with tourists, in many ways, enter into a new tourism culture and distance themselves from their society's normative authority. These men then are also free to explore new gender roles while they pursue social and economic mobility and the freedom to experience a new kind of intimate relationship. However, the demands of the role they have adopted put them in contradiction with their gender ideals. Western women bring economic superiority and ideas of female liberation that interact in complex ways with Jamaican men's tolerance of female economic independence, a tradition in their own culture (LaFont 2000, Safa 1995). Despite Jamaican women's economic independence, the predominance of female-headed households and notions of matrifocality (Prior 2001, UN 2000), men are perceived to be dominant in Jamaican culture (Barrow 1998, LaFont 1996, Stolzoff 2000). The Jamaican man's tolerance of female economic independence differs significantly from the subordinate position the man has entered into with the "affluent" tourist woman. While their cultural scripts include a model for the independence of women, the Jamaican woman does not control the man's economic opportunities. However, the men involved in romance tourism are faced with new gendered power relations in which the women control access to the financial success the men want.

While both individuals have the capacity to exert their influence over the relationship in a given circumstance, the woman possesses the disproportionate power to define the situation. Such a situated, contextual analysis (Rhode 1990) as presented here verifies that "it is in these contexts of inequities of wealth and power that one finds transformations of the native self" that incorporate the "evaluation of the West" (Bruner 1991:247). The potential for that transformation and the extent of its accommodation to Western fantasies and expectations is exhibited by these men as they manipulate their identity to fit the tourist's desire for a "natural" man. The consequence of the tourists' power is the commodification of Rastafarian culture and gender itself. Thus, romance tourism recapitulates the patriarchal structure of tourism (Enloe 1989) by reproducing the dominance relation in the tourism encounter wherein tourism functions to fulfill desires of the tourist by subordinating local culture and interests even while the women seek to challenge patriarchal power.

This situation serves to illuminate the significance of economic status for dominance and refutes conventional notions of male hegemony. Control of economic resources provides both genders the opportunity for dominance, for holding little regard for the Other's experience, needs, and feelings. Rather than the purview of men, dominance is rooted in various attributes such as economic power, physical strength, and personality characteristics that may reside with the man or the woman. Gender studies have shown that gender power is not necessarily sex-linked. This study contributes to a reconception of gender by further disentangling power and dominance from sex (Butler 1999).

The dynamics of these relationships also demonstrate that dominance and power are not static but shifting and situational, constantly negotiated and contested, a process at once global and personal. As the partners in these relationships play off traditional social and gender repertoires as well as the immediate circumstances of finance and cultural capital, the power in the relationship fluctuates between them "in relation to opposed sets of cultural values and established social boundaries" (Conway, Bourque, and Scot 1989:29).

Travel offers new opportunities for women to liberate themselves from patriarchal authority relations and redefine "woman." Feminists might celebrate as women break free of conventional constraints and gain power over their lives. However, the personal nature of these relationships may at first mask the social and historical dynamics of racial and economic hegemony embedded in them. Those social and economic inequities, as well as beliefs and stereotypes each partner holds about the Other, work to construct a relationship uncomfortably similar to the power relationship between the partners' respective societies. The agency has shifted from the characteristic nation-state and its transnational corporations to the intimately personal arena.

Breaking taboos and challenging tradition open uncharted territories of social relations. The outcome is never certain and carries with it the possibility of reproducing much of what is being challenged.

Source: Adapted from "For Love and Money: Romance Tourism in Jamaica," *Annals of Tourism Research*, 1996, 22(2):422–40. When we published the original version of this article, it drew criticism for "romanticizing" the relationships between tourist women and Jamaican men. We hope this new version will clarify our ethnographic findings and conclusions.

Acknowledgments

Although it is not possible to name them, the authors wish to acknowledge the numerous men and women in Jamaica whose kind assistance made this article possible. Winsome Anderson made invaluable suggestions on an earlier draft.

References

Abrahams, Roger D. 1983. *The Man-of-Words in the West Indies*. Baltimore: Johns Hopkins University Press.

Altman, Dennis. 2001. *Global Sex*. Chicago: University of Chicago Press.

Anderson, Patricia. 1986. "Conclusion: Women in the Caribbean." *Social and Economic Studies* 35(2): 291–325.

Barrow, Christine. 1998. "Caribbean Masculinities, Marriage and Gender Relations," in *Gender and the Family in the Caribbean*. Mona, Jamaica: Institute of Social and Economic Research.

Bond, Marybeth. 1992. "For Women Only." *justGO* 2(2).

Brodber, Erna. 1989. "Socio-cultural Change in Jamaica," in *Jamaica in Independence*, ed. R. Nettleford, pp. 55–74. Kingston, Jamaica: Heinemann Caribbean.

Bruner, Edward M. 1991. "Transformation of Self in Tourism." *Annals of Tourism Research* 18(2): 238–250.

Butler, Judith. 1999. *Gender Trouble: Feminism and the Subversion of Identity.* New York: Routledge.

Campbell, Horace. 1987. *Rasta and Resistance.* Trenton, NJ: Africa World Press.

Chevannes, Barry, and Janet Brown. 1998. *Why Man Stay So: An Examination of Gender Socialization in the Caribbean.* Kingston: UNICEF.

Cohen, Erik. 1979. "A Phenomenology of Tourist Experiences." *Sociology* 13:179–201.

Conway, Jill K., Susan C. Bourque, and Joan W. Scott. 1989. *Learning About Women: Gender, Politics and Power.* Ann Arbor: University of Michigan Press.

Davidson, Julia O'Connell, and Jacqueline Sánchez Taylor. 2002. "Fantasy Islands: Exploring the Demand for Sex Tourism," in *Sexuality and Gender,* ed. Christine L. Williams and Arlene Stein. Oxford: Blackwell Publishers.

de Albuquerque, Klaus. 1999. "In Search of the Big Bamboo." *Transition* 77, available online at www.cofc.edu/~klausda/bamboo.htm (accessed July 24, 2003).

Enloe, Cynthia H. 1989. *Bananas, Beaches and Bases: Making Feminist Sense of International Politics.* London: Pandora.

Gilmore, David G. 1990. *Manhood in the Making: Cultural Concepts of Masculinity.* New Haven: Yale University Press.

Handwerker, W. Penn. 1989. *Women's Power and Social Revolution: Fertility Transition in the West Indies.* Newbury Park: Sage Publications.

Harrison, Faye V. 1997. "The Gendered Politics and Violence of Structural Adjustment," in *Situated Lives: Gender and Culture in Everyday Life,* ed. Louise Lamphere, Helena Ragon, and Patricia Zavella. New York: Routledge.

Henry, Ben. 1988. "The Sexualization of Tourism in Jamaica." *The Star* (September 3).

Hubbard, Akintola E. 2000. "The Burden of Anansi: Caribbean Sexual Politics and the Problem of the Trickster." Unpublished paper presented at American Anthropological Association Meeting.

Keller, Evelyn Fox. 1989. "Women Scientist and Feminist Critics of Science," in *Learning About Women,* ed. J. Conway et al., pp. 77–91. Ann Arbor: University of Michigan Press.

Kempadoo, Kamala, and Jo Doezema, eds. 1998. *Global Sex Workers: Rights, Resistance, and Redefinition.* New York: Routledge.

Kempadoo, Kamala, ed. 1999. *Sun, Sex, and Gold: Tourism and Sex Work in the Caribbean.* New York: Rowman & Littlefield Publishers, Inc.

LaFont, Suzanne. 1992. *Baby-Mothers and Baby-Fathers: Conflict and Family Court Use in Kingston, Jamaica.* Ph.D. dissertation, Yale University.

———. 1996. *The Emergence of an Afro-Caribbean Legal Tradition in Jamaica.* Maryland: Austin & Winfield Press.

———. 2000. "Gender Wars in Jamaica." *Identities: Global Studies in Culture and Power* 7(2).

———. 2003. *Constructing Sexualities: Readings in Sexuality, Gender, and Culture.* Upper Saddle River, NJ: Prentice Hall.

Leed, Eric J. 1991. *The Mind of the Traveler.* New York: Basic Books.

MacCannell, Dean. 1973. "Staged Authenticity: Arrangements of Social Space in Tourist Settings." *American Journal of Sociology* 79(3): 589–603.

———. 1976. *The Tourist: A New Theory of the Leisure Class.* New York: Schocken.

Matthews, Harry G. 1977. "Radicals and Third World Tourism." *Annals of Tourism Research* 5:20–29.

Nash, Dennison. 1981. "Tourism as an Anthropological Subject." *Current Anthropology* 22(5): 461–481.

Prior, Marsha. 2001. "Matrifocality, Power, and Gender Relations in Jamaica," in *Gender in Cross-Cultural Perspectives,* ed. Caroline B. Brettell and Carolyn F. Sargent. Upper Saddle River, New Jersey: Prentice Hall.

Pruitt, Deborah J. 1993. *A Foreign Mind: Tourism, Identity and Development in Jamaica.* Ph.D. Dissertation, University of California at Berkeley.

Pruitt, Deborah J., and Suzanne LaFont. 1997. "The Colonial Legacy: Gendered Laws in Jamaica," in *Daughters of Caliban: Women in the 20th Century Caribbean*, ed. Consuelo Lopez. Springfield, Bloomington: Indiana University Press.

Rhode, Deborah L. 1990. *Theoretical Perspectives on Sexual Difference.* New Haven: Yale University Press.

Robinson, Jane. 1990. *Wayward Women: A Guide to Women Travelers.* New York: Oxford University Press.

Roberts, George W., and Sonja A. Sinclair. 1978. *Women in Jamaica: Patterns of Reproduction and Family.* New York: KTO Press.

Safa, Helen I. 1995. *The Myth of the Male Breadwinner: Women and Industrialization in the Caribbean.* Boulder: Westview Press.

Said, Edward W. 1978. *Orientalism.* New York: Pantheon Books.

Smith, Raymond T. 1956. *The Negro Family in British Guiana: Family Structure and Social Status in the Villages.* London: Lowe and Brydon, Ltd.

Stolzoff, Norman. 2000. *Wake the Town and Tell the People: Dancehall Culture in Jamaica.* London: Duke University Press.

Taylor, Jacqueline Sánchez. 2001. "Dollars Are a Girl's Best Friend? Female Tourists' Sexual Behavior in the Caribbean." *Sociology* 35(3): 749–764.

United Nations. 2000. *The World's Women 2000: Trends and Statistics.* New York: United Nations Publications.

Whitehead, Tony L. 1992. "Expressions of Masculinity in a Jamaican Sugartown: Implications for Family Planning Programs," in *Gender Constructs and Social Issues*, ed. Tony L. Whitehead and Barbara V. Reid, pp. 103–141. Urbana: University of Illinois Press.

Three: Authenticity and the Marketing of Culture

Folk tradition and communist past: Matryoshka dolls and Lenin souvenirs will later help tourists remember and narrate their trip to Russia. (Photo by Sharon Gmelch)

11

The Limits of Commodification in Traditional Irish Music Sessions

Adam R. Kaul

One important consequence of "globalization"—the accelerated inter-connectedness of far-flung people, places and things (Hannerz 1996:17)—is the fact that more and more aspects of social life have come to be defined in terms of their monetary exchange-value instead of their use-value (Shepherd 2002). In other words, things that were never before commodities have now become commodities: objects of economic value to be sold and consumed. From the beginning, the anthropology of tourism has been concerned with commodification and the implications that this has on the sustainability and "authenticity" of local cultures and customs (cf. Graburn 1976; MacCannell 1989[1976]; Greenwood 1989[1977]; Cohen 1988 for early discussions). These issues were also on the minds of the people I worked with while study-ing the impacts of tourism on performances of traditional Irish music in the small community of Doolin, Ireland. During my 14 months of fieldwork, I worked at one of the local pubs, which allowed for countless conversations with tourists as well as locals (Kaul 2004). Many tourists expressed a curios-ity about whether the musical performances they listened to were "the real thing." Likewise, local musicians constantly talked about performances, ven-ues, and audiences, and a powerful subtextual undercurrent of the notion of "authenticity" swept their discourse along. This article is an attempt to refine existing models that deal with the complex relationship between commodification, commercialization, and authenticity in tourist destinations.

Doolin is known around the world as a place to go to hear traditional Irish music played in a musical context called "the session," which is now a worldwide musical phenomenon with local variations in structure and content. In Doolin, the session is a musical context that occurs most generally in pubs but also occasionally in private houses, with three or more musicians playing jigs, reels, hornpipes, slow airs, and other genres of instrumental dance music that derive primarily from Irish and Scottish traditions. It is said that in the past, Irish "set-dancing" and traditional Irish music existed in a socially codependent symbiosis. This music is called "traditional" because it is considered a public resource that has been handed down from previous generations of musicians even though the individual authors of some tunes might be known. This music is now becoming an acceptable genre in concert settings (think, for example, of *Riverdance*) and in the recording studio, but it is by no means a classical music yet. And while people take lessons today in traditional Irish music, it is often said that a real education can only come from years of careful listening to the music as it is played by the older generations. Often that education occurs in sessions.

A session is different from a concert performance in that it is not staged. The musicians simply sit around a table in the pub, facing toward each other in a circle, and do not face outward, elevated on a stage above an audience. Ideally, sessions create a carefully balanced but permeable social boundary between the musicians and the audience across which interaction in the form

A music session in Doolin. (Photo by Adam Kaul)

of conversation, jokes, and rounds of drinks occurs. This interaction is also musical. Members of the audience often enter the musical circle of the session to "give a song," and musicians sometimes get up to join a conversation away from the session. Within the circle itself a subtly "complex system of codes and etiquettes, humiliations and value reinforcements" (McCann 2001:92) is played out, verbally and musically. Finally, while subtle status hierarchies exist within the session circle, these are achieved rather than ascribed because the session is an inherently egalitarian context where gifts, in the form of tunes, folk historical knowledge about tunes and musicians, drinks, cigarettes,[1] and conversation are exchanged under the subtle but strictly enforced rules and obligations of generalized reciprocity. For example, once people found out that my wife and I could sing, we came to realize that giving a song during a session was as much an obligation and a responsibility as it was a privilege. The session then is not simply a musical environment. It is what Mauss would call a "total social phenomenon" (1989[1924]:303), or what McCarthy calls "music as community" (1999:186, 189). So what often looks to be an incredibly casual affair is in fact incredibly complex.

Before the 1960s, traditional music was not generally popular in Ireland or elsewhere, and in towns and villages just a few miles inland from Doolin, I was told that pub owners, called "publicans" in Ireland, actively discouraged its live performance. Doolin was one of a handful of towns and villages along the west coast of Ireland that maintained a strong musical tradition (alongside strong linguistic, ritual, and oral traditions).[2] What is more, contrary to popular belief, the session is a relatively recent import to Ireland, not some "time-honored ancient" tradition (Kneafsey 2002:356). Prior to the 1960s, traditional Irish music was most often played in people's kitchens or to accompany dancing at house parties or in dance halls. It was rarely played in pubs for its own sake. However, when Irish immigrants moved to places like London and could no longer play music in their flats without disturbing their neighbors, pubs were natural alternate venues. It wasn't until after World War II that these pub sessions became a common occurrence throughout Ireland itself (Kneafsey 2003:23; Fairbairn 1994:582).Traditional Irish music has undergone many similarly dramatic contextual and technical changes during the last hundred years due to the pressures like emigration, poverty, and priestly disparagement.[3]

Another dramatic change, known as "the revival," occurred in the 1960s. Folk music(s) around the world became (re)popularized, riding a wave of social change in America, the British Isles, and elsewhere.[4] A sudden and intense interest in traditional Irish music compelled a new, young generation of fans to seek out the source of this music, which had begun to circulate via the popular recordings of a few "groups" such as the Clancy Brothers and the Furies. As one of these sources, Doolin was flooded with musical pilgrims almost overnight. Local people welcomed traditional musicians from other parts of Ireland, novice musicians, interested listeners, and hippy backpackers searching for the good life with open arms. Almost over-

Doolin, County Clare, Ireland. (Photo by Adam Kaul)

night, what could easily have been described as a depressed village in "decline" (Brody 1973) was transformed into a festival site that has lasted for decades. As local people are fond of saying, there has been one continuous session in Doolin ever since.

Locals were quick to recognize the economic opportunity that had arrived on their doorstep and quickly built up a thriving tourist "industry,"[5] complete with accommodations, restaurants, and gift shops, a full decade before the rest of Ireland came to appreciate the profitability of tourism. Although there are many tourist attractions in the area including natural landscapes such as the Cliffs of Moher, the Burren, and the Aran Islands just off the coast, the centerpiece of this local tourist industry was, and continues to be, the traditional Irish music sessions.

For around a decade between the early 1990s and into the first few years of the twenty-first century, the economy of Ireland expanded at dizzying rates, so much so that Ireland became known as the Celtic Tiger. More recently, Ireland's economy has undergone a severe downturn, but during the economic-boom era, tourism increased rapidly, and Ireland's tourist infrastructure (accommodation, transportation, and what the tourist industry calls the "tourist product") was built up. The crowds that visit Doolin changed during the era of the Celtic Tiger. By all accounts, proportionally fewer musicians and connoisseurs of this music were now in the crowds, and the pilgrimage-site feel of the place dissipated. More mass tourists—tourists with a multiplicity of motivations whose way is made easier and even predictable by a well-developed tourist infrastructure—come now to photograph and consume the sessions. As others have pointed out, mass tourism and a festival atmosphere often feed on each other (Kirshenblatt-Gimblett 1998:61). For many, Doolin is now just one of many "must-see" stops forming part of a larger holiday. As in many places, tourism is highly seasonal in Doolin. The busiest months are June through September when crowds can swell to several thousand per day, while in the winter tourists are rare. Every aspect of social life in the village is dictated by this seasonality.

The question that has formed on the lips of tourists, musicians, and concerned local stakeholders alike is an understandable but loaded one: are these sessions a "tourist commodity," and if so, are they authentic any longer? I will return to the question of authenticity in more detail later, but first I suggest that confusion emerges due to our currently conflated understanding of the processes of commercialization and commodification. Greenwood introduced the concept of "cultural commoditization" to the anthropological literature on tourism in 1977, arguing that as local behaviors and practices are marketed and sold for tourist consumption, they are divested of their original meaning (1989[1977]:179). As marketed and consumable "products" they become meaningless to their producers and therefore, inauthentic. Cohen puts a finer point on the definition of commodification by describing it as "a process by which things (and activities) come to be valued primarily in terms of their exchange value, in a context of trade, thereby becoming goods (and services) . . . stated in terms of prices from [sic] a market" (1988:380). Therefore, commodification entrenches an object or practice in a commensurable definition of value, reducing or eliminating its original functional value.[6]

I follow Williams (2002) and Shepherd (2002) in arguing that the "commodification thesis" is now so overplayed that it has become an assumed characteristic of all tourist–host interactions without much further scrutiny. A number of questions emerge. How closely related to monetary exchange must an object, behavior, or actor be in order to be considered a commodity? If money changes hand via a third party and the consumer and producer never actually engage in direct monetary exchange, can we consider this commodification? Or, as Williams asks, are there "monetised exchanges where the profit motive is absent?" (2002:525). In such cases, can the object or behavior really be considered a commodity with only an exchange value?

To begin, I propose a distinction between commercialization and commodification. First, I will suggest that commodification is a particular commercializing process whereby a produced thing or activity itself is given a consumptive market value. This returns to Cohen's definition, which argues that a commodified product, service, or behavior is one that has "come to be valued primarily in terms of [its] trade value" (1988:380). "[S]uch a manoeuvre," write Helgasson and Palsson, "requires the replacement of values and meanings that formerly excluded a thing from the sphere of commodity exchange, with the more homogenized field of significance of the market, that has at its core a single standard of commensurability" (1997:453). I would extend this one step further. The desire to create these commensurable exchange values is so intense in the process of commodification that it inevitably leads to the loss of productive control, or "creative freedom." As I argue below, it is the issue of control rather than the presence of money that is key. Second, I propose that commercialization is more a general process: it is simply the introduction or intensification of monetary exchange in relation to the production and/or consumption of a thing. If productive control remains in the hands of the producer, then an activity can become commercialized without becoming commodified. So, while all commodities are commercialized, not all commercial activities are commodified.

Furthermore, a commodified object or behavior does not need to be exchanged for money. Things that are off limits to the process of commodification are given "a special aura of apartness from the mundane and the common" (Kopytoff 1986:69). As Kirshenblatt-Gimblett points out, this "apartness" can be achieved quite literally by placing an object into a museum setting. This may turn even an everyday object into one of powerful meaning and value, although that meaning is determined by the museum exhibit itself (1998:19–23). Also, what might have a use-value in one context may become commodified and acquire exchange-value in another context or vice versa. A family heirloom, for example, might be put on the market to raise needed funds. This moves the object out of the realm of functional (and personal, sentimental) meaning into a commensurable realm of pure exchange-value as it sits in the auction house. If purchased by a collector, however, it may once again become an object with functional meaning. Exchange-values and functionality can also coexist in a balance in certain instances. For example, if the family heirloom is not sold but rather is appraised for insurance purposes, it may have both sentimental and monetary value for its owner. In other words, while profits and monetary values are an obvious place to begin an analysis of commodification, the existence of a profit motive alone does not distinguish between commodification and commercialization. Instead, the major distinction between the two processes is *control.* Are the producers themselves (in this case the musicians) free to control the performance? Can they choose what to play, how to play it, and how to represent it? Or are the musicians being controlled by some third party—a publican perhaps? Or the whims of the consumers, in this case the session audience?

Jigs for Gigs

In Doolin, musicians were always compensated for playing, typically with food, drinks, or a bit of cash. Older musicians explained to me that before the revival, music was categorized as a skill like any other, and musicians were the crafters of music. The colloquial term "musicianer" is indicative of this understanding of music as something that is performed as a service to others. When the revival hit Doolin and the crowds started pouring into the village, the musical environment began to change. One thing that did not change was the tradition of compensating musicians. As one local publican told me:

> I always gave 'em a few "bob" anyway, before anybody ever asked me for money. They'd get their food, three meals if they were there all day. And if they were going somewhere, then you'd give them a fiver or a tenner . . . anything they needed for a few pounds, you gave it to them. You didn't specify what amount, really.

He was reciprocating by paying musicians for their skilled craft, although it was never a specified amount or enough to be called a "wage" of any sort. As time wore on and the crowds swelled, the size of sessions and of their audiences took a toll on musicians and publicans. "Dancing became impossible in a jam-packed pub" wrote one early visitor to Doolin, "though there was never any lack of music—often two or three sessions going simultaneously in different corners" (Coady 1996:15). Some musicians began to look for quieter pubs to play in, away from the teeming crowds. In contrast, the publicans were growing dependent on the musicians to draw in crowds of visitors, some of whom had traveled long distances to hear a bit of music. In other words, a consumer demand had been created. The natural thing for publicans to do was to pay a few local musicians to show up at a given time to start a session off. In a short time, a new symbiotic relationship had developed between publicans, musicians, and visitors while simultaneously, the old symbiosis between musicians and dancers weakened significantly. Paying musicians ensured that a session would happen on a regular basis, what some authors have called "anchoring" (Helbig 2002:168; Vaysse as cited in McCann 2002:75) or "seeding" a session. Eventually, these payments were transformed into a wage-like payment, paid out at the end of the night. While a system of paid-for sessions contributes to a general professionalization of the music (Bohlman 1988:85–86), these payments should not be mistaken for a formal wage. Nor are paid musicians employees; rather, as Fairbairn has argued, they are given the "elevated status of desirable clients" (1992:159).

Today, musicians and publicans have created a system in which three or four musicians agree to show up on a given night each week to host a session. No more than three or four are paid to play, and normally one musician will be hired by a publican to do the "gig" once a week. That musician then decides who will be the other two or three musicians to join his or her session, and if the session is advertised in some form (verbally or in print), the evening will often simply be called "Christy and friends" or "Noel and friends." When this system first became prominent during the revival, it simply seeded the sessions. Other musicians would inevitably join in, and a larger session would form. Now, however, fewer and fewer traveling musicians come through northwest County Clare, and some nights, the pub's paid musicians will be the only ones playing.

The recognition of a lead musician (as in "Christy and friends") might be seen as the emergence of hierarchy, but this relationship existed before. In most Irish music sessions held anywhere in the world, one or two players are recognized as, what some writers have called, the "alpha" musician (Foy 1999:85). "This informal 'leader,'" Cowdery explains, "must know an enormous number of tunes and must be able to think of them and suggest them on the spot, either by calling out their titles or by authoritatively starting them" (1990:13). This role is now simply formally acknowledged by the structural relations of paid sessions.

Communality and egalitarianism are still emphasized despite the extraneous monetary realities. For example, nonpaid musicians are still encouraged to lead a set of tunes at some time during an evening. This not only builds the confidence of learning musicians, but it also emphasizes communality. While all musicians recognize that some are better players than others, and deference to the alpha musician is required, lesser talents must also be given the floor. Glassie describes the necessity of this mutual deference in the context of a *ceili*—an informal gathering of friends and neighbors for music, stories, and chat—but the description is apt here as well: "It is the responsibility of the entertaining man who occupies the ceili's center to pull others into performance, and it is the responsibility of those others, though acknowledged as lesser talents, to take their turn . . . diversifying the sport and giving the man who must do most of the work a rest" (1995[1982]:99–100).

Importantly, like all other aspects of life in northwest Clare, there is a dramatic seasonal variation in the paid session schedules in Doolin. In the summertime when tourists abound, there is a paid session every night of the week in all three pubs. The music is generally amplified so that the music can be heard throughout the large pubs. After the tourist season ends, publicans start paying for fewer sessions during the weekdays. By November, sessions are paid for only on the weekends, and eventually only two-thirds of the pubs in the village host paid-sessions at all. Therefore, as Kneafsey points out, there is a certain degree of musical dependence on tourism, and this means that a kind of "symbiotic relationship" has emerged between paid-for sessions and tourism (2003:35).

The Triangle of Consumption

The system of payments creates what I call a "triangle of consumption" in Doolin's sessions. The musicians get economic compensation from publicans for playing at given times on given nights of the week. Publicans reap large profits from tourists' consumption of alcohol and food. Tourists also consume the music, sitting or standing near the session collectively "gazing" at the musicians (Urry 2002:43), thus gaining an important Irish holiday experience. For those who have only a passing knowledge of traditional Irish music, sessions are a kind of visual and aural souvenir—one of the experiences they had to see while in Ireland. At the height of the summer tourist season, sessions in Doolin are accompanied by arrhythmic flashes from cameras. The visual/aural experience itself is a kind of consumption, and the photographs (and sometimes the recordings that tourists make) can be taken home as a more literal type of souvenir.

Of course, this triangular model is just a crude sketch, and it does not describe a balanced relationship. Nor are participants' motivations uniform. In terms of economic capital, the publicans are set to gain the most. The disproportionate profits they make in comparison to musicians are sometimes criticized by some observers and participants as exploitative. However, publicans must also be careful about the amount of money they pay out to musicians on an annual basis. A retired publican once told me,

> I wouldn't like to be in the business now. You'd want to have a good business to pay three or four musicians [every night]. At the end of the year, if you added it up, that could be most of your profit.

Certainly, the claim that most of a pub's profits go to the musicians is an exaggeration; however, the move toward a more structured system of payments has created a more competitive market, for both publicans and musicians. As might be expected, tensions emerge as a result of these paid relationships. Largely, though, everyone recognizes the necessity of this symbiosis, and the relationship between publicans and musicians is amicable if sometimes only businesslike. Publicans' motivations for hosting traditional music also vary. Some do so simply because it makes good business sense. Others are devoted connoisseurs of the music. It is important to note that money never passes between the musicians and the tourists. The publicans broker all economic exchanges in the triangle of consumption. This allows the musicians to be free from the polluting effects that direct monetary transactions would have on the perceived authenticity of their music.[7] Commercial exchanges are often perceived to be "robbed of all meaning," while "other types of exchange, particularly gift[s], do have meaning and do provide fulfilment" (Helbig 2002:226). It is the publican, a role that is often seen as the very stereotype of the Irish businessperson, who purifies the exchange by absorbing its polluting commercial aspects, thereby turning the payments into gifts.

For some musicians, the payment they receive is supplemental income. For others, although relatively uncommon, it makes up most or all of their annual earnings. In other words, a paid musician can theoretically live off his or her music although the income is only barely a living wage. This highlights the fact that musicians' motivations for playing can vary a great deal. Someone who depends on the nightly fees might play less out of enjoyment than for financial obligation. However, musicians often talked about how important it was to not start thinking about sessions as some sort of job, and in fact, many cited their desire to separate their music from paid work as the reason they kept regular day jobs. In other words, there is a real concern to maintain what Csikszentmihalyi has called the "autotelic experience" (1990:67), the desire to enjoy the music for its own sake. Due to the positive response from tourist audiences, many musicians told me that they even prefer them to locals-only audiences.

Symbolically, the tourists' consumption of what is for many an exotic musical context is arguably the most novel experience in the relationship. Their consumption takes the form of the direct experience of the music (seeing it, hearing, it and feeling it) and through photographs and the occasional sound recording, which can be re-experienced later. Now more than ever, it is difficult to ascertain just how important the musical experience is to the tourists who visit Doolin. During the revival period, which predated well-developed tourism transportation and lodging, tourists endured many discomforts in order to experience a Doolin session,[8] but today travel to Doolin is so easy and lodging is so well-appointed that a modern mass tourist in Doolin may have a plethora of motivations, or no clear motivations at all, for being present at a session.

It is also an oversimplification to presume that the distinctions between musicians and tourists are clear. Some tourists go on holiday specifically in order to play in sessions themselves. I became friends with a French tourist who eventually became an "incomer" to the village and a paid musician in the local sessions. Mass tourist crowds are never undifferentiated either, and certain tourists may feel more closely connected to the musical experience than others may. Diverse motivations, perspectives, and discursive assessments of the music (and of other tourists) all come into play. Not only is there national, linguistic and ethnic diversity among the tourist population, but some tourists know more about the locale and the local culture than others do. Some tourists know a great deal, for example, about traditional Irish music and would be able to listen to a session with discerning ears. Others will have absolutely no experience with the music and will have expectations derived from other genres like pop concerts. For these tourists, while they may enjoy it, the fast-tempo and repetitive nature of traditional music leads to a commonly heard complaint: "it all sounds the same."

These differing levels of knowledge about the session experience create different assessments of what it is "all about" as well as its authenticity. Some tourists with musical knowledge derived from pop music might find a more highly produced, "staged" performance of traditional Irish music similar to other musical experiences they may have had and thus conclude that it was more authentic. For the same reason, they might conclude that the casual social environment of a session seems unprofessional and therefore inauthentic. Conversely, a tourist with extensive experience with the session context might arrive at the opposite conclusion. Despite this diversity, however, there was an almost ubiquitous sense of disappointment among the tourists I talked to if they found out that the musicians get paid. I use the word "if" because unless they asked, no one told them. The assessment of a South African tourist is representative:

> Back in 1983 the musicians gathered spontaneously, the music was authentic, the vibe was less touristy. This time [in 2003] the musicians were obviously paid to be there.

Paid sessions are perceived to indicate a formal economic relationship that automatically marks them as commodified and therefore inauthentic. What this tourist encountered in Doolin contrasts with the widely received narrative about sessions disseminated by the tourist industry, which is that they are by nature, casual, unstructured, and "impromptu" (*Let's Go Ireland* 1996:70). The romantic assessment of the tourist above (and his subsequent disappointment) is therefore common.

Authenticity and Credibility

Lionel Trilling wrote that authenticity "is one of those words, like love, which are best not talked about if they are to retain any force of meaning" (1972:120). The academic literature is already heavy with discussions on this word. Some say it is "overdone" (Bruner 2005:209). Certainly, authenticity is a clumsy but powerful trope, and it is not always clear exactly what people mean when they use the term without looking carefully at the context. As Helbig has written, it is the "all-or-nothing nature of 'the authentic' in popular discourse" (2002:200) that is the problem. I would add that it is not just the popular discourse, but also the academic discourse, that is to blame. Bruner suggests "it may be that . . . contemporary intellectuals are the ones looking for authenticity and that they have projected onto tourists their own longings" (2005:162). At the very least, academics are certainly not immune from the same powerful and romantic narratives about "pure cultural origins" (and subsequent "commercial pollution") that often inform tourist narratives. Shepherd in fact points out that there is a powerful subtext in the literature that assumes a straightforward oppositional dichotomy between the consumption of commodified culture and some sort of cultural authenticity (2002:186).

For sure, a more nuanced understanding of authenticity is beginning to emerge, and there are several basic ways of thinking about the concept. One way to get at the meaning of authenticity is through what Wang has called "the museum approach" (2000:47, 49). In other words, one might ask, is a thing what it claims to be? This is what Bruner says people mean when they use the word to refer "to the original, as opposed to a copy" (2005:150). A determination of this kind of authenticity might arguably be impossible when considering social behaviors and performances in a tourist context. One would necessarily have to prove that they are in no way being produced for any other reason than for their supposedly original function in society. This is problematic because pure original functions are not likely to exist. Likewise, one would need proof that a behavior has not been manipulated by outside influence (however, one might delineate the "outside"), that instead, its form or performance has some sort of pure historic continuity with past forms or performances. In other words, all of the strictures that museologists use to determine the authenticity of a piece of art or an artifact would necessarily be utilized. MacCannell's analysis of authenticity in tourist contexts (1989[1976]) and Greenwood's (1989[1977]) early work on tourism are examples of this approach.[9] Various authors have pointed out the simplicity of this conflation of experiences, objects and traditions (Greenwood 1989[1977]; Selwyn 1996; Wang 2000; Kaul 2007; Bruner 2005; and in the specific context of "living histories" see Handler and Saxton 1988).

Bruner describes a second kind of authenticity: one that is "certified" by an institution or by some sort of "expert" who has the "vested authority" to deem one thing but not another authentic. One example is the reproduced village of New Salem that he describes, which was certified to be the official "authentic reproduction" (2005:150) of the village by the state of Illinois. We might call this "certifiable authenticity."

An extreme postmodern perspective argues that any notion of authenticity must be abandoned because there is not, and never has been an "absolute boundary between the real and the fake" (Wang 2000:54). I agree with Bruner that the extreme, nihilistic version of postmodernism is "a narrow and distorted view" (2005:168). Just because an objective definition of authenticity cannot be found does not mean either that all meaning is lost or that every judgment is purely subjective and equivalent. For instance, it would be ridiculous to claim that a traditional Irish musician's assessment of a particular performance of traditional Irish music is the same as that of someone who has never heard the music before. Of course, we would trust the musician's opinion over the first-time listener. Thus, everything is not relative. At the same time, we cannot simply rely on objective indicators of authenticity and discount subjective experiences altogether, even when they are uninformed by previous experience or knowledge.

An existential approach is particularly useful for analyzing these types of experiences in performance contexts like those in Doolin. Existential authenticity might be defined as an experience in which a person is completely attuned to and embedded in the phenomenological moment, the "moment of reception" (Kirshenblatt-Gimblett 1998:11). At the level of individual perceptions, phenomenologically meaningful experiences are authentic for the very reason that they are inchoate and free from any narratives that would contest them. Audience members with no prior experience of traditional Irish music performances can have what they consider to be an existentially authentic experience even though they lack the epistemological tools to assess the performance's relative quality or historical accuracy. In an entirely different context, Bruner (2005) describes how a group he worked for as a tour guide in Bali enjoyed the less historically accurate dance that was performed in a far more intimate setting than the historically accurate dance that was performed in a hotel among several hundred tourists. He argues that instead of being concerned "with issues of authenticity," they simply "demanded that it be a good performance" (2005:206–207). Another way of characterizing this would be to say that the tourists were not concerned so much with issues of objective authenticity as with having an existentially authentic experience.

Using this foundation, we can build a constructivist definition of authenticity. Meanings are created, maintained, dismantled, and changed, which means that what is or is not authentic changes as well. This seems reasonable given that cultures and the behaviors within them follow particular normative customs (Chaney 2002:203). They are "primarily traditional," yet at the same time are "continually being redesigned," "invented," or, if one prefers the dramaturgical metaphor over the technological ones, "performed" and "re-performed." For instance, the Doolin that exists today is very much a place constructed by its interaction with tourism. There has been a very conscious effort to preserve what was originally attractive about the village, including its built environment, by not overdeveloping it (Danaher 2005). Whether this issue is something to be optimistic or pessimistic about is debatable. What is certain in Doolin is that, as others have shown for other tourist destinations (cf. Mbaiwa 2004), the impact of tourism is always complex rather than simply "good" or "bad."

If authenticity is culturally constructed and context-dependent, then "authenticity should be understood as a quality of a process rather than an object," claims Chaney; "when it is invoked people are talking about how something is being done rather than the what it is (that is being done)" (2002:204). Kirshenblatt-Gimblett, discussing the (re)production of Plimoth Plantation in Plymouth, Massachusetts for tourist consumption, makes a similar point. "Authenticity," she writes, "is located not in the artifacts per se or in the models on which they are based but in the methods by which they are made—in a way of doing, which is a way of knowing, in a performance" (1998:196). This is where we are often led astray by notions like authenticity. It is not a thing that we (scholars, students, members of the public) should be looking for at all, but rather it is a process or characteristic. Although it is beyond the scope of this paper to delve into this point too much, I suggest that when the term "authenticity" is invoked (especially in the academic literature) in relation to cases like the one discussed in this article, very often what is really meant is "credibility."

The term credibility incorporates the idea that authenticity is a process of social construction while recognizing that some actors simply know better than others how to assess a quality performance. These are actors who are closer to the history of the production of an object or performance, or perhaps the producers themselves. Their assessments may not be entirely accurate or "objectively true" given their historical and contextual perspectives, but they are obviously more credible than the assessments of actors with little or no epistemological knowledge of the performance. The term credibility also does not deny the legitimacy or the co-existence of existentially authentic experiences of performances. In other words, I see no reason why a knowledgeable and informed actor (for example, a musician) might not find a particular performance very credible at all. The person might conclude that the performance was a complete "show" rather than a "real session." Simultaneously, a second actor (for example, a tourist who has never heard the music before) might conclude that the exact same performance was one of the most existentially authentic moments of his or her holiday. For me, this is simply a more pragmatic and less ideologically loaded way of thinking about the same issues.

The word "authentic" cannot be disentangled from the issue of control since one of its original meanings is, as Lionel Trilling points out, "to have full power over" (1972:131). In a case like Doolin, any discussion of authenticity, or what I would prefer to call credibility, needs to consider the amount of control the musicians have over the production of their performances. In fact, the distinction I suggest here between commercialization and commodification is important because I argue that commercial activities can coexist with legitimately credible performances if the producers maintain significant control over what gets performed. This becomes less and less possible as they lose control—in other words, as things become truly commodified.

Commodification, Commercialization, and Control

Commodification occurs when individuals lose control over the process of determining how value is assigned to the activities and things that they produce, when functional values are overridden by commensurable exchange-values. In the present case, there is no set exchange-value for tunes or sessions. Of course, the musicians are in fact paid by publicans, and in the summertime, primarily for tourist consumption. But neither tourist audiences nor publicans make a direct payment for the session as a "product" in and of itself. There is no cover charge for tourists entering the pub, and as we will see below, the publicans' payments are not so much for the music that is played as much as they are for the *fact* that music is played. Publicans do not control the means of production; they collaborate with the musicians to create a situation whereby the music can be produced. So, with regard to monetary exchange, I would conclude that the paid-for sessions in Doolin have not become commodified.

How much control do the musicians have over the production of their music in Doolin? The fact that musicians are paid to show up in order to start a session is clearly a loss of some control on their part, but outside of a few rare examples, the musicians have total control over what goes on in a session— not the publicans or the audience.[10] It is perfectly acceptable, and indeed expected, that paid musicians will invite local singers or tourists to come up and give a song or play a few tunes. They can let other musicians assume the alpha musician role and take control over the session. Their minimal responsibility as a paid musician is simply to start the session. Often, few or no unpaid musicians turn up to play, so the paid musicians must carry the night, but if a large number of unpaid musicians show up and are keen to play, the paid musicians are under little obligation to maintain any sort of leading role.

Additionally, musicians can easily quit their weekly scheduled gig if they become annoyed with the publican for any reason. This is much easier to do and more common than a publican "firing" a musician. Musicians can also get other musicians to fill in for them if they have a conflicting obligation. In these instances, the musician need not inform the publican of the substitution. Publicans have become reliant on musicians to play in the pubs, but musicians often have other income, and more importantly many other pubs that they could play in. In other words, the publican's primary concern is that there is some music. In 14 months of fieldwork in Doolin, during which time I worked in a pub, I witnessed only two nights when musicians did not show up for a scheduled gig. In both cases, the publican frantically called around to find someone to fill in at the last minute.

The musicians' loss of control is not significant enough to conclude that the traditional Irish music sessions played in Doolin are somehow commodified, inauthentic, false, or staged solely for the benefit of tourists. Indeed, musicians still find playing music meaningful, and few see any problem with the relationships inherent in the triangle of consumption. From the standpoint of most musicians I talked to, the worst threat to any sense of authenticity or credibility comes from the breakdown of the basic egalitarian social rules of the session. This includes instances when one musician dominates the session excluding other musicians or when the crowd noise prevents the typical social porosity between the musicians and the audience, rather than the commercialism that has grown up around it.

Perhaps the thrust of this argument would be clearer by comparison. There is a theme park in County Clare with old Irish cottages of various styles from the area, complete with farmyards and livestock. Visitors are able to walk into them, poke around the farm machinery, and generally be as investigative as they want to be. In the evenings, "medieval banquets" are held in a restored medieval castle, and the paying diners are entertained with music and ballads performed by musicians and singer/actors dressed in medieval-period costumes. A musician who currently plays music for these banquets told me about the program as it exists today.

> It's a very set program. It has to run within a given time. So that leaves restrictions as well.
> And the type of music they play, I feel, is totally cliché. It's down to—for example, they play "Danny Boy." But they used to do it in Irish, which is beautiful. And the tourists used to ask, "Why don't you sing 'Danny Boy'?" They had to change it back to English. And they've chosen songs that everybody can clap or join into.

This medieval banquet is similar to the reproduction of Lincoln's New Salem village that Bruner (2005) describes or Kirshenblatt-Gimblett's (1998) case study on Plimoth Plantation. There is an attempt to make the details of the performance (the acting, the costumes, the décor, the music, and the food) historically accurate or objectively authentic. On the other hand, there is a pull to satisfy the tourists' demands by playing and singing popular, but not necessarily historically accurate, songs. The performance here is tightly controlled by the management, consciously produced for a tourist audience, and is a classic example of what Edensor has called a "tourist enclave" where there is a "continual maintenance of a clear boundary which demarcates which activities may occur" (2000:328). Moreover, the representation of the music (by means of advertisements, directing the performances) is almost entirely outside of the control of the musicians. The informant above discusses how "they" make decisions about the performances, not the musicians. This is a highly commodified musical product, created not for the producers, but solely for the consumption of paying tourists. While this informant enjoys these staged performances, he told me he feels infinitely freer in other musical contexts such as when he is "busking"—playing on street corners and at tourist sites for tips thrown into a hat. It is interesting to note that when busking, the exchange of money for music is more direct than at the theme park, and yet, it is perceived by this musician to be more authentic. This highlights my point that control is in fact more important than monetary exchange.

At the other extreme might be the kind of public performance that occurs at a small old pub in the countryside between Doolin and another village nearby. Once a week for many years now, the local farmers have come out for a few drinks, to socialize and to play a few tunes. The musicians who attend this session are generally older, and a few of them are even quite renowned. However, this is a very casual affair. The music is played simply as part of a good night in quiet company. Here, there is no confused agenda, no hint of commercial motivations, and indeed no reason to play every Thursday night except for the enjoyment of doing so. Moreover, there is no advertising, or for that matter, any representation of this session in any form other than among known friends and family.[11]

Traditional Irish music has become commercialized in Doolin in the sense that monetary exchanges surrounding the music have increased. However, Doolin has not become commodified like the musical performances at the theme park nearby. The surface trappings of commercialism have painted the exterior of performances in Doolin, confusing the issue, but musicians largely maintain control over the make-up of the session. No one is telling them what tunes to play, how to play them, or to sing "Danny Boy" (in English) because the tourists request it.[12]

Conclusion

Globalization has shifted our attention towards processes that bring objects and activities once held to be outside the economic arena into the realm where they can be measured in terms of their exchange-value. This attention is warranted, but without careful scrutiny it is too often assumed that all commercial processes automatically have a negative impact on locally produced objects, activities, and performances by eroding their functional value and meaning. In this article, I have argued that a distinction needs to be made between two separate processes in this larger shift because of the varying impact they have on local people's ability to control the production of their own cultural artifacts and activities and therefore maintain their sense of functional value. Control is the key factor in the distinction between commodification and commercialization, rather than the mere existence of a monetary exchange. In particular, it is argued that commercialization can coexist, if not always comfortably, with an artist's control over the production of their art form. By contrast, commodification is the nearly complete loss of control.

The erosion of cultural meaning and legitimacy underlie many discussions of tourist consumption and social interaction between tourists and locals in tourist destinations like the one discussed here, and the concept of authenticity is often invoked. Recent critiques of this concept are justified since it is both ideologically loaded and polysemous. A more nuanced understanding is beginning to emerge, and this article is one attempt to extend the analysis. Finally, if Miller is correct that there are both benign and "unequivocally evil" forms of consumption (1995:147), then this distinction is not simply a pedantic exercise. It has great political importance for local people as they attempt to do more than simply "cope" with tourism (Boissevain 1996) by recognizing that they can marry commercial success with a sense of cultural legitimacy.

Source: Adapted from "The Limits of Commodification in Traditional Irish Music Sessions," *Journal of the Royal Anthropological Institute*, 2007, 13(3):703–719.

Acknowledgments

Support for this research was generously provided by an Overseas Research Studentship Award, and by a Radcliffe-Brown Award from the Royal Anthropological Institute. Institutional support was provided by the Anthropology Department at Durham University, the "Public Cultures in Theory and Practice" and "Anthropology in Development" Research Groups at Durham University, by Medaille College, and by Augustana College. I would like to thank the *JRAI* reviewers for their very valuable suggestions. Thanks to Sharon Gmelch who provided many useful suggestions. I am also particularly indebted to Tamara Kohn, Steve Lyon, Paul Sillitoe, Peter Dixon, Les Jessop, Ethan Paquin, and Jerry Erion for their comments. Special thanks are reserved for the people of Doolin who gave their valuable time, support, and friendship.

Notes

[1] I collected the ethnographic data that forms the basis for this article up to just a few months prior to the smoking ban that now includes all workplaces including pubs.

[2] The reputation of the "expressive culture" is so strong here that numerous folklorists, ethnomusicologists, and anthropologists have gone to Doolin over the last hundred years to collect

and document it. No doubt, this academic interest has surely had some influence on the self-preservation of local traditions by local people.

[3] This is an example of the pliability of "living" folk traditions. Indeed, traditions must constantly although conservatively change and adapt in order to survive (Kaul 2007).

[4] The revival of traditional Irish music is complex and cannot be dealt with here, but for discussions on musical revivals in Ireland and elsewhere, see Allen 1981; Blaustein 1993; Jabbour 1993; Livingston 1999; Munroe 1984; Vallely 1999.

[5] "Industry" is perhaps too strong a term. Created and run by a fiercely independent people, the development of tourism in Doolin was, and continues to be, very much a laissez-faire cooperative collection of individual business concerns.

[6] More recently, the commodification of culture has received wider attention outside of tourist settings as well (Appadurai 1996; Ateljevic and Doorne 2003; Helgasson and Palsson 1997; Kirtsoglou and Theodossopoulos 2004; Lovering 1998; McCann 2002; Nesper 2003; Schutte 2003; Shepherd 2002; Stevenson 2003; White 2000; Williams 2002).

[7] For a similar discussion about the "polluting" effects of money, but in a much different ethnographic context, see Carsten 1993.

[8] Locals were fond of telling stories about how revival tourists had to hitchhike to get to Doolin, camp in cow pastures, and do their laundry in the river.

[9] Greenwood amends his earlier "alarmist" approach in the 1989 edition of this same paper.

[10] I heard of a few rare instances in which publicans pressured musicians to play particular types of tunes or sing particular types of songs, but the explosive reaction to these incursions only highlights the fact that this is extremely inappropriate behavior. One musician famously burned his gig money after being told what type of songs to sing.

[11] My wife and I lived very close to this pub for most of a year, but it was only after about six months into the fieldwork that we first heard about this session. It is not a guarded secret or a private affair. It is simply not well-known.

[12] In fact, the commonly heard response to requests for "standards" such as "Danny Boy" is something along the lines of, "Sorry I don't know that one. Why don't you sing it for us?"

References

Allen, R. R. 1981. "Old-Time Music and the Urban Folk Revival." *New York Folklore* 7:65–81.

Appadurai, A. 1996.*Modernity At Large: Cultural Dimensions of Globalisation.* London: University of Minnesota Press.

Ateljevic, I. and S. Doorne. 2003. "Culture, Economy and Tourism Commodities: Social Relations of Production and Consumption." *Tourist Studies* 3(2): 123–141.

Blaustein, R. 1993. "Rethinking Folk Revivalism," in *Transforming Tradition: Folk Music Revivals Examined,* ed. Neil V. Rosenberg, pp. 258–274. Urbana and Chicago: University of Illinois Press.

Bohlman, P. V. 1988. *The Study of Folk Music in the Modern World.* Bloomington and Indianapolis: Indiana University Press.

Boissevain, J. (ed.). 1996. *Coping with Tourists.* Oxford: Berghahn.

Brody, H. 1973. *Inishkillane: Change and Decline in the West of Ireland.* London: Jill Norman and Hobhouse.

Bruner, E.M. 2005. *Culture on Tour: Ethnographies of Travel.* Chicago: University of Chicago Press.

Carsten, Janet. 1993. "Cooking Money: Gender and the Symbolic Transformation of Means of Exchange in a Malay Fishing Community," in *Money and the Morality of Exchange,* ed. J. Parry and M. Bloch, pp. 117–141. Cambridge: Cambridge University Press.

Chaney, D. 2002. "The Power of Metaphors in Tourism Theory," in *Tourism: Between Place and Performance,* ed. S. Coleman and M. Crang, pp. 193–206. London: Berghahn.

Coady, M. 1996. *The Wellspring of Water: A Memoir of Packie and Micho Russell of Doolin, County Clare*. Michael Coady. Self Published.

Cohen, E. 1988."Authenticity and Commoditization in Tourism." *Annals of Tourism Research* 15:371–386.

Cowdery, James R. 1990. *The Melodic Tradition of Ireland*. Kent and London: Kent State University Press.

Csikszentmihalyi, M. 1990. *Flow: The Psychology of Optimal Experience*. New York: Harper and Row.

Danaher, D. 2005. *Doolin Could Cannibalise Itself Through Holiday Homes*. Clare Champion. Ennis, Republic of Ireland. 21 January 2005.

Edensor, T. 2000."Staging Tourism: Tourists as Performers." *Annals of Tourism Research* 27(2):322–344.

Fairbairn, H. 1992. Group Playing in Traditional Irish Music: Interaction and Heterophony in the Session. PhD. thesis in musicology. Cambridge University.

_____. 1994. "Changing Contexts for Traditional Dance Music in Ireland: The Rise of Group Performance Practice." *Folk Music Journal* 6(5): 566–599.

Foy, B. 1999. *Field Guide to the Irish Music Session: A Guide to Enjoying Irish Traditional Music in its Natural Habitat!* Boulder, Colorado: Roberts Rinehart Publishers.

Glassie, H. 1995[1982]. *Passing the Time in Ballymenone: Culture and History of an Ulster Community*. Bloomington and Indiana: Indiana University Press.

Graburn, N.H.H. (ed.).1976. *Ethnic and Tourist Art. Cultural Expressions from the Fourth World*. Berkeley: University of California Press.

Greenwood, D.J. 1989[1977]."Culture by the Pound: An Anthropological Perspective on Tourism as Cultural Commoditization in Hosts and Guests," in *The Anthropology of Tourism*, 2nd ed., ed.Valene L. Smith, pp. 171–185. Philadelphia: University of Pennsylvania Press.

Handler, R. and W. Saxton. 1988. "Dyssimulation: Reflexivity, Narrative and the Quest for Authenticity in 'Living History.'" *Cultural Anthropology* 3(3): 242–260.

Hannerz, U. 1996. *Transnational Connections: Culture, People, Places*. London and New York: Routledge.

Helbig, K.P. 2002. Being "Irish": The Market, Transnationalism and the Experience of Ethnicity. PhD. dissertation. University of Pennsylvania.

Helgasson, A. and G. Palsson. 1997. "Contested Commodities: the Moral Landscape of Modern Regimes."*Journal of the Royal Anthropological Institute* 3(4):451–471.

Jabbour, A. 1993."Forward,"in *Transforming Tradition: Folk Music Revivals Examined*, ed. Neil V. Rosenberg, pp. xi–xiii. Urbana and Chicago: University of Illinois Press.

Kaul, A. R. 2004. "At Work in the Field: Problems and Opportunities Associated with Employment During Fieldwork." *Anthropology Matters* 6:2.

_____. 2007. "On Tradition: Between the Local and the Global in a Traditional Irish Music Scene." *Folklife: The Journal of Ethnological Studies* 45:49–59.

Kirshenblatt-Gimblett, B. 1998. *Destination Culture: Tourism, Museums and Heritage*. Berkeley: University of California Press.

Kirtsoglou, E. and D. Theodossopoulos. 2004. "'They Are Taking Our Culture Away': Tourism and Culture Commodification in the Garifuna Community of Roatan." *Critique of Anthropology* 24(2): 135–157.

Kneafsey, M. 2002. "Sessions and Gigs: Tourism and Traditional Music in North Mayo, Ireland; Extracts from a Field Diary (A Fictional Account Based on Actual Events, People and Places)". *Cultural Geographies* 9(2):354–358.

_____. 2003. "'If It Wasn't for the Tourists We Wouldn't Have an Audience': The Case of Tourism and Traditional Music in North Mayo," in *Irish Tourism: Image, Culture and Identity*, ed. Michael Cronin and Barbara O'Connor. Clevendon, Buffalo, Toronto, Sydney: Channel View Publications.

Kopytoff, I. 1986. "The Cultural Biography of Things: Commoditization as Process." In *The Social Life of Things: Commodities in Cultural Perspective*, ed. A. Appadurai, pp. 64–91. Cambridge: Cambridge University Press.

Let's Go Ireland. 1996. M. K. Linask and A. Crapo (eds.). London: Macmillan Reference Books.

Livingston, T.E. 1999. "Music Revivals: Towards a General Theory." *Ethnomusicology* 43(1):66–85.

Lovering, J. 1998. "The Global Music Industry: Contradictions in the Commodification of the Sublime," in *The Place of Music*, ed. A. D. Leyshon and M.G. Revill, pp. 31–56. New York: Guilford Press.

Mauss, M. 1954[1924]. *The Gift: The Form and Function of Exchange in Archaic Societies*. London: Cohen and West.

MacCannell, D. 1989[1976]. *The Tourist: A New Theory of the Leisure Class*. Berkeley: University of California Press.

Mbaiwa, J.E. 2004. "The Socio-Cultural Impacts of Tourism Development in the Okavango Delta, Botswana." *The Journal of Tourism and Cultural Change* 2(3): 163–184.

McCann, A. 2001."All That is Not Given is Lost: Irish Traditional Music, Copyright, and Common Property." *Ethnomusicology* 45(1): 89–101

McCann, Anthony. 2002. *Beyond the Commons: The Expansion of the Irish Music Rights Organisation, the Elimination of Uncertainty, and the Politics of Enclosure*. Ph.D. diss., Limerick: University of Limerick.

McCarthy, M. 1999. *Passing It On: The Transmission of Music in Irish Culture*. Cork: Cork University Press.

Miller, D. 1995. Consumption and Commodities.*Annual Review of Anthropology* 24:141–161.

Munroe, A. 1984. *The Folk Music Revival in Scotland*. London: Kahn and Averill.

Nesper, L. 2003. "Simulating Culture: Being Indian for Tourists in Lac du Flambeau's Wa-Swa-Gon Indian Bowl." *Ethnohistory* 50(3): 447–472.

Schutte, G. 2003. "Tourists and Tribes in the 'New' South Africa." *Ethnohistory* 50(3): 474–487.

Selwyn, T. 1996. "Introduction," in *The Tourist Image: Myths and Myth Making in Tourism*, ed. T. Selwyn, pp. 1–32. Chichester: Wiley.

Shepherd, R. 2002. "Commodification, Culture and Tourism." *Tourist Studies* 2(2): 183–201.

Stevenson, L. 2003. Commodification and Authenticity in the Traditional Music and Tourism Initiative. Paper presented at the Conference on Developing Cultural Tourism. University of Nottingham, December 2003. (Available online: www.nottingham.ac.uk/ttri/pdf/conference/lesley.pdf)

Trilling, Lionel. 1972. *Sincerity and Authenticity*. Cambridge, Massachusetts: Harvard University Press.

Urry, J. 2002[1990]. *The Tourist Gaze: Leisure and Travel in Contemporary Society*. Sage: London.

Vallely, F. 1999. "Revival," in T*he Companion to Irish Traditional Music*, ed. F.Vallely, p. 318. Cork: Cork University Press.

Wang, N. 2000. *Tourism and Modernity: A Sociological Analysis*. Oxford: Pergamon.

Williams, C.C. 2002. A Critical Evaluation of the Commodification Thesis. *The Sociological Review* 50(4):525–542.

White, B. 2000. "Soukouss or Sell-Out?: Congolese Popular Dance Music as Cultural Commodity," in *Commodities and Globalization: Anthropological Perspectives*, ed. A. Haugerud, M. P. Stone, and P. D. Little, pp. 33–57. Oxford and New York: Rowan and Littlefield.

12

The Maasai and the Lion King: Authenticity, Nationalism, and Globalization in African Tourism

Edward M. Bruner

Early work on the anthropology of tourism documented a variety of tourist experience in terms of a typology of tourism, including ethnic, cultural, historical, environmental, and recreational tourism (Smith 1989:4–6), as well as a typology of tourists, including explorer, elite, mass, individual traveler, backpacker, and charter tourists (Cohen 1979; Pearce 1982; Smith 1989:11–14). All tourism and all tourists were not the same, but scholars in the field tended to reduce the variety by seeking the essence of the tourist experience, as a quest for authenticity (MacCannell 1976), a personal transition from home to elsewhere (Graburn 1989), a form of neocolonialism (Nash 1989), or a particular type of "gaze" (Urry 1990). The typologies of tourism and tourists ordered the data but yielded few insights. Exceptions to the generalizations were common, rendering questionable their usefulness; one was never sure when or where the general propositions were applicable.

More recent field studies of tourism among particular peoples have tended to avoid typologies and monolithic generalizations, but still there is a predilection to homogenize local tourist displays.[1] The Maasai are represented as male warriors (Bruner and Kirshenblatt-Gimblett 1994), the Pueblo as female potters (Babcock 1990), the Balinese as living in a magical world of dance and drama (Bruner 1996b; Picard 1996; Vickers 1989), and the Tahitians as representing South Seas sensuality (Kahn 2000). In such cases, a single form of tourism becomes associated with one ethnic group in a given locality, similar to the effect that Appadurai (1988) observes for ethnography, where the connection between topic and place becomes the defining characteristic of a people, to the exclusion of other perspectives, for example, caste with India, lineage with Africa, or exchange with Melanesia. Tourism scholarship thus aligns itself with tourism marketing, in that scholars tend to work within the frame of the commercial versions of their sites. Grand statements about the nature of tourism in Bali or Africa or even more broadly in the "Third World" are sometimes the result, to the neglect of more ethnographically based and nuanced analyses of the variety of tourist displays within any one culture area.

My objective in this article is to open up the theoretical dialogue in tourism scholarship, and I do so by applying a method of controlled comparison (based on Eggan 1954), showing how one ethnic group, the Maasai, are exhibited for tourists at three different sites in Kenya. Although all three sites present a gendered image of the Maasai warrior (the personification of masculinity), a controlled comparison enables me to describe three ways of producing this image. Accordingly, I demonstrate how the breadth of meanings, ironies, and ambiguities in tourist performances emerges from a critical comparison of the processes of their production. For example, familiar concepts in the literature (such as authenticity, tradition, and heritage) are relevant in only certain touristic contexts. I emphasize the importance of the distinction—not fully appreciated in the anthropological literature—between domestic and foreign tourism, as well as the wide-ranging impact of globalization on the staging of local tourism.[2] Further, I show that historically forms of tourism are parallel to forms of ethnographic writing. Finally, I examine the sites in terms of what I call the "questioning gaze," my reference to tourists' expressed doubts about the veracity of what they are seeing and the way their questions and skepticism penetrate the commercial presentation, undermining the producer's dominant narrative.[3]

Elsewhere I have offered humanistically oriented descriptions of tourist performances privileging political complexities and local voices (Bruner 1994, 1996a, 1996b). My emphasis in this article is on the production and on the tourists, not on indigenous perceptions. My intention is to discuss each of the three sites so that the comparisons and juxtapositions between them become grist for the theoretical mill. What I say about any one site is designed to contrast with another.

By way of background, Kenya achieved independence from Britain in 1963 and has a population of approximately 30 million divided into about 42 ethnic groups. The tensions between these many ethnic groups have been severe at times. Tourism is a major source of income, the main attraction being safari runs to view the wild animals in the game parks. The Maasai, presented at the three tourist sites I discuss, are a seminomadic pastoral group with a total population of about 400,000 in Kenya; Maasai also live in Tanzania (Spear and Waller 1993).

My three Kenyan field sites are Mayers Ranch (Bruner and Kirshenblatt-Gimblett 1994), a privately produced performance organized by local entrepreneurs; Bomas of Kenya, a public production developed by the national government; and what a tour agency calls an "Out of Africa Sundowner" party at the Kichwa Tembo tented safari camp near the Masai Mara national reserve.[4] A thumbnail sketch of each site follows.

Designed for foreign tourists, the production at Mayers staged Maasai dancing in their warrior compound, chanting and carrying spears, proud and aloof. The production hid all outside influences and manufactured objects, presenting Maasai as timeless and ahistorical. Mayers reproduced a nineteenth-century colonial narrative (Knowles and Collett 1989) of Maasai men as exemplars of an African primitive, as natural man. It depicted Maasai men as brave warriors, tall and athletic, men who, at least in the past, would raid for cattle, kill lions armed with but a spear, consume raw foods such as milk and blood, and (as "Lords of East Africa") instill respect and fear in others. The producers strived for tourist realism (the aura of authenticity), and the site was designed as a series of tableaux, set up for tourist photography. The tourists viewed the Maasai from a colonial subject position, as did early explorers and ethnographers. Mayers began in 1968 and flourished until the 1980s but was eventually closed by the government, as the colonial aspects were offensive to many Kenyans. I will discuss the relations between tourism and ethnography later, but I note here that the critique of colonialism within anthropology (Asad 1975; Hymes 1972; Marcus and Fischer 1986) was part of the same worldwide anticolonial movement that led to the closing of Mayers Ranch in Kenya. Mayers is presented here as a baseline, as a superb example of postcolonial tourism that eventually gave way to newer modes of production.

Bomas is a national folklore troupe that presents the dances of Kenyan ethnic groups, including the Maasai, primarily for an audience of modern urban Kenyans. The mechanisms of production are prominently displayed. The dances are staged in an auditorium, with rows of seats and a bar in the back for the sale of refreshments. The theme of the production is Kenyan nationalism, to show that all the ethnic groups of Kenya are equally valued. Representatives of Bomas say that their aim is the preservation of Kenyan heritage, as if each ethnic culture is in the past and has to be recuperated in a museum-like setting. Bomas is an ethnic theme park for domestic tourists, a genre now found in many areas of the developing world.[5]

The Sundowner presents Maasai men dancing in the context of an "Out of Africa" cocktail party near an upscale tented safari camp on the Mara reserve. The Maasai performers mix with the tourists, who are served drinks and hors d'oeuvres by uniformed waiters. Globalizing influences are apparent, as Hollywood pop culture images of Africa and blackness are enacted for these foreign tourists as they sip champagne, alternately chatting among themselves and dancing with Maasai, all the while on safari in the African bush. These are posttourists (Feifer 1985; Urry 1990:100–102), beyond traditional tourism, who want a gracious African experience, all the comforts and luxury of home, and a good show rather than staged authenticity.

At all three tourist sites, Maasai men perform for an audience, but there are important differences. These differences are evident in the modes of transportation taken by the tourists to each site, and I describe them here, as the journey to a tourist destination is itself an inherent part of the tourist experience. Mayers is located in the Rift Valley about fifty minutes by car from Nairobi. Most tourists reached Mayers over dirt roads as passengers in a van provided by a local tour company. Bomas is located on the outskirts of Nairobi along the public bus route, and a convenient way of going is to drive or to take a city bus. Kichwa Tembo safari lodge is located by the Masai Mara reserve. In 1999, to take one example in which I participated, a group of tourists on the Intrav agency "Out of Africa" tour first visited Ngorogoro Crater in Tanzania, then went by a small charter aircraft directly from Kilimanjaro Airport in Tanzania to the Kichwa Tembo private airstrip in Kenya. The planes did not stop in Nairobi or go through Kenyan immigration or customs.[6] They flew directly from Tanzania to Kenya, over nation-states, in a seamless journey from one game park to another, indeed a transnational experience. From the perspective of the tourists, there was no border crossing, as the "nations" of Tanzania and Kenya were not really experienced. The tour was above borders, traveling not just in airspace but in global space. Travel by van, public bus, and charter aircraft characterize the three tourist attractions.

First, I summarize briefly the material on Mayers and then contrast these data with Bomas and the Sundowner. The latter sites will receive most of my descriptive and analytic attention. Although this study deals with Kenya, I suggest that the different contexts of production may be replicated in many other areas of the world where tourism is prominent. For reasons I explain in the conclusion, my claim is that my approach in this article has relevance beyond Kenya.

Mayers Ranch

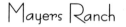

Mayers Ranch was built by the Mayers, a British family who became Kenyan citizens. The Mayers came to Kenya early in the twentieth century, eventually went into cattle ranching, drastically reduced their land holdings after Kenyan independence, and in 1968 established a tourist attraction on their land as a way of generating additional income. There have been four generations of Mayers in Kenya. Their current homestead, located in the Great Rift Valley 30 miles from Nairobi, is blessed with a natural spring and features a verdant lawn and English garden. The Mayers hired local Maasai, some from families who had worked on their cattle ranch as herders, to build a Maasai *manyatta* (compound) for young warriors who would perform their dances and enact selected aspects of their culture for tourists. After viewing the Maasai performance, the tourists would then go to the Mayers's lawn for tea and crumpets.

The transition from the mud huts and brown dust of the Maasai compound to the lush green lawn and garden adjacent to the Mayers's main house enacted a key theme in East African tourist discourse, the contrast between the primitive Maasai and the genteel British, which evokes the broader contrast between the wild and the civilized. The tourists at Mayers experienced vicariously the wildness of the Maasai and, by extension, the wildness of Africa, only to return at the end of the performance to the safety of the Mayers's cultivated lawn, to the veritable sanctuary of a British garden in the Rift Valley. The Maasai dancers never spoke directly to the tourists. They carried spears and clubs, wore a solid red cloth, covered their bodies with red ochre, and braided and decorated their hair. On the elegant lawn, the Mayers were gracious, socializing with the guests and telling stories about colonial times, while two black servants (not Maasai) dressed in white aprons and white chef's hats served tea and cookies. As white settlers, the Mayers themselves were part of the tourist attraction, nostalgic relics of a colonial era. The performance was a fastidious and carefully constructed combination of tribalism and colonialism, which the tourists told me they found fascinating and romantic.

The show at Mayers Ranch was carefully edited and produced. The Maasai performers (or actors) were not allowed by the Mayers (the directors

Maasai warriors with spears at Mayers Ranch. (Photo by Edward M. Bruner)

of the drama) to wear or display modern clothing, watches, or any industrial manufactured objects. The only souvenirs sold at Mayers were those hand-crafted by Maasai. The entire performance was produced to achieve tourist realism, an ambience of authenticity, and the appearance of the real. The Mayers directed the Maasai to act as if they were what the foreign tourists regarded as nineteenth-century tribesmen, the African primitive. The ritual performed at the Maasai village was made to seem natural, as if the Maasai were dancing for themselves and the tourists just appeared there by chance. The constructedness of the site was masked. Some of the Maasai dancers had been to school and spoke English, but during performance time they remained aloof and mute.

I first gathered data from Mayers in 1984; when I returned in 1995, I learned that the performance had been closed. During lunch at the Mayers's home, Jane and John Mayers explained to me why they had been put out of business, and they did so, of course, from their own subject position, as descendants of a white British colonial family. It was a combination of fac-tors, they said, but the primary reason was that the government felt they were exploiting the Maasai. The Mayers reported that an African-American tour group visiting the ranch to watch the Maasai performance had objected strongly, complaining about its colonial aspects—specifically that the May-ers lived in a big house whereas the Maasai lived in mud huts, and that the Mayers gave food to the Maasai as part of their compensation, which they felt was paternalistic. The Mayers's brochure said that the Maasai were a lin-guistic subgroup of the Nilotic, but other black American tourists objected strongly to the term *subgroup*, which they regarded as insulting. The key fac-tor, however, according to the Mayers and others in the tourism industry, was that many Kenyans felt the performance of Maasai warriors dancing in a European homestead was simply too anachronistic for modern-day Kenya.

After closing the tourist performance, the Mayers remained on their ranch and engaged in other income-producing activities. They missed the income from tourism, but Jane expressed a feeling of relief, saying they had felt "totally invaded" having 150 tourists come to their home on any given day. Jane agreed that a performance about tribalism and colonialism was indeed an anachronism in contemporary Kenya and felt it would be best if the Maasai were producing their own performance. Some of the Maasai who had worked at Mayers went to the hotels in Mombasa and the coast where they found employment as performers in Maasai tourist productions, and a few became involved in the sex industry, catering mainly to European women seeking a sexual experience with a Maasai man.

Rosaldo (1989) coined the phrase "imperialist nostalgia," noting that contemporary Western peoples yearn for the "traditional" cultures that the previous generation of Western colonialists had intentionally destroyed. Ros-aldo's concept is not entirely adequate for my purposes as it refers primarily to a feeling (a yearning). Cultural tourism goes far beyond this yearning, recreat-ing in performance idealized colonial images and other representations of the past, the pastoral, the original, and the unpolluted. Tourism frequently enacts imperialist nostalgia. Tourism performances, throughout the world, regularly reproduce stereotypic images, discredited histories, and romantic fantasies. The past is manipulated to serve the expectations of the tourists and the political interests of those in power, and because the Mayers, as ex-colonialists, had little power in modern Kenya, their operation could be closed. Mayers Ranch, a good example of tourism artfully produced in the postcolonial era for a foreign audience, catered to the darkest desires of the tourist imaginary, fixing Maasai people in a frozen past, representing them as primitive, denying their humanity, and glorifying the British colonialism that enslaved them.

Bomas of Kenya

The second attraction discussed in this article, Bomas of Kenya, constructs a different picture, for a different audience. Bomas, opened to the public in 1973, is a government museum of the performing arts, an encyclopedic presentation of the cultural heritage of a nation, performed by a professional dance troupe whose members are government employees.[7] Their Web site says Bomas "offers Kenya in Miniature" (Bomas of Kenya 2000). Like Mayers, Bomas has regularly scheduled daily shows. The patrons pay admission, move into a 3,500–seat auditorium for the performance, and then exit from the building to walk to the 11 traditional minivillages.[8]

Each village features the architecture of a particular ethnic group—Kikuyu, Kalenjin, Luhya, Taita, Embu, Maasai, Kamba, Kissii, Kuria, Mijikenda, and Luo—and consists of a few houses typical of that group, or as the Bomas Web site says "the original traditional Architecture . . . as built by the ancestors" (Bomas of Kenya 2000). Significantly, there is no claim that the houses are those of contemporary peoples. Handicrafts are available for purchase in each village. The crafts shown, however, are not restricted to those produced by the members of any one ethnic group but are representative of all Kenyan groups, comparable to the crafts that can be found in any souvenir shop in Nairobi. Nor are the sellers necessarily members of the same ethnic group as those in whose village the array is located. A Kikuyu seller, for example, might be found in the Maasai village. Further, no one actually lives in the villages; they are for display purposes only.

National dance troupes have been established in Uganda, Senegal, Mali, and most other African nations as part of government policy, just as performance troupes, ethnic village complexes, nations in miniature, and national museums have been established in many countries of the world. These sites differ, of course, but a general aim is to collect, preserve, and exhibit the art, culture, and history of a nation. To quote from a mimeographed information program distributed by Bomas of Kenya, "We specialize in traditional dancing and preservation of Kenya Cultural Heritage." The word *preservation* is a key. Whereas at Mayers the claim is that the Maasai are still living as they have for "a thousand years" and are essentially unchanged, Bomas talks of preserving, which implies that traditional ways no longer exist, that they are in danger of disappearing, that they belonged to the ancestors. Bomas makes a claim very different from the discourse directed toward foreign tourists. At Mayers, the Maasai occupy space in the ethnographic present; at Bomas they, and the other Kenyan groups, are in the traditional past.

At the top of the Bomas program one finds "REF: NO.BK/15/11," a reference number, typical of government documents everywhere. Other evidence of a nationalistic emphasis is easy to find. For example, the performance troupe calls itself the "harambee dancers." Coined by Jomo Kenyatta, the first president of Kenya, *harambee* is a powerful national slogan that means roughly "all pull together" (Leys 1975:75). In Kenya there are many harambee groups, sometimes called self-help or cooperative groups, and, indeed, there is a national harambee movement. The program distributed at Bomas consisted of six pages, including advertising, and described each act or scene in sequence—there were 22 in all. The last act, called the finale, was described as follows: "This is a salute in praise of His Excellency Hon. Daniel Arap Moi the President of the Republic of Kenya." Such statements render the performance of traditional dancing explicitly nationalistic.

The Bomas harambee dance troupe consists of members of many different ethnic groups, and any member of the troupe may perform the dances of any of the other Kenyan groups. At Mayers, Maasai performed Maasai dancing, but at Bomas a Kikuyu dancer, for example, could do the dances of the Maasai, the Samburu, the Kikuyu, or any group. Bomas creates an ensemble of performers from different groups who live together at Bomas as a residential community in a harambee arrangement, almost as an occupational subculture, apart from their extended families and home communities. The harambee dancers from Bomas are available for hire all over the world and have made overseas tours to the United States, the United Kingdom, Sweden, Japan, and other countries.

The troupe acts as a single functioning unit, detaching ritual dancing from its home community and putting it in a museum, a professional theater, or on the national or international stage. The troupe becomes an explicit model of the nation, melding diversity into a modern organization, disconnecting heritage from tribe. The implicit message of Bomas is that tribal dances belong to the nation. By separating cultural forms from tribal ownership, Bomas asserts that the multiethnic heritage of Kenya is now the property of all Kenyans. As an expression of nationalist ideology, Bomas speaks about tribalism as memory, in performance, where it is less threatening.

Bomas tells a story for Kenyans about themselves and appeals most to urban Kenyans. Their Web site states that visitors can see "rural Kenyan life" (Bomas of Kenya 2000). On Sunday afternoons, Bomas is crowded with local families who come with their children. Whereas the Mayers were hosts to foreign tourists and, on Sundays, to a resident expatriate British community, Bomas is host to a few foreign tourists but mostly to urban Kenyan families.[9] Businessmen meet there for conversation over beer or coffee. It is a place for Kenyans to honor their ethnicity in an urban setting, to see dances that they might not otherwise have an opportunity to witness. Bomas also arranges special shows for schools and educational institutions in the mornings, two days a week, highlighting their educational function.

For purposes of this article, it is important to understand how Kenyan tourist discourse uses such terms as *tribalism, traditional, modern, primitive,* and *civilized.* The six-page program of Bomas does not once contain the term *tribal* or *tribesmen,* and it uses the word *tribe* only twice, and then merely descriptively, as the equivalent of people or group," in contrast, *tribal* and *tribesmen* are crucial terms in tourist discourse for foreigners. The tourist brochures issued by private tour companies advertising trips to Kenya for an American or European audience use *tribal* with the implicit idea that the people so characterized are primitive and representative of an earlier state of existence. Significantly, the term used in the Bomas program is *traditional,* which contrasts with *modern.* The Kenyan audience at Bomas consists of modern urbanites, and what they witness on stage are their own traditional dances, part of a previous historical era, reflecting on their own present modernity in composite ways. Although sometimes used in the Kenyan media, the terms *tribal* and especially *tribalism* have a negative connotation in contemporary Kenya, as they have in many of the multiethnic nations of the world. The Kenyan government has long acknowledged deep-rooted ethnic identifications as a serious national problem (Chilungu 1985:15; Okumu 1975).

In brief, *tribal* is a term for foreign tourists used at Mayers, *traditional* is a term for domestic tourists used at Bomas, and *ethnicity* is a more neutral term, used by some Kenyans and anthropologists alike to avoid the derogatory or misleading connotations of *tribal* or *traditional.* The terms have different associations in touristic, ethnographic, and political discourse. Bomas, in a sense, has taken the concept of the tribe, and put it in the archives or in the museum, where hopefully, it will be safe and out of the way.

The language of the Bomas program is revealing. Here are excerpts describing two of the Bomas acts:

> The background to this item is the assassination of Nakhabuka, a young and beautiful girl of Abamahia clan in Bunyala (Western Kenya). Her jealous boyfriend shoots her with an arrow at the river, because she has married someone else. Her great spirit enters the body of one of the villagers and demands that a wrestling dance be performed occasionally in her memory.

> This item features a Giriama couple who are getting married. Unfortunately, the bride, having been bewitched just before the ceremony, threatens to refuse her man. It takes the skill of a famous medicine man to bring her back to agreement before the wedding can continue. The events of the wedding are heralded by the Gonda dance (performed mainly around Malindi on the Northern Coast of Kenya).

This is the genre of the folktale. Embedded in the Bomas program are mini folktales, dramatic narratives about everyday life. The stories are culturally and geographically specific. They refer to the Abamahia clan or to a Giriama couple and to such actual places as western Kenya or the north coast. These are real places. There is none of the generalized language of much of the tourist discourse produced for a foreign audience with its vague references to the untouched African primitive.[10] The function of such generalized references to tribesmen or to primitives is to distance the object, to depersonalize, to separate the tourist from the African. The Bomas stories, on the other hand, tell about the heritage of specific groups, ones with which the Kenyan audience can identify. That the stories tell about being bewitched, about a famous medicine man, and about spirits is part of the magical language of the folktale, but it also reflects a reality of Kenyan cultural life (Geschiere 1997).

Mayers was performed in a Maasai compound, and all Western objects were hidden from the audience. Bomas is performed in a modern auditorium that contains a restaurant and a huge bar. Before, during, and after the performance, members of the audience can order drinks. Mayers was characterized by an absence of signs; at Bomas there are signs everywhere, including ones that give the price of admission, directions to the auditorium, directions to the traditional villages, even signs that advertise Coca-Cola. Each of the villages has its own sign.

Bomas is professionally produced with such technical virtuosity that it seems like a Kenyan Ziegfeld Follies, with professional lighting, sound effects, and with the performers in matching costumes. At Bomas, the performers are clearly on stage and they smile at the audience, whereas at Mayers the Maasai were preoccupied with their dancing. At Mayers, toward the end of the dancing, the audience was invited to come on to the outdoor stage to view the performers close up, and to photograph them, whereas at Bomas there is an unbridgeable gap between the actors and the audience. The audience at Bomas does not mix with the actors on stage. Bomas gives one the feeling of being at a concert or at a theatrical production, and, indeed, Bomas employed an American producer for a time.

Mayers had a close fit between the performance and the setting and that was part of the message. Bomas has a lack of fit between the performance and the setting, and that too is part of the message. The genre of Mayers was tourist realism. The genre of Bomas is nationalist theater. Although both are studiously produced, Mayers was made to seem underproduced, and Bomas overproduced. The aim at Mayers was to mask the artifice of production. The aim at Bomas is to expose the processes of production so as to create a discontinuity between the production and what it is designed to represent. Mayers denied change. Bomas highlights change. Bomas detaches culture from tribe and displays it before the nation for all to see and share, and in the process Bomas aestheticizes, centralizes, and decontextualizes ritual. Ironically, what Bomas represents is what British colonialism was trying to achieve, the detribalization of Kenya. The British tried, but eventually failed, to turn Kenyans into colonial subjects. Bomas succeeds, in performance, in turning Kenyans into national citizens. Disjunction at Bomas is a rhetorical strategy, whereas at Mayers the strategy was to stress continuity. Mayers was a Western fantasy. Bomas is a national wish fulfillment. Mayers and Bomas are equally political and each tries to present its own version of history. Mayers was not an accurate reflection of contemporary Maasai culture, neither is Bomas an accurate reflection of Kenyan traditionalism.

Out of Africa Sundowner

Kichwa Tembo Tented Camp is described in the brochure as "luxurious enough for even the most pampered traveler," with private sleeping tents, electricity, insect-proof windows, a veranda, and an indoor bathroom with hot showers.[11] So much for roughing it in the African bush. The camp is located near the Masai Mara National Reserve, which is an extension of the Serengeti. The main attraction at the camp is game viewing from safari vehicles, but the Maasai are also prominent. There are Maasai at the private airport welcoming the incoming tourists, Maasai dancing at the camp, a scheduled visit to a Maasai village, and a briefing on Maasai culture by a Maasai chief, who began his talk to the tour group I joined by saying in English, "I think all of you must have read about the Maasai." I choose, however, to discuss the Out of Africa Sundowner party held on the Oloololo escarpment on the bank of the Mara River.

This performance introduces a new note into ethnic tourism in Kenya. The Sundowner is basically a cocktail party with buffet on a river bank in the bush. The Kichwa Tembo staff set up a bar, with a bartender in red coat, black pants, white shirt, and bow tie. The attraction is called the Out of Africa Sundowner, from the 1985 Hollywood movie starring Robert Redford and Meryl Streep, based on Isak Dinesen's (1938) book about colonial days in Kenya. *Out of Africa* (1985) was also shown to the tour group on the airplane en route to East Africa. The brochure from the tour agency describing the Sundowner says, "Standing at the precipice of the escarpment, the sun setting low amidst an orange and pink sky, it is easy to see why Africa so inspired Karen Blixen and Dennis Finch-Hatton." The brochure invites the tourists to experience the Sundowner, not from the point of view of the movie or the actors, or the book or the author, but rather from the point of view of the main characters in the story. It is all make-believe. At the Sundowner, waiters serve drinks and food to the tourists standing in groups or seated together in clusters of folding chairs. Then the Kichwa Tembo employees form a line, singing and dancing for the tourists, and the Maasai men begin their chanting and dancing. The performance is remarkable in a number of respects.[12]

During the dance, individual Maasai dancers come among the tour group, take the hands of tourists, and bring them into the line to dance with them. The other Maasai dancers smile in approval and visibly express their appreciation of the dance steps now also performed by the tourists. The remaining tourists laugh and comment; most nod in sympathy and enjoyment. A few of the dancing tourists look uncomfortable but make the best of

Smiling Maasai dancing with tourists at the Sundowner. (Photo by Edward M. Bruner)

the situation, while others rise to the occasion, dancing away, swinging about wildly, improvising, introducing dance steps ordinarily seen in an American disco. After the dance, the Maasai again mix with the tourists, this time passing out free souvenirs—a necklace with carved wooden giraffes for the women and a carved letter opener for the men. These curios are given as if they were personal gifts, but actually the tour agency at the camp buys these items for distribution at the Sundowner. It is all smiles and politeness.

At the Sundowner, the Maasai warrior has become tourist friendly. Gone is the wildness, or the illusion of wildness, or the performance of wildness, to be replaced by a benign and safe African tribesman. In Mayers Ranch, the particular appeal was precisely the tension between the wild Maasai and the cultured Englishman, but at the Sundowner that binary opposition is dissolved. At the Mayers performance, the tourists moved between two distinct spaces, the Maasai manyatta and the Mayers's lawn, the African space and the English space, the wild and the civilized. The Maasai did not enter the Mayers's area, for to do so would be a violation and would destroy the touristic illusion. At the Sundowner, however, the two spaces have merged—there is no separation between the Maasai and the tourists, but only one performance space where the two intermingle. By breaking the binary, ethnic tourism in Kenya is structurally changed (Sahlins 1981).

During the dancing at the Sundowner, the camp employees begin to sing a Kenyan song called "Jambo Bwana," written in the mid-1980s by a musical group called "Them Mushrooms."[13] The song was first performed in a tourist hotel in Mombasa, became an instant hit, and is still known through-out Kenya. Them Mushrooms moved from Mombasa to Nairobi, established their own recording studio, and have performed abroad.

The message of "Jambo Bwana" is that tourists are welcome in Kenya, which is characterized as a beautiful country without problems. One tour agent in Nairobi said it is now the "tourist national anthem" of Kenya, as it is so popular with foreign tour groups. Prominent in the song is the Swahili phrase "Hakuna Matata," which in one version is repeated four times and means "no worries, no problem." The phrase itself has a history. In the 1970s, there was political turmoil in Uganda and in the states surrounding Kenya. During this time, "Hakuna Matata," although always part of coastal Swahili language, came to be widely used as a political phrase, to say that Kenya is safe; it was reassuring to refugees as well as to the citizens of Kenya. After Them Mushrooms wrote "Jambo Bwana" in the mid-1980s, the phrase "Hakuna Matata" became more associated with tourism.

"Hakuna Matata" is familiar to tourist audiences as the title song from the Hollywood movie *The Lion King* (1994), with music by Elton John and lyrics by Tim Rice. The lyrics repeat the phrase "Hakuna Matata," defining it as follows:

> Hakuna Matata!
> What a wonderful phrase
> Hakuna Matata!
> Ain't no passing craze
>
> It means no worries
> For the rest of your days
> It's our problem-free philosophy
> Hakuna Matata! [14]

The hotel employees at the Sundowner then sang "Kum Ba Yah," an Angolan spiritual, popular in the United States as a folk, protest, and gospel song. Despite its African origins, "Kum Ba Yah" is now established in U.S. popular culture and has taken on new American meanings. The phrase "Hakuna Matata" has been similarly appropriated and is associated with *The Lion King* (1994).

At the Sundowner, the performers present "Kum Ba Yah" with a Jamaican reggae rhythm, a musical tradition that, to many North Americans, equates good times, blackness, dancing, and Caribbean vacations. [15] In other words, Africans have taken a phrase and a song originating in Africa and have performed it for the tourists with a New World Caribbean reggae beat. This musical tradition and the songs themselves, "Hakuna Matata" and "Kum Ba Yah," have been widely interpreted in American popular culture as expressions of "Africanness" and "blackness," and then have been re-pre-sented to American tourists, by Africans, in Africa. What is new is not that transnational influences are at work, that a song or an aspect of culture flows around the globe, as ethnographers are already familiar with these processes.

Nor is it new that a global image of African tribesmen is enacted for foreign tourists, as this is also the case at Mayers. What is new is that, at the Sundowner, the Americans, who have presumably made the journey in order to experience African culture, instead encounter American cultural content that represents an American image of African culture. The Americans, of course, feel comfortable and safe, as they recognize this familiar representation and respond positively, for it is their own.

This is globalization gone wild: Paul Gilroy's (1993) "Black Atlantic," transnationalism as a Lacanian mirror image, and Appadurai's (1991) "scapes" as a ping-pong ball, bouncing fantasy back and forth across the Atlantic. A reggae Lion King in the African bush. Points of origin become lost or are made irrelevant. Old binaries are fractured. The distance is narrowed between us and them, subject and object, tourist and native. Ethnography is transformed into performance, blurring the lines between genres in ways that go beyond Geertz (1983). What is left are dancing images, musical scapes, flowing across borders, no longer either American or African but occupying new space in a constructed touristic borderzone (Bruner 1996b; cf. Appadurai 1991) that plays with culture, reinvents itself, takes old forms and gives them new and often surprising meanings.

The colonial image of the Maasai has been transformed in a postmodern era so that the Maasai become the pleasant primitives, the human equivalent of the Lion King, the benign animal king who behaves in human ways. It is a Disney construction, to make the world safe for Mickey Mouse. Presented in tourism are songs that have African roots but that in North America and probably globally are pop culture images of Africa and blackness. Black Africa in the American imagination has been re-presented to Americans in tourism.

At the Sundowner, tourists receive drinks, food, a good show, an occasion to socialize, a chance to express their privileged status, an opportunity to experience vicariously the adventure of colonial Kenya, and a confirmation of their prior image of Africa. As posttourists in a postmodern era, they may also revel in the incongruity of the event, of dancing with the Maasai, of drinking champagne in the African wilderness. But what do the Maasai receive? The answer must be seen against the backdrop of what the Maasai received at Mayers and receive at Bomas. The Maasai performers at Mayers received a small daily wage for each performance in which they participated, a measure of ground maize, and a pint of milk a day. They derived additional income from the sale of their handicrafts and from the tips they received by posing for tourist photographs. They were wage laborers, as are the performers at Bomas.

The Maasai on the Mara, however, are part owners of the tourist industry and receive a share of the profits from safari tourism, but this is neither readily apparent nor ordinarily disclosed to the tourists.[16] The tourists see only what is exhibited to them in performance, but there is a vast behind-the-scenes picture. The Maasai receive 18 percent of the gross receipts of the "bed nights," the cost of accommodations at Kichwa Tembo per night per person. This can be a considerable amount as there are 51 units at the camp and the cost per night could be US$300 to US$400 in high season, or over US$100,000 per week with full occupancy (Kichwa Tembo 2000). There are a total of 22 camps and lodges on the Mara, some even more luxurious and expensive than Kichwa Tembo. The entrance fee to the Masai Mara Reserve is US$27 per person per day, and Maasai receive 19 percent of that fee. The percentages of 18 and 19 (odd figures) were the result of a long process of negotiation. The funds are accumulated and given to two county councils, and in one of these, the Transmara Council, where Kichwa Tembo is located, the funds are divided among the "group ranches," each based on one of the ten Maasai clans that own land on the reserve.

The Maasai ownership of most of the land on the reserve, as well as the land on which the camps and lodges are built, is the basis of their receiving a share of the gross receipts. Philip Leakey (a brother of Richard Leakey) reports that before the 1980s, Kenyan elite and foreign investors derived almost all of the income from international tourism (personal communication, February 19, 1999; see also Berger 1996). As a result, most Kenyans including Maasai were indifferent or even hostile to tourism, as they did not profit from it. Further, there was considerable poaching in the game parks. The depletion of the wildlife on the East African reserves posed a danger to the national heritage of Kenya and to the natural heritage of the world, not to mention that the deterioration of game threatened the entire tourism industry and with it a key source of foreign exchange. Things changed in the 1980s, as it was widely recognized that the way to gain the support of the Maasai for tourism development was to give them a stake in the industry, which the Maasai had argued for. Since then, there has been a drastic reduction in poaching on the reserve. The Maasai, who do not usually eat wild game, now have a financial interest in protecting the animals and in stopping poaching. Further, a new law was passed stipulating that anyone caught poaching in Kenya may be killed on sight.

The Maasai profit from tourism on the Mara in other ways. There are 170 park rangers on the reserve, and all are Maasai. The Kichwa Tembo package includes a visit to a Maasai village, where the villagers receive the US$10 per person admission fee as well as the profits from the sale of handicrafts. One day I counted 80 tourists, for a total income of US$800. When the Maasai perform their dances for tourists, they receive compensation. One group consisting of about 15 Maasai received US$163 per performance. Again, tourists are not usually aware of these financial arrangements. Some Maasai on the Mara are wealthy by Kenyan standards, but that wealth is not visible to the tourists. Most Maasai have used their income to increase their herds of livestock—cows, sheep, and goats—which are kept away from the tourist routes.

Maasai are employed at Kichwa Tembo not only as waiters, chefs, and security guards, but in management positions as well. Yet, the tourists do not "see" these employees as Maasai. In the hotel context, the Maasai waiters are reserved and deferential in their white uniforms, avoiding eye contact with tourists and speaking only when spoken to. If waiters were to overstep the bounds of appropriate service behavior they would be reprimanded, whereas if the same Maasai performing for tourists as warriors behaved deferentially, they would be a disappointment to the spectators. All parties understand the behavior appropriate in each position, for it is a mutually understood symbolic system, and each party to the drama performs an assigned role. Within the lodge, the tourists are usually polite to the waiters but are disinterested, for they are perceived as service employees. Kichwa Tembo camp is a space that provides the comfort, luxury, and safety on which upscale tourism depends.

In contexts in which the Maasai are performing as "Maasai," on display for tourists, it is tourist time. The Maasai men, adorned with red ochre, wearing red robes, beadwork, and sandals, and carrying sticks, change their demeanor—they become warriors. In performance, in these contexts, the tourists become voyeurs—there is a cornucopia of visualization, and the simultaneous clicking of many cameras. Ironically, in the same day a single individual might be a deferential waiter in the hotel during the serving of a meal, but a Maasai warrior, one of the "Lords of East Africa," during performance time in the evening.

The Maasai, of course, are well aware of the discrepancy between their own lifestyles and their tourist image, and they manipulate it, but there are many complexities in the situation. Some Maasai, who have in effect become performers in the tourism industry, display themselves for tourists, to be observed and photographed, and if asked, they reply that they do it for the money. They play the primitive, for profit, and have become what MacCannell (1992) calls the ex-primitive. This is the case for performers at all three sites, at Mayers, Bomas, and the Sundowner. Tourism for them is their livelihood, a source of income. On the other hand, I knew one Maasai business executive who assumed "ethnic" Maasai traits only during his nonworking hours. He dressed in Western clothing with shirt and tie during the work week in Nairobi, where he spoke English, but on most weekends, wearing jeans and a T-shirt, and speaking Maasai, he would return to his native village to become a pastoralist to attend to his extensive herd of livestock. On ceremonial occasions, he would wear traditional Maasai clothing and dance and chant in Maasai rituals. To put it another way, what touristic or ethnographic discourse characterize as Maasai "ethnic" traits, may, in tourism or in life, be displayed situationally, depending on the context, which is probably the case universally for all ethnicities. Identities are not given; they are performed by people with agency who have choices.

But boundaries are elusive. As de Certeau (1984) suggests, spatial patterns are not composed of rigid unbreakable regulations, flawlessly executed, but are spatial practices, characterized by transgression, manipulation, and resistance, as individuals appropriate space for themselves. I give two examples. While watching the dancing at the Sundowner, I noticed one man, a waiter in black pants and white shirt, who picked up a club and began dancing along with the red-robed Maasai. He was out of place, apparently a Maasai waiter who decided to join his fellow tribesmen, but it was a broken pattern.

At Kichwa Tembo, one of the tourists, an African-American woman, had taken an optional nature walk with Maasai guides. During the walk they came upon a pride of 12 lions. The woman reported that she had never been so scared in her life, but the Maasai guides urged calm and slowly moved the group away from the lions without incident. After that dramatic encounter, while resting and chatting, the woman showed the Maasai guides a picture of her grown daughter, a strikingly beautiful woman. One of the guides announced to the woman that he wanted to marry the daughter, but the woman passed it off and they continued on the nature walk. Later, back at the camp, the Maasai man came to the woman with his father, a marriage spokes-man, and offered 25 head of cattle for the daughter, with the implication of a still larger offer, a huge bride-price. The father urged the woman to consult with her own marriage brokers, and then to meet again to negotiate—a Maa-sai practice. When the woman told me about this incident, I playfully sug-gested that the least she could have done would have been to transmit the offer to her daughter and let her make her own decision. But the woman replied that her daughter was finishing her studies at a prestigious law school in California, was very driven and ambitious, and would not want to be the second wife of a Maasai villager. Boundaries are not rigid—tourists and natives do move into each other's spaces.

Maasai then are incorporated into the safari tourism industry on the Mara in a dual capacity. First, they are part owners, possibly partners, and cer-tainly beneficiaries. Second, they are also performers in a touristic drama, a secondary attraction to the wild animals on the reserve, but clearly objects of the tourist gaze. As the Maasai receive a share of the profits and a stake in the industry, the question may be asked, to what extent do they control the images by which they are represented? My observations suggest that if the Maasai now have economic and political power, they do not exercise it to influence how they are presented in tourism. As the Maasai say, they are in it for the money and are willing to play into the stereotypic colonial image of them-selves to please their clients, the foreign tourists. As one Maasai explained to me, the European and American tourists do not come to Kenya to see some-one in Western dress, like a Kikuyu. The Maasai put on the red robes and red ochre and carry clubs so the tourists will be able to recognize them as Maasai.

Who is producing the Sundowner Maasai? Kichwa Tembo tented safari camp was built by the tour agency Abercrombie and Kent, but was recently sold to another company, Conservation Corporation Africa. Regardless of the particular company involved, the Out of Africa Sundowner is produced by tour agencies and, by extension, by international tourism to meet a demand. Tourism is marketing, selling a product to an audience.

The production is skillful because the hand of the tour agency is masked in the presentation of the Maasai. It is the Maasai dancers who dis-tribute gifts directly to the tourists at the Sundowner (with gifts provided by the tour agent), it is the Maasai chief who collects the $10 fee to enter the village (but it is the tour agent who selects the village), and it is a Maasai (hired by the tour agent) who provides explanations of Maasai culture. At Mayers, the entrance fee was given to the Mayers or to their staff, and the staff provided the commentary on Maasai lifeways. It was apparent at Mayers that white Europeans were explaining and producing Africans, with all its colonial overtones. At Kichwa Tembo, however, Maasai explain Maasai culture, but briefly, as most tourists are not really interested in a deeper ethnographic understanding. In Maasai tourism generally, at Mayers, Bomas, and the Mara, there is a master narrative at work, but it is usually implicit, a background understanding. On site, textual content is less prominent than evocative visualizations, songs, dance, and movement. In a sense, the producer is more important in Maasai tourist attractions than the writer. At the Mara, a casual observer might say that the Maasai are producing themselves, but I believe it more accurate to say that the tour agents are the primary producers, with the Maasai at best relegated to a minor role. The role of the tour agent is concealed, which is part of the production.

If the Maasai at the Mara are behaving in accordance with a generalized Western representation of Maasai and of African pastoralists, then tourism in a foreign land becomes an extension of American popular culture and of global media images. The startling implication, for me, is that to develop a new site for ethnic tourism, it is not necessary to study the ethnic group or to gather local data, but only to do market research on tourist perceptions. I know these statements are somewhat conjectural, but is it too speculative to contemplate that the Maasai will eventually become (rather than just appear as) the pop culture image of themselves? I do not believe in the homogenization of world cultures caused by globalization, for local cultures always actively assert themselves, and I would argue for the long-term integrity of the Maasai. But the issue is raised, how well will the Maasai continue to compartmentalize themselves and separate performance from life? The line separating tourist performance and ethnic ritual has already become blurred in other areas of the world with large tourist flows, such as Bali. The Balinese can no longer distinguish between performances for tourists and those performances for themselves, as performances originally created for tourism have subsequently entered Balinese rituals (Bruner 1996b; Picard 1996). Where does Maasai culture begin and Hollywood image end?

Writing Tourism and Writing Ethnography

To summarize thus far, Mayers presented the tourist image of the African primitive, Bomas presents the preservation of a disappearing Kenyan tradition, and the Sundowner an American pop-culture image of Africa. The tourists at Mayers sat on logs facing the performance area in a reconstructed Maasai village, at Bomas they sit in tiered auditorium seats facing the stage, and at the Sundowner on folding chairs on the escarpment as the performance evolves around them. The performance and the setting were concordant at Mayers; are detached at Bomas; and at the Sundowner, the most global message is delivered in the most natural setting, along a river bank in a game reserve. Mayers served English tea, Bomas serves drinks at the bar, while the waiters at the Sundowner pour champagne. The binary opposition at Mayers is between the African primitive and the civilized Englishman; at Bomas it is between traditional and modern Kenyans; and at the Sundowner, the binary is dissolved because the performance presents what the tourists interpret to be their own transnational media image of Africa. The master trope at Mayers was tourist realism, at Bomas it is undisguised nationalism, and at the Sundowner it is a postmodern image.

Mayers, Bomas, and the Sundowner differ in many respects but all three sites combine tourism, theater, and entertainment. All take simultaneous account of the prior colonial status, local politics, national forces, and global international requirements. I have emphasized globalization at the Sundowner site, but there clearly are global dimensions to Mayers and Bomas. Mayers (as tourist realism) and Bomas (as national theater) are examples of transnationalism, and both arose in Kenya as an extension of the postcolonial condition, one for foreigners and the other for locals, for as Oakes (1998:11) says, both authenticity and tradition are themselves modern sensibilities. In the 1960s, Mayers reworked a nineteenth-century colonial narrative for foreigners, and Bomas is a recent variant for domestic tourists of public displays of living peoples. Such displays have a history dating back to European folk museums (Horne 1992), World Fairs (Benedict 1983), and even earlier (Kirshenblatt-Gimblett 1998:34–51; Mullaney 1983). Bomas most resembles the ethnic theme parks of contemporary China (Anagnost 1993), Indonesia (Bruner 2000; Errington 1998; Pemberton 1994), and other nations (Stanley 1998).

Viewed historically, the three tourist sites parallel three different forms of ethnographic writing. Mayers Ranch can be likened to ethnographic realism—it strived for an aura of authenticity based on a prior image of what was believed to be the authentic African pastoralist. When Mayers was opened in 1968, colonialism was gone in Kenya, a thing of the past, but there were still many British expatriates and a worldwide longing for a colonial experience—an enacted imperialist nostalgia—that Mayers produced for the expatriate community and foreign tourists.

Authenticity has figured prominently in tourism scholarship since Boorstin (1961) and MacCannell (1976). Boorstin characterizes tourist attractions as pseudo-events, which are contrived and artificial, as opposed to the real thing. MacCannell sees modern tourists as on a quest for authenticity, which is frequently presented to them as "staged authenticity," a false front that masks the real back stage to which they do not have access. For both Boorstin and MacCannell, there is a real authentic culture located somewhere, beyond the tourist view. Contemporary anthropologists would not agree with the early work of Boorstin and MacCannell, for as anthropologists now know, there are no originals, and a single "real" authentic culture does not exist. Of course, all cultures everywhere are real and authentic, if only because they are there, but this is quite different from the concept of "authenticity," which implies an inherent distinction between what is authentic and what is inauthentic, applies labels to cultures, and values one more than the other. There is no one authentic Maasai culture, in part because Maasai culture is continually changing and there are many variants. If one were to identify, say, a nineteenth-century version of Maasai culture as the real thing, one could then look further, back to the eighteenth century or to a more distant region, as the locus of the really real Maasai. It is an impossible quest.

The same vision is apparent in ethnographic realism (Marcus and Fisher 1986; Rosaldo 1989; Tedlock 2000), the basic mode of ethnographic writing until the 1960s. The classic monographs in Africa (e.g., Evans-Pritchard 1940) did not describe what the ethnographers actually observed at the time of their fieldwork but were a construction based on the prevailing anthropological vision of a pure unaltered native culture. As in anthropology, where the hypothetical ethnographic present was discredited and colonialism criticized, so too was Mayers Ranch disparaged and eventually closed. Mayers existed historically before either Bomas and the Sundowner, but it was an anachronism, doomed from the beginning.

An effort to influence the political culture of Kenya, Bomas emerged in response to those forces that led to political activism within anthropology during the 1970s, the epoch of the civil rights movement and the emergence of new nations. The genre is ethnographic activism. Bomas depicts traditional Maasai culture as fast disappearing, requiring that it be preserved in museum archives or in artistic performance. As a collective past, Maasai culture as represented at Bomas becomes part of the national heritage of postindependence Kenya. Bomas is a response to the intense nationalism that characterized many newly independent multiethnic Third World countries. The basic problem for the nation was how to express ethnicity yet simultaneously to contain it, a problem not yet resolved in many African states.

The Sundowner is an outgrowth of global media flows, electronic communication, and pervasive transnationalism. It is for foreign post-tourists, produced in the style of postmodern ethnography. Unlike Mayers, it rejects the realist genre. Unlike Bomas, it rejects nationalist rhetoric. Postmodern ethnography describes juxtapositions, pastiche, and functional inconsistency, and recognizes, even celebrates, that cultural items originating from different places and historical eras may coexist (Babcock 1999). Contemporary ethnographers no longer try to mask outside influences, nor do they see them as polluting a pure culture (Bruner 1988).

In performance, the Sundowner is more playful. It intermingles elements from the past and the present, is less concerned about points of historical origin, and does not strive for cultural purity. The comparison is not quite that neat, however, as the Sundowner tourists do occupy a colonial position and do want to view "primitive" Maasai; nevertheless, there has been a shift in the stance of the audience. Post-tourists at the Sundowner are willing to dance with the Maasai and joke with them, and they are not that fastidious about authenticity. But postmodern tourists, and ethnographers, have not entirely overcome the contradictions of their modernist and colonial pasts. Many postmodern ethnographers, it must be recognized, still struggle with an inequitable colonial relationship and vast differentials in wealth and power between themselves and the people they study. Further, ethnographers, as those who write, control how culture is represented.

That the three sites correspond to different genres of ethnographic writing is not unexpected, as both tourism and ethnography are disciplinary practices, products of the same worldwide global forces. Ethnographers are not entirely free from the dominant paradigms of their times. As an ethnographer studying tourism, ethnographic perspectives are reflected back to me by the very tourist performances that I study. The predicament, of course, is not restricted to an anthropology of tourism; it is inherent in the ethnographic enterprise (Bruner 1986).

The Questioning Gaze

I use the phrase the "questioning gaze" to describe the tourists' doubts about the credibility, authenticity, and accuracy of what is presented to them in the tourist production. The key issue is that tourists have agency, active selves that do not merely accept but interpret, and frequently question, the producers' messages (Bruner 1994; Jules-Rosette and Bruner 1994). In Bomas, authenticity both is and is not an issue—it depends on which Kenyan is speaking, as there is no monolithic local voice. Some Maasai are illiterate, others have been educated at Oxford University; some live in the game parks, others in the city; some are pastoralists, others are doctors, lawyers, and businessmen; some have a stake in the tourism industry, others have not. Urban Kenyans I know have told me they enjoy seeing their native dances at Bomas, as they do not travel frequently to their home areas, and even when they do they are not assured of witnessing a dance performance. They respect the ethnic diversity exhibited at Bomas, and they appreciate the performance as well as the entire Bomas experience. In addition to the dancing, Bomas features picnic sites, a children's playground, football, volleyball, badminton, table tennis, and a swimming pool. In other words, it is more than a display of Kenyan ethnic culture for intellectuals, ethnographers, and foreign tourists; it is a family recreational site.

Yet not all local observers share this view. Originally from Uganda, Christine Southall (a scholar specializing in East Africa) suggested to me that many Kenyan intellectuals laugh at parts of the Bomas performance, criticizing the inaccuracies in its representation of tradition and regarding its characterization of the various ethnic groups as inauthentic. In 1999, Jean Kidula, a Kenyan musicologist who has worked with the Bomas performers, explained to me that Bomas is a failed project because the original objectives were not achieved. The aim in the early 1970s was to construct a national dance troupe that would accurately perform the ethnic arts of Kenya. She feels that the dances now performed are not authentic so that Bomas has become a tourist thing, folkloristic, and commercial. The difficulty was that once the dance troupe was formed the performers began to innovate, and over the years the original tribal dance forms were changed. Kenyan people, she says, understand this but keep going to Bomas primarily because it is entertaining. To these two scholars, authenticity is important, and they criticize Bomas for not achieving it.

Commenting to me on Bomas, Jane Mayers said that "it's not true in any respect," meaning that the Maasai dance at Bomas is not necessarily performed by Maasai, that no one lives in the villages, and that their dance troupe is professional. The questions become, what is seen as true, and how does a performance derive its authority? There are different meanings of authenticity (Bruner 1994), but from my perspective, Mayers, Bomas, and the Sundowner are not authentic in the sense of being accurate, genuine, and true to a postulated original.

Anthropologists, at least in the past, have tended to regard tourism as commercial, even tacky. From the perspective of realist ethnography, tourism is a disgraceful simplification, an embarrassment, like an awkward country cousin who keeps appearing at cherished field sites (Bruner 1989; de Certeau 1984). Some U.S. anthropologists, Kenyan intellectuals, and foreign tourists might experience Bomas as being superficial and inauthentic—but that would be to miss the point. At Bomas, traditional dances are placed in such a high-tech setting and the production is so professional that the dances become detraditionalized. The modern auditorium, the bar, the signs, and the commercialism are not necessarily experienced by Kenyan visitors as an intrusion, for they serve to remind the Kenyans that they are not in a tribal village but in a national folklore museum.

Although the issue for some Kenyan intellectuals is authenticity, the issue for many Kenyan tourists, based on my interviews, is doubt about the validity of the nationalistic message of Bomas. The message of the producers is not necessarily the one received by their tourist audience. Kenyan people from all segments of society are very well aware of the reality of ethnic conflict in Kenyan society, and hence those Kenyans who visit Bomas have their doubts about the ethnic harmony portrayed there. The understanding of Kenyans in this respect is similar to the Americans who celebrate the Abraham Lincoln rags-to-riches narrative that everyone can be president, yet they know that no American of African, Native, Asian, or Hispanic descent, and no woman or Jew, has been elected president of the United States.

In this sense, Bomas is like Lévi-Strauss's (1967:202–228) definition of a myth, in that it tries to resolve a contradiction between a vision of Kenyan national integration and the reality of ethnic conflict and separatism, just as in the United States the Lincoln myth tries to resolve a contradiction between an ideology of equality and an actuality of discrimination. The function and the promise of national myths is to resolve contradictions, if not in life, then in narrative and performance. Nor is it a false consciousness, as the Marxists would have it, for most Kenyans and Americans are aware of these discrepancies.

At Mayers Ranch, many tourists had their own doubts, which they expressed to me, for the performance was too picture perfect, too neat and well scheduled, and the back stage of the performance as well as the actualities of Maasai life were too well hidden. Tourists vary, for to be a tourist is not a fixed slot to be occupied but is a role to be fashioned and performed (Jules-Rosette and Bruner 1994). Some tourists willingly surrendered themselves to the experience of the Mayers performance. One tourist told me that he was on vacation in Africa to relax, and he simply accepted whatever was offered to him. For him, there was no questioning gaze, or at least it was suppressed. Others behave as if they are in a graduate anthropology seminar. They are obsessed with issues of authenticity and question the truth value of everything. They ask, "Are these Maasai for real?"

One American student at Mayers Ranch during my visit kept muttering to herself and to anyone else who would listen that the Maasai were being exploited, which may have been the case. The African-American tourists who complained about Mayers to the Kenyan government did not see the performance as the producers intended, as a story about the English and the Maasai, but focused on skin color, as an example of whites producing blacks. This is interesting as it exports an American political sensibility to an African context (Bruner 1996a). Tourists, however, like the rest of us, have the ability simultaneously to suspend disbelief and to harbor inner doubts, and sometimes to oscillate between one stance and the other. The questioning gaze may be pushed aside, so that tourists may delight in the excitement and danger of being with the Maasai and play, in their imagination (even temporarily and tentatively) with the colonial slot into which they are being positioned. For them, Mayers was good theater, and many made a conscious effort to engage the Mayers fantasy and to identify with the plot and the characters, at least during performance time, despite inner doubts.

The Intrav tour agency that took the group to the Sundowner was skilled and sophisticated in catering to upscale tourists. It was an "Out of Africa" tour not just in the sense of the Isak Dinesen book, but in the sense of being literally "out" of Africa, above Africa, so as to protect the tourists from hassles, waits, and crowds, and to shield them from experiencing the darker side of Africa—the poverty, starvation, brutality, disease, dirt, corruption, and civil wars. The Sundowner itself went smoothly but there was an earlier instance, a memorable occasion in Tanzania, when Africa broke through the bubble. The tourists I spoke with were very disturbed about it. On a trip from Lake Manyara to Ngorogoro Crater, over a two-hour ride, the cars carrying the tourists passed a number of painfully poor Tanzanian villages. As each village came into view, emaciated children dressed in rags ran after the cars with outstretched hands, hoping for a handout, and they continued running even after the cars had passed far beyond them. The drivers did not stop, but I saw many of the tourists continuing to look back along the dusty road at the desperate children. Afterward, with pained expression, one woman tourist commented on the shocking disparity of wealth between the members of the tour group and the Tanzanian villagers, noting the contrast between our luxury and their poverty. Another said she felt ashamed to have spent so much money on a vacation while these villagers had nothing. It was a fleeting but significant moment. The tourists talked about it for days and were obviously distraught. Its significance extended beyond that one specific incident to the entire tourist itinerary, raising the larger question in the tourist consciousness, what else was being concealed on their tour of Africa? The incident materialized an inner doubt. By carefully orchestrating the "Out of Africa" tour, the agency had tried to suppress and silence parts of Africa, but they did not entirely succeed.

The tourists' identification with Africans in this instance is reminiscent of the position of the character Dennis Finch-Hatton in Isak Dinesen's *Out of Africa* (1938). In that book, Finch-Hatton, a white colonialist, casts a critical eye on the institution of colonialism, identifies with the independent pastoral Maasai, and is ultimately buried in a Maasai grave. In structural terms, he was a bridge between the civilized and the wild, flying freely over the African landscape, with the ability to move back and forth between the two domains of the binary. The tourists on the "Out of Africa" tour who participated in the Sundowner may want to be accepted, even blessed, by the primitive Maasai, if only temporarily, as a kind of absolution for the privileged position that haunts the edges of their dreams. They may relish the gifts, smiles, and dancing on the Sundowner as evidence that they are liked, or at least welcomed, by the Maasai. The African-American woman on a walking tour with the Maasai who encountered the lions may retell that story, not only as a tale of unexpected adventure (always a source of good stories for tourists) but as a way of identifying herself with the Maasai.[17]

At Mayers, Bomas, and the Sundowner, there are always doubts among the tourists about what they are "seeing," doubts that differ from tourist to tourist, but that move beyond what has so artfully been constructed for them. The questioning gaze is a penetration of the constructedness devised by the producers, but it is also more, in a number of respects. First, there is always an unpredictability of meaning about any performance, for individuals attribute their own understandings to the event, which may not be predicted in advance, and these understandings may change over time. Second, some tourists apply a frame to the activity of sightseeing and to everything else that occurs within the tour. A well-traveled tourist, for example, once whispered to me as we were about to watch a performance, "Here comes the tourist dance." It made no difference to her what particular ethnic dance was on display, except that it was presented within a touristic frame. It was a tourist dance, period. For other tourists, more inclined to surrender, an immersion in the physicality of the dance activity itself was more important than any explanation or attribution of meaning. This verges on what Kirshenblatt-Gimblett

(1998:203–248) describes as an avant-garde sensibility, where the experience itself is more important than the hermeneutics. Further, in many cases tourists simply do not understand what they are seeing and make no effort to interpret Maasai dance and culture. Even to those tourists most willing to open up to the experience and to accept the producers' fantasy, there is still, in MacCannell's terms, "an ineluctable absence of meaning to an incomplete subject" (2001:34). It is what Kirshenblatt-Gimblett (1998:72) has called the irreducibility of strangeness. Urry's (1990, 1992) tourist gaze is too empiricist, too monolithic, too lacking in agency, and too visual to encompass these varied tourist reactions. The tourist gaze does not have the power of Foucault's (1979) panopticon, for it is not all-seeing and enveloping. It is variable, and there are seepages and doubts.

In this article, I have described how the Maasai of Kenya are displayed in three tourist sites originating in different historical eras and in disparate social milieus. I emphasize that touristic representations of a single ethnic group are multiple and even contradictory. I also discuss the parallels between tourism and ethnography especially evident in the concept of the questioning gaze. I demonstrate how ethnicity, culture, and authenticity gain and lose meanings in diverse touristic and world contexts. My approach has been to study local tourist performances by the methods of ethnography, to take account of tourist agency, and then to compare systematically the various sites with attention to the national and global frames within which they are located. Constructionism, my main theoretical thrust, is not an escape from history or ethnography. Such an approach enables the ethnographer to explore similarities and differences, to embrace complexity, and to open up new possibilities.

Source: From the *American Ethnologist*, 2001, 28(4):881–908. Reprinted with permission of the author and the American Anthropological Association.

Acknowledgments

Early versions of this article were presented at a conference on tourism in September 1999 at the Department of Anthropology, Yunnan University, Kunming, People's Republic of China, and in January 2000 at the University of Illinois workshop on sociocultural anthropology. I am indebted to the participants for helpful comments, to Alma Gottlieb, Arlene Torres, Nicole Tami, Richard Freeman, Bruno Nettl, the anonymous reviewers of *American Ethnologist*, and the University of Illinois Foundation and Ann and Paul Krouse for financial support enabling my wife and me to participate in the 1999 African trip. In all of my fieldwork, my wife, Elaine C. Bruner, has been an insightful and helpful partner.

Notes

[1] Recent works on tourism include Abram et al. 1997; Boissevain 1996; Castaneda 1996; Chambers 2000; Cohen 1996; Crick 1994; Dann 1996; Desmond 1999; Handler and Gable

1997; Kirshenblatt-Gimblett 1998; Lanfant et al. 1995; Lavie and Swedenburg 1994; Löf-gren 1999; Nash 1996; Oakes 1998; Picard 1996; Rojek and Urry 1997; Schein 2000; and Selwyn 1996.

[2] Adams 1998 and Cheung 1999 are exceptions.

[3] My "questioning gaze" was inspired by MacCannell's (2001) concept of the "second gaze," which he developed in opposition to Urry's (1990) "tourist gaze." I agree with most of Mac-Cannell's critique of Urry. See also Kasfir 1999.

[4] When referring to the Maasai people, current scholarly practice is to use a double *aa*, derived from the language group Maa. The game reserve Masai Mara, a proper name, is spelled with a single *a*.

[5] In 1984, Barbara Kirshenblatt-Gimblett and I did fieldwork together at Mayers Ranch, which we published, and at Bomas, which we did not publish. I returned to Kenya in 1995 and 1999, revisited old sites, gathered new data, and initiated fieldwork on Maasai tourism on the Mara, including the Sundowner. For the past 15 years, Kirshenblatt-Gimblett has influenced my work on the Maasai and on tourism.

[6] Members of the tour group had to obtain visas, but their passports were collected by the Intrav tour guides who handled all the immigration and customs arrangements.

[7] Bomas of Kenya was initiated by the government in 1971 and opened in 1973 under the Kenya Tourist Development Corporation, a part of the Ministry of Tourism and Wildlife.

[8] As there are 42 ethnic groups in Kenya, but only 11 traditional villages in Bomas, many groups are left out, although some are represented in performance. There is no representation of minorities such as the resident Indian population.

[9] It will be helpful to examine the charges for admission to the Bomas performance. At the time of my visit, a Kenyan citizen paid about one-third the amount charged to a foreign tour-ist, and a resident child paid only about one-third of the amount paid by a Kenyan adult, making it financially feasible for many Kenyans to come to Bomas for a family outing with their children.

[10] The African Classic Tours (1986) brochure states:

> Here in East Africa, we can still view the world as our primitive ancestors saw it, in its natural state, without the influences of modern civilization. . . . Here are the living remains of prehistoric human cultures, people who still live by hunting and gather-ing: nomadic peoples living in small family groups. Here we can view the daily struggle for survival . . . and see people and wildlife living, for the most part, unaf-fected by our rapidly changing society.

[11] All quotes are from the brochure for the Intrav "On Safari in Africa" trip February 2 to 25, 1999.

[12] At this point, I must acknowledge the ambiguity of my subject position especially at the Sun-downer, for I oscillated between being a tourist and being an ethnographer, on the one hand enjoying the scene, talking with the tourists, avidly taking photographs, and on the other hand studying the event, making ethnographic observations, and writing field notes (see Bruner 1996b). All ethnographers occasionally experience a similar oscillation, between being there as a participant in another culture (merging into the ongoing activity) and the demands of being a scholar, striving for the distance and objectivity necessary to write for an anthropological audience. I have felt this tension the most in my work on tourism rather than in other ethnographic endeavors (cf. Bruner 1999).

[13] I am indebted to Mulu Muia, Duncan Muriuki, and to Jean Kidula for helpful information on the musical scene in Kenya. I also note that data was gathered by modern electronic means, by e-mail, and the Internet. Bomas, Kichwa Tembo tented camp, and Them Mushrooms all have their own Web sites.

[14] I do not know the relationship between the use of Hakuna Matata in "Jambo Bwana" and in the Elton John–Tim Rice song. Neither the lyrics nor music are the same, but the phrase, Hakuna Matata, is equally prominent in both songs.

15 Them Mushrooms also are known for reggae, and for fusions of reggae with local musical traditions. Them Mushrooms are credited with recording, in 1981, the first reggae song in East Africa, with CBS Kenya Records. Their inspiration was Bob Marley, the Jamaican reggae musician (Them Mushrooms 2000). Reggae also has a political meaning, connected to the Rastafarians.

16 Wood (1999) reports that funds flow inequitably to the Maasai chiefs and politicians, and there have been many accusations of corruption. Berger (1996) discusses these inequities, offers solutions, and shows how the Maasai are being integrated into the tourism industry in Kenya. Kiros Lekaris, Stanley Ole Mpakany, Meegesh Nadallah, and Gerald Ole Selembo have helped me better to understand how the Maasai on the Mara do profit economically from safari tourism.

17 I thank an anonymous reviewer for the *American Ethnologist* for many of the ideas in this paragraph.

References

Abram, Simone, Jacqueline Waldren, and Donald V. L. Macleod, eds. 1997. *Tourists and Tourism: Identifying with People and Places*. Oxford: Berg.

Adams, Kathleen M. 1998. "Domestic Tourism and Nation-Building in South Sulawesi." *Indonesia and the Malay World* 26(75): 77–96.

Anagnost, Ann. 1993. "The Nationscape: Movement in the Field of Vision." *Positions* 1(3): 585–606.

Appadurai, Arjun. 1988. "Putting Hierarchy in Its Place." *Cultural Anthropology* 3(1): 36–49.

———. 1991. "Global Ethnoscapes: Notes and Queries for a Transnational Anthropology," in *Recapturing Anthropology: Working in the Present*, ed. Richard G. Fox, pp. 191–210. Santa Fe, NM: School of American Research Press.

Asad, Talal, ed. 1973. *Anthropology and the Colonial Encounter*. London: Ithaca Press.

Babcock, Barbara. 1990. "A New Mexican Rebecca: Imaging Pueblo Women," in *Inventing the Southwest*, [Special Issue] *Journal of the Southwest* 32(4): 383–437.

———. 1999. "Subject to Writing: The Victor Turner Prize and the Anthropological Text." [Special Issue] *Anthropology and Humanism* 24(2): 91–73.

Benedict, Burton. 1983. *The Anthropology of World's Fairs: San Francisco's Panama Pacific International Exposition of 1915*. London: Scolar Press.

Berger, Dhyani J. 1996. "The Challenge of Integrating Maasai Tradition with Tourism," in *People and Tourism in Fragile Environments*, ed. Martin F. Price, pp. 175–197. Chichester, UK: John Wiley and Sons.

Boissevain, Jeremy, ed. 1996. *Coping with Tourists: European Reaction to Mass Tourism*. Providence, RI: Berghahn.

Bomas of Kenya. 2000. Bomas of Kenya Limited. Electronic document available at http://www.africaonline.co.ke/bomaskenya/profile.html [accessed July 2, 2001].

Boorstin, Daniel J. 1961. *The Image: A Guide to Pseudo-Events in America*. New York: Harper and Row.

Bruner, Edward M. 1986. "Ethnography as Narrative," in *The Anthropology of Experience*, ed. Victor Turner and Edward M. Bruner, pp. 139–155. Urbana: University of Illinois Press.

———. 1988 [1984]. *Text, Play and Story: The Construction and Reconstruction of Self and Society*. Proceedings, American Ethnological Society. Prospect Heights, IL: Waveland Press.

———. 1989. "On Cannibals, Tourists, and Ethnographers." *Cultural Anthropology* 4(4): 438–445.

———. 1994. "Abraham Lincoln as Authentic Reproduction: A Critique of Postmodernism." *American Anthropologist* 96(2): 397–415.

————. 1996a. "Tourism in Ghana: The Representation of Slavery and the Return of the Black Diaspora." *American Anthropologist* 98(2): 290–304.

————. 1996b. "Tourism in the Balinese Borderzone," in *Displacement, Diaspora, and Geographies of Identity*, ed. Smadar Lavie and Ted Swedenburg, pp. 157–179. Durham, NC: Duke University Press.

————. 1999. "Return to Sumatra: 1957, 1997." *American Ethnologist* 26(2): 461–477.

————. 2000. *Ethnic Theme Parks: Conflicting Interpretations*. Paper presented at the annual meeting of the American Anthropological Association, San Francisco, November 16.

Bruner, Edward M., and Barbara Kirshenblatt-Gimblett. 1994. "Maasai on the Lawn: Tourist Realism in East Africa." *Cultural Anthropology* 9(2): 435–470.

Castaneda, Quetzil E. 1996. *In the Museum of Maya Culture: Touring Chichén Itzá*. Minneapolis: University of Minnesota Press.

Chambers, Erve. 2000. *Native Tours: The Anthropology of Travel and Tourism*. Prospect Heights, IL: Waveland.

Cheung, Sidney C. H. 1999. "The Meanings of a Heritage Trail in Hong Kong." *Annals of Tourism Research* 26(3): 570–588.

Chilungu, Simeon W. 1985. "Kenya: Recent Developments and Challenges." *Cultural Survival Quarterly* 9(3): 15–17.

Cohen, Erik. 1979. "A Phenomenology of Tourist Experiences." *Sociology* 13(2): 179–201.

————. 1996. *Thai Tourism*. Bangkok: White Lotus.

Crick, Malcolm. 1994. *Resplendent Sites, Discordant Voices: Sri Lankans and International Tourism*. Switzerland: Harwood Academic Publishers.

Dann, Graham M. S. 1996. *The Language of Tourism: A Sociolinguistic Perspective*. Wallingford: CAB International.

de Certeau, Michel. 1984. *The Practice of Everyday Life*, trans. Steven Rendall. Berkeley: University of California Press.

Desmond, Jane C. 1999. *Staging Tourism: Bodies on Display from Waikiki to Sea World*. Chicago: University of Chicago Press.

Dinesen, Isak. 1938. *Out of Africa*. New York: Random House.

Eggan, Fred. 1954. "Social Anthropology and the Method of Controlled Comparison." *American Anthropologist* 56(5): 743–763.

Errington, Shelly. 1998. *The Death of Authentic Primitive Art and Other Tales of Progress*. Berkeley: University of California Press.

Evans-Pritchard, E. E. 1940. *The Nuer*. Oxford: Oxford University Press.

Feifer, Maxine. 1985. *Going Places*. London: Macmillan.

Foucault, Michel. 1979. *Discipline and Punishment: The Birth of the Prison*, trans. Alan Sheridan. New York: Vintage.

Geertz, Clifford. 1983. *Local Knowledge: Further Essays in Interpretive Anthropology*. New York: Basic Books.

Geschiere, Peter. 1997. *The Modernity of Witchcraft: Politics and the Occult in Postcolonial Africa*. Charlottesville: University Press of Virginia.

Gilroy, Paul. 1993. *The Black Atlantic: Modernity and Double Consciousness*. Cambridge, MA: Harvard University Press.

Graburn, Nelson. 1989. "Tourism: The Sacred Journey," in *Hosts and Guests: The Anthropology of Tourism*, 2nd edition, ed. Valene L. Smith, pp. 21–36. Philadelphia: University of Pennsylvania Press.

Handler, Richard, and Eric Gable. 1996. *The New History in an Old Museum: Creating the Past at Colonial Williamsburg*. Durham, NC: Duke University Press.

Horne, Donald. 1992. *The Intelligent Tourist*. McMahons Point, New South Wales, Australia: Margaret Gee.

Hymes, Dell, ed. 1972. *Reinventing Anthropology*. New York: Vintage Books.

Jules-Rosette, Bennetta, and Edward M. Bruner. 1994. "Tourism as Process." *Annals of Tourism Research* 21(2): 404–406.

Kahn, Miriam. 2000. "Tahiti Intertwined: Ancestral Land, Tourist Postcard, and Nuclear Test Site." *American Anthropologist* 102(1): 7–26.

Kasfir, Sidney Littlefield. 1999. "Samburu Souvenirs: Representations of a Land in Amber," in *Unpacking Culture: Art and Commodity in Colonial and Postcolonial Worlds*, ed. Ruth B. Phillips and Christopher B. Steiner, pp. 66–82. Berkeley: University of California Press.

Kichwa Tembo. 2000. Kichwa Tembo Tented Camp. Electronic document available at http://www.ccafrica.com/destinations/Kenya/Kichwa/default.htm [accessed June 20, 2001].

Kirshenblatt-Gimblett, Barbara. 1998. *Destination Culture: Tourism, Museums, and Heritage*. Berkeley: University of California Press.

Knowles, Joan N., and D. P. Collett. 1989. "Nature as Myth, Symbol and Action: Notes Towards a Historical Understanding of Development and Conservation in Kenyan Maasailand." *Africa* 59(4): 433–460.

Lanfant, Marie-Françoise, John Allcock, and Edward M. Bruner, eds. 1995. *International Tourism: Identity and Change*. London: Sage.

Lavie, Smadar, and Ted Swedenburg, eds. 1994. *Displacement, Diaspora, and Geographies of Identity*. Durham, NC: Duke University Press.

Lévi-Strauss, Claude. 1967. *Structural Anthropology*, trans. Claire Jacobson and Brooke Grundfest Schoepf. New York: Anchor Books.

Leys, Colin. 1975. *Underdevelopment in Kenya: The Political Economy of Neo-Colonialism*. London: Heinemann.

The Lion King. 1994. Directed by Roger Allersand and Rob Minkoff. Walt Disney Pictures.

Löfgren, Orvar. 1999. *On Holiday: A History of Vacationing*. Berkeley: University of California Press.

MacCannell, Dean. 1976. *The Tourist: A New Theory of the Leisure Class*. New York: Schocken.

———. 1992. *Empty Meeting Grounds: The Tourist Papers*. London: Routledge.

———. 2001. "Tourist Agency." *Tourist Studies* 1(1): 23–37.

Marcus, George, and Michael M. J. Fischer. 1986. *Anthropology as Cultural Critique: An Experimental Moment in the Human Sciences*. Chicago: University of Chicago Press.

Mullaney, Steven. 1983. "Strange Things, Gross Terms, Curious Customs: The Rehearsal of Cultures in the Late Renaissance." *Representations* 3:45–48.

Nash, Dennison. 1989. "Tourism as a Form of Imperialism," in *Hosts and Guests: The Anthropology of Tourism*, 2nd edition, ed. Valene L. Smith, pp. 37–52. Philadelphia: University of Pennsylvania Press.

———. 1996. *The Anthropology of Tourism*. Oxford: Pergamon.

Oakes, Tim. 1998. *Tourism and Modernity in China*. London: Routledge.

Okumu, John J. 1975. "The Problem of Tribalism in Kenya," in *Race and Ethnicity in Africa*, ed. Pierre L. van den Berghe, pp. 181–202. Nairobi: East African Publishing Company.

Out of Africa. 1985. Directed by Sydney Pollack. Mirage Enterprises Production.

Pearce, Philip L. 1982. *The Sociology of Tourist Behavior*. Oxford: Pergamon.

Pemberton, John. 1993. "Recollections from Beautiful Indonesia (Somewhere beyond the Postmodern)." *Public Culture* 6(2): 241—262.

Picard, Michel. 1996. *Bali: Cultural Tourism and Touristic Culture*. Singapore: Archipelago Press.

Rojek, Chris, and John Urry, eds. 1997. *Touring Cultures: Transformations of Travel and Theory*. London: Routledge.

Rosaldo, Renato. 1989. *Culture and Truth: The Remaking of Social Analysis*. Boston: Beacon Press.

Sahlins, Marshall. 1981. *Historical Metaphors and Mythical Realities: Structure in the Early History of the Sandwich Islands Kingdom.* Ann Arbor: University of Michigan Press.

Schein, Louisa. 2000. *Minority Rules: The Miao and the Feminine in China's Cultural Politics.* Durham, NC: Duke University Press.

Selwyn, Tom, ed. 1996. *The Tourist Image: Myths and Myth Making in Tourism.* Chichester, UK: John Wiley and Sons.

Smith, Valene L., ed. 1989. *Hosts and Guests: The Anthropology of Tourism*, 2nd edition. Philadelphia: University of Pennsylvania Press.

Spear, Thomas, and Richard Waller. 1993. *Being Maasai: Ethnicity and Identity in East Africa.* London: James Currey.

Stanley, Nick. 1998. *Being Ourselves for You: The Global Display of Cultures.* London: Middlesex University Press.

Tedlock, Barbara. 2000. "Ethnography and Ethnographic Representation," in *Handbook of Qualitative Research*, 2nd edition, ed. Norman K. Denzin and Yvonna S. Lincoln, pp. 455–486. Thousand Oaks, CA: Sage.

Them Mushrooms. 2000. Electronic document available at:
http://www.musikmuseet.se/mmm/africa/mushrooms.html [accessed June 15, 2001].
http://stockholm.music.museum/mmm/africa/mushroom.html [accessed June 27, 2003].

Urry, John. 1990. *The Tourist Gaze.* London: Sage.

———. 1992. "The Tourist Gaze Revisited." *American Behavioral Scientist* 36(2): 172–186.

Vickers, Adrian. 1989. *Bali: A Paradise Created.* Berkeley: Periplus Editions.

Wood, Megan Epler. 1999. Ecotourism in the Masai Mara: An Interview with Meitamei Ole Dapash. *Cultural Survival* 23(2): 51–54.

13

Performing Traditional Dances for Modern Tourists in the Amazon

Palma Ingles

Throughout the Amazon basin today, companies that own tourist lodges and tour boats are bringing tourists into contact with indigenous groups that previously had limited contact with people from the developed world. Tourist trips to the Amazon, often advertised as ecotours, typically offer a variety of activities including bird-watching, hiking, fishing, and visits to indigenous communities. Many of these communities were relatively isolated until recently; residents grew subsistence crops, fished, and hunted to provide most of what they needed to feed their families. For over 400 years of recorded Amazonian history, contact with outsiders has most often been a losing proposition for indigenous peoples, resulting in loss of habitat, altered lifestyles, enslavement, disease, and even death. Today, some indigenous communities continue to discourage outsiders, while others seek ways to actively participate in the tourism enterprise.

This study focused on the impacts of tourism in the Upper Amazon region of northeastern Peru. My research was conducted in four indigenous communities that host and entertain tourists, embracing tourism as a way to increase household income. Generating enough income to buy school supplies, medicines, fuel, household necessities, tools, and clothing in today's economy can be a challenge for people in these communities. Most people are small-scale farmers, growing what they need to feed their families and selling the surplus at local markets. By bringing tourists to the villages, tourism is allowing community members to earn money in exchange for having their world viewed by outsiders. Without the incentive of this added income, these communities would not participate in tourism.

Peru is one of the poorest countries in the Western Hemisphere; up to 80 percent of its 29 million people (in 2008) are unemployed or underemployed, and many live in extreme poverty. In the Amazon, there are very few paid, full-time jobs, and most of these are in the urban areas. During the last 50 years some members of the communities in which I conducted my research found temporary employment with timber companies, extracting wood from nearby forests, or with outside companies, producing jute or collecting natural rubber in the area. Others sold wild meats and animal skins, or provided live animals from the forest to buyers traveling by river. As the modern world gets closer, however, communities in the Amazon are now trying to protect their remaining forested areas from harvest by outsiders, resulting in fewer jobs for locals in the timber industry. The number of jobs available in the production of natural rubber or jute has also dramatically diminished. The sale of wild animals or their skins likewise has decreased, due in part to stricter laws but also overhunting. As a result, some economic opportunities that were once available no longer exist.

Discouraged with the limited opportunities for making a living in the forest, migration to the cities continues to increase even though, once there, many people are faced with poor, unsanitary living conditions, crime, unsafe drinking water, and a scarcity of land for growing crops. The decision of whether to stay in the forest or move to the city can be very difficult for members of indigenous communities. They weigh the challenges of moving to the city, where they may find jobs and have access to better education for their families, against the chance that they may live in abject poverty in a city slum, always struggling to provide food. Although life in the forest presents its own daily challenges, most families can usually produce enough food to eat and have access to clean water. Nevertheless, people who continue to live in communities in the forest must also seek new ways to increase their household income. For them, tourism provides new opportunities.

Tourists who come to this region for an "authentic" Amazon adventure hope that their tour will bring them in touch with the wilds of the rainforest, including the "natives" living as if frozen in time like a photograph from a 1920s *National Geographic*. Although much has changed since the 1920s, many indigenous communities in the Amazon, as in other parts of the world, are willing to entertain tourists by packaging and displaying their culture and playing the role of the unchanged "primitive," donning traditional dress, performing traditional dances, and selling locally made handicrafts.

As international tourism continues to increase in the Amazon region, more people from the developed world are visiting indigenous communities in this remote area. The resulting guest–host interactions have the potential to substantially impact small indigenous Amazonian communities economically, environmentally, and culturally. Although some of the literature concerning impacts of tourism on small-scale societies focuses on the deleterious impacts, other research highlights the benefits. The impacts within a given situation should only be evaluated within a framework that considers the location of the individual community, the goals of its members, and the opportunities that exist for economic development and sociocultural change and preservation.

Some anthropologists, social activists, conservationists, and others concerned with development issues believe that tourism is unlikely to be a sustainable form of development for rural populations in developing countries. Problems linked to tourism in less-developed countries include cultural imperialism, foreign dependency, revenue leakages, the growth of socioeconomic inequality within communities, competition for and over use of resources, cultural commoditization and staged authenticity, and more (Brohman 1996; Cohen 1988; Mansperger 1995; McLaren 1999; Nash 1989; Silver 1993; Stymeist 1996; Weaver 1998).

The marketing of staged experiences with traditional cultures appears to be more prevalent in developing than developed countries (Haralambopoulos and Pizam 1996; McLaren 1999; Silver 1993). Tourists who travel to these areas hope to see the exotic and are willing to pay a premium price for it. Some researchers assert that when elements of the culture are staged, or modified for display, they lose their meaning for the locals as well as create a false experience for tourists (Cohen 1988; Greenwood 2004[1977]; Silver 1993). Others suggest that when indigenous people portray themselves and their lifestyle as locked in time, they slow their movement toward development and modernization.

The introduction of tourism to indigenous areas is not without its impacts, but the impacts may not be all negative. Researchers in support of tourism in indigenous areas suggest that some types of tourism, especially ecotourism, ethnic tourism, or cultural tourism, may be an equitable form of development for rural populations, which are becoming more involved with a market economy and the developed world (Healy 1994; Ingles 2002, 2005; Sofield 1993; Steinberg 1997). Some research suggests that controlled tourism can offer remote communities the opportunity to make extra income, without depleting the resources of the forest around them. The production of handicrafts in developing countries can offer families the opportunity to increase their household income in a sustainable manner, without incurring added hard physical labor or increasing deforestation to grow more market crops (Beavers 1995; Deitch 1989; Healy 1994; Ingles 2002, 2005). Families in the Amazon who work with tourism may be able to earn enough extra income from the production of handicrafts to lessen their dependency on the production of market crops. In turn, this may slow deforestation of areas used for slash-and-burn agriculture, now a leading cause of deforestation in the Amazon. If tourism or ecotourism to an indigenous area is designed so that it benefits the host population, the number of tourists is kept small, and the tourism in itself does not have a negative impact on the environment, then tourism has the potential to produce favorable results.

My research focused on four indigenous Amazonian communities involved with tourism. Three of these communities are located on the Ampiyacu River, a tributary of the Amazon. Santa Lucia is a Yagua community. Pucaur-quillo is divided into two, with the Bora occupying one half and the Witoto the other. It is conceived of as two separate communities with each ethnic group having its own tribal roundhouse. The fourth community is occupied by the Yagua and is located on the Yanamano River, another tributary of the Amazon.

The first tourists to arrive in the villages of the Boras and Witotos by Amazon Tours and Cruises' riverboats came in 1973 and to the Yaguas in 1992. The three communities on the Ampiyacu entertain groups of 10 to 40 tourists for less than two hours about twice a month. In 1997, larger luxury cruise ships also started visiting the communities each year in April and May when the water is high enough to accommodate large ships. They bring 80 to 200 passengers and stop at one village on the way up the river and another as they return down river. Most tourists are Americans (58%) or Europeans (40%); only 2 percent are from Peru (Wright 2000). In 1964, Explorama Lodges built a tourist lodge across from the village of Palmares II, the Yagua community on the Yanamano River. Guides from the lodge bring tourists to the village once or twice a week during the slow season, October through April, and once or twice daily during the peak tourist season, May through September. The majority of the visitors to the lodge are Americans (62%); the rest are from Europe and South America (Jensen 2000).[1]

My goal was to understand the nature of daily life for indigenous fami-lies who derive some of their income from tourism and to determine how important this income was to them relative to their subsistence activities (hor-ticulture, fishing, hunting, and the use of other forest products). The study also sought to understand the nature of the interaction between hosts and guests in each community and the implications of tourism for cultural preser-vation and the use and conservation of natural resources. In broad terms, the study hypothesized that controlled tourism offers members of these commu-nities an opportunity to increase household income, preserve elements of their cultures (traditional dress, dances, handicrafts) that have been passed down through the generations, and help prevent the overuse or depletion of forested resources by providing an alternative income to that earned from cutting lumber and growing crops for sale.[2]

As stated earlier, for most people in the Amazon eking out even a sub-sistence-level living is difficult. Households produce income by selling or trading surplus crops and extra fish at the market or within the community, selling timber or other forest resources, and from tourism. Some families make most of their income from tourism, while others use tourism to supple-ment their other cash-producing economic activities. Many of the community members who participate in tourism earn their tourism dollars by entertaining tourists with native costumes and dance, and from the sale of handicrafts.

Boras children enjoy some of the food villagers prepare for tourists. (Photo by Palma Ingles)

The communities visited by tourist riverboats receive between US$20 to US$50 (prices in 1998) from the company per tourist group, depending upon size of the group. This money is divided between all the dancers who perform—men, women, and children. The villagers negotiate with tour conductors so that they have a say in the number of tourists they receive and the amount of money they earn. Some tourists also bring T-shirts, hats, fishing gear, flashlights, and other items to trade with villagers and spend additional money on handicrafts. This makes it difficult to determine how much money individual households make from tourism because many handicrafts are traded for new or used goods from the tourists, which do not have an assigned value. The communities benefit collectively because many tourists donate pens, paper, and books and leave money with the local school. Most villagers believe that the money tourism generates is very important for their community. If they stopped hosting tourists, they said they would have to clear more forested land for slash-and-burn agriculture in order to grow more crops for the market to replace the lost income.

As members of the communities increase their market participation, they increase the amount of land needed for cultivation. In order to find new land to cultivate (through slash-and-burn), people have to locate their gardens further away from the village. In all of the communities in this study, the newest cultivated plots were usually 45 to 90 minutes' walk from the producers' homes. Locals must then transport their crops, fish, or other goods by canoe to market. Depending on the location of the village, this may require a full day of travel. Without refrigeration or proper storage, goods must be handled quickly once they are ready. If they have abundant surplus to sell, some villagers may opt to pay local passenger riverboats to transport themselves and their goods to market, which cuts into their potential profit.

Due to the difficulty of tending market crops located so far away from the village and of transporting them to market, many women with small children welcome the opportunity to produce handicrafts for tourism instead. In many cases, all members of the family are involved in making handicrafts (e.g., baskets, bead necklaces and purses, carved animals, blowguns, and arrows), including small children. When family members return from the fields or retreat from the sun, they work on making handicrafts. Several villagers noted that handicrafts can be produced under artificial light after dark, whereas agricultural crops cannot.

The people in these communities are now dependent on certain supplies from the modern world that can be obtained only through the exchange of goods or with cash. As seen in other areas of the Amazon, as indigenous people intensify their involvement with a market economy, they are increasingly caught up in a cycle of progress and development (Colchester 1989). This is the case in the communities in this study. As households have increased their market interaction and contact with outsiders, they have increased the amount of purchased goods they rely on. Families buy supplemental foods, matches, candles, kerosene, tools, clothes, radios, batteries, and other household items. Two of the four communities now have electricity a few hours a day, produced by gas generators that families must pay for. Families also have to pay a fee to the village schools, which are partially funded by the national government, as well as buy clothes and school supplies for their children. If tourism were to stop in these communities, they would have to find other ways to bring in cash.

Most members of the communities in my study said that tourism was very important to their community and that life in their communities had improved since they started working in tourism. They support tourism as an economic opportunity and are willing to play whatever role is needed as long as tourism produces income. They also recognize that by continuing to use traditional elements of their culture for tourist entertainment, they are keeping these traditions alive, which is especially important as their communities face new challenges and change brought on by development. Handicraft production also has its roots in antiquity; when asked where they learned to make their handicrafts, most people said from their ancestors. The items they produce (such as baskets and hammocks) are based on traditional designs, although some have been altered and adapted, and are made from locally available natural materials. Every household that I visited engaged in some type of handicraft production. As I conducted my interviews, many respondents worked on their crafts as they talked, explaining the materials they were using and the process involved. Even though buyers travel the rivers, visiting communities to buy handicrafts for resale in city markets, the prices they pay are much lower than those villagers can get by dealing directly with tourists, and may not be enough to warrant the time spent. Tourists often seek out handicrafts that have some practical use in the culture that produced them, such as natural fiber hammocks, bags, and baskets, or paintings on tree bark. Without the market for these crafts that tourism provides, the knowledge of how to make them may disappear.

The Yaguas living in Palmares II sell handicrafts to tourists who stay at the lodge across the river from their village, but, at the time of this research, they were no longer performing dances or ritual ceremonies for tourists. During the busiest season for the lodge, the Yaguas may get one to three groups of tourists a day visiting their village to tour the area and buy handicrafts. The constant flow of tourists through the village during peak season is often seen by the villagers as an interruption to their daily lives. The Yaguas and the lodge are separated by a small stream. Families bathe in the stream and wash their clothes in the stream. Before the lodge was built, the Yaguas would put up fishing nets across the stream to catch fish. Once the boats servicing the lodge began traveling the stream, the Yaguas could no longer string up nets, and the boats pollute the water they depend on. During the low water season, which corresponds with the busiest season for tourism, the stream is low enough that tourists can wade across the water. Villagers complained that tourists would often wander into their village on their own, causing further disruption to villagers' daily lives. However, many say the opportunity to sell handicrafts on a regular basis is worth the trade-off.

Before the lodge opened in 1964, the village had held private three- to four-day festivals that celebrated the planting and harvesting of crops or gave thanks and recognition to the gods and spirits that were part of their belief system. On these occasions, the entire village dressed in traditional costumes and performed dances that had been passed down from their ancestors. After the lodge was built, the Yaguas began performing their dances for visiting tourists and were paid to do so by the lodge. But after the owner of the lodge stopped paying them to perform for tourists, in about 1984, they stopped. Their own interest in their ceremonies was waning; many younger villagers who had watched the dances all of their lives did not know their significance or how to perform them, and as the elders who had responsibility for planning and organizing the festivals died, the ceremonies and traditions associated with them were at risk of being lost.

Leaders of the community expressed their desire to entertain the tourists once again with native costumes and dance, for pay. When I asked some members of the community if dressing in native costumes and performing traditional dances as entertainment for tourists would help preserve their traditional culture, many said yes. They stressed the importance of dance rituals in teaching elements of their culture to the younger children and the role they played in strengthening the village's cohesiveness. With all of the pressures for change, they wanted to maintain some of the cultural practices that had been passed down through the generations. They felt that playing the part of the "primitive" for the sake of the tourists would give them the opportunity to practice their rituals on a regular basis, thereby teaching the young people about their cultural heritage. Without the regular support (i.e., payment for performance) of the lodge company, however, they would not be able to encourage enough people in the community to participate on a regular basis. The elders agreed that without a revival of some of their traditional culture now, the young people would lose the opportunity to learn forever. In response, I suggested that they negotiate with the owner of the lodge, and I spoke to the lodge owner on their behalf. The ensuing negotiations between the elders and lodge owner were successful, and they reached an agreement whereby the lodge would contribute money to buy materials for the construction of a new ceremonial house and once again pay for dance performances.

The other communities in my study continue to perform their dances and wear traditional dress for tourists. When tourists arrive, they are escorted to a ceremonial roundhouse where villagers explain facets of their life in the Amazon and provide entertainment. Most communities in the Amazon traditionally had a ceremonial roundhouse where the whole community came together for meetings, ceremonies, and festivals. Today many communities no longer have one, unless they also use it for tourism. The communities of Boras, Witotos, and Yaguas continue to use their round houses both for tourism performances and for their own ceremonies that involve everyone in the community and, at times, last several days. For these special, private occasions, they perform traditional dances, feast on a variety of foods and beverages, tell stories, and often wear native dress. The young people in these

Dancing for tourists. (Photo by Palma Ingles)

communities have shown a renewed interest in learning about their ancestors' traditions, due in part to their participation with tourism and the money it brings. Elders believe that by continuing to showcase their traditions for tourists, their children are learning about their heritage. Tourism also gives them an opportunity to embrace elements of their culture that they must sometimes shed when working in other areas of the market economy. When tourists visit local villages, they hope to encounter a culture different from their own. As a result, most tourists visiting the communities in my study are eager to learn about the villagers' traditional practices. They also happily join in the dancing when invited, photograph themselves and the locals, and bargain over the displayed handicrafts for sale. Through the presence of tourists, locals become Indians for a day and share a glimpse of their own traditional culture with people from the "modern" world.

The debate over the authenticity of performances staged by communities in less-developed countries for the sake of tourism will continue. Some researchers will continue to criticize companies involved with tourism in developing countries for practicing cultural imperialism, positing that this type of tourism is always negative for the host community. Others will support controlled tourism to less-developed areas.

In the coming years, most indigenous villages will be impacted by development. The world's population will continue to increase in the tropical and temperate zones, putting pressure on, and causing conflicts over, the earth's remaining natural resources. If indigenous people are to have a chance at protecting and preserving their territory and resources, they must be able to increase their household income to meet the economic demands of an ever-changing world. For the four indigenous communities in this study, tourism may not be the answer to long-term employment and income stability, but, for now, it offers an opportunity to increase their household income and meet some of their increasing financial responsibilities while living in the forest and without depleting their resource base. These communities are situated in areas that offer few economic opportunities, especially opportunities that are ecologically sustainable.

The introduction of tourism into indigenous communities does not take place without impacts. These impacts, whether they are economic, environmental, cultural, or social, can prove to be beneficial, deleterious, or a combination of the two. The impacts within a given situation should be evaluated within a framework that considers the location of the individual community, the goals of its members, and the opportunities that exist for economic development and advantageous sociocultural change and/or preservation. Further, the outcome can be directly associated with the type of tourism that occurs, the numbers of tourists involved, and the frequency of the occurrence. Tourism or ecotourism that interacts with indigenous communities by bringing in small groups of tourists who do not become a constant presence in the community can offer economic opportunities to communities while keeping the interruption of daily life to a minimum.

As seen in this study, tourism to indigenous villages in this area occurs in two ways; tourists arrive by boat for a short visit, or they stay near the village at a tourist lodge in the forest. The three communities located on the Ampiyacu River like their interaction with tourism because it is controlled by the villages, they know when to expect groups of tourists, and groups only come to their village once or twice a month. Although they make money by having their world viewed by outsiders, the interruption to their daily lives is minimal and brief. As one chief described to me, "We like to see the tourists arrive . . . and we like to see them leave." The experience for the Yaguas of Palmares II is different. On the one hand, the Yaguas liked the opportunity to sell handicrafts on a daily basis, in the busiest tourist season, but they felt they had given up their privacy by allowing constant interaction with tourists.

As long as tourists continue to travel to less-developed areas of the world in search of a unique tour that, at least in part, highlights the lifestyles of the "primitive," some indigenous communities will oblige if it results in increased income. Tourist entertainment not only brings in much needed income, it also offers an opportunity for locals to embrace their own cultural identity that may be threatened in a changing world. By performing traditional dances in traditional costumes, and producing handicrafts based on traditional designs, communities can continue some of the practices of their ancestors, passing this knowledge on to the younger members of their societies. Tourism, and the money it generates, may offer additional economic choices to developing communities in transition, allowing them to work with the outside world while keeping elements of their traditional culture in place.

Source: Adapted from "Performing Traditional Dances for Modern Tourists in the Amazon," *International Journal of Hospitality & Tourism Administration*, 2001, 1(3/4):143–59.

Notes

[1] Both types of tours from the United States cost about $2,500 for one week in the late 1990s.

[2] I started working in the Amazon in 1991 and have worked as a guide both with the company that owns the tourist boats and with the company that owns the lodge. Permission to work in the communities and to conduct interviews was given by the chief in each village, as well as the villagers. During my research, I traveled to each community several times for extended stays. In Palmare II, I interviewed 26 out of 32 households. (Two families were living in the city of Iquitos during my visits to the community; four households were those of government school teachers with no involvement in tourism.) The three communities on the Ampiyacu tributary work with the same tourist boat company and are similar in their host–guest interactions. For this reason a random sample of 34 out of a total 115 households in the three communities were interviewed. Personal interviews were also conducted with the heads of household. For most, I had the help of a research assistant of indigenous descent.

References

Beavers, J. 1995. Community-based Ecotourism in the Maya Forest: Six Case Studies from Communities in Mexico, Guatemala, and Belize. The Nature Conservancy, USAID/Mayafor Project.

Brohman, J. 1996. "New Directions in Tourism for Third World Development." *Annals of Tourism Research* 23(1): 48–70.

Cohen, E. 1988. "Authenticity and Commoditization in Tourism." *Annals of Tourism Research* 15:371–386.

Colchester, M. 1989. "Indian Development in Amazonia: Risks and Strategies." *The Ecologist* 19(6):254.

Deitch, L. 1989. "The Impact of Tourism on the Indians of the Southwestern United States," in *Host and Guests: The Anthropology of Tourism*, ed. V. Smith. Philadelphia: University of Pennsylvania Press.

Greenwood, D. 2004[1977]. "Culture by the Pound: An Anthropological Perspective on Tourism as Cultural Commoditization." In *Tourists and Tourism*, 1st. ed., ed. S. Gmelch, pp. 157–169. Long Grove, IL: Waveland Press.

Haralambopoulos, N. and A. Pizam. 1996. "Perceived Impacts of Tourism." *Annals of Tourism Research* 23(3): 503–526.

Healy, R. 1994. "Tourist Merchandise as a Means of Generating Local Benefits from Ecotourism." *Journal of Sustainable Tourism* 2 (3): 137–151.

Ingles, Palma. 2002. "Welcome To My Village: Hosting Tourists in the Peruvian Amazon." *Tourism Recreation Research* 27(1): 53–60.

———. 2005. "More Than Nature: Anthropologists as Interpreters of Culture for Nature-Based Tours," in *Tourism and Applied Anthropologists: Linking Theory and Practice*, ed. Tim Wallace. The National Association for the Practice of Anthropology (NAPA), Number 23. Malden MA: Wiley-Blackwell.

Jensen, P. 2000. Personal interviews.

MacCannell, D. 1973. "Staged Authenticity: Arrangements of Social Space in Tourism Settings." *American Journal of Sociology* 79:589–603.

Mansperger, M. 1995. "Tourism and Cultural Change in Small-scale Societies." *Human Organization* 54(1): 87–94.

McLaren, D. 1999. "The History of Indigenous Peoples and Tourism." *Cultural Survival* 23(2): 27–30.

Nash, D. 1989. "Tourism as a Form of Imperialism," in *Hosts and Guests: the Anthropology of Tourism*, ed. V. Smith. Philadelphia: University of Pennsylvania Press.

Seiler-Baldinger 1988

Silver, I. 1993. "Marketing Authenticity in Third World Countries." *Annals of Tourism Research* 20:302–318.

Sofield, T. 1993. "Indigenous Tourism Development." *Annals of Tourism Research* 20:729–750.

Steinberg, M. 1997. "Tourism Development and Indigenous People: The Maya Experience in Southern Belize." *Focus* 44(2):17–20.

Stymeist, D. 1996. "Transformation of Vilavilairevo in Tourism." *Annals of Tourism Research* 23:1–18.

Weaver, D. 1998. *Ecotourism in the Less Developed World.* Cab International.

Wright, P. 2000. Personal interviews.

14

The Authentic (In)Authentic: Bushman Anthro-Tourism

Elizabeth Garland and Robert J. Gordon

It was perhaps inevitable that tourism would become big business in Namibia. The World Tourism Organization touts tourism as the fastest growing sector of the world economy, with ecotourism to exotic destinations like Africa as one of the industry's brightest diamonds. And in Namibia where the diamond industry that has historically sustained the country's economic development is now reaching the end of its pipe, tourism is gaining prominence as a important new source of income. Growing at a rate of more than 7 percent per year, the tourism industry now represents the fourth largest sector of the Namibian economy, and promotion of tourism is regularly emphasized in the government's long-range plans for national economic development.[1]

While the country's principal draw for tourists is undoubtedly its remarkable natural environment (with the dramatic Namib desert in the south, the lush Okavango delta in the Caprivi Strip, and the dryland Etosha game park), tour operators and government officials alike are increasingly emphasizing the marketability of Namibia's unique cultural heritage as well. Citing exotic peoples like the ochre-covered Ovahimba and the cattle-keeping Herero, with their horned headdresses and enormous Victorian robes, the tourism industry is turning to cultural tourism as a way to distinguish Namibia from more established African ecotour destinations like Kenya and South Africa.[2]

In the context of such state-sanctioned cultural commodification, it is hardly surprising that those Namibian people labeled "bushmen"—long fetishized in ethnographies, documentaries, novels, and blockbuster films like *The Gods Must Be Crazy* and *A Far-Off Place*—have come to feature centrally in the discourse of Namibian tourism development. Indeed, tourism centered around so-called bushman people (the most famous of these being the !Kung) has arguably become the hallmark of cultural tourism in Namibia. This is evidenced by the common use of bushman-style logos by safari companies, as well as by the most prominent and successful curio shop in the capital, the Bushman Art and Afrikan Museum, which combines its status as a museum with its role as a curio vendor in order to underwrite the authenticity of the artifacts it sells.

While a modern phenomenon in terms of the degree of commercialization, present-day bushman ethnotourism, in which tourists make spatial and/or metaphysical journeys to people called bushmen, is actually only the most recent incarnation of a venerable southern African practice. Restricting discussion to what is now Namibia, its genealogy can be traced back to the nineteenth-century accounts of expeditions by explorers and naturalists like Sir Francis Galton, Charles John Andersson, Thomas Baines, James Chapman, Hans Schinz, and Siegfried Passarge, who offered elaborate, romanticized testimonies to the extraordinary hunting and tracking skills of bushmen. After the First World War, this early genre of Kalahari adventure tourism was transformed by the advent of the movie camera, most prominently by the Denver African Expedition in 1925 (Gordon 1997), and reached its apex with the made-for-television expeditions of Laurens van der Post and with a host of other similar representations since the 1970s, in which bushmen have been repeatedly depicted as beautiful, "harmless" people—perfectly adapted relics of an ancient Stone Age. Based on ostensibly real-life experiences, the veracity of these adventurers' romantic accounts has seldom been questioned. Their stories represent the rich historical lode that proponents of bushman anthro-tourism are hoping to exploit.

As lucrative as this type of tourism may be, it is also fraught with danger for the people who participate in it most directly. Many people have noted the ways in which tourism reproduces inequities of power and wealth between those who do the touring and those who get toured. Some critics have focused on the international implications of this dynamic. Cynthia Enloe, for example, writes that "tourism is as much ideology as physical movement. . . . A government which decides to rely on money from tourism for its development is a government which has decided to be internationally compliant" (1990: 28, 31). Others have traced the ways in which tourism development tends to harm those people who are already relatively disadvantaged within a given society. In the Namibian context, where so-called bushman peoples have endured centuries of oppressive and violent social policies (see Gordon 1992), it seems unlikely that the development of tourism around bushman culture could lead to anything other than further exploitation of people who are already among Namibia's poorest and most marginalized.

Such concerns notwithstanding, Namibia is a young state—having gained independence from South Africa in 1990—and idealistic government officials have looked to tourism as a potential tool for redressing the historical inequities that plague the country's population in the wake of the *apartheid* era. Hoping to generate economic benefits for the nonwhite majority of Namibians living in the "communal areas" of the country (known as ethnic "homelands" under *apartheid*), the government has undertaken a series of innovative tourism policy initiatives, devolving its ownership of wildlife to local communities that register as game-managing "conservancies," and thereby enabling rural people to develop and profit from wildlife tourism on their lands, just as white game ranchers have done for decades (GRN/MET 1995b; Jones 1995). Apropos of the issue of cultural tourism, the Government of the Republic of Namibia has also launched a campaign to encourage investors in the tourism industry (most of whom are foreign or white Namibians) to collaborate directly with local people through revenue-sharing agreements and formal joint ventures with people from the communal areas. In the handful of these collaborative ventures currently operating in Namibia, income has been generated for local communities at levels that far surpass the (traditionally low) gains from employment as wage laborers that usually accrue to people living in the vicinity of tourist enterprises (Ashley and Garland 1994; GRN/MET 1995a).

Such policy initiatives and the income generated by them certainly sound like a good thing, but the question remains: are such attempts at "progressive" tourism development enough? Can cultural tourism—tourism where the commodity being sold to tourists is not merely leisure or game viewing, but people themselves (or at least their cultural Otherness)—actually be empowering to the people who participate in it? Clearly, it is better for people to be compensated financially for their cultural commodification than for them not to be. Tales abound of "indigenous" African peoples (notably so-called pygmies) being paid little or nothing for posing for photographs and providing other "cultural" services to tourists, and surely it is better for the state to help ensure that such blatant exploitation not take place. But even in a context like Namibia, where at least some officials in the Ministry of Environment and Tourism appear to be genuinely interested in helping people benefit from and control their contact with tourists, one cannot help but wonder if culture is not similar to other African cash-producing export commodities: relatively lucrative if done well, but a losing proposition in the final, global, analysis.

As perhaps the most famous cultural Others in the world, and histori-cally also among the world's most marginalized and disempowered people, bushmen represent a good test of the possibility of ethically responsible cul-tural tourism development. By focusing on a few ostensibly progressive examples of bushman tourism in Namibia, we hope to explore what is at stake for people when they participate in marketing themselves as commodi-ties for tourist consumption. Cultural tourism, we suggest, is not merely about the exploitation or appropriation of people as cultural objects; it is also about the production of new forms of authenticity and, ultimately, new kinds of subjects as well.

Bushmen as Objects

The most obvious way to conceptualize the attraction that bushmen hold for tourists is to focus on their ascribed identity as primitive Others. Characterized in innumerable academic and popular representations as gen-tle, egalitarian, and perfectly ecologically adapted, stereotypic bushmen pro-vide a compelling, almost natural foil for the individuated materialism of the Westerners (largely Dutch, Germans, and white southern Africans) who visit them as tourists.[3] As Culler (1981) notes, the authentic Otherness of people like bushmen does not exist by itself, but is a sign relationship. It must be semiotically marked (and marketed) by means of indicators that such people live off the beaten track, are rare, are on the brink of extinction, and the like. In Namibia, this sort of authenticity marking is typically done by hyping bushmen as part of a vanishing culture: in the words of one tour book, bush-man tourism offers tourists a last-chance glance, "as the modern world closes in and a whole way of life slowly vanishes" (Haape 1993: 61).

Through films, guidebooks, glossy photo books, and postcards—and, of course, also the authoritative accounts of academic anthropologists—tour-ists are provided with evidence of what the genuine bushman product looks like. The internationally distributed *Insight Guide: Namibia*, for example, refers to the "Magic of the Bushmen" and claims that in Bushmanland,

> these last, still almost thoroughly traditional Bushmen family groups offer an image of unspoiled humane existence—without class distinctions, where men and women know and perform their own tasks. Even today, the Bushmen require only a minimum of laws. (Haape 1993: 60, 61)

Similarly, the *Spectrum Guide to Namibia* (Camerapix 1994) assures its read-ers that an estimated 2,000 Bushmen "maintain their ancient way of life, hunting and gathering":

> Natural conservationists in an ever more polluted world, Bushmen take great care of their harsh habitat, at home in a terrain where few other human beings could survive. Their incredible bushlore unfailingly leads them to water. . . . Those who continue the tribe's 20,000 years of tradi-

tions even use utensils that have not noticeably altered during the past few thousand years. (Camerapix 1994: 62)

These guides, and other commercial devices like them, serve to define or prefabricate what an authentic bushman looks like. Such imagery is then deployed by the tourism industry to sell the experience of contact with bushmen as a particular sort of desirable tourism product. Take for example a five-day tour offered in 2009 by www.responsibletravel.com, a travel agency whose name suggests its environmentally conscious orientation:

> From the Cucumber to the Elephant dance, from digging for roots to collecting berries. Such would be the experience with the Ju'Hoansi tribe in North-Eastern Namibia. Be mystified by the ancestral medicinal trances and local herb remedies prepared from the bush. Witness the expert tracking abilities and the indescribable bond that these people have with nature. Learn to appreciate life in the most basic of ways.
>   Between speaking and doing, lies a thousand miles, goes the saying. With this tour the same principle applies. One can speak and rave about the tour, but the actual experience you will get from this could be indescribable. The way of living in harmony with nature that the Ju'Hoansi tribe shows, goes beyond belief. Every single thing they have and consume comes from their immediate surroundings. They have a saying "When the wind blows, we must move." This just shows how in tune these people are with nature and their surroundings. (www.responsibletravel.com, accessed February 27, 2009)

As such promotional materials suggest, in visiting bushmen, tourists seek—and indeed often claim to find—much-needed redemption for the alienation and fragmentation of their modern lives. By coming into contact with those perceived to be their symbolic opposites, tourists gain reassurance that they are themselves worthy and whole; through exposure to the authentic Other, the Self shores up a sense of its own authenticity.

A feature story from a local South African newspaper, the *Northcliff and Melville Times* (October 1, 1985), with the remarkable title "Anita the Bushwoman," articulates well the transformative capacity ascribed to bushman tourism. In a lengthy interview, Anita van der Merwe, described in the article as a brilliant, beautiful writer, artist, and filmmaker, testifies about the time she spent with the bushmen:

> I never realized how much I depended on my looks and my achievements to establish my worth, but in the desert among these childlike and truthful people none of those things were important—only the real essence of me mattered. And when I slipped off layers of 20th century artificiality I was astonished to find, not a monster as I had expected, but the basic me which was a good and honest thing. . . . In the desert with these simple people you know who you are. You get looked at, touched—you know where you belong. There is no confusion in life. And there is no competition. You share everything.

And then, describing her return to London after leaving the bushmen, she continues:

> In London I felt so depressed and lonely, like a feather floating down the street. . . . Being a 20th century person you are so lonely—I can't explain—so out of place. In the rat race we lead such dishonest lives where we merely exit without enthusiasm or joy. I wanted to go back there forever. . . . But then came the realisation that I was not a bushman in blood or brain. Instead I try to apply what I learnt from the bushman in my life now.

For "Anita the Bushwoman," contact with "the bushman" enabled her Western self to bring to light its "real essence," an essence that she was startled to discover and was "a good and honest thing," a thing she hoped to transport from the Kalahari to her (real) life in London. As Bruner points out, such personal testimonies are part and parcel of the "master narrative structure of African tourism, (namely) that civilized persons go on tour to experience the primitive, the exotic, the erotic, and the Other, in order to recover their origin, and original state seen as pure and as yet not polluted by European civilization" (1991: 240).

For tourists like Anita, who are transparently motivated by the drive for self-discovery, the most important thing about spending time in the company of bushmen is the opportunity to gain access to their cultural difference, to their status as cultural Others. Predictably, tourism ventures that are designed to capitalize on this sort of explicit demand for bushman Otherness focus on providing tourists with evidence of the bushman's cultural uniqueness and difference from them. In Namibia, such operations typically offer tourist activities designed to display "traditional" aspects of bushman life: viewing dances and rituals, going on foraging walks or hunting expeditions with bushman guides or trackers, making or buying bushman crafts, spending time in "authentic" villages, and the like. Sometimes the pilgrimage to the Other can be upsetting, as when world-wise journalist Graham Boynton, on assignment for *Conde Nast Traveller*, found in his quest for the "Lost Tribe of the Kalahari" that "not all travel is joyous and escapist. Sometimes it forces you to confront reality." He felt as if he was "witness[ing] the last twitches of a culture in its death throes, and it was not very dignified or romantic or edifying. It did however serve to strengthen my belief that modern man's urge to pave'n mall the entire planet will lead us to destruction" (Boynton 1997:220).

Graham Boynton's and Anita van der Merwe's views on bushmen suggest a certain ambiguity surrounding issues of authenticity and emphasize the point that will be discussed shortly, namely that "authenticity" is an ideological construct, and it shares with all ideologies an inherent *double entendre*. There is a central paradox at play in such quests for "lost" tribes: they must be both completely unknown and very well-known to attract their clientele. "Lost" tribes emerge not so much from the jungle or the desert, as from the alienated, bourgeois imagination of tourists. As Dea Birkett observes:

> Lost tribes are created by us, to free our imaginations and to give us
> hope. We need them to make our own complete connectedness to the rest
> of the world tolerable. We take comfort from the presumption that there
> remain, in some distant jungle, people who do not subscribe to the
> worldwide web of relationships that has become part of our lives. As
> long as we presume they exist, there is the faint chance that we may join
> them; one day we, too, may become "lost." (Birkett 1996:47)

Boynton's observation directly speaks to this issue: when he asked his bushman guide about the cosmological significance of scars on his arm, his guide
told him that they were teeth marks obtained during a drunken brawl.

Bushmen as Producers?

One of the main reasons bushmen were expelled from the Etosha and
Kalahari Gemsbok Game Parks in the 1950s and 1960s was because Park
officials believed that they were engaging in "untraditional behavior" like
"begging." What these officials failed to realize was that "begging" was a
foraging strategy, used not only by those classified as hunter-gatherers but
also by those who see themselves as "down on their luck." So too, playing up
to tourists by dressing up in loin cloths and other stereotypically "primitive"
clothing can be seen as an elaboration of a foraging strategy, and indeed the
practice can be traced back to the 1920s (Gordon 1997). Simply put, it is
much easier to dress up and entertain tourists than to engage in a long hunt in
which the rewards are by no means certain. It is a strategy employed widely
both temporally and spatially. Nicholas Luard in his book about the
Botswana Kalahari, *The Last Wilderness,* has one of his white guides remi-
nisce about the willingness of bushmen to play the primitive role:

> "I mean, I've got this Argentinean professor of anthropology," he went
> on. "He came out here a couple of years ago looking for Bushman. I heard
> of a group. I went on ahead to set up camp. When I got there, I found the
> little buggers were all wearing T-shirts saying 'Coca-Cola adds life.' I
> only just managed to strip them off and dress the sods in hides when he
> arrived. . . ." Syd shook his head glumly. "He's been promising to come
> back ever since, I tell you, if he doesn't make it soon he'll have nothing
> left to study—T-shirts or not." I just stared at the thorn. I was thinking of
> my last visit to the desert. Late one afternoon we came upon another
> group of San. We were driving through tall grass and we stopped, and
> suddenly they materialized in front of us, peering at the truck through the
> bending stems. . . . I got out and walked with them to the camp. They'd
> encountered Europeans before, and they knew what they were expected
> to do: plait rope from fibrous leaves, carve beads from ostrich eggshells,
> make fire from sticks. I sat down. Scrupulously and with great dignity
> they went through their repertoire. I watched. There was no thought of
> payment. It was simply a ritual obligation on both sides—the San to dem-
> onstrate their skills, I, the foreigner, to observe, which was what they'd
> learned foreigners wished to do. They finished. I expressed my thanks

and handed them some cigarettes. The San have a passion for tobacco and they gave me a volley of quick handclaps in appreciation. I stood up to leave. Then I paused. The whole performance had been as decorous and genteel as a church bazaar—and just as bland. (Luard 1991:203–204)

The media critic Keyan Tomaselli, on a visit to Bushmanland in the mid-1990s, asked local Ju/'hoansi why they had allowed themselves to be portrayed as if they were in a pristine condition in the Discovery Channel's *Hunters of the Kalahari*. His respondents quickly pointed to the 10,000 rands (South African currency) that the Discovery Channel had paid for their collaboration in the film as evidence of the rationality of embracing the role of authentic bushmen (Tomaselli 1999).

In modern-day Namibia, though, even the most determined tourism providers have trouble sustaining the image of bushmen in the pristine, unchanging terms on which fantasies of them as the original cultural Others rely. The history of exploitation and oppression that has accompanied—and some have argued defined—the category "bushman" (see Wilmsen 1989; Gordon 1992) is too omnipresent in the lives of the people who bear its label to be easily concealed. Even explicit performances of bushman primitivity, staged to emphasize their authenticity as cultural objects, draw on power relations with long histories in southern Africa. Indeed, John Marshall has shown in *N!ai: the Story of a !Kung Woman*, which includes footage of the coercion used by white filmmakers in shooting the South African film *The Gods Must Be Crazy*, how these historical relations continually spill over into the present, shaping the versions of authentic bushman-ness that get produced at any given point in time.

Perhaps even more importantly, in the context of national and international efforts to empower them, people who fall under the rubric of "bushmen" are increasingly being seen and coming to define themselves as "indigenous peoples"—not primitive, untouched Others, but fully human Selves, universal subjects grappling with modernity from a historically—and culturally specific position of poverty and marginality (see Garland 1999). As indigenous peoples, bushmen cannot be conceptualized simply as objects for tourist consumption; as modernizing subjects, they must also be seen as producers, agents in the production and marketing of tourist artifacts and experiences.

The double nature of the current touristic identity of bushmen (as both primitive cultural objects and as modernizing tourism producers) has resulted in a variety of innovative forms of cultural tourism in Namibia. Unable to conceal the artifice needed to create the illusion that bushmen are pure, authentic cultural Others, bushman tourism providers have begun instead to thematize the complicated, dual position that modern-day "bushmen" are in. A new genre of tourism around bushmen has sprung up, emphasizing not only their cultural differences from Westerners (for demand for their primitive authenticity shows no signs of slacking) but also the ways they are similar to other marginal peoples in the process of incorporation into national and global political-economic systems.

Upper-end European tourists record a honey search in Nyae Nyae. Note the cattle in the background. (Image from *A Kalahari Family, Part Five: Death By Myth*, by John Marshall. Courtesy of Documentary Educational Resources)

Tasting the recovered honey. (Image from *A Kalahari Family, Part Five: Death By Myth*, by John Marshall. Courtesy of Documentary Educational Resources)

In the area of Namibia known by the *apartheid*-era term "Bushman-land," for example, most tourists who wish to visit the region's famous !Kung inhabitants currently stay at a rough campground called Makuri Camp. Built in 1994 with minimal assistance from a local NGO, Makuri Camp is owned and operated by Ju/'hoan bushmen from nearby Makuri Village. At Makuri Camp, tourists—most of whom are independent "overland" tourists with their own four-by-four vehicles—are provided with the opportunity to observe Ju/'hoan songs and dances, to go on foraging walks with Ju/'hoan women, to accompany Ju/'hoan men on hunting expeditions in the veld, and to spend time in Makuri Village just hanging out. Tourist access to such "authentic" cultural activities, however, is invariably coupled with other dynamics that disrupt the illusion of the Ju/'hoansi's cultural authenticity as primitive Others—dynamics such as debates over how high the fees should be for services provided to tourists, arguments over what to spend tourism money on, or discussions about the history of the camp, control of which has long been contested by the Nyae Nyae Farmers Cooperative, the principal community organization in the region.

Tourists at Makuri, though able to consume some aspects of Ju/'hoan Otherness, have little option but to recognize that tourism operates as a fundamentally modern economic activity for their "bushman" hosts (see, e.g., Isaacson 1996; Boynton 1997). Guidebooks increasingly help them make sense of their experience:

> For some visitors the main appeal of (Bushmanland) is its wilderness atmosphere . . . other visitors are drawn to the area by a desire to see the San (Bushmen). . . . Do not expect to encounter San in loincloths and with bows and arrows, though, as, contrary to the popular belief that these people still exist as hunter-gatherers, their way of life has changed dramatically in the past 20 years. (Olivier and Olivier 1989:233)

In recent years, organized, upmarket tour operators have begun to capitalize, in particular, on the increasing awareness that tourists have of the impact their tourism has on bushmen, by pitching their tourist ventures as helpful to local economic development. The Dutch adventure travel company Footprints, for example, regularly runs tours to Makuri Camp, advertising that it shares up to 50 percent of its earnings with the local community (Isaacson 1996). For the tourists who go on Footprints tours, bushmen have appeal both as exotic cultural Others *and* as modernizing subjects in the throws of economic development. Authentic enough to be worth visiting, the residents of Makuri also represent a prime opportunity for tourists to feel good about themselves by helping out those less economically advantaged than they.

At the other end of the luxury spectrum from Makuri Camp is the Intu Afrika Kalahari Reserve (www.namibweb.com/intuafrika.html), a foreign-owned private game park in central southern Namibia, which, given a rather unattractive location and high level of investment, has decided to append bushmen as an added draw. Inspired by the success of the Kagga Kamma

Game Reserve in South Africa (located 200 km from Cape Town and featuring some dispossessed southern Kalahari inhabitants as tour attractions), the German owners of Intu Afrika managed to lure away the anthropologist couple who served as consultants at Kagga Kamma to see if they could replicate their success and develop an upscale bushman tourist experience in Namibia.

Beyond the price range of most local tourists, Intu Afrika is a luxury venture aimed at affluent foreign tourists. While most guests at Intu Afrika stay in the luxurious main lodge, the more adventurous have the option of forsaking such comfort for an "authentic" !Kung campsite, or "boma"[4] (complete with such essential facilities as "open air" flushing toilets, hot showers, and cooking facilities), manned by a Bushman family, and located at the edge of a basin surrounded by giant camel-thorn trees. Advertising material hypes the park in terms reminiscent of the movie *Out of Africa*:

> We have a game reserve in Afrika. . . . Where the sand is blown and sifted over thousands of years of majestic waves of red dunes; Where the last few bushmen roam in freedom and harmony with the land; Where the oryx is able to survive on as little as a liter of water a year; A place that is harsh and unrelenting; Yet forgiving, resilient and able to sustain life in many unique forms to be found nowhere else on earth.

In spite of their use of romantic descriptions of "the last few bushmen" roaming "in freedom and harmony with the land" to attract customers seeking contact with pristine primitives, the owners of Intu Afrika are mindful not to appear to be exploiting bushmen as primitives outright. In an explanatory brochure, they justify their project as an exciting new minimally exploitative "joint venture" between the park and a number of bushmen recruited from the Gobabis district of Namibia and from the demobilized Smitsdrift military base in South Africa. Everyone wins, tourists are assured, in this "clear legal agreement giving bushmen a shareholding in the company and game reserve. . . . The joint venture will benefit the company, the Bushman community and the Namibian tourism industry."

Borrowing the fashionable rhetoric of "community empowerment," the brochure skillfully straddles the gap between the competing discourses of bushman primitivity and of their identity as modernizing subjects. It does so in a classically southern African manner, through an appeal to white paternalism:

> The objective of the Intu Afrika Bushman project is to empower the community to regain their dignity and pride by creating employment and cultural activities which utilize traditional Bushman skills in order to generate income for their community. These activities include game guiding, tracking, camp supervising and craft making. Many of the activities will require basic training which will be provided by Intu Afrika.

These bushmen, we are told, have "traditional Bushman skills," but are sadly lacking the "basic training" needed to turn these skills into income generators for their (brand new and completely artificial) community. Intu Afrika, and implicitly also the tourists who patronize the park, will serve as benevolent chaperones for these bushmen, ushering them from their primitive, disempowered, "traditional" state into their modern roles as partners in a legal joint venture.

Indeed, the brochure's writers come close to suggesting that tourism at Intu Afrika is the sole salvation available to modern-day bushmen. The text continues, lauding bushmen as the "true indigenous people of Southern Africa" and explaining that they were once an integral part of the Kalahari eco-system, "living in harmony with the environment but in recent years displaced." Airbrushing away the brutal nature of this "displacement" (see Gordon 1992) by attributing it to something euphemistically termed "cultural differences," Intu Afrika reports that today, these once proud people have largely been reduced to handouts, and that all efforts at development have achieved only minimal results. Then, fortunately, divine inspiration intervened: "It is here in the Kalahari in a traditional hunting area of the Bushmen, where the idea arose for members of the Bushman community to join hands with the management to develop eco-tourism for mutual benefit." And so it came to pass that in 1995 "leaders of the Namibian Bushman community" worked with the park's management to "re-establish a self-sustainable Bushman community."[5] Now, some 40 people are employed "in a variety of income generating activities such as game guiding, camp supervision and the manufacture of traditional Bushman handicrafts such as bead necklaces."

At both Intu Afrika and at Makuri Camp, "bushmen" participate in tourism ventures in a dual capacity as both objects of tourism and as tourism producers. There is little doubt that their appeal as pristine primitives—cultural Others who help define and transform the Western subjects who visit them—is the most crucial component of their attraction for tourists, and it is unsurprising that in both places, "traditional" bushman skills like hunting, gathering, singing, and craft making are the cultural features explicitly commodified for the tourist trade. While substantial differences exist between the two ventures (Makuri is much less luxurious, fees are paid directly to local residents, etc., whereas at Intu Afrika, bushmen are part of a prepaid total luxury experience), in both cases, tourists are expected to and desire to consume the trappings of authentic bushman culture.

Yet, this is clearly not the whole story, for in neither setting are the bushmen in question completely objectified as Others. Even as they are marketed, and market themselves, as "bushmen"—a category that, almost by definition, locates them as outside of modern time and space—they are simultaneously perceived to be active participants in the tourism industry, as modern subjects who choose to benefit from commodifying themselves through a range of commercial and legal transactions. Strikingly, this modernist framework for conceptualizing bushmen does not seem to undermine the one that labels them as cultural Others. On the contrary, the two discourses coexist quite comfortably. At times it even seems that the bushmen's status as Others is the very thing that makes possible their modern subjectivity—it is because of their appeal as authentic Others, after all, that people called bushmen have something to sell in the modern marketplace.

Authenticity and Meta-Tourism

Under circumstances such as these, then, what are we to make of the classic assertion by MacCannell (1976) that tourism is motivated by the quest for authenticity? As Goldman and Papson have put it, what we are dealing with here is the enigma of authenticity in the age of poseur: "as cultural production accelerates and postmodern styles (pastiche, parody, plagiarism) proliferate, recognition of the original becomes more difficult" (Goldman and Papson 1996:184). And it is true, the bushmen who participate in tourism ventures like Makuri Camp and Intu Afrika can hardly be said to be wholly authentic—that is, provided that authenticity is conceived in terms of true, unchanging, cultural Otherness and the like; and yet, they are clearly authentic enough to count as bushmen in the eyes of their customers, as the success of both operations indicates. Indeed, as we have argued above, at times the apparent inauthenticity of such modern-day bushmen—i.e., their modernity as savvy tourism producers—even seems to lend crucial credibility to tourism ventures that feature them

The coexistence of tourist discourses about bushmen as primitive Others and as modernist tourism producers begins to seem far less paradoxical once we recognize that authenticity itself has no fixed content. It is, in a sense, in the eye of the beholder. Tourists at ventures like Makuri Camp and Intu Africa don't perceive the dual identities of bushmen (as both authentic cultural Others and inauthentic modern Subjects) to be dissonant because they are continually prompted not to assess authenticity at the level of bushman cultural Otherness. With the help of tour guides and informative brochures that emphasize the "realities" of modern-day "bushman" life, these tourists are coached to believe that the only truly authentic tourism experience with bushmen is one that recognizes the reality of the bushmen's involvement in tourism.

What these tourists are being urged to practice is a kind of meta-tourism. Like those television commercials that thematize their own well-worn tropes in order to sell us products more effectively, bushman tourism in Namibia has telescoped out to a meta-level. In the place of mythic bushman authenticity, bushman meta-tourism offers tourists a sense of authenticity on a higher plane, at the level of their own perceptions. While they may regret that the bushmen they see are not as fully Other as they had anticipated, their interpretation of this regret as an inevitable component of modern-day bushman tourism enables them to reclaim even their own disappointment as an authentic part of their overall quest for bushman Otherness.

Returning to MacCannell's original insight that tourism is about the quest for authenticity (1976), our point is that tourism is about the quest, and not about the authenticity: so long as the quest can be understood to be authentic, the tourism "product" itself need not be.[6] As the cultural products consumed by tourists change, due to the warping effects of commodification (per Greenwood 2004 [1977]), or perhaps just the forces of history, the tourist quest to consume them continually shifts and redefines itself, perpetually struggling to find ways to render itself authentic, under circumstances it recognizes as ever more inauthentic. Confronted with evidence of the cultural inauthenticity of their bushman hosts, tourists to Makuri Camp and Intu Afrika merely adopt a new, meta-language in which to assert that their experiences there have been authentic after all. In the process, the quest for authenticity through tourism—the quest that motivated the tourists to seek out contact with bushmen in the first place—has been reaffirmed as a viable enterprise, even in this inauthentic age when people called bushmen are running tourist ventures.

Do Bushmen Benefit from Meta-Tourism?

By way of a conclusion, we want to turn to the question of what all of this means for the bushmen (and women!) who participate in meta-tourism ventures like those at Makuri Camp and Intu Afrika. As in the case of more conventional cultural tourism, which casts indigenous people as unchanging primitives, it is tempting to consider meta-tourism as merely an innovative version of a process that is basically about the exploitation and cultural dispossession of people who are already relatively disempowered. But the evidence from Namibia suggests that it is not so simple as this in the bushman case, for it is clear that some bushman participants in "progressive" tourism ventures gain resources and skills—cash incomes, and linguistic and cultural fluency in European ways, for example—that help them establish better positions within the larger Namibian society. Perhaps even more importantly, tourism that promises authenticity only at the meta-level, that does not attempt to conceal the ways in which tourism is changing the lives of people involved in it, offers bushman tourism providers at least a partial chance to decide for themselves how much they want to cater to tourists' desires to consume their cultural Otherness, and how much they want to assert their more modern identities as indigenous peoples or tourism producers.

By virtue of the international sophistication it fosters, meta-tourism also has at least the potential to help empower bushmen to defend themselves in the face of actions by the state that impinge upon their interests. When the Namibian Government decided, in 1997, to evict Khwe bushmen from their tourist camp operation in the Caprivi region, for example, the Khwe leader, Kippie George, was able to protest not only by visiting relevant government ministers in the capital city, Windhoek, but also by holding press conferences and briefing a local legal firm. Later he extended his protest to the international level by addressing the United Nations. Similarly, in 1996, when a number of Hai-//om bushmen were arrested for blockading the entrance to the Etosha National Park, claiming the park's land historically belonged to them, they deployed imagery familiar from meta-tourism of themselves as simultaneously "Noble Ecologists" and people who have been cruelly "Brutalized and Betrayed."

Lest we sound too optimistic about the potential of meta-tourism, however, it is important to emphasize that the benefits bushmen gain from participation in tourism come at a price. As we have argued above, the sense of authenticity that tourists gain from acknowledging the meta-realities of modern-day bushman life is itself thoroughly saturated with ideology. Though we have not developed the point here, this ideology has a specific content: it is the ideology of Western socioeconomic development. In gaining an "authentic" understanding of their hosts as both primitive bushmen and modern tourism producers, meta-tourists come to conceive of bushmen as midway through an imagined process of socioeconomic development. In what Comaroff and Comaroff refer to as simultaneous narratives "of being and becoming," (1997), developmentalism encompasses modern-day bushmen in both their primitive and modern guises, helping tourists to comprehend their dual identities in terms of a process of transformation from one state to the other. Through guidebooks and brochures that emphasize the economic importance of tourism for bushmen, tourists are encouraged to see themselves as helpful agents in this development process, recasting themselves not as exploitative consumers but as benevolent mentors and patrons to the bushmen they visit.

While developmentalist ideology may be quite helpful to bushman meta-tourists, it is at best a mixed blessing for the bushmen on whom it is heaped. A full critique of development discourse among bushmen is clearly beyond the scope of this paper (but see Garland 1999), but one basic point is that framing the modern condition of bushmen in terms of their need for development effectively erases the bloody historical circumstances that have contributed to the current situation of people so-categorized. Replacing the ugly complexity of Namibian history with a much simpler, more digestible narrative structure of progress from primitivity to modernity, development discourse enables tourists to avoid perceiving their own complicity in the disempowered, Othered position of the bushmen they visit.[7] Furthermore, so long as people called bushmen are characterized as being in the throes of a process of development, they will be denied the fully modern subjectivity that the (developed) tourists who visit them enjoy. While tourism may indeed provide bushmen with substantial benefits, it is also ensures that they remain permanently not quite like us, not yet (per Bhabha 1994). In the end, this is perhaps the most enduring effect of cultural tourism for people like bushmen. Though engaging in self-commodification may earn them certain gains, it also necessitates their continual orientation toward global economic and political systems in which they appear destined to remain third-class citizens.

Tourism is one of the main forces absorbing indigenous peoples into the modernist world system. So long as it remains permeated by a developmentalist ideology that divorces them from history and absolves their oppressors, these people who have for so long been a locus of authenticity for tourists will continue to be denied the meta-authenticity that derives from being a fully modern touring subject.

Source: Adapted from "The Authentic (In)Authentic: Bushman Anthro-Tourism," *Visual Anthropology,* 1999, 12(2–3):267–88.

Notes

[1] See, for example, the policy documents *Vision 2030* (GRN/NPC 2004), *National Development Plan 3* (GRN/NPC 2007), and *Promotion of Community Based Tourism* (GRN/MET 1995a). For recent data on the economics of tourism in Namibia, see *Namibia Tourism Satellite Account 2nd Edition* (Namibia Tourism Board 2007).

[2] Much about tourism development in Namibia indicates what Urry terms the switch to "post-Fordist" tourist consumption: (a) more information is provided than is usually the case in guidebooks; (b) there is a rapid turnover of tourist sites because of changes in fashion; (c) there has been a steady growth of "green tourism" and accommodation individually molded for the consumer; and (d) tourism has begun to be de-differentiated from leisure, culture, and education (Urry 1995).

[3] Garland (1999) expands this argument.

[4] "Boma" is a Swahili word not known locally, suggesting very much the clientele Intu Afrika is soliciting: upmarket, "Been to" East Africa tourists.

[5] There is naturally an alternative version to this account of these events. Thus, Eddie Koch of the respected *Weekly Mail* (February 17, 1995) reported on a visit to the Bushman army base at Schmidtsdrift in South Africa that:

> The owner of "Intu Afrika" called up the army base last year, and asked to borrow some bushmen who could perform their ancient traditions for tourists on his farm. . . . Since they have very little to do with their lives, five families volunteered and were dispatched by bus to their new place of employment. The problem though was that these were ordinary folk. They wore trousers and shirts and dresses. They slept on beds. They washed with soap and combed their hair. They went to church. And they did not appreciate having to sport animal skins around their loins.
>
> After a few day the irate farmer called to say he was sending them back. These people, he said, did not fit the bill. They were not short and yellow. Many looked just like other Namibians. Some drank too much. And they refused to behave like "genuine bushmen."
>
> The incident highlights the plight of a people who have been persecuted, misunderstood, shunted around and betrayed for most of their lives. "My personal feeling," says Feliciano Mario Mahango, "is that we are not seen as human beings any more. We are just sportgoed—playthings for other people."

Stuart Sholto-Douglas (personal communication with R. Gordon) who was present at the interview and worked with Mahango, points out that Mahango actually said "spotgoed," not "sportgoed," which means not sport equipment but object of ridicule and mockery. A significant difference!

[6] Indeed, one could suggest that this has always been the case for tourism around people called bushmen, in that their status as cultural Others has always been mediated by—and constructed through—the glamorous quests of Western adventurers like Laurens van der Post and John Marshall.

[7] As Taylor writes of the decontextualizing effect of tourism in England, "Uncoupling the representation from its context encourages . . . [the] audience to perceive the present in selected ways. They teach audiences by omission to fail to see the contradictions which existed in the past; or they suggest that conflicts are quickly resolved and isolated. What visitors learn . . . is 'unreal' because it is uncomplicated and sanitised to such an extent that it can neither be grasped nor truly believed in" (Taylor 1994: 247).

References

Ashley, Caroline and Garland, Elizabeth. 1994. *Promoting Community-Based Tourism Development*. Ministry of Environment and Tourism Research Discussion Paper Number 4.

Bhabha, Homi. 1994. *The Location of Culture*. London: Routledge.

Birkett, Dea. 1996. "Forest Gumption." *New Statesman* (2 August):46–47

Boynton, Graham. 1997. "The lost tribe of the Kalahari." *Conde Nast Traveller* (May):218–228, 285–293.

Bruner, Edward. 1991. "Transformation of the Self in Tourism." *Annals of Tourism Research* 18:238–250.

———. 1996. "Tourism in Ghana." *American Anthropologist* 98(2): 290–304.

Camerapix. 1994. *Spectrum Guide to Namibia*. Nairobi: Camerapix.

Comaroff, John L. and Jean Comaroff. 1997. *Of Revelation and Revolution*, vol. 2. Chicago: University of Chicago Press.

Culler, Jonathan. 1981. "Semiotics of Tourism." *American Journal of Semiotics* 1(1/2).

Enloe, Cynthia. 1990. *Bananas, Beaches and Bases*. Berkeley: University of California Press.

Garland, Elizabeth. 1999. "Developing Bushmen: Building Civil(ized) Society in the Kalahari and Beyond." In *Civil Society and the Political Imagination in Africa: Critical Perspectives*, ed. John L. and Jean Comaroff. Chicago: University of Chicago Press.

Goldman, Robert and Stephen Papson. 1996. *Sign Wars: The Cluttered Landscape of Advertising*. New York: The Guilford Press.

Gordon, Robert. 1992. *The Bushman Myth*. Boulder: Westview

———. 1997. *Picturing Bushmen: The Denver African Expedition*. Athens: Ohio University Press.

Government of the Republic of Namibia, Ministry of Environment and Tourism. 1995a. *Promotion of Community Based Tourism*. Policy Document. Windhoek, Namibia.

———. 1995b.*Wildlife Management, Utilisation and Tourism in Communal Areas*. Policy Document. Windhoek, Namibia.

Government of the Republic of Namibia, National Planning Commission. 2004. *Vision 2030*. Policy Document. Windhoek, Namibia.

———. 2007. *National Development Plan 3*. Policy Document. Windhoek, Namibia.

Greenwood, Davydd J. 2004[1977]. "Culture by the Pound: An Anthropological Perspective on Tourism as Cultural Commodification." In *Tourists and Tourism*, 1st ed., ed. Sharon Gmelch, pp.157–169. Long Grove, IL: Waveland Press.

Haape, Johannes, ed. 1993. *Insight Guides: Namibia*. Singapore: APA.

Isaacson, Rupert. 1996. "Call of the Wild: One Day He Was Sitting on the Tube the Next Hunting Wildebeest with the Kalahari Bushmen." *The Daily Telegraph* (November 2).

Jones, Brian T. B. 1995. *Wildlife Management, Utilisation and Tourism in Communal Areas*. Ministry of Environment and Tourism Research Discussion Paper Number 5.

Luard, Nicholas. 1981. *The Last Wilderness*. New York: Simon and Schuster.

MacCannell, Dean. 1976. *The Tourist: A New Theory of the Leisured Class*. New York: Schocken.

Namibia Tourism Board. 2008. *Namibia Tourism Satellite Account 2nd Edition*. Windhoek, Namibia.

Olivier, Willie and Sandra Oliver. 1989. *Visitors Guide to Namibia*. Johannesburg: Southern.

Taylor, John. 1994. *A Dream of England*. Manchester: Manchester University Press.

Tomaselli, Keyan. 1999. "Psychospiritual Ecoscience: The Ju/'hoansi and Cultural Tourism." *Visual Anthropology* 12(2–3): 183–196.

Urry, John. 1995. *Consuming Places*. London: Routledge.

Wilmsen, Edwin. 1989. *Land Filled with Flies: a Political Economy of the Kalahari*. Chicago: University of Chicago Press.

15

In a Sense Abroad: Theme Parks and Simulated Tourism

Lawrence Mintz

In British author David Lodge's novel, *Paradise News,* anthropologist Roger Sheldrake, a character described by one reviewer as a typical "theory-besotted professor," appears, in beige safari suit, en route to Hawai'i to continue his research on tourism. Sheldrake has become bored with the traditional subject matter of his discipline. He is on to something more interesting, more "hip." "Sightseeing," he enthuses, "is a substitute for religious ritual. The sightseeing tour as secular pilgrimage. Accumulation of grace by visiting the shrines of high culture. Souvenirs as relics. Guidebooks as devotional aids. You get the picture" (Lodge 1992:161).

Lodge's satire fails here only because the actual study of tourism approaches too closely his comic imagination. Scholarly writing about travel over the past decade has often compared it to pilgrimage. Titles such as John F. Sear's *Sacred Places* and Alexander Moore's subtitle for his discussion of Disney World, "bounded ritual space and the playful pilgrimage center," make the point unambiguously. Dean MacCannell, an important progenitor of this discussion, observed that the tourist seeks more than entertainment or amusement. Tourists are seeking more meaningful, even profound satisfaction, but what they actually experience is a "staged authenticity," an encounter that is essentially engineered both by the tourism industry that controls the plan of the visit and by the cultural expectations of each visitor. Cultural observers Daniel Boorstin, Jean Baudrillard, Umberto Eco, Jonathan Culler, and many others note that travel is itself in a sense a "pseudo-event," to use Boorstin's (1964) term, a "simulation" (Baudrillard 1988), a "hyperreality" (Eco 1986). Over a decade ago, Margaret J. King explained the management of experience at Walt Disney World, observing that "people have long 'understood' other cultures not through actual contact but through mediated experience and imagination" (1981:148). Such observations reflect the theoretical position that all reality is "socially constructed," that what we experience and understand is a result of decoding signs and symbols using cognitive tools (such as language) that are themselves cultural constructs.

It is the commercially designed and operated tourist simulations (i.e., theme parks) that particularly irk certain contemporary social philosophers. Critics such as Umberto Eco and Jean Baudrillard see them as disturbingly modern, or we should say postmodern, and as uniquely American phenomena. In an article on Colonial Williamsburg, critic Ada Louise Huxtable describes the restoration cum amusement environment as nothing less than the start of a "quintessentially American" process of replacing reality with "substitution." Huxtable is disturbed that it works all too well and detrimentally. She is also disturbed that theme park simulations are unabashed in their enthusiasm for the quality of the recreation: "nothing in it [the theme park] is admired for its reality, only for the remarkable simulation that is achieved; the selective manipulation of its sources is a deliberate expressive distortion that is its own art form" (1992:26).

Another source of criticism of theme park simulations is that they are "capitalist" or consumer-oriented ventures, expensive entertainments, and profitable endeavors. They are carefully planned, closely managed, technologically controlled—in short, industrialized and packaged. It is argued that they limit spontaneity, originality, individuality. In his study of Walt Disney World, Stephen M. Fjellman (1992) presents the park as a near perfect metaphor for America itself: prosperous, antiseptic, materialistic, narcissistic—powerful and controlling.

To apply a simulation of simulations to the discussion, we might note some dialogue from the popular novel and film, Michael Crichton's *Jurassic Park*, in which it is argued that real dinosaurs make lousy tourist exhibits because they move too fast to be appreciated by the human viewers. "Nobody wants domesticated dinosaurs, Henry. They want the real thing," John Hammond claims. "But that's my point," Wu responds. "I don't think they do. They want to see their expectations, which is quite different . . . You said yourself, John, this park is entertainment. And entertainment has nothing to do with reality. Entertainment is antithetical to reality" (Crichton 1990:122). Walt Disney himself understood that his park was not about "reality." Margaret J. King quotes the master as proclaiming, "I don't want the public to see the real world they live in while they're in the park . . . I want them to feel they are in another world" (1981:121).

The concerns about the meaning and effects of simulation are, of course, neither frivolous nor simple. What is the *effect* of the blurring of distinctions between original and copy, between old and new, and of radically reordering both text and context? Museums wrestle, for instance, with the problem of presenting exhibits that are composed exclusively of actual or authentic artifacts that might be incomprehensible as well as visually uninteresting; on the other hand, there are ethical and intellectual objections to offering recreations and restorations that might "work" artistically and educationally but are misleading and offensive in their "falseness." A legitimate question is raised as to whether the "real" can compete with the artificially enhanced, whether we are being conditioned to carefully structured, staged experience, with detrimental effects on our attention span, our patience for learning without amusement, our need for constant visual stimulation, our appetite for change and excitement, and so forth.

At the center of this debate lie attitudes about popular culture and its aesthetics. We have a hierarchy of tourist motives and activities that places various ambiguously defined spiritual and intellectual purposes at the top, and entertainment or amusement at the bottom. Travel that involves living and studying abroad, learning another language, making close contacts with the natives, and developing a mystical quality called "an appreciation" of the culture is deemed worthy, while various packaged tours and quick visits ("if this is Tuesday, it must be Belgium") are condemned. In a still lower circle of tourist hell is "armchair tourism," a term for media encounters (travel films, magazines, television tourism). Theme park simulations, of course, rank either just above or just below media-based travel, depending upon whether you add points because it is "live" entertainment or subtract some because they include rides and other "fun" activities.

Another cause for concern is the argument that the simulated theme park is "postmodern," disorienting in its dazzling, confusing, and facile mixture of tourist icons, parades, shows, multimedia attractions, rides, fast food, and service amenities. The food server wearing a Hollywood costume version of native dress while offering modern American fast food disguised as native fare, both of which are intended to be exotic while at the same time referencing other modern popular culture experiences, including other theme parks, leaves the visitor dangling somewhere between the excitement of new experience and the comfort zone of the familiar. Similarly, in the rapid changes of context as one moves from one attraction to another, covering a wide range of activity (touring exhibits, attending shows, enjoying rides, shopping, eating), audiences may become disoriented, overwhelmed. Such an assessment implies that the dazed spectator is therefore more vulnerable, controlled, manipulated. We need to know far more about the tourist experience, its various motives and functions, and its complex role in our society. One primary need is for more audience research, particularly qualitative, in which the participants themselves articulate their expectations and their sense of what it is they have experienced. However, it is a gross oversimplification to present the issues as one of the "real" versus "artificial" experience, or "learning" and/or "inspiration" versus recreation, amusement, or for that matter, of consumerism or leisure as a commodity. These distinctions are misleading and reductionist. Theme parks need to be explored and interpreted on their own terms, as contemporary popular culture, as participatory theater, as leisure environment, and as text.

The idea of recreating Europe or "the old country" in a nostalgic way is profoundly familiar in our culture from the accidental recreation of ethnic enclaves in our cities (e.g., Little Italys, China Towns, Little Polands, and many Irish and Jewish neighborhoods) to more consciously constructed tourist remakes such as the California Danish town of Solvang and the several Little Bavarias, Little Hollands, and Little Switzerlands dotting the landscape. We love to use European and other foreign motifs in our vernacular architecture, adding Spanish or Middle Eastern motifs to our shopping malls, gas stations, or just about anywhere we can find a place to anchor the iconic clues. Such simulations acknowledge the power of our attachment to our immigrant roots, the cultural significance we award to our parent nations, and our taste for the exotic; it coexists with our other simulations, of colonial America, of the Old West, and so forth, as means by which we establish and communicate our mythic personal, community, and national identities.

Theme parks that simulate the travel experience, most notably Walt Disney World Epcot's "World Showcase," but including such parks as Busch Garden's "The Old Country" near Williamsburg, Virginia, as well as other, less ambitious recreations of Europe, Africa, the Old West, and just about any other place a person might want to visit, present a special case of tourism. They are tours within tours, i.e., the tourist travels to the park to travel *within* the park. For that matter, in a visit to both World Showcase and The Old Country, one travels to the park, then travels within the park by cable car, boat, and monorail to reach specific destinations, and then "rides" each attraction by transport, which is either entertainment in its own right or a means of locomotion through an exhibit. In World Showcase's Norway attraction, for instance, a boat ride offers a rather tame version of a North Sea voyage while exhibiting that country's past and present through film and artifact displays. A particularly amusing case of the layering of travel within travel is provided by The Old Country's Marco Polo's journey, a ride with a Turkish motif within the Italy sector of the park. Only in America.

Perhaps the most disorienting thing about Busch Garden's "The Old Country" is its location in Williamsburg, Virginia, or as their promotional literature puts it, "surrounded by Colonial Williamsburg and Jamestown."[1] While a visit to Busch Gardens does not necessarily imply a visit to Colonial Williamsburg, it is assumed that many, if not most, tourists visit both attractions as part of the same trip. The two attractions were quite nervous about this "odd bedfellows" phenomenon when Busch Gardens opened in 1975. Colonial Williamsburg has a lot invested in its educational and inspirational potential and in the "authenticity" of its restoration and research programs.

However, they seem to have developed a comfortable relationship, fueled no doubt by the realization that they economically benefit one another. There may even be a growing if grudging acceptance by Colonial Williamsburg that in the areas of entertainment and visitor services, its functions are not really that different from those of its more clearly commercial neighbor.

Busch Gardens is one of several parks operated by Anheuser-Busch, brewers of Budweiser, Michelob, and other American mass-market beers. The first Busch Gardens, "The Dark Continent," opened in 1959 in Tampa, Florida. It was conceived as a botanical garden and zoo adjunct to the brewery, a private park built as a public service and community relations gambit. Success led to its growth into a naturalist-environmentalist theme park with an African motif, together with rides and other entertainments. The juxtaposition of the theme parks—a family ice cream and coke environment with active breweries offering brewery tours and beer samples—is potentially jarring. Unofficial amusements at the park are for teenagers to try and get a beer, and for adults to see how many free ones they can obtain.

Busch Gardens covers 360 acres, a little more than half a square mile, and serves some 2 million visitors yearly.[2] The park is divided into sectors: England's Banbury Cross and Hastings; Scotland's Heatherdowns; France's Acquataine; New France (so named so as not to violate the old country theme, but which is actually Canada); Italy's San Marco and Festa Italia; and Germany's Rhineland and Oktoberfest. Each sector uses clichéd architectural clues and familiar tourist icons to establish its national identity, thus Banbury Cross is represented by mock Tudor architecture and red London telephone booths, New France has log cabins, San Marcos has statues and fountains, and in a particularly amusing touch, France Acquataine is falling apart (e.g., artificial cracks in the sides of the buildings). Each sector offers its own selection of rides and attractions, including those for small children as well as more challenging roller coasters and other thrill rides. The rides' trappings are intended to contribute to the theme atmosphere, and names such as The Loch Ness Monster, Drachen Fire, Le Mans Raceway are used to remind revelers that they are indeed "abroad." Food options include pizza, burgers, barbeque, roast beef sandwiches, fried chicken, French fries, and other American commercial cuisine, presented as ethnic dining experiences in each country sections (pizza in Italy, barbeque in New France). Shopping for souvenirs and rather schlocky imported gifts is likewise given a national context by offering ordinary products such as cigarette lighters and coin purses decorated to appear as if they had been made in and are representative of the crafts of the "countries" in which they are purchased. Ironically, such theme park shopping might be seen as a realistic modern touch, as genuine native crafts become harder to find and to afford and are increasingly replaced everywhere by mass-manufactured junk. Rest amenities such as benches and scenic views, bridges, ponds, lakes, and pleasant park-garden settings are an important feature, and clean, efficient personal services for the comfort of the guests are readily available.

The shows at Busch Gardens have only the vaguest of themes, with the exception of Oktoberfest as discussed below. The Globe Theater offered a fascinating pastiche of Shakespeare's plays when the park first opened, became a blended magic show, light show, and extended skit, and has more recently degenerated into a variety show distinguished from others only by costume, badly rendered accent, and thinly applied motif. The concert and shows division of Busch Gardens is perhaps its weakest, though it is hard to say whether this is a failure on the part of the management or a concession to audience tastes for bland, light variety entertainment. The show in Italy, for instance, is a set of popular Italian-American classics like "That's Amore" with mercifully brief snatches of Bel Canto. The young performers are clean-cut and earnest in the classic American style.

Perhaps the most interesting attraction at Busch Gardens is Oktoberfest, an attraction reproduced from one created for the original Busch Gardens in Tampa, Florida. Oktoberfest, referring to the German harvest celebration in late September–early October that Americans tend to associate primarily with Munich and Bavaria, is held in Das Festhaus, a very large, barnlike building, nicely decorated with an attractive, gigantic stained glass window above an antique automated organ. Oktoberfesters file into a cafeteria area where they purchase platters of wurst with kraut and German potato salad or huge corned-beef sandwiches, topped off by slices of flavorless Black Forest cake and washed down by beer or soft drinks served in paper cups. They then take seats at large picnic tables encircling the stage and dance area. While dining, they are entertained by a rather authentic-looking German elder, dressed in lederhosen, drinking from a beer stein, feebly warbling "Edel-weiss" and other examples of the famed Teutonic musical genius. After a few minutes, an oompah-pah band and young dancers march in. As the band is installed in a circular bandstand that ascends into the heavens, a narrator informs the audience that they are about to experience "gemutlichkeit," the spirit of joy, abandon, and community spirit. Toward that end, visitors are encouraged to shake hands with everyone at their table within reach. After twelve minutes or so of waltzes and polkas, the audience is encouraged to participate as the dance troupe selects suitably cute partners from among the guests. Then the experience is over, and the next adventure begins.

For tourists, Busch Gardens is about having a pleasant day of varied amusements in a comfortable environment. As a place for relaxed visual stimulation, it is perhaps not as far from a European experience as it would first seem. Margaret King has observed that "in fact Americans go to Europe largely for the charming cities—for public spaces like the Italian piazza which is human and pedestrian in scale encouraging the outdoor stroll and public relaxation . . . and the sidewalk cafes which encourage 'people watch-ing'"(1981:121). Busch Gardens offers a safe, clean, comfortable simulation of the cosmopolitan ethos.

The park's diversity encourages family participation. There is some-thing for everyone from a very young child to grandparents, and it is safe to let reasonably young kids wander alone, checking in at designated times and places. Teenagers can travel in groups of peers; young couples can find privacy while surrounded by hundreds of others.

The Old Country does not overtly claim to be a learning experience or a pilgrimage. Indeed, in that sense it downplays its own theme of European travel. The various theme sectors of the park provide mild visual variety without disturbing the familiar rhythms, the comfort in formula and familiarity, and the realized expectations on which the genre depends. Visitors know what to expect in each area and from each activity, whether it is the rides or the shopping or the dining experience. Yet the park is successful in its suggestion of novelty, of variety rather than redundancy as one moves from England to Italy to France to Germany to Scotland. Though superficial, the environmental changes enhance the sense of adventure, of an escape from the ordinary world into a realm of vacation and recreation. That the same basic formula is repeated in each realm, disguised by the trappings and icons that simulate the local color, is an underlying popular culture verity. The experience is comfortingly familiar, unthreatening, immediately understood and appreciated, yet the illusion of freshness is maintained and apparently accepted. The references to the various ethnic and national identities confirm expectations; that is, they are based on familiar clichés and stereotypes. They are clearly intended to provide atmosphere rather than simulation in any active sense. At Busch Gardens the trip "abroad" is meant to be a vacation, an amusement, an opportunity for pleasure.

The "World Showcase" at Walt Disney World's Epcot is more ambitious and in a sense a more pretentious enterprise. A promotional flyer heads into the storm of simulation controversy with no quarter offered: "Situated around a 40-acre lagoon beyond Future World, the World Showcase nations are re-creations of landmark architectures and historic scenes familiar to world travelers. Built with infinite attention to detail, the mini-towns have buildings, streets, gardens and monuments designed to give . . . guests *an authentic visual experience of each land*" (emphasis added).

In any case, it is a more carefully constructed physical simulation than one would expect to find in any other theme park. The Disney organization put an enormous amount of effort and money into the materials, the design, and the construction of the World Showcase, and as Ada Louise Huxtable suggested of Colonial Williamsburg, the technological and artistic quality of the recreation might be in fact more significant than its content. The quality extends to the goods and services available. The shopping at World Showcase is of a higher order than at most theme parks, though merely by degree. It still involves souvenirs and gifts; just better quality. The fast food is also the same but better than one finds elsewhere. World Showcase's gourmet restaurants, however, claim to provide an "authentic" touristic experience. L'Originale Alfredo di Roma Ristorante, the Biergarten, Restaurant Marrakesh, Chefs de France, and Bistro de Paris lay claim to originality and top quality. The view of this writer is that while they do not quite make it, they come amazingly

China in Florida: part of Epcot's "World Showcase." (Photo by Walter Gmelch)

close considering the challenges they face. Any gourmet restaurant would be daunted by having to serve as many seatings with as many meals and by the time constraints posed by tourists with agendas and priorities other than the dining experience. There are also financial limits; while the restaurants are much more expensive than those at any other theme park, they are still considerably less expensive than most first-class gourmet establishments. As providers of "theme park fare," the restaurants at World Showcase are remarkably admirable.

World Showcase does not rely on exciting rides or participatory games and activities. Rather, it offers tours and exhibitions, in a most interesting way paralleling the definition of tourism that stresses information and inspiration as paramount goals. The tourist visiting the park's Mexico sector, for instance, is cast in the role of a tourist, given a brief and very superficial survey of that country's history, and an equally brief introduction to its tourist attractions, which are dwarfed by the enormous, adjacent Mexican bazaar. This creates the impression that Mexico's primary reason for existence is the revenue opportunity it provides for tourists to spend money. The presentation of the dominant national image in the other lands is generally less demeaning than it is in the Mexico sector, but the basic theme is that the countries of the world are places that are interesting for us to see—charming diversions for our shopping and dining pleasure.

Whatever lessons about native cultures are to be learned are self-gleaned from reading the annotations on some of the artifact displays. The films that are the highlights in several of the sectors are visual treats, especially the Circle-Vision 360 presentations "Wonders of China" and the "Impressions of France," but they too rely on the spectacular sensory effect rather than any significant social or cultural communication. We see the countryside, some of the landmarks, and faces of the people while listening to music and soothing narration. Despite the well-publicized fact that World Showcase employs natives of the various lands (who are issued special green cards by the U.S. Immigration Service toward that end), there is no real opportunity to engage in a serious encounter with the people or the culture of any of the simulated lands. The only sector where the visitor learns something about the culture, society, politics, or people to be encountered is the American Adventure. Although even here there is much less learning than in any *National Geographic* article, to say nothing of a more extensive stay abroad. (But as suggested earlier, the case may be made that the theme park experience is closer to the actual package tour experienced by many American tourists on a "trip of a lifetime" to Europe.) For all of its quality of detail, World Showcase is neither more informative, more stimulating, more inspiring, nor more fun than Busch Gardens. It seems a quiet respite from the more exciting Magic Kingdom or the newer MGM and Universal Studios parks and from the intellectual appeal made by Epcot's Future World. Here again tourism emerges as a pleasant, amusing vacation activity rather than anything invested with a higher purpose.

The question is: why should tourism be anything more than a pleasant, relaxing, entertaining experience? If we make some largely false assumptions about the value of tourism and then reason from them that theme park simulations fail to provide a "proper" tourist experience, and/or if we speculate that the simulations replace people's impulse for actual tourism or more extensive travel, we can conclude that the time spent at them is not well spent. If we wonder why trips to these parks, especially to Walt Disney World, nevertheless seem to be so highly valued, so prominent, and even monumental in the lives of American consumers, we will not find an answer by uncovering a hidden or overlooked profundity in the theme park formula. Indeed, evaluating the simulated tourism experience according to a false set of standards and assumptions about the meaning of tourism inevitably misleads. If instead we focus on what parks actually deliver, on their mildly stimulating, formulaic, predictable, safe, clean amusement; on the opportunity they provide for shopping for worthless but inexpensive goods and for eating convenient and comforting if mediocre food, we can properly understand the nature of simulated tourism. "It's the entertainment, stupid."

Source: Adapted from "Simulated Tourism at Busch Gardens: The Old Country and Disney's World Showcase, Epcot Center," 1998, *Journal of Popular Culture* 32(3):47–59.

Notes

[1] Most of the facts about Busch Gardens cited here come from the company's promotional literature, c. 1989. According to a spokesperson, they were still basically accurate as of 1993.

[2] Epcot provides a library and an information service office for educators, primarily for teachers using the park's resources for future-studies or for cultural studies rather than for study of the Disney parks per se. However, there are also some clippings and other general information, mostly from press releases, which provide useful materials on the history and details of the construction and operation of all of the Disney theme park enterprises.

References

Baudrillard, Jean. 1988. "On Seduction: Similacra and Simulations." *Selected Writings*. Stanford: Stanford University Press.

Boorstin, Daniel. 1964. *The Image: A Guide to Pseudo-events in America*. New York: Harper.

Crichton, Michael. 1990. *Jurassic Park*. New York: Knopf.

Culler, Jonathan. 1981. "Semiotics of Tourism." *American Journal of Semiotic* 1(1–2): 127–40.

Eco, Umberto. 1986. *Travels in Hyperreality*. San Diego: Harcourt, Brace.

Fjellman, Stephen J. 1992. *Vinyl Leaves: Walt Disney World and America*. Boulder, CO: Westview.

Huxtable, Ada Louis. 1992. "Inventing American Reality." *New York Review* 3 Dec: 24–29.

King, Margaret J. 1981. "Disneyland and Walt Disney World: Traditional Values in Futuristic Form." *Journal of Popular Culture* 15(1): 116–140.

Lodge, David. 1992. *Paradise News*. New York: Viking.

MacCannell, Dean. 1976. *The Tourist: A New Theory of the Leisure Class*. New York: Schocken.

———. 1992. *Empty Meeting Grounds: The Tourist Papers*. London: Routledge.

Moore, Alexander. 1980. "Walt Disney's World: Bounded Ritual Space and the Playful Pilgrimage Center." *Anthropological Quarterly* 53:207–18.

Sears, John F. 1989. *Sacred Places: American Tourist Attractions in the Nineteenth Century*. New York: Oxford.

Urry, John. 1990. *The Tourist Gaze: Leisure and Travel in Contemporary Societies*. London: Sage.

Four:
Tourism and Identity

Australian Aboriginal plays the digeredoo for tourists at Circular Quay, Sydney. (Photo by Sharon Gmelch)

16

Through a New Mirror: Tourism and Identity in the Amazon

Amanda Stronza

> *People become aware of their culture when they stand at its boundaries.*
> — A. Cohen (1985)

> *The Ese eja, we know the science of the natural world and how to live. We have the legacy of our ancestors, the ones who know. The mestizos are in zero. If they know anything, it is because of us. We the natives know everything, all of the animals, and because of the moon and the sun, we are never lost. We are timid, but our minds are always working.*
> —45-year-old Ese eja man from Infierno

Tourism is often a catalyst of change in the ways people perceive themselves and others. When tourists and locals meet, their encounters are like windows that double as mirrors: each side uses the other to peer into a new world while at the same time casting back impressions and reflecting on themselves through the eyes of the other. Expectations of how each side "should" look are often based on ethnic stereotypes, nostalgic ideals, and the promising pictures in brochures. In the wake of such gazing, hosts and guests on both sides are likely to walk away affected, their views of themselves and of the other somehow altered.

The purpose of this article is to describe the ways in which tourism has affected perceptions of identity and culture in the mixed-ethnic Native Community of Infierno in the southeastern Peruvian Amazon. The members of Infierno partnered with a private tourism company in 1996 to build, comanage, and share profits in an ecotourism lodge called Posada Amazonas. Using ethnographic data gathered between 1996 and 2006, I interpret transformations of identity in the community and how perceptions of self and other are changing in the context of tourism. I pay particular attention to what Pierre van den Berghe has called re-creations of ethnicity as locals reflect on what (they think) tourists want to see. In so doing, I emphasize the relational and dynamic qualities of ethnic identity.

Nearly 7,000 tourists pass through the community of Infierno every year, though they stay at Posada Amazonas, an ecolodge located far upriver from where most of its residents live. (Photo by Amanda Stronza)

Tourism, Culture, and Ethnicity

Many anthropologists have interpreted tourism's effects on ethnicity and cultural identity (Chambers 2010; Gmelch 2004; Nash 1996). Nuñez (1963) described tourism as a "laboratory situation" for testing how cultural perceptions and relations shift when hosts and guests interact. A number of seminal works have shown how ethnicity is represented, perceived, and reinvented through the tourist gaze (Bruner 1987; Bruner and Kirshenblatt-Gimblett 1994; MacCannell 1984; Urry 1990). Some have argued that tourism can represent a first wave of globalization that overpowers or altogether obliterates local traditions and values (Mowforth and Munt 1998). Others have shown that tourism can lead to a renaissance of native culture by instilling new pride in local communities (van den Berghe and Keyes 1984; van den Berghe 1994; Grunewald 2002; Ingles 2001) or by encouraging creative forms of self-representation (Bendix 1989; Leong 1989; Cohen 1979, 1988; Evans-Pritchard 1989).

The mechanisms by which tourism alters culture and identity are debated. Erisman (1983) has suggested the large influx of foreign goods, people, and ideas to host destinations drive change. In this view, markets and the "commodification of culture" are primarily to blame for identity loss (Greenwood 1977, but see revisions in 1982, 1989). Though local residents may gain economic benefits from tourism, they do so by catering to the needs of outsiders; as they serve others, they may lose a sense of themselves. An alternative view posits that feelings of identity shift in response to the conveyance of tourists' expectations—or the "gaze." This understanding begins with the premise that tourists are preoccupied by a search for the authentic, or "the pristine, the primitive, the natural, that which is as yet untouched by modernity" (Cohen 1988:374; see MacCannell 1976). As tourists gauge their satisfaction of a trip based on how well their perceptions of authenticity match their experiences in a destination, the logical response for locals is to mirror back brochure behaviors (Adams 1984; Rossel 1988; Silver 1993). These responses may shift significantly over time as locals gain increasing experience with tourists (Pi-Sunyer's 1989[1977]). Maoz (2006) has introduced the term "the local gaze" to describe a more complex, two-sided mirror between the gazes of tourists and locals. In the two-way exchange, tourists themselves tend to "live up to the expectations and images the locals have of them" (p. 229).

Van den Berghe and Keyes (1984) argued that tourism is always a form of ethnic relations. Especially in tourism that brings people of different ethnic groups together, locals may modify, revive, or invent "new" customs and traditions to appeal to tourists' desires for authentic cultural displays. Over time, the displays have a tendency to develop their own "reconstructed" authenticity (MacCannell 1984). For example, Esman (1984) found that tourist versions of Cajun culture are now interpreted by many Cajuns as authentic and traditional even though much of it has been created specifically for tourists. Xie (2003) has similarly described how traditional dance forms of bamboo beating in China co-evolved with tourism development. Even if locals are not playing up the exotic or brochure-ready displays of their ethnicity, tourism can exert a strong influence on local conceptions of self (Picard and Wood 1997). Schiller (2001) observed that Dayak identity in East Kalimantan has evolved in a dynamic relationship with tourism. Using the metaphor of "the play of mirrors," Caiuby Novaes (1997) wrote that self-image among the Bororo Indians of Brazil was shaped by their interactions with non-Bororo. A member of the Tla-o-qui-aht First Nations tribe in Canada commented, tourism "makes me think about my culture every single day" (Mazurkewich 2007).

But what is ethnicity in these analyses, and how does it become authentic or fake in the eyes of tourists? Graburn (1976) suggested that tourists tend to recognize ethnicity as "a small bundle of overt features"—clothing, architecture, dances, arts. These are what get exaggerated by tourism, and sometimes feed back into a host community, changing locals' sense of who they are, or who they think they should be (or at the very least, who they think outsiders think they should be). Evans-Pritchard (1989) described a Native American woman who felt she had to "look 'Indian' in order to be accepted as authentic by the tourists" (p. 97). Cohen (1979) wrote of locals who "played the natives" for tourists. In these ways, tourism becomes a kind of a stage for local plays of culture and ethnicity.

The notion of "playing up" ethnicity is possible only if ethnicity is defined as something changeable and subject to manipulation. Yet, ethnicity is often treated as primarily a biological product of inheritance, passed down through blood and genes. Jackson (1995) noted that people are often described as *possessing* ethnicity, just as an animal has fur or claws. Field (1994) argued that ethnic traits are often seen as "the essences of being Indian that function as Cartesian coordinates against which the degree of 'Indianness' of a group can be determined" (p. 238). Here ethnicity is something people acquire early in life as part of their normal development and socialization, not something they reconstruct or invent later in life.

Yet, most anthropologists and other social scientists have long ago disposed of these static and primordial conceptions of ethnicity. We know ethnicity to be a social construction. Weber (1968) called ethnic groups those that "entertain a subjective belief in their common descent. . . . It does not matter whether or not an objective blood relationship exists" (p. 389). Ethnicity in this light is less something someone *has,* like blue eyes or brown skin, and more something someone *does* with varying levels of consciousness. Stephens (1996), for example, argued that ethnicity is a creative and improvisational process of consciously creating and re-creating what it means to be Sioux, Welsh, or Aymara. Throughout Amazonia, Lepri (2006) argues, identity is primarily processual rather than inherited. Anyone, she explains, can through his or her actions "become a proper Piro, Cashinahua, or and so forth" (p. 70). Paulson (1997) portrayed a Bolivian woman who changed her ethnicity in the course of just one day, depending on the task at hand. Valdivia (2005), too, provides examples of how Amazonian peoples in Ecuador articulate their ethnicity (or "indigeneity") in relation to tourism and other forms of market integration.

These notions of mutable ethnicity follow on Barth's (1969, 1994) seminal work, which posited that ethnicity is continuously created in instrumentalist ways to construct and maintain boundaries. Such boundaries can be subjective, ideological, symbolic, and not necessarily identified by outsiders. Their purpose is essentially to keep insiders in and outsiders out as members of the ethnic group compete or mobilize to achieve some advantage (see also Despres 1975).

Discussions of ethnic boundaries and boundary maintenance are inextricably linked with Benedict Anderson's concept of "imagined communities" among ethnic groups or nations. Communities are socially constructed by the people who identify themselves as part of a group and who coalesce around certain perceptions, images, and discourses (Anderson 1983). Though such communities may be imagined, they are not false, as perceptions define the very boundaries of collective identity (Nagel 1994). In the context of tourism, this perspective highlights the power of members of a host community to construct identities for themselves (and their visitors). In this way, the tourist gaze can ultimately be a tool of power, wielded by locals, to imagine their own "community" through their interactions with others.

Case Study: Ecotourism in a Mixed-ethnic "Native Community"

The *Comunidad Nativa de Infierno*, a mixed-ethnic village of 150 families in the lowland rain forests of the Peruvian Amazon, is an especially apt place to track and interpret changes in ethnic relations associated with tourism. Over the past decade, the members of Infierno have partnered with a private tourism company, Rainforest Expeditions, to build, comanage, and share revenues in a highly profitable ecotourism lodge called Posada Amazonas (Stronza 1999). The communal–private partnership is a legally binding 20-year contract, which began in 1996 and will end in 2016. The members of Infierno share all rights and responsibilities with Rainforest Expeditions, and the community owns the lodge and its infrastructure outright.

Posada Amazonas has won several international awards, including the United Nation's Equator Initiative Award, for its efforts to bring the ideals of ecotourism to practice (http://www.equatorinitiative.net/). Ecotourism is broadly defined as nature-based tourism with three special features: (1) it minimizes the negative environmental, economic, and social impacts often associated with mass tourism, (2) it delivers a net positive contribution to environmental conservation, and (3) it improves the livelihoods of local people (Charnley 2005; Stronza 2001).

The lodge consists of an architecturally designed complex of thatched buildings that can accommodate 60 guests at a time. The number of tourists to Posada Amazonas has steadily increased from 2,000 in 1998 to 4,000 in 2002 to more than 7,000 in 2007. In 2005 alone, the lodge generated profits of $110,000 for the community. Seventy to 80 percent of the profits are divided among families for personal use, and the remainder are used for communal projects, including a secondary school, water tank, and new river port (Gordillo et al. 2008). Profits are also channeled to increased social support in the form of an emergency health fund, care for the elderly, and loans for higher education in Lima.

Infierno and Posada Amazonas are located in the province of Tambopata, several hours by motorized canoe from the capital of Madre de Dios,
Puerto Maldonado (population ~40,000, see figure 1). The community com-
prises 9,558 hectares on both sides of the Tambopata River. It lies within the
buffer zone of the Tambopata National Reserve, and near the Bahuaja-Sonene
National Park. The members of Infierno have a mixed economy based on
fishing, hunting, and gathering with some horticulture. They travel to the
market in Puerto Maldonado to sell produce and buy manufactured goods.

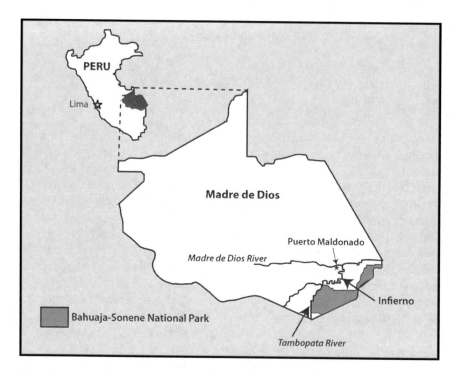

Figure 1: Department of Madre de Dios, Peru; Native Community of
Infierno; and Bahuaja-Sonene National Park

Despite its title and legal designation by government decree as a com-
munally owned "native" territory, Infierno is culturally diverse. The members
comprise three main ethnic groups: Ese eja, ribereños, and Andean colonists.
The cultural and ancestral heritage of the Ese eja is tied with the lowland rain
forests of what is today southeastern Peru and northwestern Bolivia. The Ese
eja distinguish among themselves by referring to their place of origin, generally the river where they were born or have lived most of their lives
(Ocampo-Raeder 2006). The Ese eja of Infierno are Bahuaja Ese eja, or the
"Ese eja from the Tambopata River." Two other groups of Ese eja are associ-

ated with the Heath River in Madre de Dios, and the Madidi River in Bolivia (Alexiades 1999; Peluso 2003; Lepri 2006).

The ribereños are people of mixed heritage who represent some of the earliest immigrants to the Peruvian Amazon (Chibnik 1994). Their name implies proximity to rivers. The ribereños arrived for a variety of different reasons—as part of the rubber boom, and later in search of opportunities in extractive industries like timber, gold, or Brazil nut harvest. The Andean colonists—or *colonos*—in Infierno settled in the area during the 1980s and 1990s. They maintain cultural and economic ties with the Andes. Many continue to speak Quechua, visit family in Cusco, Puno, and Arequipa, and send remittances.

Though the groups are different, ribereños and *colonos* in Infierno tend to refer to themselves collectively as *mestizos*. "Mestizo" is a Spanish word that implies mixed ancestry (Rudel et al. 2002). Herrera (2007) argues that "mestizo" is a complex social phenomenon that needs to be understood in terms linked to colonialism, as mestizos are those who have "been assimilated to the larger national-society" (p. 6). In Madre de Dios, "mestizos" include a wide range of people of Brazilian, Bolivian, Chinese, Japanese, and Yugoslavian descent as well as Coastal and Andean Peruvians (Ocampo-Raeder 2006).

Understanding how the mestizos and Ese eja came to share communal land requires some background. Until the 1970s, no indigenous communities were recognized in Peru. The national government granted individual parcels within native territories to "anyone who cared to colonize the area" (Gray 1997:77). This changed in 1974 when the Law of Native Communities stated that Amazonian indigenous peoples were to have their lands demarcated and recognized as inalienable territory. When this law led to a title of "native community" in Infierno in 1976, the Ese eja joined with ribereños and families of mixed indigenous and Andean descent who were already living in the area since the rubber boom. Information about why non-Ese eja members were included varies. According to some elders, the Ese eja were coerced by government representatives. Apparently, support for public works was conditioned on a certain number of inhabitants. The Ese eja had only 14 families, and they needed 20 to solicit a school.

Minutes from meetings in which local leaders began negotiating terms for the new "native community" reveal early concerns about ethnic differences between the families, and how these would play out in a shared community. In 1975, a government representative acknowledged "two classes" of people, and asked, "Why cannot these two forces unite? The natives also can be absorbed with the mestizos" (CNI, Libro de Actas, February 1975). In that meeting, an Ese eja elder announced that he did not want to join the "mestizos" because they "deceive us and look at us badly." A younger Ese eja leader spoke up, "Why don't we join with the mestizos so that we can have more power? Today we are all brothers, and we are all equal. The bad treatment and the naming of 'the Indian' to humiliate us has finished." One of the mestizos responded, "Yes, there is discrimination, but there is no reason to call anyone 'Indian' if we are all one race."

Notes from a meeting three months later reported that "all is well" in reference to the new settlement, save for "a lack of confidence in working together with the mestizos because some of them have committed abuses" (CNI, Libro de Actas, May 1975). By the following year, the government had built a new school, and the Ese eja and mestizo families agreed to form one community. Yet, a persistent and underlying tension remained, as the following comment from the minutes revealed: "Between the mestizos and the natives, there are disagreements, and because of these, the community will not be able to develop in the best way. It was agreed: the natives will work on one side [of the river] and the mestizos will work on the other side, where the school is" (CNI, Libro de Actas, June 1976).

Over the following years, the founding members of Infierno gradually accepted several new families of Andean colonists. These migrants became official members of the community and were granted rights to extract and produce from communal lands. Ocampo-Raeder (2006) estimated the population of Infierno in 2000 as approximately 380, with 36 households identified as Ese eja, 44 as ribereños, and 25 as Andean colonist. It is difficult to give an exact population figure at any time as the communal census includes only people who are official members of the community. Gordillo and his colleagues (2008) estimated the population of Infierno as approximately 600. In addition to the original primary school and medical post of 1976, the community now includes a kindergarten and secondary school, a meeting house and handicrafts studio, connectivity via an unpaved 19 km road to Puerto Maldonado, a water tank tower, three bodegas, and the ecotourism lodge, Posada Amazonas.

A Longitudinal Study of Ethnicity and Ecotourism

I began the research in the same month Infierno and Rainforest Expeditions signed the contract to launch their joint venture. Between 1996 and 2006, I have lived in the community and collected qualitative and quantitative ethnographic data in five major time periods, totaling 28 months. In the first period, when the community and company were planning Posada Amazonas, I conducted participant observation and a series of stakeholder interviews to understand early expectations and concerns about tourism development. In the second period, as the lodge was being built, I collected baseline data on people's household economies and their values about ethnicity, culture, and tradition. When the first groups of tourists began to arrive, I returned to ask the same questions I had asked in previous years, in addition to some new questions. When the lodge was fully functional and people began to focus on other concerns in the community, I returned to work in an applied capacity, leading focus groups and workshops to envision needs and priorities for the future. Subsequently, I joined with community leaders in Infierno over the course of a year (2002–2003) to share and compare lessons learned in Posada Amazonas with other community-based lodges in Ecuador and Bolivia. Most recently, I returned to carry out follow-up interviews during the 10-year anniversary of the signing of the contract, when the partnership was at its halfway point.

Much of the focus of this research has been on livelihood changes associated with tourism and effects on conservation, community development, and perceived quality of life (e.g., Stronza 2007). However, I have also sought to understand changes in reported feelings of identity, and in definitions, descriptions, and displays of Ese eja and mestizo culture.

The data presented here come from four main sources: (1) participant observation and detailed fieldnotes of meetings, discussions, focus groups, and key events during the periods of 1996–1999, 2002–2003, and 2006; (2) in-depth interviews with participants in the lodge and a purposive sample of 115 men and women in 68 community households in 1998 and 2003; (3) written surveys with 120 tourists in 1997; and (4) content analysis of marketing materials for Posada Amazonas. To build generalizations from the more qualitative ethnographic data, I coded field notes and interviews for topics and emergent patterns. When I found cases that diverged from the patterns, I re-examined and evaluated the data in the light of those cases. I conducted all of the interviews in Spanish without interpretation. Spanish is the dominant language in Infierno though some speak Ese eja at home, especially elders. All of the Ese eja in Infierno are fluent in Spanish.

Ethnicity before Tourism

Questions concerning identity and ethnic relations and how they might be altered in the context of tourism moved to the forefront of the research even before the lodge came under construction. The notion of ethnic identity is difficult to avoid in Infierno. Concerns over who belongs in what group, what people think of each other, and how they get along are at the core of both casual conversations and formal meetings. Of 65 men and women who responded to the question "What is the worst problem in Infierno today?", 16 percent identified "conflicts between ethnic groups," and another 26 percent pointed to the "lack of organization and willingness to work together." In fact, concerns over ethnic conflict and lack of organization topped other serious problems, such as "lack of economic opportunities," "lack of potable water," and "lack of quality education." Even among the people I talked to outside of the community, the fact that Infierno is a *mixed* community often came up as the first distinguishing characteristic.

Aside from the fact that everyone talks about ethnicity in Infierno, at least two things warranted better understanding of people's notions of identity and how they were changing in the context of tourism. For one, most people who knew Infierno described it as rife with conflict over ethnic differences between the Ese eja and mestizos. A predictable comment was, "Infierno [meaning "Hell"] lives up to its name." Others described the community as "hornet's nest."

Based on all that I had heard and read, I expected to find, or more precisely *see,* conflict and ethnic difference in Infierno. I imagined distinguishable camps—the Ese eja looking and acting different on one side, and the mestizos on the other. Yet, when I arrived in 1996, I found it difficult to discern much of any conflict or, for that matter, see major differences between the groups. With time, I learned that people did (and do) maintain a strong subjective sense of identity and affiliation. Though people were not openly fighting or shouting, the differences that had accumulated over more than two decades of sharing the same territory were deeply felt and embedded in people's memories.

Infierno was often described as having *lost* its indigenous identity. Invariably, the community was characterized as the most "Westernized," "modern," "acculturated," or simply "changed" of the native communities in the region. Indeed, Infierno is just 30 minutes by road from the urban center of Puerto Maldonado, and half the community is comprised of mestizos. Even within Infierno, the Ese eja frequently identify themselves as different from Ese eja (*nativos*) of other communities in the region. With a combination of shame and wonder, they often remark that other Ese eja still keep their traditional ways. They live differently, ("only pure Ese eja among them"); they do things differently ("they still hunt only with bows and arrows"); and they talk differently ("even the *children* speak the language fluently"). One mestizo from Infierno observed: "Now they [the Ese eja] have their radios, they listen to the news, they have their watches, and nice shoes. The real ones, the old ones who died, were Ese eja. They did not know about money, they spoke their language, they did not know anything. The Ese eja in other communities—*they* are the real ones."

It was common to hear that the natives in Infierno had lost their authenticity, or that they were somehow not "real." Yet, when the community signed the contract with Rainforest Expeditions, many onlookers outside of the community were quick to protest, arguing that the influx of tourists to Infierno would destroy Infierno's ethnic identity. Here was an irony: on the one hand, the natives of Infierno were perceived as having little identity left to lose, but on the other hand, something about their identity was still worth saving from the Westernizing influences of tourism.

Like Oil and Water

Ocampo-Raeder (2006) has described a cultural resilience among the Ese eja in Infierno. Even though they differ from other Ese eja in the region, she argues, they maintain "important memories, practices, and information about the Ese eja way of life" (p. 69). This insight was certainly reflected in responses to my question, "What does it mean to be Ese eja [or mestizo]?" No one needed to think very hard or very long to be able to explain the differences between their two overarching ethnic categories. Many respondents differentiated the groups by referring to work. A 36-year-old mestizo who had migrated to Infierno from the Andes said, "The Ese eja are the same as the mestizos, but their work is different. The Ese eja like meat and hunting. The mestizos like agriculture more. The Ese eja do not work much in the *chacra* [farm], only in *pedazos* [pieces], and not all year. The Ese eja are comfortable with just what they have. We are thinking about old age, about being prepared for the future. The Ese eja do not think about old age. For example, they do not have fruit trees or cattle." Similarly, an Ese eja man said, "The mentality of the native is to work for the day. We think only about hunting to eat today, and not to invest money for the future. The mestizos are thinking about having more. They have their radios and they have money, so they are not missing anything at home. They put more into the chacra." Implicit in these distinctions is the idea that farming is true work and foraging is not, and that farming implies a person is concerned for the future, whereas foraging is a day-to-day existence. As a 38-year-old Ese eja woman explained: "The Ese eja live from fishing, they walk in the forest. The mestizos do too, but not much—they worry more about working."

A second group of respondents brought up differences in perceived intelligence. Generally, people said the mestizos were smarter, in part, because they had a better command of the language. As a 37-year-old Ese eja man explained, "The mestizos participate more; the Ese eja are more humble. The mestizos have more knowledge." A mestizo of the same age who had been born in Infierno explained, "The natives are ashamed to speak their own language." A third group pointed to physical differences between the Ese eja and the mestizos. A 30-year-old mestizo man described the Ese eja as noticeably different "in the face, in the hair, in the language. They do not talk like we do, and they have another class of words." Similarly, a 63-year-old mestizo said of the Ese eja: "Their noses are turned, and their faces are different."

The level of consensus was strong, even across categories of gender, age, and ethnicity. The same stories emerged, regardless of who was doing the telling; that is, the mestizos and the Ese eja, the men and the women, the young adults and the elders had very similar ideas about what it means to be Ese eja or what it means to be mestizo. Stereotypes had become well entrenched in Infierno, and perceived ethnic differences were already assumed, felt, and discussed on a normal basis before tourism became a factor in Infierno.

In general, people said the Ese eja do not plan for the future, but instead, they worry only about meeting today's needs; they do not farm, but they do hunt; and, they are knowledgeable about the forest. The consensus about the mestizos was that they are savvier, especially in terms of language, and, because they speak well, they dominate in meetings. Also, the mestizos were described as ambitious, thinking only about themselves and not about the community as a whole. These perceptions correspond with those described in Isabella Lepri's (2006) work among the Ese eja of Bolivia. She found that the Ese eja construct a self-identity in relation to mestizos (*dejja*) and see themselves as "ignorant, backward, cowards, dirty and poor," and the mestizos as "educated, clean and they own 'things'" (p. 73).

As with most stereotypes, I found evidence to counter the perceptions. Though people said the Ese eja had problems with language, several Ese eja men of different ages speak Spanish fluently and often vociferously in community meetings. Though people said the Ese eja did not engage in agriculture and/or the market economy, many Ese eja farmers sell farm produce on a regular basis to the river taxis and markets in Puerto Maldonado. Though the Ese eja were described as the ones who hunt (and not the mestizos), several mestizo men hunt regularly, and several Ese eja men pointed out they rarely hunt at all.

On the other hand, some of the stereotypes did have empirical basis. A comparison of mean annual incomes and mean number of hectares cleared for agriculture showed that the Ese eja in general earned less income per year and cultivated fewer hectares of annual crops on average than did the mestizos (see tables 1 and 2). Differences were significant at a p-value < 0.05. Included were only households in which men and women were both either Ese eja or mestizo. See Ocampo-Raeder (2006) for thorough analysis of these differences.

Table 1   Mean Annual Income: Ese eja and Mestizo (non-Ese eja)

Ethnic Group	Number of Households	Mean Annual Income	Standard Deviation
Non-Ese eja	49	US$3,348	US$2,258
Ese eja	51	US$2,280	US$1,856

t-stat = 2.530; p-value = 0.013

Table 2   Number of Hectares Cleared: Ese eja and Mestizo (non-Ese eja)

Ethnic Group	Number of Households	Mean Number of Hectares Cleared (1998)	Standard Deviation
Non-Ese eja	51	2.045	1.682
Ese eja	51	1.280	0.868

t-stat = 2.885; p-value = 0.005

The facts and fictions regarding "how the Ese eja are" or "how the mestizos are" have been passed on through at least two generations in Infierno. The alacrity with which people responded to interview questions and the consensus among the answers attests to the prevalence of stereotypes. Like all stereotypes, the ideas seem to have some foundation, and 20 years ago, the differences must have been much more marked. Yet, whether or not the stereotypes remain empirically true today in Infierno has done little to diminish their hold on people's imaginations and prejudices. One man mused, "Like oil and water, the mestizos and Ese eja will never mix."

Tourists' Perceptions

Though ethnic differences were a source of great concern to people in Infierno, the question remained whether they would matter to tourists, too. Would tourists have certain expectations about the people they were meeting on their visits? Did they have perceptions about who was "real" and who was "not real" in ways that matched people's ideas in Infierno? Conran (2006) has argued that Western tourists perceive the Other as persons to be "intimately experienced" rather than as an object of their gaze. Would tourists be disappointed to learn that their experiences in Posada Amazonas were not always with Ese eja natives? I suspected that the answer to this question and tourists' expectations would ultimately affect how people in Infierno characterized themselves.

I distributed surveys to tourists in Tambopata before Posada Amazonas was built, described plans for the community lodge, and asked the respondents to rank how important it would be to know that a native Ese eja versus a local mestizo was assuming different roles in the lodge. The 5-point Likert scale examined the degree to which it "mattered a lot" or "did not matter at all" whether a person performing a specific job at the ecolodge was Ese eja (figure 2). Chhabra and his colleagues (2003) used a similar scale to gauge authenticity as perceived by tourists attending a Scottish heritage festival.

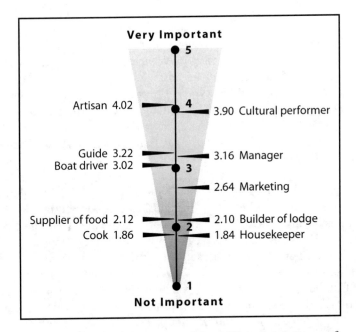

Figure 2: Tourists' Responses (N = 120) to Importance of Ese eja vs. Mestizo Identity of Ecolodge Job Holders

For positions such as housekeeper and cook, most tourists said they did not care whether the person carrying out the work was an Ese eja. For positions such as guide or artisan, most tourists said they did care. These latter positions are more strongly dependent on knowledge of local culture. The notion of authenticity in these positions is more important to tourists than it is in other positions. An implication of these scores is the idea that authenticity and culture are associated with the Ese eja and perhaps not with the mestizos.

Review of the tour company's marketing material showed that they were, in some ways, upholding these ideas. In the brochures and Web sites, Posada Amazonas was said to be located in the "Ese eja Indian Community" or the "Ese eja Native Community." While it is clear that the "Native Community of *Infierno*" is an unappealing name for a lodge (few tourists would jump at the opportunity to spend their vacation in "Hell"), the marketing material is notable not only for omitting a word, but also for inserting "Ese eja."

To a large extent, the joint owners of Posada Amazonas have downplayed cultural aspects relative to the wildlife and natural history. Early in the partnership's history, the owners of Rainforest Expeditions explained: "We do not intend for the project to use the community or the people themselves as the focus of attraction for tourists. Rather, we want to work with the community to develop the natural resources they have as a tourist attraction. We hope to capitalize on their natural resources more than on their cultural resources." This statement is supported by some of the marketing materials. One magazine advertisement for Posada Amazonas contained color photographs of macaws, capuchin monkeys, giant otters, and a Harpy eagle with a caption that read: "*Come meet some of our most frequent visitors.*" The small gallery could have included an image of an Ese eja man holding a bow and arrow—a flourish that would be typical of other Amazon lodges—but it did not. Below the pictures, the caption continued: "*In Posada Amazonas, you will find the perfect balance between wildlife and the richest tropical forests in America in a comfortable, secure, and authentic lodge. . . .*" Though the word "authentic" appeared, there was no insinuation that "authentic" implied "Ese eja."

It is true that Posada Amazonas is home to many species of wildlife that are attractive to tourists. Yet what distinguishes the lodge from others is the fact that it is locally owned. This participatory feature alone would be enough to attract some tourists, but "local" can be made even more appealing to tourists by characterizing the local as not just local, but *indigenous*. Perhaps for these reasons, articles about Posada Amazonas in the popular press emphasize the fact that the lodge is comanaged by native, Ese eja (not mestizo) members of Infierno. A 2003 issue of *Outside* magazine identified Posada Amazonas as one of the "top ten ecolodges" of the world. Their description follows:

> At the edge of an old-growth forest the size of Connecticut, Posada Amazonas is run and staffed mainly by members of the native Ese'eja community. Ese'eja means "true people," and these *indigenos* [sic] are

expert river navigators who support themselves by hunting, preparing forest medicines, and gathering wild Brazil nuts to sell to tourists. Because of the lodge's community ownership, guests have ample opportunity to "go local." This might mean taking ethnobotanical walks—during which Ese'eja guides explain which seeds and barks are traditionally used for hammocks, fans, arrows, and medicines—or visiting the neighboring 1.8-million-acre Tambopata National Wildlife Reserve to search for giant river otters and parrots. (Singer 2003)

Though more than half of Posada Amazonas' staff people are not Ese eja, they are omitted from the information presented to tourists. In summary, as evident from the discourse of community members, tourists, Rainforest Expeditions, and the popular press, "culture" and "ethnicity" seem to be the domain of the Ese eja. By contrast, the mestizos tend to be perceived as devoid of culture, at least of the kind that might be marketable for tourism.

Ethnicity after Tourism: New Reflections

The visitors from California squinted in the late morning sun as they watched the performance from their seats on the school's wooden porch. Quechuan music streamed from the small boom box while the young performers from Infierno danced, their palm skirts rustling in unison. Like so many small warriors, the boys lifted half-sized bows and arrows above their heads as the girls carrying squash gourds skipped in time. Each child wore the bright orange tail feather of a scarlet macaw. The performance was presented as a gesture of gratitude to the students from the U.S. who had brought a telescope and other new supplies from their own school to Infierno. Standing on the last step of the porch, Don Rolando, an elder Ese eja man, watched the dance for a few moments, then turned to walk away, his head shaking: "That is not anything Ese eja."

Later that evening, the students gathered in the lodge to talk about their visit to the community. A young woman spoke first, "I was a little uncomfortable looking down at the kids. I guess it made me feel too important."

"Yeah," another added, "it seemed like they were a little uncomfortable too. I wondered if they were just acting for us, I mean, in a way that they thought we wanted them to be."

"I think it was nice they danced for us," offered one of the parents sitting in the back. "They obviously put a lot of preparation into it."

"True," conceded another student, "But what I liked best was playing soccer with everybody afterward. That felt more real."

Because Posada Amazonas is a locally managed tourism project, people in Infierno are not only the subjects of brochures, they are also active participants in determining what is being said and depicted about them. This is in contrast to many tourism cases where locals have little or no control. For example, Yea (2002) found that host communities in Sarawak were highly dissatisfied with their level of control in tourism, particularly their lack of ability to confer or deny for themselves "destination status." The lack of participation is especially problematic in that it creates and sustains inequitable, exploitative relationships (p. 189).

The fact that the local members of Infierno are managing their own images became especially apparent to me one afternoon when I was showing a stack of photographs to Diego, a young Ese eja man who had been involved in Posada Amazonas from the beginning. One of the photographs portrayed Gustavo, an Ese eja man in his 40s, dressed in a traditional tunic called a *cushma,* clutching a bow and arrow, and looking directly at the camera. Diego studied the picture for a few moments, and then, holding it to the light, declared, "This is great for the brochure!"

The "brochure ready" photograph that was meant for personal use. (Photo by Amanda Stronza)

I was immediately taken aback, for I had not considered using the photograph for a brochure. Though I could see that it was a provocative image, it was one that Gustavo had requested I shoot for his own use, not for public display. Later, I thought about Diego's comment, and how much it revealed, in so few words, his consciousness of public image, his awareness of tourists' desire for the authentic, and his knowledge of the fact that Infierno had become a place to be seen, and in that way, consumed. I realized also that not everyone in Infierno perceived things in the same way Diego had, and perhaps that was precisely the point. Diego had been involved in tourism from the beginning; his involvement had already influenced his sense of self and his desire to project the "right image" to tourists—one that would be perceived as ethnically authentic and adorned with the appropriate accoutrements of Ese eja culture.

Diego may represent an extreme case of heightened awareness about tourists' expectations of authenticity, but he is not alone in Infierno. As Posada Amazonas has gained success, and as the community has received more attention from tourists, photographers, researchers, and other outsiders, people in Infierno have begun to talk more about reviving their culture, especially their Ese eja culture. In the 10 years since the introduction of tourism, people seem to have gained a new appreciation for Ese eja identity, and in various ways, they seem to be playing up their ethnicity. The words of Rosa, a mestizo mother of five children with mixed ethnic heritages, summed it up simply: "We cannot disappoint tourists who have come to see Indians." Another woman of Ese eja origin added, "We're living like any community, and not like the native community that we are. Now we want everyone to know our origins."

Many tourism scholars have described this phenomenon. MacCannell (1992) wrote of "ex-primitives," or those who adapt to modern life by acting primitively for others, through staging their culture. Adams (1997a) described how the Tana Toraja of Indonesia were "re-examining their rituals and consciously reshaping their traditions and past" (p. 317). Grunewald (2002) argued that the Pataxo of Brazil are not Indians "just for tourists." In the realm of tourism, "they mold and remold themselves, in accordance with expectations that they themselves pose" (p. 1018).

Yet, new pride in Ese eja identity represents a turn of events in Infierno. For years, the Ese eja were told their beliefs and practices were antiquated and backward. Many were made to feel embarrassed, foolish, or ashamed to speak their own language, live by their most traditional practices, or simply look and behave in ways that were distinctly Ese eja (Alexiades and Lacaze 1996; Chavarría and García 1993). With tourism, however, the Ese eja are considering the possibility that a return to the past may be the best path to a prosperous future.

Now that tourism has become more important to the livelihoods of many families in Infierno, the Ese eja seem to be gaining a newfound sense of pride and entitlement. Coupled with this is mounting concern among the mestizos that the Ese eja might be especially favored by tourists. The result has been a redrawing of ethnic

Schoolchildren from the community practice their dance performance. (Photo by Amanda Stronza)

lines between those who are "truly native" and those who are not. Though the Ese eja and the mestizos have been living together for more than two decades, and although they agreed to build and manage Posada Amazonas together, now they are having new debates about who has a right to what resources and, more pointedly, who is most deserving of benefits from tourism.

An increased sensitivity to ethnic heritage and a vocalized need to define who's who may be linked, in Barth's (1969) instrumentalist fashion, to the economic benefits from ecotourism. There are several indicators of this trend. The first relates to "cultural rescue." One man described cultural rescue as important to live up to how Infierno had marketed themselves as the Ese eja community. "We want to acknowledge the cultural differences between us," he said, "In fact, that could be another kind of attraction." He then suggested that they would need to dress appropriately, adding, "Though we won't be wearing our traditional costumes *everyday*." Interest in cultural rescue appeared in discussions about the need to learn from Ese eja elders. Two years after the lodge opened, more people were speaking with urgency about collecting tape recordings and photographs. An elder who knew many of the traditional songs and stories of the Bahuaja Ese eja had died in 1997, and there was a sense that time was running out. One man said, "Those who were born here are not Ese eja. They act like mestizos. They don't speak the language, only Spanish. There are only a few of us who still speak. Little by little, we are finishing."

Concerns about loss of Ese eja memory and language would be repeated to me again and again, especially after 1998. This was a difference from my first year in Infierno, 1996, when most people told me they could speak only a few words of Ese eja, that they were not as fluent as their grandparents or neighbors. Just two years later, many people assured me they were strongly fluent. I could attribute this to the several things: (1) they were always fluent, but ashamed to say; (2) they were never fluent, but wanted to be or had become so in later years; (3) they were never fluent, but wanted others to think they were. Any of these answers provides evidence that a revaluing of cultural identity had occurred in just a matter of just a few years.

A second indicator of increased interest in Ese eja culture is discussion of intellectual property. Though the Ese eja leaders said they did want tourists to visit the community, they were also apprehensive. In particular, they reported feeling wary of commercializing or exploiting their cultural traditions for consumption by tourists. One Ese eja leader offered this insight: "The tourism project should not collect knowledge of the Ese eja. It would not be good for us because the lodge is part of Western society. They would take our knowledge and then gain the most from it. We must be prepared to do cultural rescue for ourselves, collecting stories and songs for our own children."

The treatment of Ese eja culture as intellectual property had existed in Infierno even before tourism began, and these concerns about commodifying culture and who has a right to share cultural knowledge of the Ese eja with agents of the outside world were debated before any marketing brochures were created or tourists came with expectant gazes. The grassroots indigenous federation in Puerto Maldonado was instrumental in introducing the concept of intellectual property to Infierno and to other native communities in the region. When Rainforest Expeditions and Infierno signed the partnership, the leaders of the federation were some of the most emphatic in their concerns to protect Ese eja culture from the commodification and potential expropriation that could occur in the context of tourism. The advice of indigenous rights organizations and activists in Peru has continued to influence how people in Infierno talk about culture as property and its potential "use" (and misuse) in tourism.

A third trend, and this is perhaps the most significant indicator of renewed pride in Ese eja culture, is the fact that even mestizos in Infierno have begun to identify themselves as natives. Such a premium has been attached to Ese eja identity that even people who have not a drop of Ese eja blood, or who have never defined themselves as Ese eja, had begun to characterize themselves as native. This switch of identity was especially surprising when a man who began calling himself a native in 1998 was the same man who had highly derogatory words to say about the Ese eja in 1997. In fact, everyone in his family had negative descriptions of the Ese eja in comparison with the mestizos. One comment, from his father, for example, was, "When the Ese eja sell something, their money disappears quickly because they drink a lot. Sometimes then they have to steal."

The man's change of heart about the Ese eja and, ultimately, his change in self-identity occurred when he began working at Posada Amazonas in a position that gave him a tremendous amount of daily exposure to tourists. After discovering that tourists wanted to learn about his traditions as a native of the region, he found it advantageous to accommodate their perceptions of who he was. Indignant when I questioned his decision and motives, he said, "Well, I was born here, and so I've always considered myself a native." Of course, his point was valid: it did not matter that he was not Ese eja—he was nonetheless *native*. He knew enough about local flora and fauna, social history, and mythology of the area to fill several hours of conversation with tourists. He was not void of culture, and it did not make sense for him to dilute somehow the perceived authenticity of his being by revealing to tourists that he was not precisely "native" in the way that they thought he was.

Not only people working at the lodge, but also some community members who rarely interacted with tourists, were beginning to consider a change in their identity. At a meeting to plan for the future of development in Infierno, a leader of the "cultural rescue" initiative addressed the importance of including mestizos. He had sensed that there was growing resentment about the exclusiveness of the Ese eja-only endeavor. Addressing the mestizos, he said, "We want to involve everyone. Little by little, the Ese eja culture can be adopted by everybody." At that, a mestizo in the group responded, "Yes, we can dance like Ese eja, use the clothes, learn to speak the language." And another mestizo added, "Yes, I feel completely Ese eja. We've been living as one family for 25 years now."

Medina (2003) reported similar identity shifts in a Belizean village where locals grew cognizant of the fact that tourists were according higher value to "things Maya" than to "things Mestizo" (p. 362). In response, mestizo villagers began to associate with Maya identity, regardless of whether they actually spoke Mayan or had much lived experience with Maya culture. Van den Berge (1995) found that tourism prompted local mestizos in Chiapas, Mexico, to modify their attitudes and behaviors toward Indians, especially as they sensed that maybe there was something "interesting" that the well-heeled tourists from developed countries were noticing about the Indians that they had been missing. Nagel (1994) too has argued that people respond to shifting ethnic incentive structures by asserting minority status or even changing their ethnicity.

Finally, an indicator of ethnic consciousness and boundary maintenance in Infierno is mounting tension and talk of dividing the community. Though the playing up of ethnic tradition by the Ese eja is a positive trend in that it has lead to a resurgence (or, for some, a first-ever feeling) of ethnic pride, in other ways, it has exacerbated old tensions in the community. The tourism lodge does not mark the first time ethnic conflict has arisen in Infierno. Nearly two decades ago, the mestizos and the Ese eja discussed splitting over debates about who had rights to a loan from the Agrarian Bank. Notes from the community's logbook of 1979 also indicate that one of the community members asked the general assembly if the mestizos could separate from the Ese eja.

Though the conflicts are deeply rooted, tourism seems to be causing an accentuation of difference in the community. Neither the mestizos nor the Ese eja want to stop working together in Posada Amazonas, yet when the lodge first opened, both sides thought the other was receiving preferential treatment. One Ese eja man said that the mestizos should have no right to work in the lodge, that the lodge should belong only to the Ese eja. When I asked about the mestizos who signed the contract and help build the lodge ("Should they benefit as well?"), he said, "We can pay them for their time, but after that, they should be excluded from the project." The mestizos, in turn, argue that they invested the labor, and now the Ese eja are being favored. As one woman clarified, "The mestizos helped more in building the lodge, but now the Ese eja are being hired."

Despite the perceptions, designation of staff positions at the lodge is not determined along ethnic lines. All members of the community, regardless of ethnic origin, dominate language skills and all have vast knowledge of natural history (for guiding). Furthermore, the visible or physical differences between the Ese eja, ribereños, and colonists are relatively minor, or at least not obvious to tourists. Partly because the ethnic tensions are high enough to warrant vigilance, the hiring patterns at the lodge are quite equal between the groups.

In 2000, the Ese eja proposed a solution to the mounting ethnic rivalries. They suggested separating from the mestizos, and moving upriver. As a group, they said they had decided that their children may attend school with mestizos as always, but in the evenings, they would return to the Ese eja-only sector of community. The question of who would be included in the Ese eja portion of the divided community, and how they would decide, or even *who* would decide is unclear. Some leaders said they would follow rules of patrilineal descent. This accommodates many of the leaders who have parented children with non-Ese eja women. Yet, even among the leaders, the rules are confusing: some people who are not Ese eja by descent would be entitled to join the Ese eja enclave if they "share similar beliefs."

Other ethnographers have reported similar interethnic conflicts sparked by tourism. Schiller described competition among natives and migrants as a "disturbing side effect of culture tourism in Kalimantan" (2001:414). Adams wrote of "intensified interethnic competition, rivalry, and suspicion" among some South Sulawesi groups as an unanticipated consequence of tourism promotion (1997b:174). Some ethnic groups were spotlighted for tourist promotion, but not others—just as the Ese eja have been noted, but not the mestizos.

The four indicators of renewed (or new) pride in Ese eja culture I have mentioned are: (1) heightened concern for cultural rescue and learning language, stories, and songs from elders; (2) interest in presenting various aspects of Ese eja culture to tourists, coupled with debates over intellectual property rights; (3) adoption of Ese eja identity by non-Ese eja members of the community; and (4) discussions of dividing the community.

Conclusion

In the previous vignette, an elder Ese eja man commented with some frustration that the dance presented to tourists was "not anything Ese eja." The backstory of that invented dance took place one afternoon in Infierno, shortly after the day's classes had finished.

The teacher met with the Ese eja and mestizo members of the Family Parents Association. A big item on the agenda was to plan a performance for a special group of visitors (students from an international exchange program). The parents started the meeting by talking about what costumes the children should wear. The general idea was to present a dance as a show of gratitude to the visitors who had made donations to the school. Several parents suggested designs and materials, and their ideas seemed to emanate from some reservoir of perceptions about what the guests might want to see. What kinds of palms or seeds or feathers should be used? How should the boys' costumes differ from the girls'? Fifteen minutes into the discussion, the teacher pulled from her bag a cassette tape decorated with the photograph of an Indian man. "He may be from Pucallpa [an Amazon town in Peru]" she contemplated aloud. And then holding up the picture, she reminded everyone, "They must also have their bows and arrows." At that point, Pablo, an Ese eja man who had begun to sell bows and arrows to the tourists, murmured from the back, "But they have to be from this area, what the Ese eja really use."

Anthropologists have argued that the gaze of tourists is influential in shifting the ways locals look, behave, and feel. The case of Infierno suggests that hosts can and often do play a proactive role in determining what happens in host–guest interactions. Especially when making decisions about how to portray themselves, community members have expressed particular ideas about what the tourists want. Diego's comment that the photograph of the Ese eja man wearing a cushma is "perfect for the brochure" reveals that people are thinking explicitly about images and expressions of ethnicity. In addition, the mestizo guide's decision to call himself a native illustrates conscious attempts to match tourists' expectations.

Over the course of just a few weeks in Infierno, and in different kinds of interactions with outsiders, I watched people demonstrate tremendous creativity in matching behaviors to visitors' expectations. With a group of foundation donors, community members proudly played up their role of lodge owners, content with the direction tourism was taking in their community (though, privately, they had a number of concerns about who was participating and who was gaining). With visiting schoolchildren, they performed a dance, dressed in what they hoped would be perceived as typical Amazonian Indians—this role to match the lesson plans of teachers. For a Native American woman who was visiting from the U.S. to share stories about cultural rescue among her people, the members of Infierno played up their own role as crusaders in rescuing a languishing language and set of traditions. For guests who were visiting from another part of the Amazon, people apparently felt no need to change much of anything—the expectations from other Amazonians were minimal and so too were the efforts to play up.

The fact that people in Infierno are shifting the outward manifestations of their identity does not necessarily imply that they have lost a sense of who they are ("really are"), or their ability to distinguish what is genuine from spurious. Especially in places where tourism is invited rather than imposed, as in Infierno, locals can remain conscious of what is real and staged even as they manipulate their culture to attract more tourists. Pablo's recommendation to use bows and arrows that are "really used" by the Ese eja reflects a concern for authenticity even as he helps fabricate a cultural display for tourists.

Because ethnicity is mutable, people may carry "a portfolio of identities" that are more or less salient vis-à-vis various audiences (Nagel 1994:154). Lepri (2006) explains that Ese eja notions of identity are "multiple, sometimes contradictory, and they vary in the encounters with different Others" (p. 68). Further, the trend to play up or embellish cultural identity in Infierno has not been the result of tourism alone. As Greenwood suggested, "All viable cultures are in the process of 'making themselves up' all the time. In a general sense, all culture is 'staged authenticity'" (1982:27). With this in mind, Taylor (2001) reminds us to consider the "sincerity" with which locals stage and perform their own culture.

Perhaps the members of Infierno have been "making themselves up" for many years, or at least as long as the mestizos and the Ese eja have shared the same land and tried to reconcile the differences among them. They are now and perhaps always have been a community in transition. Anyone who spends enough time in Infierno certainly gets the sense that it is possible to see culture changing and being re-created on a daily basis. People seem always to be shifting their identity. I was reminded of this one day when tourists weren't even around.

It was a Sunday, and the members of a mestizo community upriver were in Infierno, about to engage in a champion soccer match with Infierno's team, *Los Angeles de Infierno*. One of the fans from the other team asked Felipe, a star player from Infierno, "What are you doing wasting your time with these natives of Infierno?" Felipe responded without even a pause: "I was born, raised, and educated in Infierno. I've always considered myself to be a native as well." Later in the game, fans for the other team yelled out some derogatory comment about how poorly "the natives" play. In unison, a group of three women from Infierno's side, two of them Felipe's sisters, called back indignantly, "We are *not* natives!"

It simply is not clear who is who in Infierno, and people seem to be deciding this from moment to moment, situation to situation, depending on the audience and what's at stake. What is clear is that tourism has prompted people to talk openly about the differences between them, the changes they are experiencing, and the fairness of ethnically defined rights and privileges. As an indirect and perhaps unintended result of tourism, a few fundamental questions concerning identity, culture, and community have seeped into everyday debates and conversations in Infierno. These include the question of what culture is and who has it, how and why ethnic differences define people, whether ethnic diversity is a strength or a weakness, what traditions are meaningful and why, and how things have changed over the past 25 years.

Source: Adapted from "Through a New Mirror: Reflections on Tourism and Identity in the Amazon," *Human Organization*, 2008, 67(3):244–257.

References

Adams, Kathleen M. 1984. "Come to Tana Toraja, 'Land of the Heavenly Kings' Travel Agents as Brokers in Ethnicity." *Annals of Tourism Research* 11:469–485.

———. 1997a. "Ethnic Tourism and the Renegotiation of Tradition in Tana Toraja." *Ethnology* 36(4):309–320.

———. 1997b. "Touting Touristic 'Primadonas': Tourism, Ethnicity, and National Integration in Sulawesi, Indonesia," in *Tourism, Ethnicity, and the State in Asian and Pacific Societies*, ed. Michel Picard and Robert Wood, pp. 155–180. Honolulu: University of Hawaii Press.

Alexiades, Miguel. 1999. Ethnobotany of the Ese'eja: Plants, Health, and Change in an Amazonian Society. Ph.D. Dissertation, The City University of New York.

Alexiades, Miguel N., and Didier Lacaze. 1996. "FENAMAD's Program in Traditional Medicine: An Integrated Approach to Health Care in the Peruvian Amazon," in *Medicional Resources of the Tropical Forest: Biodiversity and its Importance to Human Health*, ed. M. Balick, E. Elisabetsky, and S. L. Laird, pp. 341–365. New York: Columbia University Press.

Andeson, Benedict. 1983. *Imagined Communities. Reflections on the Origin and Spread of Nationalism*. London: Verso Editions.

Barth, Frederik. 1969. *Ethnic Groups and Boundaries*. Boston: Little Brown.

———. 1994. "Enduring and Emerging Issues in the Analysis of Ethnicity," in *The Anthropology of Ethnicity: Beyond 'Ethnic Groups and Boundaries,'* ed. H. Vermeulen, and C. Govers, pp. 11–32. Amsterdam, Holland: Het Spinhuis.

Bendix, Regina. 1989. "Tourism and Cultural Displays: Inventing Traditions for Whom?" *Journal of American Folklore* 102:131–146.

Bruner, Edward M. 1987. "Of Cannibals, Tourists, and Ethnographers." *Cultural Anthropology* 4(4):438–445.

Bruner, Edward M., and Barbara Kirshenblatt-Gimblett. 1994. "Maasai on the Lawn: Tourist Realism in East Africa." *Cultural Anthropology* 9:435–470.

Caiuby Novaes, Sylvia. 1997. *The Play of Mirrors: The Representation of Self Mirrored in the Other.* Austin: University of Texas Press.

Chhabra, Deepak, and Robert Healy, Erin Sills. 2003. "Staged Authenticity and Heritage Tourism." *Annals of Tourism Research* 30(3):702–719.

Chambers, Erve. 2010. *Native Tours: The Anthropology of Travel and Tourism,* 2nd ed. Long Grove, IL: Waveland Press.

Charnley, Susan. 2005. "From nature tourism to ecotourism? The case of the Ngorongoro Conservation Area, Tanzania." *Human Organization* 64(1):75–88.

Chavarría, M. C., and Alfredo Garcia. 1993. *Estudio socio-economico para la ampliacion territorial de la comunidad nativa Infierno, Puerto Maldonado, Peru.* Direccion Subregional Agricultura Madre de Dios (DSRA-MD), Federacion Nativa del rio Madre de de Dios y Afluentes.

Chibnik, Michael. 1994. *Risky Rivers: The Economics and Politics of Floodplain Farming in Amazonia.* Tucson: University of Arizona Press.

Cohen, Anthony P. 1985. *The Symbolic Construction of Community.* London: Routledge.

Cohen, Erik. 1979. "The Impact of Tourism on the Hill Tribes of Northern Thailand." *Internales Asienforum* 10:5–38.

———. 1988. "Authenticity and Commoditization in Tourism." *Annals of Tourism Research* 15:371–386.

Conran, Mary. 2006. "Commentary: Beyond Authenticity: Exploring Intimacy in the Touristic Encounter in Thailand." *Tourism Geographies* 8(3):274–285.

Despres, Leo. A. 1975. *Ethnicity and Resource Competition in Plural Societies.* Chicago: Aldine.

Erisman, H. Michael. 1983. "Tourism and Cultural Dependency in the West Indies." *Annals of Tourism Research* 10:337–361.

Esman, Marjorie R. 1984. "Tourism as Ethnic Preservation: The Cajuns of Louisiana." *Annals of Tourism Research* 11: 451–467

Evans-Pritchard, Deirdre. 1989. "How 'They' See 'Us': Native American Images of Tourists." *Annals of Tourism Research* 16:89–105.

Field, Les W. 1994. "Who are the Indians? Reconceptualizing Indigenous Identity, Resistance, and the Role of Social Science in Latin America." *Latin American Research Review* 29:237–256.

Gmelch, Sharon. 2004. *Tourists and Tourism: A Reader.* Long Grove, IL: Waveland Press.

Gordillo, Javier, and Carter Hunt, and Amanda Stronza. 2008. "An Ecotourism Partnership in the Peruvian Amazon: The Case of Posada Amazonas," in *Ecotourism and Conservation in the Americas: Putting Good Intentions to Work,* ed. A. Stronza and W. H. Durham. Wallingford, UK: CAB International.

Graburn, Nelson, ed. 1976. *Ethnic and Tourist Arts: Cultural Expressions from the Fourth World.* Berkeley: University of California Press.

Gray, Andrew. 1997. *Indigenous Rights and Development: Self-determination in an Amazonian Community.* Oxford, England: Bergahn Books.

Greenwood, D. J. 1977. "Tourism as an agent of change: A Spanish Basque Case." *Annals of Tourism Research* 3:128–142.

———. 1982. "Cultural 'Authenticity.'" *Cultural Survival Quarterly* 6(3):27–28.

————. 1989. "Culture by the Pound: An Anthropological Perspective on Tourism as Cultural Commoditization," in *Hosts and Guests: The Anthropology of Tourism*, 2nd ed., ed. V. Smith, pp. 171–185. Philadelphia: University of Pennsylvania Press.

Grunewald, Rodrigo de Azeredo. 2002. "Tourism and Cultural Revival." *Annals of Tourism Research* 29(4):1004–1021.

Herrera, Jessica. 2007. "A Little Lizard among Crocodiles" Ecotourism and Indigenous Negotiations in the Peruvian Rainforest. Master's thesis. University of Manitoba, Winnipeg, Canada.

Ingles, Palma. 2001. "Performing Traditional Dances for Modern Tourists in the Amazon." *International Journal of Hospitality & Tourism Administration* 1(3/4):143–159.

Jackson, Jean E. 1995. "Culture, Genuine and Spurious: The Politics of Indianness in the Vaupés, Colombia." *American Ethnologist* 22:3–27.

Leong, W. T. 1989. "Culture and the State: Manufacturing Traditions for Tourism." *Critical Studies in Mass Communication* 6:355–375.

Lepri, Isabella. 2006. "Identity and Otherness among the Ese Ejja of Northern Bolivia." *Ethnos* 71(1):67–88.

MacCannell, Dean. 1976. *The Tourist*, 2nd ed. New York: Schocken Books.

————. 1984. "Reconstructed Ethnicity Tourism and Cultural Identity in Third World Communities." *Annals of Tourism Research* 11:375–391.

————. 1992. *Empty Meeting Grounds.* London: Routledge.

Mazurkewich, Karen. 2007. "Tourism on 'the Rez' is Helping Native Bands Wean Themselves from Welfare and Preserve their Culture." *Montreal Gazette*, http://www.canada.com/montrealgazette/news/travel/story.html?id=e05e8c9a-f24f-4e97-9b4c-8ccf518db4d4 (accessed July 7, 2007)

Maoz, Darya. 2006. "The Mutual Gaze." *Annals of Tourism Research* 33(1):221–239.

Medina, Laurie K. 2003. "Commoditizing Culture: Tourism and Maya Identity." *Annals of Tourism Research* 30(2):353–368.

Mowforth, M., and Munt, I. 1998. *Tourism and Sustainability: New Tourism in the Third World.* London: Routledge.

Nagel, Joane. 1994. "Constructing Ethnicity: Creating and Recreating Ethnic Identity and Culture." *Social Problems* 41(1):152–176.

Nash, Dennison. 1996. *Anthropology of Tourism.* New York: Pergamon.

Nuñez Jr., Theron A. 1963. "Tourism, Tradition, and Acculturation: Weekendismo in a Mexican Village." *Ethnology* 2:347–352.

Ocampo Raeder, C. 2006. Ese Eja Signatures: A Systematic Assessment of the Effects of Indigenous Resource Management Practices on an Amazonian Forest. Ph.D. Dissertation. Stanford University.

Paulson, Susan. 1997. "Bolivia and the Politics of Development in the 90s: Class, Gender and Ethnicity in Local Arenas of Power," Paper presented at Latin American Studies Association, Guadalajara, Mexico, April 17–19, 1997.

Peluso, Daniela M. 2003. Ese Eja Epona: Woman's Social Power in Multiple and Hybrid Worlds. Ph.D. dissertation. Columbia University.

Picard, M., and R.E. Wood, eds. 1997. *Tourism, Ethnicity, and the State in Asian and Pacific Societies.* Honolulu: University of Hawaii Press.

Pi-Sunyer, Oriol. 1989[1977]. "Changing Perceptions of Tourism and Tourists in a Catalan Resort Town," in *Hosts and Guests. The Anthropology of Tourism,* 2nd ed., ed. V. Smith, pp. 187–199. Philadelphia: University of Pennsylvania Press.

Rossel, Pierre. 1988. "Tourism and Cultural Minorities: Double Marginalization," in *Tourism and Cultural Minorities: Double Marginalisation and Survival Strategies,* ed. P. Rossel, pp. 1–20. Copenhagen: Document IWGIA.

Rudel, Thomas K., and Diane Bates, Rafael Machinguiashi. 2002. "Ecologically Noble Amerindians? Cattle Ranching and Cash Cropping among Shuar and Colonists in Ecuador." *Latin American Research Review* 37(1):144–159.

Schiller, Anne. 2001. "Pampang Culture Village and International Tourism in East Kalimantan, Indonesian Borneo." *Human Organization* 60(4):414–422.

Silver, Ira. 1993. "Marketing Authenticity in Third World Countries." *Annals of Tourism Research* 20:302–318.

Singer, Natash. 2003. "Resort to Virtue: The World's 10 Best Eco-Lodges." *Outside Online* March http://outside.away.com/outside/destinations/200303/200303_resort_virtue_6.html (accessed November 12, 2007).

Stephens, Lynn. 1996. "The Creation and Re-creation of Ethnicity: Lessons from the Zapotec and Mixtec of Oaxaca." *Latin American Perspectives* 23:17–37.

Stronza, Amanda. 1999 "Learning Both Ways: Lessons from a Corporate and Community Ecotourism Collaboration." *Cultural Survival Quarterly* 23(2):36–39.

———. 2001. "The Anthropology of Tourism: Forging new Ground for Ecotourism and Other Alternatives." *Annual Review of Anthropology* 30:261–83.

———. 2007. "The Economic Promise of Ecotourism for Conservation." *Journal of Ecotourism* 6(3):170–190.

Taylor, John P. 2001. "Authenticity and Sincerity in Tourism." *Annals of Tourism Research* 28(1):7–26.

Urry, John. 1990. *The Tourist Gaze: Leisure and Travel in Contemporary Societies*. London, Newbury Park: Sage.

van den Berghe, Pierre. 1994. *Quest for the Other: Ethnic Tourism in San Cristóbal, Mexico*. Seattle: University of Washington Press.

———. 1995 "Marketing Mayas: Ethnic Tourism Promotion in Mexico." *Annals of Tourism Research* 22(3):568–588.

van den Berghe, Pierre, and C. Keyes. 1984. "Introduction: Tourism and Re-Created Ethnicity." *Annals of Tourism Research* 11:343–352.

Valdivia, G. 2005. "On Indigeneity, Change, and Representation in the Northeastern Ecuadorian Amazon." *Environment and Planning* 37(2):285–303.

Weber, Max. 1968. *Economy and Society*. New York: Bedminster Press.

Xie, Philip F. "Bamboo-beating Dance in Hainan, China: Authenticity and Commodification." *Journal of Sustainable Tourism* 11(1):5–16.

Yea, Sallie. 2002. "On and Off the Ethnic Tourism Map in Southeast Asia: the Case of Iban Longhouse Tourism, Sarawak, Malaysia." *Tourism Geographies* 4(2):173–194.

17

Negotiating Gender Relations and Identity between Locals and Tourists in Turkey: Romantic Developments

Hazel Tucker

> We say eyewash. European girls are washing the eyes of the men. They're uncovering their legs, showing their arms, and putting on lipstick. Turkish women, especially Göreme girls, they don't know—of course they know lipstick by now—but they don't use it. And of course we go to the fancy one, nice one, pretty one, open one. She can speak with me about herself and I can speak openly with her. Because she is free and I am free, but that one [the Turkish one] is not free.

This extract from an interview with a local man explains how the Muslim men in the Turkish village of Göreme are being drawn into relationships with tourist women that contrast with the kinds of relations they have with local women. Placed against the context of local gender roles and relations in this way, this type of tourism relationship—local men's relationships with tourist women—is presented almost as an inevitability, as an opportunity difficult to miss: "she is free and I am free, but the Turkish one is not free."

This type of tourism relation is becoming extremely prominent in Göreme, a popular destination known for its caves and "fairy chimney" rock formations. An ever-increasing number of short-term "romances," as well as long-lasting relationships and marriages, are taking place between local men and tourist women. A triangular set of relations thus unfolds between tourist women, local men, and local women, giving rise to many important issues concerning not only the interaction between global and local but also the links between gender and power. The "romantic developments" in the title of this chapter are twofold. First, this refers to the growing presence of romance, or at least an ideal of romance, in the local setting through and because of these romantic liaisons.[1] Second, there is a development of tourism business taking place in Göreme that is generated specifically from these relationships.

Sex relations in the tourism context are embedded in the cross-cultural complexities of gender, sexuality, and power (Bowman 1989, 1996; Hall 1992; Ryan and Hall 2001). The close level of interaction between villagers and tourists is an important factor in the villagers' experiences with tourists; that closeness allows the villagers, in part at least, to redress power inequalities inherent in the tourist–host relationship by asserting their own control over tourists' activities and experiences. Sex relationships might be a further way in which these men can regain a sense of control over their tourist guests that is otherwise experienced as diminishing as the level of tourism continues to rise. This is precisely the way that sex relations between tourist women

Göreme village, Turkey. (Photo by Hazel Tucker)

and "host" men were explained by Bowman in his assertion that: "'Fucking tourists' in Jerusalem in the eighties was . . . a means of imagining and acting out a power that, in fact, the merchants did not have," because it provided them with "a field in which to play out scenarios of vengeance against foreigners who, in their eyes, oppressed them both economically and socially" (1989:79). Zinovieff (1991) painted a similar view of Greek men's sexual relationships with tourist women, arguing that the men's tricking, lying, and sexually conquering tourist women is a way of symbolically counteracting ideas of the women's and the West's underlying superiority.

However, like many studies of tourist–host encounters, these accounts fail to provide a balanced view of both tourist and host narratives and how they relate to each other. Rather, they tend toward an overconcentration on the purpose and strategy of the men involved in such relationships, while playing down the voices of the women. Moreover, attempts to describe and explain these relationships seem repeatedly to look for their structure and function, thus neglecting the possibility of excitement and attraction. In other words, these relationships, along with most other contexts of cross-cultural courtship and marriage (see Breger and Hill 1998), are usually presented in terms of their outcome and as a means to a particular end. They are seldom viewed, particularly where the men involved are concerned, as processes in which the "antistrategy" of emotion may play a part (Kohn 1998).[2] Moreover, these relationships are often conveyed through the idiom of male "predator" and female "victim," thereby reiterating the gender stereotypes of rational and strategic men versus emotional and weak women (Seidler 1987). By contrast, I aim to develop an understanding of both the reasons and the emotions evoked by these tourism relationships and their implications for gender identity in Göreme.[3]

Fun and Romance

The tourism business is largely the domain of men in Göreme, and although the tourism realm is therefore the men's place of work, it also represents a zone in which the men feel relatively free from much of the restriction normally present in Turkish village life. It is in this arena that tourist women and local men first meet, and where the men find themselves to be both the victims of the tourist's "eye-washing" presence and the lucky inhabitants of a tourist "paradise." While male tourists are accepted and welcomed, newly arrived women generally receive a great deal more attention.

There is a belief among some village men that they are more handsome, more willing, and better in sexual relations than men in the tourists' home environments; they deduce from this that foreign girls actually go to Göreme for sex. The answer one young Göreme man gave to me when I asked why many tourist women come and have relations with Göreme men was: "Because we are handsome and young, you know, nice tak tak. We can do it

24 hours!" The fact that so many tourist women do have relations with the men is clearly enough to prove the men's sexual prowess and thus to heighten their sexual identity. With busloads of new arrivals every day, tourism in Göreme has produced a sense of paradise for local men. Some men even referred to the Quran in conversations about this topic, telling of where it says that in heaven there will be 40 women around each man. Göreme is like that now, they said; "It's raining girls here!"

Similarly, the charm that the Göreme men display to new arrivals clearly appeals to the tourist women's sense of their own attractiveness, and in doing so heightens their sense of their own sexual identity. A woman from the United States said of her experiences in Göreme: "I don't get looked at, at home. Then I come here and I've got 10 guys all looking up admiringly at me. If there is any girl here who says she doesn't like it, she's lying. Any girl who didn't make the most of it and have a good time here would be stupid." This was also expressed by two women from New Zealand who told me that although they had heard that women are hassled a lot in Göreme, they found no problems there, especially after Istanbul. They added, "You get chatted up here, but it's no big problem," and "it's nice to get a bit of attention; I felt quite bubbly when I was first here." Moreover, as the American woman suggested, some women who "don't get looked at" at home because they may not satisfy standards of beauty or ideal weight, for example, can find themselves being the object of much amorous attention from Turkish men. So, just as the tourist women reflect back a positive self-image onto the men regarding their sexual identity, the men enhance the women's positive image of themselves: "They are so charming—they make you feel like a queen." This, together with the financial and cultural powers usually associated with the tourist in relation to the local people in the tourist setting, serves to enhance, for the time that she is on holiday at least, her own sense of personal and sexual power.

Furthermore, the sense of enchantment surrounding these meetings is strengthened by the context in which they take place. The women are in a magical land of fairy chimneys and caves, and the men are in the tourist realm where they are free to play and experiment with roles and identities. The liminal nature of both women's and men's experiences in this tourist realm allows for and promotes a sense of romantic and sexual freedom that might be more restrained in their "home" contexts. He is in his new paradise where uncovered and "free" women are plentiful. She has arrived in an enchanting landscape where she is charmed by numerous attractive and attentive men.

Of course, the women are usually aware that the men must have a family life somewhere "behind the scenes," and for some women this point feeds into their ideals of the exotic in their interactions with the "local."[4] Conversely, many women have no interest in anything other than the fun and play of the tourist realm; fixed in the "holiday" mode, they prefer to ignore the potential complications of the background of the men they meet. The tourist

Fairy chimneys in "Love Valley," near Göreme. (Photo by Hazel Tucker)

realm of central Göreme, together with the backdrop of fairy chimneys and caves, thus provides a magical and bewitching context within which these liaisons take place.[5]

However, the interactions between village men and tourist women are not without problems. After receiving warnings from family and friends, seeing special notes for women in the backpacker guide books, and being "hassled" by men in Istanbul, some women then experience men's advances in Göreme as annoying hassles. The term "hassle" is a common expression across Turkish and English spoken in Göreme, used and understood to mean chasing foreign women. It is a term used by the local men in reference to their chasing tourists and is also used with more negative connotations attached by tourists themselves in reference to their being chased, either sexually or for their business in restaurants or shops. In Göreme, though, the men working in tourism are by now well aware of the negative connotations attached in tourist discourse to the term "hassle," and they pride themselves on their not hassling tourists to the same extent as men in other Turkish tourist destinations.

Some women's rejections of the attention they receive may stem from a more general desire to interact with the local people they meet on their trip in a way that somehow includes "real" selves rather than mere stereotypes. One Australian woman told me in conversation, for example:

I'm not saying I'm cleverer than other women, but, I can just see straight through the crap; I just don't trust them. It's all this "I love you, you're beautiful" and so on, but I haven't fallen for it. They're always after something else, and I don't think that one of them isn't. I don't trust them. I could have gone for them, but I didn't want to get involved. And they're too intense—all this "I'll kill myself" stuff.

Many women doubt that the attention a man shows them in the tourism domain is based on attraction and choice of them in particular, and they reject the advances they receive; this choice, itself perhaps is as a way of redressing the imbalance of power they sense in interactions with these seemingly over-bearing men. The men's behavior, on the other hand, is a response to the "eye-washing" of the beautiful and free tourist women, and it is also a direct manifestation of certain aspects of the traditional gender relations in the village.

Traditional Gender Relations

The traditional gender relations in Göreme, like other Central Anatolian villages, are such that men and women do not meet except with close kin or in marriage. The women's domain is within the realm of the household, and to socialize in public, or *gezmek* (being out and about), "even with her husband," is possible only at particular formal occasions such as weddings or engagement parties. The behavior of tourist women is thus deeply inappropriate to local ideas about gender identity and behavior. Being a tourist is the ultimate in being out and about, and so even before considering the behavior of tourist women when they are actually in the village, the fact that many of them are traveling independently of their menfolk back home is an anomaly in the local view. The villagers have had to stretch the boundaries of their gender repertoires a long way to grasp the concept of touring women and have succeeded in doing so to varying degrees and depending on the level of contact and experience they have had with tourists.

Villagers are generally able to separate themselves from the tourists on moral grounds. Women's identity is primarily based on Islam, and knowing that the tourists are generally not Muslim enables them to position tourists clearly as "other" and thus allows them to accept the tourists' uncovered hair or their short sleeves and trousers. To villagers, tourists are *giaours* (infidels), and whatever tourists do, whatever they wear, villagers know, or believe, that it is all right for them to do so in their own country. This ability to separate the giaours from themselves has enabled them largely to get used to tourists' infidel behavior:

The people have got used to it. Everyone has really got used to it; they don't get uncomfortable anymore. But they say, for example, the very old ones, they say, "Look, how they are coming; they are very young but they can come here. Our girls are by our sides all of the time, but they can come here. How do their families give them permission [*izin*]?"

Some people talk like that. But for us it is not a problem, we've got used to it, to the tourists. And now my mother says sometimes, you know, when I wear jeans sometimes, she says "You *gezmek* like a *gavur*." (Göreme girl [translation])

Only tourist women gezmek, and that indeed is precisely why the men are drawn to them. This was explained by a Göreme man in his telling me:

In our eyes, in our heads, the women would always help the husband, everywhere—clean, cook—this is what we think about the woman. OK, you could take her out, but she doesn't want to go out, she doesn't like to go out. She is shy, because she hasn't eaten in a restaurant maybe all her life. . . . Sometimes the man needs to do this because we are seeing it from Europeans. They are very happy, having dinner together, going to a bar, drinking. They look very happy. I think we learn from these guys [the tourists]. Also we want to do things like that, what they're doing. So you go and ask your wife, she doesn't want to come, so you have to look for a girl. That's the reason to hassle girls.

The men are consequently learning new ways of relating to women, though of course they are well aware that their fun in the bars and "pansiyons" (the local term for small tourist accommodation establishment, or guesthouse) is always played out against the context of the village. The young men in particular are accused by their elders of turning their backs on their religion and tradition. One man explained: "Formerly there was no tourism in our life. People were going to the gardens to work, and adults were going to the mosque and children were going with them after school. Now what's going on? . . . If boys are with European girls and getting drunk in pubs, it is impossible for them to read the Quran and practise Islam." [translation] There is clearly a generational difference in the ways in which local men behave in and respond to the tourism processes. Many of the middle-aged men who had their fun with tourist women 10 or 15 years ago are, today, considered to have returned to a way of life more appropriate to village tradition. The younger men, on the other hand, who have only known tourism and who are growing up with the bars and plentiful "available" tourist women, are increasingly drawn by the pulls that tourists and tourism present to them. They are drawn away from religion and also away from the codes regarding gender relations that are traditional in Turkish village society.

Marriage (*evlilik*) in Göreme is an arrangement made strictly between the families of the boy and girl, though the children themselves are increasingly being given a say in who they would like to marry, as they are in more urban areas of Turkey. So that the girl's shame and the honor of her family are kept safely guarded until the day of her marriage, there is no "courting" between unmarried boys and girls except perhaps for occasional chaperoned meetings between engaged partners. Ideally, marriage candidates are selected by parents and ultimately decided on by the patriarch of each family, the selection criteria being predominantly based around issues such as hard work and good temperament for a prospective bride, and family wealth and honor associated with the boy.

When asked whether love ever featured in choice of marriage partner, a typical reply from villagers was: "No, if they're lucky, love will come later." Younger villagers' answers were more mixed, however, suggesting an emerging ideal of romantic love in the dreams of adolescents. As with other societies where arranged marriage is the norm, love, while not considered entirely separate from marriage, is not considered as a primary reason for the marriage union.[7] Nevertheless, the concept of romantic love has long held a central place in Middle Eastern poetry (Magnarella 1974), and Turkish music is filled with the desperation of *karasevda* (doomed love, or literally, black love). Moreover, romantic love is becoming increasingly visible for Göreme villagers, not only through the behavior of tourists but also through exposure to Western films, television, and travel/migration. When I visited the homes of Göreme women in the afternoons, they would often be sitting enthralled by a love entanglement being played out in a Turkish soap opera on TV. If I asked how the women felt as they watched life situations that were so different from their own, they shrugged and said that "for others it is like that, but in Göreme it is like this." Hence, while the beginnings of an ideal of romantic love seem not too distant, the parameters of emotion in traditional marriage rules remain firmly in place.

Furthermore, because of the strict codes of shame and honor, women must remain within the parameters of traditional gender roles and relations. Men, on the other hand, particularly with their ready excuse of working in tourism, are relatively free from traditional village gender codes while they are in the tourism realm. Men are drawn toward what is on offer to them in the tourism realm, and they are expanding their repertoire of possibility regarding gender relations: through entertaining and socializing with tourists, the men learn new patterns of courtship; they go out with and socialize with women in a way that is not possible within traditional gender relations and in a way they have not done before. A young pansiyon worker who has a tourist girlfriend told me:

> Before we didn't have any chance. We couldn't go out with Turkish girls; we couldn't go to bars; we couldn't have fun; we couldn't meet each other; we couldn't know each other.... Turkish girls are slowly going out—in Istanbul and Ankara they are, but not here, not in Göreme. But here it is also good, really. It is good to share everything with the tourists.

The men are thus learning how to go about courtship and have a girlfriend. So, what started off for both the man and the tourist as a part of the play and fun in the liminal tourism realm, turns into something long-term.

Long-Term Relationships

The presence in Göreme of long-term tourist girlfriends has steadily increased in recent years. Tourists stay for varying amounts of time depending on the success of their relationships, and some women come back repeatedly from year to year after spending winters in places such as London where they can earn money to live on throughout the following summer. An increasing number of tourist women have become permanent residents in the village, either by marrying a villager or having long-term plans in that direction. The women are of various nationalities; many of them are from Australia and New Zealand, others from Northern Europe, North America, South Africa, and Japan. All of them work in tourism businesses: some investing in and running pansiyons with their partner, others earning their keep by serving in bars or sitting outside travel agencies or restaurants in order to "catch" customers. Only very occasionally does a woman stay and work in the village without having a local boyfriend—simply because she enjoys being there. Such women are usually "hassled" so much that either they give up and start a relationship or they leave.

Following are some women's accounts of how they ended up long-term in Göreme:

> I stayed another week and then I had to catch a flight back to Sydney for my best friend's wedding, and Mustafa asked me to stay, and I'm like "I can't," and he said, "Well if you go, you're not going to come back cause I leave for the army in four months. . . ." And I went "Ah, I'll just miss the wedding." So I rang Rebecca . . . and I said to her, "Look, I've met this guy and I really think there's something huge between us, that I'm falling in love with him already." But we'd only been here a week, but I said, "There's something big between us; he's asked me to stay, and I know you're going to be really disappointed but this is something I have to do, and I want to do." And for the first time in my life I did something for me.

> We had all intentions of going to the Middle East until we got on the bus that morning. We just thought, "What are we doing on this bus?" And after two and a half hours, we're like, "No come on, let's go back." The only thing that was stopping us from doing it was losing face with people we'd told we were going to the Middle East. That was the only thing—which is just so dumb! Because traveling is all about meeting people, and that's what we'd done—we'd found people that we loved—and came back! And a lot of the people we'd met here seemed a lot closer than a lot our friends in London, even my friends at home. Some friends you've known for life don't feel like friends like this.

Most women's accounts of why they stayed in or returned to Göreme combine an expression of romantic commitment to a particular man with an attraction to a lifestyle they perceive to be possible in Göreme as a place. Many of the Australian and New Zealander backpackers in particular are undertaking long trips in Europe, many for around two years in duration, before they embark on their life career. Unlike most of the northern European travelers, therefore, they have no fixed strings pulling them home after their holiday in Turkey. These long-term travelers express a desire to escape from the drudgery and "normal" expectations of a career back home. They are thus more than open to the notion of diverting the path of their lives by exploring unusual and exotic possibilities. One Australian woman explained:

> The concepts of what we've grown up with as a normal life—you work, you save, you buy your house, you buy your car, you get married, you have kids, those fundamental things that you're brought up with doing, getting your pension fund and everything like that. They are not like that here; they are not established; they don't know; that's why it is sort of not reality, because it's just different from everything you'd be doing at home.

An alternative life in Göreme is attractive because, not only does it promote a sense of freedom, it is also a chance to purposefully reject norms and expectations present in the women's home life. As one of the women quoted above added, "For the first time in my life I did something for me." They frequently express a pride in their having ignored or gone against parents' wishes and friends' warnings not to "get involved with a guy from the Middle East." They are actively rejecting overprotective and restrictive relationships in their home environment through their escape to and survival in a somewhat forbidden and exotic world. Thus, these women's decisions to stay in Göreme clearly combine a romantic ideal about the life and love they might have there with a strategic choice concerning their own lives.

Local men also see their long-term involvement with a foreign girlfriend as something of an escape from the ties and restrictions surrounding traditional gender relations. One young man explained this in the following:

> I have a girlfriend, a foreign girlfriend and we suit each other very well. So I don't think that I could find the same characteristics of her in a Turkish girl. The foreign girls think more freely than the Turkish girls; it is easy to communicate. And we don't care about the culture, tradition, religion. We don't care about any of them. But if I want a Turkish girl, it would start with her parents; her parents would have been involved in our relation, it's our tradition. Of course there are many reasons to be attracted to my girlfriend, but I knew also that nobody will be involved in our relation, neither her family, nor my parents. They can say something, they can try to be involved in our relation, but she told me and I told her that we don't care, we didn't care about anybody else.

The language with which these relationships are discussed is filled with notions of freedom, choice, and the defiance of restrictive structures in place in both the women's and the men's home societies. By entering into a long-term romance with the foreign "other," both the men and the women are at once embarking on something new and something perceived to be emancipating. As with the "fun" part in the earlier days of a woman's stay, long-term relationships continue to be played out largely in the tourism realm of the village, in the pansiyons, restaurants, shops, and bars. The women frequently congregate together, providing familiar and easy company for each other, and discussing the latest "drama," such as a fight that occurred the previous evening in the disco or a clampdown by the Jandarma on their illegal work.

The young men, their boyfriends, have come to call them "the local girls," indicating that they are no longer tourists or guests, and suggesting that they should begin to adhere to village gender codes. It is in this regard that, as the relationships progress, problems and conflicts emerge between the couples, as well as among the men and their relationships with each other. Tensions are clearly created between the traditional and the new regarding gender relations and ideals within the village context, and throughout the summer in particular, there are often fights in the bars and discos in Göreme. Fights are sometimes against tourist men who are seen to interfere with a local man's chances with a tourist girl, and sometimes between local men when one man sees his "possession" of a particular girl being challenged by another man. Once belonging to a particular man, a woman's sexuality is potentially dangerous, as she has the power to provoke trouble between men. This was described by one man in the following way:

> All the women are coming over—it's changing everything. Women came, they stayed here, and there are many problems going on in town, fighting and killing because of the tourists. It wasn't like this before. Tourist women, they sleep with another guy, and they sleep with another guy tomorrow and then they all have to face each other tomorrow. And it's starting to make problems for the guys—especially the young guys. They are active, they are young. They want to go out and they want to meet a woman, and it's getting worse and worse every year. It's no good. But you can't tell the women, "Stop doing this," and you can't tell the men, "Stop doing this."

Unlike local women, tourist women have the power to choose, to reject, and to play among local men. Unaware of the codes in the scheme of local gender relations, tourist women can behave in ways that provoke often violent disputes among the men, as well as misunderstandings between themselves and their boyfriends. An example of this came from a woman from South Africa I met one day in a pansiyon, who told me of her experiences with a Göreme man she had been seeing for about 10 days. She was very tense and told me almost immediately that she was "having problems with a guy." She said that the problems had started when she had gone for what she considered a harmless walk with a tourist guy she had met in her pansiyon. This had angered her Turkish boyfriend, though she did not understand why. She went on:

> He was very charming for the first few days, but now he's turned very possessive. He's treating me like a possession. He won't let me go out; he tells me to sit and shut up, what to wear. He told me to change before I went out to the bar one night—told me I couldn't go out like that here. He won't let me smoke; he told me not to talk while we're eating. He won't let me go out alone—even down the street. It's archaic, he's really a peasant! He's got all his spies out. They all know that I'm with him, he's told everyone, and he says, "This is my town," with the idea that I have to do what he says or else.

Misunderstandings of this kind frequently occur between tourist women and Göreme men. As soon as a woman is considered to be attached to a man, her interaction with other people in the village becomes limited and she finds herself subjected to rules and conditions that she does not understand. These are the rules and conditions, or a confused version of them at least, that exist within the context of local gender relations, and they not only restrict the sense of play and freedom that the tourists initially expected from their stay in Göreme but can lead to disputes between partners. The South African woman quoted above had, from the "local" perspective, behaved in a way that would be potentially damaging to her boyfriend's pride and honor. He had therefore acted to save his pride and honor, which involved playing a heavy hand and subjecting her to his, and the village's, rules. He acted to remove any sense of power her sexuality might have had, leaving her feeling sour and with no choice but to leave the village. Similar situations occur time and time again throughout the summers in Göreme, some happening a few days into the relationship and some after a few months. As a further illustration, a Canadian woman talked of her experiences like this:

> It was fun when I came. I had fun with him. He never made a pass at me and we used to go for walks, and then we'd go out for dinner, and then we'd dance all night. But then it became work. I think at first Turkish guys are attracted to the free spirit of the foreign women, but then they start to impose rules, like don't wear short T-shirts, so it cramps you . . . and now it's lost its charm, it's worn thin. They become more controlling of you, and then they go out and do things with other people that they used to do with you, and leave you to do all the work.

Such situations, or their outcomes at least, lie behind the accounts of touristic sexual liaisons between local men and tourist women elsewhere. These accounts have portrayed the men as strategically abusing their tourist "victims." Zinovieff (1991), for example, places a strong emphasis on the way Greek men cast women out after the conquest, since they are using their sexual conquests with tourist women largely as armor in their competitive relationships among their peers. In Göreme, too, games and competitions occur among the men regarding their sexual conquests in the tourism realm. I heard groups of men judging newly arrived girls on whether they were likely to be "easy" or "difficult" (to get into bed) in order to then make bets with higher kudos for scoring a "difficult" one. I also heard men teaming up to go out to the bars to get "chicks" for the night. Some men and boys in the village have achieved a high status among their peers because of their skill and the number of their accomplishments in this sphere.

However, it was pointed out by some men that competitions and showing off have lessened during the past few years, because tourist women have gradually become more plentiful and so it has become more common or "normal" to have sexual relations with them. With the exception of the younger men, for whom these activities are new and exploratory and so still play a role in achieving status among peers, if men tell each other what they did with a tourist girl last night, the reply is, "So what?" The relationships have thus become valued in themselves rather than being wholly part of a male system of prestige. When the relationships break down, such as the situation described above of the South African woman, it is not necessarily because they were always intended as short acts of conquest for the men concerned. Rather, it is because of tensions and conflicts emerging from clashes in the codes and understandings concerning gender roles and relations between the two partners.

It is perhaps because of their concentration on male narratives "after the event," therefore, that the portrayals of such relationships from Bowman (1989) and Zinovieff (1991) repeatedly place a template of rational strategy over male behavior and contrast that to the "weakness and femininity" associated with emotion (see Seidler 1987). Bowman (1989) tells of the way groups of Palestinian men in Jerusalem who are "feminized"—weakened by their economic and political positions—are able to regain a "masculine" position through sexually dominating the women of the "dominators." It is certainly likely that as a single woman researcher in Göreme I was unable to obtain quite the same male narratives of sexual conquests as Bowman could in Jerusalem. Moreover, there is no doubt that the negotiation of power and "rights" between tourists and their hosts is always in process. The men's assertions of control over their tourist girlfriends, therefore, may be similar to the villagers' broader assertions of control over the tourists in their village generally, as achieved through the pronouncing of tourists as "guests." Furthermore, parallels may be drawn between Bowman's Palestinians and the men working in Göreme's tourism businesses who come from other parts of Turkey, especially Kurdish men from the southeast. Those men undoubtedly experience disempowerment regarding the Turkish political arena, and, as outsiders, they are also in a weak position relative to Göreme villagers. It is interesting to note that Kurdish men were generally the group in Göreme who were most strongly accused of "ripping off" foreign women in village male discourse.

Nevertheless, it is doubtful that relations with tourist women function in the same way for the Göreme men. Being on home ground in their village, their pride and power in gender as well as economic relations are not so evidently in the balance as they are for "outsider" men. The Göreme men thus seem to be exploring the new experiences of charming, courting, and socializing with girls. Concurrently, however, as the relationships become long-term, the tensions and conflicts experienced in the juggling of relations and gender codes between the tourism and the "back" realms of the village grow more intense.

Caught in the Middle

Since these tourism relationships are a "new" development, there arises the uncertainty and the lack of parameters and codes of practice that accompany any form of social change. As a couple's relationship becomes more long-term, for example, the women have certain ideals and expectations regarding how much time they should spend together and how they should live their lives. The men, too, may develop ideals of living and sharing time with their girlfriends, but they are less able to express these desires because of the pressure of village behavioral codes on them. Thus, the men find themselves caught up in the tensions that exist between the tourism and traditional realms:

> In Göreme everybody knows each other; it's too small, and also our families look at us. Normally in the house we never touch, we never kiss, we never sit close. We never touch in the home with family. For example, if I was married, and my wife was sitting here, we would never touch because they see it. It doesn't look good. That's shameful for us, shame. . . . In Göreme, we can't walk together in the center, or near the cafe, because everyone will see us. The old people, they can't do anything to us, but they tell people. It's shameful. They tell that he is having a tourist girl, they are gossiping. And they are saying to my father and mother "How will you find a Turkish girl for him?," because I am all the time going with tourists.

Gossip and shame act as strong social controls in Göreme society, and the men experience the intensities of this form of control when they contravene village tradition by "all the time going with tourists." The men feel somewhat torn between the values and expectations of the tourism realm and the "back" of the village.

Further tensions arise between the tourist women and the traditional realm, as well as between the local women and the tourism realm. The social controls of teasing and gossip, as well as the occasional firmer reprimand, press the tourist women into having some awareness of the many rules and expectations of them in the village. With their activities occurring mainly in the tourism realm, tourist girlfriends usually maintain something of an uncomfortable awareness of the "back" areas of the village and the women who are related to their partners. This was evident from the tourists' frequent questions to me, in my position as a link between the two realms, concerning what the local women thought of their presence in the village.

A tourist woman's respect among the people of Göreme is lacking from the outset because of her being "open" (acik) and associated with infidelity. Many of the women's reticence to learn Turkish is another barrier in their communication with villagers. Furthermore, if tourist women wish to remain living in the village in the long-term, they must also work hard at gaining respect through learning to behave appropriately within the village. Some of the women do try, however uncomfortable they feel, to spend some time with their partner's family. Others are shamed into keeping away, feeling much more comfortable in the tourist sphere of Göreme. When I told one Australian girl that I had just been speaking with her boyfriend's mother, she assumed that the mother must have said bad things about her. I asked her why she assumed this. "Because I never go up there—they're too scary!" she answered.

I had met this mother while I was with a group of women making bread in their neighborhood. I had asked them what they thought about all the tourist girls coming and staying in Göreme. "We don't like it!" the mother exclaimed. "Would you like it if your children went with 'others'? We can't get on. We have a lot of work, bread, grapes—we are always working, and our men are going around with tourist girls!" [translation] She expressed concern that she and her son's tourist girlfriend could not understand each other and so would not get along in the future in the same way that she would with a Turkish daughter-in-law. She was concerned in the same way for her son and the danger for him in the new and unknown quantity of his long-term involvement with a tourist girl. Unlike Turkish daughters-in-law, tourist girlfriends can always leave, and she talked of this and other young men's hurt in the past when their girlfriends had left them and not returned. The concerns of these women emphasized the ideas held by villagers that foreigners are dangerous and threatening to their relatively closed village order.[8]

Yet there have been approximately 20 marriages to foreign/tourist women over the past 15 years, and the numbers continue to increase by one or two every year. Marriage to a foreigner is more or less condoned within the village. Brides are in any case very often incomers from other places, be they other villages, provinces, or countries (through migration). However, tourist women are recognized as being unable or unwilling to come into their husband's family as a Turkish daughter-in-law would, and as a partaker of women's work within the household. The structures of households and gender relations are therefore changing significantly, though it is important to note that changes in family and household structures were already occurring through outward migration from the village.

Complaints, heard particularly from elderly people in the village, concerning the young men's relationships with tourists tend to refer more to a general absence of marriages, and thus brides (*gelin*), due to the men's newfound play and courtship with tourist women. The concern is that men are marrying at an increasingly later age, and households are consequently left with no gelin for an elongated duration. Another concern is that men who work in tourism and experience the "fun" of foreign girls will carry on with this play even if they do comply with their parents' wishes to marry. As the young man quoted above said about his situation, "They are saying to my father and mother 'How will you find a Turkish girl for him?' because I am all the time going with tourists."

Through networks of gossip, women in Göreme are well aware of what takes place in the tourism realm. However, while men's relationships with foreign women might be socially problematic, they may be more accepted by women and the village as a whole on economic grounds. Women accept their husbands' staying out late and going to discos with tourists largely in the understanding that they are working. It has been learned through the past years of running tourism businesses in the village that tourism is about entertaining people, which involves taking tourists out to dinner or for a dance at the bar. The stretching of sociocultural boundaries is thus justified, to an extent, for economic reasons. Some foreign women told me of being invited to their boyfriends' house and meeting their wives. A few foreign women have even moved into the man's home, or pansiyon, to live with him and his wife. The man would usually tell his tourist girlfriend that he had been forced into the marriage by his family when he was very young and that he had never loved his wife and no longer had relations with her. That seems to satisfy the foreign women who, because of their own ideals of love-marriage, consider his loveless marriage to be void. The greatest problems come, of course, when men who are married to a foreign woman continue to behave this way and keep going out with other tourists.

Men married to Turkish women, for the most part, receive less "trouble" from their wives when they play with tourist women. Although conversations among village women about their husbands' infidelity are expressive of some contempt, their tone generally remains light-hearted and jovial. Since marriage in village tradition does not primarily include an ideal of love, jealousy in the sense that many of the tourist women imagine to be an issue, is not prevalent. This was confirmed by a village girl who, in conversation about marriage and jealousy, told me: "Everyone marries, but they don't know love; they can't find love; they cannot love them, because they are not a good person, but they are obliged to live together. For that reason, they do not get jealous. Whatever is done, let it be done. It is not important at all in that case." [translation]

Hence, the men's "playing" with tourists for short-term flings is generally tolerated. However, the gossip that ensues about such relationships can be more hurtful to village women than the actual behavior of their husbands. When I asked one village woman, for example, what the Göreme women thought about the tourist women having relationships in the village, she told me:

> They all ask, "Will they marry? Will she take your husband?"—They said it about me a lot. My husband went out with foreign women, especially one for a long time, and everyone said, "He will marry her." But I knew he wouldn't, because we're happy like this. And we became friends, me and the girl, we slept in the house together, we ate together, I liked her a lot. But all the gossip—everyone saying she'll take her husband from her—that she wouldn't go. I know he did everything, I see everything and I know everything, of course I do. [translation]

These words also indicate some village women's fears concerning the possibility that their husbands might actually leave them to be with a foreigner more permanently. It is largely accepted that the men will have their play with tourist women, but it becomes a different story altogether when a woman's husband develops a relationship that might continue into the future. Because a woman is completely dependent financially on her husband, it is devastating for her and her children if her husband leaves to be with another woman. On this, one village girl said:

> They [the wives] can't say anything, because when they get divorced their family doesn't want to take them back. It is difficult, very difficult, because their family will ask what happened, and they will say my husband was unfaithful to me. "That's natural" their family will say. "It is normal" they will say. So they cannot come back, women cannot divorce. It is very difficult. [translation]

The foreign women are not necessarily blamed for these occurrences. As one girl, whose father had left to live with a German woman some years ago, said: "We don't like them [foreign women], because they are breaking up families, but many of the men in Göreme don't tell them that they are married. Then by the time she finds out, she either doesn't believe it or she doesn't care." [translation] It is highly dishonorable for a man to leave his family in this way. Hence, some men attempt to bring together their wife and their girlfriend under one roof; a man can then have the best of both worlds. Likewise, the (economic) devastation caused to a woman if her husband leaves her explains her accepting a foreign girlfriend into the home. What takes place within a marriage tends to be less concerned with emotion and more with the economics of the situation.

Developing Business through Romance

Foreign women are sometimes welcomed into families either as providers of wealth, which comes from their investments and work in tourism businesses, or as providers of a way for the men they marry to go to their home country to work. As it was noted earlier, local entrepreneurs have come to believe that they will sell more rooms, meals, tours, and so on if they have a tourist woman working for them to "catch" potential customers. Similarly, many of the long-term tourist women are asked either by their boyfriends or by other men to invest money and enter into partnership in their tourism business. In contrast to local women, then, whose value is in their domestic and garden work and procreation capabilities, foreign women are forging new gender roles in the village where their presence, work, and investments are seen as increasing the economic opportunities of tourism business.

Tourists' money or work is responsible for developing many of Göreme's tourism businesses. This process began with the first marriage between a villager and a tourist woman 15 years ago. The ideas and styles of these often successful businesses are used as prototypes by other entrepreneurs. Examples of style elements introduced by "tourist managers" in pansiyons include: dormitory rooms that are cheaper to stay in because they are double rooms; communal areas with floor cushions where tourists can "hang around" and meet with each other; laundry services; book exchange systems; and so on. Tourists have also opened cafés that sell cappuccino coffee, chocolate brownies, and Vegemite sandwiches. Turks who work in these businesses learn how to make these "tourist foods" and may later open their own business selling similar items. Longer-term tourists are therefore frequently the innovators in Göreme's tourism business.

As noted earlier, tourist women's narratives concerning their staying and investing in "romantic" Göreme demonstrate that they made an active choice to do something for themselves. They are attempting to improve their own lives by escaping the social and financial pressures that they perceive to be present in their home environment. The longer a woman stays in Göreme and the more involved they become with a Göreme man, however, the more she inevitably becomes involved in the social and financial pressures associated with her partner's home life. One woman who runs her partner's pansiyon said, for example: "His whole family is taking money out of my pocket. I'm getting used for work. I mean I'm not doing anything that I wouldn't normally do anyway, but when it comes to being fair, I'm putting all the hard labor in, and then most of it goes to his family." Another woman, who was working in a bar unconnected with her partner's business, said:

> I know it's their duty to look after their family and give them money and all that, but I find it very hard cause if he's got any money it goes to his family. He's never got any money, cause he's paying for them, and I find that very hard to cope with. So that's what makes me think that I can't come back here and work and just live to support his family, cause that's not the way it works for me. You work for yourself, and you work for your kids' education, or to make your business better or whatever, but with his family, it's never going to work like that.

In other cases, tourist women have invested quite large sums of money in the businesses of their partners. A problem for them is that they cannot obtain any legal status regarding their investment, and if their relationship later breaks up, they have little power to take back their financial investments. What starts as a woman's decision to invest in bettering her own lifestyle often turns later into a situation in which she feels trapped and largely disempowered in relation to both her partner and the whole Göreme context. One Australian woman who had been in the village for two years told me that:

> In the short-term relationships, the tourists are in control, because they're here for a short time and then they're off. But in the long term, the men are in control because somewhere along the line it enters into some sort of business relationship. And whether it's cultural or financial or whatever, the men tend to control. Even women who I'd thought of as being fairly strong seem to be dominated by the men in that sense.

This woman was reflecting on her own situation in which she feared having lost tens of thousands of dollars to a villager. From the villagers' point of view, the fact that many women have entered into these joint business ventures has led to a belief that, when capital is lacking, the simple answer to building up a tourism business is to "just meet a tourist girl and get her to invest in a business together, telling her that you can make good money together."

The village women, too, while being marginalized through the men's romantic liaisons with tourists, are tolerant for the sake of potential economic gain. It has been frequently noted in discussions on gender and development that, as the development of capitalism and entrepreneurship occurs, traditional gender roles limit women's access and rights to any property and business for themselves, thus serving to reinforce women's dependency on men (Scott 1997; Sinclair 1997; Starr 1984). This has certainly been the case in Göreme with the growth of small tourism enterprises. It follows that a way for Göreme women to include themselves and to have more control over the economics of the household might be to gain a daughter-in-law (over whom the mother-in-law has most direct and everyday control) who has financial resources. Thus, a local woman's access to financial resources may be gained through the touristic liaisons of her son, or in some cases, even her husband. Thus, as mentioned above, while these touristic relationships can be socially problematic for local women and villagers generally, they may be tolerated or even sought for economic reasons. This point was demonstrated in encounters I had with some of the poorer families of the village; mothers would suggest that I (as a representative of tourist/Western wealth) marry their sons, and on one (rather unpleasant) occasion, it became clear that a wife was trying to place me together with her husband. It is always expected that any honorable man will provide for his family; since both men and women see foreign women as being rich, local men and women often see foreign women as a possible route to economic salvation.

In addition, as with most other case study accounts of sexual/romantic liaisons between tourist women and local men, marriage to a foreign woman might be seen by the male partner, and possibly his family also, as a means of escape to the woman's home country and a prosperous future. Unlike the situation in the 1960s and 1970s, it is fairly difficult today for villagers to obtain a visa and legitimately migrate to northern Europe or another "Western" country. Marriage to a foreigner makes this a little easier, and one day I heard a group of teenage boys wandering through the streets singing "No woman, no visa" to the tune of Bob Marley's "No Woman No Cry."

These, of course, are the key scenarios that give rise to popular as well as anthropological portrayals of the men in these relationships as the strategic "players," and the women, stricken by romance, as the hapless victims of the men's exploitative tactics. While these men do dream of escaping to a richer land, and they soon learn from others around them that to court and then marry a foreign woman is the easiest way to achieve this, it should be remembered that alongside this, the foreign woman is also acting out of choice and strategy for a happy future.

In more recent years, however, with a number of village men having been to northern Europe and Australia to work with their foreign wives, the view of prosperity in a foreign land does not appear as rose-colored as it used to. Many young men have returned with stories of finding it hard to gain employment there and of being treated badly among a hard and cold people. Along with this disillusionment often comes the breakdown of the marriage, and so the men have returned alone and disappointed. With tourism continuing to develop in their home village, then, it is gradually becoming consid ered a better prospect to stay and, if need be, obtain a foreign partner's help in the starting and running of a tourism business in the village. Since the tourists are often in an economically stronger position than the villagers are, they must be willing to invest in their life in the village together with their partner; "If you're going to make a life together, that's normal isn't it? I mean, you get married, and most people get married for life, so you think 'this is my life,' so you're going to put money in."

Today, then, after stories of unhappiness and lack of work in those foreign lands from where the tourists come, many couples are choosing to stay in Göreme to build businesses together in tourism. Along with the innovative ideas that these foreign residents have regarding the tourism business, and the changes to the landscape of Göreme's tourism that result from those ideas, the women's work in this realm is demonstrating and creating a new type of gender role in the village. Instead of entering her husband's home and working within the household in the traditional way together with her mother-in-law, the new wife is working together with her husband in the tourism business. The husband's family gains economically from their new type of gelin—not from her work within the household, but from the financial gains she brings in from the tourism realm. Her work in the tourism realm is condoned because it is understood that that is what she knows best. After all, she is a tourist herself.

Moreover, the tourist women themselves, because they are working in tourism, find a reasonably comfortable place halfway between the tourism realm and the traditional realm. While they are expected to spend some time with their female relatives and to attend family occasions such as weddings and religious holidays, whenever they wish to escape back to their more familiar cultural environment, they have the ready-made excuse that there are tourist customers to attend to. The presence of foreign women and the romantic relations they develop with local men are thus forging new ideas about gender in the village, starting with their romantic liaisons where young local men are learning about the possibility of courtship and romance and ending with marriage and the development of new business in the village along with a new type and role of the gelin.

Developing Romance: Changing Village Life and Identities

In this article I have discussed the ways in which gender identities and ideologies are renegotiated and molded at different points of the intimate relationships between Göreme men and tourist women. Rather than merely studying partners' retrospective narratives after relationships have taken place, which tend to emphasize misunderstanding and abusive power relationships usually in favor of the men, I have viewed the relationships as processes throughout which the expectations and power of each partner are constantly negotiated. Looking at how the relationships begin in the fun and playful context of the tourism realm, and following them through to longer-lasting relationships and marriage, allows us to see the choices and strategies of both the men and women involved, together with the part that the antistrategy of romance and emotion plays throughout. By renegotiating gender conditions set in their home context, men in Göreme are experiencing and developing a new taste for romance, as well as exploring ways of using that romance to develop tourism business in the village. Similarly, foreign women are choosing to stay and negotiate new roles for themselves in the village, new roles that themselves challenge and rework the values and ideologies regarding gender identities throughout the wider context of Göreme society.

Concurrently, problems and misunderstandings do occur between "romance" partners because of clashing concepts of gender identities and expectations. As the foreign woman's status changes from that of "tourist" to "insider," so it becomes necessary and expected that her behavior corresponds with the traditional gender relations of the village. Foreign women therefore consider themselves to be more empowered in the earlier stages of their relationships. As the relationships move toward the possibility of marriage and lifelong commitment, the identity and status of each partner in relation to each other, as well as their status in relation to the context of gender ideologies in the village, can become problematic.

Some young men are learning from these difficulties; after years of fun and play with tourists, they decide to marry a Turkish girl. One young man who, after many tourist girlfriends, had finally married a girl from the village, told me:

> Maybe we've lost some of our culture, our traditions, but still we have some. I've lived with tourists all this time, learned about them, their very different culture—even if I have some of your culture now, it's very different. You can't tell a Western woman, "No, you must stay at home, you can't go alone to the disco." Anyway, they don't listen, they just leave.

This man, however, married a village girl whom he chose carefully for her nontypicality regarding the usual conformity to gender identity in Göreme. He wished to marry a girl who understood village expectations but who would also be able to fit in with what he had learned regarding courtship and socializing through his relations in the tourism sphere. Many men in their twenties are now following a similar path, choosing to marry a Göreme girl, but one who is more educated and "open" because she grew up in a Turkish city or in northern Europe after her family's migration. These men have realized that marriage to a foreigner is likely to eventually break down. However, they also wish to marry someone who might gezmek together with them, eating in restaurants, going on holiday, and even traveling abroad.

The Göreme men's gender repertoires have thus expanded to include a blend of both local and tourist gender ideologies, a blend that is also serving to gradually rework gender roles and identities of local women in the village. Through the romantic developments between tourist women and local men, tourism is creating something very new in Göreme, not only through change in terms of economics and livelihood, but in the gender roles and relations that are at the very center of villagers' lives.

Source: Adapted from *Living with Tourism: Negotiating Identities in a Turkish Village*, 2003, London: Routledge.

Notes

[1] A discussion of the use of the term "romance" versus "sex tourism" to describe such relationships is provided by Herold et al. (2001). Previously, Pruitt and Lafont (2004[1995]) had chosen the term "romance tourism" to describe the relationships that tourist women had on holiday in Jamaica, as opposed to the "sex tourism" more widely discussed in relation to tourist men (Cincone 1988; Hall 1992; Lea 1988).

[2] Kohn (1998) raises this issue with reference to inter-ethnic marriage in Nepal, pointing out that the anthropological literature on marriage has tended towards a neo-functional leaning, leaving no room for the "simple attraction" of the exotic other. Commenting on Bourdieu's (1990) account of the "game" of marriage, Kohn argues that: "the whole emphasis on strategy as the impetus for marriage does not leave room of the aesthetic spark, the romantic and wholly reckless anti-strategy of love, especially across culturally constructed 'boundaries'" (1998: 69).

[3] The discussion here is based on interviews and focus groups with Göreme men and women as well as tourist women.

[4] As Pruitt and Lafont (2004[1995]) and Meisch (1995) point out with reference to romantic relations in Jamaica and Ecuador respectively, close liaisons with a local man may be viewed by some tourist women as a key to her own access to local culture: "What could be more backstage, and offer a more intimate experience of a culture, than being invited into someone's bedroom and bed?" (Meisch 1995:452).

[5] The Mayor of Göreme often used language of magic and bewitchment to explain the presence of so many tourist girlfriends and brides in the village. Kohn (1997), citing Schneider (1993), also discusses the bewitching forces which draw tourists into gradual residency on a Scottish island.

[6] It is important to note that rural village life makes up approximately one-half of modern Turkish society, and that there are vast differences between marriage and gender practices and ideologies between the rural and the urban settings. Göreme is said by villagers to be extremely "conservative" with respect to gender relations, even in comparison to Avanos town that is only ten kilometers away. Today, young "courting" couples are a common sight around university campuses and in cafes and parks in Turkish urban society.

[7] See, for example, Fruzzetti (1982) and Trawick (1990).

[8] See Cohen (1971), Meisch (1995), Pruitt and Lafont (2004[1995]) and Zinovieff (1991).

References

Bourdieu, P. 1990. *In Other Words*, Oxford: Polity Press.

Bowman, G. 1996. "Passion, Power and Politics in a Palestinian Tourist Market," in *The Tourist Image: Myths and Myth Making in Tourism*, ed. T. Selwyn. New York and London: John Wiley.

———. 1989. "Fucking Tourists: Sexual Relations and Tourists in Jerusalem's Old City." *Critical Anthropology* IX:77–93.

Breger, R. and R. Hill, eds. 1998. *Cross-Cultural Marriage*, Oxford: Berg.

Cincone, L. 1988. *The Role of Development in the Exploitation of Southeast Asian Women: Sex Tourism in Thailand*, New York: Women's International Resource Exchange.

Cohen, E. 1971. "Arab Boys and Tourist Girls in a Mixed Jewish Arab Community." *International Journal of Comparative Sociology* XII:217–233.

Fruzzetti, L. M. 1982. *The Gift of a Virgin*, Delhi: Oxford University Press.

Hall, C. M. 1992. "Sex Tourism in South-east Asia," in *Tourism and the Less Developed Countries*, ed. D. Harrison. London: Belhaven.

Herold, E., R. Garcia, and T. DeMoya. 2001. "Female Tourists and Beach Boys: Romance or Sex Tourism?" *Annals of Tourism Research* 28(4):978–997.

Kohn, T. 1998. "The Seduction of the Exotic: Notes on Mixed Marriage in East Nepal," in *Cross-Cultural Marriage*, ed. R. Breger and R. Hill. Oxford: Berg.

———. 1997. "Island Involvement and the Evolving Tourist," in *Tourists and Tourism— Identifying with People and Places*, ed. S. Abram, D. Macleod, and J. Waldren. Oxford: Berg Press.

Lea, J. 1988. *Tourism and Development in the Third World*, New York: Routledge.

Magnarella, P. J. 1974. *Tradition and Change in a Turkish Town*, Cambridge, MA: Schenkman.

Meisch, L. 1995. "Gringas and Otavalenos—Changing Tourist Relations." *Annals of Tourism Research* 22:441–462.

Pruitt, D. and S. LaFont. 2004. "For Love and Money—Romance Tourism in Jamaica," in *Tourists and Tourism*, ed. S. Gmelch. Long Grove, IL: Waveland Press.

Ryan, C., and C. M. Hall, eds. 2001. *Sex Tourism: Marginal People and Liminalities*, London: Routledge.

Schneider, M. 1993.*Culture and Enchantment*, Chicago: University of Chicago Press.

Scott, J. 1997. "Chances and Choices: Women and Tourism in Northern Cyprus," in *Gender, Work and Tourism*, ed. T. Sinclair. London: Routledge.

Seidler, V. (1987) "Reason, Desire, and Male Sexuality," in P. Caplan (ed.), *The Cultural Construction of Sexuality*, London: Tavistock.

Sinclair, T. 1997. "Issues and Theories of Gender and Work in Tourism,' in *Gender, Work and Tourism*, ed. T. Sinclair. London: Routledge.

Starr, J. (1984) "The Legal and Social Transformation of Rural Women in Aegean Turkey," in *Women and Property—Women as Property*, ed. R. Hirschon. London: Croom Helm.

Trawick, M. 1990. "The Ideology of Love in a Tamil Family," in *Divine Passions: The Social Construction of Emotion in India*, ed. O. M. Lynch. Delhi: Oxford University Press.

Zinovieff, S. 1991. "Hunters and Hunted: Kamaki and the Ambiguities of Sexual Predation in a Greek Town," in *Contested Identities*, ed. P. Loizos and E. Papataxiarchis. Princeton, N.J.: Princeton University Press.

18

Sherpa Culture and the Tourist Torrent

James F. Fisher

Tourists come to Khumbu not only because they want to see and experience Mt. Everest and the Himalayas but also because they like the Sherpas or like what they have heard or read about them. Khumbu offers tourists the rare opportunity (rare because, in Blake's phrase, "men and mountains meet" so much more closely there than elsewhere in the Himalayas) to experience culture and nature, and their combination—high human adventure at the top of the world.

A kind of mutual admiration society exists between Sherpas and Westerners, and just why this should be so is an interesting question in itself. What is involved is the set of stereotyped images each group has of the other. Westerners have developed a positive image of Sherpas: that of an egalitarian, peaceful, hardy, honest, polite, industrious, hospitable, cheerful, independent, brave, heroic, compassionate people. This image begins on the basis of literary evidence, which has by now assumed epic proportions, and is reinforced, when everything goes well, by personal experience in the course of a trek.[1] Of course, the image captures only one side of the Sherpa personality.

This image reflects not only what Westerners think about Sherpas but also what Sherpa culture itself values in human beings. So far as it goes, the image captures one side of the Sherpa personality—but only one side. Like all people, Sherpas wear masks. They have a public, onstage side that they want the rest of the world to see, and a private, backstage side that is more unadornedly true to themselves. Although the qualities that characterize the public side are also present—and are in fact rooted in the private side—so are other, less praiseworthy, types of behavior.

One of the difficulties Sherpas experience when working on a tourist trek—a twenty-four-hour-a-day job—is maintaining the onstage image full-time, a task that would vex a saint. Successful trekking Sherpas realize that they are, in part, paid professional actors and entertainers. Their stories and dances and songs are genuine enough, but they are also what clients want. And what clients pay for, they get. Only when the trek is over and the back-stage self can be safely unveiled at home do the Sherpas engage in the drink-ing binges and general hell-raising that may go on for days.

In addition to alcoholism there are other less salutary sides to Sherpa character. For example, because of their international mobility Sherpas can easily smuggle contraband such as gold and drugs. This activity can provide money to support lifestyles of ever-escalating luxury, comfort, and ease. It can also land the Sherpas in foreign jails. But none of this backstage behavior is included in the official image so ubiquitously brandished.

The original image Sherpas held of Westerners, before the airstrip was built at Lukla in 1964, was one of technologically sophisticated, generous, wealthy, irrationally adventurous, egalitarian, and well-intentioned, if not always physically strong, people. This more or less coherent image was formed on the basis of contact with a small number of relatively homoge-neous people, mostly mountaineers and the occasional hardy trekker. But in post-Lukla times this image has given way to a less clearly focused one that has emerged out of the Sherpas' experiences with thousands upon thousands[2] of tourists—everyone from the psychotic French woman who had to be strait-jacketed and evacuated to the American who has taken the vows of a lama to the German divorcee in search of romance. Although the original positive image still holds, foreigners are now equally likely to be thought crude, stum-bling, demanding, arrogant, unpredictable, and cheap. Where foreigners are concerned, Sherpas have learned to have no stable expectations. So much for unitary images.

Westerners are enchanted with Sherpas because the qualities the Sher-pas are thought to possess are not only those Westerners admire but also pre-cisely those they feel they should embody but conspicuously lack or do not adequately measure up to. So Sherpa society, or the Western image of it, rep-resents a dramatic realization of what Westerners would like to be them-selves, hence their frequently breathless enthusiasm for the Sherpas. There is also probably a measure of admiration for what Westerners regard as the lib-eral Sherpa sexual ethic.

Although the causes, strength, and justification of the mutual admira-tion may be debated, there is clearly an affinity between Westerners and Sherpas, as evidenced by the high rate of intermarriage. As of the mid-1980s there had been forty or so cases of marriage between Westerners and Sherpas, almost all relatively uneducated villagers from Solu or Khumbu (Fürer-Haimendorf 1985). And there have been many more informal liaisons, primarily between Sherpa trekking leaders *(sardars)* and their Western female clientele. (Similar liaisons occurred in the Alps in the nineteenth century.) These liaisons reverse the more typical tourist situation elsewhere in the world, where single tourists are apt to be males traveling in pursuit of interests both exotic and erotic.

Mountains and Mountaineering

Although it is the environment of Khumbu that attracts Western tourists, their perception of that environment, ironically, is fundamentally incompatible with that of the Sherpas. The most general Sherpa term for beautiful *(lemu)* can apply to the physical features as well as the personal qualities of human beings, both men and women. It can also apply to inanimate objects and to the environment as a whole. But while a field or forest might be *lemu,*

The Himalayas as near Khumbu. The peak in the upper left is Everest. (Photo by James Fisher)

the giant snow peaks towering in every direction over Khumbu are never considered *lemu*. Their lack of color (their whiteness) is seen as uninteresting (though religiously significant)—not a surprising judgment in view of the Sherpa preference for vivid colors evident in such disparate contexts as religious paintings and women's aprons. A snow peak elsewhere might be admired for its shape, and Pertemba, one of the foremost Sherpa sardars of his time, says that one of the pleasures he derives from climbing is the beauty of the different views from high on a mountain. But in general, familiarity has bred indifference rather than awe, and the shape of the Khumbu snow and ice peaks is just too boring to be considered *lemu*. Even the dramatic setting of Tengboche Monastery is said to have been selected without regard to its beauty. It was chosen by name, sight unseen, because the footprints of Lama Sangwa Dorje, a seminal figure in Sherpa history who was born about 350 years ago, had been embedded in rock when he stopped there.

Sherpas pay close attention to their environment nonetheless, and not just to those features of it that are economically important. They often find familiar shapes in mountains or villages, much as Westerners find them in clouds. To Sherpas, Phortse looks either like a *damar*, a percussive rattle lamas use during rituals, or like an animal hide stretched out to dry. And together the villages of Khumjung and Khunde resemble a horse whose rider is Khumbi Yul Lha, the peak that rises above them.

Sherpas are generally mystified that Westerners come to Khumbu at such great expense and in such great numbers, whether to trek or to climb. Even the most experienced sardars admit they cannot fathom why Europeans climb, though they make guesses. One hunch is that they climb for fame, since the books they write always include plenty of pictures of themselves. But Sherpas also know that books are bought, so a second hypothesis is that people climb to make money. One sardar, for example, thought this was the case with the British mountaineer Chris Bonnington since he has written (and presumably sold) so many books; but the same sardar believed that fame drives Reinhold Messner (the first climber to ascend all fourteen 8,000-meter peaks) to the summits. Another sardar wondered whether science was not the prime motivation, while still another held that climbers climb to clear their minds from the worries of office work. If he were an office worker, this sardar told me, he might well need to clear his mind too, but if so he would do it by going on a weekend picnic rather than by climbing.

Eight of Khumbu's most experienced and illustrious sardars unanimously agreed that virtually the only reason they climb is that they need the high income they cannot earn any other way. As one put it, if he had the education to qualify for a good office job, he would unhesitatingly choose that line of work. Sherpas see no intrinsic point in climbing: neither fame (though that is welcome since it helps them get their next climbing job more easily; it also accounts for the multiple ascents of Everest), nor challenge, nor adventure. Climbing is simply a high-paying job. None of the eight sardars expressed much enthusiasm for a hypothetical all-Sherpa expedition because they could not imagine any earnings accruing from it. Even though they enjoy the camaraderie and the scenic views and take pride in a job well done, these reasons alone would never motivate them to move up a mountain. The "First Sherpa Youth Mt. Everest Expedition" of 1991 suggests contrary sentiments, but the participation of skilled Sherpa climbers who were paid for that expedition corroborates the view of the eight sardars.

Women are for the most part left behind during a climb with the difficult task of managing the household, but those affected see the inconvenience as a relatively minor one, for which they are compensated by the pay earned by their husbands. Sherpas see danger as by far the most negative feature of climbing. Their friends' deaths, one after the other over the years, make them vividly aware of the risks. Their wives and parents, although they welcome the earnings, universally oppose expedition work because of the danger. But the climbing Sherpas' view is that danger comes with the territory; they just hope they can learn enough from the deaths of their friends to avoid their mistakes. They judge that climbing is a hard but good job in which the benefits balance the risks—a view probably shared by Nepal's other big foreign exchange earners, the Gurkha soldiers who are paid to fight and die for Britain and India. Climbing Sherpas compare deaths on a mountain favorably with those of soldiers and taxi drivers, whose lives are not insured, unlike their own. Those who feel that the difference in pay and the perks do not justify the greater risks of climbing choose trekking, although many do both, depending on the vagaries of opportunity and their own fluctuating financial needs.

Sardar Pertemba, like many climbing/trekking Sherpas, abandoned his studies and started working earlier than he might have because of the English he had learned at his village school (he also points out that knowing English will not get you to the top of the mountain). Although Pertemba likes both climbing and trekking, the work he enjoys most is the teaching he has done at the government mountaineering school in Manang. Most Sherpas learn to climb not from foreign mountaineers but from other Sherpas, usually between base camp and camp 1 on their first expedition. Pertemba thinks Sherpas need a mountaineering school in Khumbu to train young Sherpas properly and systematically in mountaineering techniques. Such a school would also generate income locally for experienced climbing Sherpas.

Although Sherpas do not consider mountains aesthetic monuments, they are not indifferent to all peaks. Some, like Khumbi Yul Lha, rising behind Khumjung-Khunde, are sacred by virtue of the deities that reside on them. Sherpas were reluctant to climb Karyolang, because of its sacredness, during the first all-Nepal expedition to that peak in 1975. They had no such compunctions about Kwangde, the second objective of the expedition, and proceeded to the top, as it turned out, of the east peak, which they mistook for the summit. Whether for spiritual reasons Sherpas would have been reluctant to attempt the summits of Khumbu in 1907, when they first began climbing in Sikkim, is an interesting but unanswerable historical question. Certainly no such general reluctance exists today. Not only the mountains but also some of their spirituality may have eroded over the years.

Khumbu must now be one of the most thoroughly mapped regions on the face of the earth,[3] with vernacular names for virtually all prominent features of the landscape, but this detailed nomenclature is often a creation of foreign cartographers. When I visited Everest base camp in 1964, Kala Pathar (Nepali for "black ridge"), now one of the most popular trekking destinations in Nepal, was unnamed.

All this increasing specificity of geographical detail is evidence of the reversal of values that historically made Solu, with its lower elevation, more fertile fields, and more salubrious climate, the more highly valued land. According to one account, the earliest Sherpa pioneers settled first in the more hospitable climate of Solu, and the latecomers or impoverished Solu Sherpas had to settle for the harsher, more rugged landscape of Khumbu. Now, however, Khumbu is the center of prosperity, thus demonstrating that a "natural resource" acquires worth only when it is culturally constituted—i.e., when technology, values, and a market for it simultaneously converge.

Social Implications

Sherpa and Western concepts of pollution constitute yet another example of cultural incompatibility. The Sherpa concept of pollution, called *tip* (see Ortner 1973), has nothing to do with the environmental effects of discarded tin cans and plastic bottles that concern so many Westerners—porters and Sherpas are responsible for the bulk of non-toilet paper litter. Sherpas do not care one way or the other about this Western-style pollution because their concept of pollution concerns only the self, or human creations and artifacts, such as houses. *Tip* is a feeling, a moral state of mind, and is not generated ultimately from empirical observation of the natural world. For example, pollution can have religious causes, such as an imbalanced relationship with deities or contact with supernatural beings. Or it can be induced socially by contact with certain kinds of people, such as low-caste Nepali blacksmiths *(Kamis)*, of whom there are a few families in Namche and one in Khumjung, or members of the Tibetan butcher class, another low-ranked group. Westerners would surely, if they were aware of these discriminations, moderate their views of egalitarian Sherpa society. They would be even more likely to modify their views if they realized that they themselves are a source of tip and that at least until very recently Thame Sherpas returning from an expedition had to be purified before they were allowed back in their houses. But since all Westerners must come to the Sherpas via the far more obviously hierarchical Hindu societies to the south, they are lulled into ascribing an egalitarian ideology to the Sherpas that simplifies, if it does not downright distort, the ethnographic facts.

But I do not want to leave the impression that Sherpas and their clients pass like ships in the night, completely misperceiving one another. The Sherpa-trekker relationship is, as these things go in the world of tourism, an unusually long and intensive one. As in any person-to-person interaction, however, only behaviors relevant to the encounter are exhibited. We never play all our roles at the same time. Nevertheless, Sherpas and their clients get to know one another over an extended period of time, rarely less than a week, often a month or more.

Exigencies of living break down what might otherwise be a formal, distant relationship: the Sherpas are in their element, perfectly acclimatized, doing well what they have always done naturally—walking, carrying loads, enduring cold weather. The Westerners, by contrast, are usually out of shape, tired, plagued by sore muscles and blisters, and gasping for air. Sherpas are paid to be helpful under these conditions, and they are. They are even heroic, as the many stories of Sherpas who have died trying to rescue their clients on high peaks attest. And they are cheerful, hardworking, and eager to please, so in the end a relationship of trust and respect is built that would be impossible with a guide on a half-day tour of Kathmandu.

Westernization

Are Sherpas being Westernized? By many visible indexes they are. First, they wear Western-style clothing—pants, shirts, down jackets, and climbing or hiking boots. (Women's clothes have not changed from the indigenous Tibetan style, thus conforming to the female sartorial conservatism that has generally been the rule all over South Asia.) It is significant, however, that Khumbu Sherpas wear either Sherpa clothes (even the best-equipped mountaineering Sherpa wears the traditional Tibetan coat on ceremonial occasions, such as weddings) or Western dress but never the Nepali national dress. When His Majesty King Birendra visited the government yak farm at Syangboche in 1974, the *pradhan panchas* (mayors) of both the Khumiung and Namche *panchayats* (village councils) greeted him with sport coats and neckties, not *daura-suruwal*, the national dress. (At a formal reception in Kathmandu for members of the Nepal-China-Japan Everest Expedition in 1988, attended by the king, however, Sherpas did wear daura-suruwal.)

Similarly, although Sherpas recognize the importance and desirability of mastering the national language in both its spoken and written forms, a Sherpa who uses too much Nepali in an otherwise purely Sherpa conversation in Khumbu is felt to be putting on airs.

Through association with trekkers as well as extensive travel abroad in the lands from which the trekkers come, Sherpas have gained a wide knowledge of modern hygiene, several Western languages (and Japanese), and material culture generally. The tradition of drinking Tibetan salt-and-butter tea has largely disappeared in Sherpa homes (because of the high price of butter and the uncertain supply of Tibetan tea). Western ways are admired because Western contacts have opened new channels of mobility and access to power, wealth, and prestige. Sherpas honor the West because their experience of it has been so overwhelmingly positive financially.

My own view is that such matters as clothing styles and diet are relatively superficial; much more important is the Sherpas' success in maintaining a cultural identity that is strongly and exclusively Sherpa. Sherpas tend not to be self-deprecating; whatever they are, they are mostly proud of it. Even those Sherpas who have achieved the greatest success, through mountaineering accomplishments or university educations, think of themselves primarily and uncompromisingly as Sherpas.

Part of the reason for this tenacious cultural identity is the mutual admiration of Westerners and Sherpas that I have already mentioned. Sherpas are so massively reinforced at every point for being Sherpas that they have every reason not only to "stay" Sherpa but even to flaunt their Sherpahood. One might say that tourists pay Sherpas in part for being Sherpa, or at least for

By 1988 Lama Sarki (pictured here with his wife) had married and opened a lodge in Phakding, a few hours' walk up the valley from Lukla. Although he has not followed his religious calling, he is still regarded as a reincarnate lama as indicated by his name. (Photo by James Fisher)

performing the role that accords with the popular image of Sherpas. The term "Sherpa" has now become a label for anyone who helps manage a trekking group, regardless of ethnic background. Even ethnicity has become a prize to be claimed, and the advantages of Sherpa status is not lost on other groups in Nepal. Tamangs, for example, frequently try to pass themselves off as Sherpas in an ethnic, not just job category, sense. This process of "Sherpaization" counters the momentum of the much-vaunted Sanskritization (emulation of high Hindu caste behavior) that has absorbed the upward-mobilizing energies of the subcontinent for centuries.

As evidence of the reinforcement Sherpas have received for their pride and independence, a number of the more successful among them in recent years have dropped the honorific suffix *saheb* and address their Western clients by their first names—something no house servant, hotel servant, or tour guide in Kathmandu would dream of doing. Westerners often react favorably to being treated as equals, even by someone waiting on them hand and foot. But some of them, accustomed to or expecting more traditional hierarchical relations between servant and master, are taken aback by the I'm-just-as-good-as-you Sherpa personality.

Because the "tourist Sherpas" still identify themselves very much as Sherpas, no class of marginal people—neither fully Sherpa nor Western—has developed, as it often does in such contact situations. The sexual differentiation that exists between Sherpa men and women is largely being maintained by differential access to education and jobs: there are occasional Sherpani [Sherpa women] "cook-boys" but only one Sherpani sardar so far. On the other hand, the three Sherpanis who have summitted Everest in recent years have shattered the traditional separation of high-altitude male Sherpas from low-altitude female Sherpas. The "tourist Sherpa" is not marginal to his society at all but fully accepted within its fold. Even Sherpas who live ten months of the year in Kathmandu keep their houses and fields and often their families in Khumbu. One Sherpa who has lived in Kathmandu for more than fifteen years, ten months of the year, now holds a high and trusted position (as *cho-rumba)* in the civil-religious hierarchy in his village. He is able to return to his village during the *Dumje* festival, in early summer, when his presence is essential. Even though he is hardly ever in his village, his status there does not diminish. On the contrary, his success in the travel business in Kathmandu has endorsed and enhanced it.

Intensification

Rather than becoming Westernized or nationalized, then, Sherpa culture has been intensified. That is, Sherpas have come to value some of their traditions even more than they did prior to the advent of tourism. For example, although nowadays Sherpas rarely commission the carving of prayers on stones to be placed on the prayer walls at the entrance of villages, there seems to be no lessening of faith in Buddhist doctrine, and interest and participation in the many Buddhist rituals are as strong as ever. Some Sherpas claim that interest in religion has deepened, and some of the most successful and "Westernized" Sherpas are among the most devout.

Certainly the most educated Sherpas are still committed Buddhists who believe in and rely on their lamas' liturgical and ecclesiastical powers. The Tengboche rimpoche was able to raise US$20,000 in two days, a considerable sum in 1981, for a new *gompa* (Buddhist temple) in Kathmandu. Kalden Sherpa, owner of a flourishing trekking company, considered himself a Christian in 1963 (Hillary 1964) after two years in a Catholic boarding school, but he is now one of the most generous supporters of Tengboche Monastery; he personally financed the higher studies of four *thawas* (novice monks) at this Kathmandu gompa.

Sherpas not only have maintained their cultural identity and intensified it but also have contributed to making generally Tibetan lifestyles respectable in Nepal among Hindu and Hinduized Nepalese. In the first place, the status of hero is accorded anyone who has climbed Mt. Everest—recognition in the press, praise by the prime minister, and an audience with the king, thus turning the job of high-altitude porter into a distinguished and honorable occupation. Through spring of 2002, 244 Nepalese Sherpas had climbed Everest (some with multiple ascents, including one who has climbed the peak twelve times—without ever using oxygen), along with 14 non-Sherpa Nepalese (nine Tamangs, two Gurungs, two Chhetris, and one Newar), and ten Darjeeling Sherpas. There have been a total of 1,648 ascents of Everest, by 1,195 individuals.

Sherpa success at high altitudes coincided with a surge of interest in things Tibetan after the great publicity given the Dalai Lama's retreat from Lhasa in 1959. Then after the 1962 China-India border war, when India placed severe restrictions on travel by foreigners into the Indian Himalayas and closed such traditional centers of Tibetan culture as Kalimpong to Westerners, Kathmandu became a place not only for foreigners to experience the culture of Tibetan refugees but for Bhutanese, Sikkimese, and Tibetan nobility and entrepreneurs (and, increasingly as time went on, rich Tibetan refugees) to live and work. Being wealthier than most Nepalese, they frequented the more elegant hotels and restaurants in their traditional dress. Thus their costume ceased to be identified only with the lowly Bhotias (Nepali for person of Tibetan culture) and became accepted as the standard apparel of wealthy, sophisticated, influential people.

As all these developments combined to raise the status of Sherpas in the eyes of their countrymen, the female dress of Sherpas or Tibetans changed from an object of scorn, from the Hindu point of view, to high fashion—worn in the fashionable restaurants, hotels, and discotheques of Kathmandu, and on board Royal Nepal Airlines Corporation aircraft (and those of other private airlines) on international and domestic flights by women who would not have dreamed of wearing anything but a sari a few years before. A telling case in point is that of a Namche Sherpani who married a wealthy Newar and moved to Kathmandu in the late 1950s. During her first few years in Kathmandu she wore a sari, trying to blend in with her husband's milieu. By the 1970s she had reverted to her Sherpa dress, although this time with a more modish, tailored cut. By the late 1980s her tastes had become eclectic—sometimes she wore a Sherpa dress, sometimes a sari, sometimes slacks, blue jeans, or a Western dress.

Political Implications

Although Sherpa culture is being intensified rather than adulterated, tourism is nevertheless accelerating the last stage of nation building in what would otherwise still be a remote and inaccessible area. Until 1964, when then Crown Prince Birendra made one of the first landings at Lukla to dedicate the new school at Chaurikharka, no high-level government official had ever visited Khumbu. Now the King and other high officials have visited Khumbu many times. In 1964 the government's presence in Khumbu was represented by a post office and police checkpost in Namche. By 1978 two airstrips had been added along with a meteorological station, a government yak farm, village panchayat secretaries from outside Khumbu, a medical center, a bank providing such services as savings accounts and cashing of travelers' checks, a police checkpost in Thame, and a national park that includes all of Khumbu (excluding, technically, the villages themselves).

Sherpas have viewed most of these institutions as either helpful or harmless. But initially, at least, the primary feeling about Sagarmatha National Park (Sagarmatha is the Nepali word for Everest) was one of fear. The main impact of the park so far has been to enforce strictly the law against cutting green wood for fuel, and since no realistic alternative has been provided, Sherpa concern is understandable. Much of the fear is based on rumors about even worse regulations still to come, such as one that would prohibit Sherpas from gathering leaf litter in the forests.

The traditional forest wardens *(shing nawas)* had ceased functioning by the early 1970s as the astronomical sums tourists paid for firewood had led to massive cutting that systematically undermined the forest wardens' authority. In 1982 honorary forest wardens were appointed from each panchayat ward, but they did not have much effect because they were given no authority to levy fines. All this is in dramatic contrast to 1964, when firewood was free for the asking to any overnight visitor in Solu-Khumbu.

The consumption of wood is strongly influenced not only by numbers of tourists but also by their trekking style. Seventy percent of Khumbu trekkers in 1978 belonged to organized groups, which carry their own tents and food, while 30 percent stayed in local lodges—teahouse trekkers, as they are known in the trade (Bjonness 1979). The big groups use more wood because they are big (there are two or three porters or Sherpas for each tourist) and because their Sherpas make their own, usually inefficient, cooking fires and keep their clients cozy with bonfires. Teahouse trekkers, on the other hand, require fewer support personnel and keep warm inside the lodges. As year-round lodges have sprung up almost all the way to Everest base camp, Khumbu trekkers are increasingly likely to be the individuals and small groups who patronize them. Kerosene is so prohibitively expensive compared with firewood that only hotels and lodges can afford to use it. Moreover, national park officials can monitor fuel use and enforce regulations much more readily in fixed sites than they can among nomadic trekking groups.

Sherpas say that the national park is now their forest warden. The traditional rule that enjoined Sherpas from cutting green trees applied only to forests near the villages, and the fine for breaking it (a bottle of beer) was mild. National park officials attempt to enforce the rule everywhere, far from the villages as well as near them, and punishment for infractions includes heavy fines and imprisonment.

Sagarmatha National Park has an impact even in areas where it does not belong. When the national park dedicated a new trekkers' lodge on the grounds of Tengboche Monastery, a chicken was sacrificed—not as part of the dedication ceremonies but by some Nepalese officials on their own. Officially or unofficially, the sacrifice of an animal near a monastery, of all places, was resented by the lamas, who refuse to kill even insects.

The deterioration of local political institutions cannot be explained by the existence of the national park alone. Even if the local Village Development Committees did not feel preempted by the park, tourist jobs have lured away virtually everyone with leadership abilities. To serve effectively in Village Development Committees, it is generally necessary to reside in the area. But as one influential local leader put it, anybody with any ambition, brains, or ability is off working for tourists most of the time, so there are too few competent people left to serve on the Village Development Committees. The result is that Village Development Committee members are either capable leaders who are often absent from Khumbu, residents with little interest in politics, or, in one case, the wife of a local leader who serves as a surrogate for her politically important but frequently absent husband.

Both factors—the supremacy of the national park and the lack of leaders who stay put in Khumbu long enough to take an active part in political affairs there—have led to a fragmentation of village interests, with different individuals or groups promoting separate aims: the Everest-View Hotel, the trekking companies, the Himalayan Trust, the Village Development Committees, the national park, and so on. Whatever forces united a village politically in the past seem to have weakened in the face of all the external interests that now assert themselves. This fragmentation of interests is reflected in the lack of consensus on the importance of keeping animals out of the fields of Khumjung.

Demographic Consequences

The major demographic consequence of tourism is the large outflow of young men from Khumbu for the better part of the year. There are two reasons for this emigration: one is to avoid the inflated social obligations that bankrupt those not involved in tourism (the "social budget" is now estimated to exceed the "domestic budget.") The other is to earn the money trekking and mountaineering jobs bring in.

One consequence of the long seasonal absences among the Sherpas is a lower birth rate and a concentration of births nine months after the summer monsoon season. Other demographic consequences of tourism and mountaineering include high mortality rates for young men: through spring 2002, 153 Sherpas died on mountaineering expeditions in Nepal, including 59 on Everest (this figure excludes the many Sherpas killed on K2, Nanga Parbat, and elsewhere outside of Nepal.) The great majority of these were Khumbu Sherpas, and the mortality rate among adult males is therefore quite high. But the existence of polyandry (although younger Sherpas now scorn the custom) and the easy remarriage of widows diminish the effects such deaths might have on the birth rate.

A much greater difference in the birth rate has been effected by the family-planning techniques made available through the Khunde Hospital. Contraception has recreated the relatively low fertility conditions that polyandry had produced before; the former results in fewer children per family, the latter in fewer families. Sherpas simultaneously love children and view them as difficult and demanding to raise, an attitude that provides a traditional basis for an interest in family planning.

The practice of family planning measures seems to be influenced by the degree of participation in tourism. In Khunde, with only seven exceptions, all fertile women who had living husbands and two or more living children were practicing some form of birth control. Of these, fourteen had accepted IUDs, and three were taking pills. By contrast, in Phortse not a single woman had accepted a loop, three had received long-lasting injections (Depo-Provera), seven had tried pills but six of these had stopped taking them (some of whom had since become pregnant), and nineteen were not practicing any form of contraception. The fact that only seven women were not practicing contraception in Khunde, compared with nineteen in Phortse (two villages of about the same size) can be explained by the degree to which the inhabitants of each village have been drawn into the modern world through tourism and mountaineering.[4] The economic importance of children declines quickly in an economy based on tourism rather than agriculture or transhumant nomadism.

A final demographic consequence is the dispersal of the population to previously unoccupied areas of Khumbu or to sites once occupied only seasonally and now inhabited permanently. One example is the Syangboche area, site of the airstrip that serves the Everest-View Hotel. Only one family has moved here on a permanent basis (a recently prospering Kami family from Namche), but many other Sherpas stay in Syangboche for longer periods of time at the hotels, lodges, and tea shops that have sprung up there. If a piped-water system is ever devised to supply water to Syangboche (water at present must be carried from Khumjung-Khunde or from a seasonal spring above Namche), the Syangboche settlement will no doubt grow considerably.

With the opening of teahouses and hotels by entrepreneurs in such places as Phungi Tenga (at the bottom of the hill leading to Tengboche), Pheriche, Dingboche, Lobuche, and Gorak Shep—all formerly inhabited only in the summer months but now occupied the year round—the population has further dispersed. A different example of the same phenomenon is the concentration of Sherpas in an area of Kathmandu called Jyatha Tole, now known only half-jokingly as Sherpa Tole. By the late 1980s the more financially successful Sherpas were moving out of the cramped and congested bazaars of the capital to its airier and more fashionable suburbs.

Conclusion

The immediate future promises more of the same. If one or another of the dire events mentioned earlier, such as an oil embargo, were to transpire, most Sherpas would be able to return to their traditional means of livelihood; they even state that they would be happy to do so. Whether they really would be happy cannot be known before the event, but the more important point is that they have not burned their economic or psychological bridges behind them. Those who have been sufficiently educated would have the option of obtaining office jobs in Kathmandu and elsewhere.

According to the law of evolutionary potential, the more general an adaptation of an organism or population to its environment, the greater its potential to evolve into something else; the more specialized the adaptation, the fewer the options available for further growth. Such specialized adaptations are inherently fragile, but Sherpas are fortunate in that their economic options remain open. Unlike inhabitants of other parts of the world heavily involved in tourism, most Sherpas will be able, if necessary, to return to their traditional ecological niche, even if the hotel and shop owners of Namche and along the trails will have useless buildings and facilities on their hands.

There is little scope for the further growth of tourism in Khumbu now, primarily because airlines are severely limited in the number of tourists they can transport to Lukla and Syangboche. The completion of the Lamosangu-Jiri road has probably brought a few more trekkers, but it has not broken the transportation bottleneck. The number of tourists as of the late 1970s was just under 4,000, up from 20 in 1964. In 1985 the number had reached about 5,000; by 1986 it had climbed to 6,909, and by 1999, 22,000. In Namche, hotels keep springing up to accommodate the increasing numbers of teahouse trekkers, but if lodges are overbuilt, profits will be split into an increasing number of shares, or some businesses will prosper at the expense of others.

I have argued that religious belief remains intact, but the population of the monastery at Tengboche has not. By 1978 there were so few monks that the Tengboche rimpoche had to import four from Thame just to have enough personnel to perform Mani-Rimdu, the biggest monastery celebration of the year. By 1985 the pendulum had begun to swing the other way. Substantial contributions from foreigners and increased receipts from tourist lodges owned by the monastery (in such places as Namche and Lobuche) resulted in improved living facilities, which made the monastic life feasible for more monks than it had been when each monk had to be self-supporting.

No carved stones for the *mani* walls have been commissioned for years, and Sherpas say there are fewer readings of sacred texts (a day's reading still costs nine *manas* of rice, but nine manas cost much more now than formerly). Some Sherpas think religion as a belief system is stronger now than in the past. I have yet to find a university-educated or tourist Sherpa who does not believe in reincarnation or prostrate himself before the rimpoche to receive his blessing. If the prolonged absence of Sherpas from their villages continues, a time may come when many of them will have had little experience of Buddhist rituals such as Mani-Rimdu. This could result eventually in a weakening of religious sentiment. But in each of the three years from 1985 to 1987 an elaborate ritual (*boomtso*, literally "one hundred thousand offerings for the well-being of mankind") was held at Tengboche whose costs included NPR300,000 for the performance and NPR75,000 for a helicopter to import a renowned Nyingmapa lama. (NPR is the official international code for Nepal's currency, the rupee. In 1991, US$1.00 = NPR30.80.) These funds, plus donations to the visiting lama, were collected from Khumbu villagers, despite a general feeling that the sums were extravagant and a financial strain on individual villagers.

To flourish, a religion like Buddhism requires full-time practitioners, particularly specialists who can maintain levels of purity and religiosity that lay villagers cannot possibly aspire to. The danger to Buddhism in Khumbu lies not in the threat from other ideologies—indeed none seems to be even faintly competitive. The efforts of Christian missionaries to proselytize Sherpa students in the high schools elsewhere in Nepal have been ineffectual and even resented. The danger to the practice of Buddhism at its present high level (in 1989 there were twenty-five monks at Tengboche along with twenty-five novices in the new school) would lie in the dwindling numbers of monks in the monasteries (if the pendulum were to swing back once again), which could ultimately result in an insufficient critical mass of clergy. There is no guarantee the novices will stay, and three of the eight thawas sent at great expense for further studies at Boudhanath dropped out of the order.

In the short run tourism is enormously popular with the Sherpas of Khumbu. Although an occasional older Sherpa mutters ominously about what the future may bring, even such mutterings in effect acknowledge the blessings that abound. The Tengboche rimpoche told me that tourists are somewhat like the torrents of rain that plague the north Indian states of Bihar and Uttar Pradesh that border Nepal: the floods come every year, and there is not much anyone can do about them. Whatever misgivings exist are overshadowed by the knowledge that most Sherpas have never had it so good. But if it is good, it is good in the way that a political honeymoon is good—the course of subsequent events needs careful attention.

Source: Adapted from *Sherpas: Reflections on Change in Himalayan Nepal*, 1990, University of California Press.

Notes

[1] Perhaps because of the sense of humor of tired trekkers who had hoped to escape from questionnaires in the Himalayas, the book tourists cited most frequently in my 1978 survey was *Tintin in Tibet*.

[2] Goodman reports 22,000 visitors to Khumbu in 1999; the numbers have declined since then due to the Maoist insurgency and the events of "9/11."

[3] See the May 2003 issue of the National Geographic for an unprecedentedly detailed map of Mt. Everest.

[4] The Sherpa medical assistant at Khunde Hospital reports that Phortse women are too shy to ask for loops and are reluctant to ask for any other form of contraception, whereas for Khunde women such devices are accepted as an everyday fact of life. It is true that the hospital is located in Khunde and not in Phortse, but more than mere physical proximity is involved, since for any Phortse woman it is only a two-hour walk to Khunde—no great distance by Khumbu standards. Many Phortse women come within a few minutes of Khunde on their trips to the weekly bazaar at Namche on Saturdays, when the clinic is closed.

References

Bjonness, I. M. 1979. "Impacts on a High Mountain Ecosystem: Recommendations for Action in Sagarmatha (Mount Everest) National Park." Unpublished report.

Fisher, James F. 1990. *Sherpas: Reflections on Change in Himalayan Nepal*, foreword by Sir Edmund Hillary. Berkeley: University of California Press.

Fürer-Haimendorf, Christoph von. 1984. *Sherpas Transformed: Social Change in the Buddhist Society of Nepal*. Bangalore, India: Sterling Publishers.

Goodman, Anthony Richard. 2002. *Away from the Honey-pot: Potential for Redistributing Visitors in Solu-Khumbu District, Nepal*. M.S. thesis in Protected Landscape Management, International Centre for Protected Landscapes, University of Wales, Aberystwyth.

Hillary, Sir Edmund. 1964. *Schoolhouse in the Clouds*. Garden City, NY: Doubleday.

Ortner, Sherry. 1973. "Sherpa Purity." *American Anthropologist* 75:49–63.

19

Tourism in Ghana: The Representation of Slavery and the Return of the Black Diaspora

Edward M. Bruner

Recent literature on diaspora, borderlands, hybridity, and exile has taken us ever further from the concept of culture as stable and homogeneous and has opened up new theoretical and research vistas (Gupta and Ferguson 1992; Rosaldo 1989). The postmodern world is characterized by vast transnational flows of people, capital, goods, and ideas (Appadurai 1991), as the series of recent symposia devoted to the topic attest (e.g., Harding and Myers 1994; Lavie and Swedenburg 1996). As with many new intellectual currents, the first wave of enthusiasm is followed by more critical assessments and efforts at conceptual clarification. Paul Gilroy (1993:205–212) and James Clifford (1994), for example, thoughtfully reexamine the term diaspora by comparing the Jewish and the black diaspora experiences and trajectories. As George Marcus (1994:424) suggests, what we need in this field is theory that constructs our objects so that they may be studied by fieldwork and the more traditional methods of ethnography.

The literature on diaspora and hybridity has on the whole neglected tourism, perhaps because tourist visits are thought to be temporary and superficial. But travelers such as migrants, refugees, exiles, expatriates, émigrés, explorers, traders, missionaries, and even ethnographers may also travel for limited periods of time. To develop traveling theory, we need to know more about all patterns of travel (Clifford 1989), including tourism (Bruner and Kirshenblatt-Gimblett 1994). My essay contributes to this emerging discourse by describing the meeting in the border zone between African American tourists who return to mother Africa, specifically to Elmina Castle on the coast of Ghana, and the local Akan-speaking Fanti who receive them.[1]

Elmina Castle. (Photo by Edward M. Bruner)

In recent years, Ghana has become an economically promising West African nation (Carrington 1994) that now encourages a nascent tourist industry in the Central Region as a route to economic development.[2] Attractions include pristine beaches, a rain forest, and local cultures and rituals, but the star features are the historic castles of Elmina and Cape Coast, which were used as staging areas for the mid-Atlantic slave trade. Elmina Castle was constructed in 1482 by the Portuguese (van Dantzig 1980). One of the great medieval castles, it was the first major European building in tropical Africa and has been designated a World Heritage Monument under UNESCO. In 1993, there were 17,091 visitors to Elmina Castle; 67 percent were residents of Ghana, 12.5 percent were Europeans, and 12.3 percent were North Americans. An important and growing segment consists of blacks from the diaspora, and includes many African Americans. Some are upscale tourists in organized tour groups, others are independent travelers. Some make the journey on a budget, and still others prefer to stay in African homes and to eat local food, for a more intimate African experience. In general, however, they are a class-privileged and more educated segment of the larger African American population, consisting mainly of those with the money and the leisure time to make the long and expensive journey.

The Struggle over Meaning

As part of the tourism development project, much effort has gone toward the rehabilitation of the historic castles and the construction of a museum in Cape Coast Castle. The increased attention has precipitated discussion over the interpretation of the castles, particularly over which version of history shall be told (cf. Bruner and Gorfain 1984).

What most Ghanaians want from tourism is economic development, including employment, new sources of income, better sanitation and waste disposal, improved roads, and a new harbor. Expectations are high. The regional planning agency wants the tourist dollars to remain in the Central Region for the benefit of the community.

Funds from tourism have already begun to flow into the local community, and there are numerous plans for small-scale business enterprises that depend on the tourist trade. Many young people in Elmina want to tap into the market by offering themselves as local guides. Some have plans for selling food and crafts, others want to provide home stays and even to organize performance groups for the tourists. Local people may benefit from such contacts with tourists in ways besides the financial remuneration. In addition to money, they may receive presents, and some have become pen pals or gone abroad with tourists. The young Africans benefit most; those over 45 years of age interact with foreign tourists much less frequently. While Ghanaians see tourism primarily as a route to development, the African American tourists have a different perspective.

African Americans focus on the dungeons at the 500-year-old Elmina Castle because, understandably, the slave trade is of primary interest to them. Indeed, many African Americans come to Ghana in a quest for their roots, to experience one of the very sites from which their ancestors may have begun the torturous journey to the New World. It is for them a transition point between the civility of their family in Africa and the barbarism of slavery in the New World. One woman is reported to have fasted in the dungeon for three weeks and afterward stated that she achieved a spiritual reunion with her ancestors.

For many African Americans, the castles are sacred ground not to be desecrated. They do not want the castles to be made beautiful or to be whitewashed. They want the original stench to remain in the dungeons. In Dr. Lee's eloquent words, a return to the slave forts for diaspora blacks is a "necessary act of self-realization," for "the spirits of the Diaspora are somehow tied to these historic structures" (Report 1994:3). Some diaspora blacks feel that even though they are not Ghanaians, the castles belong to them.

Tourists in Elmina Castle, view from the women's dungeon. (Photo courtesy of Frank Fournier)

Richard Wright presents the meaning of the slave dungeons to African Americans in his book *Black Power,* where he describes his own return to Ghana and his visit to Elmina Castle. He refers to the "awe-inspiring battle-ments of the castle with [their] somber but resplendent majesty," and says that Elmina is "by far the most impressive castle or fort on the Atlantic shore of the Gold Coast" (1954:340). Reflecting on the slave dungeons, he pictures

> a tiny, pear-shaped tear that formed on the cheek of some black woman torn away from her children, a tear that gleams here still, caught in the feeble rays of the dungeon's light—a shy tear that vanishes at the sound of approaching footsteps, but reappears when all is quiet, a tear that was hastily brushed off when her arm was grabbed and she was led toward those narrow, dank steps that guided her to the tunnel that directed her feet to the waiting ship that would bear her across the heaving, mist-shrouded Atlantic. (1954:341–342)

Balancing this sadness is the sense of strength and pride many African Americans feel at the recognition that their ancestors must have been strong people to have survived these inhuman conditions (Jones 1995:1).

Most Ghanaians, on the other hand, are not particularly concerned with slavery. Although there was domestic slavery in Africa, that experience was different from the one undergone by those who were transported to the New World and suffered the indignities of the black diaspora. For Ghanaians, Elmina Castle represents a part of Ghanaian history, from the Portuguese who built Elmina in 1482 primarily to facilitate trade on the Gold Coast, to the

Dutch who captured the castle in 1637, to the British who gained control of Elmina in 1872, through to Ghanaian independence in 1957. After independence, Elmina Castle served various functions: it was the home of the Edinaman Day Secondary School, the office of the Ghana Education Service, the District Assembly, and a police training academy before it became a tourist attraction. From trading post to slave dungeon to military fortification to colonial administrative center to prison, school, and office, Elmina Castle has had, over a period of 500 years, a long and colorful history. First came the Portuguese, then the Dutch, followed by the British, and now the tourists.

Generally Ghanaians focus on the long history of Elmina, while diaspora blacks focus on the mid-Atlantic slave trade, which reached its height between 1700 and 1850. Ghanaians want the castles restored, with good lighting and heating, so they will be attractive to tourists; African Americans want the castles to be as they see them—a cemetery for the slaves who died in the dungeons' inhuman conditions while waiting for the ships to transport them to the Americas. Ghanaians see the castles as festive places; African Americans as somber places. Of course, some Ghanaians did express the hope that the restoration would not change the character of the castles and the dungeons.

In interviews and focus groups, many Ghanaians noted that African Americans become very emotional during visits to the castle and dungeons. From a Ghanaian perspective, they become almost "too emotional," which suggests that the Ghanaians do not understand the feelings of diaspora blacks. Obviously, Ghanaians have not shared the diaspora experience, and they may not have read works by such writers as Maya Angelou, Richard Wright, or Eddy L. Harris. In black diaspora literature, there is an almost mythic image of Africa as a Garden of Eden. For black American men in that popular literature, a return to Africa is a return to manhood, to a land where they feel they belong, where they can protect their women, and where they can reconnect with their ancestry. The kings and queens and paramount chiefs of West Africa represent royalty and dignity, resonating powerfully in the diaspora imagination. In Africa, black people are in control, are free and independent, as opposed to the condition of being a disempowered minority in America. These themes pervade black diaspora literature: "Africa as motherland. Africa as a source of black pride, a place of black dignity" (Harris 1992:13). Often the identification is intimately personal: "Somewhere deep in the hidden reaches of my being, Africa beats in my blood and shows itself in my hair, my skin, my eyes. Africa's rhythms are somehow my rhythms, and Africa speaks to me its languages of love and laughter" (Harris 1992:27). Or as Maya Angelou writes, "I was soon swept into an adoration for Ghana as a young girl falls in love" (1986:19).[3] In addition to Maya Angelou, other African American intellectuals such as W. E. B. DuBois and the anthropologist St. Clair Drake have taken up residence in Ghana.

Kwame Anthony Appiah, a Ghanaian philosopher now teaching at Harvard University, describes some of the differences between the African and the black diaspora understandings of race in his book *In My Father's House*. He writes that many African Americans, raised in a segregated society and exposed to discrimination, found that "social intercourse with white people was painful and uneasy" (1992:6). But since Africans "came from cultures where black people were in the majority and where lives continued to be largely controlled by indigenous moral and cognitive conceptions, they had no reason to believe that they were inferior to white people and they had, correspondingly, less reason to resent them" (1992:6–7). Although there was resentment and resistance against colonialism, he continues, "the experience of a colonized people forced to accept the swaggering presence of the colonizer" must be seen in its African cultural context, for even educated African children "were fully enmeshed in a primary experience of their own traditions" (1992:7). Appiah is correct that the struggle against colonialism was conducted from within the base of a secure African family system and an active African religious tradition, although there were changes due to the colonial presence. However, colonial penetration was not so deep that it led to a failure of self-confidence or to alienation, a claim Appiah supports by reference to the works of such African writers as Chinua Achebe, Wole Soyinka, and Camara Laye. Interpreting the African and the diaspora experiences as similar, Appiah writes, would be to misread the psychology of postcolonial Africans.

Conflicting Interpretations

In addition to the tourists and the ordinary Ghanaian citizens, museum professionals have an interest in the castles. Members of the Ghana Museums and Monuments Board and their Smithsonian consultants strive for authenticity and historical verisimilitude (Bruner 1994). They want the castles to be represented and interpreted as "accurately" as possible. But the 500-year history of Elmina Castle raises a difficult question: Which period will be presented for any given section in the restored castle? Particular rooms and locations changed in function over time. The site of the Portuguese church inside Elmina Castle—one of the oldest Catholic places of worship in Ghana—was converted by the Dutch in 1637 into a slave auction market. The restoration could emphasize the early church, the place used for the selling of human beings, or the transition from place of worship to slave market. As a solution to the problem of restoring a castle that changed over five centuries, one museum professional suggested constructing a 15th-century Portuguese room, followed by a 17th-century Dutch room and then a 19th-century British room, but others felt this might compromise the integrity of the restoration.

Which story shall be told? Vested interests and strong feelings are involved. Dutch tourists are interested in the two centuries of Dutch rule in Elmina Castle, the Dutch cemetery in the town, and the old Dutch colonial buildings. British tourists want to hear about colonial rule in the Gold Coast. Many Ashanti people have a special interest in the rooms where the Asantehene, their king Prempeh I, was imprisoned in Elmina Castle in 1896, after the defeat of the Ashanti forces by the British army. The king was later exiled to the Seychelles Islands and only returned to Ghana in 1924. He is important to all Ghanaians as a representation of resistance to British colonialism.

The government guides at the castle are aware of and sensitive to their varied audiences. They know that all visitors are not alike and that different groups may bring their own constellation of interests. The guides cater to these varied interests by shifting the emphasis of the tour. If a group expresses a special concern with the architecture of the castle, for example, the guides will emphasize that aspect.

The difficulty arises when different claims are made simultaneously. The problem became so intense that the National Commission of Culture held a conference on May 11–12, 1994, to decide on guidelines for the con-servation program.

A restaurant-bar had been opened above the men's dungeons in Cape Coast Castle. The museum professionals saw the castle as a historic monu-ment and museum, and, as in similar institutions in other areas of the world, they wanted to have a restaurant where the tourists could go for rest and refreshments. Their view was that the restaurant would make the castle a more pleasant place, so that the tourists might stay longer, have a more leisurely visit, and thereby learn more. But objections were raised that it was inappro-priate to have a restaurant at a cemetery, that it was a desecration of a sacred site. The recommendation of the commission was that "facilities for restau-rant, restrooms and shops could be located outside Elmina and Cape Coast Castles but appropriate musical performance and religious services should be permitted in the monuments" (Report 1994:ii). The restaurant was closed.

An African American view has been expressed by Imahküs Vienna Robinson in a widely circulated newspaper article entitled "Is the Black Man's History Being 'White Washed?'"[4] Robinson is an American from New York who has moved permanently to Ghana with her husband, to a home on the coast with a view of Elmina Castle. The couple has established an organization called One Africa Productions, dedicated to the reuniting of Africans from the diaspora with Africans from the continent, and, for a fee, they also conduct performances in the dungeons, primarily for African Amer-ican tourists. In addition, they have other development programs and contrib-ute to the support of a local village. In her article, Imahküs Robinson describes the first time she visited the Cape Coast dungeons in 1987.

> As I stood transfixed in the Women's Dungeon, I could feel and smell the presence of our Ancestors. From the dark, damp corners of that hell-hole I heard the whimpering and crying of tormented Mothers and Sisters being held in inhumane bondage, never knowing what each new day . . . would bring. Strange white men that kept coming in to look at them, feeling them, examining their private parts as if they were some kind of animals; removing them for their own sick pleasures, while awaiting the Devil ships that would take them into a four hundred (400) year long hell.[5]

After describing her own transformative experience in the dungeon, she comments on the restoration, "And here I am today witnessing the 'White Wash' of African History. But I cannot sit in idleness and watch this happen without sounding an alarm. . . . Restore, preserve, renovate, maintain? Exactly what is being done?" Robinson is objecting specifically to new glass windows, to the walls of the castle being covered with fresh paint, and most important, to finding that the Men's Dungeon had been "painted a bright yellow."[6] She continues about the dungeon, "Gone was the musty, lingering smell of time and of Black male bodies, the lingering feel of the spirit of these ancestors who had been forcibly removed from their 'Mother' land."

The recommendation of the May 1994 conference was that the cultural heritage of all the different epochs and powers should be presented, but also that the area symbolizing the slave trade be given reverential treatment. In keeping with this, there was a proposal to change the name from Elmina Castle to Elmina Castle and Dungeons, and the same for Cape Coast.

From the perspective of the Ghana Tourist Board and the tourism industry, an admittedly economic perspective, the issue, at least in part, is one of tourism marketing. In May 1994, for example, 500 members of the African Travel Association, including many American representatives, held their convention in Ghana. Tours and visits to the castles were arranged as part of a conscious marketing and advertising effort. If the African American market only or primarily is targeted, the emphasis could be to satisfy that market. But if the market is a broader American and European one, then the emphasis might be placed differently. Beyond marketing efforts, of course, there are larger issues of historical representation, and the key question becomes, What is best for Ghana?

The Representation of Slavery

Aside from the struggle over presentation and interpretation, there are other impacts of tourism. The attention of diaspora blacks to the dungeons and the slave experience has the potential consequence of introducing into Ghanaian society increased tension between African Americans and Ghanaians, and possibly a heightened awareness of black-white opposition, a sensitive and possibly controversial issue.

The Robinsons and other African Americans are not asking that only the slave dungeons be discussed by the government guides; they have no intention of suppressing history and want the guides to present the entire history of the castles. They understand that Africans themselves were active participants in the slave trade, that at first the Gold Coast was a slave importing area, that the Europeans established positions on the coast and did not themselves conduct slave raids into the interior. It was other African peoples who brought the slaves to sell to the Europeans on the coast. There was domestic African slavery and an earlier period (1400 to 1600) of Arab slave trading across the Sahara to the Middle East and the Mediterranean.

But emphasizing the dungeons and the slave trade calls attention to the European whites as oppressors and the diaspora blacks as victims. The opposition between blacks and whites certainly exists in Ghanaian society but it is not currently prominent. All parties recognize that Africans and diaspora blacks have had a different historical experience, but some groups of African Americans, including the Robinsons' One Africa, see the need to "educate" the Ghanaians about slavery and life in the diaspora. To help achieve this goal, on June 19, 1994, the Robinsons sponsored a ceremony in Cape Coast Castle called Juneteenth to commemorate the last day of slavery in America, which was June 19, 1865. In addition, American blacks have gone into schoolrooms to teach Ghanaians about these subjects. The youth of Elmina—and other areas of Ghana—are very taken with the black American lifestyle, which they regard as current and "cool," and are open to its influences. What one point of view sees as education might also be considered a rewriting of Ghanaian history.

The situation is full of ironies. When diaspora blacks return to Africa, the Ghanaians call them *obruni,* which means "whiteman," but the term is extended to Europeans, Americans, and Asians regardless of skin color, so it also has a meaning of foreigner. This second meaning is also ironic, since the diaspora blacks see themselves as returning "home." So the term obruni labels the African Americans as both white and foreign, whereas they see themselves as black and at home. A white South African will be called an obruni, but black South Africans, as well as blacks from other countries of Africa south of the Sahara, such as Nigeria, Burkina Faso, or Kenya, will not be called obruni but will be referred to by another term which means "stranger." Some African Americans who live or work in Ghana have confided to me that they find it especially galling that they are called obruni but a black person from Nigeria, who is also a foreigner, is called simply a stranger.

When we asked the people of Elmina who the tourists are, they mentioned, among others, Americans, Dutch, British, Germans, and Portuguese. (The Portuguese built Elmina Castle in 1482, though there are not many tourists from Portugal these days.) The term obruni is applied to all. It suggests that in Elmina conceptualization, the entire stream of foreign visitors over the last 500 years, including African Americans, is seen as similar. We in the West make many fine distinctions between traders, missionaries, colonialists, ethnographers, and tourists, and the Elminas do understand these differences. But the differentiations we make between types of travelers, between black brothers and white oppressors, between Europeans and Americans, are merged by the Ghanaians into a single inclusive category: we are all obruni.

Many Ghanaians have told me that they consider some African Americans to be racist.[7] They include the Robinsons in this group, though during my discussions with the Robinsons I did not hear one word of racism or hate against any other person or group. One reason for the accusation is that the Robinsons' company, One Africa Productions, puts on a performance in the castle dungeon called "Through the Door of No Return—The Return," a reen-

Juneteenth celebration, 1994, Cape Coast Castle. (Photo by Edward M. Bruner)

actment of the capture of the slaves. When the performance is held for an African American tour group, the Robinsons exclude whites, on the not unreasonable basis that the African Americans are paying for the performance and feel more comfortable that way. The African American tourists understandably want to share the moment among themselves, as it is their historical experience. On other occasions, the Robinsons do allow whites to participate.

"Through the Door of No Return—The Return" is a fascinating performance. After a tour of the castle, the group assembles in the dungeon, where they hold hands, light candles, pray together, usually weep together, pour libation as a homage to the ancestors, and then pass through the door that the slaves went through to the slave ships taking them to the Americas. For the slaves, after going through that infamous door, there was no return, and it was the beginning of diaspora history. But in the Robinsons' reenactment, once the tour group gets to the other side, they sing "We Shall Overcome" and the Negro National Anthem, which are diaspora songs. Then they reenter the castle, singing and dancing African songs to the beat of the drums, festive songs, to celebrate their joyous return to mother Africa. Another production company enacts a different "Through the Door of No Return." In the version of a Ghanaian tour operator in Accra, the performance ends after going through the door, and there is no reentry to the castle, or symbolically, no return to Africa. Thus, the African American production and perspective end with a return to Africa, while the Ghanaian production and perspective end with the slaves going through the door and not returning. The different performances and endings enact different versions of black history and dramatically reveal the disparate understandings of African Americans and Ghanaians.[8]

A further irony is that when African Americans return to Ghana, they find a kind of racism that they already have overcome in America. For example, if there is a long line of people waiting in a shop and a white person enters, the shopkeeper will frequently serve that white person ahead of the Ghanaians. A further complexity is that it was peoples of Ghana who captured the slaves and sold them to the Europeans in the castles, so that from an African American perspective, one could say that the Ghanaians were not only their brothers and sisters but also their oppressors. Thus an African American tourist who meets a Ghanaian may secretly wonder, Did his ancestors sell my ancestors?[9] Further, some Ghanaians, seeing that diaspora blacks are prosperous and educated, feel they were in a sense fortunate in being taken as slaves, because now they are economically well off and have a higher standard of living than the Ghanaians![10] African Americans too may ask, What would my life have been like had my ancestors not been taken as slaves but remained in Africa?

Another view expressed was that the African American interest in slavery and the dungeons focuses on one event and one time range in the past, as opposed to a return to all the expressive cultural aspects of contemporary African culture. In this perception the return should be multifaceted and fully open to all dimensions of the present-day African experience. This concern is reflected in current African American scholarship. Slavery in America was once treated as part of Southern history, but in the last 25 years, with revisionist scholarship, the darker side of slavery has been more fully exposed and revealed. Price (1983), for example, correlates Saramakas's statements about their past in slavery with ethnohistorical sources. David Scott (1991), however, is critical of this effort to verify an authentic past rooted in slavery, and proposes to change the problematic to ask how the figures of "Africa" and of "slavery" are utilized by contemporary peoples to construct a history, to provide an identity, and to create narratives and practices. Rather than aim for an ever-more-accurate reconstruction of slavery, Scott shifts the problematic to ask about the meaning of slavery to contemporary peoples.

At the May 1994 conference in the castle, a prominent African American referred to Anthony Hyland, an architect working on the restoration, as a "white slave master." In Elmina a diaspora black, after visiting the dungeons, physically attacked a Dutch tourist. One Ghanaian woman, who had seen the Robinsons' production of "Through the Door of No Return—The Return," told me that after viewing the performance she wanted to go out and strangle a white person.

After my return from Ghana, while writing this essay, I read a *New York Times* article written by Michael Janofsky entitled "Mock Auction of Slaves Outrages Some Blacks" (1994). At Colonial Williamsburg, an enactment of a slave auction had been scheduled; four slaves were to be sold to the highest bidder. The performance had been organized by the African-American Department of Colonial Williamsburg, which includes 13 black museum professionals.[11] The director of the department, a black woman, argued that open display and discussion was the only way for people to understand the degradation of slavery, a horror that had to be faced. She asked, If museums depict the Holocaust of Jews, why not a slave auction of blacks? But critics said the "slave auctions are too painful to bring to life in any form" (Janofsky 1994:7), and the Richmond branch of the NAACP reported that their phones were ringing off the hook in protest and outrage. The performance of the slave auction was canceled. America has not yet come to terms with slavery or its representation.[12]

Who Owns the Castles?

Aside from the issue of representation and interpretation, there is the question of who should control the castles. The Ghana Museums and Monuments Board is the designated custodian of all national monuments, but traditional chiefs also have a claim. In my meeting with the Council of Chiefs of Edina (Elmina), they noted that artifacts and furniture from Elmina Castle had been relocated to museums and sites elsewhere in Ghana, and they wanted the objects returned. The chiefs complained that when the African Travel Association brought 500 travel agents and officials to the area, they did not even pay a courtesy call on the Elmina traditional chiefs, who felt embarrassed and offended. Further, they said that CEDECOM (Central Region Development Commission), the regional planning agency, does not inform them of its plans for tourism development, even though that development is taking place in their area of jurisdiction. The chiefs also suggested that the land on which Elmina Castle is located belongs to them, to the stool (the emblem of the traditional chiefs), so they should get royalties. This very issue is what precipitated warfare between the British and the Ashanti in 1872 after the transfer of the West African settlements from the Dutch to the British. The Ashanti claimed that Elmina belonged to them, therefore, the British should pay them ground rent. The British refused, so in 1873 the Ashanti attacked. The people of Elmina at the time sided with the Ashanti, so the British demanded that the Elminas give up their weapons. When they refused, the British bombarded and destroyed the part of Elmina located along the sea coast, adjacent to the castle. That section of Elmina has never been rebuilt and is now an archaeological site. Since 1873, all the residents of Elmina have lived on the other side of the Benya River, away from the castle. We could say that British military might moved the local population away from the castle, so that the British and the Elmina peoples were separated by the river.

The process of separation has continued to the present. Before the restoration, in the area surrounding the castle, there was a market with small stands and food stalls. All of these sellers and market people have been relocated away from the castle grounds. Previously the markets served the needs of the local residents, but now the castle serves the tourists. In our focus group discussions there was no objection to the removal of the food sellers, and in fact the majority of Elminas approved of it. They understood that the castle area had to be cleared and cleaned for the tourists.

When I first went to Elmina Castle in June 1994, I was shocked to find a sign at the entrance to the castle that read, in English and in Fanti, "THIS AREA IS RESTRICTED TO ALL PERSONS EXCEPT TOURISTS." The local people, the residents of Elmina, were not to go beyond the castle wall and were restricted from entering the castle grounds. It was explained to me that this was to keep the locals from defecating in the area around the castle and on the beach, and also to protect the tourists from being hassled. Elmina residents are able to enter the castle only as tourists—they are supposed to pay a 300 cedis (about U.S. 30 cents) admission fee, though the guides told us that not all do so. One Elmina resident, refusing to pay the entrance fee, stated that the castle and the land belonged to the Elmina people, so why should they pay an admission fee? Some African Americans also refuse to pay the fee, saying they didn't pay to leave here, so they shouldn't have to pay to come back. To return to my argument, the Elmina people have again been separated from the castle, their castle, which has been dedicated completely to tourism. The local people not only are excluded from their major tourist site but have become the objects of tourism themselves, for the tourists look at and photograph the people as well as the sites.

As one enters the grounds and approaches the castle at Elmina there is a second sign—a huge one—which lists the donors and agencies involved in the restoration project (the Monuments and Cultural Heritage Conservation project) as follows: United States Agency for International Development (USAID), United Nations Development Programme (UNDP), Shell (Ghana) Limited, Ghana Museums and Monuments Board, International Council on Monuments and Sites (U.S. Chapter), and Smithsonian Institution. Finally, in a smaller type size at the bottom, it states that the project is being implemented by the Central Region Development Commission and the Midwest Universities Consortium for International Activities (USA). The latter, MUCIA, includes my university, the University of Illinois.

These signs suggest that the people of Elmina are restricted from entering the castle and that the project has been given over to a blue ribbon list of international aid agencies and is controlled by their staff and hired consultants, of which I am one. The United States is mentioned in the sign three different times. The government of Ghana is not mentioned except through two of its agencies, which are themselves dependent upon USAID and United Nations money. So who "owns" the castle? Who has the power to represent one of Ghana's greatest historical monuments?[13]

Tourism as Commerce

Ghanaians generally welcome tourists but, in the focus groups, some tourists were considered "ruffians," "dirty," and "drug addicts," and some of their behavior was considered "shocking." A 46-year-old female said some tourists are "really dirty," and some "look like madmen." A 44-year-old male said, "The way some of them dress, the way some of the men have their earlobes pierced, the very short dresses of some of the women which expose their private parts, are what I don't like about them." A 19-year-old female said, "Some are Rastafarians and I think they do not normally bathe. We don't like that." There is also distrust, and I quote from the transcriptions of the focus group discussions:

> Some [tourists] are CIA agents, but come under the cover of tourism and help their government to deal with African governments. They normally help their government to over-throw African governments. Our government should watch these people very well. [male, age 36]

> My worry is that we are near the sea. And we receive a lot of foreign boats on our shores. And in these days of many stories about wars, we could be taken unaware by enemies. Before we could do anything, we would be surrounded by enemies. [male, age 18]

There are also aggressive acts toward tourists, mugging and stealing, to such an extent that the local government has assigned guards to protect the tourists. We heard over and over again about the need for protection of the tourists.[14] The district chief executive expressed the hope that the tourists coming to Elmina would register with the Ghana Tourist Board, who would then inform the assembly, who would then know of their coming so that they could be guarded.

The term protection appeared repeatedly, so we probed for shades of meaning to better understand how the word was being used locally. We found three meanings: first, it means protection in the sense of guarding against theft; second, it means protection in the sense of guiding and helping the tourists find their way in Elmina town; third, it means protection from harassment and from the annoyance of those who come up to the tourists requesting money, or a pen, or an address. A protector then is not only a guard but a cultural broker, a mediator between the citizens and the tourists. When a tourist walks through the town accompanied by a guard-guide-protector, then that tourist is much safer, as the other residents of the community recognize the Elmina person serving as protector and do not disturb the tourist.

Above all other negatives, however, there is one behavior most offensive to the local Ghanaians.[15] The people of Elmina object strenuously when tourists take photographs without permission. We heard this sentiment frequently in the focus group discussions and interviews.

> I am ever ready to destroy the camera of any obruni who takes my picture without my permission. [male, age 40]

> One tourist at one time took a picture of a fisherman who was changing his clothing. This was not good. At that time I even called a police officer to intervene but he did not mind me. We wish this attitude of tourists should be checked because we blacks cannot take such pictures in Europe or America. [male, age 37]

> They take pictures without the consent of the people. Some intentionally take pictures of naked and badly dressed people. These pictures give a bad impression about us when they are sent abroad. [female, age 63]

> Some tourists take pictures without our consent. I once struggled with a tourist who took my picture without telling me. I seized the camera and removed the film from it. I had wanted to destroy the camera but I did not. We want them to make us aware before taking our picture so that we may charge them because in their countries, people pay for everything. [female, age 19]

There are two factors involved in the strong objections to tourists taking photographs without permission. One view expressed is that tourists take photographs of naked children and dirty places, and the tourists return home displaying a very negative image of Elmina and Ghana. The issue here is the poor representation of the Elmina people, a derogatory image. The second factor is that the taking of photographs is not reciprocal. Citizens have complained that those taking the photos return home and sell the photographs for a profit, but the people of Elmina get nothing in return. The observation was made a number of times about a local person traveling abroad who saw pictures of Elmina people on calendars, postcards, and in magazines. It was asked, If the photographers profit why shouldn't their subjects?

The concern about photography on the part of Ghanaians is indicative, almost metaphoric, of the pervasive commercial nature of the transactions between tourists and locals in Elmina. Little children continually ask for money, as do many adults. One constantly hears the phrase, "Obruni, money money." The illiterate, less-educated people ask for money directly, while educated persons also request payment, but do so in a more subtle and indirect manner. Ghanaians resent the image of African poverty reported by Westerners, yet the practice of begging for money from Westerners is widespread, possibly a consequence of the tremendous disparity in wealth between the tourists and the locals. Asking for payment may, however, be a cultural characteristic—in some situations, those in Elmina ask for money from other members of their own community. A local elder as well as one of our research assistants had both completed papers for their B.A. degrees at the University of Cape Coast. Their papers were on Elmina festival and culture, and in both cases they had to pay for the information they received.

The consequence of this practice from the tourist perspective is that it exposes the commercial nature of tourism. We know that tourism is a business, indeed an industry, and that the tourists do have to pay for their experience, but the commercial aspect is frequently disguised. When tourists go on organized group tours they usually pay for everything in advance, and thereafter no money changes hands except for drinks and incidentals. The touristic experience is bought, but there are few reminders of this on the organized tour. Individual budget travelers too have the myth that they do not pay for their touristic adventures and that they become "friends" of the local people. Many tourists believe the myth, encouraged by the tour operators, that they are guests and that the locals are their hosts. But if in Elmina tourists are constantly asked for money, for everything, including photographs, it reminds the tourists that they are not guests but are paying customers. It destroys the illusion that the tourist is simply a visitor and an adventuresome traveler. For those African Americans who return to Africa for self-realization, or to experience the slave dungeons, the commercial nature of the encounter may be disappointing.

We speculated further about the mercantile nature of tourist-local interactions in Elmina. A member of our research team thought that as politicians in Elmina pay for votes, and missionaries pay for converts, why shouldn't tourists pay for photographs? After all, this is capitalism, and isn't tourism the commodification of social relations and experience? The citizens of Elmina may have it right, that tourism is a business, based on exchange, and to trade money for photographs is appropriate and realistic.

There are other objections to the behavior of tourists. Locals are offended when tourists walk through the town in swimming suits, or bikinis, or when they wear see-through clothing. Giving or receiving with the left hand is considered impolite in Ghana, yet tourists do it. We received some comments, especially from older people, that it was inappropriate for tourist couples to walk hand in hand, or to touch or kiss in public. A Ghanaian woman will usually walk behind her husband. But some of the Elmina youth did not object to this aspect of tourist behavior, and they found themselves explaining to their elders that touching or kissing in public is just part of Western culture, and that the Elmina folk should learn to understand it. Still others said that for couples to walk together and to touch each other showed affection, respect for one's partner, that it was better than the Elmina way, and that in this regard, the people of Elmina could learn from the tourists.

Cultural Revival

A final consequence of tourism is that the tourist interest in Ghanaian culture has led to an increase in Ghanaians' own interest in their culture. As anthropologists know, most people in most societies take their culture for granted and do not ordinarily think about it. However, in times of change, controversy, ritual, or performance, people are led to examine their culture, and the coming of the tourists has a similar result. Especially in crafts and in performances such as dancing, drumming, and musical group performances, there is a revival due to the attention tourists pay to these long-standing "traditional" practices.

> Tourism has even made us more conscious about our culture. It has made us revive some of our cultural practices like dancing, drumming, dressing, and even our festivals. You know, most of the tourists express interest in these aspects of our culture. [male, age 38]

> Yes, these days, because of the tourists, the chiefs dress nicely and better than in the past. [female, age 19]

Tourism not only enhances Ghanaian interest in their culture, it supports local festivals and enhances the display of the power of the chiefs. We have a vast literature in African social anthropology on the decline of the power of chiefs as a consequence of colonialism and modernization. Renato Rosaldo (1989) has coined the phrase "imperialist nostalgia" to refer to Western longing in the imagination for what the imperialists had destroyed in a previous era. But what has been destroyed in colonialism has been recovered and enacted in tourism (Bruner and Kirshenblatt-Gimblett 1994).

The festivals of Ghana are among the main ritual performances and tourist attractions. I attended the 1994 Fetu Afahye, the annual festival in the Oguaa traditional area, in the town of Cape Coast. The activities of the afahye were spread over 17 days culminating on September 3 in a procession (*durbar*) of the *asafo* companies (military organizations) and the traditional chiefs marching through the town, ending in Victoria Park. Asafo membership is inherited patrilineally although the Fanti have dual descent. It would be beyond the scope of this essay to describe the festival other than to say that it serves many functions. It is a libation to the 77 Oguaa gods for the harvest from the earth and from the sea, a spiritual renewal for the community, a display of the traditional social organization, a period for renovation of the shrines, a time of family reunion, and a weeklong period of carnival and merrymaking—celebrated by boat races, a state ball, dances, political speeches, a masquerade, a church service, a beauty queen contest, a marathon walk, a concert, and a football (soccer) match. For a week, there is singing, drumming, and dancing in the streets of Cape Coast. It is a festive occasion for the entire community, but it has not had unbroken historical continuity.

In 1932, the colonial government banned the festival and seized all firearms because of a clash between two of the military organizations. The asafo companies had always been competitive, but in 1932 the situation got out of hand. The Ghanaian government removed the ban in 1964, and the afahye has been conducted since that time. According to one history of the festival, told to me by Nana Awuku, a traditional chief and business leader, the 1970s were the peak time for participation and energy in the festival.

Since the 1980s, the festival at Cape Coast has been in decline. Fewer people attend and many appear to be losing interest in the afahye. One factor has been the erosion of the authority of the traditional chiefs, which began with the treaty of 1844, when authority was transferred from the chiefs to the British. Since Ghanaian independence, the government has taken over many of the functions previously performed by the traditional chiefs. Nkrumah further transferred power from the traditional chiefs to the central government with the regulation that the central government had to give its approval for the installation or removal of a traditional chief. In Elmina, their festival, the bakatue, was not performed from 1979 to 1988, as there was no paramount chief. Another factor causing the decline has been the charismatic Christian movement, which has been very powerful in Ghana. They ask, How can one be Christian and believe in fetishism, spirits, and ancestor worship? During the height of the 1994 Fetu Afahye, a Christian group held a religious meeting in Cape Coast, in direct competition with the festival. A third factor has been the economic one.[16] In 1993, only four traditional chiefs participated in the festival, primarily because of the cost. In a comparable festival held in Elmina, one chief spent 700,000 cedis (U.S.$700), and in the Cape Coast afahye another chief spent 1,000,000 cedis (U.S.$1,000), an enormous sum by Ghanaian standards. The chief had to hire drummers and members of his retinue for the procession. A visitor might look with awe at the large following of the chief, at the adoration displayed, and might marvel at the display of African tradition. But these days, adoration and tradition have to be purchased. It cost one chief 250,000 cedis (U.S.$250) just to purchase a cow, necessary to feed his "followers."

Chiefs and others can no longer afford the festivals, one of the most spectacular tourist attractions in the Central Region. In 1994, in order to encourage the participation of the traditional chiefs in the procession, CEDE-COM provided a monetary subsidy to the chiefs, which increased participation from four chiefs to nine. It is ironic that the agency of government specifically charged with change and development finds itself supporting traditional chieftaincy in order to encourage tourism. In a sense, CEDECOM is reconstructing the institution of the chieftaincy, not as a locus of political authority, for that has long since eroded, but as display, as performance for tourism.[17] They see their task as one of supporting the Fetu Afahye without diminishing its character as an "authentic" celebration. Major support for the afahye is also provided by commercial sponsors, such as Embassy Cigarettes, Fan Milk, and Accra Brewery.

These governmental and commercial subsidies do not imply that the festival has become completely commodified or that it has lost its meaning to all the people. The festival still has traditional significance, rooted in indigenous social structure. The ritual and spiritual components, such as the pouring of libation and sacrifices at the shrines, are still performed by ritual specialists, even in places where the community-wide celebratory aspects of the festival are in decline.

Though charismatic Christians may not participate in the afahye in Cape Coast, many others do. Over time, the religious and societal aspects of the festival have been supplemented by new additions, such as the beauty contest and the town ball. And the carnivalesque features, the pure enjoyment, are apparent. Once at the Fetu Afahye I found myself dancing in the street, and I looked across the road at an old woman selling in the market, who was also dancing in front of her stand, smiling at me. Ours eyes met. We both kept dancing separately but we continued to look at each other, as if dancing together, across the road. It was a joyous moment.

Final Thoughts

Gilroy, in his important book *The Black Atlantic*, distinguishes between the essentialist view of blackness and the more constructivist and synchronistic concept of an emergent black Atlantic culture, one that he calls a rhizomorphic, fractal, transcultural, and international formation, that combines elements from Africa, the Caribbean, America, and Britain (1993:4). I applied this distinction to my data. In their discourse, the Robinsons and many African Americans (while on tour in Ghana) proclaim a black essentialism. The very term of the Robinsons' company—One Africa Productions—claims that all blacks are Africans. Though some live on the African continent while others live in the diaspora and may be African Americans, they are all one people, one Africa. The Robinsons focus on a common origin, on the essential unity among all blacks, and on historical continuity, thereby erasing hundreds of years of separate experience. This is what they say, but it is different in their practice, in their lives, and in their performances. Their ceremony, "Through the Door of No Return—The Return," starts with the tears of slavery in the dungeons on the Gold Coast, turns to

American diaspora nationalist songs, and ends with festive contemporary African music, clearly a blend of historically disparate elements. It constructs a three-part narrative of initial horror, diaspora resistance, and joyous return. Thus, while the Robinsons' texts are essentialist, their practice is constructivist. Ghanaians, on the other hand, do not share an essentialist view of blackness, for although they are very aware of the similarity in skin color, it is not for them the single overriding classificatory criterion for the sorting of human beings, for they see the returning African Americans primarily as foreigners, as Americans, as wealthy, and as tourists. In my view, not to "see" African Americans as black provides a liberating corrective for an American society beset with racial problems, where race, defined solely by skin color, is widely perceived as a "natural" and biologically given categorization.

In conclusion, we ask again, who owns Elmina Castle—the diaspora blacks who left as slaves, the Elmina citizens and the traditional chiefs who remained in place, the USAID and other international aid agencies who support the restoration and provide the interpretive perspective, or the tourists to whom the castle has now been dedicated? This is a rhetorical question, but the castle has not been simply a passive place. Elmina Castle may have been built initially as a European colonial intrusion on the Guinea Coast, but subsequently the castle has made its own claims to power and monumentality. Dominating the countryside, a massive structure on the edge of a humble fishing village, the castle takes on properties of its own and imposes its own meanings on the surrounding area. Elmina Castle is a bastion of power, a site to be struggled over, a transition point between the passage of goods and peoples from the interior of Africa to Europe and the New World. By their very nature, castles are dominant localities that define boundaries, that tell us who has the right to be inside the castle, within the center of power, in control, and who is outside, on the periphery. Castles are a dynamic presence, places that produce movement between home and abroad, sites for the construction of narratives of time and narratives of space. Old castles have long histories, stories of combat and battle, honor and degradation, beauty and cruelty, civilization and barbarism. Who owns the castles? Who has the right to tell their story?

Source: "Tourism in Ghana: The Representation of Slavery and the Return of the Black Diaspora," *American Anthropologist*, 1996, 98 (2): 290–304. Reprinted with permission of the author and the American Anthropological Association.

Acknowledgments

I hesitated to write about this topic, given its sensitivity and my own subject position, but after reading early drafts of this paper, African American colleagues and specialists in African American studies felt the data were useful and encouraged me to publish. I thank Kal Alston, Timothy Daniels, Alice Deck, Faye V. Harrison, Alma Gottlieb, Alejandro Lugo, Emily Osborn, Richard Price, Enid Schildkrout, Arlene Torres, the members of my cultural studies reading group at the University of Illinois, and Dominic Kofi Agyeman, who made important contributions to this study.

Notes

[1] Methodologically, this paper takes the castle as a site for analysis, but other papers in my larger project focus on the ethnography of a tourist performance in Kenya (Bruner and Kirshenblatt-Gimblett 1994), a historical theme park in Illinois (Bruner 1994), and the interaction between anthropologists, tourists, and indigenous peoples in Bali (Bruner 1995, 1996). My aim is to study a global transnational process, tourism, in its performative local manifestations.

[2] I was in Ghana in June and again in September 1994 for a total of approximately six weeks, as part of a USAID contract administered by MUCIA (Midwest Universities Consortium for International Activities) through the Tourism Center at the University of Minnesota. I acknowledge that this was a short time for fieldwork, but I had considerable help in the field. J. B. Lomo-Mainoo and Ben Anane-Nsiah of the Ghana Tourist Board were my local hosts. I assembled a research team consisting of Dominic Kofi Agyeman of the Sociology Department at the University of Cape Coast; his assistant Henry D. K. Baye; my wife Elaine C. Bruner; and Joanna Mensah and John Akofi-Holison, university students and residents of Elmina. Our team interviewed members of many segments of the Elmina community, including government officials, traditional chiefs, the queen of the fishmongers, the chief fisherman, the priest and priestess of Benya shrine, the heads of asafo companies (military organizations), the chairman of the bakatue (festival) planning committee, owners of bars and hotels catering to tourists, tour guides, and ordinary citizens. In addition, we set up six focus groups in Elmina consisting of 59 individuals ranging in age from 15 to 70, about equally divided between men and women. The focus group discussions were conducted in the Fanti language, transcribed, and then translated into English.

[3] The romantic notions are there, but Angelou, Harris, and other African American writers returning to Africa also describe their disillusionment with the poverty, sickness, heat, hardship, and even the brutality of modern Africa.

[4] Imahküs Robinson gave me a typed copy of her article dated January 1994, but I was unable to obtain the newspaper citation.

[5] I do not claim that the Robinsons represent the voice of all African Americans who travel to Ghana, but the Robinsons are prominent in local discourse, they establish relationships with African American visitors, and they are articulate spokespersons for one stream of diaspora thought.

[6] The question of whether or not to paint the castles was discussed in the local newspapers, and I raised the issue with the Council of Chiefs of Edina (Elmina) at a meeting in the House of Chiefs. The chiefs were in favor of Elmina Castle being painted without, however, covering up the faces of the atrocities of the slave trade.

[7] See Appiah 1990 for an analysis of the many meanings of racism.

[8] Faye V. Harrison, in her review of this paper for the editors of the *American Anthropologist,* made some comments so relevant to issues discussed here that I obtained her permission to quote her directly, rather than to simply paraphrase her words. She writes as follows:

> The independent and quite controversial film, *Sankofa,* produced and directed by Ethiopian filmmaker and Howard University professor Haile Gerima, begins its storyline in one of Ghana's "slave castles" with a tour group being shown the dungeons. A beautiful (blond wig-wearing) black fashion model who's being photographed on the outside of the castle becomes curious when she sees the tourist group descend into a dark tunnel, so she follows them. Her path takes her across time into the 17th or 18th century. The film accomplishes what the Robinsons' performance does, except in much more graphic terms and imagery! I remember coming out of the theater needing to be debriefed for my return to 20th-century everyday life. The intensified anger and

hostility I felt toward racial oppression stimulated me to think and talk through complexities and nuances that the film erased. In light of "Tourism in Ghana," what's
interesting about the film is that it was produced largely for an African American audience, but the director and scriptwriter were African as were many of the cultural
agents who made the project feasible. This is an instance when a diasporic return
home was the result of a transcultural and transnational collaboration. The film could
not have been produced without the meeting in the borderlands conjoining the
diaspora and continent.

Harrison's comment is in the theoretical tradition of Paul Gilroy (1993), to which we shall
turn later in this paper. See Bruner (1996) for a discussion of the concept of border zone as
applied to tourism. Relevant also is the difference between texts produced by writers and
intellectuals and ethnographic data gathered from ordinary citizens.

[9] The silence about slavery in Ghanaian public discourse may reflect shame and embarrassment, even guilt, about the Ghanaian role in the slave trade. Sly reports that in December
1994, "a group of Ghanaian chiefs performed a ceremony of atonement for their ancestors'
role in slavery for a group of visiting African-Americans" (1995:29A).

[10] This formulation may be so jarring to an American sensibility because it speaks of wealthy
African Americans who return to Ghana almost as if they were like European immigrants
who became successful in the New World and returned for a visit to the old country to display their newfound prosperity. It blurs the distinction so crucial to the American experience
between slavery and migration, between forced involuntary servitude and a voluntary journey to seek a better life. The Ghanaian formulation leads us to further problematize the concept of travel and traveling theory (Clifford 1989).

[11] For the larger context of the politics of representation of race at Colonial Williamsburg, see
Gable et al. 1992.

[12] There may be more public performances about slavery than I had realized. Charisse Jones
reports that within the last decade many African Americans have "begun to re-examine slavery—reflecting upon it in film and music, remembering it through ritual and ceremony,
assessing its legacy from universities to neighborhood study groups" (1995:1). Particular
expressions are enumerated documenting the "transition from feelings of shame and denial
about slavery to an embrace of that painful past" (1995:14). Jones writes that there has been
an increase in performances about slavery within the U.S. black community. My point, however, may still be valid—that America has not yet come to terms with slavery as a national
rather than simply as a black or ethnic tragedy, and that we have not yet fully acknowledged
the necessity for a truly national catharsis. As I write these words, the O. J. Simpson trial and
the Million Man March have precipitated renewed discussion of race relations in America,
but I ask, How can America come to terms with racism if we don't yet have ways of representing and talking about the single most significant experience in black American history,
the experience of slavery?

[13] As part of the tourism development project, a team from the Smithsonian Institution produced the exhibits at the West African Museum at Cape Coast Castle, and their challenge
was to balance the conflicting political currents to which they were exposed. According to
observer Enid Schildkrout, who is a specialist in Ghana as well as a museum professional,
the voice of the diaspora "dominated the script of the exhibition," at the expense of the voice
of the Ghanaians (personal communication, 1995).

[14] I do not have firm statistical data on the precise incidence of crimes against tourists in Elmina.

[15] Ruth Behar (1993) reports similar findings.

[16] Recent economic studies in Ghana include Mikell 1989 and Clark 1994.

[17] The institution of chieftaincy, of course, is influenced by many factors other than tourism
development, for example, local politics and economics.

References

Angelou, Maya. 1986. *All God's Children Need Traveling Shoes*. New York: Vintage Books.

Appadurai, Arjun. 1991. "Global Ethnoscapes: Notes and Queries for a Transnational Anthropology." In *Recapturing Anthropology: Working in the Present*, ed. Richard G. Fox, pp. 191–210. Santa Fe: School of American Research Press.

Appiah, Kwame Anthony. 1990. "Racisms." In *Anatomy of Racism*, ed. David Theo Goldberg, pp. 3–17. Minneapolis: University of Minnesota Press.

———. 1992. *In My Father's House: Africa in the Philosophy of Culture*. New York: Oxford University Press.

Behar, Ruth. 1993. *Translated Woman: Crossing the Border with Esperanza's Story*. Boston: Beacon Press.

Bruner, Edward M. 1994. "Abraham Lincoln as Authentic Reproduction: A Critique of Postmodernism." *American Anthropologist* 96:397–415.

———. 1995. "The Ethnographer/Tourist in Indonesia," in *International Tourism: Identity and Change*, Marie-Francoise Lanfant, ed. John B. Allcock, and Edward M. Bruner, pp. 224–241. London: Sage.

———. 1996. "Tourism in the Balinese Borderzone," in *Displacement, Diaspora, and Geographies of Identity*, ed. Smadar Lavie and Ted Swedenburg. Durham: Duke University Press.

Bruner, Edward M., and Phyllis Gorfain. 1984. "Dialogic Narration and the Paradoxes of Masada," in *Text, Play and Story: The Construction and Reconstruction of Self and Society*, ed. Edward M. Bruner, pp. 56–79. (Proceedings of the American Ethnological Society Annual Meeting, 1983.) Long Grove, IL: Waveland Press.

Bruner, Edward M., and Barbara Kirshenblatt-Gimblett. 1994. "Maasai on the Lawn: Tourist Realism in East Africa." *Cultural Anthropology* 9:435–470.

Carrington, Tim. 1994. "Ray of Hope: Amid Africa's Agony, One Nation, Ghana, Shows Modest Gains." *Wall Street Journal* (January 26):A1.

Clark, Gracia. 1994. *Onions Are My Husband: Survival and Accumulation by West African Market Women*. Chicago: University of Chicago Press.

Clifford, James. 1989. "Notes on Travel and Theory." *Inscription* 5:177–188.

———. 1994. "Diasporas." *Cultural Anthropology* 9:302–338.

Gable, Eric, Richard Handler, and Anna Lawson. 1992. "On the Uses of Relativism: Fact, Conjecture, and Black and White Histories at Colonial Williamsburg." *American Ethnologist* 19:791–805.

Gilroy, Paul. 1993. *The Black Atlantic: Modernity and Double Consciousness*. Cambridge, MA: Harvard University Press.

Gupta, Akhil, and James Ferguson. 1992. "Beyond 'Culture': Space, Identity, and the Politics of Difference." *Cultural Anthropology* 7:6–23.

Harding, Susan, and Fred Myers, eds. 1994. "Further Inflections: Toward Ethnographies of the Future." Special issue. *Cultural Anthropology* 9(3).

Harris, Eddy L. 1992. *Native Stranger: A Black American's Journey into the Heart of Africa*. New York: Vintage Books.

Janofsky, Michael. 1994. "Mock Auction of Slaves Outrages Some Blacks." *New York Times*, October 8:7.

Jones, Charisse. 1995. "Bringing Slavery's Long Shadow to the Light." *New York Times* (April 2, front section):1, 14.

Lavie, Smadar, and Ted Swedenburg, eds. 1996. *Displacement, Diaspora, and Geographies of Identity*. Durham: Duke University Press.

Marcus, George E. 1994. "General Comments." *Cultural Anthropology* 9:423–428.

Mikell, Gwendolyn. 1989. *Cocoa and Chaos in Ghana*. New York: Paragon.

Price, Richard. 1983. *First Time: The Historical Vision of an Afro-American People.* Baltimore: Johns Hopkins University Press.

Report of the Proceedings of the Conference on Preservation of Elmina and Cape Coast. 1994. Castles and Fort St. Jago in the Central Region Held in the Cape Coast Castle, May 11–12.

Rosaldo, Renato. 1989. *Culture and Truth: The Remaking of Social Analysis.* Boston: Beacon Press.

Scott, David. 1991. "That Event, This Memory: Notes on the Anthropology of African Diaspora in the New World." *Diaspora* 1(3):261–284.

Sly, Liz. 1995. "Ghana Planning to Restore Castle." *Dallas Morning News* (April 9):1A, 29A.

van Dantzig, Albert. 1980. *Forts and Castles of Ghana.* Accra, Ghana: Sedco.

Wright, Richard. 1954. *Black Power.* New York: Harper and Brothers.

20

Rites of the Tribe:
The Meaning of Poland for
American Jewish Tourists

Jack Kugelmass

Frankfurt airport, summer 1987. When I enter the plane, I find myself seated beside a Jewish family from Brooklyn. The father, an old Hasid with black suit and long white beard, seems like a relic from an age gone by, which is how he must appear to the other passengers in the plane. But the children look a little better placed in this century: the son, wearing a blue blazer, gray pants, tie and homburg, is in his late twenties and clean shaven. He is in business. The daughter, who is in her thirties, is stylishly dressed in white and pink. She is a professor of Jewish studies and is fluent in Polish. The father is very proud of his children's secular education. For him, that too is a link to the past: before the war, his sister was a professor in Cracow. The father is a survivor of Bergen Belsen and he is taking his son and daughter to visit the graves of his ancestors. They have brought with them enough food for the eight-day trip. The son assures me that his sister is a gourmet cook and has prepared everything they will need.

Once the plane is in the air and passengers can move about, the father becomes quite a hit, especially among the older passengers unaccustomed to seeing Hasidim on, or even heading to, Polish soil. While the father converses with other passengers in Polish, the daughter passes a note to him in English. He looks at it, laughs, and then shows it to me. The note reads: "What did the Polack say when his wife gave birth to twins? 'Who's the father of the other one?'"

As we approach Warsaw, the son looks out the window and comments to his father and sister, "Look how beautiful it is. Poland's a beautiful country!" They both laugh. Looking at the greenery below, I'm a little bewildered by the comment. I ask what he sees that's so special. "Oh," he replies, "I'm just referring to a family joke. We have an uncle who went to Poland with his son and the first day in the hotel room he looked behind a picture on the wall and spotted a microphone. He's a very paranoid person, so throughout the trip he kept saying to his son, 'Look how beautiful Poland is. It's such a beautiful country!' Finally on the last day of the trip they were running out of kosher food and the son was hungry and exhausted because there was very little he would eat and he yells, 'I can't stand this place!' The father got upset. He started shouting at the son, '*A gantse vokh hob ikh gemakht vi ikh glaykh dos plats, itst afn letstn tog du makhst af mir a kholere.* [All week I've pretended that I like this place and now on the last day you're making a plague on me.]'" In a few moments the plane touches down. As it does, the father murmurs, "*Borukh ha-Shem* [Blessed be God]." The son does the same and I do too. I ask if it's appropriate to say *Shekhiyanu* (a prayer thanking God upon experiencing something for the first time). "No," the son replies. "I don't think so. Not for this."

From Yehudit Hendel's *Near Quiet Places: Twelve Days in Poland:*

> I tried to get out of it on some pretext. I was scared and my first impulse was to refuse. Why? I thought. How? What? But suddenly it all began to move and soon I couldn't think about anything except going to Poland. Suddenly I felt I had to go to Poland and yet, at the same time, I felt a tremendous hesitation about going to Poland. All the baggage we drag around with us from Poland. . . .
>
> And suddenly I was plunged into a vortex of dread and regret and memory and longing to forget and hatred and streets and house numbers and will you get to Lodz, will you be in Czestochowa and maybe you'll go to the cemetery in Lublin maybe you'll find my father, maybe you'll go to the cemetery in Krakow maybe you'll find my mother. Heavy sacks we all drag on our back and big stories and small stories, a thousand rocks pour down all at once from that volcano extinguished long ago that died and wasn't buried. Why do you have to go to Kaluszyn, the stranger from Jaffa repeated. Ten thousand Jews there were in Kaluszyn, one remained. Right after the War, he went back to Kaluszyn and started running along the railroad tracks, he went crazy running along the railroad tracks and a Pole passing by shot him and he was the last corpse of Kaluszyn after the war, on the railroad tracks.[1]

A number of years ago, two Warsawian Jews arrived in New York and paid a visit to the YIVO Institute for Jewish Research. They stopped in front of my office and read the cartoon one of my students had posted on the door.

The drawing depicts a group of dark-skinned "natives" scrambling to hide their television, stereo, and various other modern appliances. Another native, acting as the lookout, peers out the window and, having just spotted two approaching white people wearing pith helmets and bush jackets, shouts frantically, "Anthropologists!" "Anthropologists!" My visitors commented that with the increasing flow of Jewish tourists to Poland they had begun to feel just like those natives, constantly being scrutinized by others on their performance of Jewish rituals.

In this essay, I shall examine the meaning of tourism with special reference to the current Jewish fascination with Poland. The thesis I shall argue is that tourism is not necessarily the activity of buffoons, nor is it only an act of cultural colonization; not only is mass tourism part and parcel of the secular rites of modern society, its public culture,[2] but it sometimes has significant cultural and religious implications for those who participate in it.

The vast majority of Jews who travel to Poland do so in organized tour groups. Probably the smallest in numbers yet the most striking by way of appearance (I once listened to a non-Jewish Pole tell of seeing "an authentic *foreign* Jew with black hat and side curls!") are Hasidim, who now flock to the burial sites of famous rabbis, particularly in southeastern Poland.[3] Such tombs are littered with photocopied *kvitlekh* (handwritten petitions) on behalf of a sick relative, an unmarried daughter, an unemployed child. Pilgrims to the tomb of Rebbe Elimelech in Lezajk bring back his guarantee that they will repent before their death. Their tours are extremely short—sometimes no more than 48 hours—and very insular: in Cracow they have appropriated a synagogue to themselves and restored a ritual bath; in Warsaw the only group that ventured to the Nozyk synagogue in the six weeks I visited the place organized their own *minyan* (ritual quorum) in a separate room, purposely avoiding an existing service.

A much larger number of group travelers are on synagogue or communal organization group tours. These people are chiefly interested in visiting concentration camps or the sites of Jewish resistance during the Holocaust. Unlike the survivors and their children, who always return to the site of their or their parents' youth, institutional tours rarely make any attempt to see the physical remains of *shteytlekh* (typically small market towns that once characterized much of the Jewish settlement pattern in Poland) that still dot the Polish landscape.[4]

Although I do not have precise figures on the size of current Jewish tourism to Eastern Europe (my guess is that we are speaking of a figure somewhere in the tens of thousands), the numbers were clearly on the increase well before the end of communism, and the fact is that by the mid 1980s no visitor to the area could look through a camera viewfinder and be assured that another American or Israeli will not suddenly appear to mar the "pristine" view. Major Jewish institutions both in America and in Israel now sponsor guided tours for members to various parts of Eastern Europe, particularly Poland, Czechoslovakia, and Hungary. These tours run the gamut of

Jewish institutional life, from the most secular and academic to the ultra-Orthodox. Their origins lie, however, in Jewish communal fund-raising. In 1948 Henry Montor of the United Jewish Federation chartered a TWA airplane and took 35 communal leaders on a four-week mission to the displaced persons camps in Europe and then to Israel to see the process of absorption then underway. These leaders subsequently spearheaded local fund-raising drives.[5] In recent years, the United Jewish Appeal (UJA) had begun to send an increasing number of groups to Poland, while some American synagogue groups and literally scores of nationally organized youth groups such as the Conservative movement's United Synagogue Youth and the Orthodox movement's B'nai Akiva have done likewise. The displaced persons camps are a thing of the past, and with the resurgence of fund-raising tours the focus within Eastern Europe is now primarily the death camps.[6] The symbolism remains the same. The tours are structured around the themes of Destruction and Redemption. Almost all groups conclude their travel to Eastern Europe with a longer tour of Israel. Little wonder then that even a Jewish singles' tour goes to the usual places, although in their case Redemption is through the implicit possibility of marriage and reproduction, hence the trip concludes in Eastern Europe.

Various designated historical sites existed in Poland long before the current wave of Jewish tourism: the Ghetto Heroes Monument, the Anielewicz bunker, and Treblinka. Long before the end of communism, Poland had made concerted efforts to woo Jewish visitors, in particular

Participant in United Synagogue Youth Group writing note to the dead, Treblinka. (Photo by Jack Kugelmass)

through the training of Orbis guides and the setting up of Jewish desks with special brochures at tourist offices. Efforts had been made to renovate historically significant buildings and to erect monuments and markers at various sites. Tykocin in northeastern Poland has a reconstructed seventeenth-century synagogue, now a museum; the Great Synagogue in Cracow has been renovated and turned into a museum, while the surrounding square is undergoing renovation and reconstruction; the Nozyk synagogue in Warsaw was renovated in the early 1980s. More recently, stone monuments have been erected in the Warsaw Ghetto to form the so-called memory route, and a large monument has been constructed at the Umschlagplatz; both projects were designated by the government to open as part of the commemoration of the forty-fifth anniversary of the Warsaw Ghetto Uprising. The seventeenth-century synagogue in Lancut, with its magnificent polychrome walls, underwent extensive if slow renovation. In addition, the ongoing restoration of Kazimierz Dolny and the completed renovation of Sandomierz—two sixteenth-century towns—add important sites for Jewish visitors.[7]

The state's awareness of Jewish tourism is also evident in the objects available for sale in Cepelias, the government-owned folk art outlets. In Cracow, in the summer of 1987, one store had in its window a wooden Jewish figurine holding an actual piece of Torah! Although such figures (usually holding texts clipped from the *Folks-sztyme* (the state-sponsored, and, therefore, communist Polish Yiddish newspaper) have their roots in peasant culture, at 5,000 zlotys (five dollars at the black-market rate)—at that time the equivalent of a week's salary for the average Pole—the sculpture is clearly intended for the tourist market. A Cepelia in the nearby covered market had in stock enormous quantities of mass-produced Jewish peddlers. Two years later, the private stalls in the market had begun to cash in on the fad: one shop had about two dozen Hasidic figurines holding Hebrew texts clipped out of prayer books; other shops had much poorer carvings of peddlers and other Jewish types. In the summer of 1989 the store with the peddler and Torah scroll had mass-manufactured miniature Jews on springs so that with a little push they would *shokl* (rock back and forth) in the manner of Orthodox Jews praying. Some years later, I came across something even more striking. In the marketplace in Cracow, I found wooden figurines of a terrified Jewish family with children huddling deep within their parents' clothing. The image clearly evoking experiences all too common during World War II, now resurfacing in a rather sympathetic guise—a good indication of how much Poland's emerging Holocaust consciousness is tied to Jewish tourism.

Jewish figurines are not as common in Warsaw's Old City as in Cracow. Here, however, they are not to be found in Cepelias but in the market square, where certified artists sell directly to the public. In 1987, I bought a hand-carved figure of a Jew with his arms extended palms outward and shrugging his shoulders. The price was one dollar, and it was the only carving of its kind that I could find in Warsaw. Today one sees "lines" rather than unique works of art and the prices start at ten dollars. Wares in the market

square include groups of hand-carved *klezmorim* (Jewish musicians), generally next to other non-Jewish musicians and Christ figures. Some are representational; others are caricatures or even abstract. In evidence also are
paintings of Jewish figures such as "ghetto rebbes," match sellers, and, of
course, klezmorim; one stall carries a line of caricatures, including a blatantly
Shylockian moneylender counting his gold coins.

Non-Jewish artists made all these objects. Most of the vendors are
young men in their twenties and thirties: when asked about the objects they
make they are likely to refer to family stories and the memory of Jews, particularly Jews in hiding during the war—a very common theme in contemporary
Polish discourse. The artist who makes the "ghetto rebbes," however, is in his
eighties, and his work is based on what he himself has seen. He refers to himself as a "philo-Semite" and has a portfolio of Jewish subjects he can reproduce on demand. The market also has various Jewish books for sale, all
recently published translations of Sholem Aleichem, Itsek Manger, Bashevis
Singer, the Talmud, and various Holocaust memoirs. Some are still available
in bookstores, and the market is a more direct way for private entrepreneurs—
increasingly evident as Poland moved toward a free-market economy—to
reach Jewish, that is, foreign Jewish, consumers. Except in the market in the
Old City, the only Jewish items for sale in the summer of 1989 were large
quantities of brass Hanukkah menorahs copied from antique Polish models.
These could be seen in jewelry shops and Cepelias near Western hotels.[8]

Paintings of Jewish moneylenders on sale in the Old City, Warsaw. (Photo by Jack
Kugelmass)

Not all tourists rely on the market to acquire things. For scholars, especially before the end of communism, the best buys in Poland were microfilms of prewar Jewish publications available from the National Library and other archives; the more daring would keep their eyes open for prewar ritual objects. Although these could be bought at the government-owned art store Desa, because they are prewar they could not be removed from the country legally. Their value is less monetary than sentimental: for American Jews they are metonymic representations of Polish Jewry, and buyers are convinced that through their acquisitions they are rescuing the last traces of a destroyed people.[9] For example, while visiting Przemysl, the town of his great-grandfather, Arthur Kurzweil, at the time a young genealogist, meets a Pole who has acquired a substantial collection of Judaica:

> Then the old man showed me something which stunned me—a little necklace with an amulet hanging from it. On one side of the amulet was a miniature painting of Moses holding the Tablets. On the other was tiny Hebrew writing, almost all of which was too small or too unclear to read. Through the son, the old man told me that he found this in the ghetto after the war.
>
> I had to have that necklace. I kept imagining it hanging around the neck of a young Jewish woman, and that on her way to the death camp she'd discovered it was missing. Here it was now, just another curio; another item in an antique collection.
>
> I had to have that necklace. It needed a new home, perhaps around the neck of a free Jewish woman in America, perhaps on my shelf.[10]

The narrative reaches its climax when the Pole shows him a Torah, then takes it away only to return with a small piece of it he has cut out. Horrified by the desecration, the author leaves with the amulet and Torah fragment, convinced that the text of the fragment contains a message that he, a descendant of one of the town's former inhabitants, was fated to receive.

The desire to salvage vestiges of prewar Jewry may even go beyond artifacts to the actual remains of people. At Treblinka, one Jewish synagogue youth tour group leader collected pieces of bone from the surrounding fields. These he placed in a plastic container with the intention of burying them in Israel at the next stage of the tour!

Whereas some entrepreneurial non-Jewish Poles profit from the influx of Jewish tourists, the advent of the tour buses, especially before Poland's economy opened to the West, also proved to be a boon for many members of the Polish Jewish community. Tourists were an opportunity to do business—to rent an apartment, change money, or ask for donations—and those visitors who showed a lack of interest in such dealings were quickly ignored by the formerly solicitous coreligionists. Of course, success in such solicitation depends a good deal on the presentation of self as destitute. Consequently, there was much in the interaction of American tourists and Polish residents that resembled the characters of the above-mentioned cartoon. In Cracow I was told of one congregant who kept a spare change of clothes near the synagogue. A quick change in costume created the illusion of two people instead of one, thereby enabling him to double his money from each tour group. In Warsaw's Nozyk synagogue, rumors abound that not all who related their tales of woe were Jewish. Indeed, one could see an occasional congregant "reading" from an upside-down Hebrew prayer book.

Not surprisingly, these encounters are often rather distressing for the tourist, particularly for younger people who are accustomed to the American system of neighborhood synagogue class and age spatial separation; they are inclined to interpret what they see as peculiar to Poland. In one case, a United Synagogue Youth group had arranged for members of the group to read from the Torah during the Sabbath services. Following these *aliyes,* the young women from the group, who had occupied the second-level balconies (the synagogue is Orthodox and thus enforces a separation of men and women during prayer), showered the young men with candies—a traditional East European Jewish custom. The candies were chocolate covered, an item rationed at that time in Poland, and a number of congregants wandered around the synagogue scavenging the scattered chocolate from the floor. The service itself proved to be rather contentious, with the synagogue's officials reluctant to give the group the full participation its leader had requested and even prearranged. Disgusted with the congregation's behavior, the group leader was determined to have future groups spend the Sabbath in Cracow, where the congregation is much smaller, less knowledgeable in Jewish tradition, and less likely to interfere.

Although some groups prefer to keep such encounters to a minimum, others carefully orchestrate them by arranging meetings with select members of the Jewish community, particularly with young members of the intelligentsia, who are invariably asked by the visitors to justify their remaining in Poland. The older members of the community are less offended by the question. They are more openly cynical about Poland and the country's treatment of Jews, so their answers are straightforward—usually connected to family obligations and age. The younger members find their ties to the land and their very identities as Polish Jews challenged. They are proud of their country even if they acknowledge its darker side. Some, such as one young mathematician, use the encounter to explain the positive features of contemporary life in Poland and the close connections he and others feel with members of the Catholic intelligentsia. The message is not an easy one for American Jews to accept, and it requires frequent repetition. One man, who ran a Jewish travel agency in Warsaw, was particularly offended by the question despite his ready acknowledgment that Poland remains, in his view, an extremely anti-Semitic country. He turned the question around and asked the visitors, "Why do you stay in America? Why don't you move to Israel?" When asked the typical tourist question by a group of young Orthodox Jews from England, a man who ran the Jewish cultural club in Cracow explained that in Poland he could decide for himself how he should act as a Jew. When asked whether he would be happier if there were more Jews around, he was quick to respond,

"No. Not if they're anything like those *schnorrers* [beggars] who hang around the synagogue!"

The schnorrers, a direct result of increased Jewish tourism, were once a source of profound embarrassment for younger Polish Jews. They haunted the synagogues and other remaining Jewish monuments, and they gave foreigners the sense that all Polish Jews are destitute. To counteract this image, the intelligentsia were careful to define their interaction with tourists on more-equal terms. They would not solicit financial contributions for themselves, although they were quite happy to receive luxury goods such as tea, coffee, special foods, and even old clothes. Some would accept money if it were intended to further the work of "the committee," the group of Jewish and non-Jewish intellectuals whose organization, the Committee for the Preservation of Jewish Monuments in Poland, has been active in the restoration of tombstones in the cemetery of Warsaw and in other cities and towns throughout the country. In addition, they were always glad to receive Jewish books and published material unavailable in Poland. For them, the presence of foreign Jews is vital to their often only recently acquired Jewish identity, and because of it, they were ready to forgive numerous indiscretions made by naive or insensitive visitors.[11]

In describing relations between Iranian-born Jews and Jewish visitors to that country, Laurence Loeb notes that while traveling abroad Jews will "actively seek contact with local co-religionists and their institutions, especially the synagogue. It is a noteworthy pattern of Western Jewish tourist culture that Jews, who are totally disinterested in Jewish life at home, become avid anthropologists abroad."[12] If Loeb's statement is correct for Poland, it is so only in regard to visiting synagogues. But to think of American Jewish tourists in Poland as anthropologists goes beyond even the most critical interpretation of the nature of anthropological inquiry.

Jewish visitors go to Poland to see the past, and the category applies not only to the relics of the place but also, by way of contagion, to all who live nearby. Whereas tourists generally engage in a form of popular ethnography,[13] there is something unique about Jewish tourism in Poland. Jewish tourists see nothing quaint about the local culture either Jewish or non-Jewish; their interest is the dead rather than the living. They go as antiquarians rather than ethnographers; consequently, they bring back with them no experiences that deepen their knowledge of the local culture. The experiences they remember are likely to be those that enhance an already existing negative opinion. Indeed, they are the experiences they expect to have in Poland, and because they confirm deeply held convictions, they are almost a desired part of the trip.

Most tourists go places to have a good time. Even for those who go on so-called adventure travel tours to see the more-remote corners of the globe, there is still a balance between leisure and learning in which leisure very much has the upper hand. But when Jews go to Poland, leisure does not figure in their calculations of distance, sites, and expenditures of time. One Jewish Pole, who had established a tourist company to deal with foreign Jewish travelers to Poland, was considering including stays at the mountain resort town Zakopane and other scenic locales in his package tours, but he soon tempered the idea for lack of interest.[14] A sophisticated non-Jewish Pole, familiar with the itinerary of Jewish tour groups, was convinced that their frightful pace was intentionally designed to instill a negative sense of place. Since American Jews are known to have very strong biases against Poland long before they go on such excursions, the question one must ask is, why do they go? There are various reasons at work here, and I shall attempt to outline what they are.

Even the most innocent of journeys lays claim to space. "The very carrying out of a tourist itinerary," writes Donald Home, "is a form of appropriation" transforming the unfamiliar into home turf.[15] But the case of Jewish tourism to Poland is not one of an innocent journey but of actively contested history. I recall, for example, standing at the site of the crematorium in Birkenau. The Polish guide, an educated man in his late fifties and rather sympathetic to the subject of Jewish history, was lecturing a Jewish group. Waiting for a pause in his talk, a woman began to question him about the Jewish population of Oswiecim before and after the war. The guide maintained that relations between Jews and Poles were good: the victimization of Jews was a German rather than a Polish problem. Other visitors prodded further, determined to extract from him some admission of what they already knew: that anti-Semitism was indeed a Polish problem before and after the war. The imminent departure of the buses for Cracow rescued the guide from a conversation he preferred not to engage in. This same anger on discovering firsthand the obliteration of Jewish memory and the blatant rewriting of history appears in almost any account of travel to Eastern Europe.[16] Kurzweil writes that in Przemysl,

> I learned about the town museum devoted to the history of the area. I went there eagerly, to learn what I could about the place my family had lived in so long. In the entire four-story building though I should have expected it I was shocked to find only two tiny showcases of Jewish items. A skullcap, a menorah, candlesticks, a megillah. Here, where several thousand Jews had lived, where Jews from the area were kept in a ghetto before being taken to a death camp, the Jewish presence was recognized only by a few relics in a dusty corner.[17]

Jews have long felt that Polish public culture was reluctant to give proper recognition to the degree of Jewish suffering during the war. This reluctance was particularly evident in the Auschwitz museum, which was established as a Polish national shrine: until its recent makeover and the installation of photo/text panels, exhibits at the site significantly overlooked the Jewish presence at the camp. While Jews were present collectively through exhibits about torture and the display of confiscated prayer shawls, displays of individual biographies, such as in a pavilion that features the portraits of scores of individuals and highlights the martyrdom of Polish political prisoners, make no reference to Jews. The one individual who stands out in the pavilion is Father Kolbe, who volunteered to die at Auschwitz in place of another. Kolbe, however, was the editor of a virulently anti-Jewish publication before the war—something not mentioned. Although there is a Jewish pavilion at Auschwitz, it was constructed long after others had been established for various occupied countries, including the so-called German Democratic Republic, or East Germany and Austria whose pavilion's entryway mural greets visitors with the slogan, "Austria: Hitler's First Victim!" Many Jews respond to this by visiting the nearby death camp Birkenau, a largely unreconstructed site generally ignored by other tourists. Other Jews are determined to make their presence felt at Auschwitz. A subtle protest is evident in the large numbers of *yortsayt* (memorial) candles placed by visitors, along with bouquets of flowers with Hebrew-lettered banners, at the wall of execution. The wall is like an *axis mundi* of People's Poland, legitimizing the Communist state by tying it to the suffering of Polish political prisoners.

Often the protests are less subtle. A historian I know led a Smithsonian-sponsored tour of mostly Polish Americans and arranged a visit to the Great Synagogue in Cracow. A Polish guide was giving what my friend considered a highly informed and sympathetic survey of the history of the synagogue when suddenly an Israeli tourist jumped in front of her and began to harangue the visitors: "Don't believe a word she is saying. Had these people helped them during the war this place wouldn't now be a museum. Instead there would be living Jews to pray here!" Such obtrusiveness is hardly unique. Visitors to Auschwitz and other concentration camps are likely to spot groups of young Israelis carrying their national flag as they head from pavilion to pavilion, and in the summer of 1989 specially organized groups of European and American Jews protested at the Carmelite convent just outside the wall. Although most Jews do not intend to cause a violent confrontation, they do intend to provoke. Young observant Jews march through the streets on the way from synagogue to their hotels wearing *yarmulkes* rather than less-marked headgear and singing Hebrew or religious songs. Their intention is to be as visible as possible, to reclaim, even if only symbolically, territory that had once belonged, if not to their own, then at least to other people's parents and grandparents.

Much of this seems to be a Jewish meditation on power and powerlessness. These demonstrations are a way of reflecting on the past and perhaps, too, a way of rectifying history. Little wonder, then, that tourists are hyperconscious of the gaze of Poles. In describing her experiences as a participant in the 1988 Jewish students' "March of the Living" from Auschwitz to Birkenau (held on Israel's official day of commemoration of the Holocaust), one participant recalls the group's arrival in Warsaw:

> We then were flown to Warsaw by the Polish airline. It was an extremely shaky flight, but we made it in one piece. Outside the Warsaw airport,

the Orthodox boys prayed the Mincha service. Polish soldiers, young and
old, stood around laughing and pointing during the service. They said,
Zhid, Zhid ("Jews, Jews"). That would be the first of many hostile acts
directed toward our group during the tour of Poland.

And then later,

On Yom Ha'Shoah, every one of us who marched from Auschwitz to the
crematoria at Birkenau saw the hatred in the eyes of the Polish people.[18]

Or the following example: A young woman from Montreal, the child of survivors, was horrified to hear a Polish woman comment while watching a
group of Orthodox American Jews protesting the Carmelite convent, "Look
at all the noise they make now. But during the war all they could do was
shiver and be quiet!" The comment confirmed everything her parents had
told her about what to expect in Poland.[19] Indeed, for some, such encounters
constitute a direct way of linking the self to a collective past. Concluding a
description of his recent journey tracing Hasidic landmarks in Poland, Paul
Fenton writes that in Plock,

I had hoped to find the tombs of my ancestors in the cemetery, to kneel
and pray for those of our family who had perished violently among the
first victims of Nazi brutality. Instead my hopes were met with the spectacle of the football field, which now occupies the spot of the age-old
cemetery. As we walked along the side of the field I discovered the
debris of a tombstone with some Hebrew lettering. What desecration!
Even the memorial monument which had been erected in a corner of the
sports field by a handful of survivors of the *Shoah* had been severely
vandalized. As we stood there, plunged in tearful thought, a book of
Psalms in our palms, a group of youngsters jeered while passing *Zhid,
Zhidka* (Jew boy, Jew girl). Though I had never ever heard that cry
before, the blood froze in my veins as if I had perceived some horrific
echo resounding from the depths of time through the collective memories of generations of cowering ancestors.[20]

This sense of experiencing "collective memories" suggests that contested history is not the only factor bringing American Jews to Poland. An
underlying dilemma of modern culture is that despite the increasing prevalence of a two-dimensional universe, made possible through the growth of
electronic media, humans remain sensual beings, and they are ill at ease with
information that can be perceived only as a representation of itself. This is the
thrill, it seems to me, of seeing personalities "in the flesh." The mythic
becomes tangible; skepticism dissolves. Most American Jews are of East
European descent: their ancestral homes, if conveyed to them at all through
the narratives of parents and grandparents, lack the clarity of place that only
direct experience can provide. Even names of places of origin are often
obscured, either because they were not passed down to succeeding generations or because they were passed down only in their Yiddish form.[21] In the
words of the French Jewish historian Rachel Ertel:

> Over the years Poland remained a forbidden land to me. It would perhaps be fairer to say that it simply didn't exist, at least not in a material sense. The Poland I carried within me, like the weight of the dead, spoke Yiddish. The names of its cities, towns, and villages, its streets and rivers, were Yiddish names one cannot find on any map. A country made up of words, of false and true memories, not even mine—I did not have any—, not even those of my relatives, who never spoke of them: impersonal collective memories that obliterated all reality—a phantasmagorical Poland. A phantom Poland. A Poland from which I could not remember having been rescued by the Extermination. [22]

Divorced from place through migration, and determined to put the past far behind, an image of the shtetl as primitive and rural emerged long ago, and the trope has wide currency in the popular imagination. Its source is partly the negative stereotyping of the Old Country in the rotogravure section of the *Forverts* (the principal Yiddish immigrant newspaper in the U.S.) and in the romanticized images in paintings by Chagall, the drawings of Yudovin, and, of course, the Broadway musical *Fiddler on the Roof.* Such images speak to the post-Holocaust resurrection of the shtetl as an idyllic Jewish enclave.[23] The romanticization allows for a sense that through such journeys one enters cosmogonic space, a place inscribed with tribal memory.

For many American Jews, Eastern Europe had become so remote in its memory culture that precise knowledge of locality of residence of grandparents or great grandparents is quite uncommon. Moreover, not all areas have been accessible, particularly (until recently) those towns that after the war became part of the Soviet Union. So most Jews going to Poland are going for reasons having less to do with memory culture that is specific to a particular family than with memory culture that pertains to a much larger collectivity. And this memory culture has typically conflated time into the few short years of the Holocaust, and place into a few of its principal camps of extermination—Auschwitz, Treblinka, and Majdanek.[24] I say most, because at least since the 1990s, there are increasing numbers who go precisely to trace their family roots. These are part of the general U.S. genealogical craze, inspired, in part, by the 1970s television miniseries *Roots.* For them a trip to Poland or Ukraine offers an opportunity to acquire documents from local administrative offices, to visit and photograph ancestral homes, and sometimes to meet an elderly person who remembers parents or grandparents. The latter is particularly the case for the children of survivors who often make this journey to see where a parent was hidden during the war and to meet those who were instrumental in his or her rescue.

Of course, all people have a need to experience mythic time and space; pilgrimages sensualize history, both sacred and secular. For visitors the ability to experience narrative or image in the flesh is part of the thrill of being in Eastern Europe. Sense of place, as Yi-Fu Tuan suggests, "achieves concrete reality when our experience of it is total, that is, through all the senses as well as with the active and reflective mind."[25] The continuing appeal of pilgrimage stems from the need to peer behind the surface representations to reexperience culture as fully three-dimensional, as real. Ironically, it is rarely reality that the pilgrims see.

Tourism, thanks in part to the transformations it produces within the host society, has a peculiar tendency to constitute the world it seeks to present.[26] The tourist is increasingly presented with theme-park reenactments of local cultures, both domestically through commodity culture in shopping malls, theme-park stores, and restaurants, and abroad in such places as Club Med. This may sometimes suit the needs for privacy of the host community, but it also provides a processed and therefore easily digestible experience for the guests.[27] Warsaw's Nozyk synagogue is an excellent case in point. An example of what Richard Schechner refers to as the "restoration of behavior," a piece of reality extrapolated and reformulated through subsequent performances, the synagogue is undoubtedly much more lavish, with its polished marble floors, wooden pews, and oriental rugs, than it ever was before.[28] Next to it are the community's "canteen" and theater—both offering clean, new, almost elegant venues for Polish Jewish and American Jewish contacts.

Of course, those who travel to re-created places and moments in history are often seeking a reality that is more real than the real.[29] Events witnessed on television, for example, are much easier to accept than those we witness firsthand: unprocessed experience generally lacks a dramatic structure to make it meaningful. Without the authoritative voice of the narrator, experience seems to lack legitimacy. Hence we have the endless barrage of statistics in televised sports;[30] a similar phenomenon is apparent in weather reporting. The problem of the authoritative voice is particularly acute for minority cultures, and particularly so for minority cultures that, having experienced considerable social mobility, are successfully integrated economically into the social mainstream. To some degree, marginal groups fend off the authoritative voice and create an oppositional culture with its own system of meaning. Uncertain of who they are and where they stand vis-à-vis oppositional and hegemonic culture, American Jews keep seeking a mirror through which to know the self. Perhaps this is why Jews have become one of the great tourist peoples of the modern world,[31] playing anthropologist to their more primitive coreligionists across the globe.

Why go to Poland and why the increase in Jewish travel there now? What is the appeal of staying in Warsaw's Hilton Intercontinental or the Holiday Inn, the so-called tourist bubbles enabling visitors to be "physically 'in' a place but socially 'outside' the culture,"[32] of seeing "the past" representationally, that is, through recently constructed monuments and museums? Moreover, why go somewhere with the intention of *not* having a good time? For Jews, visiting Poland and the death camps has become obligatory: it is ritualistic rather than ludic—a form of religious service rather than leisure. Indeed, it is the very seriousness of such visits that ultimately distinguishes Jewish travel to Poland from tourism, that tells us we are dealing not just with a matter of rite rather than festival[33] but also with something completely devoid of a trace of festival. I believe that those who go, particularly those who travel in tour groups—the majority of Jewish travelers to Poland—do so to participate in a secular ritual that confirms who they are as Jews and, perhaps even more so, as American Jews. I use the term secular ritual here for several reasons: to make a clear distinction with the traditional ritual of pilgrimage, which has a long-standing place in East European Jewish culture, including appropriate prayers and prescribed modes of behavior. These secular rituals do not comply with traditional forms but rather appropriate them and in part invent whole new meanings. Participants in a United Synagogue Youth tour at Treblinka, for example, are handed small index cards and told to scatter throughout the site and to write a note to someone who died in the camp—an act clearly copied from the Hasidic custom of writing kvitlekh; to point out the relative cosmological shallowness of such secular rituals. Traditional ritual's sense of efficacy derives from an elaborate cosmology; secular ritual is much narrower in scope. Indeed, the movement away from traditional cosmology in general among Jews is something I will discuss further below; to distinguish such collective behaviors from the merely personal or idiosyncratic.[34]

Despite substantial evidence of the acculturation of groups in the modern world, there is equally compelling data to suggest that group distinctiveness persists. One strategy for survival is the invention of new traditions, even the fabrication of new cultures. Jews have been active in this endeavor since the emergence of a secular national Yiddish and Hebrew culture in Eastern Europe more than 30 years ago. They have continued to reinvent traditions even after the near demise of language-based Judaism in America. Not only do these traditions, which I call the "rites of the tribe" because of their largely ethnic rather than religious basis, serve to situate actors within a sociopolitical framework (as opposed to a cosmological one), but they also contain within themselves rhetorical strategies both to represent the traditional and to inform participants how they should experience it. Ironically, their very inventedness may lend them an aura of authenticity, particularly in an iconoclastic age. To a much greater extent than traditional religious rituals, the rites of the tribe tend toward the spectacle: the transcendent and the contemplation of divinity, although present in part, are of secondary importance. The mechanical eye of Man has replaced God.[35] Indeed, the lens of the camera has become the means of entering the "Great Time." Little wonder, then, that a tour group to Birkenau would pause just outside the gate for a group video portrait before entering the camp.

What is particularly striking about these rites is their appeal to large segments of American Jewry. I include among these rites dining at kosher-style restaurants, visiting Israel, buying books on Jewish subjects, and going to Jewish museums. And there is an iconic dimension to the rites that includes the purchase and display of kitsch paintings of Israeli soldiers praying or Hasidim dancing at the Western Wall.[36] Thus, there is a continuing and perhaps growing tension within American Judaism between the Great Tradition and popular practice. The study of Hebrew and Aramaic holy texts, for

Montreal synagogue tour group outside Birkenau. (Photo by Jack Kugelmass)

example, is well beyond the intellectual reach or patience of people accustomed to a world in which their nonethnic native tongue, English, is dominant. Even a vernacular liturgy is problematic. Contemplative or petitionary prayer lends itself to poetry; technical and instrumental modern culture is most at home in prose. Increasingly, prose, too, is giving way to other forms of discourse, particularly those based on the still and moving image. Although American Jews are the largest consumers of books among American ethnic groups, like all Americans they spend the bulk of their leisure time watching television, not reading; the spectacle is paramount not only because of the power of the reproduced image over the reproduced word but also because of television's very lack of poetry, which gives it instant accessibility.[37] Rites must fit the cultures that perform them: the rites that American Jews have preferred over the past few decades—family feasts and marches on behalf of Israel or Soviet Jewry—are nonpoetic and therefore unambiguous. They borrow their mode of discourse from television, not only because they lend themselves to pageantry, but also because, like all successful American media productions, they are condensed, entertaining, and very charged emotionally.[38] Rather than television replicating culture, it is culture that replicates the world of television.[39]

Although feasts, whether in delicatessens or as part of family-centered holiday celebrations, provide a major way for American Jews to practice Judaism, their very festiveness mitigates their potential for catharsis. Marches, whether on behalf of Soviet Jewry or within Eastern Europe and Israel, have a more serious, even self-sacrificing quality to them. Participants are frequently required to engage in practices that they avoid in their every-day lives: attending services three times daily, eating strictly kosher food pre-packaged in Western Europe, attending lectures and evening discussions, and enduring sometimes arduous travel schedules. Such practices contribute to their "time out of time" quality. Their very liminality suggests to participants that what they are experiencing is important.[40] Indeed, both organizers and participants call the journeys "missions." At the same time, the shared nature of the experience has tremendous potential for generating catharsis. Partici-pants are encouraged to discuss what they have seen, to talk about their feel-ings, either during the travel time between the site and the hotel or later in the evening, during group discussions.

There is a force here pushing participants away from disengagement and pulling them toward putting themselves in the place of Holocaust vic-tims. At Auschwitz-Birkenau, a member of a Montreal synagogue group watched her fellow participants march toward the destroyed crematoria. As they walked, she could see the men at some distance. Crossing her vision was a barbed wire fence, and she commented to others near her that for a moment she imagined the men actually imprisoned in the camp. Such catharsis is far more likely to result from these rites than from the traditional liturgy. Even a lone traveler can experience such catharsis. Reflecting on the previous day's tour of Cracow and Kazimierz, Jeffrey Dekro writes:

> Last night I was transported from 1987 to earlier times: before the war and even back to the eighteenth and nineteenth centuries. In that way I have become part of Polish hasidic life, and I also enter the world of my grandparents Dora and Josef.
>
> Today we go to Auschwitz. By the time we enter, I have changed from being a "surviving grandson" to being equal, arriving at the gates from the past in the past. Only now can I finally die with Josef, Dora, and my father Hans. Later as I walk back through the camp entrance at Birkenau, I am reborn, in my present life. As witness, not as survivor.[41]

If Eastern Europe is able to provide such a meaningful backdrop for staging Jewish rites, why is its value only recently discovered? Here, I think, we need to consider a number of issues. An important factor must certainly be the genealogical craze that began with the airing of the television series *Roots* and continues unabated among various ethnic groups in the United States. This should come as no surprise, given Fredric Jameson's assertion that the tendency of postmodern culture is toward pastiche and nostalgia.[42] Another factor is the recent responsiveness, if not the very solicitousness, of East European countries themselves. Floundering economically and pressed for hard currency, these countries see Western tourism as a relatively simple way to generate income. Here then lies an obvious if not entirely happy mar-riage: moribund national economies' thirst for cash and the Jewish search for roots. Finally, there is the recent emergence of the Holocaust as a subject of popular Jewish discourse, indeed, as one of the tenets of what Jonathan Woocher refers to as American Jewish civil religion.[43]

Although discussions of the Holocaust have long found their place in Jewish educational activities and even in liturgical innovations, the subject itself has emerged from the confines of synagogue adult education programs to university lecture halls and even television. The airing of the made-for-television film *Holocaust* and the annual showing of Holocaust-related documentaries on National Educational Television have undoubtedly made the subject less parochial and more an acceptable subject of popular and even ecumenical discourse. And the response to the 9½-hour documentary *Shoah,* a film consisting entirely of recent footage, did two things simultaneously: It contemporized the Holocaust by bringing victims and witnesses together in Poland, thereby demonstrating to millions of viewers that mythical time could be experienced even now. It did what Joshua Meyrowitz suggests has become symptomatic of the impact of the media on social behavior generally since the 1960s—it realigned the sense of place. Poland ceased to be remote. Through repeated airings on the Public Broadcasting Service of this and other films in which Poland is a backdrop, Poland became a familiar place, encapsulated and contained both literally and metaphorically within a living-room box.[44]

The reason for earlier neglect of the Holocaust stems in part from the lack of an accessible (in English rather than Yiddish) literature of destruction immediately after the war which could have transformed family trauma into history,[45] and in part from the Jewish identification with hegemonic culture in the years during and immediately after the war. Its recent emergence as a cornerstone of American Jewish civil religion is, as Charles Silberman suggests, generally connected to the rise in Jewish nationalism immediately before and after Israel's June War in 1967.[46] However, the media's interest in the subject reflects, I think, the postwar emergence of American Jewry as an increasingly central group within American society and culture, a prominence apparent in the increasing "outness" of Jewish characters in American television and cinema, but even more blatantly in the construction of a Holocaust memorial on the National Mall in Washington.[47] Yet, it also reflects the emergence of a postmodern ironic sensibility in which the mythic underpinnings of society are open for scrutiny. If there is anything that seems paradigmatic of this sensibility, it is the spectacle of noncombatant extermination that characterized World War II.[48] Visits to the sites of mass death are for all people a way to experience the mythic birthplace of the postmodern, to witness cosmogonic time: Auschwitz, after all, is Poland's major tourist attraction.

Still, Auschwitz has special meaning for American Jews, and its current appeal may have as much to do with contemporary issues as it does with the past. Herbert Gans argues that the Holocaust has come to serve "as a need for the threat of group destruction." The need stems from increasing intermarriage, a decline in religious observance, and the fear that a lack of overt anti-Semitism has made the boundaries between Jew and non-Jew too permeable.[49] Charles Silberman argues that American Jews are extremely nervous about the degree of success they have achieved in America. They are particularly afraid that the very security of their lives in the United States poses a threat to group survival—that without anti-Semitism Jews will lose their group solidarity. In the words of Jacob Neusner, "The central issue facing Judaism in our day is whether a long-beleaguered faith can endure the conclusion of its perilous age."[50] Seen in this context, it is clear that the attraction of the Holocaust in general—and, because of it, of Poland in particular as a place of pilgrimage—is that it represents a much simpler past.

Although pilgrimages to Poland began as inducements for securing donations from a wealthy and often nonobservant elite within the Jewish community, it is striking how common they have become. So much are they part of the lifetime of the Jew that increasingly Jewish children are sent on them as part of their religious or ethnic education, and even fund-raising tours now promote multigenerational participation.[51] Some years ago, an American Jewish family arranged to have their son's bar mitzvah in Cracow. The event was turned into a documentary film titled *A Spark among the Ashes*. In the summer of 1989 an American Jew married a Polish-born convert to Judaism at the Nozyk synagogue and the ceremony was broadcast on NBC and CNN! These examples point to two interrelated aspects of what Herbert Gans refers to as the emergence of "symbolic ethnicity": one is the heightened value placed on rites of passage in Jewish ritual, since they are generally less demanding than calendrical rites; the other is the tendency for ethnics in general to express their identity by trips to the old country. A problem with Gans's model, however, is that it lacks an underlying sociopolitical explanation; cultural symbols, as Abner Cohen suggests, are often intricately tied to political and economic conflict.[52] The case I would like to make is that the expansion of rites connected to the Holocaust, in particular the rite of pilgrimage to the death camps, emerged simultaneously with and at least to some degree in response to two conflicts with profoundly disquieting implications for American Jews; one is international, the other domestic.

Of course, the international situation that most deeply affects American Jewry is the Arab–Israeli conflict. Although the association of one another with Nazis is a rhetorical strategy exploited rather shamelessly by both sides, the evocation of the past has more concrete value in the Israeli case, since Nazism for Jews conjures up much more than political loathing. For Arabs the term is a referential symbol, a type of name-calling; for Jews it is a condensation symbol, conjuring up deep emotion and tribal memory.[53] One cannot help thinking that the increasing popularity of such events as the March of the Living, a pilgrimage to the death camps involving thousands of North American Jewish schoolchildren, is growing in direct proportion to the ambiguousness of the Middle East situation; that is, as long as Israel was perceived as a David against Goliath, there was no need for a ritual to convince participants and spectators of the vulnerability of the Jewish people. But with the increasing perception of Israel as Goliath—the use of stones by the Palestinians is also a rhetorical strategy—there is increasing need for Jews to formulate a counterrhetoric. Certainly, the attraction of the Holocaust is its very lack of ambiguity.

Of equal concern to American Jews is the possible rise in popular anti-Semitism in the United States. Here the cause for pilgrimage is not anti-Semitism in general, since invoking the Holocaust, if anything, gives a sense of succor to those who would do Jews harm. The Holocaust has much more meaning when evoked as a rhetorical strategy to counter accusations of Jewish powerfulness, particularly when they are directed against Jews by a group or groups staking its or their own claim on powerlessness. Seen in this context, the purpose of the pilgrimage is not just a reminder of the past for contemporary Jews but also an attempt to make it actual, to be used rhetorically as a statement that despite current success, Jews do not have, nor did they ever have, political power. Consequently, Jews are in fact a vulnerable and discriminated-against minority.

The contrast is most evident, I think, when we look at how European Jews commemorate the Holocaust. To the best of my knowledge, until recently, at least, there were no regularly organized pilgrimages to Poland, even though many European Jews are, like American Jews, descendants of East European Jewry. Of course, most European Jews have their own Holocaust experience to commemorate, which they do in a manner that fits their respective national cultures. West European Holocaust memorials are typically devoted to Jewish members of the resistance, as are Polish Jewish memorials. Unlike its European counterpart, American public discourse on history, probably since the Vietnam War, has legitimized the victim and increasingly recognized and celebrated various modes of opposition. The Vietnam War Memorial in Washington, designed by Maya Lin, is a case in point. As "an abstract image of sacrifice," the monument's very ambiguity is an open text leaving possible a multiplicity of readings.[54]

The recent construction of a memorial at the site of the Umschlagplatz, where Jews were assembled before deportation just outside the Warsaw Ghetto, speaks to the fact that over the past few years Polish Jewry has increasingly fallen into the cultural orbit of American Jewry. Not only was its commission by the Polish government an indication of its desire to court American Jews, but its style of commemoration, particularly the listing of representative Jewish first names to commemorate the ordinary rather than the extraordinary, is distinctly non-Polish,[55] and evokes Maya Lin's memorial. In one other example of superb public art—Treblinka—among the tens of thousands of stones representing the Jewish populations of towns and cities destroyed by the Nazis, there is one stone on which the name Janusz Korczak is inscribed. So, in a sense, there is an ambiguous reading possible here of the monument's iconography. The Jewish reading is of mass extermination; the Polish reading is of the lone hero in the face of countless nonheroic deaths.

By evoking the Holocaust dramaturgically, that is, by going to the site of the event and reconstituting the reality of the time and place, American Jews are not only invoking the spirits of the tribe, that is, laying claim to their martyrdom, but are also making past time present. And in doing so they are symbolically reversing reality: they are transposing themselves from what they are currently perceived as—in the American case highly privileged, and in the Israeli case oppressive—and presenting themselves as the diametric opposite of privilege, as what they in fact were. Indeed, it is this image of the self that remains central to the American Jewish worldview.

In stressing the political component of the rite of pilgrimage, I do not mean to suggest that there is anything cynical at work here. On the contrary, those who perform these rites do so out of conviction, because they offer a way out of a difficult moral dilemma and allow Jews to steer a course somewhere between hegemonic and oppositional culture. The increasing introduction of African American spirituals into the text of the Passover Haggadah is a similar case in point.[56] Moreover, these rites are performed primarily for fellow Jews: they are intra- rather than intertribal. They have the same agenda as all rituals, namely, to bridge fundamental discontinuities in life: those between American and East European Jewry, between postwar and prewar Jewry, between the living and the dead, between power and powerlessness. They are an attempt to counteract fragmentation and the loss of belief that modernity itself has brought on and the possibility that such disbelief will cause the complete demise of the tribe. They are also about memory, the attempt to retain some connection to a past as if even the memory of loss could have a salutary effect on contemporary culture.[57]

Pierre Nora writes that *lieux de memoire,* or sites of memory-museums, archives, festivals, and the like,

> are fundamentally remains, the ultimate embodiments of a memorial consciousness that has barely survived in a historical age that calls out for memory because it has abandoned it. They make their appearance by virtue of the deritualization of our world—producing, manifesting, establishing, constructing, decreeing, and maintaining by artifice and by will a society deeply absorbed in its own transformation and renewal, one that inherently values the new over the ancient, the young over the old, the future over the past.

As Nora argues, there are lieux de memoire because there are no longer *milieux de memoire,* or real environments of memory.[58] There is something terribly disconcerting about this substitution of sites for context. Sites are more like causeways than bridges: they plow through rather than span differences. Indeed, a tendency to place Poland and its people, both Jews and non-Jews, into a master narrative in which their cultural and historical specificity is completely removed is quite evident during the pilgrimages. Furthermore, it is very disconcerting that these rites pay homage to the martyrdom of Polish Jews at the expense of attempting to retrieve what the culture had achieved, not to mention expressing any curiosity about the vitality of postwar Polish Jewry and the struggle to maintain Jewish culture in contemporary Poland. In the face of historical and social discontinuity, American Jewish memory culture has frozen Poland in time and turned its inhabitants into figures in a vast *tableau vivant.*

Of course, these pilgrimages alone are not to blame for dismissing Polish Jewry. Judaism's great tradition weighs against too much local variation, particularly when it veers away from rabbinic precepts. Jews also have a transnational little tradition made possible through continuing migration, intermarriage among Jewish subgroups, and various cultural productions including "how to" books on making bar mitzvahs and weddings and celebrating holy days. One might also speak of the folk categories of the American Jewish worldview, particularly the great chain of being through which national and even denominational subgroups are located in terms of past, present, and future: Eastern Europe is the past, America is the present, and Israel is the future. Given such ranking, the increasing incorporation of Polish Jewry into American Jewish or Israeli cultural hegemony on one side and Polish Catholic hegemony on the other is likely to lead to the demise of a uniquely Polish Jewish culture. Increasing pressure is placed on young people in general and the intelligentsia in particular to migrate—either to Israel or to the United States—in order to acquire greater Jewish knowledge and "to live as Jews." And so the trope of the past threatens this community with ultimate extinction.[59]

Rather than Poland inscribing itself on its pilgrims, the reverse is the case. Here we have a museum very much invented by its public. Indeed, the case presented indicates the need for various metaphors to classify a museum's relationship with its community. Shrine and academy suggest a role as repository of sacred objects and ultimate Truth. Such institutions require a resident priesthood to formulate the canon, place the icons in the appropriate settings for adulation, and create an appropriate liturgy. The public is privileged to enter such institutions; they are expected to show sufficient awe, and unless they are aficionados, they are not expected to have any input on the canon and its presentation. But some museums are as much theater as shrine. Their objects are like props, silent evocations of powerful sensations. The text, however, is not scripted like liturgy, nor is the public expected to behave with awe. Lacking a resident priesthood, the text is performance rather than script, unique in some ways for each group of visitors.

Perhaps, then, stage rather than shrine is the more accurate metaphor for looking at Poland and its Jewish public. The very fact that Polish Jewry was nearly extinct until very recently weighed heavily in favor of the stage metaphor: shrines need a priesthood. For American Jews, Poland is filled with ready-made props—ruined synagogues, doorposts with impressions from *mezuzahs,* cemeteries hidden within overgrown vegetation, and crumbling remains of death camps. These objects are deafening in their silence, and until recently largely scriptless; almost no one in Poland is capable of writing texts and labels to the country's Jewish monuments.[60] Moreover, its viability as stage is enhanced by the country's nearly complete lack of actors who might contest the presence of these foreign visitors, or attempt to wrest control of the performance. What American Jews are performing is, if not their actual identity, then at least an attempt to piece together the icons of the past, to retrieve or reclaim them and to reassemble them, albeit within a framework that inscribes their meaning through the present rather than the past.

Given the dimensions of the Holocaust and the challenge it poses to Jewish thinking, particularly nonrabbinic thinking, to explain it, these rites have very special meaning, since they do what endless study and discussion cannot do. They create meaning. As Sherry Ortner suggests, by shaping and systematizing otherwise abstract and diffuse cultural orientations, performance itself is meaningful.[61] Although the same claim for a discursive thrust could be made for even the most nostalgic reflections,[62] these rituals are unusual because they are much less oriented toward the present via the past than they are toward the future via the past. Very much like rehearsals, their work, to borrow a phrase from Richard Schechner, "is to 're-present' a past for the future (performance-to-be)."[63] In part a meditation on the past, and in part a scripted play about the present, the rites I have described are also rehearsals of what American Jews are intent on becoming or, perhaps more accurately stated, intent on not becoming. How ironic. Poland, long relegated to the past by American Jews, has suddenly emerged as a stage on which to act out their future.

Source: Adapted and updated from "The Rites of the Tribe: The Meaning of Poland for American Jewish Tourists," *YIVO Annual*, 1993, 21:395–453.

Notes

[1] Yehudit Hendel, "Near Quiet Places: Twelve Days in Poland," in *Lillit*, Spring 1990, p. 17.

[2] Donald Home, *The Public Culture: The Triumph of Industrialism* (London: Pluto Press, 1986).

[3] Shifra Epstein, "Photographing a Contemporary Hasidic Pilgrimage to Poland," *Jewish Folklore and Ethnology Review* 10 (1988): 21–22.

[4] Individuals do sometimes leave the tours for half a day in order to visit their family's home village, town, or city. Also, not all the tours are ideologically motivated in quite the same way. Some are sponsored by cultural institutions; the Hebrew University recently planned a tour of the Lublin area with special reference to the world of Bashevis Singer; Yad Vashem organizes tours of Holocaust sites for historians; and the Jewish Museum of New York organized a tour in conjunction with its photographic exhibition on Russian Jewry led by the historian Zvi Gittelman.

[5] Charles Silberman, *A Certain People: American Jews and Their Lives Today* (New York: Summit Books, 1985), 197.

[6] Tours organized by the UJA and other Israel-oriented groups are almost exclusively devoted to touring death camps. The Joint Distribution Committee, which sponsors relief efforts in Poland, focuses its tours more on contemporary Polish Jewish life.

[7] But the restoration was undertaken primarily for historical and architectural reasons rather than to attract Jewish tourists. Besides the physical monuments, there are in Poland a number of academic activities of specific Jewish interest. Various international conferences have been organized dealing with the Holocaust; the National Museum in Cracow recently mounted an enormous art exhibit dealing with the Jew in Polish painting; Warsaw's Jewish Historical Institute has a long and important history in postwar Polish academic efforts and includes a permanent exhibition space devoted to the Holocaust; and more recently, the Jagiellonian University has established the Center for Jewish Research. During a period of major financial crisis within Poland generally and the university in particular, the institution procured and

renovated a building for the center in the hope that additional help for the purchase of books and office equipment would come from private sources, particularly foreign Jews.

[8] These menorahs apparently came about through the entrepreneurship of an American Jew who commissioned the work from Polish craftsmen.

[9] For a discussion of this concept in tourism generally see Beverly Gordon, "The Souvenir: Messenger of the Extraordinary," *Journal of Popular Culture* 20 (Winter 1986): 141. Of course, in the case of an artwork, the object takes on special meaning, no matter how humble once inside its new owner's living room. As Gordon notes, the object "becomes transformed into a significant icon. It becomes sacralized in the new context, and is imbued with all the power of the association made with its original environment."

[10] Arthur Kurzweil, "Report from Przemysl: No More Jews," *Present Tense,* no. 3 (1981): 15.

[11] Most members of the intelligentsia are young, and they are able to gain access to hard currency by working abroad for periods of time. Consequently, tourism for them is not a business but a way to maintain contact with friends. After the war and the destruction of East European Jewish life, there arose two centers of Jewish cultural life: New York and Jerusalem. Poland is now at the border of both. Since the liberalization of travel and the wooing of Jewish tourists, the country has become a convenient stopover for both American and Israeli academics traveling between the two centers. Despite the prohibitive cost of Western books, the homes of Jewish intellectuals are virtual public libraries, their address books are "who's whos" of world Jewish intellectuals. A Polish ethnographer who works on Jewish subjects and is closely tied to the network of visiting Americans and Israelis described her social calendar over the summer as a constant series of dinner invitations to expensive restaurants from foreign visitors. When I mentioned to her that I was uncertain whether I would see a mutual friend in Cracow, since I hadn't been able to reach him by telephone and I wasn't sure of his whereabouts, the ethnographer assured me that he never leaves the city during the summer months. "After all, it's the season!"

[12] Laurence Loeb, "Creating Antiques for Fun and Profit: Encounters between Iranian Jewish Merchants and Touring Coreligionists," in *Hosts and Guests,* ed. Valene Smith (Philadelphia: The University of Pennsylvania Press, 1989), 187.

[13] This is a concept John MacAloon has developed in regard to the festival component of the Olympic Games in his article "Sociation and Sociability in Political Celebrations," in *Celebration: Studies in Festivity and Ritual,* ed. Victor Turner (Washington, DC: Smithsonian Institution Press, 1982), 262.

[14] A *New York Times* article on tourism in Poland would suggest that the travel agent has not completely abandoned his efforts:

> Piotr Kadlcik, director of the Our Roots travel agency, said he hopes his company can help Jewish tourists learn more about Poland and its Jewish heritage. "A lot of American Jews and Israelis think of Poland as a wasteland for Jews, with only cemeteries," he said alluding to the Holocaust. "We want to show them that it's just not true. We want to show them just what it means to be Jewish in Poland today."
>
> Gabrielle Glaser, "In Poland, Tourism with Apologies,"
> *New York Times* 30 July 1991, C1.

[15] Home, *The Public Culture,* 249.

[16] In his article "Journey to the East: Different Communists—Different Jews," *Present Tense* 3 (Spring 1976): 65, Sigmund Diamond describes his reactions to the Archaeological and Ethnographic Museum in Vilnius: "At the door was a guidebook in which we were requested to write our comments. I saw names from India, Laos, Egypt, Iraq, and the republics of the U.S.S.R.—and of two Lithuanians from Chicago. I wrote: 'A lovely museum, but in an ethnographic museum why is there no mention of the work of all the ethnic and religious groups in Lithuania? Professor Sigmund Diamond, Columbia University, New York, USA.' A petty thing, but I felt better."

[17] Kurzweil, "Report from Przemysl," 15.

[18] Leah Oko, "'The March of the Living'; A Trip to the Edge and Back Again," *Lifestyles* 17, no. 97 (Winter 1988): 30.

[19] And it brought to life her mother's story about her decision to leave the country when, in postwar Lodz, a woman thinking her to be a non-Jew commented that the Germans should have executed all Poles who hid Jews.

[20] Paul Fenton, "Hasidic Landmarks in Present-Day Poland," *European Judaism* 23 (Autumn 1990): 29.

[21] The article "Tenacious Pursuit of Lithuanian Roots Is Richly Rewarded," *Dallas Morning News,* 10 June 1990, describes some of the problems encountered in trying to decipher an aging parent's memory of a town's name and location.

[22] Rachel Ertel, "Voyages en Pologne." *Politiques de l'oublie.* A special issue of *Le Genre humain*, 1988:55.

[23] As Deborah Dash Moore argues in her article "The Construction of Community: Jewish Migration and Ethnicity in the United States," in *The Jews of North America,* ed. Moses Rischin (Detroit: Wayne State University Press, 1987), 108, "When World War Two destroyed the remnants of home, the world that had been abandoned, modern Jews were left bereft of the foil of an imagined past they could reject."

[24] Indeed, in an attempt to counteract that, one youth group decided to include rarely visited camp Sobibor in its itinerary. When participants learn that they alone visit this camp, they are very pleased. A camp should not be neglected.

[25] Yi-Fu Tuan, *Space and Place* (Minneapolis: University of Minnesota Press, 1977), 18.

[26] Barbara Kirshenblatt-Gimblett, "Authenticity and Authority in the Representation of Culture: The Poetics and Politics of Tourist Productions" *Deutscher Volkskundekongress* 1 (1989): 59–69. This is particularly so because the very logic of tourism as an encounter with the exotic imposes upon its subjects a quality that may not be, indeed, could not be, in keeping with their, that is, the natives', reality. Moreover, because of the economic asymmetry between the tourist and the subject, the latter has a vested interest in presenting his or her world in a manner in keeping with the tourist's expectations. This is particularly true for marginal members of the host culture, for example, elderly people divorced from the more dynamic sectors of the economy, or for entrepreneurial types who recognize the profit to be made by acting as cultural brokers between the host culture and tourists. See, e.g., Smith, *Hosts and Guests,*69.

[27] Smith, 69, discusses a case in which Eskimos in Alaska create a Siberian house with artifacts, draft a traditional story, and rehearse a dance. She also mentions the discomfort of tourists when locals frequent the hotel bar.

[28] Richard Schechner, *Between Theater and Anthropology* (Philadelphia: University of Pennsylvania Press, 1985).

[29] In his book, *Travels in Hyperrealtty* (New York: 1986), Umberto Eco makes this point regarding the touristic productions of the Southwest.

[30] Todd Gitlin, "Prime Time Ideology," in *Television: The Critical View,* ed. Horace Newcomb (New York: Oxford University Press, 1987), 518.

[31] According to Silberman, *A Certain People,* 199, Jews travel abroad more than any other ethnic group. Two in five adult Jews have been to Israel at least once, and the same proportion have been to Italy. Almost one Jew in five has been to Israel two or more times.

[32] Smith, *Hosts and Guests,* 6.

[33] As Roger Abraham notes:
> Festivals and rites still seem part of the same human impulse to intensify time and space within the community and to reveal mysteries while being engaged in revels. Cultural objects and actions become the foci of community actions carried out in common, when the deepest values of the group are simultaneously revealed and

made serious. But in our secularized world there is a felt need to distinguish between holy work and revelry. While rites in contemporary culture are still often accompanied by festivities, and a festival often has a designating rite at its core, surely we have progressively associated rituals with being "for real" and festivals with "fun."

> Abraham, "An American Vocabulary of Celebrations," in
> *Time Out of Time: Essays on the Festival*, ed. Allesandro Falassi
> (Albuquerque: University of New Mexico Press, 1987), 177.

[34] According to Sally Falk Moore and Barbara G. Myerhoff:

In the repetition and order, ritual imitates the rhythmic imperatives of the biological and physical universe, thus suggesting a link with the perpetual processes of the cosmos. It thereby implies permanence and legitimacy of what are actually evanescent cultural constructs. In the acting, stylization and presentational staging, ritual is attention-commanding and deflects questioning at the time. All these formal properties make it an ideal vehicle for the conveying of messages in an authenticating and arresting manner.

> Moore and Myerhoff, "Introduction," to their *Secular Ritual*
> (Amsterdam: Van Gorcum, 1977), 7.

[35] John Berger, *About Looking* (New York: Pantheon Books, 1980), 53.

[36] For the most part, the ultra-Orthodox do not participate: delicatessen Judaism is not their culture. Although they do make pilgrimages to Eastern Europe, theirs are not to appropriate history but to resume a prewar tradition of petitionary visits to the graves of famous sages. Even Yom Hashoah, the annual commemoration of the Holocaust, is ignored. Their day of commemoration is Tisha B'Av, the annual day of commemorating all great catastrophes in Jewish history.

[37] In *Amusing Ourselves to Death: Public Discourse in the Age of Show Business* (New York: Penguin Books, 1985), Neil Postman discusses the impact of television on American culture, particularly the movement away from serious discourse—which he associates with a typographical culture—to entertainment, the slick depthlessness that characterizes the electronic/image medium. Although his chapter on religion focuses on the televangelists, the point he makes has broader application to how religion in America has adjusted to the cultural hegemony of television and, in doing so, has degraded itself: "The spectacle we find in true religions has as its purpose enchantment, not entertainment. The distinction is critical. By endowing things with magic, enchantment is the means through which we may gain access to sacredness. Entertainment is the means through which we distance ourselves from it" (122).

[38] In discussing television's syntax, Robert R Snow points out that television news emphasizes moments in time, particularly emotional moments, rather than stressing historical sequence. The idea is that given the importance of news film or tape, emphasis is placed on involving the viewer in the emotion of the moment rather than interpreting events as part of a chronological sequence with historical significance. While the emphasis on emotional moment is an inflection device, the impact has implications for the syntax of news over the long run. The notion that some news is old and not worth reporting stems in part from the position that if the event is connected to some prior event and now lacks emotional punch, it is irrelevant. Over time, viewers may lose a sense of history as they orient primarily to what's happening now, just as they do when viewing an entertainment program. Snow, *Creating Media Culture* (Beverly Hills, CA: Sage,1983), 130.

[39] This, of course, is the gist of Postman's argument that in succeeding typography, television has created a cultural revolution, and—given the special character of the medium, its preoccupation with entertainment—it is a revolution with very negative consequences for serious cultural discourse. Although I agree with much of his argument, I believe that he gives too much weight to the characteristics of the medium and not enough analysis to the special character that the medium assumes under the conditions of late capitalism. Less negative

about television's possibilities than Postman, Snow nevertheless argues: "Television format has become a form of communication that is gradually being adopted by other media, by people in their interpersonal encounters, and in the major institutions of society. Gradually the reality presented by television is becoming the paramount reality in society" (ibid., 166).

40 See Barbara Myerhoff and Stephen Mongulla, "The Los Angeles Jews' 'Walk for Solidarity': Parade, Festival, Pilgrimage," in *Symbolizing America,* ed. Herve Varenne (Lincoln: University of Nebraska Press, 1986).

41 Jeffrey Dekro, "First Time Home: Poland Leaves Its Mark on a Visitor," *Reconstructionist* 54 (Oct.–Nov. 1988): 11.

42 Fredric Jameson, "Postmodernism and Consumer Society," in *Post-modernism and Its Discontents: Theories, Practices,* ed. E. Ann Kaplan (New York: Verso, 1988).

43 Jonathan Woocher, "Sacred Survival: American Jewry's Civil Religion, *Judaism* 34 (Spring 1985): 151–62.

44 The same thing happened to Poles. When *Shoah* was aired on Polish national television, the film sparked a broad national debate on the Jewish view of Polish behavior during World War II. For the first time in more than 40 years, Poles and Jews sparred with one another almost face-to-face, although they were really thousands of miles apart. The controversy seems also to have increased Polish curiosity about the Jewish place in the country's past: the American film *Fiddler on the Roof* was aired twice on national television, and traveling productions receive rave reviews throughout the country. For an analysis of the impact of television on contemporary sense of place, see Joshua Meyrowitz, *No Sense of Place: The Impact of Electronic Media on Social Behavior* (New York: Oxford University Press, 1985).

45 Nathan Glazer's argument as cited in Herbert Gans, "Symbolic Ethnicity: The Future of Ethnic Groups and Cultures in America," in his *On the Making of Americans: Essays in Honor of David Riesman* (University of Pennsylvania Press, 1979), 207.

46 Silberman, *A Certain People,* 182–185.

47 *Judith* Miller, *One, by One, by One* (New York: Simon & Schuster, 1990), 234.

48 E.g., Susan Sontag writes:

One's first encounter with the photographic inventory of ultimate horror is a kind of revelation, the prototypically modern revelation: negative epiphany. For me, it was photographs of Bergen-Belsen and Dachau which I came across by chance in a bookstore in Santa Monica in July 1945.

Nothing I have seen—in photographs or in real life—ever cut me as sharply, deeply, instantaneously. Indeed, it seems plausible to me to divide my life into two parts, before I saw those photographs (I was twelve) and after, though it was several years before I understood fully what they were about.

Sontag, *On Photography* (New York: Dell, 1977), 19–20.

49 A similar process appears to be taking place among certain young Armenians some 60 years after the Turkish slaughter. Gans, "Symbolic Ethnicity," 207–8.

50 Quoted in Silberman, *A Certain People,* 24.

51 Initially the March of the Living was organized to include thousands of Jewish schoolchildren from across North America. So successful was the event that rabbis who participated as group leaders have begun to take their congregations on a similar pilgrimage, and the event is repeated with other schoolchildren.

52 Gans, "Symbolic Ethnicity," 204–205; Abner Cohen, *Urban Ethnicity* (London: Tavistock, 1974).

53 See Edward Sapir's distinction between the two types of symbols, as cited in Murray Edelman, *The Symbolic Uses of Politics* (Urbana: University of Illinois Press, 1985), 6.

54 Harry W Haines, "'What Kind of War?': An Analysis of the Vietnam Veterans Memorial," *Critical Studies in Mass Communications* 3 (Mar. 1986): 17.

[55] What I mean by this is that as abstract design, it lends itself to multiple readings. Polish public culture until recently was very much imbued with state social realist symbolism, a symbolism that eschewed multiple readings and relied on representational art.

[56] See Anita Schwartz, "The Secular Seder," in *Between Two Worlds: Ethnographic Essays on American Jewry,* ed. Jack Kugelmass (Ithaca, N.Y: Cornell University Press, 1988).

[57] I am reminded here of an oft-repeated very powerful Hasidic story about this very issue, a story that combines place, memory, and rescue. In the story the eighteenth-century founder of Hasidism, the Baal Shem Tov, would fend off danger to his fellow Jews by going to a place in the forest, lighting a fire, and reciting a prayer. In each succeeding generation, memory dissipated, so that when Israel of Rizhin tried to overcome misfortune he could no longer perform any of these rites: all he knew was the story about place, the fire, and the prayer. According to the Hasidic tale, that knowledge was sufficient. Indeed, it is this very premise that enables American Jews make such an easy bridge to their past. The fact that the story appears in Elie Weisel's *Souls on Fire: Portraits and Legends of Hasidic Masters* (New York: Random House, 1972), 167–68, and various other publications, suggests its place within popular American Jewish literature.

[58] Pierre Nora, "Between Memory and History: *Les lieux de mémoire,"* *Representations 26* (Spring 1989): 12, 7.

[59] Given how small the Jewish community is in Poland and its near total intermarriage with non-Jews, the alternative may in fact be assimilation into Polish culture and society.

[60] In Tarnow, e.g., the surviving *bima* (raised area where Torah is read) from the destroyed main synagogue recently received a commemorative plaque. Donated by Jews living abroad, the plaque included Polish and Hebrew inscriptions. The Polish, clearly a translation, was grammatically incorrect.

[61] Sherry Ortner, *Sherpas through Their Rituals.* (New York: Cambridge University Press, 1978), 5.

[62] See Suzanne Vromen's "The Ambiguity of Nostalgia," *YIVO Annual* 21 (1993): 69–86.

[63] Schechner, *Between Theater and Anthropology,* 51.

Five:
Tourism's
Many Implications

Tourists climb the steep sandstone steps of Angkor Wat, Cambodia. (Photo by Sharon Gmelch)

21

Sailing into the Sunset: The Cruise-ship Industry

Polly Pattullo

The first journeys across the Caribbean Sea were made by Amerindian canoeists who settled the island chains, paddling north from the river systems of the Orinoco and the Amazon. Hundreds of years later the Spanish explorers arrived, and when other European powers joined the fight for control of the Caribbean, it was the sea, not the land, that saw their greatest battles. The sea became an economic highway for slavers, traders, buccaneers, and fishermen; then it became a passageway for escaped slaves, indentured laborers, and settlers; and later still, it was a watery flight path for emigrants and boat people. These shipping channels (except for those traditionally used by Caribs and fishermen) were linked with the economic and political power blocs of Europe and North America rather than with each other, for each harbor was a juncture of imperial arrival and departure.

Caribbean ports are still working places. Container ships arrive with imports from tableware to tractors, mostly from the United States, or cars from Japan, and they depart with bananas from Martinique or St. Vincent for Europe. Now, however, by far the biggest vessels in port are cruise ships, also from the United States, on pleasure journeys that no longer pay attention to those old colonial lines. Crisscrossing the Caribbean Sea, these great white whales come and go more quickly than the banana boats loading up alongside them. There is time, though, for seven hours or so on land—arriving in the morning and departing in late afternoon.

Down the gangway come the cruise-ship passengers, straight into a pur-pose-built, duty-free shopping mall, or into streets packed with tourist shops. Just like at the last port of call, most terminals have pizza joints, ice cream parlors, souvenir shops, perhaps a casino or two, and hoardings [billboards] with familiar transnational names: Dollar Rent A Car, Colombia Diamonds, Benetton, Gucci, and Little Switzerland. There is time to fit in shopping, an island tour, or a trip to a beach or to the cruise line's private island. Ranks of minibuses line up to whisk the tourists away on their prebooked, prepaid tours arranged by the cruise lines with chosen ground operators. Those who have failed to book can take their chances and get a cheaper deal with the many freelance taxi drivers and tour guides.

The most popular ports of call are the ones with the best duty-free shop-ping and casinos. The shops are ice-cold and imitate Fifth Avenue: the gifts, under glass, are much the same whether in Ocho Rios or Antigua—jewelry, perfumes, or china figurines of pastel-colored cottages or simpering milk maids. Each destination is in competition with the next to provide a shoppers' paradise. St. Kitts, for example, with its modest duty-free mall in Basseterre, must try to compete with St. Maarten, its flashy Americanized neighbor, stiff with shops and casinos. "We would like to see a greater turnover so we are upgrading our duty-free outlets," said an official from the St. Kitts division of tourism. Armed with leaflets on shops recommended by the cruise ships, cruisers know which are the best and cheapest destinations. Not St. Kitts, for sure, and even Antigua is not a star attraction. A young couple in Antigua's duty-free Heritage Quay did not plan to spend much money there. They were saving it for St. Thomas, in the U.S. Virgin Islands (USVI). "We might as well go back on board and get some breakfast." They had heard that shopping was better in St. Thomas where the average expenditure in 2000 was US$259.80 compared to US$27.70 in Antigua.[1]

By afternoon, the passengers drift back to the ship, with their pur-chases, to eat (food is included in the cruise price) or to join those who have never left, preferring to glimpse the island from the rails. The last somewhat drunken stragglers, with T-shirts reading "Drink Till You Sink," are scooped up the gangway. Soon, the quayside will be almost empty, as shopkeepers count their takings and taxi drivers give up for the day. Only beggars and scavenging dogs remain as the ship disappears over the horizon, lights twin-kling on its way to another sunset at sea.

The Cruise Boom

The Caribbean cruise business is booming; it grows still larger as the numbers and sizes of ships visiting ever-bigger terminals increase. "The untapped potential in the Caribbean—where we're putting more tonnage over the next several years—is vast," claimed Julie Benson of Princess Lines, a subsidiary of P&O Cruises, in the mid-1990s.[2] A decade later that boast seemed well founded with the industry running at a remarkable capacity of more than 90 percent, far higher than land-based tourism. The 1990s saw particularly spectacular growth. At least 28 new ships were delivered to the cruise companies; most were destined for the Caribbean. The biggest companies, Royal Caribbean Cruise Line (RCCL), Carnival Cruise, Holland America, and Princess, led the way. RCCL had three ships on order, all with a capacity for more than 1,800 passengers; Princess had spent almost US$1 billion on three ships, one, *Grand Princess* at 105,000 tons, was the biggest liner ever. Carnival also had added eleven ships to its fleet by 1996, and spent US$400 million on the Italian-built boat, *Tiffany*. Disney Corporation also entered the cruise market, with its first ship in operation in 1999. Even the smaller companies had increased their fleets, building vessels for three hundred or so luxury-market passengers or for those in the even more select sail-ship market.[3]

The emphasis, however, is on size—and the bigger the better. Of the new ships built between 1995 and 2001, nearly 80 percent had 1,500 or more berths. The largest, *Mariner of the Sea,* built for Royal Caribbean International at a price of US$520 million, has a tonnage of 140,000, and a capacity for 3,835 passengers and more than 1,000 crew. Another giant, *Carnival Glory,* which launched its seven-day cruises in mid-2003, boasts fourteen passenger decks with twenty-two bars and lounges, a 15,000-square-foot health club, four swimming pools, and three restaurants, including an upscale "steakhouse-style" supper club serving prime U.S. beef.[4]

The lido deck on Royal Caribbean's *Explorer of the Seas*. Note how most deck chairs face inward, away from the sea. (Photo by Robert Wood)

The Caribbean has nearly half of the world capacity of cruise "bed days." However, its share of the cruise business has declined from a peak of 60 percent of all bed days out of North America in 1991 to 48 percent in 2000. According to the Caribbean Tourism Organization (CTO), this is because the cruise industry has "sought to add itineraries for the burgeoning capacity." Even if its share has decreased, its awesome volume of business continues to expand. In the Caribbean itself, cruise tourism has grown much faster than land-based tourism—from 7.8 million passenger arrivals in 1990 to 14.5 million in 2000, an increase of 8.6 percent per year, compared to an average annual increase of 4.7 percent for stay-over arrivals. The Bahamas, a traditional cruise destination close to Florida, was the busiest port of call, with 2.5 million cruise passenger arrivals in 2000. The next most popular destination was the U.S. Virgin Islands (1.7 million), followed by Cozumel (1.5 million) on the Mexican coast, Puerto Rico (1.3 million), the Cayman Islands (1 million), and Jamaica (907,000).[5]

Many destinations have recorded spectacular growth. St. Lucia, for example, had 58,000 cruise arrivals in 1986 but nearly half a million in 2000, when Dominica recorded 239,000, up from 11,500 in 1986. Other islands with an expanding cruise-ship market were St. Kitts & Nevis, Aruba, and Curaçao.[6] Belize and the Dominican Republic were late, but expanding, entries and even Haiti, abandoned by the cruise-ship industry in 1993 when sanctions against its military regime were announced, was back on the itinerary by 1995. Only Trinidad, perhaps, with an industrial rather than a tourist base to its economy, has not seen a massive rise in cruise visitors, along with some of the very small islands that do not have cruise facilities, such as Anguilla, Saba, and St. Barthelemy.

Most cruises begin in either Miami or Port Everglades in Florida or in San Juan, Puerto Rico. Of non-American bases, Aruba, Antigua, and Martinique also play their part, all being significant airline hubs for the European market. From these starting points, the ships crisscross the Caribbean Sea, dropping into islands here and islands there as they see fit, depending on the duration of the cruise and the range of attractions that the destinations can muster.

Rocking the Boat

Yet while the cruise lines steamed ahead, unloading more and more passengers off bigger and more luxurious ships on to the docksides of small Caribbean states, fundamental questions began to be asked by the mid-1990s about the benefits of the cruise industry to the Caribbean and its people, and its long-term effect on the region's own land-based tourism.

Taxation has been a thorny issue. Departure taxes for both airline and cruise passengers have traditionally been set by individual governments. This head tax is one way in which the cruise industry contributes to the expenses involved in providing appropriate port or airport facilities. In the case of the cruise tax, this ranged in 2000 from US$1.50 in Guadeloupe and St. Maarten (an increase from zero in the mid-1990s) to US$15 in Jamaica and the Bahamas. Intercountry rivalry and what are considered to be differences in the quality of facilities offered to cruise ships by each destination were said to explain such a discrepancy.[7]

To eliminate such discrepancies, in January 1992 the Organization of Eastern Caribbean States (OECS) agreed to adopt a standard head tax of US$10 to take effect in October of that year. The decision did not please the cruise lines. "To solve the hotel problem by raising taxes on cruise ships is stupid and punitive," said Bob Dickinson, president of Carnival Cruise Lines.[8] Retaliation was not long in coming. The RCCL announced that it would drop St. Lucia, one of the seven OECS states, from its itinerary; the *Nordic Prince,* which had made eighteen calls to St. Lucia in 1991, also decided to go elsewhere. The boycott of St. Lucia resulted in calls of solidarity from other CTO members, but in the end they were empty promises.

The OECS position was, however, strengthened when Caricom, the wider regional organization, also came up with a plan to adopt a unified tax (Jamaica had already taken the lead). It was to be set at US$5 in April 1994, to be raised to US$7.50 in October of that year, and to US$10 by 1995.[9] For the Caribbean this was a major step forward, since earlier discussions about increasing the head tax had only taken place bilaterally, giving the cruise operators the built-in advantage. The operators could play one country against another by threatening to skip one destination for another with a lower tax. This time the region as a whole seemed to be flexing its muscles. As Jean Holder said: "The concept of the minimum tax, set at a reasonable level, was intended to enable the weak destinations to earn a little much-needed revenue, to create some Caribbean solidarity and thus effect an adjustment to the strategic advantage that is held largely by the cruise lines. Its success is dependent entirely on each country keeping the agreement."[10] Caricom's move raised the possibility of a regional approach, not just about the head tax but also about other important issues surrounding the cruise industry. St. Lucia's prime minister, John Compton, expressed the opinion that the region would "no longer accept mirrors and baubles for the use of its patrimony."[11]

The tax issue was symptomatic of the tensions between the cruise ships and the region's land-based tourist industry. Those on the side of the cruise ships expressed barely disguised contempt for the Caribbean's hotel industry. Without the cruise industry, said Joel Abed in *Travel Trade News*, "to both promote and present its attractions and facilities to potential vacationers, the Caribbean resort industry, as we know it today, would all-too-quickly become a virtual tourist desert."[12] Bob Dickinson of Carnival expressed his position only marginally less aggressively. "They're not only biting the hand that feeds them, they're yanking off the whole arm."[13]

The tax row provoked similar outbursts of passionate rhetoric from the region. There was a general distrust of what was considered to be imperious behavior by the cruise lines. Yet despite this, and the agreement made at the highest level in Caricom, the unified passenger head tax was not achieved within the agreed time span. (St. Lucia even aborted its decision to raise the head tax in 1994 according to the OECS decision.) Indeed, as has been seen, it has yet to be achieved.

Royston Hopkin, then president of the Caribbean Hotel Association, conceded in the wake of the row: "The cruise-ship lobby is very strong and the governments have been very weak. The cruise lines sweetened the governments who were not united. We gave our best shot, but by the time the heads of government got to it the three-tier system was introduced and this weakened our position." The Caribbean's failure dismayed many sections of its tourist industry. It demonstrated the inability of the region to take a unified stand and also showed just how powerful the cruise industry's grip was. Peter Odle, then president of the Barbados Hotel Association, was another aggrieved hotelier. "I was against cruise ships from the beginning," he said. "The Caribbean will not realize the cruise business is a disservice until it's nearly too late. The cruise ships are using our most precious asset—the sea—polluting it like hell and not making any significant contribution to our economy. And instead of taking a firm stand, the governments are all over the place; there is a lack of political will." Similar sentiments were expressed by Allen Chastenet, a former director of the St. Lucia Tourist Board: "If anyone is sucking the Caribbean dry it is the cruise ships."

A further row developed in 1997 when the Organization of Eastern Caribbean States, representing seven islands in the eastern Caribbean, decided to impose an environmental levy of US$1.50 per capita on all visitors, including those from the cruise ships, entering its member countries. The fee would help pay for a waste management project, partly financed by the World Bank and aimed at improving the collection of waste from sources such as cruise ships. The Florida-Caribbean Cruise Association (FCCA) objected, saying that its ships had "zero discharge" and that each vessel "usually" had "about US$10 million worth of waste disposal facilities, including incinerators, pulpers, and compactors." It argued that an across-the-board levy was not needed. Finally, the FCCA agreed to pay. It was a rare victory for regional unity.[14]

The CTO has continued to take the position that Caribbean governments have the right to take action to make the competition between land and sea tourism more equitable.[15] On the other hand, it has also recognized that the Caribbean doesn't hold many cards in relation to the cruise industry. "The cruise lines have the ability to move their ships and they do move them when they are not happy," said Jean Holder in 2000.[16] From the shore, foreign cruise lines are seen as having built-in advantages over land-based tourism—cruise ships generate greater local revenue and employment per passenger—but these advantages are used, it is argued, at the expense of the Caribbean, in a particularly rapacious manner.

Despite the row over head taxes, cruise ships do not pay as many taxes as the land-based industry, where taxation either doubles the price of many purchases or restricts the hotelier to buying regional products only. Hotels must also pay corporation tax and casino tax profits. In contrast, cruise ships are seen as moveable feasts that sail away into the sunset, their bars and casinos untaxed. Raising money to build hotels is problematic even though construction work employs local labor and supports local financial institutions. In contrast, cruise-ship contracts go to overseas shipyards largely in Europe, where long-term, low-interest loans are also available. Furthermore, more and more hotels are now owned by Caribbean nationals; no cruise ships are owned by Caribbean nationals.

The contrast continues. Caribbean hotels provide jobs for locals, with work permits required for the employment of non-nationals. Cruise lines operating in the Caribbean, on the other hand, are free to employ whom they wish. Their ships are not registered in the United States, their home base, but use flags of convenience to avoid U.S. labor laws, taxes, and regulations. Thus, as the president of the Carnival Corporation, whose ships are registered in Panama, wrote in his book, *Selling the Sea*: "Of course, ships registered in these flag-of-convenience nations pay lower wages and taxes on an aggregate basis than those registered in the United States (or Norway or Italy for that matter). But that makes it possible for them to offer cruises at much lower cost than if their ships were registered in countries with restrictive hiring policies" (Dickinson and Vladimir 1997).

Many lines employ European officers, with North American and western European staff in areas like business and entertainment, supported by a Third World crew. Around fifty countries may be represented as cruise employees. The officers on the Carnival's *Fantasy*, for instance, are Italian, while what is called its "international" crew is drawn from Latin America, India, and the Philippines. Crew members, often from the poorest parts of the Third World, are paid low wages, work in shoddy conditions, and endure an authoritarian management code, according to a 2002 study. "Conditions for workers below deck haven't improved in decades," said Tony Sasso, a Miami-based inspector with the International Transport Workers Federation. "Many are reluctant to come forward and complain. To most people, workers on cruise liners are nonentities. They have an almost invisible existence." In contrast, work in the land-based industry may seem more attractive with many employees being paid union rates and benefiting from trade union representation. This may be one reason why so few Caribbean nationals have jobs on cruise ships. Meanwhile, other nationals—from the Philippines or Bangladesh, for example—find the wages better than at home.

The proportion of Caribbean products purchased by cruise lines also remains small. Caribbean supplies to the cruise industry are estimated at between 1 and 5 percent of total requirements. According to the FCCA, member cruise lines spent US$51.2 million on Caribbean supplies in 1993. Technical inputs such as petroleum products, parts, and chemicals represent US$30 million (59 percent of the total expenditure), while handling services such as warehousing and stevedoring at ports account for US$7.1 million, or 14 percent of the total expenditure. Just over a quarter of the cruise lines' expenditure in the Caribbean was on food and drink (US$13.8 million), of which half was on beer and liquor. Foods included fruit and vegetables, dairy products, bread, water, spices, seafood, coffee, and sugar.[17] If this figure is at all accurate, only US$6 per passenger was spent on food and drink grown and produced within the Caribbean.

The list of significant Caribbean suppliers is short: Bico Ice Cream and Pine Hill Dairy, both of Barbados; Dominica Coconut Products; Commonwealth Brewery of the Bahamas; Tropical Beverages of Trinidad and Desnoes & Geddes; Red Stripe Beer, Jamaica.[18] Toilet paper from Trinidad and Tobago also joined the list after what the managing director of Savvy Traders Ltd. called "a long and frustrating battle." The result is that not only are most cruise ships supplied by U.S. companies, but that fresh produce from outside the region is also flown or shipped into the Caribbean during a cruise. Thus, in one ludicrous example, a barge from Venezuela filled with bananas was seen to supply the cruise ships in St. Lucia, one of the Caribbean's major banana producers. Since the tax row, however, the FCCA has been seen to play a more sensitive role. There have been opportunities for purchasers and Caribbean producers to talk to each other at trade shows and conferences. Such meetings, said the FCCA, enabled these companies "to strengthen their contacts within individual cruise lines, make new contacts and learn from other successful suppliers of cruise lines."[19]

The difficulties (quantity, quality, regularity of supply, delivering on time) faced by Caribbean producers are similar to, and even greater than, those they face in supplying the land-based industry. In a commitment to high standards, the cruise lines make tough demands on their suppliers. Part of the RCCL's mission statement, for example, pledges "to locate, buy, and deliver the highest quality of specified goods and services at the fairest overall cost possible in a timely manner."[20] The supplies must be competitive with products from Hong Kong and Taiwan; they must be on time and they must be delivered in an appropriate condition. They must also fit U.S. tastes. According to RCCL's head of purchasing, American cruise passengers expect steak from grain-fed cattle and products, such as yogurt and cereal, that have familiar brand names. Such demands are beyond most Caribbean producers.

From this low base, selling Caribbean goods to the cruise lines has proceeded painfully slowly. It began in the early 1990s with a CTO initiative that, according to Jean Holder, brought together the Caricom Export Development program and cruise lines to discuss their needs. Even the successful and efficient Dominica Coconut Products, now a Colgate-Palmolive subsidiary, took three years to sign a contract with the RCCL to supply three million bars of soap a year.[21] Most producers and tourist boards have been only vaguely aware of the needs of the cruise lines and even less able to deal in the quantity and the quality required. The small scale of many producers and the lack of developed regional exporting and marketing groupings have further limited the opportunities.

One successful link-up between producers and cruise ships shows just how small—and rare—such occasions are. In 2001 up to 10,000 tons of tomatoes from St. Kitts-Nevis found their way each week onto the dining tables of Royal Caribbean International ships. The contract was the result of collaboration between the producers, shippers, cruise lines, and the Republic of Taiwan's agricultural mission on St. Kitts-Nevis. It was trumpeted as a major achievement, with further opportunities for other crops to reach the cruise shippers sometime in the future.[22] Yet the cruise lines have always made it clear that servicing their ships is "no easy task "and "cannot be taken lightly." "This is a very price competitive business, often with very little differentiation in price. The key difference is who has what we need and who can deliver it 100 percent accurately," said the director of purchasing for Carnival Cruise Lines in 1998.

Despite what appears to be an uneven match between sea and land tourism, regional governments continue to give the cruise ships their blessing, boasting of the increase in passenger arrivals over the years. Responding to the needs of bigger ships, for example, the host countries have to expand and improve port facilities. The FCCA is in no doubt as to its requirements: "Ports must be welcoming, modern, and comfortable in order to effectively accommodate upwards of 3,000 guests and crew arriving at the same time. Services must be first-class, and ground excursions must be efficient, dependable, and offer visitors the best of the destination," is the FCCA's line. In an article, "Keeping up with the Megaships," it continued: "When the passengers disembark they should receive the same seamless attention and service that they do on board the cruise ship."[23]

The ships tie up at ports that have been especially deepened, widened, and modernized by local governments. To be able to offer a home porting facility (using a cruise destination as an arrival and departure point, as in San Juan, Puerto Rico, for example) is another reason behind port improvements. But San Juan has faced criticism from the cruise industry. While Puerto Rico had spent money on land-based facilities, similar developments had not taken place at the port, the FCCA complained. The cruise industry had been treated with "an astonishing indifference" with the infrastructure lagging behind the needs of the ever-increasing size and numbers of cruise ships, and San Juan had become "unappealing." This remained the case until early in 2001 when a new administration had, according to the FCCA, decided to stop the drift to indifference and to begin a "new sense of welcome" for all those future cruise-ship visitors.[24]

This sort of criticism from the FCCA makes both old and new cruise destinations scramble to invest millions of dollars on new facilities. In the eastern Caribbean, all the islands have sprung into action to improve their cruise facilities. Dominica spent US$28 million on a dock extension at its Roseau port and on a wharf and terminal building at the Cabrits, a national park on the north of the island, to boost its cruise-ship arrival figures. The facilities opened in 1991, and in that year alone cruise arrivals increased from 6,800 to 65,000. St. Kitts, too, has sought to expand its cruise business. In 1994, a US$16.25 million loan agreement was signed with the Bank of Nova Scotia to construct a new cruise-ship berth, separate from the dust and cargo of the old port.[25] In 2002, it opened later than planned, the construction twice having been demolished by hurricanes. In 1995, St. Vincent also announced a cruise-ship berth development at its capital, Kingstown, to be funded by the Kuwaiti Fund and the European Investment Bank.[26] The latest destination to publicize a major upgrade of what is called its "cruise-tourism product" is the USVI. A US$30 million expansion of its second pier was announced in 2002. "If it is not built, St. Thomas, which is now number 4 in the world in cruise-ship destinations, within a decade will drop to number 10," said Gordon Finch of the Virgin Islands Port Authority.[27]

Even larger islands with established cruise-ship facilities sometimes have to run to keep up. The logistics of providing such facilities and service for these megaships is an enormous challenge. Ocho Rios in Jamaica, a popular cruise-ship destination, was, by the beginning of the twenty-first century, considered to have an inadequate port for the forthcoming mega-liners. A lack of cleanliness at St. Vincent's capital, Kingston, and harassment of visitors led to cruise cancellations; similarly, the Princess Line decided to drop Jamaica from its itineraries in the 2001–2002 season citing "very poor comments from visitors." The Caribbean is constantly addressing such problems—many of which require massive investment to overcome. It's not easy being a host to the cruise-ship industry.

Big Spenders?

The cruise lines also have another winning card: their very own islands. Cruise lines can reduce the number of days in port by buying or leasing their own island or by anchoring off a deserted stretch of beach. As *Caribbean Travel News* noted: "Increasingly, the trend is for cruise lines to go one step further from taking their passengers around the Caribbean islands—and to give them one all to themselves."[28] This policy was begun in the early 1980s by Norwegian Cruise Line, which owns Great Stirrup Cay in the Bahamas, now "remodeled" with a wider beach, a barbecue area, and water sports. Part of the point is that the islands are uninhabited. Holland America's 1997 brochure about Half Moon Cay, also in the Bahamas, paints an appropriate picture for the cruisers: "Half Moon Cay recalls the idyllic Caribbean of 30 years ago. There are no hassles. It's just you and a balmy island with a white-sand beach, coral reefs, and a clutter-free arrangement of attractive facilities designed for casual roaming." One inference is that it's desirable because it has no inhabitants—no needy locals to get in the way of the fantasy. By the end of the twentieth century, six out of the eight major cruise lines operating in the Caribbean owned their own private islands (Wood 2000).

On these islands, the cruise lines show off their private beaches, where what is called "cruise-style service" is on hand with barbecue and bar provided by cruise staff. Princess Cruises own Princess Cay on Eleuthera, Bahamas, ("For total tropical tranquility, it's hard to beat this land of lotus-eaters")

Explorer of the Seas taken from a beach at Labadee, Royal Caribbean's "private island," which is actually a peninsula of Haiti. (Photo by Robert Wood)

and Saline Bay, Mayreau, in the Grenadines ("every castaway's first choice"). The RCCL owns Coco Cay, also on the Bahamas, and leases Labadee in Haiti, an isolated promontory on the north coast where tourists spend a day on a beach surrounded by a high wall patrolled by guards. When cruise lines create their own version of paradise, they avoid port fees and passenger head taxes while protecting their customers from the less than paradisical reality of much of Caribbean life.

Desert-island days, days at sea, island tours booked through the cruise ship: all are ways in which cruise lines can persuade customers to buy their services and thereby control the quality and quantity of the holiday experience. Another way is to attract customers to spend money on board in the shops, boutiques, and bars, available at all times (except when the ships are in port) and often at competitive prices compared to goods sold on land. The Princess line brochure states: "There's no need for you to be in port to go shopping. Both *Canberra* and *Sea Princess* carry a remarkably comprehensive selection of goods . . ." As an Economist Intelligence Unit (EIU) report on the Caribbean pointed out: "Onboard shopping, which by definition is duty-free, is being promoted increasingly aggressively as a means of maximizing their share of a passenger's overall holiday expenditure."[29] This continues to affect the land-based duty-free outlets, which find that the outlets on the cruise ships can outbid them.

The *Fantasy* of Carnival Cruise Lines is a typical giant cruise ship that provides its customers with just about everything they could desire. Sailing out of Cape Canaveral bound for Nassau and Freeport, its 2,634 passengers have paid as little as US$249 in 2002 for a three-day cruise. It has two dining rooms, nine bars and lounges, including Cleopatra's Bar (decorated with hieroglyphics and Egyptian statuary) and the Cat's Lounge with its tables in the shape of bottle tops and cats' eyes glinting from the ceiling. There is a casino and concert hall for "Las Vegas-style revues," and 1,022 "accommodation units," most of which convert to "king-size beds," while twenty-eight have bathtub whirlpools. There are three outdoor swimming pools, a 500-foot banked and padded jogging track, and a health club. The belly of this gleaming ship boasts two glass elevators that surround the Spectrum, a twirling lump of colored geometric kitsch.

The cruise industry continues to introduce more elaborate and more unusual attractions in its ships. Appealing to a broader market of cruisers—away from the stereotypical image—cruise ships have introduced ice-skating rinks, rock-climbing walls and basketball courts. No Caribbean island can compete with such an array of delights. "This is a tremendously dynamic industry. It's great value for money; everyone can afford a cruise. Everything is done for you and the marketing is tremendous. The passengers see the ship as the destination," claimed Robert Stegina of the *Fantasy*. Or as a Carnival spokesman said: "People do not come to us to visit the Caribbean, but to be on our boats."[30] If this is so, what then is left for the land destinations? How much do customers spend on land if the ship becomes the economic centerpiece of the holiday?

Cruise lines argue that they make a major contribution to the economic well-being of the region. Their reasoning is affirmed in periodic reports commissioned by the FCCA. The latest report, "The Economic Impact of the Passenger Cruise Industry on the Caribbean," drew its material from surveys of passengers and crew undertaken in the first quarter of 2000. It reported that passengers and crew accounted for a total annual economic impact of $2.6 billion throughout the Caribbean of which $1.4 billion was in direct spending and $1.2 billion indirect. It estimated that a typical ship, carrying 2,000 passengers and 900 crew members generated almost $259,000 in passenger and crew expenditure during a port visit. In a survey of ten ports, average spending per passenger per call totaled $104 ranging from $173.24 in the U.S. Virgin Islands to $53.84 in San Juan, Puerto Rico. Crew members spent an average of $72 per port and were similarly most attracted to goods and services in the USVI. Other figures showed that cruise-related indirect expenditure generated 60,000 jobs throughout the Caribbean.[31]

The CTO's own figures for what passengers spent at various ports in 2000 shows a different pattern. While the USVI scored highest in passenger spending, the estimate here is $259.80 in the U.S. Virgin Islands. At the bottom of the CTO's scale is St. Vincent with a passenger spending of $16.20. Whatever the statistics, most of passenger onshore expenditure was on duty-free shopping, with much less on tours and attractions and little on food. In 2000, however, the CTO reported on "the gradually increasing economic contribution from the cruising sector." It commented that while cruise passenger expenditure was just under 6 percent of all visitor expenditure at the beginning of the 1990s, this had increased to 12 percent in 2000. Statistics threw up an infinite variety of claims in that decade; the EIU similarly plumped for a total cruise-ship contribution of 6 percent in 1990.[32] The Bahamas, the largest of the cruise destinations, put the industry's contribution at 10 percent in 1993, while Jamaica's 1994 OAS report concluded that cruise-ship passengers contributed 3.6 percent of tourist expenditure, "more than a quarter of which was for goods at in-bond stores that contribute little to the economy."[33]

Big Business

Conflicting statistics, major leakages of spending, especially of duty-free goods, and a generally low contribution to the overall income generated by tourism in the Caribbean are themselves indicators of the economic limitations of the cruise industry. But even more fundamentally, who earns the money spent by the cruise industry? Who benefits from the government's expenditure on port and shopping facilities and such expenses as extra police security?

The cruise-ship disembarkation points, with their car rentals, taxi services, helicopters, and tour-operator booths all under one roof, are largely controlled either by transnational chains, by local elites, or by established expatriates. These groups make private contracts with the cruise lines to act as their agents; they also own many of the retail outlets. The Bridgetown Cruise Terminal, for example, which opened in January 1994, is a joint venture between the port authority, three local companies (Cave Shepherd, Harrison's, and Beer & Beverage Ltd.), and the public (25 percent of the shares). Its financial structure was criticized by commentators, including Professor Hilary Beckles of the University of the West Indies at Cave Hill, who commented: "Those three companies have used their position to franchise to the duty-free outlets. They have restructured the white corporate structure of Broad Street [the capital's main shopping area] and duplicated it at the cruise terminal." Indeed, there are replicas of local streets and a chattel-house village—all accessible without leaving the terminal. While the chairman of the Port Authority, Edmund Harrison, denied any such monopolization of the terminal, opportunities for the smaller entrepreneur appear to be limited.

The extent of the interlocking of interests between cruise ships and local big business at the expense of local small business is at the heart of the debate about the cruise industry's economic contribution to the region. Complaints by small businesses in the Cayman Islands, for instance, illustrate this issue. In 1994, taxi drivers, water-sports businesses, and tour operators threatened to hold demonstrations against cruise ships if their grievances were not addressed. The main complaint of the Committee against Cruise

Ship Abuse of Local Water Sports/Taxi Owners was that cruise lines pre-booked passengers on island and water-sports tours with a few, foreign-controlled companies. "Small operators like us do not have the financial resources, marketing infrastructure, or contacts to approach the cruise lines in Miami," said the committee's chairman, Ron Ebanks. Cruise passengers were charged US$30 by the cruise ships for a snorkeling trip that was minutes from the cruise dock, where equipment could be rented at the site from local suppliers for US$8. Ebanks also charged that cruise ships told passengers not to use local taxis but to take a tour sold on board.[34]

There have been similar complaints from small retailers in Nassau and Freeport in the Bahamas, where T-shirt sellers claim that cruise-ship staff accompany cruisers on shopping trips, recommending certain stores that pay for advertising space or are big enough to offer concessions. The retailers allege that shopping is controlled by the few large outlets that have made financial deals with the cruise lines. Such difficulties, together with occasional insults and patronizing behavior from some cruise officials, have further reinforced suspicions that the cruise industry is a foreign-controlled body that seeks to make deals to its own advantage rather than in partnership with the Caribbean. While the immediate bitterness sparked off by the tax row has simmered down, even the CTO's diplomatic Jean Holder remarked that while some cruise lines seek a partnership in cooperation, others "seem to see the Caribbean simply as an area of exploitation for profit."[35]

On the other hand, many of the islands now have a population that has come to depend on the cruise-ship visitors. In Dominica, for example, where by the end of the 1990s the banana industry was in disarray, many people in the informal economy had turned to finding a source of income in tourism, and, in particular, the cruise ships. The CTO recorded average spending per cruise visitor to Dominica of $27.10 in 2000, the third lowest of all reported destinations after St. Vincent and Grenada. During the tourist season, four boats a week tie up in the capital, Roseau. Across the road, at the converted old marketplace, the place is crammed with vendors' booths selling crafts that vary little from one booth to another. If the tourists only buy sporadically, it is better than nothing and "better than staying at home," according to one vendor. For other vendors, like the Rastafarian who sells attractively printed T-shirts and incense sticks, every little dollar counts as it does for the women who provide the ice for the vendors at the entrance to one of the island's main sites. Whatever the tourist brings, however little, makes a difference.

Whatever the temperature of the relationship, cruise companies remain fierce and powerful competitors. They also spend large sums in promoting themselves. In 1993 alone, the two giant companies, Carnival and Royal Caribbean, spent almost US$82 million. (Compare this to the US$12 million spent on the CTO's first regional U.S. ad campaign in 1993.) Behind the campaigns is the "concept," spelled out by Bob Dickinson of Carnival Cruise Lines, when he listed six aspects of the cruise "product" that, he said, were superior to a land-based holiday: value for money; a "trouble-free" environment; excellent food; the "romance of the sea"; superior activities and enter-tainment; "an atmosphere of pampering service" (1993:118).

These factors are emphasized in cruise advertising, a constant presence on North American television and in magazines and newspapers. Indeed, cruise-ship brochures dazzle with descriptions of a life of luxury on board. "Sail with us in 1994, and you'll discover a world of attentive service and courtesy you simply cannot find ashore," boasts a P&O brochure. As the FCCA's executive director, Michelle Paige, told *Caribbean Week,* the passen-gers require excellent service on land because they are accustomed to the high standards on board. The Caribbean, she said, "could do a better job of providing a better service."[36] The Princess brochure, for instance, exudes self-congratulations: pampering includes a "fluffy white bathrobe" and "deli-cious petit fours to welcome you to your cabin and a foil-wrapped chocolate left on your pillow each night." Then there is the gala buffet, which, accord-ing to the same brochure, is an "ingenious display of gastronomic artistry that's a tribute to the skills of ice-carving and sugar-sculpture . . . But for sheer flamboyance, nothing can match the Champagne Waterfall, a glittering pyramid of 600 glasses with bubbly cascading from top to bottom. Mag-nifique! And the perfect introduction to the night ahead." Such flourishes have little to do with the Caribbean but if the ship is the destination, the Car-ibbean itself loses relevance except as a vague and shimmering backdrop. Or, as Carnival's Bob Dickinson, put it: "The limited number of countries and ports offered is not a deterrent to Carnival customers; after all the ship is the attraction, not the port of call" (Dickinson 1993).

Both the covert message of the cruise industry and its upfront promo-tional material compare cruise tourism favorably to land-based tourism. "Should anyone be in doubt that the cruise ships are in competition with us, the attached photocopy of a Royal Caribbean advertisement should set their mind at rest," was the curt memorandum sent by John Bell, executive vice-president of the Caribbean Hotel Association, to his board of directors and member hotel associations. The advertisement was headed "Why a Hotel Should Be Your Last Resort," and the introductory blurb began:

> There's not a lobby on earth that can stack up to the Centrum on a Royal Caribbean ship. Now compare all that a Royal Caribbean cruise offers versus a typical resort and you'll stop pretty quickly. There just is no comparison . . . A Royal Caribbean cruise ship is a resort of the very first order. Choosing anything less should be your last resort.

The cruise lines combine that sort of aggressive promotion with a hard-sell system to retailers. Nearly all cruises in the U.S. market are sold through travel agents who are visited by armies of sales representatives. The commis-sion on sales paid to the agents tends to be higher than that paid for hotel-based holidays. At the same time, the cruise business has been offering dis-counts, anxious to fill the berths and so maintain its high occupancy rates. Carnival's pricing strategy is budgeted for an amazing 100 percent occupancy, which means that for the moment prices can be kept down. Caribbean hotels are unable to respond.

While some cruise analysts have pondered the wisdom of the rampant expansion in ships and berths, the big cruise lines continue to report healthy figures. In the third quarter of 2002, for example, Carnival announced profits of $500.8 million. Increasingly the giant lines are becoming an oligarchy as economies of scale push out the smaller operators. The second and third largest cruise operators, Royal Caribbean and P&O Princess Lines, were discussing a merger in 2002; this would make them the biggest single cruise line overtaking Carnival Cruise Lines—with its forty-three ships and five in construction (at an estimated value of $2.3 billion). And the passengers, mainly American, keep on coming, and no longer just the old and the rich. The market is changing: the young are being targeted by advertising and are responding. Cruises now attract honeymooners and families, and other "niche" markets; there are conference cruises; theme cruises around sports, music, and education; and so on. The populist Carnival Cruise Line announces in its online information that around 30 percent of its passengers are under 35, with 40 percent between 35 and 55, and 30 percent over 55.

The cruise lines argue that they market the Caribbean as well as the ship. A cruise, they say, provides an introduction to the region, a floating showcase for the charms of the Caribbean. One study suggested that up to 25 percent of stay-over tourists had first sampled their holiday choice from the rails of a cruise ship. Another survey indicated that 40 percent of cruise passengers would like to return to the Caribbean for a land-based holiday. The Caribbean often misses opportunities to entice cruisers back to dry-land holidays, say the cruise lines. According to the FCCA's Michelle Paige, destinations do not package themselves as well as they could or advertise their attractions. "If we don't make the passengers feel comfortable, they are going to get right back on the ship."[37] The FCCA's 2000 survey also asked the tourists whether they would be likely to return to ten named destinations on a cruise or on a land-based holiday. The answers showed that the passengers were more likely to return on a cruise than on a land-based holiday. Between 59 percent (Bahamas) and 90 percent (USVI) wanted to return on a cruise. Only Jamaica and the USVI (and Cozumel in Mexico) scored above 60 percent as places where the passengers would be likely to return as stay-over visitors, with only 39 percent, for example, likely to return to St. Kitts.[38] The CTO's strategic plan of 2002 calls for an increase in the conversion of cruise-ship tourists to stay-over tourists.

Possibilities of partnership, stressed by both the CTO and the FCCA in their more conciliatory moods, have begun to be explored in marketing, employment strategies, sourcing, and so on. There is also much talk within the region of a more concerted approach towards the unresolved problems presented by the cruise industry. These more conciliatory tones, perhaps born of desperation, were made official at the end of the Caricom tourism summit in 2001 when a further attempt to ease the tensions between the sea and land industries was launched. A Caribbean cruise committee, cochaired by the tough-talking Paige and the equally robust figure of Butch Stewart, was formed in an attempt to promote "effective collaboration" and to maximize benefits to the region. Yet the introduction of some sort of licensing system for cruise ships, in which contracts and guidelines would be observed on both sides, seems far away. In the meantime, the cruise lines are often perceived as using the Caribbean islands as a chain of low-charge parking lots, coming and going as they see fit. The problem is that without them there would be more hardship and less opportunity for those hundreds and thousands of people who watch for the great white whales to appear over the horizon each morning.

Fishing, Sailing, and Water-sports Tourists

Of course, the cruise lines are not the only users of the Caribbean Sea. There is a growing group of tourists who also use the sea as the focus of their holiday for water skiing, surfing, windsurfing, fishing, sailing, and diving or snorkeling. Fishing and sailing, chartered and bareboat, remain the up-market pursuits. Fishing, in particular, has been a sport for tourists from the early days, and it remains particularly popular in the Bahamas where record catches are made in deep-sea game fishing, while in the shallows, fishing for barracuda and bonefish is popular.

The British Virgin Islands, one of the region's largest water-sports destinations, stresses the attractions of its unspoiled islands and cays. "One can imagine no better holiday for a fisherman than cruising in a motorboat among the islands, with a tent for shore at nights, with food and conversation enriched from the day's catch," enthused a circular from the West India Committee in 1921. Then, there was no mention of sailing, but by 1958, *McKay's Guide* mentioned that the islands had "wonderful sailing in the waters off their coasts" and advised: "With time on your hands in St. Thomas and a liking for the sea, you couldn't do better than to charter one of the many boats available for the purpose, and cruise among these islands for as many days as you can spare." Ten years later, another guidebook commented that "this part of the Caribbean is becoming known as a yachtsman's paradise." The British Virgin Islands has forbidden obtrusive development, but encourages marinas and secluded luxury resorts. The main focus of development has been the yacht charter business, which began in 1967. There are now more than 500 yachts for hire out of the British Virgin Islands, which makes it one of the largest bareback [self-skippered] charter fleets in the world. Charter yacht tourists outnumber hotel tourists and spend more money than them (Lett 1983:35–36). Much of the business is in flotillas where beginners in groups of 12–15 sail in small dinghies under expert supervision.

Modern-style marinas now dot the Caribbean, hangouts for a largely young, American clientele, who pay handsomely for a week's charter. For the yachties, the Caribbean is the fashionable place to be in the winter months, when the sailing elite of the world converges on Martinique after the Route du Rhum transatlantic run or on St. Lucia for Christmas following the Atlantic Rally for Cruisers. The regatta season then moves on to St. Maarten, Puerto Rico, and the Virgin Islands before ending in April, with Antigua's Sailing Week at English Harbor, where Nicholson's Yachtyard, an expatriate stronghold, was one of the first charter bases in the Caribbean in the 1940s. Marinas are big business, and Jamaica has a new project on hand: a marina at Port Antonio, one of the oldest tourism locations in the Caribbean. Promoted as a "megayacht destination," it will, according to the Port Authority of Jamaica, "compare favorably with any waterfront tourism development in the world." It will accommodate the range of craft: from "boutique" cruise ships to the megayachts of the megarich. The argument is that Port Antonio will benefit from such upscale visitors. "The last yacht that came here for a week bought £670 [US$1,120] worth of flowers every day," said Noel Hylton, the president and chief executive of the Port Authority.[39] The opportunities—for linkages into the local economy—are there.

Fishing, sailing, and windsurfing tourists are different from the beach-based tourists. They tend to be more upscale, and are traditionally socially and racially a select group (in an island like Barbados, this is still the case). However, at another level, they are more informal than other tourists. On Bequia, for example, the yachties, who cultivate a lotus-eating manner, hang around St. Elizabeth Bay and its bars, owned by bare-footed expatriates. While the tourist establishment eyes the boat people with some suspicion (they may be rich but they are scruffy) the yachties themselves appear less affronted by authentic Caribbean life than nervous package tourists. And they can make a significant, and direct, contribution to island economies, depending on local suppliers for provisions. In many cases, farmers supply direct to sailors at the marinas. In the British Virgin Islands two types of trading go on: There is the merchant who supplies the flotillas with fruit and vegetables from the United States, shipped in on containers from Florida. The alternative is to buy from individuals who provide Caribbean fruit and vegetables to the more discerning boat captains and owners from a boat-to-boat shop. In Grenada, a small farming cooperative relies on business with sailors for its success and expansion, while for the yachties at the uninhabited Tobago Cays in the Grenadines, young men from Union Island arrive by boat to sell whatever service is required.

Much of the ownership of water-sports businesses, however, remains in expatriate hands. This is partly because of the capital expenditure involved and partly because of the ambivalent nature of the relationship of Caribbean peoples to the sea. While the sea is all around them, and while as fishermen and boatbuilders they are linked to it, they have not traditionally seen it as a place to be exploited for sport. Hence, water-sports tourism has originally been run by and for white foreigners; with some exceptions this remains largely the case, along with such subsidiary businesses as ships' chandlers and marine supermarkets. In the water-sports s business, outsiders dominate both as employers and employees. The yacht charter owners tend to give jobs to other expatriates, often well-connected young men who spend the winter seeking work around Caribbean marinas. So says Jeremy Wright, who owns Boardsailing BVI and is chairman of the Caribbean Windsurfing Association: "My business employs outsiders due to the skills required in looking after the tourists who arrive with differing abilities. I occasionally employ locals yet find that they generally do not get that excited in the teaching and the beach operation side of things. This is the opposite to the outsider who, of course, loves the chance to work in this environment."

Diving and snorkeling have also emerged as an important niche market, for the Caribbean has some of the best diving in the world. Islands like Bonaire and the Cayman Islands, for instance, are both long established and have promoted themselves almost exclusively as dive destinations. New destinations, like Dominica, are also beginning to gain reputations. Divers, like yachties, are adventurous, relatively wealthy and, most important, conscious of the environment. In the Bahamas, the Exuma National Park, administered by the Bahamas National Trust, has developed a "support fleet" of yachties, who each contribute US$30 a year to its upkeep. Nick Wardle, of the National Trust, says that the well-being of the park, the first in the Bahamas, relies on goodwill and that the scheme is a strong replenishment exercise. "The Park is remote; we want to keep it like that. No one is allowed to take anything from it." The Exuma National Park has become a model of its kind and prompted the Bahamas government to announce the protection of 20 percent of the Bahamian marine ecosystem in 2000.

The Caribbean Sea is the resource of all who use it. Yet it is under threat from a range of environmental problems, from dumping to sewage disposal and the destruction of reefs, and all its users, whether cruise ships or jetskiers, are to some extent to blame. The only way to regulate the operations of cruise ships and to protect the marine environment would be to create regional regulatory bodies embracing every state. The CTO has, on many occasions, appealed to the region "as a matter of urgency" to put together a joint environmental plan to regulate behavior, enforce regulations, and punish offenders. Other organizations have also called on the region to establish a body to safeguard the marine environment. Meanwhile, the use of the Caribbean Sea for transporting nuclear waste has made the region even more aware that its waters are a vital component of its patrimony. As Jean Holder points out, the Caribbean has "few resources left that give us any real bargaining power."[40] One of those is the Caribbean Sea.

Source: From *Last Resorts: The Cost of Tourism in the Caribbean*, 2003. Reprinted with permission of the author and the Latin American Bureau.

Notes

[1] Caribbean Tourism Organization, 2000.

[2] Associated Press, London, 25 December 1994.

[3] *New York Times*, New York, 15 June 1994.

[4] Florida-Caribbean Cruise Association, *Caribbean Cruising*, Second Quarter 2002.

[5] Caribbean Tourism Organization, *Caribbean Statistical News*, Barbados, 2001.

[6] Ibid.

[7] Ibid.

[8] *Trade News Edition*, 7 June 1993.

[9] Jean Holder, "Getting the Most from Cruise Tourism for the Caribbean," address to conference at Coopers Lybrand International, Barbados, 1993.

[10] Ibid.

[11] *Caribbean Week*, Barbados, 26 June 1993.

[12] Ibid.

[13] Holder, op. cit.

[14] Caribbean Insight, December 1997.

[15] Ibid.

[16] IPS agency, November 2000.

[17] Florida-Caribbean Cruise Association (FCCA) Newsletter, July 1994.

[18] Ibid.

[19] Ibid.

[20] Edward Bollinger, Vice President of Purchasing, Properties and Logistics, RCCL, address given to the CTO, San Juan, Puerto Rico, 9 July 1992.

[21] *Caribbean Week*, 12–25 November 1994.

[22] Florida-Caribbean Cruise Association, *Caribbean Cruising*, second quarter 2001.

[23] Florida-Caribbean Cruise Association, *Caribbean Cruising*, second quarter 2002.

[24] Florida-Caribbean Cruise Association, *Caribbean Cruising*, second quarter 2001.

[25] *The Democrat for St. Kitts*, 25 March 1994.

[26] *Caribbean Insight*, London, January 1995.

[27] *Daily Nation*, Barbados, 15 April 2002.

[28] *Caribbean Travel News Europe*, Summer 1993.

[29] Economist Intelligence Unit (EIU), *Tourism in the Caribbean*, London, 1993.

[30] *Santo Domingo News*, 25 August 1995.

[31] Florida-Caribbean Cruise Association, *Caribbean Cruising*, second quarter 2002.

[32] EIU, op. cit.

[33] Organization of American States, *Economic Analysis of Tourism in Jamaica*, Washington, DC, 1994.

[34] Caribbean News Association (CANA), 5 November 1994.

[35] Holder, op. cit.

[36] *Caribbean Week*, 12–25 November 1994.

[37] CANA, 26 May 1994.

[38] Florida-Caribbean Cruise Association, *Caribbean Cruising*, second quarter 2002.

[39] Focus on Jamaica, *The Times*, 6 August 2002.

[40] Jean Holder, "Regional Integration, Tourism and Caribbean Sovereignty," mimeo, 1993.

References

Dickinson, Robert. 1993. "Cruise Industry Outlook in the Caribbean," in *Tourism, Marketing and Management in the Caribbean*, ed. Dennis Gayle and Jonathan Goodrich, p. 188. London.

Dickinson, Robert, and A. Vladimir. 1997. *Selling the Sea: An Inside Look at the Cruise Industry*. New York: Wiley.

Lett, James W. 1993 "Ludic and Liminoid Aspects of Charter Yacht Tourism in the Caribbean." *Annals of Tourism Research* 10.

Wood, Robert. 2000. "Caribbean Cruise Tourism: Globalization at Sea." *Annals of Tourism Research* 27(2).

22

The Janus-Faced Character of Tourism in Cuba

Peter M. Sanchez and Kathleen M. Adams

While a group of American tourists rested and sipped sugar cane nectar following a boat tour of limestone caverns outside Viñales, Cuba, a two-year-old member of the entourage delighted in discovering a friendly puppy. As the toddler frolicked with the Cuban dog, several locals gathered to watch the playful scene. An older man, the puppy's owner, turned to the girl's American parents and queried, "Why don't you adopt him and take him back to the United States, since she likes him so much?" The father answered politely, "Well, we would love to but we already have a dog." With a mischievous sparkle in his eyes, the Cuban responded by recounting to all within earshot that he knew an employee at Havana's luxurious Hotel Nacional who witnessed a middle-aged North American woman bring a skinny Cuban dog back to her room. There she fed it steak and paid veterinarians to administer shots and vitamins. Eventually, the woman flew back to the United States, taking the now-plump and pampered Cuban dog with her. For weeks, the refrain of the workers at the Hotel Nacional was, "Gee, why can't I become a dog?" This type of wry humor abounds in Cuba. The average Cuban lives in hardship, as the basic requirements of life are scarce. At the same time, Cuba is under siege by foreigners, many of whom stay in opulent government-owned hotels and dine at restaurants where food is abundant and varied. This duality of existence has created a serious strain on Cubans who have already

419

experienced long-term deprivations. Although tourism is increasingly important to the Cuban economy, observers cannot help but wonder if the island can survive this capitalist abundance amidst socialist scarcity.

Many developing nations, socialist and nonsocialist, have turned to tourism as a vehicle for nation-building. While tourism carries the allure of being a quick way to earn hard currency, capital is usually a means for achieving a much broader nation-building agenda that may include national integration, strengthening of the state, self-determination (sovereignty), and social equity and justice. Thus, nation-building is herein seen as a broad plan that includes economic, political, social, and ideological goals. Tourism is salient in this regard, as it allows developing nations to exploit their scenic and heritage resources, potentially instilling civic pride, while simultaneously generating new revenue, principally for the achievement of more important goals.

This article explores the uneasy marriage between socialism and tourism in an economically challenged nation. It focuses on Cuba as a case study for examining what we term the "Janus-faced" character of tourism. Allcock and Przeclawski (1990) first noted the contradictory tendencies between socialism and tourism, and this article further explores these paradoxes. While tourism initially appears as an economic panacea—for example, in 1990 it earned Caribbean countries "six times the revenue of all traditional agricultural exports" (Edwards 2005:5)—the industry has potentially ruinous side effects that can undermine a developing (particularly a socialist) country's nation-building aspirations. Our study both documents the complex ways in which tourism development interfaces with the cultivation of a loyal socialist citizenry and also explores how Cuba has sought to use tourism to build international sympathy and political support. In short, we aim to examine the extent to which national goals, particularly social justice visions, are realized, challenged, or contorted in the process of developing tourism in a socialist, developing nation. We suggest that while tourism has helped Cuba weather a severe economic storm, the unpleasant face of tourism may be undermining the support that the Cuban people have had for socialist ideology.[1]

In recent years, scholars have devoted increasing attention to tourism's political and sociocultural dimensions (Hall and Jenkins 1995; Teo, et al. 2001; Enloe 2001). As Hall observed, however, with a few exceptions, most politically oriented studies "focus on notions of prescription, efficiency and economy rather than ideals of equality and social justice" (1994:7–8). Inspired by this charge, we seek to spotlight tourism politics, social justice, and inequality. Our study asks: How does Cuba attempt to use tourism to advance international support for its own social justice visions? Domestically, how is tourism in Cuba intertwined with social equality and inequality, and with support for the Cuban government? For counties that include social justice and equality on their agendas, tourism must be examined closely to assess whether it assists or undermines these nation-strengthening goals.

In addressing issues of social inequality, the nexus between tourism and "racial" relations is particularly salient. As van den Berghe (1980) observed, international tourism is generally superimposed on local systems of ethnic relations and can profoundly affect indigenous ethnic hierarchies. Only recently, however, have scholars started exploring the salience of van den Berghe's observations for nations embracing tourism as a strategy for revenue and nation-building (Adams 1998; Picard and Wood 1997). For instance, Wood has underscored that, although various institutions mediate the relationship between tourism and ethnicity, generally none are more central than the state (1997:2). As Wood emphasizes, state policies intersect with tourism development and ethnic/racial politics, "shaping the range of ethnic options available to groups and the construction of otherness produced by a variety of local actors" (1997:6). In Cuba's case, as argued here, tourism is subtly entwined with racial stereotyping. Moreover, hiring practices and tourist dollar flows underscore the dormant racial hierarchies of the Batista era—hierarchies that socialism sought to erase (cf. De La Fuente 1998).

While tourism in Cuba poses threats to national integration and independence, it also offers opportunities to enhance images of the nation and its accomplishments. As shown in other locales, tourism has been used by states to project positive images abroad. Leong chronicled how Singapore has touristically mined ethnic cultures for not only economic development but also national image management (1989). And Richter documented how the Marcos government used tourism to foster a favorable international image of the Philippines (1989). Likewise, apartheid-era South Africa conscripted tourism to project an enhanced image of the nation to visitors from countries inclined to impose trade sanctions (Pizam and Mansfield 1996). This article chronicles how Cuba has drawn on tourism to foster both respect for its socialist accomplishments and sympathy for the injustices suffered at the hands of Cuba's antagonistic northern neighbor, the United States. As will be shown, however, the state has had an uphill struggle since the less attractive face of tourism works against the accomplishment of these goals.

Despite the prominence of political agendas and ironies in Cuban tourism, surprisingly few researchers have spotlighted these themes. While some scholars (cf. de Holan and Phillips 1997) analyze the economic dimensions of Cuba's decision to pursue tourism, and others examine the sociopolitical ramifications of sex/romance tourism in Cuba (cf. O'Connell-Davidson 1996; Cabezas 2004), the intersection between international tourism to Cuba, Cuban sentiments about socialism, and the government's attempts to channel foreigners' political sensibilities via tourism policy remain understudied. Seaton's examination of tourism's effects on political culture within Cuba is an exception. Seaton argues that poor governments most in need of tourism as a source of revenue are "most likely to be subverted by it politically" (1999: 307). His findings regarding Cuba's domestic situation resonate with those herein; although, unlike this study, Seaton does not address the flip side of Cuba's political use of tourism to woo foreign audiences.

As the Cuban government attempted to rebuild the nation economically, politically, and ideologically, after the collapse of the Soviet bloc, partly via the tourism industry, the unpleasant "face" of tourism emerged very quickly in ways that undermined some of the government's goals. This article examines this paradox, chronicling both the external political sympathy the Cuban government seeks to inspire via tourist-oriented displays and the internal challenges to the socialist vision triggered by Cuba's opening to international tourism.

Tourism in Cuba

Cuba has experienced four periods during which tourism became important to the island's economy. This article addresses the most recent, fourth tourism boom, which was inspired by economic crisis and necessity. When the Soviet bloc disintegrated between 1989 and 1991, Cuba lost its preferential trading relationship with communist countries. In 1995, an official in Cuba's Finance Ministry explained to one author the stark realities of the time. He noted that, while prior to 1991 Cuba could send one negotiating team to Moscow and devise a comprehensive trade deal with the entire Communist bloc within a couple weeks, after the USSR's fall, Cuba was informed that it would henceforth have to negotiate trade deals with each country individually. Additionally, Russia and former Soviet republics now insisted on paying market prices for Cuba's sugar and other products, while also insisting that Cuba pay market prices for all goods and services purchased from them. The economic effects on Cuba were dramatic and devastating. Cuba experienced an unprecedented drop in real Gross Domestic Product for three consecutive years: –25% in 1991, –14% in 1992, and –20% in 1993 (Pastor and Zimbalist 1995:11).

As a result, after 1991, Cuba desperately needed hard currency and many basic products, including food. The economic crisis, termed the "special period in time of peace" by Castro, also meant that Cuba's health and educational systems, the pride of the revolution, suffered. In desperation, the government implemented dramatic economic changes (directly contradicting socialist and revolutionary values) designed to increase economic efficiency and to promote the tourism industry, much as China and other socialist countries had already done (Zhang et al. 1999:478; and Matthews and Richter 1991:125). Foreign investors were allowed to establish joint ventures with the Cuban government in almost all sectors of the economy, save for health and education. Eventually, the Cuban government sanctioned a limited number of wholly owned foreign ventures. In 1993, Cuba allowed U.S. dollars to circulate in the economy and, ironically, dollars soon became the dominant currency. Cuba also legalized a number of small private businesses. Cubans were allowed to rent out rooms, *casas particulares*, to tourists or Cuban-Americans visiting relatives on the island. And Cubans were permitted to establish small private restaurants, *paladares*, in their homes.

Tourism became the preferred panacea for surviving the economic crisis. The result was a dramatic rise in hotel construction and foreigners visiting Cuba. In 1990, 340,000 foreigners visited Cuba, but by 2000 the figure jumped to 1,774,000 (Centro de Promoción de Inversiones 2005). In 2004, Cuba broke the two million mark, with 2,048,572 foreign arrivals (Grogg 2005). Cuba's goal is to receive 6.2 million tourists and to add 70,000 hotel rooms by 2010 (Centro de Promoción de Inversiones 2005).

While the Cuban state was able to weather the economic crisis by turning to tourism, the influx of foreigners and the advent of semi-capitalist economic ventures have reintroduced to Cuba the more unpleasant face of tourism—prostitution, drugs, and corruption—reminiscent of the 1950s, which threatens to undermine many of the Cuban government's national goals, including the preservation of socialism.

Socialism or Tourism? When Karl Marx Meets Adam Smith

When Cuba entered its contemporary economic crisis in 1991, the regime's new slogan became "socialism or death!" The slogan could just as well have read "socialism or tourism?" Instead, the Cuban government embarked on a program to embrace both socialism *and* tourism, as it opened its economy to foreign investment while steadfastly attempting to retain its socialist economic and political system. To promote tourism, however, the government had to make fundamental economic changes, such as inviting foreign investment and legalizing the U.S. dollar, significantly challenging the character of Cuban socialism. These changes have led to new inequalities and to the return of some of the problems—corruption, drugs, racism, and prostitution—that once characterized the Batista dictatorship (Barbassa 2005:17). Private incentive and entrepreneurship, whether legal or not, is now a salient characteristic of the Cuban economy. Much of this individualism takes place in the tourist sector where Cubans struggle to get hard currency through various means not sanctioned by the government. Until 2004, the U.S. dollar was king, but after the Bush administration imposed tighter rules on travel and U.S. currency entering Cuba, Cuba banned the U.S. dollar, and now the convertible peso has taken its place.

Recognizing the potential threat of tourism to revolutionary ideals, Cuba attempted initially to limit the contact between foreigners and Cubans. At first, the government focused its tourism expansion on the Varadero Beach complex, and similar areas, where it could isolate tourists more easily from as many Cubans as possible. But as hotels mushroomed around the country and growing numbers of tourists arrived, it became increasingly difficult to enforce tourism segregation. Consequently, Cubans came into contact with tourists and began to experience the pernicious dimensions of tourism.

Perhaps one of the most paradoxical outcomes of the tourism boom is the increasingly visible economic inequality in a socialist county, described by Jackiewicz as a "huge class divide" (2002). Although a political elite existed in Cuba since the early days of the revolution, tourism has contributed to the emergence of a nascent *petite bourgeoisie* whose members are becoming conspicuous consumers. Those with access to tourism-industry-derived hard currency can live far more comfortably than those without it. And, since the government can no longer provide for all basic needs and has accepted the notion of unemployment, many Cubans lacking access to hard currency now live in the kind of poverty visible in other developing countries. Cubans running paladares or casas particulares, working in hotels, or selling products illegally to tourists all have access to hard currency and have managed to weather the economic crisis much better than those outside the tourism sector. For example, in Cuba, a doctor earns less money that a bell-hop at an internationally oriented hotel, as many hotel workers told the authors during interviews. Wood and Jayawardena (2003:153) report that while a general practitioner in Cuba earns roughly U.S.$20 per month, a hotel manager earns approximately U.S.$40 per month and a restaurant waiter earns U.S.$20, plus another U.S.$17 in tips. Consequently, many professionals (including communist party members) have abandoned government jobs to enter the tourism industry.[2] These tourism jobs may be perceived as "demeaning" from a professional perspective, but they are financially rewarding. One hotel worker, previously employed as a mechanical engineer, related to the authors that his hotel bellhop job had resulted in both a larger income and the chance to travel abroad, indirectly giving him access to more money. Likewise, a recent study observes that the tourist industry offers a venue in which workers can meet foreigners who may facilitate travel to other nations or who may become marriage partners, thus enabling the worker to gain more currency and, potentially, the opportunity to leave the country (Cabezas 2006:508). In effect, then, the emerging tourist industry has undermined the Cuban government's goal of egalitarianism. Adding insult to this phenomenon is the fact that the merit-based economic structure has been partly inverted by menial jobs in the tourist industry becoming more desirable than professional and high-level government jobs.

Although racism persisted in Cuba despite the efforts by the revolution to eradicate it, the existence of heightened racism is clear from various interviews with Cubans. Furthermore, ethnographic experiences show that the economic pressures of the "special period" have exacerbated the racism that survives on the island. For instance, one of us (Sanchez, a Cuban-born scholar) witnessed conflict erupt between a "white" tourist-industry translator and three Afro-Cuban scholars who were speaking to an American study group visiting the Santiago *Centro Cultural Afrocubano* in 1995. Answering a question posed by one of the Americans, the scholars stated that, despite the efforts of the revolution, racism still existed in Cuba. The translator, however, did not translate their meaning, leaving out their conviction that racism was still prevalent in Cuba. The scholars responded quickly, telling the translator that her translations were "incorrect." The translator curtly replied to the Afro-Cubans, "I don't know the language of your people's research," disparagingly implying that blacks used different terminology than whites. One Afro-Cuban scholar promptly rebutted with a Cuban saying, "He without blood from Congo has blood from Carabalí," suggesting that all Cubans have blood from Africa. The authors witnessed similar racial tensions many times on all three research visits.

Racism has a long history in Cuba, and clearly it has not been eradicated by the revolution. The presence of the bourgeoning tourist industry has exacerbated racist attitudes and racial discrimination. Not only do fairerskinned Cubans have easier access to more visible and prestigious positions in the hotel industry (Cabezas 2004:995), but many white Cubans are uninhibited about expressing racial biases, both among themselves and to foreign visitors. Often it is subtle, such as sliding the index and middle fingers back and forth over one's forearm to signify someone dark; but sometimes it is disturbingly direct, as in the example above, or by constantly suggesting to tourists that crime in Old Havana is perpetuated by blacks (which may be true to some extent but only because blacks are generally poorer than whites, serving as clear evidence that racism is still present on Cuba). For instance, while strolling in Old Havana at night one white Cuban woman cautioned one of us in racist terms: "Not all Negroes are thieves, but all thieves are Negroes." A young, black male, in fact, complained to one author that while all Cubans are supposed to be able to attend university, at the University of Havana, the student body is "principally white." He stressed that the same was generally true with tourism-industry jobs.

At the Hotel Sevilla, for example, our survey of the bellhops in May 2004 found that all were white and university educated. And, although chambermaids were not necessarily university educated, they tended to be fairskinned. This pattern was repeated time and again. In a total of three trips to Cuba, spanning nine years, we found that almost all workers at the front desks of Havana and Varadero hotels oriented towards international tourists were predominantly "white."[3] In a study of racism in Cuba, De la Fuente quotes a black Cuban singer as saying: "Tourism firms look like South African companies in the times of Peter Botha. You go there, and they are all white. And I wonder: Where am I, in Holland?" (1998:7). In keeping with our findings, Cabezas also observes that "Afro-Cubans are excluded from front line service positions with direct customer contact" (2006:513). Certainly, Afro-Cubans can be found in the tourist industry and sometimes they occupy key positions, but overall, while they represent a significant segment of the Cuban population, they are underrepresented in the high-level and best-paying positions in the industry. Racial preferences in tourism-related hiring appear, then, to have exacerbated inequality and racism. This inequality, within a socialist system, threatens to erode domestic support for the Cuban government. While they may fear the alternative and still view Castro's revolution positively, many Cubans we interviewed were often quite critical of the government's policies and lamented their current paradoxical experiences and hardships. Thus, tourism has also increased ethnic divisions in Cuba. Rather than helping build and integrate the nation and strengthening the state, tourism has helped in part to do the opposite in Cuba—yielding more social division and tension.

Another form of emerging inequality is that between Cubans and foreign tourists. In most developing countries, mainstream tourists enjoy more luxurious lifestyles than most local citizens. However, in socialist Cuba, a society infused with ideals of equality, national pride, and accomplishment, the contrast between the struggling Cuban and the lavish-living tourist is particularly disturbing. Most Cubans, even those with dollars, cannot stay at the principal tourist-oriented hotels, unless they are honeymooning or have received rewards from the state for some accomplishment. As a tourist official we interviewed reported, even when a Cuban couple or worker is allowed to stay in a tourist hotel, it is often at a less desirable hotel, and the government can shorten their stay or move them to a lesser hotel if foreign tourists need the room. While foreigners cavort in Cuba's opulent hotels, play golf on manicured courses in the Varadero resort region, and dine in elegant hotel restaurants, Cubans must stay principally in less-lavish hotels for domestic tourism. Moreover, even when invited by foreign visitors, Cubans for many years were not permitted to go beyond the lobby of hotels meant for foreigners. On various occasions during all three of our visits, the authors witnessed Cubans become enraged by this humiliating inequality and discrimination. According to an official at the Center for Promotion of Foreign Investment (who confirmed this practice), the reason for this policy is that Cuba desperately needs hard currency. When a foreigner stays at the prestigious Hotel Nacional, the government charges in dollars; but, for honeymooning Cubans, payment is in pesos. This explanation, while economically sound, does not address the policy of barring Cubans from entering hotels catering to foreigners and its attendant, negative social ramifications.

Recent changes, if fully implemented, will allow Cubans to stay at any hotel. In recent years, Cubans have been allowed to dine at restaurants frequented by tourists. However, they had to pay in dollars (now convertible pesos), meaning that the vast majority of Cubans do not or cannot go to these restaurants. This deliberate and de facto segregation highlights the emerging inequality in Cuba and effectively locates Cubans below foreigners in the international social hierarchy—a reality that is palpably askew in a socialist society, as almost all Cubans interviewed underscored. Tourism has, in effect, helped turn Cubans into second-class citizens, an undesirable outcome for a government attempting to promote self-determination, national pride, and equality. Again, for a state using tourism for nation-building, tourism's economic benefits may pale in comparison to the resurgent unpleasant face of the tourist industry.

To the emerging inequality, tourism has added new forms of corruption. Although all corruption certainly cannot be tied to the tourism industry and Cuba is heralded as one of the least corrupt countries in the world (Chavez 2005:13), the presence of more foreigners on the island has helped increase the willingness of some Cubans to engage in criminalized activity in order to acquire tourists' hard currency. In this regard, from the state's perspective, almost all Cubans have become criminals. *Resolver*, "to resolve" or "deal with," is a term widely used by Cubans that refers to any instance where a Cuban takes care of a difficult situation. Since most Cubans are in difficult situations every day, "resolver" is a way of life on the island. While resolver suggests great cunning and ingenuity, it also often refers to some degree of illegal activity. During the course of interviews and participant observation, the authors heard many stories of how tourism workers engage in resolver. For instance, one tourism worker recounted how her brother, who worked at a cigar factory, would conspire with other workers to sneak out cigar bands from the factory. The bands were essential since they would authenticate a cigar as being "made in Cuba." With bands secreted out of the factory, ordinary cigars could look authentic enough to sell to tourists, and all workers involved would share the profits. Another worker with access to dollars, because of his job in the tourist sector, purchased house paint on the black market. When a state inspector visited his home, the official fined him for possessing paint that he was not supposed to have. From the states' perspective, this individual either stole the paint from the state or bought it on the black market, both illegal actions. These two examples illustrate the wide range of activities that can be termed as efforts to resolver. Almost every Cuban we talked with about the hardships in Cuba shared similar stories. These types of illegal resolver activities have clearly reached epidemic proportions in Cuba: they are so pervasive that the state can only make superficial attempts to combat them.

Another tourism-related phenomenon that brings in currency and has the potential to undermine the egalitarian revolutionary narrative is *jineterismo*. *Jinetero* means jockey, and was most likely initially applied to prostitution. However, the word is now applied much more broadly to cover any kind of activity, often illegal, resulting in acquiring hard currency from tourists; essentially the hustling of foreigners. It can represent a range of commodified and often sexually tinged services, including prostitution, courting a foreigner for a meal or marriage, or simply serving as an attractive guide for dollars (now convertible pesos). The Cuban, in the wit implied by the expression, takes the foreigner for a ride.

Prior to the revolution, prostitution was seen as the product of corrupt U.S.-imposed capitalism. The revolution, it was envisioned, would erase Havana's reputation as the "brothel of the Caribbean" (Pattullo 1996:90). Socialism, it was assumed, would eradicate sex work, since equality and personal-dignity would replace exploitation. The dire economic crisis of the 1990s and the rise of tourism, however, revitalized commoditized sexual encounters in Cuba. When tourists began to return in large numbers during a period when Cubans were struggling to survive, the incentive for young women and men to become involved in sex work was too strong to resist (Trumbull 2001). By 1995, *jineteras*, as well as jineteros, walked the streets and approached tourists at hotels openly. The Cuban government has made several attempts to curb prostitution, by rounding up and fining sex workers, but it continues to thrive, although not as blatantly as in the mid-1990s. In 1996, for instance, Cuba's Central Committee publicly denounced the "humiliating" dimensions of tourism, noting prostitution as a key problem, along with eroding values prompted by citizen access to tourism dollars (Schwartz 1997:211). In the same year, the government attempted to crack down on organized prostitution networks in Havana and Varadero Beach (Schwartz 1997). In 2004, at a meeting with representatives of the Cuban Women's Federation in a Havana neighborhood, the authors were told that the community of 125,000 residents had 213 prostitutes in 2003. The federation had worked with these prostitutes and the number had dropped to 87 in 2004, although the improvement was partly because 16 had fled Cuba. Despite some gains in reducing prostitution, the continuing existence of commoditized sexual services in socialist Cuba is an embarrassment for the government and militates against the solidifying socialist ideology and attaining national goals. One should note, however, that for those engaged in jineterismo, these activities are yet another avenue to resolver.[4]

Hustling tourists is no longer the sole domain of the lone entrepreneur. State employees, whether working at a hotel or for one of the island's travel agencies, like Havanatur, are increasingly participating in jineterismo, as well. For example, a state-employed tour guide may steer a group to a particular *paladar* or organized event, earning a kickback from the restaurateur or venue director. A hotel security guard or bellhop may accept a fee for a sex worker to enter a hotel to visit a guest. A bus driver may take a group on a nonscheduled side-trip, for a tip. The authors did not observe these practices in 1995, but they were pervasive in 2004. In essence, jineterismo is thriving and seems to be expanding to include state workers.

One individual told us that even party officials who run state-operated restaurants are able to take part of the "profit" in order to augment their base salaries. Even the military is involved in the tourist industry and its enticing profits. For instance, *Gaviota* is a state-operated tourism concern that is controlled by the Cuban armed forces (*Economist* 2004). Thus, Cubans who are involved in illegal activities and hustling now include party and military officials. While it is understandable that government officials would want to cash in on the tourism bonanza, these pseudocapitalist enriching endeavors invariably undermine the government's stated core values. As more and more citizens, government officials, and party elite become engaged in jineterismo and profiteering, socialism in Cuba risks becoming pure rhetoric, with a decreasing chance for survival now that Raul Castro is in power and after Fidel Castro's death.

Not surprisingly, in summer 2004, a major shake-up at the Ministry of Tourism occurred. Several key officials lost their jobs, including the minister of tourism, and the positions were filled by players from *Gaviota*. According to the *Economist*, "The military takeover of tourism is part of a broader campaign against corruption," since Raul Castro had recently said that the tourist industry was resulting in a "lack of respect" for Cuba's communist party and the state (*Economist* 2004). It is clear that the Cuban government understands fully that the contradictions inherent in the tourist industry are dangerous for socialist Cuba's values and regime. Although tourism is certainly not the only explanation for increased corruption, it is nevertheless a recent important contributor. If corruption continues and increases, achieving the goals of nation-building, social justice, and egalitarianism will become more difficult.

Socializing the Tourists (and the People): Socialism 101

Recognizing that tourism has fueled ideological contradictions, Cuba's government has attempted to politicize tourism as much as possible to gain both internal and external support. As in most countries, the Cuban government promotes its political achievements and values in various ways through the tourist industry. Most Cuban tours include visits to the Museum of the Revolution, where foreign tourists learn of Castro's July 26 revolutionary movement that destroyed the Batista dictatorship. Here, the pedigree of Castro's revolutionary movement is the focal point. In the galleries of this celebrated museum, tourists and Cuban schoolchildren meander through three floors of displays. The initial displays on the top floor trace Cuba's history and are infused with egalitarian, socialist ideology. For instance, the colonial phase, during which the cultures of indigenous populations became "extinct," is represented as a period in which "feudal methods of capitalist market production are introduced" along with slave labor and the "birth of more advanced social groups that fought for economic and political emancipation." Displays in this section celebrate rebellious indigenous leaders, such as Cacique Guama who is heralded as the "maximum expression of the rebelliousness of our inhabitants against the Spanish conquerors in the 16th century." As one moves through subsequent displays covering more recent centuries, the overarching story celebrates many historic instances of Cubans' continued and heroic resistance to a series of external, largely capitalist, oppressors. U.S. visitors to these galleries who read the display copy are invariably prompted to reflect on how these representations of history contrast sharply with what their American schoolbooks had taught them. For instance, on the 2004 study tour we led to Cuba, our American students clustered in a gallery dedicated to the 1898 commencement of the "Yankee Military Occupation" and read with astonishment the following caption in English:

> "Despite resistance from the more enlightened sectors of our people, the Yankee imperialist intervention [of 1898] succeeded in establishing itself and opened the way for the transformation of the former colony of Spain into a neocolony of the U.S."

When discussing the Museum of the Revolution, a number of the American travelers we interviewed commented not only on this "eye-opening" socialist lens on American intervention in Cuba but also on subsequent displays that, among other things, recounted the CIA's 1971–1974 efforts to introduce a pig fever virus (reputed to have killed over a million Cuban pigs); and celebrated the educational and health care advances accomplished during Cuba's socialist era. Other galleries that appeared to consistently draw the focused attention of foreign tourists included a room devoted to "Che" Guevara and his comrades. In this way, Cuban museums socialize not only Cuban schoolchildren but also prompt foreign tourists to reflect on the Cuban experience with new eyes.

International tourists also frequent Playa Girón on the southern coast, where the Cuban government's victory over a CIA-supported Cuban-exile invasion force at the "Bay of Pigs," as it is known in English, is glorified. In Santiago, the old Moncada barracks, where Castro carried out his first military operation against Batista's army on 26 July 1953, is now a museum that again pays tribute almost exclusively to the 26-July movement. Revolutionary posters, billboards, and murals abound in Cuba, and tour buses often pause to facilitate tourist photos of these monuments. In short, the tourist in Cuba, both domestic and foreign, is continually reminded of the revolution and Cuba's socialist ideology.

While these sorts of nation-building, socializing tourist sites are hardly unique to Cuba, what is distinctive is the government's use of tourism to publicize and generate international sympathy, and even social activism, on behalf of Cuban causes. In 2004, the political cause being highlighted for tourists was that of five Cubans convicted of espionage in the United States in 2001. These five men, according to the Cuban government, were infiltrating Cuban-American groups in Miami that had been involved in acts of "terrorism" in Cuba. From Cuba's perspective, these men are heroes who were protecting their country and the global community via their efforts to end international terrorism. In contrast, to the U.S. government they were "spies" pursuing intelligence-gathering activities for a foreign government on U.S. soil. Throughout Cuba in 2004, poster displays and memorial statues were prominent in spots frequented by international tourists. Five-starred stone and cement memorials to the five men were common, bordering parking lots at tobacco farms, nature parks, and rum and cigar factories on the tourist circuit. As tourists alighting from their buses and taxis spotted these intriguing shrine-like memorials, their curiosity was invariably piqued and their Cuban guides promptly offered them introductory lessons on the "Cuba Five." Likewise, guides show videos about the injustices faced by these "five heroes" to foreign tourists on long bus rides. Many hotels catering to international tourists also prominently displayed multilingual petitions for tourists to sign, demanding that the United States free these men. Hundreds of foreign tourists had signed the petitions we examined, declaring sympathy toward the five men and solidarity with Cuba. Of course, it is easy for tourists to sign a petition in support of the Cuba Five or Cuba's political system. But will this support translate into understanding more activist roles on their return home?

Revolutionary photos on display at the Hotel Nacional, Havana's classic hotel. (Photo by Peter Sanchez)

A typical monument to the Cuba Five. This display is adjacent to the entrance to a tobacco farm that is a routine stop for international tour groups. This monument is the first thing foreign tourists see as they alight from their buses and follow the path into the main building of the tobacco farm. (Photo by Peter Sanchez)

Other ways in which Cuba attempts to engender support for the government and socialism include health tourism (see Goodrich 1993) and tour stops to showcase specific local health care facilities. At Frank País Orthopedic hospital foreigners can obtain expert medical care at considerably less expense than in other countries. Numerous medical facilities in Cuba provide similarly low-cost specialized health care to foreigners. Tours of these facilities further highlight Cuba's medical and health accomplishments and thus help to dispel negative images of Cuba and socialism.

Tourists are also routinely taken to destinations showcasing the ecological accomplishments of the socialist government. At the Las Terrazas ecological community, a popular destination (particularly for solidarity tours), located about 30 minutes from Havana, tourists are able to observe an economically self-sufficient, sustainable commune (Winson 2006:15–17). The ultimate message is that socialism can work given the proper conditions. All commune residents work and live in the preserved biosphere and produce all they consume. Local musicians greet and serenade tourists. Tourists can stay overnight at the ecological community's lodge, stroll in the hilly terrain, and learn about coffee growing and processing from collective members. Tourist sites such as these, along with the many others that highlight the revolution and socialist ideals, serve as potential counterweights to the pernicious effects that increasing individualism and capitalism have on Cuba.

Some "pro-Cuba" tourism originates from abroad. In the United States and in other countries, numerous organizations sponsor and organize educational and solidarity trips to Cuba. These trips also pursue the goal, directly or indirectly, of promoting support for Cuba's socialist government. For example, Global Exchange, based in San Francisco, is one U.S.-based group that has traditionally organized such trips. The group's Web page states that the primary goals of the organization are to end the U.S. government's classification of Cuba as a terrorist country, end the U.S. embargo against Cuba, and end U.S. travel restrictions against Cuba (Global Exchange 2005). Likewise, in Canada, Cuba Education Tours organizes trips to Cuba to "advance learning, friendship, dialogue, and understanding." This organization rejects U.S. policy and supports the goals of Castro's government, stating on their Web site: "100% literary, free education and health care for all in Cuba" (Cuba Solidarity 2005). Finally, the New York-based Center for Cuban Studies, founded by a group of scholars, promotes educational trips to Cuba "to counter the effects of U.S. policy" (Cuba Update 2005). These organizations, and others, take people to Cuba to showcase both the benefits of the Cuban revolution and the pernicious effects of U.S. policies. Although the Cuban government publicizes these tours, often the "average" Cuban plays no role, so it is hard to determine whether Cuban citizens are fully aware of the international sympathy and support for Cuba. Generally, Cubans who are eking out an existence are still left with growing inequality, lack of government services, and a parade of wealthy tourists, spending seemingly unlimited quantities of cash. All this takes place on an island where sensibilities about equality, community, social justice, and dignity have been instilled for almost five decades. Much of the way in which Cuba politicizes tourism, therefore, influences foreigners much more than Cubans.

The immersion course we ran for students in Cuba in 2004, for example, could be categorized as solidarity travel in that students from the United States visited Cuba to learn about its political system, culture, and society, which almost always results in a greater appreciation for a country that is often criticized heavily by the U.S. government and media. Our 14 students visited the Museum of the Revolution, met with representatives of the Federation of Cuban Women, visited Frank País Hospital, visited the Las Terrazas ecological community, and engaged in activities that often highlighted the benefits and accomplishments of the Cuban system. At the end of the course, the students filled out an open-ended questionnaire that asked them to note the most important things they learned and to express how their image of Cuba changed on the trip. The survey's two most pertinent, open-ended questions were: What is your impression of Cuban culture, people, and society; and what is your impression of the Cuban political system? Without exception, the students stated they had generally a negative impression of Cuba before the immersion experience. Thus, although these students were open to visiting Cuba and learning of its system, they were, nevertheless, like most Americans in their willingness to accept the negative image of Cuba prevalent in the United States. All the students, however, expressed very positive views of the Cuban people in the post-trip survey, characterizing them as "friendly," "generous," worthy of respect, and very committed to the "goals of the revolution."

When discussing their impression of the political system, however, students were much more willing to express negative sentiments. Students expressed concerns about living conditions, the system's unfairness (particularly resulting from tourism), poor implementation of principles, apathy, the lack of transportation, and so forth. One student wrote, "I now believe the Cuban political system is in grave danger." Thus, while the students enjoyed their immersion experience and visited many locations highlighting the benefits of Cuba's socialist system, none of the students expressed clearly positive opinions toward the system, in its current manifestation. If other "solidarity" tourists are leaving with the same impressions, then the government's efforts at gaining support are not having the desired effect.

Regarding the system's survival, however, what Cuban citizens think is much more important than what foreigners think. And what Cubans think is conditioned significantly by the emergence of tourism and its attendant ironies. Even before the Soviet Union's collapse in 1991, the Cuban government had already begun to prepare for the coming economic shock that led to the "special period." Cuban officials realized that with the pending loss of Soviet subsidies and preferential trade agreements, Cuba would have to find new avenues for earning hard currency. Tourism was an obvious option so the government quickly began to develop Varadero Beach as a destination, building hotels and an airport via joint ventures with foreign companies. As early as 1989, Castro was promoting the importance and value of the tourist industry. In a television interview broadcast by Tele-Rebelde immediately before the inauguration of the new airport at Varadero, Castro told the viewers that Cuba's natural beauty is a "patrimony of humanity" and "people throughout the world are eager to have fresh air, fresh water, to escape from the poison in the environment, the toxins that have accumulated." More pragmatically, Castro added: "At the same time, it [tourism] will serve as a very important source of income for the country" (FBIS 1989.) By 1993, Castro conceded that tourism was not a panacea, particularly in terms of its effects on Cuba's ideology. In an interview televised by Cubavisión, Castro said:

> Tourism has many positive aspects and some negative aspects. We try to develop the positive aspects of tourism and to avoid the negative aspects. What do we try to avoid? We have not established gambling, casinos, and all that. . . . This is not a country full of drugs and we maintain a strict and rigorous policy in this regard. (FBIS 1993)

Castro neglected to mention sex work and jineterismo, but by 1993, these tourism ills had emerged and would continue to fuel the Janus-faced character of Cuba's tourism. The Cuban government, from the outset, put a positive face on tourism despite the fact that Cuba's political elite would not have given much thought to developing tourism if not for the economic crisis. Necessity turned Cuba's leaders into supporters of an industry closely associated with the evils of global capitalism and a bourgeois lifestyle. Tourism, after all, had been a plague encouraged by the Batista regime that had "infected" Cubans and disgraced the nation. Now tourism, the government argued, would represent Cuba's gift to a world suffering from capitalism.

The greatest challenge for the Cuban government, however, is to sell this Pollyannaish view of tourism to its own citizens. As discussed above, most Cubans who are exposed to the tourist industry have strongly mixed feelings about tourism. They enjoy the access to cash that enables some of them to live better than their fellow citizens and fraternize with foreigners. Yet, many are frustrated and offended by the corruption, inequality, and humiliation that tourism has helped to generate. Cubans, in many ways, have had to sell themselves and their country for access to hard currency. And now, increasingly, some Cubans are living an almost bourgeois lifestyle. Although opinion polls pertaining to whether Cubans are persuaded by the government's positive rhetoric do not exist, the authors' conversations and interviews would suggest that most Cubans are generally resentful of what tourism has done to the island, where sun, sand, and sex are increasingly viewed as the exclusive domain of the foreigners and newly privileged Cubans. Almost all of the Cubans we interviewed, including government officials and tourism workers, spoke of tourism in disparaging ways. According to most Cubans we spoke with the most negative aspect of the tourism industry by far is the inequality it has helped to fuel, both financially and in terms of the opulent and free lifestyle of the foreign tourist. Perhaps these are sentiments that exist only in areas where tourism is pervasive, such as Havana and Varadero. This is small consolation, though, since tourism is prevalent in Havana and other larger cities where most of the Cuban population resides. We surmise, therefore, that Cuba's political elite will have a difficult time at best in moderating the negative effects of tourism.

Conclusion

Tourism in Cuba has, to some extent, helped to "save" the economy by providing much needed hard currency. The Castro government in the early 1990s experienced a serious crisis that had grave political repercussions. Castro introduced major economic changes in order to survive, but despite these changes, in the fall of 1994 alone, roughly 30,000 fled the island and there were clashes with the police near the Malecón. The government, nevertheless, survived that crisis. The economy grew, and, while Cuban life is still challenging, some degree of normalcy emerged, as hard currency continued to arrive via tourism. More recently, Castro's exit from power and the taking of the reins by Raul, has not led to a collapse of the Castro government and revolution, demonstrating the strength of the state and its economic strategies, like the focus on tourism. On the other hand, tourism has created serious contradictions that have not been ameliorated and threaten to undermine the government's most important national goals—mainly, the preservation of socialism. Continuing inequality, racism, prostitution, and corruption threaten to lessen support for Castro's government and Cuba's ideology. The government has attempted to deal with the contradictions by using tourism as a vehicle for support. But the government's attempts to lasso tourism to highlight the values of the revolution and to foster international support may be nothing more than window dressing when compared with the deleterious effects of tourism on the government, national goals, and socialist ideology.

More broadly, the Cuban case illustrates some of the potential contradictions that can arise in the uneasy marriage between tourism and nation-building for developing nations and socialist nations in transition. While it can certainly contribute to a country's coffers and enhance pride in citizenship, tourism can also fuel or regenerate ethnic divisions, economic inequalities, and corruption, all of which may undermine the authority of the state. Under such a scenario, the Janus-faced character of tourism may well prevent developing states from achieving their nation-building goals. And, nation-states that pursue social justice as one of their chief national goals may want to weigh more carefully the decision to embrace tourism as a vehicle for fueling national development, fostering international sympathy, and building a loyal citizenry.

In the small beach community of Guanabo, in Playas del Este, live Silvio and Nora, brother and sister, both retired. They are Afro-Cubans, octogenarians, and former professionals. Silvio was a musician, son of Aniceto Diaz who introduced the *danzonete* to Cuba's already rich music repertoire. Nora was a black female lawyer in 1950s Havana but suffered a breakdown in the 1990s. They live in their small, run-down home that they won in a newspaper lottery in the mid 1950s, cook their food on a counter-top camping stove, and rely on a dated, rusting refrigerator. Their kitchen is devoid of food and condiments; ironically even the sugar jar is empty. Their pensions from the state are meager and, unlike Cubans with relatives involved in tourism or sending remissions from abroad, Silvio and Nora have no access to hard currency. Consequently, they cannot afford to purchase "luxury" items such as soap, toothpaste, toilet paper, and the like. They are gaunt. Silvio and Nora represent the government's last hope for support. The revolution was made for people like them. If *they* lose faith and confidence in the system, then, with or without tourist capital, the revolution may not outlast Fidel and Raul Castro.

Source: Adapted from "The Janus-faced Character of Tourism in Cuba." *Annals of Tourism Research*, 2008, 35:27–46.

Notes

[1] The research for this article is based on three trips to Cuba, over a span of nine years. Sanchez is Cuban born. He returned to Cuba in 1995 on a short-term group research trip during which he conducted preliminary research on the emerging non-governmental organizations, met with representatives from 14 organizations, and conducted interviews with dozens of Cubans in Havana and Santiago. He returned for additional research in 1996, and again in May 2004, when Sanchez and Adams took 14 students on a Cuba immersion course. On this more recent trip, the authors met with representatives of 19 organizations and government agencies, attended community events, and interviewed workers and managers at hotels and tourist restaurants in a variety of Cuban tourist destinations.

[2] One should note that not only tourist dollars enabled the emergence of this petite bourgeoisie, but also remissions sent by departed family members to kin remaining in Cuba.

[3] Classification of race is different in Cuba and the United States. Many Cubans classifying themselves as white would be perceived as "black" by people in the United States.

[4] Brenner (2004) discusses parallel themes in Haitian and Dominican women's sex tourism work, terming it an "advancement strategy."

References

Adams, K. M. 1998. "Domestic Tourism and Nation-Building in South Sulawesi." *Indonesia and the Malay World* 26(75):77–97.

Allcock, J. B., and P. Przeclawski.1990. "Tourism in Centrally-Planned Economies." *Annals of Tourism Research* 17:3.

Barbassa, J. 2005. "The New Cuban Capitalist," in *Capitalism, God, and a Good Cigar*, ed. Lydia Chavez, pp. 17–30, Durham: Duke University Press.

Brenner, D. 2004. *What's Love Got To Do With It? Transnational Desires and Sex Tourism in the Dominican Republic*. Durham: Duke University Press.

Cabezas, A. 2004. "Between Love and Money: Sex, Tourism, and Citizenship in Cuba and the Dominican Republic." *Signs: Journal of Women in Culture and Society* 29(4):987–1012.

———. 2006. "The Eroticization of Labor in Cuba's All-Inclusive Resorts: Performing Race, Class and Gender in the New Tourist Economy." *Social Identities* 12(5):507–521.

Centro de Promoción de Inversiones. 2005. Oportunidades de Inversión, Turismo, Estructura Sectoral (.zip) <www.cpi-minvec.cu/op-turismo-esp.htm>

Chavez, L. 2005. "Adrift: An Introduction to Contemporary Cuba," in *Capitalism, God, and a Good Cigar*, ed. Lydia Chavez, pp. 1–14, Durham: Duke University Press.

Cuba Solidarity. 2005. Cuba Education Tours <www.cubasolidarity.ca>

Cuba Update. 2005. History and Purpose, Center for Cuban Studies <www.cubaupdate.org/more.htm>

De Holan, P., and N. Phillips. 1997. "Sun, Sand and Hard Currency: Tourism in Cuba." *Annals of Tourism Research* 24:777–795.

De La Fuente, A. 1998 "Recreating Racism: Race and Discrimination in Cuba's 'Special Period.'" *Cuba Briefing Paper Series*, Number 18, July. Georgetown University, Center for Latin American Studies.

Economist. 2004. "Tourists, by the Left," March 372 (July 31):33.

Edwards, J. 2005. "Building the Tourism Mega-Cluster: What Works and What Doesn't. Strategic Considerations of Building a Tourism Mega-Cluster." <http://64.233.167.104/search?q=cache:XYvz6cUo6K8J:www.intracen.org/wedf/ef2005/Tourism_Mega_Cluster_Papers/7Discussion_paper_Jennifer_Edwards.pdf+%22times+the+revenue+of+all+traditional+agricultural+exports%22&hl=en&ct=clnk&cd=1&gl=us>

Enloe, C. 2001. *Bananas, Beaches and Bases: Making Feminist Sense of International Politics*. Berkeley: University of California Press.

FBIS. 1989. "Castro Discusses Tourism with Reporters." *Daily Report*, Report No. LAT-89-186, September 27.

———. 1993. "Castro Holds News Conference on Tourism." *Daily Report*, Report No. LAT-93-109, June 7.

Global Exchange. 2005. *Programs in the Americas: Cuba* <www.globalexchange.org/countries/americas/cuba>

Goodrich, J. 1993. "Socialist Cuba: A Study of Health Tourism." *Journal of Travel Research* 32 (Summer):36–41.

Grogg, P. 2005. "Tourism-Cuba: Record Number of Visitors, Despite Odds." *Inter-Press Service News Agency*, January 18 <www.ipsnews.net/africa/interna.asp?idnews=27080>

Hall, C. M. 1994. *Tourism and Politics: Policy, Power and Place*. New York: John Wiley.

Hall, C. M., and J. Jenkins. 1995. *Tourism and Public Policy*. London: Routledge.

Jackiewicz, E. L. 2002. "'Bowling for Dollars': Economic Conflicts and Challenges in Contemporary Cuba." *Yearbook of the Association of Pacific Coast Geographers*. Honolulu: University of Hawaii Press.

Leong, W.1989. "Culture and the State: Manufacturing Traditions for Tourism." *Cultural Studies in Mass Communication* 6(4):355–375.

Matthews, H. G., and Richter, L. K. 1991. "Political Science and Tourism." *Annals of Tourism Research* 18:120–135.

O'Connell-Davidson, J. 1996 "Sex Tourism in Cuba." *Race and Class* 38 (July):39–48.

Pastor, M., and A. Zimbalist. 1995. "Cuba's Economic Conundrum." *NACLA: Report on the Americas* 29(2):7–12.

Pattullo, P. 1996. *Last Resorts: The Cost of Tourism in the Caribbean*. London: Cassell.

Picard, M., and R. Wood, eds. 1997. *Tourism, Ethnicity and the State in Asian and Pacific Societies*. Honolulu: University of Hawaii Press.

Pizam, A., and Y. Mansfield, eds. 1996. *Tourism, Crime, and International Security Issues*. West Sussex: John Wiley.

Richter, L. 1989 *The Politics of Tourism in Asia*. Honolulu: University of Hawaii Press.

Schwartz, R. 1997. *Pleasure Island: Tourism and Temptation in Cuba*. Lincoln: University of Nebraska Press.

Seaton, A. V. 1999. "Demonstration Effects or Relative Deprivation: The Counter-Revolutionary Pressures of Tourism in Cuba." *Progress in Tourism and Hospitality Research* 3(4):307–320.

Teo, P. et al., eds. 2001. *Interconnected Worlds: Southeast Asia Tourism in the 21st Century.* Cambridge: Pergamon Press.

Trumbull, C. 2001 "Prostitution and Sex Tourism in Cuba." <http://lanic.utexas.edu/project/asce/pdfs/volume11/trumbull2.pdf> (accessed May 20, 2009).

Van den Berghe, P. 1980. "Tourism as Ethnic Relations: A Case Study of Cuzco, Peru." *Ethnic and Racial Studies* 3(4):375–392.

Winson, A. 2006. "Ecotourism and Sustainability in Cuba: Does Socialism Make a Difference?" *Journal of Sustainable Tourism* 14:6–23.

Wood, P. and C. Jayawardena. 2003. "Cuba: Hero of the Caribbean? A Profile of its Tourism Education Strategy." *International Journal of Hospitality Management* 15(3):151–155.

Wood, R. E. 1997 "Tourism and the State: Ethnic Options and Constructions of Otherness," in *Tourism, Ethnicity and the State in Asian and Pacific Societies*, ed. Michel Picard and Robert E. Wood, pp. 1–34. Honolulu: University of Hawaii Press.

Zhang, H., et. al. 1999. "An Analysis of Tourism Policy Development in Modern China." *Tourism Management* 20:471–485.

23

Giving a Grade to Costa Rica's Green Tourism

Martha Honey

Costa Rica is the poster child for ecotourism. This brand of nature-based tourism, which seeks to be low impact and provide tangible benefits for both the environment and host communities, is widely said to be the fastest growing sector of the tourism industry. And tourism, in turn, rivals oil as the world's largest industry. Today, nearly every country in Latin America that is promoting tourism is also promoting some form of ecotourism. In no other country, however, has the experiment with ecotourism been as extensive as in Costa Rica. It seems that every traveler in the United States who is interested in nature has been to, or is heading for, Costa Rica. Costa Rica's ecotourism boom, while largely positive, has not been without a series of problems, conflicts, and conundrums over its direction and its effects.

Beginning in the late 1980s, Costa Rica was transformed from a staging ground for the covert U.S. war against Nicaragua and a testing ground for U.S. free trade and privatization policies into a laboratory for "green" tourism. More than any other event, President Oscar Arias's 1987 receipt of the Nobel Peace Prize for his role as the architect of the Central American Peace Plan propelled Costa Rica onto the world stage, securing its image as a peaceful country and marking the start of the ecotourism boom.

In the 1990s, Costa Rica jumped to the head of the ecotourism queue, surpassing older nature travel destinations such as the Galapagos Islands,

439

Kenya, and Nepal. In 1992, the U.S. Adventure Travel Society dubbed Costa Rica the "number one ecotourism destination in the world." By 1993, tourism had become Costa Rica's number one foreign exchange earner, surpassing coffee and bananas.

As a journalist based in Costa Rica in the 1980s and early 1990s, I witnessed firsthand Costa Rica's transformation from the southern front for the contras into an ecotourism mecca. Costa Rica illustrates that, most fundamentally, tourism can only thrive in an atmosphere of peace. But while regional peace accords and the dismantling of the contras and local CIA operations improved conditions on the ground in Costa Rica, it can be argued that, as a result, the country changed less than did its international image. Arias's Central American Peace Plan helped the world to view Costa Rica through a different lens—in part because once the region's wars ended, journalists began turning their attention to stories about what made Costa Rica unique. The reality was that Costa Rica had the right stuff—the right political, socio-economic, infrastructural, geographic, and natural ingredients—to permit it to successfully ride the crest of the ecotourism wave.

Student tourists walk above the forest canopy across a suspended bridge at Sky Walk Monteverde, Costa Rica. (Photo by R. Hays Cummins)

Costa Rica's main building block for ecotourism has been, as in many other countries, its national park system. Officially created in 1969, the national park system grew rapidly so that by 1990 it included 230 different protected areas with varying restrictions and permitted uses, including tourism. Today, more than 25 percent of Costa Rica's territory is under some form of protection. Worldwide, the average is just 3 percent. Some 13 percent of Costa Rica falls under the rubric of national parks and other strictly protected areas. In recent years, national parks and their surrounding buffer areas have been reorganized into nine regional conservation areas or megaparks. These are complemented by hundreds of private nature reserves; more than 110 of these contain "ecolodges" and/or provide tourism activities such as hiking, bird watching, rainforest canopy walks, and butterfly farms. As Amos Bien, a biologist and founder of Costa Rica's first genuine ecolodge, Rara Avis, writes, "This mosaic of large, pristine national parks with smaller private reserves with visitor facilities provided the fertile ground necessary for ecotourism to be born in Costa Rica."

While the country's name—Rich Coast—comes from Christopher Columbus's mistaken belief when he landed in 1502 that the land was full of precious minerals, in recent decades this misnomer has seemed appropriate as scientists, conservationists, and tourists discovered its vast ecological richness. As part of the narrow isthmus joining North and South America, Costa Rica has flora and fauna from both continents as well as its own endemic species. This West Virginia-sized country boasts more bird species (850) than are found in the United States and Canada combined, more varieties of butterflies than in all of Africa, more than 6,000 kinds of flowering plants (including 1,500 varieties of orchids), and over 35,000 species of insects. Costa Rica's extraordinary natural wonders are encapsulated in the statistic that the country contains 5 percent of the world's biodiversity within just 0.035 percent of the earth's surface. Costa Rica is, as former minister of natural resources Alvaro Umana put it, a biological "superpower."

However, Costa Rica's national parks and biodiversity have been supplemented by other ingredients lacking in many developing countries: its longstanding and well-functioning democracy, its political stability, the abolition of its army in 1948, strong social welfare programs, its respect for human rights, and its (generally) welcoming attitude toward foreigners, particularly the gringo variety. Costa Rica has one of the highest standards of living, the largest middle classes, the best public health care systems, the best public education through the university level, and the highest literacy rates in Latin America. The country has produced an outstanding coterie of scientists and conservationists and has for decades attracted scientists and researchers from around the world. More than a hundred local and international environmental NGOs have branches in the country. Costa Rica is physically compact and easy to get around in, with adequate amounts of paved roads, telephones, and electricity. It has a pleasant climate. And it's just a few hours' flight from the United States. The combination of these qualities made Costa Rica uniquely prepared to rapidly move into ecotourism.

On these stable foundations, Costa Rica's ecotourism industry grew. Until the mid-1980s, Costa Rica's tourism sector was modest, largely locally owned, and geared to domestic and regional visitors. Between the mid-1970s and mid-1990s, the number of foreign visitors nearly doubled and gross receipts grew more than 11-fold. By 2000, Costa Rica, with a population of only four million, was receiving over one million visitors a year. Government exit surveys conducted at the airport showed that about 60 percent of tourists were motivated primarily by ecotourism; another 20 percent reported visiting a national park or ecotourism facility during their stay. The country was earning over $600 million from ecotourism and nature-based attractions.

And, propelled by ecotourism, environmentalism has taken root in the national consciousness just as a tradition of nonmilitarism (not having an army) had done earlier. When my family and I first moved to Costa Rica in 1982, environmentalism was confined to a small cadre of scientists and national park officials. I recall, for instance, that buses in San José carried signs saying something like: "Don't litter. Throw your trash out the window." Today, however, ecotourism has become part of "self-identity," as Chris Wille, an official with the Rainforest Alliance puts it. "Ecotourism has helped create the self-image of Costa Ricans. That's tremendously important. There's a lexicon of environmentalism here, right up to the president."

Three decades ago, "ecotourism" was not part of the lexicon in Costa Rica or anywhere else. The origins of ecotourism can be traced to the late 1970s, when conventional, mass, packaged tourism, epitomized by cruise ships and high-rise beach hotels, came under criticism on a number of fronts. Developing countries that had moved into tourism as a way to earn foreign exchange and reduce poverty, found they were gaining little. Most of the profits, particularly from prepaid packaged tours, never entered the country or "leaked out" as foreign investors repatriated their profits, paid high salaries to expatriate managers, and imported luxury goods, vehicles, and building materials to replicate First-World lifestyles in some of the world's poorest locations. An increasing consolidation within the tourism industry made it easier and more convenient for travelers to pay for nearly everything—airline tickets, hotels, car rental, and sometimes meals—before they left home. The smaller and less industrialized a country, the more foreign exchange had to be expended to meet the demands of the international tourism market. In some cases almost everything used in a tourist facility was purchased overseas. The World Bank estimated that the "leakage" of tourism dollars from developing countries averages 55 percent; other studies found the leakage from some areas could run as high as 80 percent to 90 percent.

Parallel with this was the growing realization of the darker side of mass tourism. While tourism has been popularly portrayed as the benign, "smokeless industry," many countries found that poorly regulated mass tourism brought not only environmental destruction and pollution but also social ills such as prostitution, crime, black marketeering, gambling, drugs and, increasingly, sexually transmitted diseases. In the 1970s, social ills associated with mass tourism helped spur the "responsible tourism" movement, supported by Protestant churches and centered in Thailand, with a focus on countering child prostitution.

Ecotourism also grew up in the womb of the worldwide environmental movement that took off in the 1970s. In Latin America, particularly in the Amazon region, scientists and environmentalists were becoming increasingly alarmed about the rapid destruction of the rainforest through logging, ranching, oil drilling, mining, and human encroachment and settlement. The rise of the environmental movement helped increase public awareness that rainforests are vital as both reservoirs of biological diversity and suppliers of oxygen necessary to maintain a balance in the earth's atmosphere. Gradually, ecotourism, along with various forms of sustainable harvesting of trees and plants, was proposed as alternative economic activities to protect the rainforest.

Parallel with this, there was a growing realization among parks officials, scientists, and community development activists that the concept of park management through cordoning off parks—either literally with fences or figuratively with police forces—and barring access to local people was not working. Seeing no tangible benefits from either parks or nature tourism, angry and hungry rural communities, who had often been forcibly expelled to create the parks, turned to poaching of wildlife, particularly elephant and rhino in Africa. Beginning in the late 1970s and early 1980s, some parks officials, scientists, and community activists began to call for a new approach to give local people tangible benefits from parks. They argued that protected areas and wildlife would only survive if there were harmony, not hostility, between people and parks.

In a groundbreaking 1976 article, Costa Rica–based biologist Gerardo Budowski wrote that the relationship between tourism and conservation can be variously one of conflict, coexistence, or symbiosis, and he went on to outline ways in which tourism can be used to support conservation. The emphasis, described in the prolific writings of Mexican architect and ecotourism expert Hector Ceballos-Lascurain, was that the rainforest could be saved in part through low impact, locally run tourism by turning tourists into environmentalists and by building an activist constituency among the traveling public committed to environmental protection. In the mid-1980s, University of Pennsylvania biologist Daniel Janzen, who has worked for decades in Costa Rica, argued that parks would only survive if there were "happy people" living around them. Janzen put this philosophy in practice in Costa Rica's Guanacaste National Park where, as new cattle lands were incorporated into the park, he invited the cattlemen and their herds to remain inside the park. He proposed turning ranchers into rangers and incorporating them as part of the park staff.

Only with time did these various experiments and intellectual strands come together under the ecotourism label. While definitions vary, the most widely accepted is that first promulgated in 1991 by The International Ecotourism Society (TIES): "Responsible travel to natural areas that conserves the environment and improves the welfare of local people." The core tenet is that, done right, ecotourism can, on balance, be positive in its impacts, i.e., it can provide tangible benefits for both conservation and host communities and it can be educational as well as enjoyable for the traveler. Properly understood, ecotourism is not simply a niche market within the tourism industry but rather a set of principles and practices closely linked to the concept of sustainable development.

Over the years, ecotourism proponents have further expanded the definition arguing, for instance, that the architecture of ecotourism sites should be both low impact ("tread lightly on the earth") and should convey a "sense of place," incorporating local customs, culture, styles, and materials. Others stress that ecotourism must also adhere to international norms and conventions regarding human rights and fair labor standards, as well as respect local democratic social movements. This includes honoring calls for tourism boycotts, such as the African National Congress's call for a boycott of apartheid South Africa in the 1970s and 1980s and, today, the call by Burma's pro-democracy movement for a tourism boycott against the ruling military junta.

During the 1990s, propelled in part by the United Nations' 1992 Earth Summit in Rio de Janeiro and a rapidly growing tourism industry, ecotourism exploded. In 2002, the United Nations declared the "International Year of Ecotourism" and staged the World Ecotourism Summit—a signal that this concept had taken on global significance. The significance of ecotourism can be measured in other ways as well: the expansion of university departments and degrees in eco- and sustainable tourism, the dozens of national ecotourism societies and scores of international meetings dealing with this alternative form of tourism, and the hundreds of millions of dollars flowing from the Inter-American Development Bank and other international aid and lending institutions as well as from environmental NGOs into projects with ecotourism components.

More volume and international recognition, both around the globe and within Costa Rica, has not, however, necessarily meant better quality. While ecotourism is described as "win-win" for the environment and conservation, host communities and developing countries, the traveling public and the travel industry, the reality is more complex. Because definitions and standards have been weak, far too much gets put under the big green tent labeled "ecotourism." Instead, what is currently being served up as ecotourism includes a mixture of three rather distinct phenomena: "greenwashing" scams, ecotourism "lite," and real ecotourism. In Costa Rica all three varieties have taken root, jousting to capture pieces of the tourist market.

Costa Rica's ecotourism panorama is marked by both contradictions and potential. Visitors to Costa Rica find an ecotourism industry full of creativity and experimentation as well as crass opportunism, marketing ploys, and downright scams. Although the image is of a country of small ecolodges and beach cabinas, government investment policies have favored larger and foreign-owned hotels.

Beginning in the mid-1980s, Costa Rica passed legislation providing investment incentives for hotels, air and sea transportation companies, car rental agencies, and tour operators. The Costa Rican Institute for Tourism's (ICT) incentives and tax exemptions favored foreign investors and applied only to facilities with more than twenty rooms. "These restrictions often preclude local people from qualifying for incentives," wrote geographer Carole Hill in 1990. Experts estimated that by the early 1990s, 80 percent of the country's beachfront property had been purchased by foreigners. Between 1990 and 1994, 13 new four- and five-star hotels were built, involving investments of nearly $1 billion. While in the early 1980s there were virtually no foreign-owned hotel chains, by early 2000 many international hotel chains, including Sheraton, Holiday Inn, Hampton, Melia, and Barcelo, had either built or bought hotels in Costa Rica.

Some of these big hotel projects have brazenly sought to put on the "eco" mantle. One of the most controversial projects has been Papagayo, a megaresort along a dry and barren peninsula in Guanacaste province. The original developer was Mexico's Group Situr, which laid out plans for a giant resort complex a la Cancún: vacation homes, condos, shopping centers, golf courses, marinas, and hotels for up to 30,000 rooms—more than twice the total number of rooms in the entire country. Despite much public outcry and charges that public officials were being bribed, the Costa Rican government in 1995 gave a "green" light to this $3 billion project, the largest to date in all of Central America. Situr's first hotel was a stucco complex named Caribbean Village, an incongruous choice since it overlooked the Pacific Ocean. Equally inappropriate was the large sign out front reading Ecodesarrollo Papagayo ("Ecodevelopment Papagayo"). In an interview at the site, Arnoldo Estaril, Situr's infrastructure coordinator, told me that the name was fitting because "we're going to plant trees and do an aviary for birds and a butterfly farm." Environmental activist Leon Gonzalez retorted, "Everybody calls themselves 'eco developments,' but Papagayo is a city!"

Around this same time, another near-city masquerading as ecotourism was slated for development along Playa Grande, an important leatherback turtle nesting beach on the Nicoya Peninsula, also in Guanacaste. I became aware of the project through an article in a 1995 architectural magazine entitled "Green Luxury" which bragged, "ecotourism will meet the high life in a luxury beach resort." The project's architect and main developer, Yves Ghiai, an Iranian based in San Francisco, boasted that "environmental considerations are an integral part of the design" including a system of yellow lights designed not to disturb the leatherbacks as they lay their eggs. "[T]esting found the yellow lights to meet reptilian and human needs alike." Nonsense, scientists later told me in Costa Rica: Any lights on a beach will scare away turtles looking for a nesting area. Nonsense, also, said the project's administrator in Costa Rica who admitted he knew nothing about any of the environmental innovations described in the article—solar panels, electric golf carts, etc. And, he added, the yellow lights were intended to keep away mosquitoes, not protect the turtles. He showed me the plans for the project: an enormous beachfront complex with condos, restaurant, shops, a casino and nightclub, hotel, marina, and yacht club. As ecotourism expert Anne Becher, who helped devise Costa Rica's first eco-rating program, put it, "The only thing green about some of these places is the color of the dollars they are earning." Fortunately, the "Green Luxury" project provoked a public outcry and it was shelved. But struggles to block such developments continue at Playa Grande and elsewhere.

Today, everything in Costa Rica seems to carry "eco" in its name. There is, for instance, "Eco-Playa" (a typical beach indistinguishable from other gray-black sand beaches), "Ecological Rent-a-Car" (which rents the same vehicles as Hertz, Budget, or Avis), "eco-gas" (super unleaded), "eco-musica" (songs with environmental themes), and innumerable ecolodges, ecosafaris, and ecological cruises. Many of these tourism enterprises can be categorized as ecotourism "lite," meaning that the company's green rhetoric far outstrips the reality of its adherence to sound ecotourism principles. The classic example of this in Costa Rica as elsewhere is the growing number of major hotel chains that offer guests the "eco-option" of not having their sheets and towels laundered every day. Such sensible but relatively minor environmental innovations are advertised with claims such as "Keep your towels and help save the world!" The reality is that it is the hotels that are saving sizeable sums on their laundry bills.

Or consider the new Four Seasons Hotel, which is scheduled to open as part of the Papagayo complex in early 2004. Billed on the Four Seasons Web site as bringing "casual luxury and unsurpassed service to this pristine jungle setting," it is actually situated on dry and denuded former cattle grazing land. Although still under construction, it is also being billed to the travel press as ecologically responsible because plans for the golf course include using a special type of grass that can be watered with a combination of sea and recycled wastewaters. However, this all-inclusive resort will bring only modest revenue to Costa Rica, with vacationers paying for their packages overseas and not needing to venture into Costa Rica since everything (except a rain forest!) is available at the resort.

Some smaller lodges, too, have little more than the patina of ecotourism. One of the most notorious examples is Villas del Caribe (this one correctly named for its Caribbean coast location), built by Canadian multimillionaire businessman and U.N. official Maurice Strong, the architect of the U.N.'s 1992 Earth Summit. The Rio Summit was opening just as Strong's company, Desarrollos Ecológicos (Ecological Development), was putting the finishing touches on the $35 million, 12-suite beach resort. While billed as environmentally sensitive for its recycling, composting, and nature walks, one researcher who took a close look concluded that it had "very modest offerings of ecotourism." Even more troubling to local residents and Costa Rican environmentalists, Strong did not have clear title to the land: the luxury hotel was built within the Gandoca-Manzanillo Wildlife Refuge, where development is restricted, and the Kekoldi Indian Reserve, where construction must be approved by the Indian association. It was not, and Costa Rican Indian leaders were livid about Strong: "He's supporting Indians and conservation around the world, and here he's doing the complete opposite," declared Demetrio Mayorga, president of the Kekoldi Indian Association.

Despite many hypes and shams the green brush is dragged over, Costa Rica also contains scores of genuine ecotourism businesses that are working to be low impact, good environmental stewards, socially responsible, culturally respectful, and beneficial to the surrounding communities. Costa Rica's original ecolodge, Rara Avis, was built by Amos Bien, a New York biologist and ecotourism expert who, since his arrival in 1977, has put down deep roots in the country. Beginning in 1983, Bien took out a bank loan and built Rara Avis, a modest lodge on a private reserve, with the intent of demonstrating to area farmers that rainforest left intact could be more profitable than clear-cut land. He also has sought to provide tangible benefits to area residents through employment and profit-sharing, purchasing supplies locally, awarding student scholarships, offering free tours for local school children, and making in-kind donations to the local clinic and schools.

As ecotourism has grown, whole rural communities of Costa Rica—Monteverde, Tortuguero, the Osa Peninsula, to name a few—have been converted into ecotourism centers. They include small-scale lodges situated in or near private or public reserves and offer a variety of nature hikes, white water rafting, and other outdoor activities. Costa Rica has also developed some of the world's best naturalist guides who deftly interpret the ecological, cultural, and political panorama. Many middle- and lower-middle-class Costa Ricans have managed to move into auxiliary businesses associated with ecotourism, including opening tour agencies or restaurants featuring local dishes, renting riding horses, or building butterfly "farms" or a few guest cabinas. While there are shortcomings and conflicts in all these communities, on balance, ecotourism has brought more income to many Costa Ricans, raised environmental awareness, and provided more funds for conservation projects, national parks, and private reserves.

The New Key to Costa Rica, the country's oldest and most respected guidebook, has long specialized in highlighting genuine ecotourism businesses. Most are locally owned or owned by longtime foreign residents, thereby ensuring that most of the profits stay within the country. Beginning in 1992, the guide's authors, Beatrice Blake and Anne Becher, began a pioneering "green-rating" system with the aim of helping to protect high standards within nature-based, small-scale, and often locally owned lodges. With input from other environmentalists, academics, lodge owners, and tour operators, they created an eight-page survey to measure environmental, economic, and sociocultural impacts of accommodations. Based on on-site inspections and interviews with hotel managers, workers, and community representatives, the *New Key* authors began awarding eco-logos—one to three "suns"—to those hotels that passed a certain number of the criteria.

In 1997, Costa Rica's tourism ministry, the ICT, unveiled its own certification program. Like the New Key survey, the ICT's Certification for Sustainable Tourism (CST) program grew out of a mounting concern that the "golden goose" of ecotourism was being killed by mass tourism, greenwashing, and ecotourism "lite." Tourism officials as well as sectors of the tourism industry were worried that, unless the government began setting rigorous standards, Costa Rica would lose its ecotourism edge. According to a 1998 evaluation, many of the 104 hotels that had signed up to be assessed were resentful of other facilities that "also use such terminology but do not really put into practice basic environmental principles or contribute to the quality of life in their communities." From the outset, the CST was designed to take in a broader swath of the market than simply ecotourism. Its principle creator, ICT official Eduardo Lizano, felt strongly that tourism in Costa Rica was moving beyond small ecolodges and that if the country were to remain competitive internationally, the new, lamer, more conventional, and often more luxurious hotels also needed to abide by responsible environmental and social principles.

Unlike the homegrown, low-budget *New Key* survey, the CST program has been backed with political muscle and financial resources. A CST audit includes 153 yes/no questions covering the physical-biological environment, hotel facilities, customer satisfaction, and socioeconomic issues, including respect for the surrounding community and nature. Accommodations voluntarily apply for certification, which includes an on-site audit by a team of experts. The first round of audits is free. Certified facilities are awarded logos—one to five leaves—by a seven-member National Accreditation Commission. Although several hundred hotels have applied for certification, political infighting within ICT slowed the process so only 59 hotels so far have been certified. Of these only five have been awarded four leaves; none have yet achieved a top score of five leaves.

In 2002, tourism ministers from the other Central American countries officially accepted CST as the model to be used throughout the isthmus, and currently a number of South American governments, including Brazil, Ecuador, Peru, and Chile are creating certification programs modeled along the lines of the CST. It has also been welcomed by many within Costa Rica: former Costa Rican President Rodrigo Carazo, whose ecolodge in a private reserve features traditional Costa Rican architecture and art, said, "I never thought they could do what they are doing. Tourism ministers always think in terms of number of hotel rooms. When they began to talk about paying attention to the environment, I thought they were going to be rejected by the hotels. But this did not happen and CST is growing bigger and stronger." Even the Four Seasons Papagayo project is being forced to build with an eye on the CST program and incorporate some showcase eco-reforms so that it might be able to get certified.

Despite these obvious successes, there have been problems. In addition to bureaucratic haggling, the CST is poorly marketed, leading some hotels to wonder if it's worth the effort. The CST is, however, working to develop and expand the program to include tours and guides. Finally, there is a longer term and very sensible plan to move CST outside the tourism ministry and set it up as either an NGO or a for-profit entity.

Despite Costa Rica's international reputation, some recent studies are indicating that ecotourism so far has fulfilled only partially its objectives of providing significant resources for national conservation efforts and benefits to local communities. A recent study around the Corcovado National Park by Caroline Stem and a team of Cornell University professors reported "mixed" findings "regarding ecotourism's effectiveness as a conservation and community development tool." The study, to be published in the *Journal of Sustainable Tourism*, concluded that "ecotourism would be most effective as a component of a broader conservation strategy," i.e., if there was stronger and clearer national planning and policies.

When stacked against other land-based, foreign-exchange-generating activities such as cattle ranching, banana growing, and logging, Costa Rica's ecotourism industry does appear more economically and environmentally viable than the others. During the first half of the 1990s, tourism grew at 17 percent per year. While this has slowed considerably due to a combination of internal and external factors, the future still looks relatively bright. Projects such as Papagayo, however, raise the wider question of whether tiny Costa Rica can afford, in the long run, to have it both ways: to promote itself as a leading ecotourism/nature tourism destination sprinkled with small-scale rainforest lodges and beach front cabinas, along with dozens of hotel chains and a growing number of megaresorts catering to mass tourism. In the long run, many Costa Ricans fear, the country's unique ecotourism image will be lost, with other countries, particularly Belize, taking on the ecotourism mantle. The move toward creating a strong certification model is important, but certification is only one tool. The government also needs to work to bring its regulations and legislation into line with its country's international reputation and its innate strengths. Ecotourism, not mass or conventional tourism, is most in keeping with Costa Rica's geographical size, its extraordinary biodiversity, and its political and social history.

Source: From "Giving a Grade to Costa Rica's Green Tourism," *NACLA Report on the Americas*, 2003, 36(6):39–46. Reprinted with permission of the author and the North American Congress on Latin America.

24

Power Disparities and Community-Based Tourism in Vietnam

Melissa Stevens

Counterpart International is one of many international nongovernmental organizations (INGOs) now partnering with local communities and organizations to implement sustainable development projects. Its mission statement captures the central goal of the more neopopulist[1] of these organizations: "Giving people a voice in their own future through smart partnerships offering options and access to tools for sustained social, economic, and environmental development" (Counterpart International 2007). Even a seemingly straightforward and positive mission statement like this, however, can become complicated and confused when applied on the ground, unless the project is designed in a way that addresses the inherent power differentials that exist between stakeholders. It takes careful planning and considerable effort to ensure that all voices, including those of vulnerable populations, are heard during the planning process. This paper examines how Counterpart International and its local Vietnamese partners approached the issue of power disparities when planning a community-based tourism project. It also points to ways INGOs can work toward their boarder development goals of inclusion and empowerment even before a project has been fully implemented.

Background

Power Disparities in Community-based Tourism

The World Tourism Organization defines sustainable tourism as that which "meets the needs of present tourists and host regions while protecting and enhancing opportunity for the future" (UNWTO 1996). Community-based tourism is a form of sustainable tourism that is usually understood to be small-scale, destination-focused tourism in which the community has primary control over decision making and profits (Timothy and Tosun 2003, Drake 1991).

Most community-based tourism projects involve partnerships between destination communities and international nongovernment organizations. The role of the INGO is usually that of a consultant and facilitator that provides local people with information, skills training, networking opportunities, and start-up capital with the ultimate goal of community empowerment. Scheyvens (2003) has identified four dimensions of community empowerment: economic, social, psychological, and political. A successful community-based tourism project should encompass all four. It should generate income and employment for local people; strengthen community cohesion by providing funds for social development; foster community optimism, confidence, and self-worth; and give local people a stronger political voice and more control over resources. However, the achievement of these goals depends on many factors. One of the most important, and the one this paper focuses on, is making sure that all stakeholders, including subgroups within a local community, have a voice in project planning and decision making.

The principles of "participation" and "inclusion" inherent in the *concept* of community-based tourism are not necessarily inherent in all community-based tourism *projects*. However noble the intentions of those involved, projects are implemented within existing and deeply entrenched power structures—between international and local partners as well as among local actors. Consequently, community-based tourism has the potential to exacerbate and perpetuate inequalities rather than minimize them and foster benefit sharing (Cater 2006). The INGO is usually one of the most powerful or influential players in community-based tourism projects; few local participants can match it, either economically or politically. On many occasions, the power disparities between INGOs and local communities are perpetuated by the community itself. Hierarchies established between "First World" and "Third World" nations historically through colonialism and currently through neocolonialist[2] development and trade practices have conditioned communities in developing countries to take a passive role in planning and development while depending on the INGO to actively lead (Stronza 1999). Furthermore, when INGOs initiate a community-based tourism project, they usually do so through established channels of power. Often they are legally unable to access a community except through these channels. As a result, they form their initial partnerships with the political elite rather than with the more marginalized populations who are the real target of their development plans.

Other power disparities occur at the local level. Even within small communities internal power hierarchies exist, usually based on gender, class, or economic standing. Generally, traditionally powerful actors will automatically assume a disproportionate role in decision making and in defining project goals, while the less powerful and more vulnerable will become involved on a lesser level, if at all. The risk is also that marginal individuals or groups within a local population will not benefit from a community-based tourism project, yet they will be burdened with its costs (Chambers 2010). For example, people from wealthy households—larger homes with better amenities—are more likely than people from poorer households to become home-stay or guesthouse operators. Consequently, they will benefit economically from tourism, while poorer households in the community will be affected only by its costs, including increased prices for essential goods and loss of privacy. Such inherent inequalities exist even before an INGO appears on the scene and cannot be ignored if a community-based tourism project is to be truly inclusive. As Hall (2003) has pointed out, the interests of the "powerful" are inevitably better represented than those of the vulnerable.

Deconstructing the Concepts of Community-based Tourism

Concepts central to the goals of community-based tourism development, such as "sustainability," "community," "inclusion," and "participation," are socially constructed, which means that each stakeholder group, including the INGO, tends to define them based on its own experience and interests. Whose definition is used to establish project goals depends largely on whose "voice" is strongest, and marginal members of the community often lose out unless the partnering organizations who are implementing the project actively seek their participation.

"Sustainability" is usually defined broadly, leaving plenty of room for interpretation and misunderstanding. Butcher has concluded that those using the concept "are usually asserting a distinctive position rather than a universally agreed viewpoint" (2007:2). Likewise, Mowforth and Munt assert that "there is no agreement over the exact nature, content and meaning of sustainability. It is a contested concept in all senses of the word. Different interests—supranational and transnational organizations, INGOs, socio-environmental organizations, social classes and so on—have adopted and defend their own language (discourse) of sustainability" (1998:40). Cater has pointed out that there are important political implications in considering, "Who defines what sustainability is? How is it to be achieved? And who has ownership of its representation and meaning?" (2006:24).

Any community-based tourism project must also address what is meant by the term "community." How this concept is operationally defined will determine who participates and who benefits from a project. Usually, "community" is spoken of as if it were an objective entity. In reality, its conceptualization is subjective and culturally constructed. It is usually defined by a project's initiators and therefore may bear little relationship to local conceptions or structures. Unfortunately, INGO staff members seldom view themselves as culturally shaped stakeholders (or as having a vested interest in ensuring a specific project outcome). Project goals and the strategies used to achieve them typically are informed by one set of ideologies—those of the INGOs—even though the projects themselves are implemented in a different cultural context. Even when local people take on leadership roles, "the power of Western ideology may still hold sway under the guise of 'conventional' wisdom adopted by professionals worldwide" (Cater 2006:28). For example, in 1980 the conservation organizations WWF and the International Union for the Conservation of Nature and Natural Resources (IUCN), and the United Nations jointed authored *The World Conservation Strategy*, one of the first supranationally authored documents developed to arrive at strategies for sustainable development (IUCN, UNEP, and WWF 1980; Butcher 2007). Its strategies were often misapplied in cases where locally developed solutions would have been better. All too often, notes Cater (2006), INGOs regard such strategies as "universal templates" to apply to any project development and make only minor adjustments to fit the local situation.

The merits of community involvement are seldom debated in sustainable tourism projects; local participation is assumed to be desirable. What is questioned, however, is *how* local populations should be involved and *if* their "involvement" means "control" (Mowforth and Munt 1998:103). Full community participation has both advantages and disadvantages, and the appropriate level and method of local participation should be determined early in a project (Drake 1991). Using terminology coined by Pretty, community participation ranges from "manipulative participation," in which local involvement is largely a pretense, to "self-mobilization," in which the community independently takes the initiative and decides how it will incorporate INGO assistance (cited in Mowforth and Munt 1998:241). In most cases, however, control lies with donors, and it is their interests that shape project agendas since local communities usually must rely on outside funding solicited by an INGO. As Butcher points out, when "communities are invited to participate, it is usually only in the implementation of ecotourism projects, rather than in shaping the development agenda behind them, and hence real choices may be narrowly defined" (2007:62). Mac Chapin (2004) created a controversy in the conservation world when he scathingly accused large conservation INGOs of neglecting their target populations in favor of their donors' interests by promoting cost effective, large-scale approaches to development. As Mowforth and Munt point out, when outsiders tell locals how to solve their problems it can also be "pretentious and patronizing" and "suggestive of neo-colonial attitudes" (1998:246).

Scholarly discussions of the actual power relationships between INGOs and local communities in development projects have often painted a picture that is antithetical to the mission statements of the INGOs under study

(Butcher 2007; Cater 2006; Mowforth and Munt 1998). Such critiques are necessary if we are to improve our methods and approaches. So far, however, it seems that little attempt has been made to use these critiques to examine how well INGOs succeed in adapting their development strategies to the local culture and circumstances. I hope to open further dialogue along this vein with the following case study from Vietnam.

Community-Based Tourism in Quang Binh Province, Vietnam

I identify myself as a cautious advocate of community-based tourism. Such projects have the potential to provide income assistance, to encourage positive multicultural exchange, to promote conservation initiatives, and to empower communities. Yet, I am cautious because of the complexity of the issues involved. Community-based tourism is not a panacea for the ills of a destination community, nor is it an easy way to accomplish development goals. Many factors, some of which are unique to an individual destination, need to be considered when attempting to determine a project's feasibility and how community-based tourism planning and development should proceed (Stronza 2001).

Phong Nha-Ke Bang (PNKB) National Park is located in Quang Binh Province, in central Vietnam. In 2003, it received UNESCO World Heritage status due to the impressive record of the earth's geologic history found in the park's limestone caves and karst formations. Most of the area's 52,000 inhabitants are of the Kinh ethnicity, Vietnam's majority population, and practice subsistence agriculture. They live in the park's buffer zone, an area encompassing about 755 square miles. This population is growing rapidly, however, and "poverty is widespread, with many people dependent upon the exploitation of forest products as part of their livelihoods" (UNEP and WCMC 2003[2001]). Presently, many area residents illegally remove timber from the park's forests and also hunt wild game there, which they sell to restaurants. Both practices are dangerous and unsustainable. Counterpart International, the INGO I worked with, together with its local partners, is working to develop community-based tourism businesses in this buffer zone. Tourism businesses, it is hoped, will provide an alternative and environmentally sustainable source of income, replacing these forest extraction practices and supplementing the income that families produce through traditional agriculture. The project is also meant to further the broader goals of biodiversity conservation and community development (Counterpart International Vietnam 2007).

Counterpart has been working with local authorities in the national park's buffer zone communities since 2004, focusing on three areas: sustainable agriculture (establishing "forest gardens"), health (awareness building and training), and micro-finance (supporting green businesses). The latter

A tourist boat near the entrance of Phong Nha Cave in Phong Nha-Ke Bang National Park. (Photo by Melissa Stevens)

includes community-based tourism. One of Counterpart's local partners is the Quang Binh Women's Union, which is a chapter of Vietnam's Women's Union, a national organization with the mandate to ensure that Vietnamese women have a voice in local and national politics (Vietnam Women's Union 2005). The Quang Binh Women's Union is promoting sustainable development and conservation projects, and as a result of its partnership with Counterpart, a "Green Future Fund" has been created to provide micro-enterprise training and development among its members in three communes.[3]

In discussing ideas for a new development project, the Women's Union expressed an interest in tourism in order to benefit from the proximity of Phong Nha-Ke Bang National Park. The park currently attracts a modest number of domestic tourists and fewer international tourists, but visitor numbers have been increasing annually since 1990. The Vietnam National Administration of Tourism promotes the park as an international tourist destination; and national park officials, private investors, and other local and international organizations are working to develop projects that will expand tourism offerings (UNEP and WCMC 2003[2001]). A commercial airport linking Quang Binh Province with other national airports in Vietnam opened in 2008. At the time of the community-based tourism project's initiation, however, the park provided a limited number of jobs, most of which employed local people as boat operators, photographers, and concession stand vendors.

Counterpart suggested using a community-based tourism model, and in 2007 it commissioned a third party to conduct a feasibility study. This study found that there was wide support for tourism development both within the proposed destination communities in the park's buffer zone and from Western tourists visiting other areas of Vietnam (Counterpart International Vietnam 2007; Ellman 2007). The Quang Binh Province People's Committee also expressed its wish to engage in "rapid yet sustainable" economic development in the province, with tourism development as one of its mainstays. Given all these developments, it was considered an opportune time for local communities to become involved in community-based tourism development.

Counterpart International has implemented community-based tourism projects in other countries, but its Vietnamese arm had never before been directly involved in tourism planning or development. To explore what methods and tools it might use, Counterpart Vietnam turned to the Netherlands Development Organization (SNV), an INGO with similar neopopulist ideals. SNV had been instrumental in introducing the concept of community-based tourism in Vietnam and regards resident "ownership" as the ultimate goal of community-based tourism projects. It also stresses the importance of establishing a definition of "community" that is accepted by all residents and of setting up representative organizations that are built and accepted by all stakeholders (Butcher 2007).

I worked on the Quang Binh community-based tourism project as a temporary consultant for Counterpart and as an anthropologist knowledgeable about community-based tourism. (At times, I also provided a Western tourist's point of view.) My direct involvement occurred during the summers of 2007 and 2008, in the project's initial stages when its goals and agenda were being formulated but before most implementation had taken place. My roles were to conduct background research that would contribute to the project's design, to initiate dialogue with community members, and to build community consensus. As Counterpart's community-based tourism "expert," I was responsible for demystifying the concept of "community-based tourism" and for explaining its principles to local stakeholders. To prepare for this task, I reviewed other community-based tourism projects in Vietnam and interviewed local and regional officials to determine their level of support and to learn about the country's current tourism development policies. I also interviewed community representatives to assess their knowledge of tourism, and conducted participant observation within the park's buffer zone villages and with Western tourists.

After this preliminary research was completed, a group study tour of community-based tourism projects in Sa Pa and Mai Chau in northern Vietnam was organized in order to learn firsthand about the experiences of other community home-stay operators. Counterpart staff, including myself, and four representatives from two of Quang Binh's communes (the chair of a commune farmers' association, the chair of a commune people's committee, and two chairs of village people's committees) participated in the study tour and in our informal group analysis of what we had learned.

In Quang Binh, I also conducted household interviews with villagers to promote the participation and inclusion of local residents who did not hold official positions of power. These interviews focused on villagers' assessments of local needs and assets, their knowledge of and attitudes toward tourism, and the rewards they hoped that community-based tourism development would bring. Residents hoped to increase their household's income, to spend more time at home, to pay for their children's education, to bring international attention to their struggles, and to learn more about the rest of the world. These goals differed from those of other stakeholders in the project, although there was overlap. Counterpart's goals, for example, were to increase local household incomes but also to increase community participation in local planning processes and to reduce household dependence on the forest as an income source. The primary goals of government officials were economic development and heightening Quang Binh Province's visibility at the national level. Tourists represent one powerful stakeholder group that was not directly involved in Quang Binh's planning process, although interviews with Western tourists in other areas of Vietnam had revealed that they were interested in community-based tourism, especially if it allowed them to learn more about the lives of rural Vietnamese, participate in adventures such as kayaking and biking, view natural areas, and learn traditional skills such as cooking and rice-wine brewing.

Two boys carry loads of lumber on their bikes outside Phong Nha-Ke Bang National Park. (Photo by Melissa Stevens)

One fact my interviews also revealed was that community members needed and wanted more information on what community-based tourism meant. Most villagers had limited or no experience with tourists; to them the concept of community-based tourism was new and abstract. To build a unified understanding of the concepts of sustainable tourism and community-based tourism and how their principles could be translated into businesses, Counterpart organized an all-day workshop. Representatives of all three of the involved communes, including members of the Women's Union, attended the workshop. Counterpart staff, myself included, national park staff, and study tour team members, all made presentations that were followed by a question-and-answer session.

A second objective of the workshop was to have local people identify potential community-based tourism attractions and activities such as bird watching, trekking to a waterfall, and brewing rice wine. This was accomplished using a free-listing exercise in which all village attendees participated. Once people's ideas had been solicited, the identified activities were ranked according to desirability principles that had been established earlier in the workshop. These principles were ease of development; market potential; profitability; shared community benefit; environmental impact; and existing assets, resources, and skills. These were applied to each suggested attraction or activity during group discussions. Then representatives from each of the three communes presented their final ratings of potential tourism sites and activities within their commune to the entire group.

Since the time of my direct involvement and research, the project has produced a pilot home-stay operation in the village of Chay Lap with plans to extend home-stay offerings and provide biking, kayaking, and trekking services. The current home-stay provides lodging in a traditional Kinh wooden house on one family's farm in the village. Other households in the community provide locally farmed ingredients and meals that show off the regional fare. These services are co-managed by the newly formed Chay Lap Village Tourism Management Board and the Phuc Trach Commune and Bo Trach District People's Committees, with the assistance of Counterpart International.

Addressing the Problem of Power Disparities

The development of this community-based tourism project is an ongoing and evolving process. Counterpart prides itself on being a locally inclusive organization that focuses on building partnerships rather than simply providing aid to communities in need. The organization's Vietnam offices are primarily staffed with Vietnamese nationals, and most people in its provincial office, located in Dong Hoi City, come from Quang Binh Province. Staff members have worked hard to develop good rapport and a positive working relationship with their local partner, the Quang Binh Women's Union. They also have acquired an in-depth knowledge of local community assets and needs. Throughout the planning process, Counterpart relied on local knowledge and local definitions of strengths and needs. Nevertheless, as pointed out earlier, inherent power disparities between different stakeholder groups inevitably exist.

For Counterpart to operate legally as an INGO in Vietnam it has to respect and utilize established systems of governance. Project planning had to begin from the top down. Counterpart's consensus-building strategy was to first seek the participation of provincial authorities and work through the power structure, building understanding and initiating dialogue in a politically sensitive manner. Then it worked to consider fully the needs and goals of every stakeholder group so that all could be represented in its project implementation plan. A variety of stakeholder groups were identified. These included the government, from provincial to commune level, since official permission was needed to develop tourist businesses. Other stakeholders included Counterpart's own staff, the Quang Binh Women's Union, Phong Nha-Ke Bang park officials, villagers living within the park's buffer zone, and future tourists. As the planning process progressed, residents of neighboring villages were also defined as stakeholders since they, too, would be affected by any community-based tourism development in the area.

To address the uneven balance of power among these various stakeholders, Counterpart explicitly sought the opinions of vulnerable populations, namely, villagers and Women's Union members. It used an established system of village governance—the village meeting—to do this, which proved effective since it utilizes egalitarian decision-making methods. Village meetings are a locally respected and well-utilized arena for sharing information and building consensus. Meetings are called well in advance using loudspeakers that can be heard throughout the village. Counterpart used these meetings to discuss the project, to field questions, and to receive feedback from residents. Of course, there are flaws in any method of participation. Even though village meeting halls are centrally located, older and infirm residents may be unable to travel to them. While meeting times are meant to be convenient for most residents, some people will always have to be absent. Additionally, not all attendees may feel comfortable speaking candidly in a public setting. Meeting organizers—village leaders and Counterpart staff—nevertheless attempted to make the meetings as inclusive as possible. I also made myself available for individual discussions afterward.

Even though the concept of community-based tourism was introduced from the outside, by Counterpart, the operational definitions of "community" and "participation" were derived from residents' own usage as revealed during interviews. As the primary interviewer, I focused on how residents viewed other groups in relation to themselves and at how they self-identified as "community" members. One result of these interviews, as mentioned, was that previously excluded surrounding villages were added as stakeholders. "Participation" was defined on the basis of how interviewees said they wished to become involved in the project. Most people expressed a desire to be actively engaged in the planning process through contributing ideas and by voting on decisions.

The all-day workshop described earlier was important in encouraging community participation. Most stakeholder groups were represented at the workshop, and everyone was given the opportunity to present information and to engage in the question-and-answer session or otherwise contribute their ideas and opinions. Participants from the study tour to community-based tourism projects in northern Vietnam reported on the results of their interviews at this time and reflected on their own experiences as "tourists." During the workshop, it emerged that many people feared that the project might never come to fruition. Other studies had previously examined the tourism potential of the park and surrounding areas, yet had yielded little. Counterpart staff used this opportunity to stress that community-based tourism projects rely on contributions and input from all stakeholders to succeed. Participation is a process and "ownership" of the project will not be established quickly, but ultimately, Counterpart would like to see local people take full control of their tourism businesses.

A difficult objective in all community-based tourism planning is balancing the desires and needs of tourists with those of local residents. Most large-scale tourism developments around the world focus on the interests of tourists and all but ignore local residents, sometimes forcibly removing them from their homes in the interest of tourism development. Community-based tourism development, in contrast, attempts to benefit the local population while still attracting and meeting the needs of tourists. It goes without saying that in order for the Quang Binh Province tourism initiative to be economically viable, its tourism offerings must be attractive to tourists. Fortunately, many of the amenities tourists want match those desired by local people, such as the desire of both to have accessible roads and sanitary waste management. When desires conflict, creative solutions are called for. The traditional Kinh "Five Dragon" wooden house is aesthetically pleasing to Western tourists, reinforcing their romantic notions of "authentic" culture. But these houses are not practical for rural residents today, especially in the rainy season. One of the most frequently articulated needs that emerged during household interviews was the desire for a new concrete house. These large structures are much easier to maintain but not very attractive to tourists. The head of Counterpart's Vietnamese office suggested using the traditional compound structure of the Vietnamese Kinh household as a model and constructing a traditionally-styled "Five Dragon" guesthouse along side the family's own house that could be a modern concrete structure if the family so desired. This solution also addressed the desire of future home-stay operators to maintain a separation between family and guest areas.

Conclusion

Despite the fact that community participation and inclusion are central goals of any community-based tourism development model, power disparities exist, both between the INGO and the community and within the community itself. These affect how much different segments of the community will participate in the formation of goals and in defining responsibilities. Finding ways to include a community's less powerful and more vulnerable populations in the decision-making process is complicated but not impossible.

To begin with, INGOs must recognize that they come to the table with a disproportionate amount of power and that they are the creators of strategic concepts like "sustainability" and "community," the meanings of which local people may only partly understand or share. As this case study illustrates, however, many INGOs are aware of the local power structure and of their own position and have developed methods to address the power disparities that exist and to promote the inclusion of vulnerable populations so that the final community-based tourism project is truly community owned and controlled. Having said this, more analysis is needed of INGO methods and of the insights offered by critics in order to increase the effectiveness and the success of community-based tourism projects.

Anthropologists are often called on to be cultural brokers and interpreters as well as advocates for vulnerable populations. Anthropological methods are designed to seek out the emic voice that is often missing during the formation of goals in development projects controlled by outside agencies. Without wanting to step fully into a postmodern critique of the role of an anthropologist in such projects, the anthropologist is also a stakeholder in such enterprises and part of the power structure. Anthropologists bring a perspective affected by their own cultural ideologies and biases, and they usually have research agendas and hopes of "discovering" something significant and worthy of publication. They are not immune to acting on their own interests over those of the target population, and may do so without realization. To guard against this, I reiterate MacCannell's appeal for self-examination and explicit acknowledgement of personal biases and ideological premises in order to maintain transparency in an ethical manner when working with both INGOs and destination communities.

Source: Written expressly for *Tourists and Tourism*.

Notes

[1] Neopopulism emphasizes "the *local*, the *community* and their *control* over their own distinct development in the face of the market, state and supranational bodies," with a specific focus on "participation and on 'bottom up' planning" (Butcher 2007:32).

[2] Neocolonialism refers to the ways in which economically powerful states continue to exert economic control over other states through indirect means including trade policies.

3 Vietnam has several levels of regional governance. Provinces (similar to states in the United States) contain several districts that, in turn, contain several communes. Communes contain several villages, towns, or cities. Each level has its own governing body called a People's Committee, which is headed by a chairperson. The pilot community-based tourism project described in this paper is located in Chay Lap Village, in Phuc Trach Commune, in Bo Trach District, which is in Quang Binh Province.

References

Butcher, Jim. 2007. *Ecotourism, NGOs and Development*. London: Routledge.

Cater, Erlet. 2006. "Ecotourism as a Western Construct." *Journal of Ecotourism* 5(1&2):23–39.

Chambers, Erve. 2010. *Native Tours: The Anthropology of Travel and Tourism*, 2nd ed. Long Grove, IL: Waveland Press.

Chapin, Mac. 2004. "A Challenge to Conservationists." *World Watch* 17(6):17–31.

Counterpart International. 2007. Counterpart Mission Statement. Electronic document, http://www.counterpart.org/Default.aspx?tabid=327 (accessed November 28, 2007).

Counterpart International Vietnam. 2007. *Developing Community-Based Tourism Initiative in the Bufferzone of Phong Nha-Ke Bang National Park, Quang Binh Province, Central Vietnam. Terms of reference*. Dong Hoi, Vietnam: Counterpart International Vietnam.

Drake, Susan P. 1991. "Local Participation in Ecotourism Projects," in *Nature Tourism*, ed. Tensie Whelan, pp. 132–163. Washington, DC: Island Press.

Ellman, Eric. 2007. *Life in the Bufferzone: Can "Cultural/Heritage Tourism" Rescue Nature in Vietnam?* Rapid Appraisal Report. Dong Hoi, Vietnam: Counterpart International Vietnam.

Hall, C. Michael. 2003. "Politics and Place: An Analysis of Power in Tourism Communities," in *Tourism in Destination Communities,* ed. Shalini Singh, Dallen J. Timothy, and Ross K. Dowling, pp. 99–113. Oxon, UK: CABI Publishing.

IUCN, UNEP and WWF. 1980. *World Conservation Strategy: Living Resource Conservation for Sustainable Development*. Gland: International Union for the Conservation of Nature.

MacCannell, Dean. 1992. *Empty Meeting Grounds: The Tourist Papers*. London: Routledge.

Mowforth, Martin and Ian Munt. 1998. *Tourism and Sustainability: New Tourism in the Third World*. London: Routledge.

Scheyvens, Regina. 2003. "Local Involvement in Managing Tourism" *In Tourism in Destination Communities,* ed. Shalini Singh, Dallen J. Timothy, and Ross K. Dowling, pp. 229–252. Oxon, UK: CABI Publishing.

Stronza, Amanda. 1999. "Learning Both Ways: Lessons From a Corporate and Community Ecotourism Collaboration." *Cultural Survival Quarterly* 23(2):36–39.

———. 2001. "Anthropology of Tourism: Forging New Ground for Ecotourism and Other Alternatives." *Annual Review of Anthropology* 30:261–283.

Timothy, Dallen J., and Cevat Tosun. 2003. "Appropriate Planning for Tourism in Destination Communities: Participation, Incremental Growth and Collaboration," in *Tourism in Destination Communities,* ed. Shalini Singh, Dallen J. Timothy, and Ross K. Dowling, pp. 181–204. Oxon, UK: CABI Publishing.

UNEP and WCMC. 2003[2001]. Protected Areas and World Heritage: Phong Nha-Ke Bang National Park. Electronic document, http://www.unep-wcmc.org/sites/wh/Phong_nha.html (accessed April 25, 2007).

Vietnam Women's Union. 2005. Basic Information of Vietnam Women's Union. Electronic document, http://hoilhpn.org.vn/newsdetail.asp?CatId=66&NewsId=819&lang=EN (accessed November 30, 2007).

UNWTO. 1996. *Agenda 21 for the Travel and Tourism Industry: Towards Environmentally Sustainable Development*. Madrid: World Tourism Organization.

25

Rethinking Tourism

Deborah McLaren

"Welcome to Paradise . . . before it's gone" is macabre. Do we really want to destroy paradise, make it go? Current high-consumption forms of tourism are *not* sustainable. Realistic information must be made easily available. As we travel, we need to ask ourselves, "Why am I traveling? How can I help change the destructive aspects of the travel industry?"

I asked these questions of several responsible tourism advocates. Virginia Hadsell, founder of the Center for Responsible Tourism, told me that despite the efforts of the worldwide responsible tourism movement that began to emerge in the 1970s, the negative impact of irresponsible tourism has increased. She sees some hopeful signs, however, as the issue of irresponsible tourism is being placed on the agenda in many parts of the world. Increasingly, from many quarters, the rights of indigenous peoples, concern for the deteriorating environment, the homogenization of cultures, and the rights of women and children are being addressed—and often connected with the tourism industry.

Over the past few decades, the world has truly shrunk, in a large part because of tourism. As citizens of the global North, we can fly to Rio de Janeiro tomorrow and float down the Amazon the day after. Our ability to see the world close up has made us more concerned about international problems. News about environmental threats to the rain forests, the plight of the people who live there, human rights abuses around the world, and the increasing poverty and economic gaps between citizens reach us speedily each day.

Issues like the uncontrolled power of corporations and the destruction of the planet have become central in many of our lives. Yet in some ways the rapid rate at which information is being thrown at us makes it almost too much to comprehend. We feel overwhelmed, sometimes jaded, by the surplus of information. We see the problems but remain unsure how to effect change.

Numerous "alternative" types of tourism are evolving, and the real danger is that travelers will simply consume these new products, places, and peoples without recognizing the urgent need for a critical reevaluation of global tourism and their participation in it. To rethink tourism is to challenge the travel industry at every level, including the booming new forms of travel, which, even if well intended, have many of the same detrimental effects as conventional tourism. Olivier Pouillon, a tourism activist who works in Indonesia, warns, "Stop looking for alternatives or technical solutions to tourism. When you scream ecotourism, agritourism, and alternative tourism, it makes people forget to look at what is wrong with tourism." Tourism scholar and activist Shelley Attix asks,

> Why are we "activists" afraid of the "t" word? Tourism industry people aren't. If we are concerned about what tourism is doing and come from different backgrounds—business, indigenous sovereignty, environmental—then we should talk instead of waiting until there is a crisis. It is very difficult, except in strategic boycott situations, to shut down tourism. We have to keep alliances strong and prepare for transitional efforts. We need to train young people to be managers and handle policy decisions during these transitions from mass tourism. We have to make plans in terms of finances and management skills to take over the helm and make big changes. We're making the "t" word so bad that no one wants to talk about it, and that's counterproductive.

The remedy is within tourism itself. To counter tourism's economic, social, and environmental devastation, we must learn to recognize corporate tourism's messages and methods. Tourism has provided us with fantasies. At the same time, it provides potentially free public relations that may help to encourage rethinking of the industry and create alternatives. Tourism provides people-to-people contacts and an opportunity to utilize the ability to communicate with one another, to meet, and to organize. On a global level, this can help foster an appreciation for rich human, cultural, and ecological diversity and can cultivate a mutual trust and respect for one another and for the dignity of the natural world.

You and I are tourists, even if we are traveling to learn about or change the world. Unless we are willing to stay at home, reject the transportation systems, communication lines, and technologies and the tremendous amount of resources that we consume each time we travel, we need to understand not only our participation in the promotion of the global tourism industry but also its importance and potential as a tool for change. Tourism can raise awareness of and action for the global nature of problems like poverty, pollution, and cultural erosion. Close human relationships and activities liberated from preoccupations with profits and bottom lines are crucial to this awareness. In the past three decades, there has been a return to social responsibility and social idealism. This value shift is reflected to a small degree in the tourism industry (in the tourism-for-peace movement, for example) in the consciousness of the cross-cultural impact a travel experience has for both a visitor and the communities visited. The trend in travel is for more tourists and locals in alliance with schools, NGOs, religious groups, the media, cities, and governments to work to stop the paving of paradise.

So where do we start? With ourselves. We can read, learn, make personal changes, be more involved in our own communities, pressure governments and corporations, denounce exploitation, change policies, and investigate the global forces transforming our lives. We can discuss, educate, and organize. I believe that most tourists understand that there are many things wrong with tourism. What we need is a clear outline for change.

The first requirement is for more tourism research and analysis. This can occur as activism goes forward. Travelers from the global North can link with people in other places to make progress on issues that concern us all. By building on experiences and developing relationships and networks, we can challenge international trade and tourism policies, misinformation produced by the travel industry, and exploitative practices. We can make sure that monies from tourism go to the local economy.

Many developing countries are on the brink of abandoning traditional organic practices and moving toward more capital-intensive methods of development. The responsible tourism movement can draw attention to development policies that are undemocratic and promote reliance on the global economy as opposed to local resources. In many places around the world people are building sustainable communities that focus on the well-being of the community, rely more on renewable energy, discourage consumption, and create less pollution.

The Need for Education

While there has been a fair amount of critical analysis of tourism from the academic community, most tourism education focuses on hospitality management, training, and operations. Critical studies in economics, political control, culture, the North-South dichotomy, and the way tourists view themselves have contributed important insights.

According to Luis Vivanco, "Many tourism programs are designed to reproduce the industry, validate its basic capitalist paradigms, and create the next generation of managers. Will they allow for more critical, deconstructive work to happen under their umbrella? My guess is that if it's allowed, truly critical social scientific and political perspectives will be marginalized by the business and technique-focused emphasis of the industry." Real changes in tourism will not be created until people from diverse communities, backgrounds, and disciplines take a more integrated approach. Anthropologists, political scientists, and sociologists must connect with tourism management and training programs to share information, challenge unsustainable practices and unfair labor, and develop critical analysis.

A few programs do exist that are not completely industry-focused. Texas A&M is an example of an interdisciplinary approach to tourism in the United States. The University of Waitago in New Zealand has a very unique program in tourism that is completely interdisciplinary and based in geography, and offers some critical analysis. At the same time it hopes to serve the Maori, the indigenous peoples of New Zealand.

Women of all colors are urgently needed to look at gender issues in tourism and change policies that exploit, discriminate, and cause violence to women. Support for tourism gender studies at universities and colleges will support education for women to work in tourism in areas other than as prostitutes, waitresses, maids, bar attendants, and housekeepers.

There needs to be tremendous support for indigenous students of tourism. While it is necessary to understand Western systems in order to tackle the issues of tourism, it is important to remember that Western education has produced the systems that are threatening the planet. Educational programs must introduce and integrate lessons from indigenous ecological values and traditional and subsistence economics. I encourage students to research tourism, to undertake an analysis of advertising strategies or investigate the corporate responsibility of a tourism company. When educational programs encourage critical thinking and opportunities for people from diverse perspectives, they can create the tools, information, and education for those who are affected to change tourism. The global tourism industry must be persuaded to set aside some of its trillions of dollars in profits to advance the education of young people around the world to rethink tourism.

Tourists as Activists

The Center for Responsible Tourism suggests tourists ask themselves: Is this trip necessary? "Tourism has become a supermarket of illusions, exotic lands promising to satisfy secret desires. Ask yourself, why am I buying this trip? What do I leave behind? How many trips does it take to renew my soul and body? What do I do with my experiences when I return home?"[1] As tourists questioning tourism, the role we play, and the impact of our very presence in destination communities, we can start by considering the amount of natural resources it takes to transport us to our destination, to get us around while we are there (whether the oil used by airplanes and cars or the energy for the lights and air conditioning in the hotel room), where our waste is going, whether the locals have adequate water resources, how much land has been "reconstructed" for the place we stay, and whether residents have been moved to make room for us. Who owns the hotels, and where do our dollars go? We tourists can make some powerful political choices by voting with our feet and our pocketbooks.

As tourists, we must make educated economic choices and support small-scale, locally owned and operated businesses. Get involved in your own community so that when you travel you will have a reason to be involved in other communities and will *stay involved*; acknowledge the modern realities of indigenous and rural communities and learn to respect, not romanticize, other cultures. Support responsible tourism organizations. Subscribe to their magazines and newsletters. Volunteer. Study. Learn about local currency programs and how you can start one in your community. Pressure large tourism companies to do more than greenwash. Organize a "reality tour" of your own community to examine environmental, economic, or social justice issues. Invite teachers, students, local community members, your family, city officials, religious leaders, local businesses (including those in tourism), and others to participate. Make activism a goal of the tour. Contribute funds to support more integrated, diverse critical tourism studies.

Travelers can act responsibly by seeking out accurate information about the places they intend to visit. In the United States and elsewhere, many indigenous organizations will provide a list of recommended readings by authors they believe accurately describe their culture and history. Environmental and social justice groups that work with native and indigenous peoples will have information about important current issues. Indigenous peoples face any number of issues, ranging from health care and uranium mining cleanup to sovereignty rights and free trade agreements. In the United States, travelers can support the protection of sacred religious sites. Many such places have been turned into tourist destinations, rock-climbing walls, and even resorts. Sacred Sites International Foundation advocates for "the preservation of natural and built sacred places. We believe that protecting sacred sites is key to preserving traditional cultures and time-honored values of respecting the earth."[2]

While social activists are developing new tourism strategies, concerned tourists are changing their focus from relaxation to activism. Global Exchange, a San Francisco organization, has been a leader in people-to-people tourism. Their reality tours explore grassroots movements, offering travelers an opportunity to meet people behind the scenes, from Zapatistas in Chiapas and young people in Cuba to women organizers in South Africa and Vietnamese facing injustices created by capitalism. Tourists are now monitoring elections in Mexico, speaking out on behalf of indigenous peoples being forced from their lands by oil companies, and trying to uphold human rights in Bosnia. They are sharing information about fair trade, organic farming, or permaculture, and less consumptive technologies.

Deborah Tull joined a reality tour organized by Bard College:

> I spent nine months traveling, meeting local people and helping out. I still have questions about what we did—did it really make a difference?

Some places I could see that yes, it did. However, in other places I felt we were contributing to problems. Yet, overall, we traveled in a different way—meeting and learning from local people involved in important issues. It certainly changed my perceptions about tourism. It actually changed my life. I will never see tourism in the same light, I will never travel in a conventional way. I've talked to a lot of friends, family, and my teachers about it and believe I have been influential.

Travel Industry Changes

Some segments of the travel industry are more aware of environmental and human rights issues and are actively involved in reform. A growing number of small tour operators are rethinking their industry. Although many alternative ideas claim to benefit local people, we must not lose sight of the fact that tour operators are in the business to make money, and the tourist is the paying consumer they cater to. Tourism researcher Barbara Johnston warns against some tourism ideas that are emerging:

> Alternative tourism represents an industry whose ventures capitalize on the increasing global concern with disappearing cultures, lifestyles and ecosystems. . . . [However], the vision of responsible tourism includes more than this potentially exploitative relationship. Responsible tourism encompasses those ventures that are consciously designed to enhance the socio-environmental milieu of the host while educating and entertaining the guest. These ventures sell the "exotic" to gain money, labor, and/or foreign presence—all in an effort to restore the degraded environment while attacking the roots of social inequity. (Johnston 1990:31)

Many ecotourism projects are extremely misleading and exploitative. Some may be well intentioned but are misguided attempts to sell nature and culture. One example of a tour company that not only follows responsible tourism guidelines but also monitors the global travel industry is The Travel Specialists (TTS). A member of Co-Op America, a fair-trade organization, TTS serves as a link between concerned travelers, tour operators, tour programs, and local community projects. It evaluates other travel programs, promotes responsible tourism, and monitors the impact of tourism on local communities and the environment. TTS established the Eagle Eye Institute, a program to get urban youth out of the cities and into nature for hands-on learning experiences. The group also publishes a newsletter that includes travel opportunities, suggested readings on responsible tourism, and updates about the travel industry.

The Alaska Wilderness Recreation & Tourism Association (AWRTA) is a statewide model of how local business and industry, conservation, and communities—including native communities—come together to improve the tourism industry. AWRTA, a nonprofit trade organization, promotes the recognition and protection of Alaska's recreation and tourism resources and the businesses that rely on them. AWRTA's mission is to support the stewardship of the wild in Alaska and the development of healthy, diverse travel businesses and communities by linking business, community, and conservation interests. AWRTA promotes the recognition and protection of Alaska's recreation and tourism resources including scenic qualities, wildlife, fisheries, wilderness, wildlands, and rivers. AWRTA also developed an innovative funding mechanism for environmental and conservation groups. The *Dollars a Day for Conservation* program, aimed at tour operators arranging travel to Alaska, can help clients and the habitat and wildlife they enjoy by putting their money toward conservation efforts. It is a voluntary program and asks tour operators to simply introduce the concept to their clients and "passing through" their donations. AWRTA consists of members from native communities and therefore offers travelers to Alaska more realistic expectations and connections to native cultures.

More Natural Experiences

The real argument for environmental protection through any form of tourism requires a departure from the global marketplace economy that exploits the natural world. It is almost impossible to do this within the context of the global tourism industry, which gobbles up resources. We must expect to pay for the environments we visit. In the global North, we pay taxes to keep up our sewer systems, water, and even national parks. In many other countries, there is no such public support. If you plan to travel, factor in the cost of the environment and public services into your trip. Better yet, set aside funds especially for this purpose and donate them to an environmental organization or community development project. But it is important to understand as well that Western solutions to saving the planet are not always compatible with those of the people who live in wilderness areas. For example, conservation—a Western concept—is an idea that land should be preserved in its natural state. Under conservation statutes new parks, wildlife refuges, wilderness areas, and monuments have become protected lands. The designation of wilderness lands may actually impinge on indigenous ways of life because limitations are placed on traditional and subsistence activities. Instead of developing new sites, new destinations, we should consider the pressing issues related to tourism that are already on our doorstep, investigate the "corridors" and peripheral areas of protected lands.

Local Action

Local people in destination communities are speaking out and taking action against exploitative tourism. Some paint murals on walls near tourist resorts to graphically illustrate their anti-tourism sentiments. Others have developed educational programs for residents and designed regional tourism strategies to protect their natural resources and limit the numbers of tourists and developers who enter their lands. Still others are setting up their own travel companies that promote responsible tourism through people-to-people links, some of which focus on human rights; they are developing tour programs that recruit scientists and volunteers to work directly with them to preserve their environments. Native people are taking over operations of parks—their ancestral homelands—and training others to do the same. While they share the use of these areas with tourists, their own communities are the first priority. They are establishing local currencies that keep dollars within the communities. Some are working with universities and local governments to come up with new policies on land planning and use in their regions. Some programs are even assessing the reasons *why* record numbers of stressed tourists are escaping from urban environments. Many programs examine the impacts of tourism upon their environments, teach tourists about the impact of their mere presence, and invite them to take action to help offset the damage. There are even projects for individuals or organizations in the United States and Europe to help purchase land in the global South to set aside as protected areas for wildlife and for local people.

Indigenous peoples are resisting tourism with increasing strength. The Maasai in Africa, the Mayans in Chiapas, the Quechuas in the Amazon, many Native Americans in the United States, and many others are resisting irrational development of their lands in the name of ecotourism. These groups have organized opposition both from within their own countries and in the international community, and their voices are being heard. Responsible tourism groups, environmentalists, and others have responded by providing support and publicizing injustices. Concerned citizens rallied in 1996 to oppose the construction of a sprawling resort in the heart of India's Nagarhole National Park, one of the world's biological "hot spots" and home to indigenous peoples. The opponents denounced the development, organized locally with tribal people, and called upon responsible tourism organizations around the world to help publicize their plight. In 1997 the Indian courts ruled against the resort, at least for the time being. Unfortunately the hotel continues to press for development and the community members live in a precarious situation. Rural communities are organizing to address conflicts caused by tourism. Chris Beck explains one such project in Alaska.

The Talkeetna Community

Since 1998, visits to the small, end-of-the-road-town Talkeetna increased dramatically. Talkeetna traditionally has been a destination for modest numbers of climbers, anglers, and independent sightseers. These travelers come for spectacular views of the Alaska Range, proximity to Denali National Park and Preserve, and the town's historic and colorful character. In recent years, the opening of two new hotels led to a rapid increase in package tourist visits. Annual visitation is up at least threefold, from about 30,000 to 120,000 annual visitors.

Many townspeople are feeling overwhelmed by the sudden rush of tourism. In a town of less than 700 residents, as many as 1,000 visitors per day has led to congestion, parking problems, and new commercial development. Perhaps most important, many people have the sense that they're losing the things they most like about their town—a sense of contact with history, the natural world and their neighbors.

To respond to these changes, the town is currently in the middle of an ambitious tourism-planning project. One goal of the project is to address the immediate side affects of rapid tourism growth—for example, finding ways to reduce congestion by parking motor coaches and RVs on the edge of town, rather than having them drive through the middle of the community. Another goal of the project is to establish, for the first time, land use controls so future development is compatible with the town's funky/rustic/historic character. Finally, the project is working to build better lines of communication, and improved decision-making capacity, both within the community, and between the community and "outside" interests such as major cruise lines.

It is essential to create links within communities. Foreign-owned or -operated tourism companies could help support local agriculture and more sustainable practices by buying local goods and services such as food and transportation. They could recognize the harm in building cluster sites and make sure broad planning in the area included agricultural lands and other lands used by locals.

The Media

Most travel advertising of destination communities is created in the global North or by private industry and government tourist offices in the global South. This medium dominates the planet and promises paradise while other sectors of the media discuss how backward, poor, and degraded these same locations are. Any argument to rethink tourism must see through this corporate vision and its methods of propaganda. While responsible tourism organizations and tourism scholars have provided the best critiques of global tourism, the mainstream media are taking notice, especially with the growing concern about threats to national parks and protected areas. More travel writers, newspapers, and magazines are responding to the alerts about negative tourism activities and providing more realistic accounts of the life of locals, the dismal conditions that tourism has helped create, and the anti-tourism campaigns launched by grassroots groups everywhere.

Clay Hubbs, an educator, started the alternative travel magazine *Transitions Abroad* in the mid-1970s to provide information on economical, purposeful international travel opportunities—travel that involves learning by living, studying, working, or vacationing alongside the people of the host country. Hubbs describes his magazine's mission:

> A lot of tourists have a consumer attitude—what can I get, instead of what can I learn. We have to put aside our own cultural biases and learn as much as possible from the people we visit. I find that if you stay long enough, learn the language, you get a sense of who locals are as "peo-

ple." Through the magazine we are providing people-to-people links and small-scale programs, and with the numbers of people traveling "independently" mushrooming, it is obvious that people benefit and the travel industry does not.

Indigenous brochures describe cultural taboos and warn tourists from certain areas. Internet services speak to broad issues that affect both travelers and people in local destinations. Ron Mader, who coordinates the Internet service Planeta.com, told me, "It seemed to me that there were all of these groups not talking to each other about 'ecotourism.' I set up Planeta to run both positive and critical articles on ecotourism in the Americas and to hear from many people throughout the hemisphere. Many have been excluded from the governmental arena or the larger circles of powerhouse NGOs."

New and interesting media tools for tourists abound. One is *On This Spot: An Unconventional Map and Guide to Lhasa*, published by the International Campaign for Tibet. It provides uncensored stories behind Lhasa's tourist sites and commemorates dozens of places and events that the Chinese government is trying to hide from tourists and the international community. The map explains the contemporary political situation and gives the exact locations where Tibetan prisoners of conscience are held today. Linking travelers with Tibetan support organizations around the world, this map is a great example of a rethinking tourism tool.

The Green Tourism Association, based in Toronto, is the first such city to offer a written green tourist guide and a companion green map to show people all the best ways to experience a rich and sustainable urban existence. *The OTHER Guide to Toronto: Opening the Door to Green Tourism* (and the accompanying *The OTHER Map of Toronto*) provides resources that links tourism to the environment and celebrate the green city.

What can you do to encourage the media and marketers to present a more realistic image of tourism and its effects? Don't buy travel magazines that are simply advertisements for corporations and reject the "awards" they give themselves. Support the alternative press that does not depend upon corporate funds and offers critical analysis of travel. Educate your local news media. As a tourist, researcher, or activist, you can write about your tourism experiences. Always make sure to include resource information to link people, and illustrate how the issues you learned about on your travels are related to you and your community. For example, a traveler to the Amazon wrote about irresponsible, exploitative oil and gas development and linked her story to increased consumer demand for petroleum in the United States.

Human Rights

On several occasions the United States has sought to use tourism as a political weapon. As Linda Richter, a tourism scholar who has researched politics and tourism in Asia, wrote, "The United States demonstrated opposition to the regimes of the People's Republic of China and Cuba by forbidding travel to those countries for many years. Now it is symptomatic of the desired change in political relationships that the United States has lifted the travel ban on the People's Republic of China (and) allowed some travel to Cuba" (1989:6). By opening the doors of free trade, countries are "rewarded" with an expanding force of superconsumers, the tourists. They are also "rewarded" with expanding infrastructures, technologies, imports and exports, Western homogenization, and all the other tools of capitalism, consumerism, and globalization.

Despite the "rewards," some countries continue to oppress people. Individual tourists, as opposed to tour groups, have played a role in documenting some of the abuses simply by being part of the community. According to tourism analyst Ronald Schwartz, following demonstrations in Tibet in 1987, tourists who witnessed the events "became the principal source of information to journalists denied access to Tibet and gathered material on arrests, torture, and imprisonment for human rights organizations. A loosely knit network that arose in the first few days following the demonstrations continued to function for more than two years, recruiting new volunteers [tourists] to take the place of those who left" (1991:588). They also provided medical treatment to wounded Tibetans who were afraid to go to government hospitals. Yet Schwartz emphasizes that this was a special group of independent travelers who might have been concerned about human rights in Tibet in the first place. Such "engaged" tourists have not simply stepped out of their own societies, leaving behind obligations and seeking relaxation and luxury: "The ease with which travelers from different nationalities, a group of strangers, were able to create a clandestine organization and pool their skills . . . is remarkable. But their ready agreement on goals and tactics suggests a common culture of shared perceptions and values" (589). Engaged tourists share skills and values that belong to a larger social world.

Monitoring Corporations

Some corporations are taking steps to become more responsible, but only after facing tremendous pressure from the public. The public is needed to monitor and challenge corporations at every level. Community resistance to tourism corporations has been mostly unsuccessful. Nevertheless, resistance is increasing, and workers in the tourism industry are also organizing to resist. Any argument to rethink tourism calls for investigation of the power of international tourism corporations in order to get large corporations out of the local planning process and reduce their local political influence and control. In the United States, disclosure laws mean that information about global tourism corporations is fairly easy to obtain. The U.S. Securities and Exchange Commission requires corporations to file quarterly and annual reports. Any environmental liabilities—significant remediation or cleanup—must be reported. It is much more difficult to investigate overseas corporations. The best way is to locate and work with a grassroots group in the destination country. Friends of the Earth publishes the booklet *How to Research Corporations*. Other groups like the Multinational Monitor and Transnational Resource Action Center (TRAC) can also assist in investigating corporate actions and responsibility, and may help publish your own investigative work.

Travelers can learn more about corporate responsibility, oppressive governments, and actions against human rights abusers from the numerous publications that monitor human rights, corporations, the environment, and government actions. *Boycotts in Action* (BAN) provides information about boycotts of corporations, countries, and organizations, including tourism and travel-related corporations. A dedicated hiker told me, "People underestimate the power they wield. I became an environmental activist to save the places I love. It makes me angry to see politicians 'selling' wilderness areas, designing bills with loopholes allowing for construction of roads, power lines, and pipelines. I write about my experiences to encourage others to get involved. There is no doubt it is effective. Public pressure is the only way to make sure politicians don't sell out to private interests."

Tourism Revisited

In rethinking tourism, we must analyze the role we tourists play in promoting current destructive practices. With pressure, the industry can be reshaped so that profits from tourism are distributed more equitably. We must reduce consumption and respect natural limits rather than merely think "green." Technology is not neutral but interacts with society and nature. It is essential to replace environmentally and socially obsolete high technology with more appropriate, less-consuming, and traditional technologies.

This task is enormous. The developed world is in a state of denial about such severe problems. It is unlikely to change voluntarily; it will have to be forced by community groups in the global South and by cross-border organizations everywhere. A more generous spirit and greater volunteerism with respect to tourism issues goes hand in hand with a condemnation of the elitist, materialistic view that tourists are entitled to purchase other environments and cultures. Travelers must be willing to be on equal footing with locals, to try to understand cultures widely disparate from their own, to contribute to the community (perhaps through manual labor or professional expertise).

Those of us in the North who reject the advance of commercialized global culture and those from the South who are victimized by it vociferously oppose the continued devastation of the environment and indigenous populations. We need to take a hard look at the travel industry, at the self-exploitation of communities, and the roles we play as individuals. This inner journey of reevaluation won't be easy, but it is essential.

Some say it is too late. At a conference to rethink current economic directions, a former executive of one of the largest travel companies in the world was asked if he could see an alternative future. He replied, "There is no way to stop economic globalization because tourism and travel have already created globalization." Yet because of global grassroots movements for change, it may be possible to develop a deeper understanding of the course we're on and the role of global tourism. There are alternative strategies and movements, and there are alternatives to tourism.

Tourism has become politicized within global institutions, nations, communities, industry, the environment, and within almost all of us, whether we are tourists or persons affected by tourism in our community. The field begs for more research, monitoring, linking, policymaking, and change. Meanwhile, despite the slowdown caused by the September 11, 2001 terrorist attacks, global tourism is growing at a phenomenal rate—particularly in areas deemed "safe" such as the Arctic. There is an urgent need to rethink tourism and ecotravel and stop the paving of paradise.

It has been almost twenty years since my first trip to Jamaica. My continual journey through "tourism" over those years has been one of learning—sometimes frustrating, always challenging, often delightful, and in many ways transformative. When I think back to the day when I rode horseback among the shantytowns and hills near Montego Bay with a local guide named Joseph, one thing seems clear to me: in many ways we were both searching for dignity and an opportunity for self-realization. Throughout the world, among different cultures and classes, people are looking for self-determination. The world we are now born into and the society we know measures humans in terms of their economic worth. Human potential is enormous and largely unrealized. Western-style capitalism and consumerism have undermined the possibility for people to make their own choices about their lives and to have opportunities for their futures. Tourism continues to play a tremendous role in spreading the corporate empire. However, it is an industry that is different from many others. One of its primary functions is to develop human relationships. I see that as a chance to rethink and change our future. *That* would be paradise.

Source: From *Rethinking Tourism and Ecotravel*, 2003. Reprinted with permission of the author and Kumarian Press.

Notes

1 Quoted from "Third World Travel—Buy Critically," brochure adapted from a TEN publication and distributed by the Center for Responsible Tourism, Berkeley, CA.

2 Quoted from Web site for Sacred Sites International Foundation, 1442A Walnut St. #330, Berkeley, CA 94709, 510-525-1304, e-mail sacredsite@aol.com, Web address www.sitesaver.org.

References

Attix, Shelly. 1993. *Ecotourism: A Directory of Marketing Resources*. Pearl City: University of Hawai'i Press.

Hubbs, Clay. Annually. *Alternative Travel Directory*. Amherst, MA: Transitions Abroad Publishing.

Johnston, Barbara. 1990. "'Save Our Beach Dem and Our Land Too!' The Problems of Tourism in 'America's Paradise.'" *Cultural Survival Quarterly* 14(2):30–37.

Richter, Linda. 1989. *The Politics of Tourism in Asia*. Honolulu: University of Hawai'i Press.

Schwartz, Ronald. 1991. "Travelers Under Fire: Tourists in the Tibetan Uprising." *Annals of Tourism Research* 18(4):588–604.

Appendix A: Contributors

Jon G. Abbink is Senior Researcher at the African Studies Centre, Leiden, the Netherlands, where he heads the research group on political culture and social movements in Africa. He is also Professor of African ethnic studies at the VU University, Amsterdam. He has carried out field research in Israel and Ethiopia. His research interests are political change and ethnic relations in Africa, political culture in Northeast Africa, and the anthropology and history of Ethiopia. He became interested in tourism research while doing fieldwork in southern Ethiopia, where he was struck by the ambivalent response of local people, seeing tourists as a "necessary evil." His books include *Mytho-légendes et histoire: l'énigme de l'ethnogenèse des Beta Esra'el* (1991), *Meanings of Violence: A Cross-Cultural Perspective* (edited with G. Aijmer, 2000), *Rethinking Resistance: Revolt and Violence in African History* (edited with K. van Walraven and M. de Bruijn, 2003), and *Vanguard or Vandals: Youth, Politics and Conflict in Africa* (edited with I. van Kessel, 2005).

Kathleen M. Adams is Professor of Anthropology at Loyola University Chicago. She is also Adjunct Curator at the Field Museum of Natural History. She has conducted research in Indonesia, San Juan Capistrano (CA), and is beginning a new project in Italy. Her research interests include tourism, identity politics, art/visual anthropology, museums and cultural heritage. She is the author of *Art as Power: Recrafting Identities, Tourism and Power in Tana Toraja, Indonesia* (2006), and co-editor of *Home and Hegemony: Domestic Work and Identity Politics in South and Southeast Asia* (with Sara Dickey, 2000). She has

479

also published articles on tourism, ethnic relations, arts, and cultural representations in a variety of edited volumes and peer-reviewed journals, including *American Ethnologist, Ethnology, Ethnohistory, Museum Anthropology, Cultural Survival Quarterly, Annals of Tourism Research*, and *Tourist Studies*. She has been teaching the anthropology of tourism since the late 1980s and credits her academic interest in tourism to growing up in one of San Francisco's most heavily toured neighborhoods.

Denise Brennan is Associate Professor in the Department of Anthropology at Georgetown University. She is the author of *What's Love Got to Do with It? Transnational Desires and Sex Tourism in Sosúa, the Dominican Republic* (2004). Currently she is writing a book on the resettlement of formerly trafficked persons in the United States, *Life after Trafficking: Resettlement after Forced Labor in the United States*.

Edward M. Bruner is Professor Emeritus of Anthropology and Professor Emeritus of Criticism and Interpretive Theory at the University of Illinois. He was past president of the American Ethnological Society and the Society for Humanistic Anthropology. He became interested in tourism in the mid-1980s while leading a student group on a round-the-world year abroad program, where he realized that anthropologists and tourists are found together, everywhere. "Tourism haunts the anthropological enterprise," he says. His edited volumes include *Text, Play, and Story* (1984) and *The Anthropology of Experience* (1986). His most recent book is *Culture on Tour: Ethnographies of Travel* (2004).

Frederick Errington is Distinguished Professor of Anthropology at Trinity College, Hartford CT. He is a sociocultural anthropologist who has engaged extensively with people in Papua New Guinea, Indonesia, the American state of Montana, Fiji, New Zealand, and Australia. His interests have long been in the different ways in which people make meaning for themselves, often under difficult and changing circumstances. He has written about "cargo cultures," religious change, aesthetics, gender, class formation, and global engagements (including tourism). In collaboration with Deborah Gewertz, he co-authored *Cultural Alternatives and a Feminist Anthropology* (1989); *Twisted Histories, Altered Contexts; Articulating Change in the 'Last Unknown'* (1991); *Emerging Class in Papua New Guinea* (1999); and *Yali's Question: Sugar, Culture, and History* (2004). *Yali's Question* was written initially to be presented as the Louis Henry Morgan Lectures at the University of Rochester. Most recently, he and Gewertz completed *Cheap Meat* (2009), a book about the trade in fatty meat from New Zealand and Australia to (some of) the Pacific Islands. They are now embarked on a new project about the history and sociocultural significance of instant noodles.

James F. Fisher is the John W. Nason Professor of Asian Studies and Anthropology, Carleton College, Minnesota. He has published *Trans-Himalayan Traders* (1986), *Sherpas* (1997), and *Living Martyrs* (1998). He became interested in tourism after participating in an expedition in the Himalayas led by Sir

Edmund Hillary. "One of our objectives was building the Lukla airstrip in northeast Nepal, which shortened the trip to the Mt. Everest area from two weeks to 45 minutes, thus opening the flood gates to tourists and forever changing the lives of the Sherpas who live there."

Elizabeth Garland is an Assistant Professor of Anthropology at Union College. Her work focuses on the symbolic and political-economic position of Africa within the world system, and in particular on the lived experience of development and environmentalism in postcolonial East and Southern Africa. She first became interested in the cultural dimensions of tourism when an interest in African wildlife led her to work for a variety of ecotourism ventures around the edges of several African national parks. She is currently completing a book on wildlife conservation, tourism, and the neoliberal state in Tanzania.

Deborah Gewertz is the G. Henry Whitcomb Professor of Anthropology at Amherst College. Over the years, she has pursued research in Papua New Guinea, Fiji, New Zealand, and Australia. Her interests are in social history, the history of anthropological thought, and global food systems. She has written about ethnohistory, gender, sociocultural change, class formation and global engagements (including tourism). Long collaborating with Frederick Errington, she coauthored *Cultural Alternatives and a Feminist Anthropology* (1989); *Twisted Histories, Altered Contexts; Articulating Change in the "Last Unknown"* (1991); *Emerging Class in Papua New Guinea* (1999); and *Yali's Question: Sugar, Culture, and History* (2004). *Yali's Question* was written initially to be presented as the Louis Henry Morgan Lectures at the University of Rochester. Most recently, she and Errington completed *Cheap Meat* (2009), a book about the trade in fatty meat from New Zealand and Australia to (some of) the Pacific Islands. They are now embarked on a new project about the history and sociocultural significance of instant noodles.

George Gmelch is Professor of Anthropology at the University of San Francisco and the Roger Thayer Stone Professor of Anthropology at Union College. He has studied nomads, return migrants, commercial fishermen, Alaskan natives, Caribbean villagers and tourism workers. He is the author of ten books; two of his most recent writings have been on baseball (*Inside Pitch: Life in Professional Baseball*, 2006/2001, and *Baseball without Borders*, 2006). He is currently doing research on wine tourism in California's Napa Valley.

Sharon Bohn Gmelch is Professor of Anthropology at the University of San Francisco and at Union College. Her work focuses on visual anthropology, gender, ethnicity, and tourism. She is the author of seven books including *Nan: The Life of an Irish Travelling Woman* (1991/1986), which was a finalist for the Margaret Mead award, and most recently, *The Tlingit Encounter with Photography* (2008). She is currently doing research on wine tourism in the Napa Valley and a cross-cultural study of tour guides and their role as cultural mediators. She became interested in tourism while directing anthropology field schools in Barbados where the impact of tourism was inescapable.

Robert Gordon is Professor of Anthropology and African Studies at the University of Vermont. He has done fieldwork in Namibia, Lesotho and Papua New Guinea and is the author of several books including *Law and Order in the New Guinea Highlands* (with Mervyn Meggitt, 1985), *The Bushman Myth and the Making of a Namibian Underclass* (2000/1992), and *Picturing Bushmen* (1997).

Nelson H. H. Graburn obtained his BA in the Natural Sciences and Anthropology at Cambridge University, his MA at McGill University, and his PhD at the University of Chicago, both in anthropology. He has taught in the Department of Anthropology at the University of California, Berkeley since 1964, and at the International Institute of Culture, Tourism and Development, London Metropolitan University, since 2007. He had done research among Canadian Inuit on cultural change and the emergence of tourism and commercial arts since 1959, on Japanese tourism since 1974 and Chinese tourism since 1991. His interest in the invention and commoditization of Inuit sculptures and prints let to the publication of *Ethnic and Tourist Arts* (1976) and to his contribution "Tourism: The Sacred Journey" in Valene Smith's *Hosts and Guests* (1977). He is a founding member of the International Academy for the Study of Tourism and of RC-50, the Research Committee on International Tourism of the International Sociological Association, and faculty founder of U. C. Berkeley's Tourism Studies Working Group.

Martha Honey is Director of the Washington, D.C., office of the Center for Responsible Travel (CResT), a policy-oriented research NGO affiliated with Stanford University. Her numerous publications include *Hostile Acts: U.S. Policies in Costa Rica in the 1980s* (1994), *Ecotourism and Certification: Setting Standards in Practice* (2002), and *Ecotourism and Sustainable Development: Who Owns Paradise* (2008/1999). For two decades, she lived and worked as an international journalist based in Tanzania and Costa Rica. She holds a PhD in African history.

Palma Ingles is an anthropologist for NOAA Fisheries in St. Petersburg, Florida, where she conducts research with fishermen and fishing communities. She did her dissertation research on conservation and tourism in the Peruvian Amazon and worked as a tour guide on tourist boats in the late 1990s. She continues to do research and run tours in the Amazon on her vacations. She is currently working on a book on the impacts of tourism in the Amazon as well as designing a book of her photographs from her 18 years of work in the Amazon.

Adam R. Kaul is an Assistant Professor of Anthropology at Augustana College in Rock Island, Illinois, where he helped found the college's Anthropology program. He conducted his major fieldwork in the west of Ireland in a small village in County Clare where he studied tourism, traditional music, and the changing social structures. He has published several articles about this research, and more recently a book entitled *Turning the Tune* (2009). He became interested in studying tourism when he was backpacking around Ireland himself as a young man, shortly after graduating from college. "Tourism is riddled with all of the deep ironies, contradictions, and tensions that we see in a world of increasing global cultural interaction," he says.

Jack Kugelmass is Professor of Anthropology and the Sam Melton Professor and Director of the Center for Jewish Studies at the University of Florida. He received a BA from McGill University, an MA and PhD from the New School for Social Research. He previously taught at the Max Weinreich Center for Advanced Jewish Studies and at the University of Wisconsin-Madison. Among other books he is the editor of *Jews, Sports and the Rites of Citizenship* (2006), *Key Texts in American Jewish Culture* (2003), author of *The Miracle of Intervale Avenue: The Story of a Jewish Congregation in the South Bronx* (1996) and coauthor of *From A Ruined Garden: The Memorial Books of Polish Jewry* (with Jonathan Boyarin, 1998). He is currently working on a book on twentieth-century Yiddish travelogues. He was the editor for two terms of *City & Society*, the journal of the Society for Urban, National, Transnational and Global Anthropology.

Suzanne LaFont is a Professor of Anthropology at City University of New York, Kingsborough Community College and School of Professional Studies. Her books include *The Emergence of an Afro-Caribbean Legal Tradition in Jamaica* (1996), *Women in Transition: Voices from Lithuania* (1998), *Constructing Sexualities: Readings in Sexuality, Gender, and Culture* (2002), and *Unravelling Taboos: Gender and Sexuality in Namibia* (edited with Dianne Hubbard, 2007). She has also published several articles in scholarly journals and chapters in edited manuscripts, including the forthcoming "Not Quite Redemption Song: LGBT Hate in Jamaica," in *Homophobias: Lust and Loathing Across Time and Space*. Her research interests are the interrelatedness of sexualities, gender, power, and human rights.

Orvar Löfgren is Professor of European Ethnology at the University of Lund, Sweden. His recent books include *On Holiday: A History of Vacationing* (1999), *Magic, Culture and Economy* (edited with Robert Willim, 2005), and *Off the Edge: Experiments in Cultural Analysis* (edited with Richard Wilk, 2006). Tourism interests Löfgren "as a laboratory of modernity, an arena where people have been able to experiment with new aspects of their identities and social relations and also develop cultural skills like daydreaming and mind-traveling."

Dean MacCannell is Professor Emeritus of Environmental Design and Landscape Architecture at the University of California at Davis. His book, *The Tourist: A New Theory of the Leisure Class* (1976), was one of the earliest contributions to tourist studies. He was a founding member of the International Tourism Research Academy and Research Group 50 (the sociology of tourism) of the International Sociological Association. He teaches seminars on tourism theory at A.I.L.U.N. in Italy and at Colombia National University in Bogotá. His new book on *The Ethics of Sightseeing* is with the University of California Press.

Deborah McLaren is a sustainable tourism consultant and the former director of Indigenous Tourism Rights International (aka the Rethinking Tourism Project) in St. Paul, Minnesota. She is the author of *Rethinking Tourism and Ecotravel*

(2003/1998). She has an MA in social ecology, with an emphasis and research focus on tourism and globalization. She is concerned about the ability of researchers and academics to adequately disseminate tourism research results to indigenous and rural communities—"often the focus of the research yet rarely the recipients of the information."

Polly Pattullo is a British journalist who works for the *Guardian* newspaper in London. She is the author of three books about the Caribbean including *Last Resorts: The Cost of Tourism in the Caribbean* (2003) and *Fire from the Mountain: The Tragedy of Montserrat and the Betrayal of its People* (2000). Her most recent book is *The Ethical Travel Guide* (with Orely Minelli, 2009). She is interested in social justice issues and tourism, particularly ecotourism, having closely observed its impacts—both negative and positive—in Dominica.

Deborah Pruitt's interest on the impact of tourism on people's hopes for their futures grew out of her experiences while living in Jamaica and studying grassroots organizing for social change and development. She is a faculty member at the Western Institute for Social Research in Berkeley. Her thriving consulting practice in nonprofit capacity building and executive team building called Group Alchemy Consulting enables her to apply insights from cultural anthropology to social change efforts.

Lawrence E. Mintz is an Associate Professor Emeritus at the University of Maryland where he taught courses on popular culture and American humor from 1969 to 2007. He was the developer and director of the Art Gliner Center for Humor Studies, and editor of *Humor: International Journal of Humor*. He became interested in tourism watching visitors navigate the tourist voyage during a year living in Paris and by defending his enthusiasm for Walt Disney World and other theme parks against the usual academic criticism.

Peter M. Sanchez is Professor of Political Science at Loyola University Chicago. His research interests include democratization, U.S.–Latin American relations, and social movements. He has conducted field research in Cuba, the Dominican Republic, El Salvador, Guatemala, Panama, and Peru. In the 1997–1998 academic year he was a Senior Fulbright Scholar in Panama where he taught U.S.–Latin America relations at the University of Panama and conducted research on the final disposition of the 1977 Panama Canal Treaties. He is the author of *Panama Lost? US Hegemony, Democracy, and the Canal* (2007). He is currently working on a book, *Priest Under Fire*, focusing on the life of a priest from El Salvador who joined the popular movement during the civil war and after the peace accords was elected three times to the National Assembly. Professor Sanchez's research has been published in journals such as *American Behavioral Scientist, Annals of Tourism Research, Harvard Journal of Hispanic Policy, International Politics, Italian Geopolitical Review, Journal of Developing Areas*, and *The Latin Americanist*, as well as chapters in several books.

Melissa Stevens is a PhD student in anthropology at the University of Maryland, College Park, where she also teaches a course on anthropological approaches to sustainable development. Her research interests include community-based tourism, local participation in development, the political economy of tourism and sustainable development, and Vietnam and East Africa. While earning her Master of Applied Anthropology degree at the University of Maryland, she worked with Counterpart International to plan a community-based tourism project in Vietnam. The pilot project has recently begun hosting its first tourists. Her research examined the effects of power disparities between stakeholder groups on the ways in which community-based tourism concepts such as "community" and "participation" are operationalized. She plans to explore the same issues at a community-based tourism site in East Africa for her dissertation research.

Amanda Stronza is an environmental anthropologist and Assistant Professor in the Department of Recreation, Park, and Tourism Sciences at Texas A&M University. Her book *Ecotourism and Conservation in the Americas* (edited with William H. Durham, 2008) features detailed case studies on ecotourism from tour operators, researchers, community leaders, and environmentalists. Since 1993, she has conducted ethnographic research on one village in the Peruvian Amazon, studying longitudinal effects of ecotourism on local livelihoods, natural resource use, and cultural identity. She is PI on an NSF-Cultural Anthropology project titled, "Cross-Cultural Analysis of Community Participation in Ecotourism" and she serves as Co-Director for the NSF-IGERT program in "Applied Biodiversity Science: Bridging Ecology, Culture, and Governance for Effective Conservation."

Jill D. Sweet is Professor Emeritus of Anthropology at Skidmore College, Saratoga Springs, New York. She is the author of *Dances of the Tewa Pueblo Indians: Expressions of New Life*, 2nd edition (School of American Research Press, 2004). Between 1972 and 1981 Sweet earned her MA and PhD in Anthropology from the University of New Mexico as well as her BA and MFA in Dance from the University of California Irvine. In 1979, Sweet was named Weatherhead Fellow and Resident Scholar at the School of American Research, Santa Fe, NM. In addition to her books, Sweet has written numerous articles on tourism and dance among the Pueblo Indians.

Hazel Tucker is a Senior Lecturer in the Department of Tourism at the University of Otago, New Zealand. She has a PhD in Social Anthropology from Durham University, UK, and has conducted extensive fieldwork in tourism and social change in central Turkey. She is author of *Living with Tourism* (2003, Routledge) and co-editor of *Tourism and Postcolonialism* (2004, Routledge). She has also published on heritage construction and interpretation, host–guest relationships in tourism, and tourist experiences and performances in the package tour sector of New Zealand.

Appendix B: Films about Tourism

AMAZON EXCHANGE: EFFECTS OF ECOTOURISM ON INDIGENOUS CULTURE
Eli Pyke and Amanda Stronza (2004, 57 minutes) Spanish and English
Available from The International Ecotourism Society (TIES) (www.ecotourism.org)

Amazon Exchange is a documentary film on the cultural effects of ecotourism on
indigenous Amazonian communities. It involves two case studies: Posada
Amazonas, a Peruvian jungle lodge owned jointly by a Lima tour agency and
the local community Infierno, and Chalalan Ecolodge, a Bolivian company
started with the aid of Conservation International and now owned and operated
by the community of San Jose de Uchupiamonas. In the film, members of each
community that participated in a series of workshops called "Treque
Amazónico" share their experiences and views in the area of community-based
ecotourism. Issues involved include community development, conservation,
and business management.

ANONYMOUSLY YOURS
Gayle Ferraro (2003, 60 minutes)
Available from Berkeley Media LLC (www. berkeleymedia.com) and Aerial Pro-
ductions (www.aerial-productions.com)

This sophisticated and compelling documentary on sex trafficking in Southeast
Asia places a human face—through the stories of four young women in Myan-
mar (formerly Burma)—on an institution that enslaves as many as 40 million

women worldwide. Shot clandestinely, it exposes viewers to trafficking methods, the factors that make children vulnerable, the psychological and physical harm done to victims, and the pervasive corruption and poverty that allows sex trafficking to thrive. In the words of one reviewer: "This film touches the viewer emotionally but it also challenges us intellectually."

BANGKOK GIRL (AKA FALANG: BEHIND BANGKOK'S SMILE)
Jordan Clark (2005, 50 minutes)
Available from High Banks Entertainment (www.highbanks.ca)

This documentary provides a glimpse into Thailand's notorious sex tourism industry through the experiences of a 19-year-old bar girl named Pla who has been working in the bars since age 13. Pla seems to have avoided selling her body—a remarkable revelation given her surroundings—but it may not last. The introduction of *falangs* (foreigners) to Thailand has forever changed the city, the economy, and Thai people's lives and desires.

CANNIBAL TOURS
Dennis O'Rourke (1987, 77 minutes)
Available from Direct Cinema Limited

Cannibal Tours is two journeys. Depicted first are European and American "ethnic" tourists on a luxury cruise up the Sepik River in Papua New Guinea. The second journey (the filmmaker's underlying text) is a metaphysical one—an attempt to discover the place of the Other in the Western popular imagination. Why do "civilized" people want to visit the "primitive"? It is also a powerful film about the role photography plays in tourism.

CAN'T DO IT IN EUROPE
Charlotta Copcutt, Anna Weitz and Anna Klara Åhrén (2005, 46 minutes), English and Spanish
Available from First Run/Icarus Films

In the opening scene, a dust-covered sledge hammer drives a chisel into the rock wall of a Bolivian silver mine. At an Internet cafe in Potosi's central tourist district two men talk excitedly about their upcoming tour of the mines. Potosi receives 50,000 visitors each year. What brings European and American adventurers to this impoverished Bolivian mountain town? The filmmakers follow a group of 29 tourists on their excursion into the still-functioning silver mines. They also interview a bilingual tour guide from a mining family and Potosi's Director of Development, who believes that—in order to attract visitors—the work conditions must never be modernized. June Nash's classic ethnography, *We Eat the Mines and the Mines Eat Us*, provides excellent background information. *See also* MINED TO DEATH.

Cashing in on Culture: Indigenous Communities and Tourism
Regina Harrison (2002, 28 minutes)
Available from Berkeley Media LLC (www. berkeleymedia.com)

Ecotourism and "ethnic" tourism, designed specifically to bring affluent and adventurous tourists into remote indigenous communities, are among the fastest-growing types of tourism worldwide. Filmed in the small tropical forest community of Capirona, Ecuador, this film is a case study of the many issues and potential problems—cultural, economic, and environmental—surrounding eco- and ethnic tourism. The film is also a case study of community-based tourism in that its tourism is managed by the Quechua-speaking Capirona Indians who took eight years to decide to admit tourists into their villages. How do indigenous communities, in the context of global tourism and business interests, set up and run successful tourist operations without compromising their own cultural traditions and despoiling their environment?

Coney Island
Ric Stone, Buddy Squires and Lisa Ades (1991, 60 minutes)
Available from PBS (www.shop.pbs.org)

Before there was Disneyland, there was Coney Island. Produced for public television (PBS), the documentary uses archival photographs, newsreel footage, and interviews to reveal the development and appeal of New York's famous tourist playground from its birth in the mid-1800s until its demise after Word War II. In addition to its beaches, Coney Island at its peak consisted of three vast amusement parks offering an assortment of rides (it was the birthplace of the roller coaster) and spectacles including huge moving panoramas showing the creation, the end of the world and Hell, and reenactments of the Boer War and the fall of Pompeii. There was also a miniature town, known as Lilliputia, inhabited by 300 little people. Good supplemental materials are available through the PBS Web site (http://www.pbs.org).

Destination: Tourism
Dafna Kory (2007, 20 minutes)
Available from Berkeley Media LLC (www. berkeleymedia.com)

Bodh Gaya, the world's most popular Buddhist pilgrimage destination, is located in one of India's poorest states. Visitors to this UNESCO World Heritage site are typically shocked by the extreme poverty there, and the Buddhist tradition of almsgiving motivates them to donate money. As a result, Bodh Gaya has developed a sophisticated charity "industry" that caters to and depends on tourists and tourism. For four winter months there are tourists, and therefore work. The rest of the year is marked by desperate unemployment. In addition, dozens of foreign-owned and foreign-operated monasteries function like all-inclusive resorts, monopolizing tourism services and inflating real-estate values. Village schools are entirely funded by tourist donations and their students have become a "Kodak moment" for the visiting Buddhist pilgrims. The film reveals the complexities of "religious tourism," the ethical dilemmas of charity and philanthropy, and the realities of seasonal livelihoods in poor countries.

GOA UNDER SIEGE

Magic Lantern Foundation (1999, 30 minutes)
Available from Tourism Concern (www.tourismconcern.org.uk)

The film discusses the many impacts of tourism on Goa's residents, from the introduction of the drug culture to the stress that tourism places on the local water supply. The conflict between residents who have mobilized to gain a voice in the tourism industry and those of governmental officers in India interested in development is apparent. Although the production quality is not as high as it could be, the video comes with useful supplemental materials (i.e., printed film narration and citizen's tourism manifesto).

THE GOLF WAR

Jen Schradie and Mall DeVries (2000, 39 minutes)
Available from Bullfrog Films (www.bullfrogfilms.com). *See also* www.golfwar.org

Peasant farmers and fishers in a beachfront community in the Philippines have been tilling their land for generations. But, the government decides to follow a U.S. Agency for International Development-funded report's recommendations that the area be developed for tourism. The government's plan to transform farmland and fishing grounds into a luxury beach resort sparks a dramatic conflict when villagers actively resist the building of golf courses and yacht marinas. Tracking down both armed guerrillas and tourism boosters, the filmmakers reveal a larger, national battle over land and revolution in what the *Los Angeles Times* called a "bombshell of an expose." Although about a different tourism development, see Sally Ann Ness's *Where Asia Smiles: An Ethnography of Philippine Tourism* (2002).

THE GOOD WOMAN OF BANGKOK

Dennis O'Rourke (1992, 82 minutes)
Available from Direct Cinema Limited (www.directcinema.com)

The film, which Dennis O'Rourke labels a "documentary fiction film," explores sex tourism in Bangkok largely through the experiences and commentary of a woman named Aoi. It also includes explicit nude scenes of Thai sex workers dancing, the comments of male sex tourists, and a recurring interview with a woman relative in Aoi's home village. The nature of O'Rourke's involvement with Aoi has been the subject of critical commentary. According to O'Rourke, "The film includes a character—'the filmmaker'—who reflects me and others of my race and class, gender and profession, *but who is not me* (the person who was/is me was/is very different; because every day and every night I had to make the film). Through the description of this character, I took the rhetorical but sincere position that 'the filmmaker' was implicated and guilty along with the sex tourists." An essay by O'Rourke appears in *The Filmmaker and the Prostitute*, ed. Chris Berry, Annette Hamilton, and Laleen Jayamanne (Sydney: Power Publications, 1997).

HEADING SOUTH (VERS LE SUD)
Laurent Cantet (2005, 108 minutes), French and English
Available from Studio Canal (www.studiocanal.com)

This French feature film, starring Charlotte Rampling, Karen Young, Louise Portal, and Ménothy Cesar, depicts with sensitivity and seriousness the experiences of three middle-aged white women in the late 1970s, who travel to Haiti for the purposes of "romance" tourism with young black men. Their experiences and perspectives are juxtaposed with class issues and the deteriorating political climate of Haiti at the time. The film reveals the complex attitudes and emotional needs on both sides.

HOLI-DAYS
Randi Steinberger (2002, 50 minutes)
Available from Tell-Tale Productions (http://tell-taleprod.com)

Holi-days documents the contradiction between modern travelers' and pilgrims' expectations and their actual experiences in Jerusalem, Florence, and Las Vegas. It captures, in the words of one reviewer, "their theme-park similarities. Jerusalem seems a carnival of religious intensity and Florence a diorama of Renaissance culture, each retailing its past for the entertainment of visitors; like Vegas, they're tourist towns now." Las Vegas is filled with spectators enjoying its ability to replicate the physical icons of global travel: the Eiffel Tower, the Canals of Venice, and the Statue of Liberty, to name a few. As one tourist in the film happily exclaims, "I'm never going to Paris . . . so I think it's worth it to see it here." *Holi-days* suggests that the change tourists seek can be as profound as a religious epiphany, as superficial as a successful shopping spree, or as life transforming as winning the big jackpot.

THE HUMAN ZOO
Ko Ko Gyi (2008)
Available from Probe Media Foundation's Imaging Our Mekong
(www.newsmekong.org/humanzoo)

The film shows Burmese Kayan or Padaung refugees trapped in tourist villages in northern Thailand. The title comes from the common nickname given to the villages, which are run by Thai nationals who reap most of the profits from tourism. Famous for the distinctive brass rings that women and girls wear around their necks, the Kayan have been locked into a dependency on tourism for 20 years. The Thai government denies them both Thai citizenship, which would give them freedom of movement and the right to work, and exit visas, which would allow them to take part in the United Nations resettlement program. The government claims they are economic migrants who earn a good living from the tourist trade, rather than refugees fleeing conflict.

IN AND OUT OF AFRICA
Lucien Taylor and Llisa Barbash (1992, 59 minutes)
Available from Berkeley Media LLC (www.berkeleymedia.com)

This film explores authenticity, taste, and racial politics in the transnational African art market. It follows a Nigerian art trader, Gabai Baare, from rural Côte d'Ivoire to Long Island, New York, where he bargains for a sale. As objects change hands, they transform in meaning as well as in economic value. At the core of the film are the stories Baare tells about the art objects as he mediates between the values and aspirations of African producers and American consumers.

INCIDENTS OF TRAVEL IN CHICHEN ITZA
Jeffrey Himpele and Quetzil Castaneda (1997, 90 minutes)
Documentary Educational Resources (www.der.org)

This ethnographic video depicts the attempts of New Agers, the Mexican state, tourists, and archaeologists to "clear" the ancient Maya city of Chichen Itza in order to create their own idealized and unobstructed visions of the "Maya," while the local Maya themselves struggle to occupy the site as vendors and artisans. During the spring Equinox, when a shadow representing the Maya serpent-god Kukulkan appears on a temple pyramid, more than 40,000 New Age spiritualists and secular tourists from the United States and Mexico converge on the site to witness this solar phenomenon. The New Agers appear as exotic ritualists on display for both secular tourists and for local Mayas. It also shows how resident Mayas struggle against the Mexican state that regularly "sweeps" them from the tourist zone.

INNOCENTS ABROAD
Les Blank (1991, 84 minutes)
Available from Flowers Films (www.lesblank.com)

American filmmaker Les Blank and editor Chris Simon join American tourists on a whirlwind and often funny tour of Europe. A Globus Gateway "European Horizons" tour bus leaves London with 40 mostly retired people in the hands of British tour director Mark Tinny. They cover 3,000 miles and 24 European cities in 14 frantic days. The film's overall impression is one of excited travelers having the adventure of a lifetime while relying on the security provided by an organized tour. The perceptions of Americans looking at Europeans is matched by the varied responses of Europeans they encounter working in popular tourist destinations.

Life & Debt
Stephanie Black (2001, 86 minutes)
Available from New Yorker Films (www.NewYorkerFilms.com)

Life & Debt looks at the impact of globalization on Jamaica. Through images and narration by Jamaica Kincaid (based on her book, *A Small Place*), it contrasts the reasons tourists come to Jamaica with what they do not see and know about real conditions on the island. Excellent interviews with former Jamaican Prime Minister Michael Manley, deputy director of the IMF Stanley Fisher, and others reveal the devastating impact free trade, NAFTA, the business practices of multinationals, and lending policies of the IMF and World Bank have had on the country's economy.

Mined to Death
Regina Harrison (2006, 38 minutes)
Available from Berkeley Media LLC (www. berkeleymedia.com)

Working at an elevation of 16,000 feet, Quechua-speaking miners in Potosi, Bolivia, dig out zinc, tin, and silver much like their Incan ancestors did more than five centuries ago. This documentary explores their lives and work as the veins of ore in the sacred mountain of Sumaq Orqo become increasingly depleted. Today, 28 indigenous mining cooperatives eke out a living on the mountain. Commentary by the miners, their wives, and their children powerfully conveys the hardships and tragedies of life in the Andes. A few miners now guide tourists who come to experience firsthand the perils of the mines: noxious gases, unprotected paths, extreme heat and cold, and little to eat or drink for several hours while walking through the bowels of the earth. Interviews with European and American tourists reveal their conflicted emotions after witnessing these harsh conditions. Complements the film *Can't Do It in Europe*.

The Toured: The Other Side of Tourism in Barbados
Julie Pritchard Wright (1991, 39 minutes)
Available from Berkeley Media LLC (www.berkeleymedia.com)

This documentary, made by an American anthropology student/filmmaker, shows tourism from the point of view of some of those working in the industry. Bajans talk about the realities of making a living in a tourist economy and witnessing one's traditional culture change under the impact of foreign visitors. The occupation most highlighted is that of the "beach boy" who becomes sexually and "romantically" involved with women tourists. It also includes interesting comments from one of the women.

Traveler's Philosophy: Giving Time, Talent, and Treasure
Peter Jordan and Charlene Music (2008, 25 minutes)
Available from Center for Responsible Travel (www.responsibletravel.org)

This documentary showcases successful examples of travel philanthropy. Examples include micro-enterprises inspired and supported by a luxury hotel, tourist/local community service projects, and providing financial support for wildlife management in Costa Rica.

TREKKING ON TRADITION
Jennifer H. Rodes (1992, 44 minutes)
Available from Berkeley Media LLC (www. berkeleymedia.com)

This film explores the effects of mountain tourism or trekking on a small village in rural Nepal. It examines the views of both the trekkers (Europeans and Americans) and the Nepalese, and weaves a complex patchwork of conflicting dreams, aspirations, and frustrations.

Appendix C: Tourist Guidelines

The following guidelines, written for tourists by various NGOs and indigenous peoples, are a few of those available.

Traveler's Code for Traveling Responsibly: Guidelines for Individuals

Cultural Understanding

- Travel with an open mind: cultivate the habit of listening and observing; discover the enrichment that comes from experiencing another way of life.

- Reflect daily on your experiences and keep a journal.

- Prepare: learn the geography, culture, history, beliefs, and some local language; know how to be a good guest in the country or culture.

Social Impacts

- Support the local economy by using locally run restaurants and hotels, buying local products made by locals from renewable resources.

- Interact with local residents in a culturally appropriate manner.

- Make no promises that you cannot keep (photos, college admission).

- Don't make an extravagant display of wealth; don't encourage children to beg.

- Get permission before photographing people, homes, and other sites of local importance.

Environmental Impacts

- Travel in small, low-impact groups. Stay on trails.

- Pack it in, pack it out; assure proper disposal of human waste.

- Don't buy products made from endangered animals or plants. Become aware of and contribute to projects benefiting local environments and communities (a social benefit as well).

Adapted by Tourism Concern (www.tourismconcern.org.uk).

Tourism Concern's Guidelines

- Save precious natural resources. Try not to waste water. Switch off lights and air-conditioning if you go out.

- Support the local tradespeople and artisans. Buy only locally made souvenirs where possible. But do help safeguard nature by avoiding souvenirs made from ivory, skins, or other wildlife.

- Recognize land rights. Tribal peoples' ownership of the lands they use and occupy is recognized in international law. This should be acknowledged irrespective of whether the national government applies the law or not (governments are among the principal violators of tribal rights). When in tribal lands, tourists should behave as they would on private property. (From *Survival International*'s code.)

- Always ask before taking photographs or videotape recordings of people. Don't worry if you don't speak the language—a smile and a gesture will be understood and appreciated.

- Please don't give money or sweets to children—it only encourages begging and demeans the child. A donation to a recognized project, health center, or school is a more constructive way to help. (If you have a guide, ask for details.)

- Respect for local etiquette earns you respect. In many countries, loose and lightweight clothes are preferable to revealing shorts, skimpy tops, or tight-fitting wear. Similarly, kissing in public is often culturally inappropriate.

- Learning something about the history and current affairs of a country helps you understand the attitudes and idiosyncrasies of its people and helps prevent misunderstandings and frustrations.

- Be patient, friendly, and sensitive. Remember—you are a guest.

The Achuar Visitors Behavior Requests

- Though culture and traditions may appear odd, please don't criticize them. Follow the Achuar community rules and learn about their extraordinary culture.

- Ask your Achuar guide if is possible to take photographs or video-tape recordings. Avoid close-up shots and offer people money for a photograph.

- The Achuar feel pleased when you buy their handicrafts. All communities have a fixed price. Avoid purchasing items made from feathers, animal skins, or insects.

- Please avoid any physical contact with community members.

- Do not give money, presents, or sweets to the kids. If you have educational materials that you would like to donate, please give them to the resident manager.

- Do not enter an Achuar house without an invitation.

- The Achuar are jealous people. If you are a man, you should never look directly at a woman's face.

- Because the Achuar house is divided by gender, do not go to the *ekent* or female area on the east side.

- *Nijiamanch,* the manioc beer, is always offered. If you do not like it, you should at least pretend to drink it. Refusing might be considered an insult.

- Please do not take animals or plants out of the reserve area.

- Donations to the FINAE, the Achuar organization, the different projects, or scientific research can be coordinated through the Pachamama Alliance. Please ask the resident manager.

Kapawi Ecolodge and Reserve; www.ecuador-wildlife.com/jungle/kapawi.html

Tourism—Simply . . . a Guide to Better Tourism

- Don't rely on guidebooks. Learn as much as you can from other sources (indigenous writers, independent newspapers, films, and so on). Try to understand the different cultures of the place you're visiting on their own terms and behave appropriately. For example, don't visit religious places semi-clothed.

- Look at your own mindset. Try to understand why people behave differently: concepts of time, for example, vary between cultures. Don't demand special privileges, like better access to transport and services.

- Don't steal pictures. In some cultures it's more than invasive to have your picture taken. Ask if it's okay for you to take someone's photograph and be ready to offer or exchange something you have.

- If you make a promise to send a letter or photograph then keep it.

- Use locally produced goods and services—from your choice of airline to the food you eat.

- Respect the local environment. Try to be a guest rather than a colonizer.

- Don't go somewhere if you think that being a tourist there supports a repressive regime.

- Ask yourself—why am I going? Consider using international networks that can help you to stay with local families rather than in hotels.

New Internationalist 245 (July 1993). Some points adapted from *Guide Notes for Responsive Travel* published by Centre for the Advancement of Responsive Travel (CART).

Treading Softly: A Guide to Eco-Friendly Travel in Vietnam

Dear Traveler,

Welcome to Vietnam—a country that evokes a multitude of images and emotions—a nation small in size but expansive in heart and soul.

Vietnam's contrasts and diversity—its many ethnic groups and its rich cultural, historical, and ecological heritage—attract thousands upon thousands of tourists each year. However, it is a fragile land that has borne the brunt of human and natural disasters. Years of war, subsequent reconstruction of the country, high population growth, poverty, and now the push toward rapid industrialization and a market-oriented economy have had environmental and social consequences.

Tourism, too, has had a negative impact, affecting even the most distant corners of the country with its cultural and environmental footprint. The aim of this guidebook is to show how you, as a visitor, can play a part in helping to protect Vietnam from the negative impacts of tourism.

By treading softly on the country's environment and respecting its people, you can minimize your impact while gaining the maximum enjoyment from your traveling experience, and take home an abundance of happy memories. You will also contribute positively, by thoughtful example, to a more sustainable tourism industry in Vietnam.

Protecting the Future

Tourism, one of the planet's biggest industries, has been a major driving force behind globalization. Every corner of the planet has become a potential tourist destination, and some of the world's most fantastic landscapes are now nationally and internationally protected as a direct result. The idea of sustainable tourism has evolved out of concern about the negative impacts of tourism. Sustainable tourism aims to protect the environment and respect peoples and their cultures while enhancing the socioeconomic benefits of tourism. Importantly, sustainable tourism should contribute to improving the quality of life of host communities. Protecting destinations in your lifetime—so that you, your children, and future generations will also have the opportunity to revisit—is a must. Here's how you can help . . .

Getting You on Side

First and foremost, it is important to realize that what you do makes a difference. By being a responsible and sensitive traveler, you can raise awareness of others in the tourism sector, be they tour operators, guides, or your fellow holidaymakers; be they from the country you are visiting or abroad. It doesn't cost a lot and it doesn't require a revolutionary adjustment. Small changes can add up to a significant overall positive impact.

Vietnam has only comparatively recently opened up to international tourism, which is now a major foreign exchange earner. While Vietnam can learn from the experiences, both positive and negative, of other countries—you can help by showing your support for sustainable tourism. You can vote with your money, choosing to patronize hotels, airlines, resorts, and tour operators that advance energy and environmental conservation and are committed to global principles of sustainability. You are not the only visitor to Vietnam—your impact on the environment is multiplied a millionfold by other people every year.

Every tourist and every host community will have a different concept of crowding, environmental degradation, invasion of privacy, noise, and so on, and a different level of tolerance. If you are aware of being crowded, or of not enjoying your visit due to pollution or noise, then you have touched upon your carrying capacity. Think of others—both tourists and hosts—and the possibility that their tolerance level may be lower than yours.

Temper Your Expectations with Reality

Tourists strive to have "authentic" experiences when they travel. They want to experience "untouched paradise" or "traditional" cultures, while often expecting the same comforts they would have at home. Fantasy often turns to disappointment when tourists arrive at their destination and find it "modernized" or "spoiled." Think about how realistic this expectation is when so many people are traveling with similar expectations.

The truth is, cultures are rarely stagnant, but constantly changing and adapting. Development usually brings increased options for communities, be they in the form of electric pumps, plastic buckets, fluorescent lights, televisions, new concrete toilets, or modern clothing. Unfortunately, when visitors no longer consider a community "authentic," tour operators are forced to move on, taking away valuable income and impacting other areas.

Yet modern life in Vietnam is also fascinating! Accept that you cannot expect to preserve living culture as in a museum. Accept the people you visit as they are, whether they are wearing traditional dress or baseball caps. Culture is more than clothes, crafts, and dances—dig deeper to discover the inner expression of culture and tradition.

It's also worth mentioning that "exotic," "innocent," "graceful," "virginal," "pure," and other such tired stereotypes of Vietnam do not paint a realistic picture and are, in fact, demeaning in their simplicity and connotations. Remember that no society or people is perfect or pure. Each has its shortcomings and foibles, and Vietnam is no exception.

Low-Impact Tourism

Although there are commonsense ways in which you can avoid creating negative impressions and damaging the environment, it's still easy to make mistakes when you are new to a place. Here are some Vietnam-specific guidelines that, if appropriately followed, should make your trip more enjoyable and ensure that you leave behind a positive impression and only the softest of footprints.

Be an Environmental Ambassador

Home to one-tenth of the world's mammal, bird, and fish species, Vietnam has a unique environment. Scattered throughout the country are around 100 protected areas that encompass a huge variety of ecological systems that include coral reefs, islands, beaches and dunes, wetlands, mountains, forests of every description, limestone landscapes and caves, river deltas, and lakes. Among these protected areas are 11 national parks managed by the Forest Protection Department, which represent some of the jewels of Vietnam's natural heritage. Vietnam's 11 national parks are: Ba Be, Ba Vi, Bach Ma, Ben En, Cat Ba, Cat Tien, Con Dao, Cuc Phuong, Tam Dao, Tram Chim, and Yok Don. In addition to these 11 national parks, the country has four UNESCO World Heritage Sites—the Ancient Capital at Hue (December 94), Ha Long Bay (December 94), Hoi An (January 99) and the Cham Monument at My Son (January 99), and one UNESCO/MAB Biosphere Reserve named Can Gio Mangrove.

Numerous flora and fauna species are also unique to Vietnam—40 percent of Vietnam's plants grow nowhere else—while seven of the 12 large mammals that have been described in the last century were discovered in Vietnam. Sadly, the environment is under threat. In 1943, natural forest covered an estimated 43 percent of the country. At the end of 2000, total forest cover, including both natural forest and plantations, had dwindled to 33 percent. Tourism provides an economic reason for conserving natural resources and, if sustainable, can encourage the protection of the country's biodiversity.

Helping to Conserve Vietnam's Precious Biodiversity

Many species of Vietnam's wild fauna and flora are under threat from both domestic consumption and the illegal international trade. Though it may be "an experience" to try wild meat such as bear, muntjac, bat, monkey, and python, ordering these foods will indicate your acceptance of these products and add to their demand.

- Be careful when consuming wild products such as bush meat and traditional medicine, as these may have come from endangered or threatened species. When offered wild meat, be sure that it is derived from sustainable management practices that can, in fact, contribute to the conservation of wild animals and rural development. In case of doubt, however, the best policy is to politely refuse it.

- In the case of tourist souvenirs, do not buy products made from endangered plants or animals, such as elephant ivory, tortoiseshell, and wild animal skins. Again, unless you are certain the species is not endangered, never buy live or stuffed animals, however tempting, and forgo the coral you will no doubt see on sale in the markets. Vietnam's coral and ornamental fishes are being severely depleted by destructive harvesting practices.

- Remember that virtually all countries in the world are parties to the CITES Convention, which regulates the trade in endangered species of wild fauna and flora. Accordingly, importing many wildlife products without special permit is illegal and you could be severely fined in your own country.

Rubbish, Waste, and Energy Use

Environmental awareness in Vietnam is generally low. You can help change this subtly by example—for instance, not dropping litter even if someone tells you it's okay to do so. By setting a quiet example, practicing the 3 Rs—reduce, reuse, recycle—and explaining the reasons for your actions to others, you can play a positive role in protecting the environment and the natural and cultural resources of Vietnam.

- Make sure you properly dispose of any rubbish you generate. There are few public rubbish bins in Vietnam, so this may mean carrying it with you for a while.

- If no toilet is available, make sure you bury your waste, and avoid sites near waterways. Burning or carrying toilet paper and hygienic items out of natural areas is a must.

- Carry a toilet roll and a couple of airtight plastic bags with you in case you need to take your rubbish with you.

- Never use shampoo or soap in rivers, lakes, or the sea. Vietnam's waterways are precious resources, and in some of the country's drier areas water is a very scarce commodity.

- Please turn off your air conditioner, fans, lights, and other electrical appliances when you leave your hotel or guesthouse.

- Try to reduce the use of air conditioners in cars and encourage drivers to turn off the engine when stationary.

Coral Reefs and Limestone Caves

Vietnam is home to a large expanse of stunning limestone landscapes—of which Halong Bay in the north is the most famous—and coral reefs, both of which have suffered severe damage in recent years. Coral reefs in particular have been damaged due to dynamite fishing, boat anchorage, mining for concrete production, and sale to tourists.

- When visiting coral reefs do not touch live coral, as this hinders growth—some species, such as "fire corals" are also able to cause a harmful sting.

- Do not anchor boats on coral reefs. If your tour operator does this, try to convince him or her to anchor in a sandy area. Indicate that you are willing to swim the extra distance to the coral.

- When exploring limestone caves, don't touch the formations, as it hinders growth and turns the limestone black. Never break off stalactites and stalagmites in limestone caves—they take lifetimes to regrow.

Walking and Trekking in Natural Areas

While walking and trekking are preferable to 4WDs as a means of exploring national parks and other protected areas, the constant flow of tourists can still have a negative impact on the fragile ecological balance of these places. Remember that you are just one of thousands who will visit and impact an area.

- Keep to designated trails when out walking, both for your safety and the protection of the environment. There are reasons why certain trails are used.

- Follow the rules and regulations of the protected area you are visiting. For example, never make fires, avoid making unnecessary noise, and do not take samples from nature (flowers, mushrooms, frogs, etc.).

- Pay particular attention to the guidelines for rubbish discussed above. Do not dispose of rubbish or cigarette butts in the wild as they may take many years to break down (if ever).

Culture: A Matter of Etiquette

Traveling in Vietnam is not always relaxing. It can be unpredictable, intense, and frustrating, but it is rewarding. Being demanding and loud, however, will get you nowhere. Remember the importance of "face"—the subtle but important quality of personal dignity in Asian countries.

- Try to learn about the local culture before you travel and broaden your experiences beyond the guidebooks. Guidebooks can make or break a guesthouse or hotel by concentrating people in certain places. Guidebooks are also often out of date by the time they are distributed. Be willing to try alternative options.

- Learn some of the local language. Even basics such as "hello," "goodbye," and "thank you" will be appreciated

- Respect cultural differences and don't look down on or try to change them.

- Be careful when showing affection in public. Relationships in Vietnamese society are fairly traditional, so in general it's best to limit affection to holding hands—especially in rural areas.

- Avoid patting or touching people on the head—it's the symbolic high point in Asia.

- Be aware of the importance of the ancestral shrine in Vietnam. Avoid backing up to, pointing your feet at, or changing your clothing in front of it.

What to Wear

To be sure of not causing offense, it is best to respect local dress standards and dress modestly, especially in the countryside.

- There are no areas where nude or topless swimming or sunbathing is appropriate.

- Women should try to avoid wearing low-cut or tight sleeveless tops and brief, clinging shorts. It is advisable to wear a bra at all times. Men should avoid walking around bare-chested.

- At religious sites, do not wear shorts or sleeveless tops and remember to remove your shoes.

Questions, Privacy, and Humor

Vietnamese concepts of privacy are very different from those of Westerners, as they are accustomed to living and sharing in a close-knit community and in crowded conditions.

- Don't be offended by the (very Vietnamese) fascination with your personal details—How old are you? Are you married? Do you have children? and so on—questions that you may consider private. You may find the answer "not yet" *(chưa)* to the question of marriage or children a useful one.

- Don't be taken aback if people are intrigued by your size, especially if you are tall or well built. The Vietnamese are a small, slight people and may openly display their amazement at Western bulk. Remember this when selecting your clothing!

- Talk to the locals and make friends. The people of Vietnam are friendly and hospitable. They love it when they hear a foreigner try to speak their language.

Snap Happy

Vietnam is a photographer's dream—from the vivid greens of the rice paddies and cloud-shrouded mountains to the bustle of open-air markets and street life, there are endless photographic opportunities. However, nobody enjoys being followed by a camera, so remember to ask permission before taking photographs—and respect a refusal.

- Don't hound men and women in traditional ethnic dress for the "perfect colorful shot" if they appear shy or avoid your camera, and remember that videos are even more intrusive.

- Try not to get into the situation of paying for the right to take photos, as it encourages a begging mentality.

- If you promise to send back a photo, make sure you are sincere in your offer.

Just Say No

It's in your own interests to respect local regulations and practices concerning drugs and alcohol. Drugs are illegal in Vietnam and their possession and usage carry harsh penalties.

- Be careful about alcohol consumption, especially when visiting rural and ethnic minority areas, where as a tourist you may enjoy privileged status.

- Remember that tourism can fuel the demand for alcohol and drugs and lead to increased consumption/use by locals, encouraging social problems.

Getting Personal

Be aware that in some communities it may be taboo to conduct an intimate relationship with a local.

- Don't assume that what is acceptable at home is acceptable everywhere. Vietnam is still a largely traditional society and getting involved with a local may cause offense.

- Remember also that the recipient of a foreigner's attentions can be seriously affected within their local communities in terms of their well-being, social standing, and reputation.

Out and About: Buying Local

By using locally produced goods and services, you can contribute financially to the community you are visiting and help turn tourism to the country's benefit.

- Drink and eat local food when you can.

- Use local transport and local shops.

- Offer to repay hospitality in cash or in kind to avoid exploiting the goodwill of others. At the same time, try to avoid paying for simple acts of kindness in cash—for example, being given directions.

- Hire a local guide when visiting protected areas or historical sites. This way you will contribute to the local economy, learn more about the area, and have the opportunity to meet local people.

Giving Money or Gifts

Giving money away to both children and adults promotes a begging mentality and culture. It also highlights the income gap and strips away people's self-esteem. By avoiding cash handouts you can play a part in discouraging the development of a society that equates every human action as a potential moneymaking scheme.

- Avoid giving children money or gifts; it is better to pay for a postcard, map, or a shoeshine.

- Giving chocolate or sweets is a bad idea, as many people do not have access to dentists and knowledge of dental hygiene is poor.

The Hard Sell

Vietnam is a developing country and one that has experienced a long period of war, so poverty is obvious and unavoidable. Be prepared to be approached by street sellers, shoe shine boys, etc., or followed by empty *cyclos* expectantly awaiting your patronage, especially in Hanoi, Ho Chi Minh City, and other large towns.

- If you are approached by a street seller, be firm but polite and calm in turning them away, even if you are irritated by a day filled with similar approaches.

- Take a *cyclo* when you can, as they are a great way to see a city and view street life at close quarters. *Cyclos* are today losing out to taxis and *xe om* (motorbike taxis), so you'll also be supporting a threatened trade.

- Certain streets have been made off-limits to *cyclos*, so your driver may have to take an indirect route to your destination.

- Negotiate prices in advance before accepting either goods from street sellers or getting on a *xe om* or into a *cyclo*.

The Sex Trade

In Asia, prostitution is an unfortunate fact of life. The link between tourism and prostitution is undisputed. Be aware that prostitution is illegal in Vietnam. Be careful not to act in any way that could be seen as encouraging this, especially where children are concerned.

- Don't buy sexual services; remember that the relationship between tourists and prostitutes is almost always unequal and tends to be exploitative.

- The sexual exploitation of children is a significant problem right across Asia. However, several countries now have laws that enable the trial at home of tourists who have committed crimes of pedophilia abroad. If you observe anyone known to you involved in child prostitution, you might consider reporting him or her to the police when you get home.

Before You Go

As you head off on holiday, it is important to think about the main reason for your trip to Vietnam, whether it's adventure, biodiversity, new cuisine, history, art, and culture, meeting new people, or simply cultivating a golden tan. It's equally important to realize that everything you do while you're away has a consequence for somebody, or something, else.

Enjoying your time in Vietnam will be easy. But by following the *A to G Green Guide*, you'll also be doing something active toward ensuring a long-term future for both tourism and the environment. In return, you'll be rewarded with a richer traveling experience and the respect of the people of this fascinating country.

Treading Softly was produced as part of the "Support to Sustainable Tourism Project" executed by SNV (Netherlands Development Organization) Vietnam together with IUCN (World Conservation Union) Vietnam.